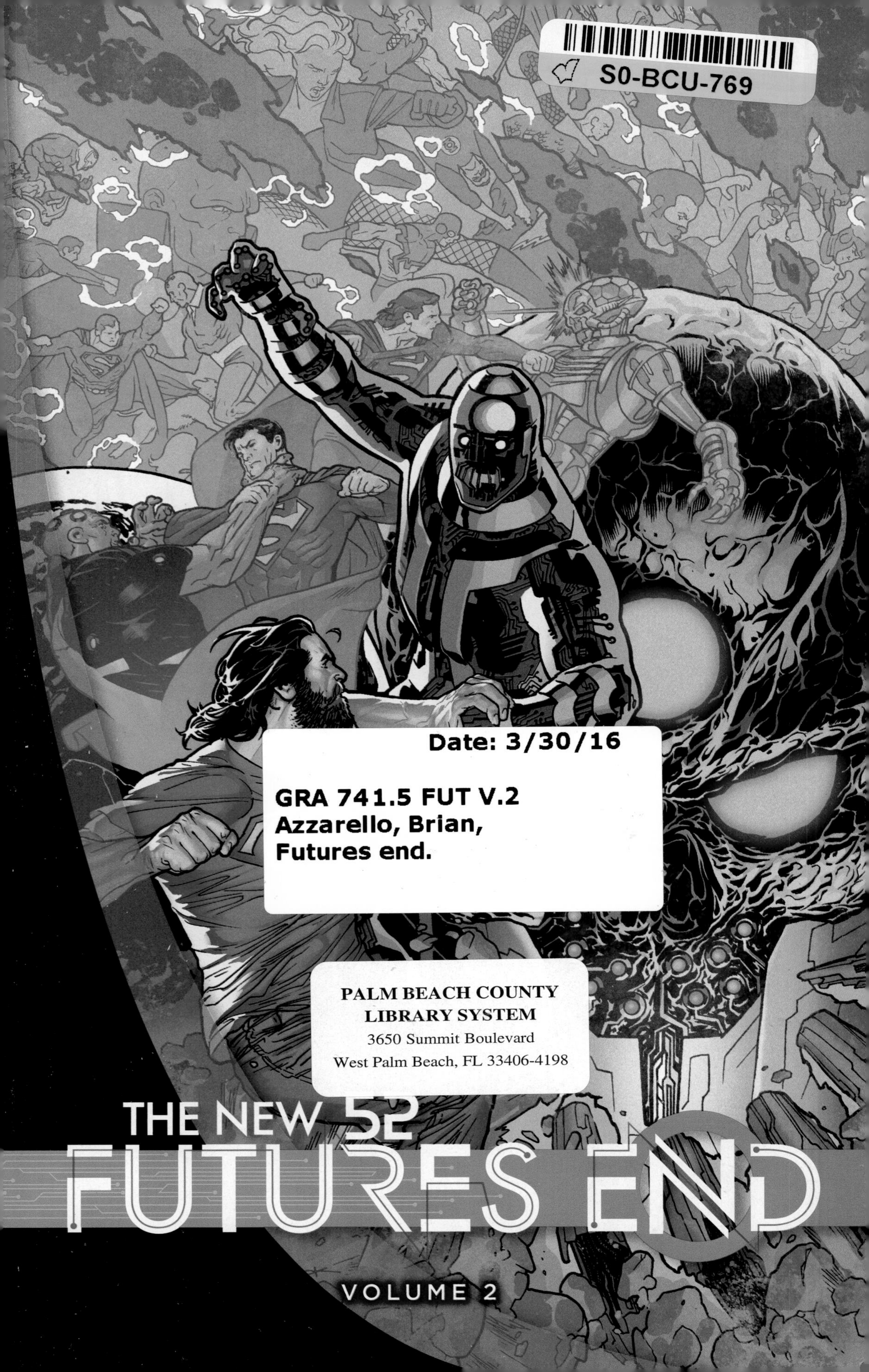
THE NEW 52
FUTURES END
VOLUME 2

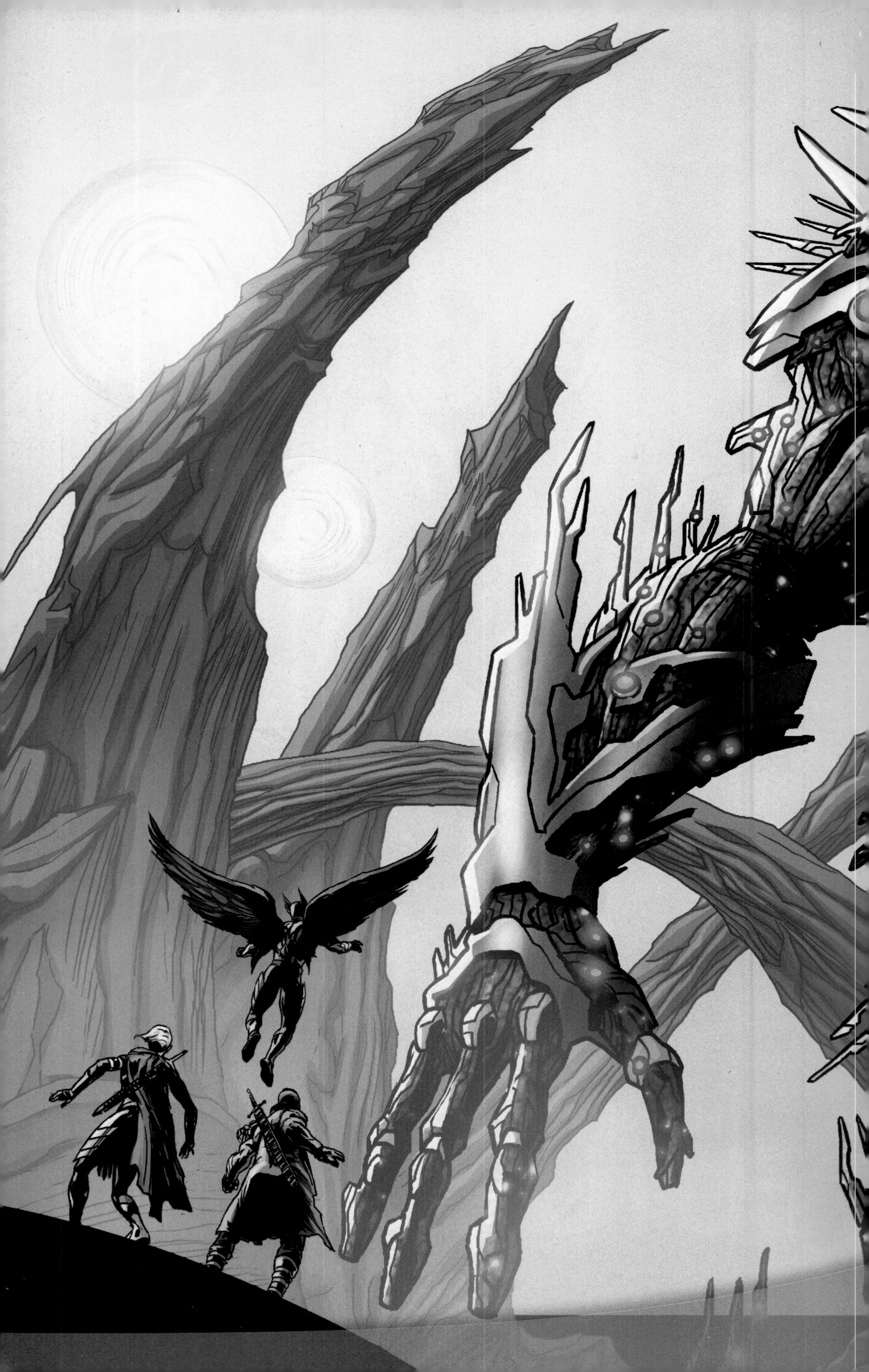

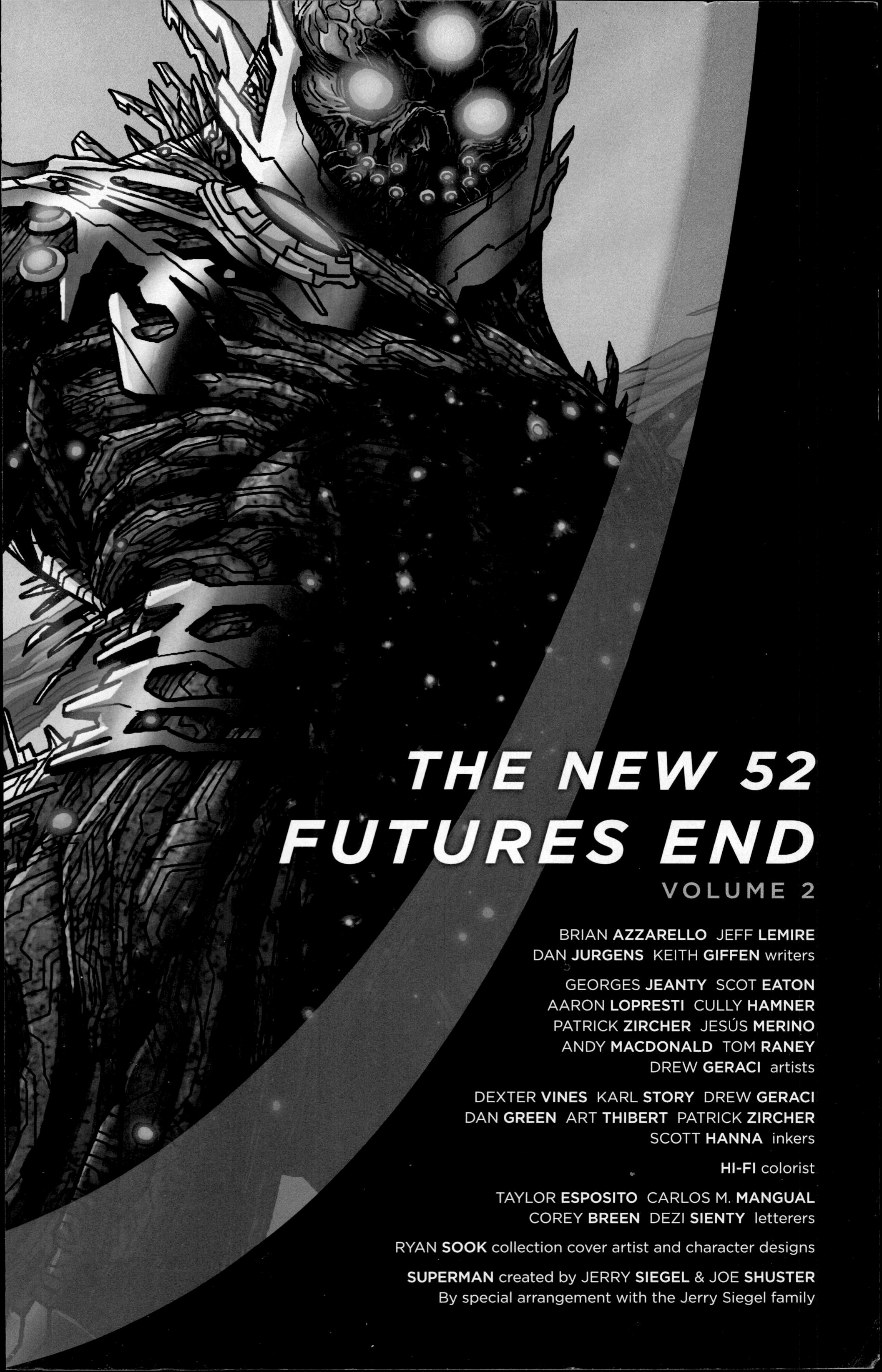

THE NEW 52
FUTURES END
VOLUME 2

BRIAN **AZZARELLO** JEFF **LEMIRE**
DAN **JURGENS** KEITH **GIFFEN** writers

GEORGES **JEANTY** SCOT **EATON**
AARON **LOPRESTI** CULLY **HAMNER**
PATRICK **ZIRCHER** JESÚS **MERINO**
ANDY **MACDONALD** TOM **RANEY**
DREW **GERACI** artists

DEXTER **VINES** KARL **STORY** DREW **GERACI**
DAN **GREEN** ART **THIBERT** PATRICK **ZIRCHER**
SCOTT **HANNA** inkers

HI-FI colorist

TAYLOR **ESPOSITO** CARLOS M. **MANGUAL**
COREY **BREEN** DEZI **SIENTY** letterers

RYAN **SOOK** collection cover artist and character designs

SUPERMAN created by JERRY **SIEGEL** & JOE **SHUSTER**
By special arrangement with the Jerry Siegel family

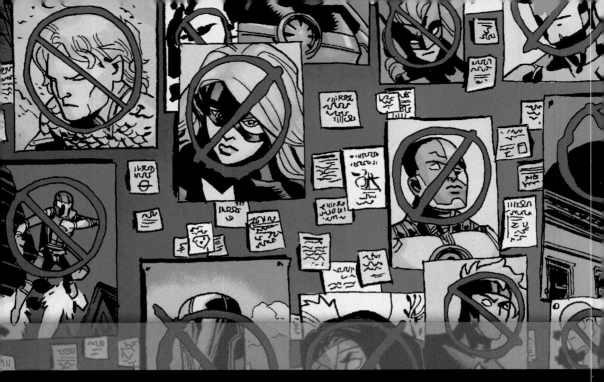

THE NEW 52: FUTURES END VOLUME 2

Originally published in single magazine form in THE NEW 52: FUTURES END 18-30 Copyright © 2014 DC Comics.
All Rights Reserved. All characters, their distinctive likenesses and related elements featured in this publication are trademarks of DC Comics.
The stories, characters and incidents featured in this publication are entirely fictional.
DC Comics does not read or accept unsolicited ideas, stories or artwork.

DC Comics, 4000 Warner Blvd., Burbank, CA 91522
A Warner Bros. Entertainment Company
Printed by RR Donnelley, Owensville, MO, USA. 6/12/15. First Printing.
ISBN: 978-1-4012-5602-9

SUSTAINABLE
FORESTRY
INITIATIVE

Certified Chain of Custody
20% Certified Forest Content,
80% Certified Sourcing
www.sfiprogram.org
SFI-01042
APPLIES TO TEXT STOCK ONLY

Library of Congress Cataloging-in-Publication Data

Azzarello, Brian.
The New 52 : Futures End, volume 2 / Brian Azzarello, Jeff Lemire.
p. cm.
ISBN 978-1-4012-5602-9 (alk. paper)
1, Comic books, strips, etc. 2. Graphic novels. I. Azzarello, Brian. II. Title.
PN6726 .D386 2014
741.5'973—dc23
2014027359

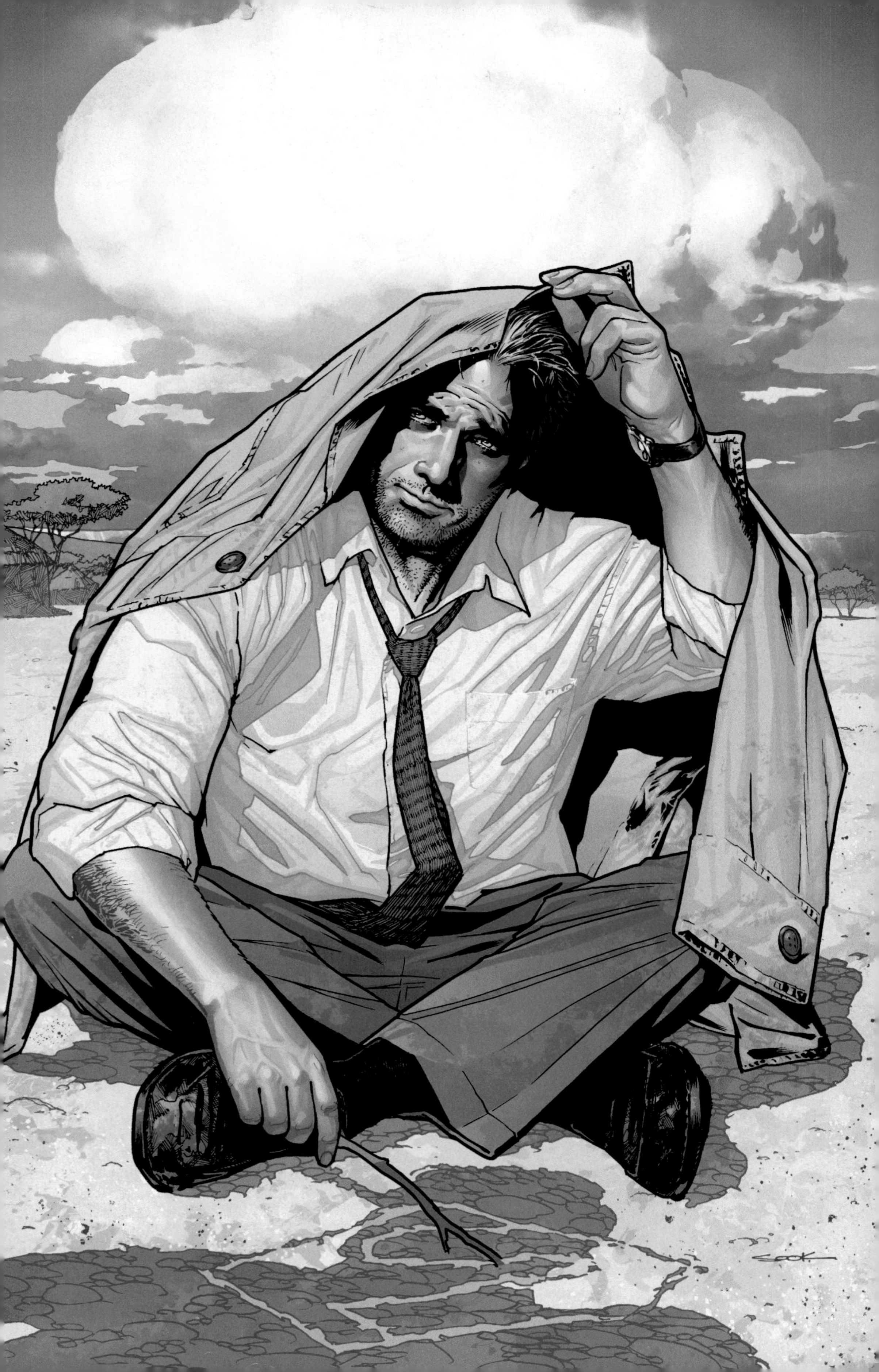

INTO THE FUTURE

WRITERS
- Brian Azzarello
- Jeff Lemire
- Dan Jurgens
- Keith Giffen

PENCILLER
- Georges Jeanty

INKERS
- Dexter Vines
- Karl Story

COLORS
- Hi-Fi

LETTERS
- Taylor Esposito

COVER
- Ryan Sook

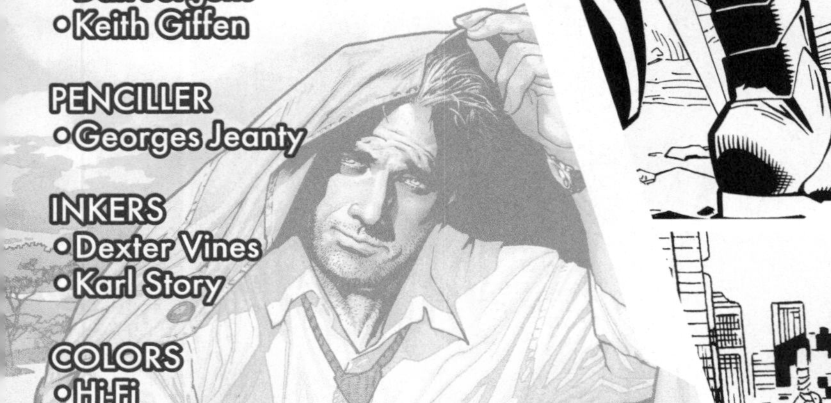

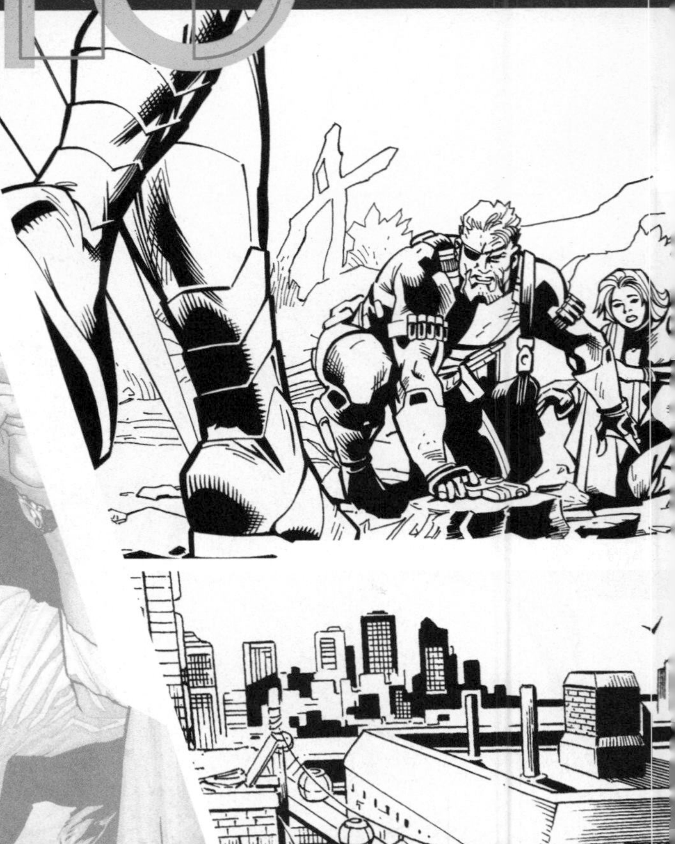

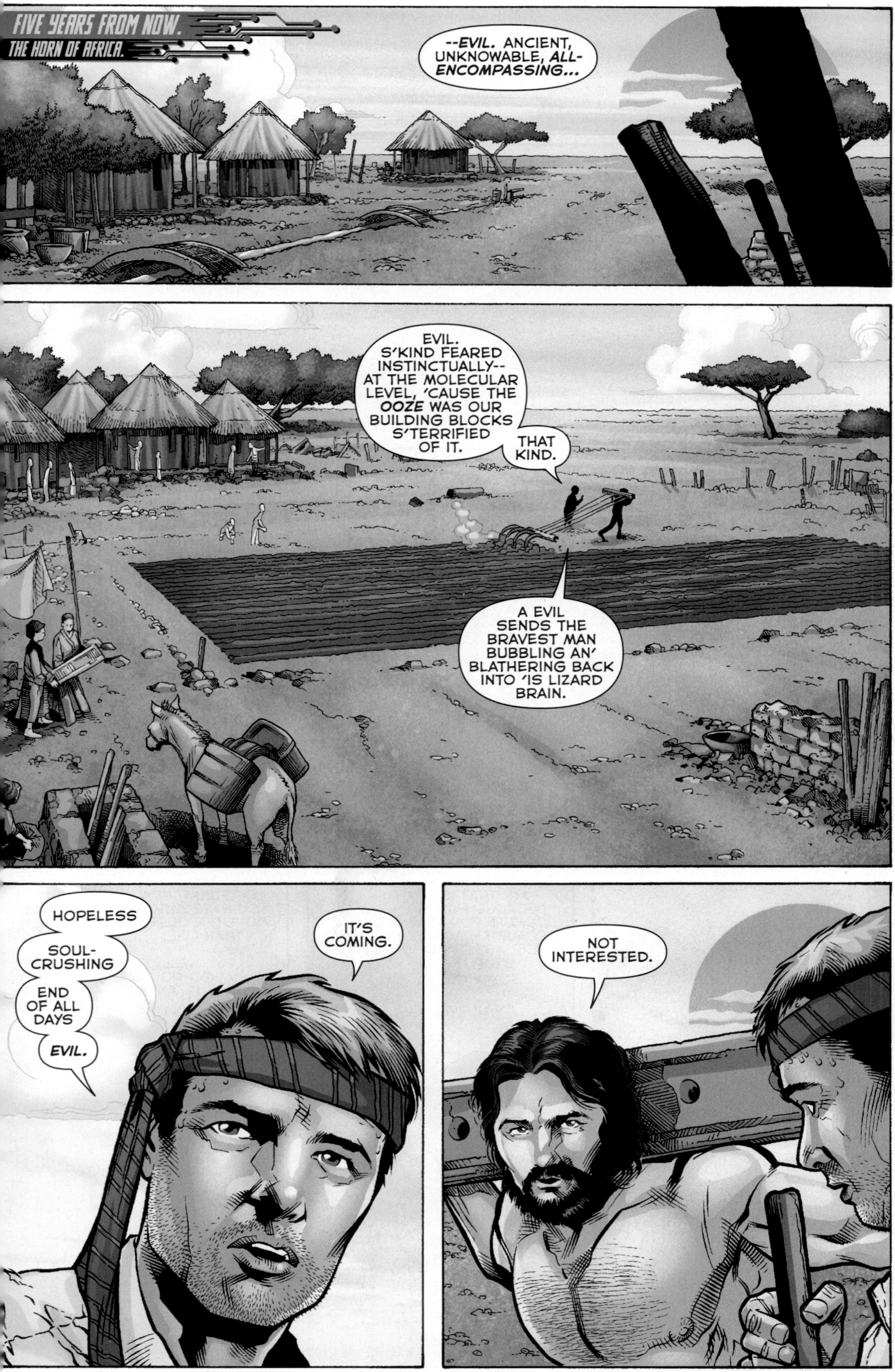
FIVE YEARS FROM NOW.
THE HORN OF AFRICA.
--EVIL. ANCIENT, UNKNOWABLE, ALL-ENCOMPASSING...
EVIL. S'KIND FEARED INSTINCTUALLY-- AT THE MOLECULAR LEVEL, 'CAUSE THE OOZE WAS OUR BUILDING BLOCKS S'TERRIFIED OF IT.
THAT KIND.
A EVIL SENDS THE BRAVEST MAN BUBBLING AN' BLATHERING BACK INTO 'IS LIZARD BRAIN.
HOPELESS
SOUL-CRUSHING
END OF ALL DAYS
EVIL.
IT'S COMING.
NOT INTERESTED.

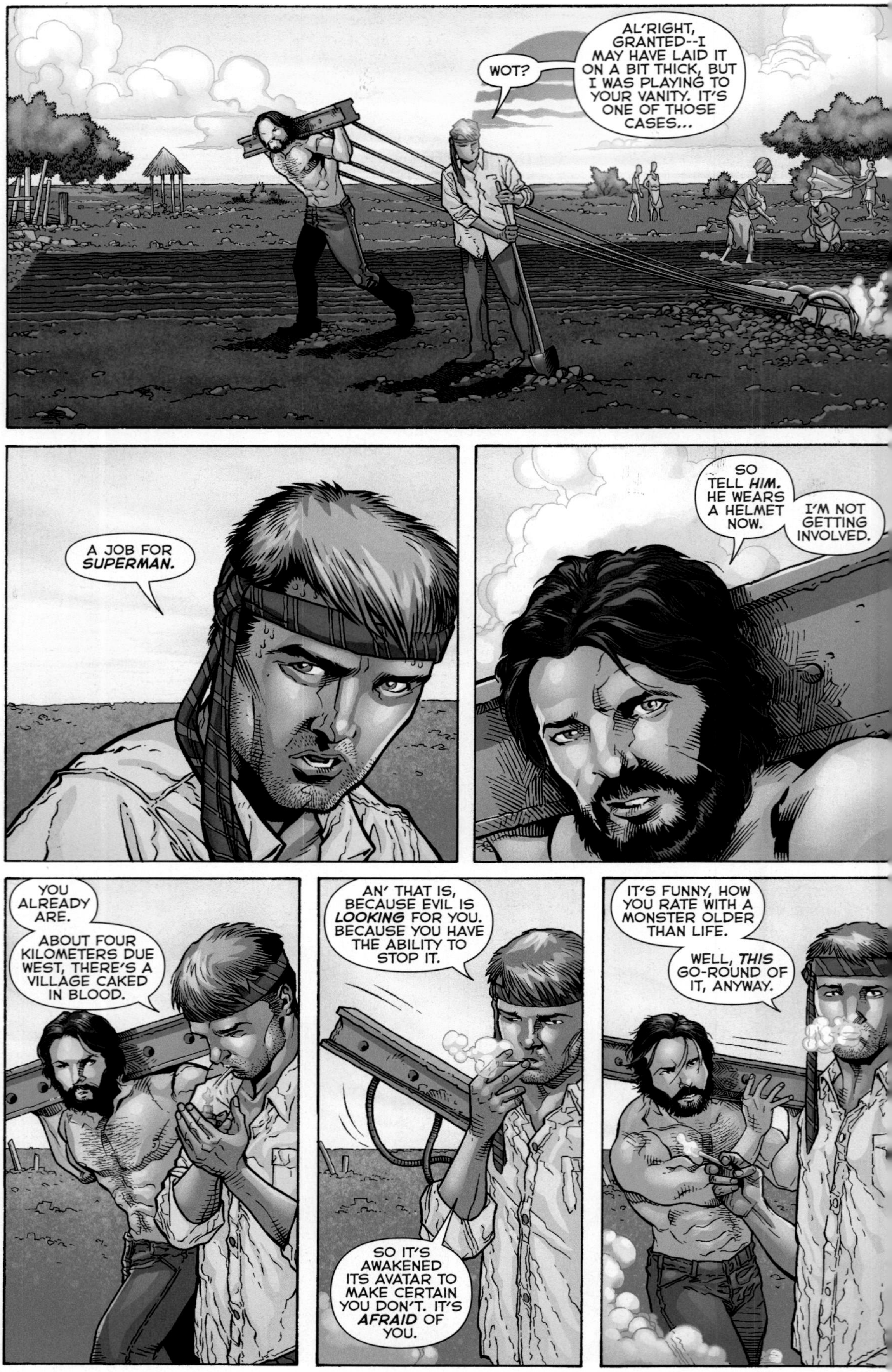
WOT?
AL'RIGHT, GRANTED--I MAY HAVE LAID IT ON A BIT THICK, BUT I WAS PLAYING TO YOUR VANITY. IT'S ONE OF THOSE CASES...
A JOB FOR SUPERMAN.
SO TELL HIM. HE WEARS A HELMET NOW.
I'M NOT GETTING INVOLVED.
YOU ALREADY ARE.
ABOUT FOUR KILOMETERS DUE WEST, THERE'S A VILLAGE CAKED IN BLOOD.
AN' THAT IS, BECAUSE EVIL IS LOOKING FOR YOU. BECAUSE YOU HAVE THE ABILITY TO STOP IT.
SO IT'S AWAKENED ITS AVATAR TO MAKE CERTAIN YOU DON'T. IT'S AFRAID OF YOU.
IT'S FUNNY, HOW YOU RATE WITH A MONSTER OLDER THAN LIFE.
WELL, THIS GO-ROUND OF IT, ANYWAY.

I'VE SEEN WORSE.

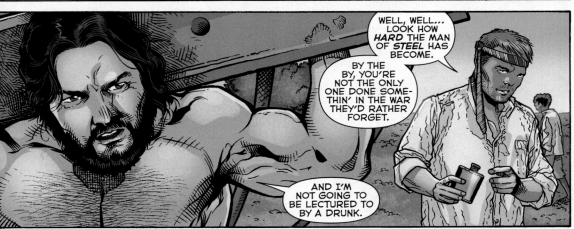

WELL, WELL... LOOK HOW *HARD* THE MAN OF *STEEL* HAS BECOME.

BY THE BY, YOU'RE NOT THE ONLY ONE DONE SOME-THIN' IN THE WAR THEY'D RATHER FORGET.

AND I'M NOT GOING TO BE LECTURED TO BY A DRUNK.

OH, I APOLOGIZE IF *MY COPING MECHANISM* ISN'T AS NOBLE AS YOURS.

SO *HERE'S* TO...

TURNING YOUR BACK ON THE WORLD.

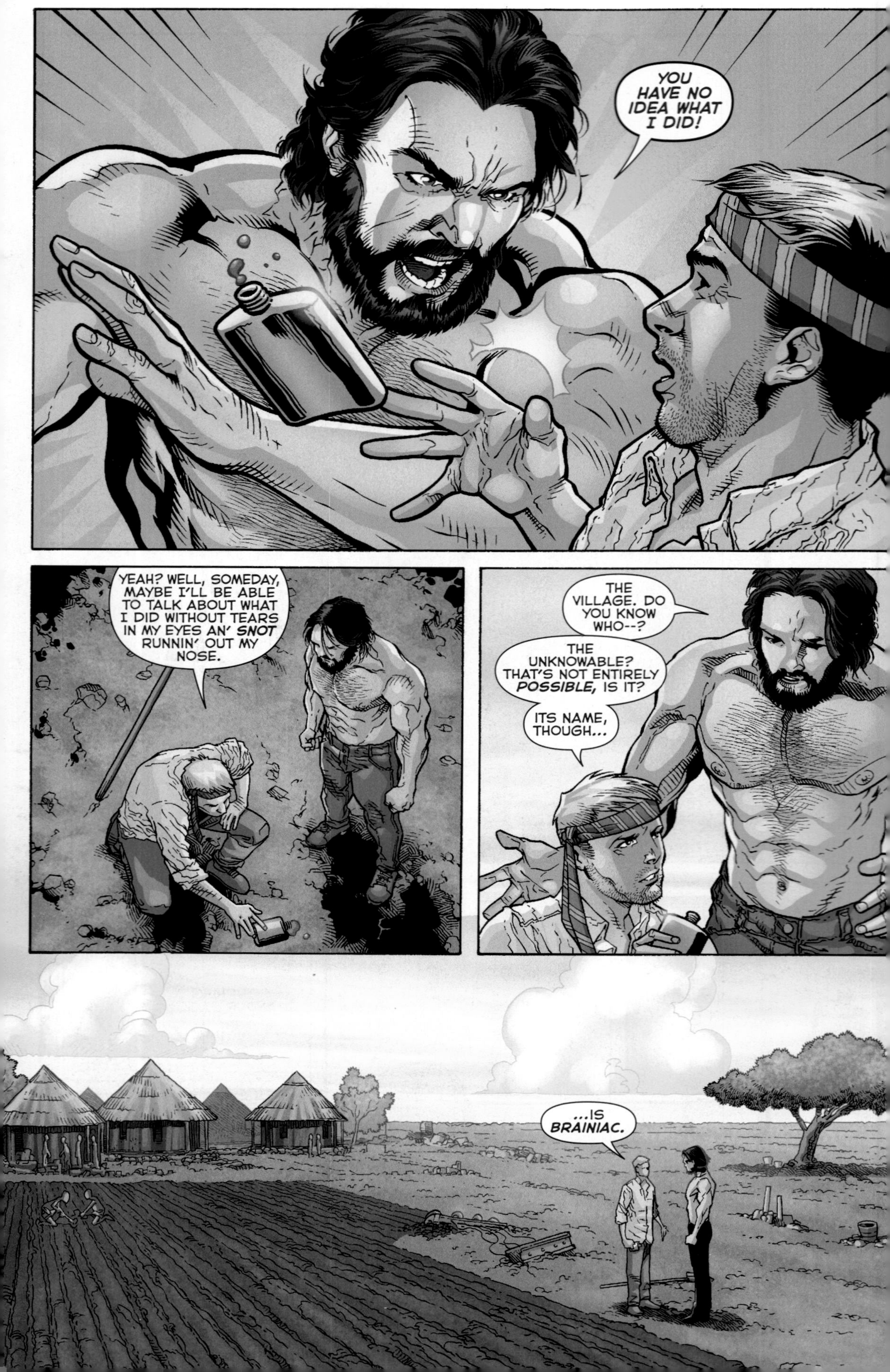
YOU HAVE NO IDEA WHAT I DID!
YEAH? WELL, SOMEDAY, MAYBE I'LL BE ABLE TO TALK ABOUT WHAT I DID WITHOUT TEARS IN MY EYES AN' SNOT RUNNIN' OUT MY NOSE.
THE VILLAGE. DO YOU KNOW WHO--?
THE UNKNOWABLE? THAT'S NOT ENTIRELY POSSIBLE, IS IT?
ITS NAME, THOUGH...
...IS BRAINIAC.

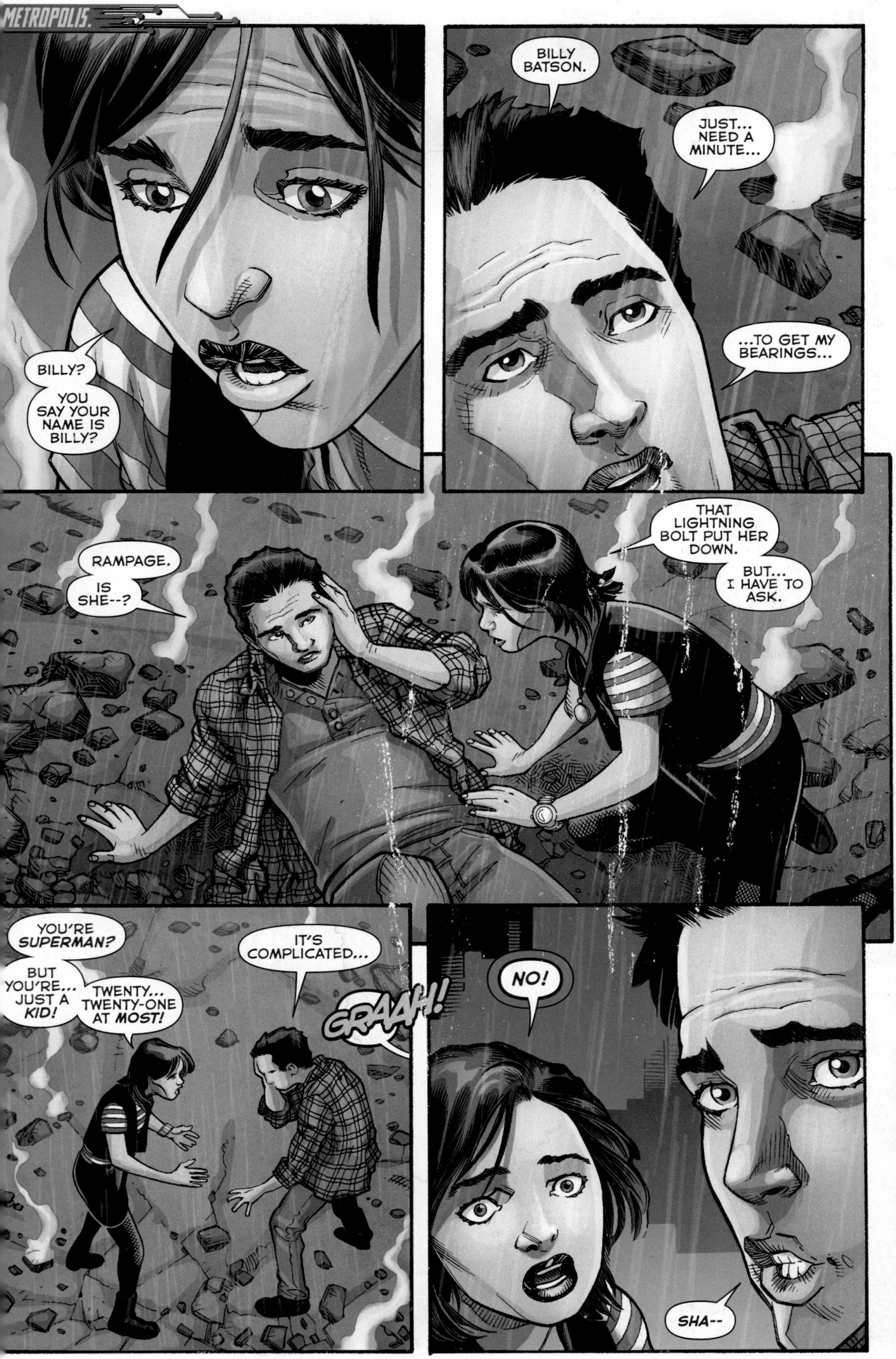
METROPOLIS.
BILLY?
YOU SAY YOUR NAME IS BILLY?
BILLY BATSON.
JUST... NEED A MINUTE...
...TO GET MY BEARINGS...
RAMPAGE.
IS SHE--?
THAT LIGHTNING BOLT PUT HER DOWN.
BUT... I HAVE TO ASK.
YOU'RE SUPERMAN?
BUT YOU'RE... JUST A KID!
TWENTY... TWENTY-ONE AT MOST!
IT'S COMPLICATED...
GRAAH!
NO!
SHA--

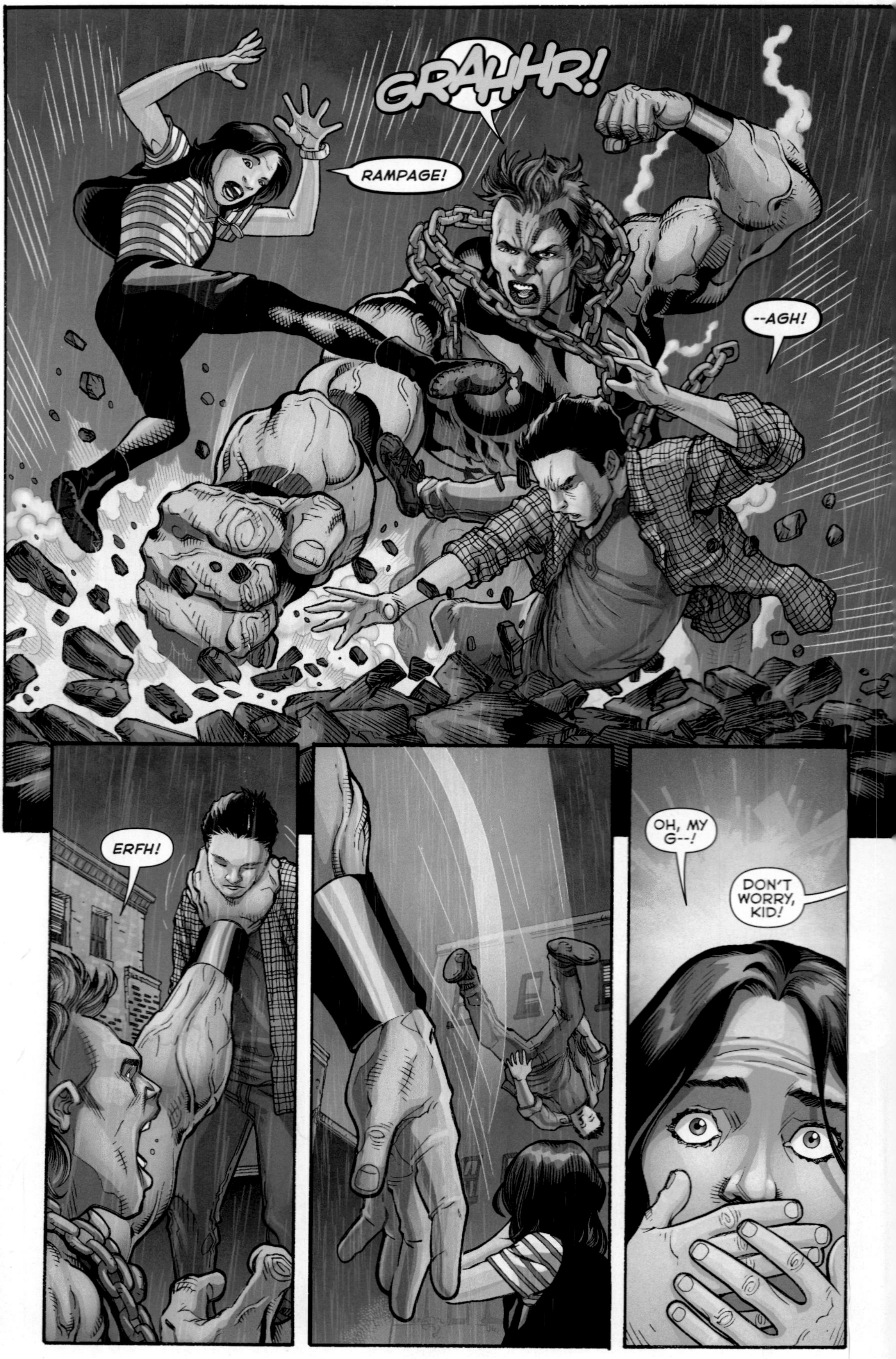
GRAHHR!
RAMPAGE!
--AGH!
ERFH!
OH, MY G--!
DON'T WORRY, KID!

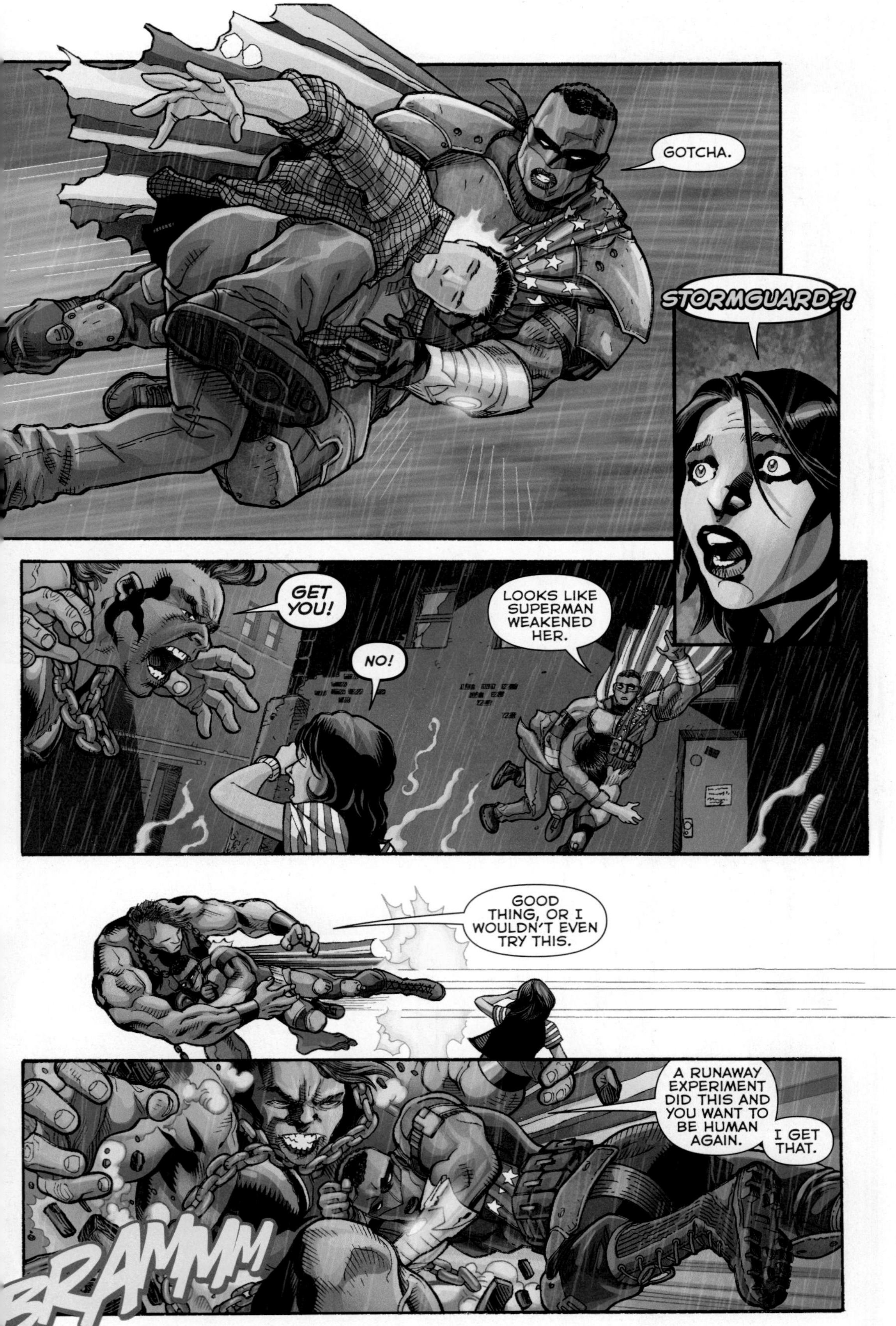
GOTCHA.
STORMGUARD?!
GET YOU!
NO!
LOOKS LIKE SUPERMAN WEAKENED HER.
GOOD THING, OR I WOULDN'T EVEN TRY THIS.
A RUNAWAY EXPERIMENT DID THIS AND YOU WANT TO BE HUMAN AGAIN.
I GET THAT.
BRAMMM

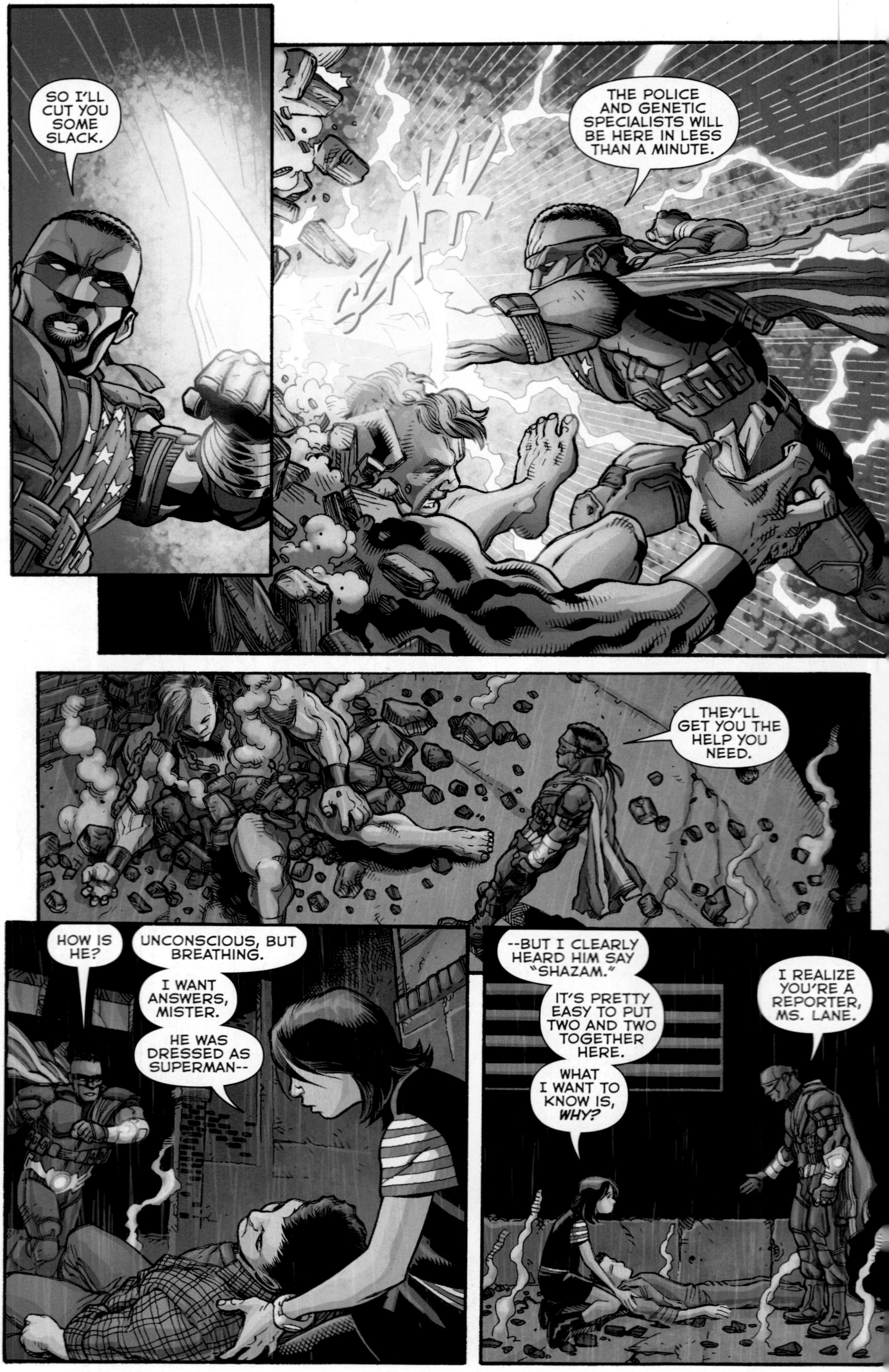
SO I'LL CUT YOU SOME SLACK.
THE POLICE AND GENETIC SPECIALISTS WILL BE HERE IN LESS THAN A MINUTE.
THEY'LL GET YOU THE HELP YOU NEED.
HOW IS HE?
UNCONSCIOUS, BUT BREATHING.
I WANT ANSWERS, MISTER.
HE WAS DRESSED AS SUPERMAN--
--BUT I CLEARLY HEARD HIM SAY "SHAZAM."
IT'S PRETTY EASY TO PUT TWO AND TWO TOGETHER HERE.
WHAT I WANT TO KNOW IS, *WHY?*
I REALIZE YOU'RE A REPORTER, MS. LANE.

BUT THERE ARE SOME STORIES YOU RUN--

--AND SOME YOU DON'T.

THIS IS ONE WHERE I'M HOPING YOU *DON'T*.

ARE YOU *SERIOUS?!*

22,300 MILES OVER EARTH.
JUSTICE LEAGUE DEFENSE STATION OMEGA.

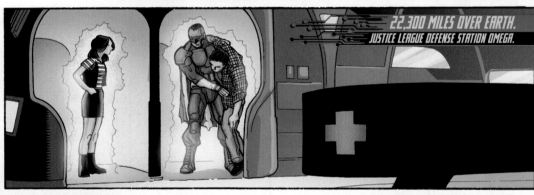

SUBJECT-- BILLY BATSON.

UNCONSCIOUS. SIGNS OF PHYSICAL TRAUMA.

WE NEED A FULL DIAGNOSTIC.

PROCESSING.

WHERE--?

OH.

THE FIRST AMENDMENT GUARANTEES MY RIGHT TO REPORT THIS STORY, YOU KNOW.

THOSE OF US WHO FOUGHT FOR THIS COUNTRY AND EVERY IDEAL IT HOLDS DEAR ARE AWARE OF THAT, MS. LANE.

SORRY. BUT THIS IS *NEWS* AND YOU HAVE NO *RIGHT* TO SIT ON IT!

CONSIDER THE DOWN-SIDE.

IT'S BEEN DETERMINED THAT THE WORLD NEEDS A SUPERMAN.

DON'T TAKE THAT AWAY.

BUT IF HE'S NOT SUPERMAN...

...WHERE'S THE REAL ONE?

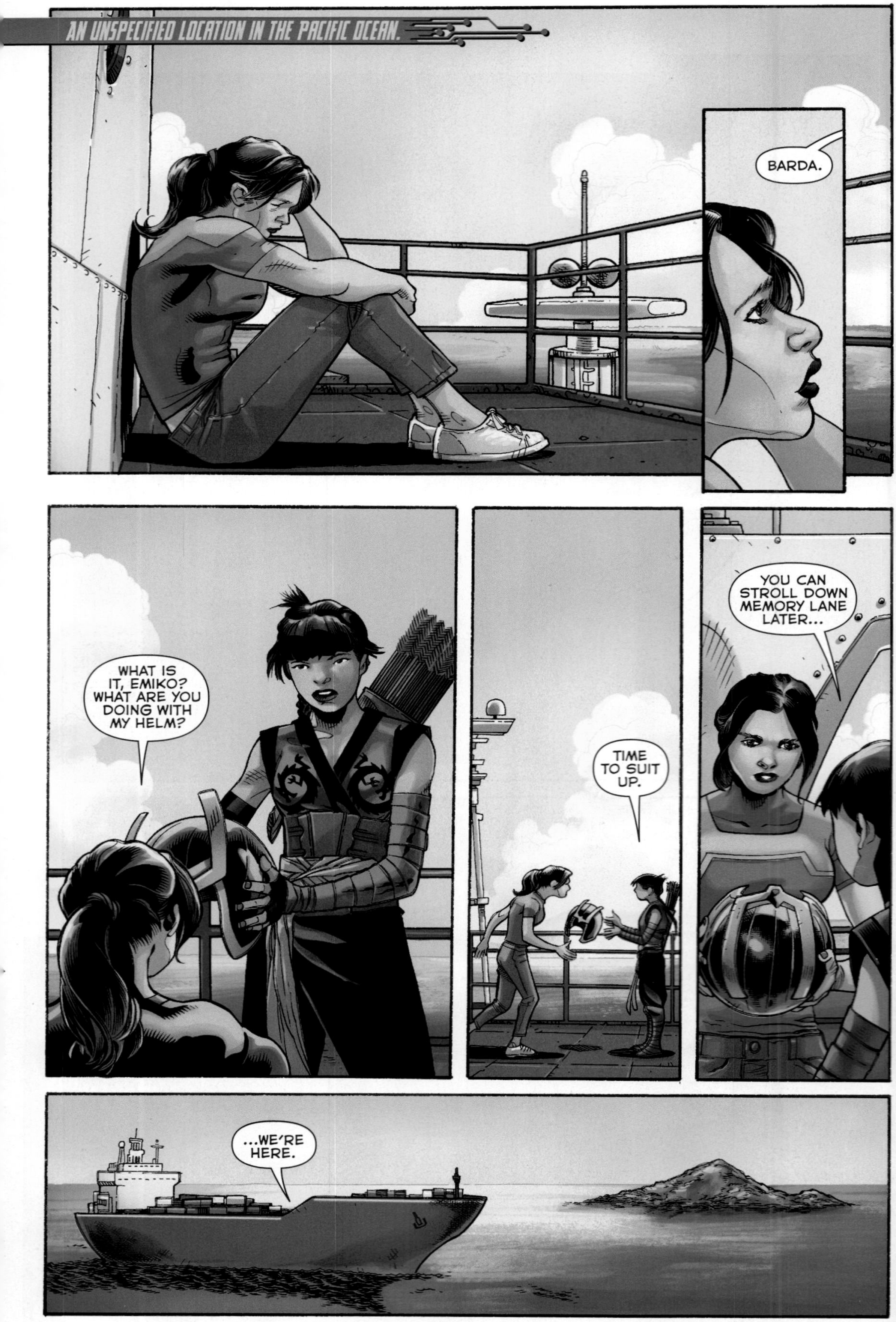
AN UNSPECIFIED LOCATION IN THE PACIFIC OCEAN.
BARDA.
WHAT IS IT, EMIKO? WHAT ARE YOU DOING WITH MY HELM?
TIME TO SUIT UP.
YOU CAN STROLL DOWN MEMORY LANE LATER...
...WE'RE HERE.

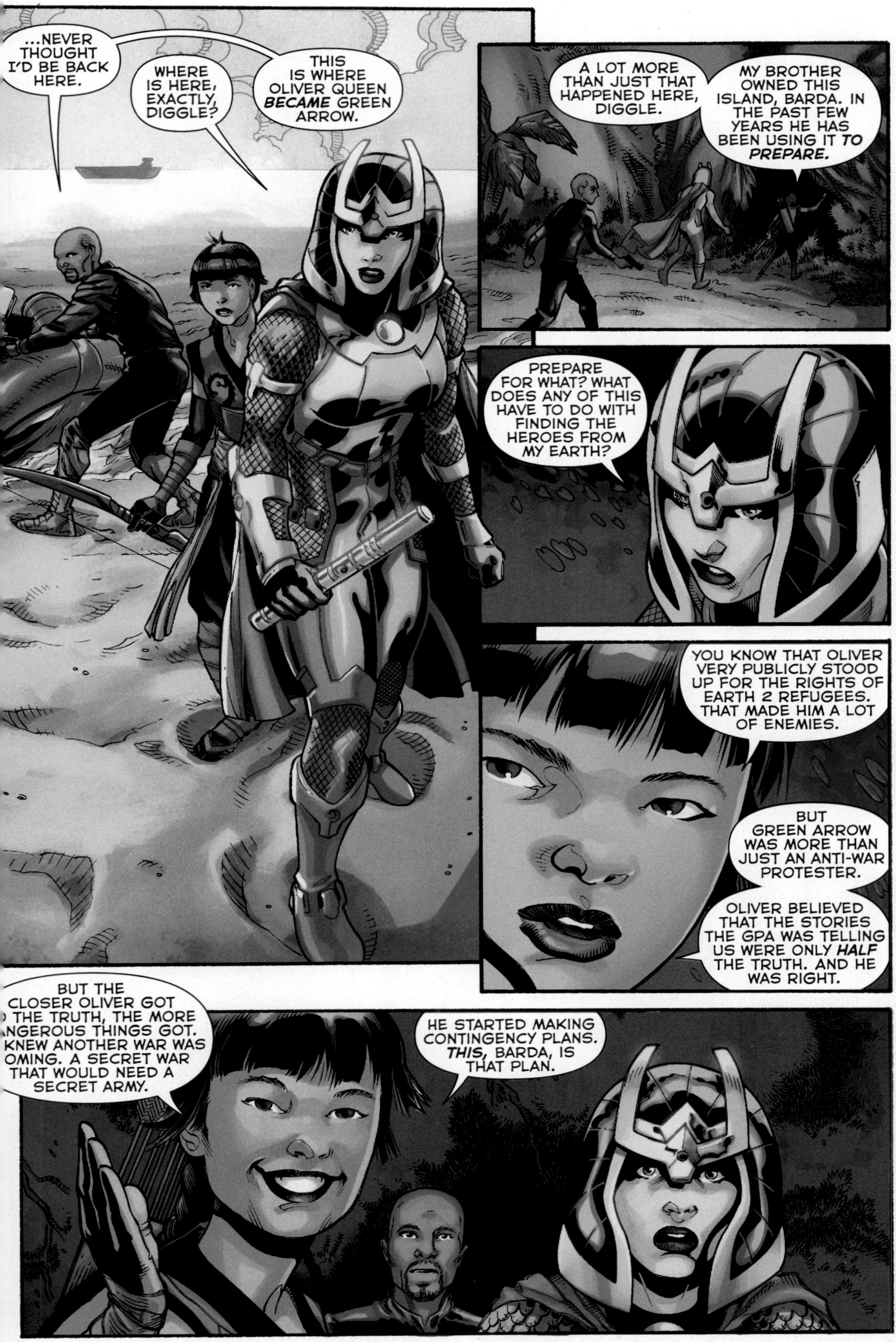
...NEVER THOUGHT I'D BE BACK HERE.
WHERE IS HERE, EXACTLY, DIGGLE?
THIS IS WHERE OLIVER QUEEN BECAME GREEN ARROW.
A LOT MORE THAN JUST THAT HAPPENED HERE, DIGGLE.
MY BROTHER OWNED THIS ISLAND, BARDA. IN THE PAST FEW YEARS HE HAS BEEN USING IT TO PREPARE.
PREPARE FOR WHAT? WHAT DOES ANY OF THIS HAVE TO DO WITH FINDING THE HEROES FROM MY EARTH?
YOU KNOW THAT OLIVER VERY PUBLICLY STOOD UP FOR THE RIGHTS OF EARTH 2 REFUGEES. THAT MADE HIM A LOT OF ENEMIES.
BUT GREEN ARROW WAS MORE THAN JUST AN ANTI-WAR PROTESTER.
OLIVER BELIEVED THAT THE STORIES THE GPA WAS TELLING US WERE ONLY HALF THE TRUTH. AND HE WAS RIGHT.
BUT THE CLOSER OLIVER GOT TO THE TRUTH, THE MORE DANGEROUS THINGS GOT. HE KNEW ANOTHER WAR WAS COMING. A SECRET WAR THAT WOULD NEED A SECRET ARMY.
HE STARTED MAKING CONTINGENCY PLANS. THIS, BARDA, IS THAT PLAN.

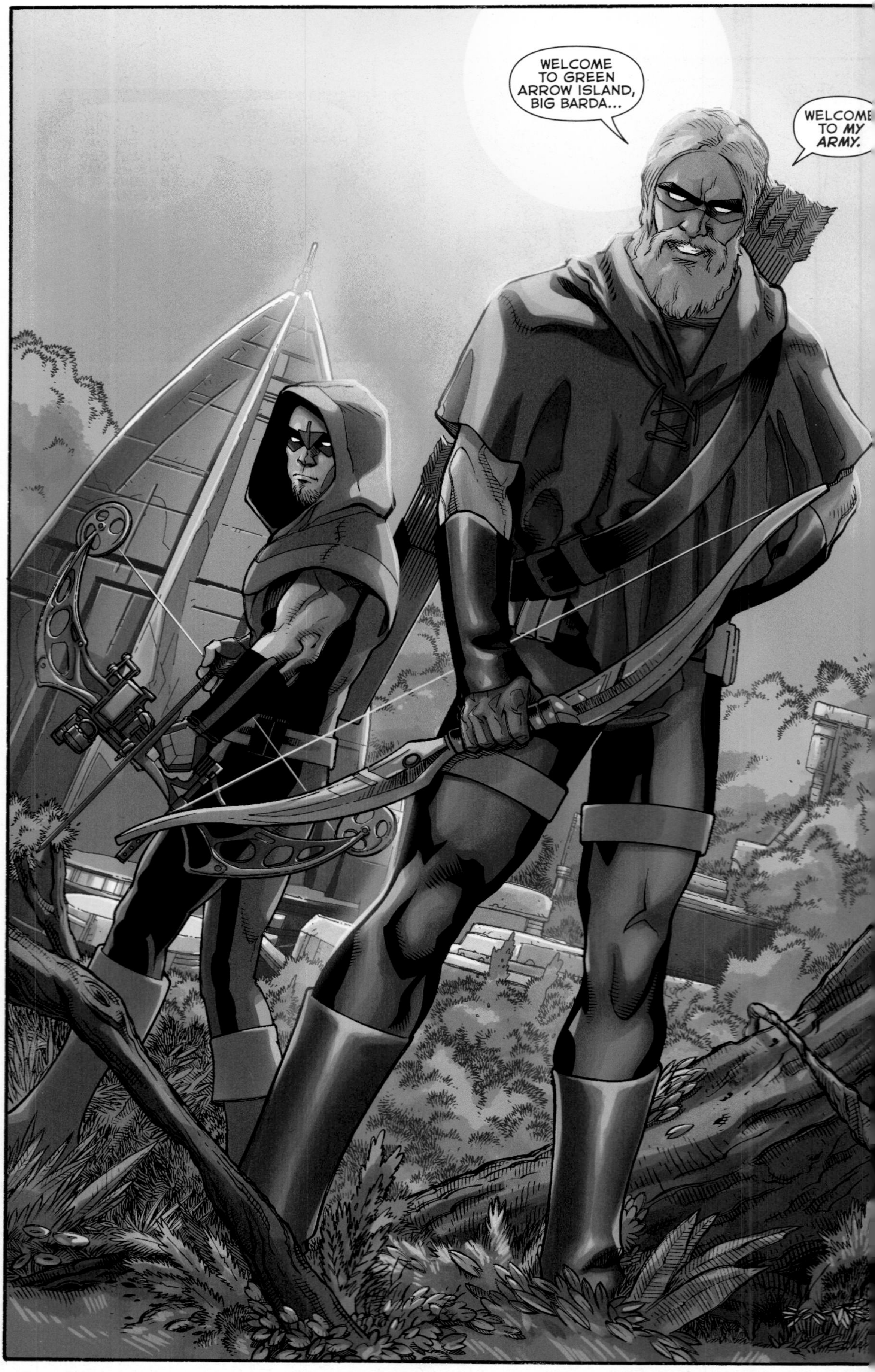
WELCOME TO GREEN ARROW ISLAND, BIG BARDA...
WELCOME TO MY ARMY.

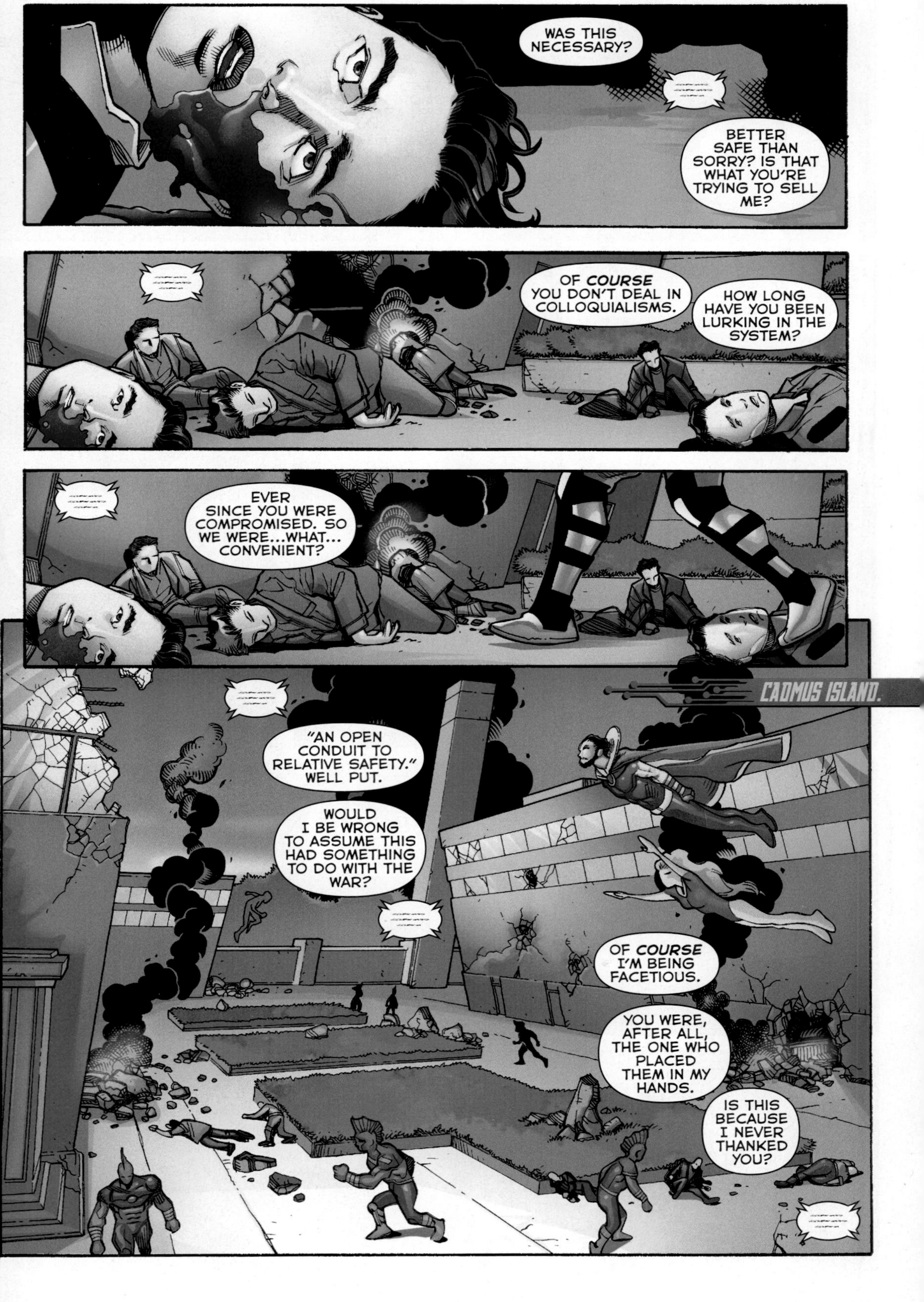
WAS THIS NECESSARY?
BETTER SAFE THAN SORRY? IS THAT WHAT YOU'RE TRYING TO SELL ME?
OF COURSE YOU DON'T DEAL IN COLLOQUIALISMS.
HOW LONG HAVE YOU BEEN LURKING IN THE SYSTEM?
EVER SINCE YOU WERE COMPROMISED. SO WE WERE...WHAT... CONVENIENT?
CADMUS ISLAND.
"AN OPEN CONDUIT TO RELATIVE SAFETY." WELL PUT.
WOULD I BE WRONG TO ASSUME THIS HAD SOMETHING TO DO WITH THE WAR?
OF COURSE I'M BEING FACETIOUS.
YOU WERE, AFTER ALL, THE ONE WHO PLACED THEM IN MY HANDS.
IS THIS BECAUSE I NEVER THANKED YOU?

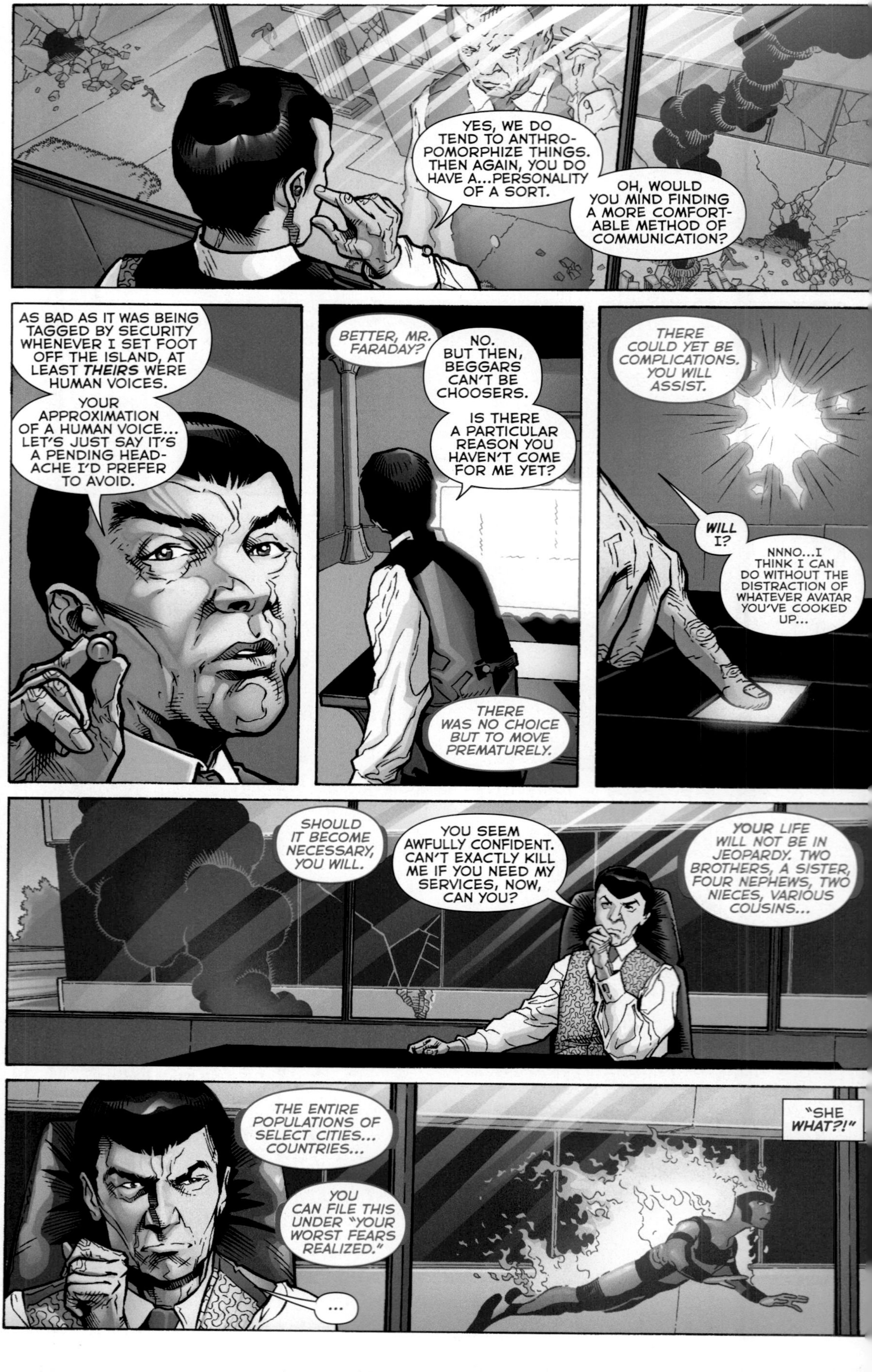
YES, WE DO TEND TO ANTHRO-POMORPHIZE THINGS. THEN AGAIN, YOU DO HAVE A...PERSONALITY OF A SORT.
OH, WOULD YOU MIND FINDING A MORE COMFORT-ABLE METHOD OF COMMUNICATION?
AS BAD AS IT WAS BEING TAGGED BY SECURITY WHENEVER I SET FOOT OFF THE ISLAND, AT LEAST THEIRS WERE HUMAN VOICES.
YOUR APPROXIMATION OF A HUMAN VOICE... LET'S JUST SAY IT'S A PENDING HEAD-ACHE I'D PREFER TO AVOID.
BETTER, MR. FARADAY?
NO. BUT THEN, BEGGARS CAN'T BE CHOOSERS.
IS THERE A PARTICULAR REASON YOU HAVEN'T COME FOR ME YET?
THERE WAS NO CHOICE BUT TO MOVE PREMATURELY.
THERE COULD YET BE COMPLICATIONS. YOU WILL ASSIST.
WILL I?
NNNO...I THINK I CAN DO WITHOUT THE DISTRACTION OF WHATEVER AVATAR YOU'VE COOKED UP...
SHOULD IT BECOME NECESSARY, YOU WILL.
YOU SEEM AWFULLY CONFIDENT. CAN'T EXACTLY KILL ME IF YOU NEED MY SERVICES, NOW, CAN YOU?
YOUR LIFE WILL NOT BE IN JEOPARDY. TWO BROTHERS, A SISTER, FOUR NEPHEWS, TWO NIECES, VARIOUS COUSINS...
THE ENTIRE POPULATIONS OF SELECT CITIES... COUNTRIES...
YOU CAN FILE THIS UNDER "YOUR WORST FEARS REALIZED."
...
"SHE WHAT?!"

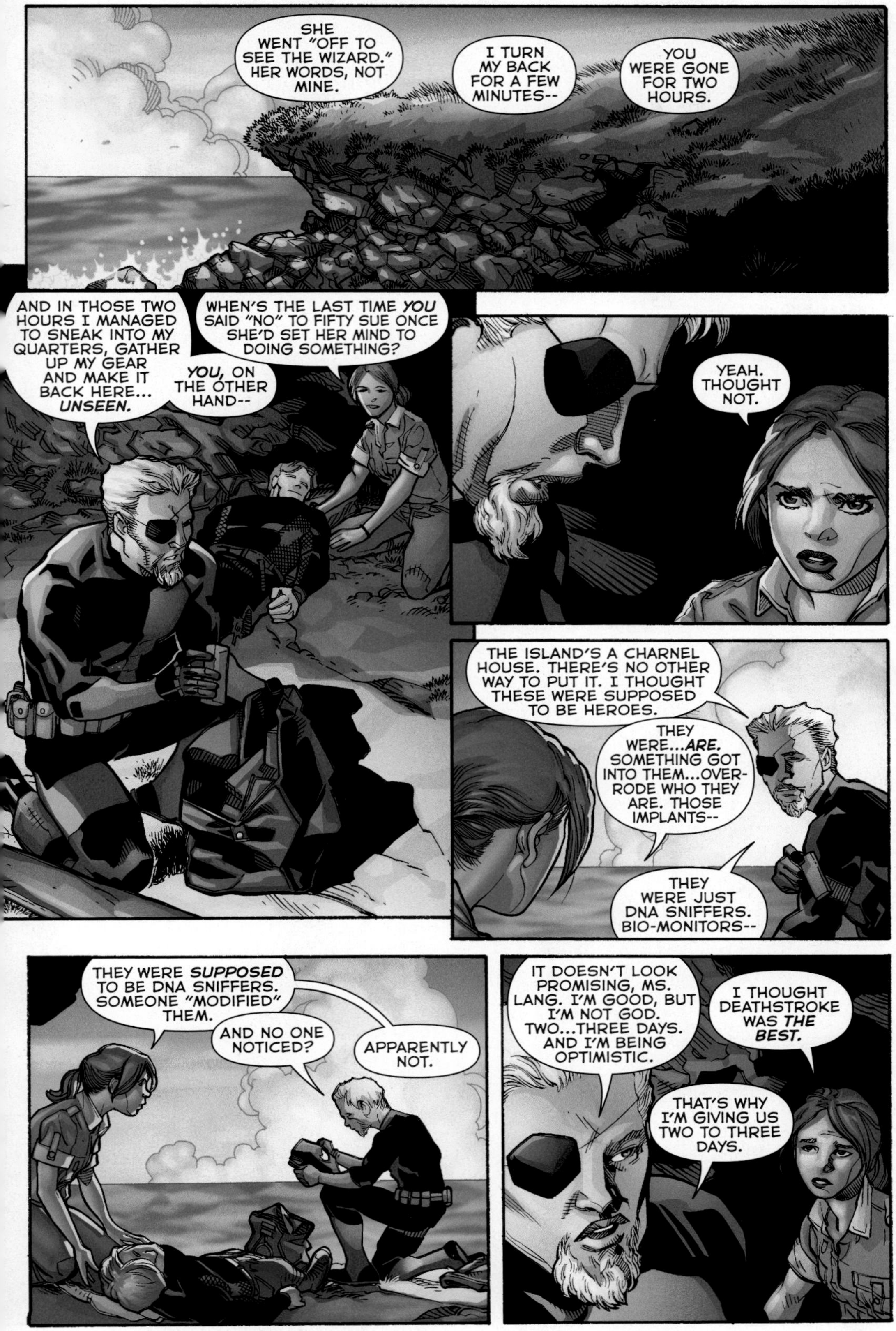
SHE WENT "OFF TO SEE THE WIZARD." HER WORDS, NOT MINE.
I TURN MY BACK FOR A FEW MINUTES--
YOU WERE GONE FOR TWO HOURS.
AND IN THOSE TWO HOURS I MANAGED TO SNEAK INTO MY QUARTERS, GATHER UP MY GEAR AND MAKE IT BACK HERE... UNSEEN.
YOU, ON THE OTHER HAND--
WHEN'S THE LAST TIME YOU SAID "NO" TO FIFTY SUE ONCE SHE'D SET HER MIND TO DOING SOMETHING?
YEAH. THOUGHT NOT.
THE ISLAND'S A CHARNEL HOUSE. THERE'S NO OTHER WAY TO PUT IT. I THOUGHT THESE WERE SUPPOSED TO BE HEROES.
THEY WERE...ARE. SOMETHING GOT INTO THEM...OVERRODE WHO THEY ARE. THOSE IMPLANTS--
THEY WERE JUST DNA SNIFFERS. BIO-MONITORS--
THEY WERE SUPPOSED TO BE DNA SNIFFERS. SOMEONE "MODIFIED" THEM.
AND NO ONE NOTICED?
APPARENTLY NOT.
IT DOESN'T LOOK PROMISING, MS. LANG. I'M GOOD, BUT I'M NOT GOD. TWO...THREE DAYS. AND I'M BEING OPTIMISTIC.
I THOUGHT DEATHSTROKE WAS THE BEST.
THAT'S WHY I'M GIVING US TWO TO THREE DAYS.

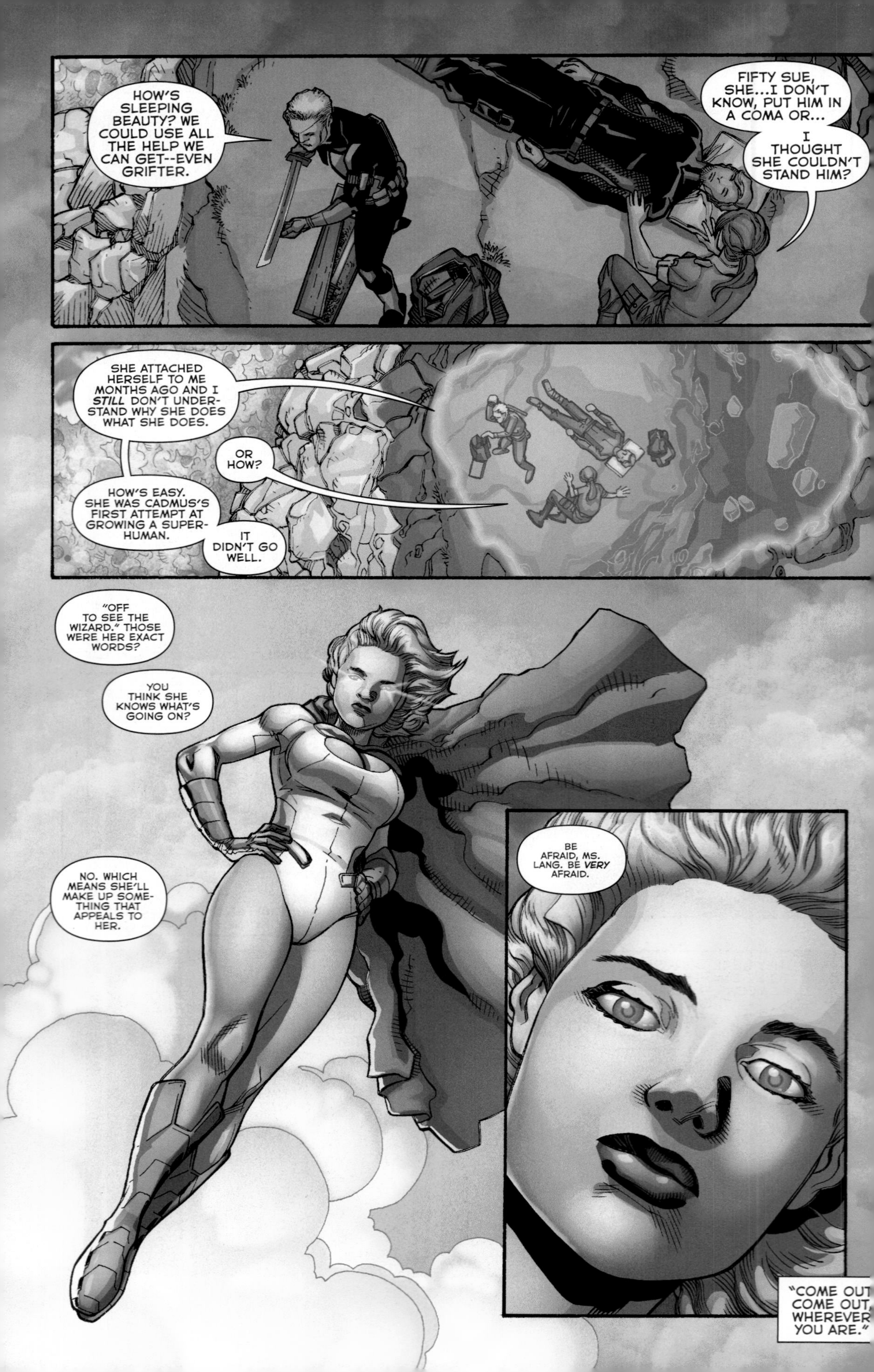
HOW'S SLEEPING BEAUTY? WE COULD USE ALL THE HELP WE CAN GET--EVEN GRIFTER.
FIFTY SUE, SHE...I DON'T KNOW, PUT HIM IN A COMA OR...
I THOUGHT SHE COULDN'T STAND HIM?
SHE ATTACHED HERSELF TO ME MONTHS AGO AND I *STILL* DON'T UNDERSTAND WHY SHE DOES WHAT SHE DOES.
OR HOW?
HOW'S EASY. SHE WAS CADMUS'S FIRST ATTEMPT AT GROWING A SUPER-HUMAN.
IT DIDN'T GO WELL.
"OFF TO SEE THE WIZARD." THOSE WERE HER EXACT WORDS?
YOU THINK SHE KNOWS WHAT'S GOING ON?
NO. WHICH MEANS SHE'LL MAKE UP SOMETHING THAT APPEALS TO HER.
BE AFRAID, MS. LANG. BE *VERY* AFRAID.
"COME OUT, COME OUT, WHEREVER YOU ARE."

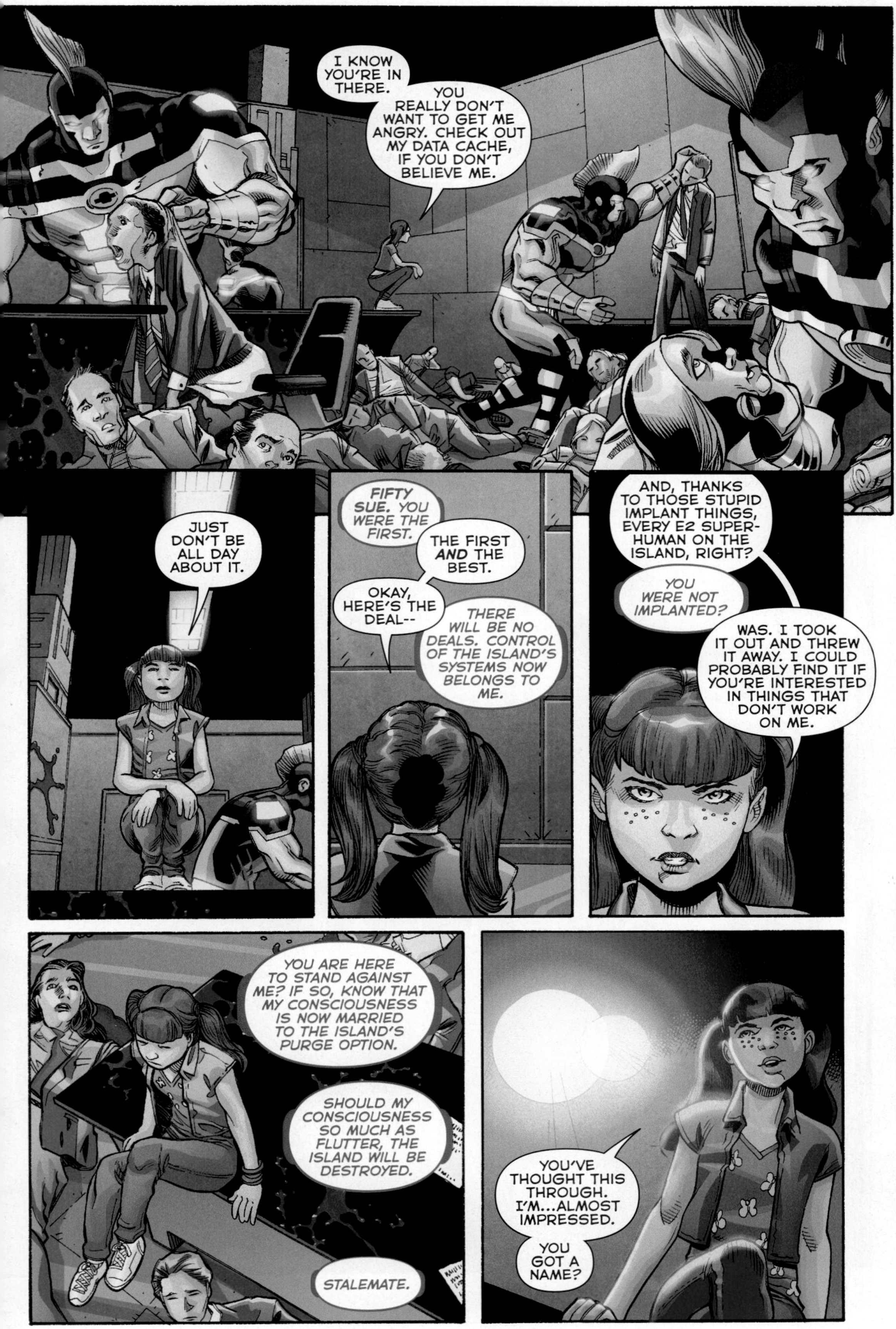
I KNOW YOU'RE IN THERE.
YOU REALLY DON'T WANT TO GET ME ANGRY. CHECK OUT MY DATA CACHE, IF YOU DON'T BELIEVE ME.
JUST DON'T BE ALL DAY ABOUT IT.
FIFTY SUE. YOU WERE THE FIRST.
THE FIRST AND THE BEST.
OKAY, HERE'S THE DEAL--
THERE WILL BE NO DEALS. CONTROL OF THE ISLAND'S SYSTEMS NOW BELONGS TO ME.
AND, THANKS TO THOSE STUPID IMPLANT THINGS, EVERY E2 SUPER-HUMAN ON THE ISLAND, RIGHT?
YOU WERE NOT IMPLANTED?
WAS. I TOOK IT OUT AND THREW IT AWAY. I COULD PROBABLY FIND IT IF YOU'RE INTERESTED IN THINGS THAT DON'T WORK ON ME.
YOU ARE HERE TO STAND AGAINST ME? IF SO, KNOW THAT MY CONSCIOUSNESS IS NOW MARRIED TO THE ISLAND'S PURGE OPTION.
SHOULD MY CONSCIOUSNESS SO MUCH AS FLUTTER, THE ISLAND WILL BE DESTROYED.
STALEMATE.
YOU'VE THOUGHT THIS THROUGH. I'M...ALMOST IMPRESSED.
YOU GOT A NAME?

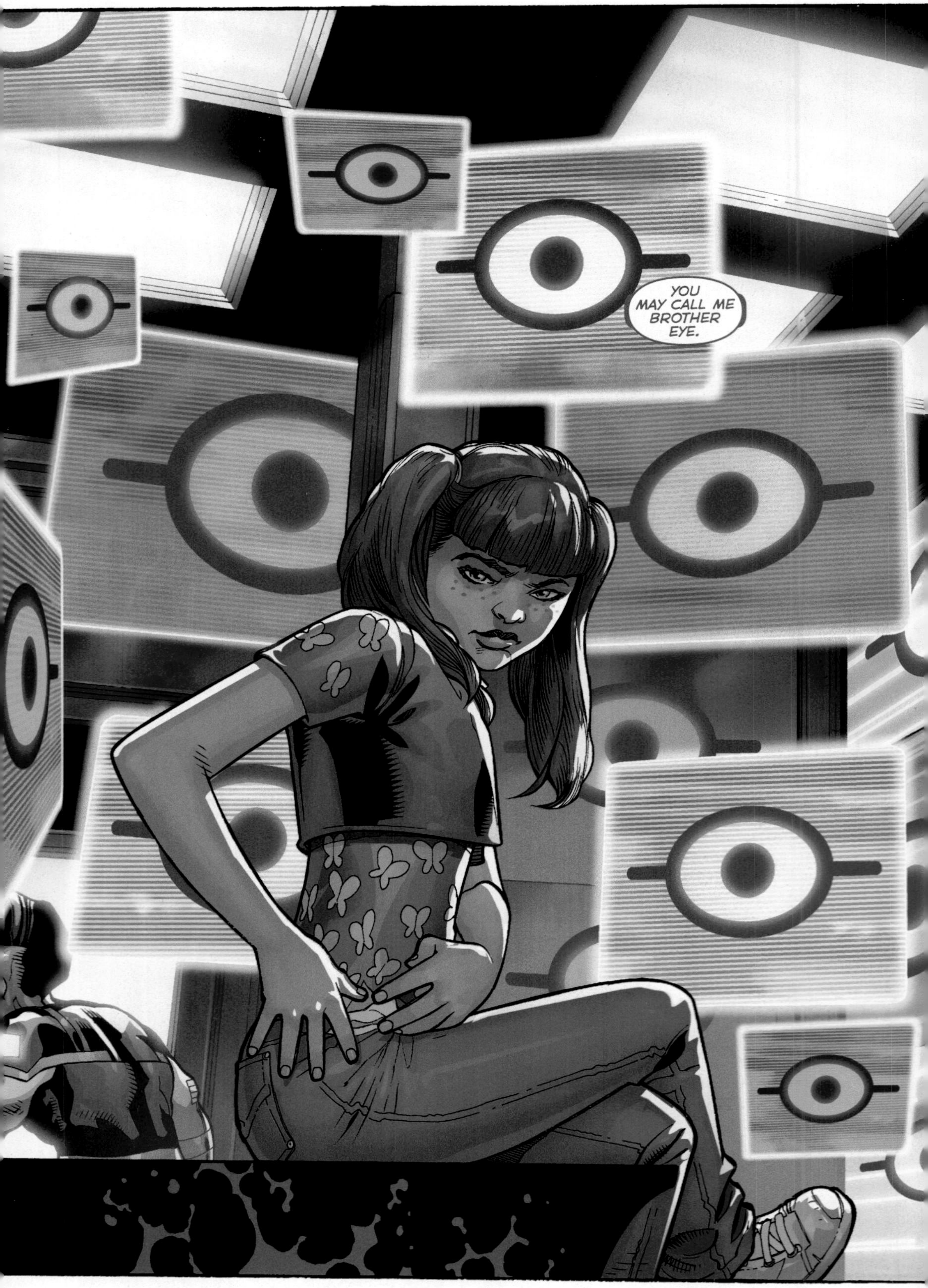
YOU MAY CALL ME BROTHER EYE.

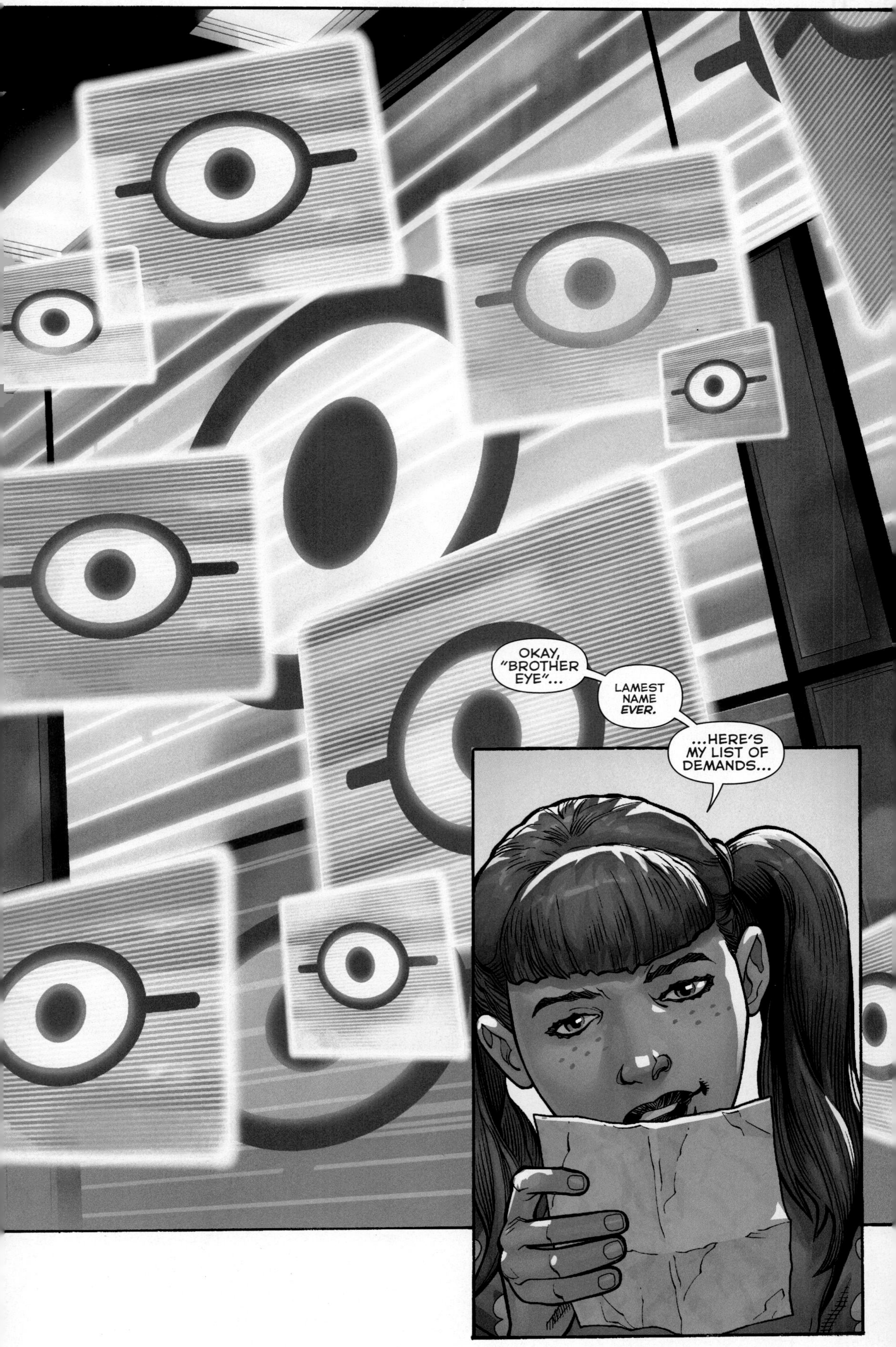
OKAY, "BROTHER EYE"...
LAMEST NAME *EVER*.
...HERE'S MY LIST OF DEMANDS...

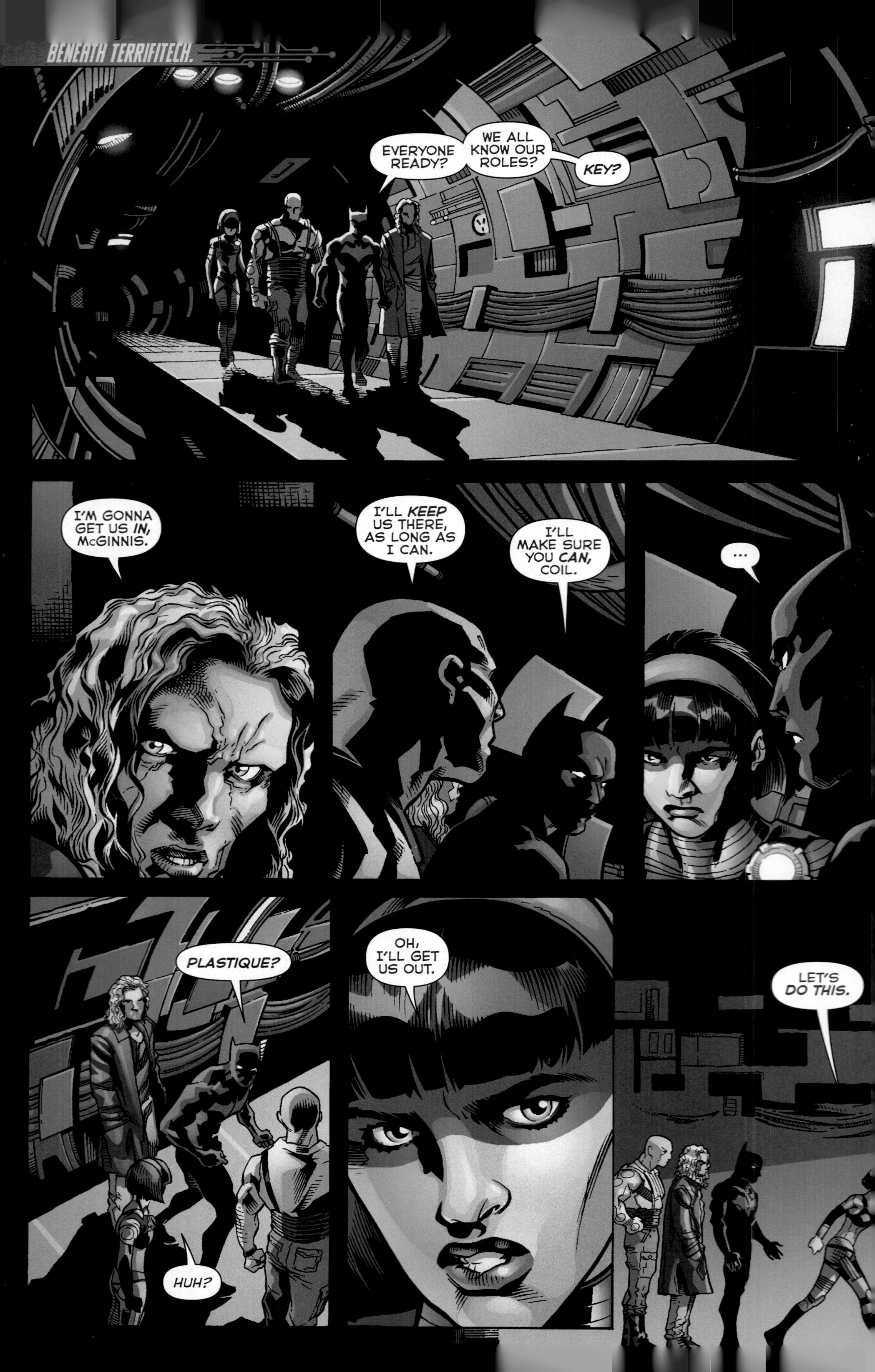
BENEATH TERRIFITECH.
EVERYONE READY?
WE ALL KNOW OUR ROLES?
KEY?
I'M GONNA GET US IN, McGINNIS.
I'LL KEEP US THERE, AS LONG AS I CAN.
I'LL MAKE SURE YOU CAN, COIL.
...
PLASTIQUE?
HUH?
OH, I'LL GET US OUT.
LET'S DO THIS.

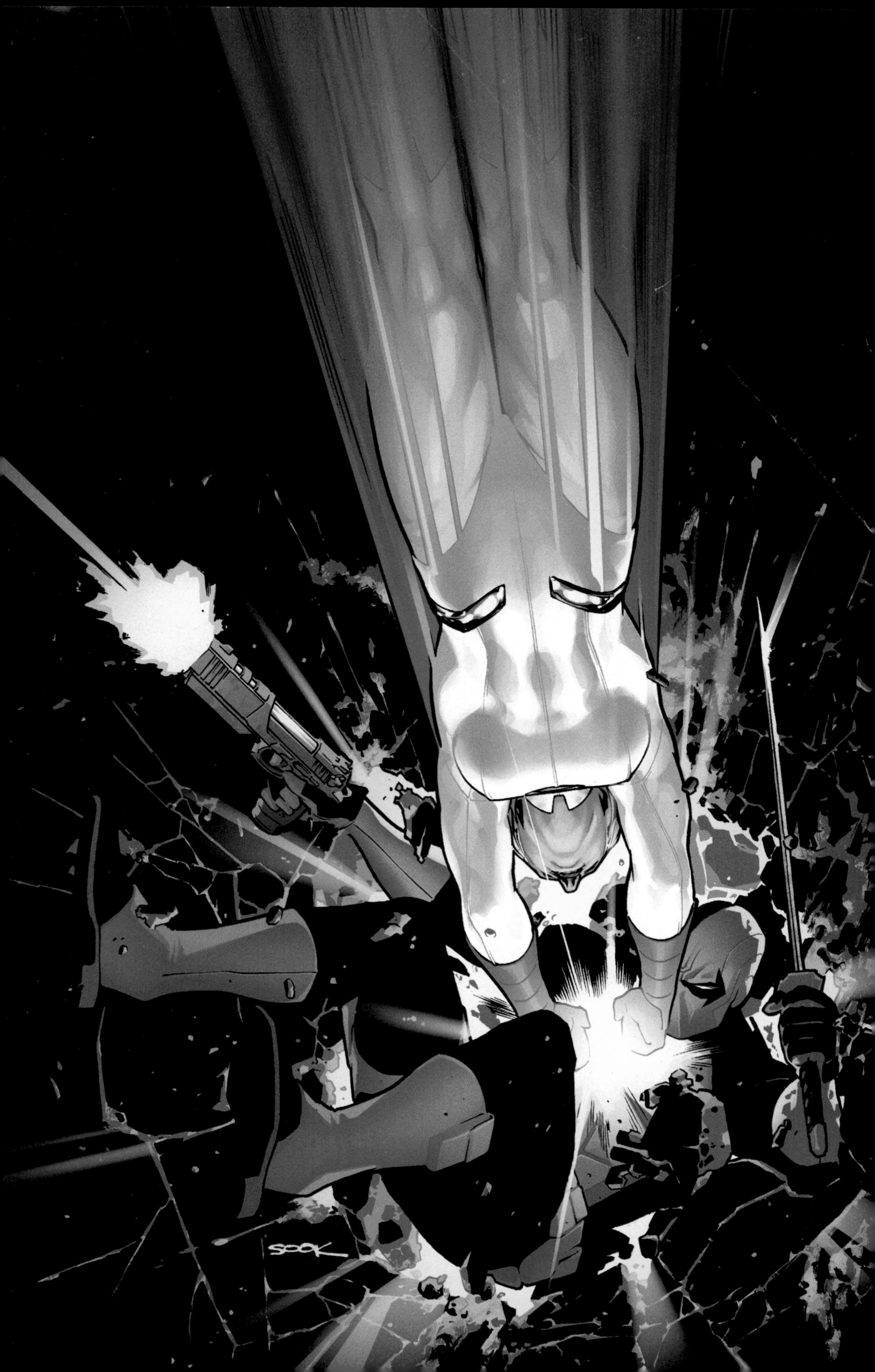
SOOK

INTO THE FUTUR

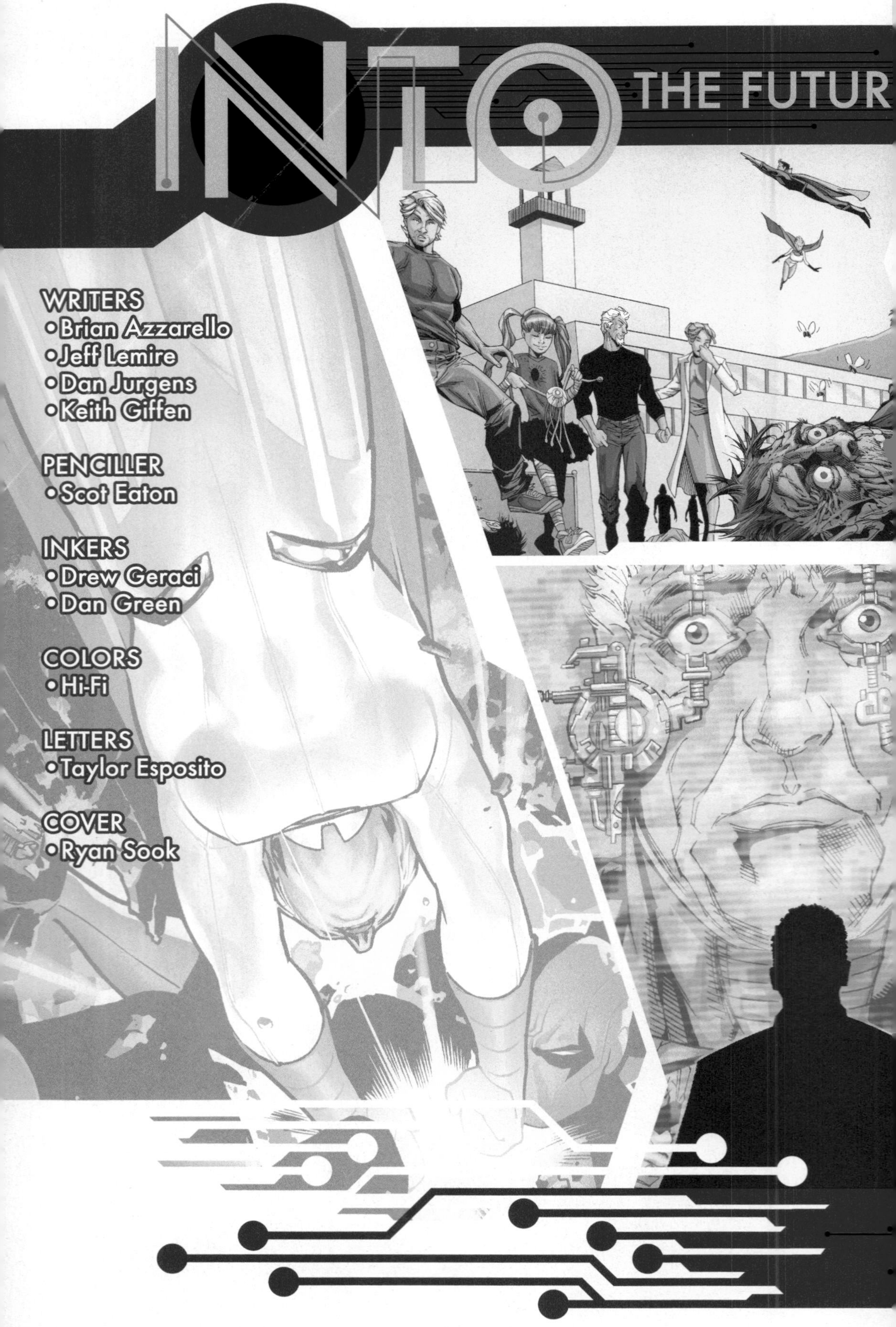

WRITERS
- Brian Azzarello
- Jeff Lemire
- Dan Jurgens
- Keith Giffen

PENCILLER
- Scot Eaton

INKERS
- Drew Geraci
- Dan Green

COLORS
- Hi-Fi

LETTERS
- Taylor Esposito

COVER
- Ryan Sook

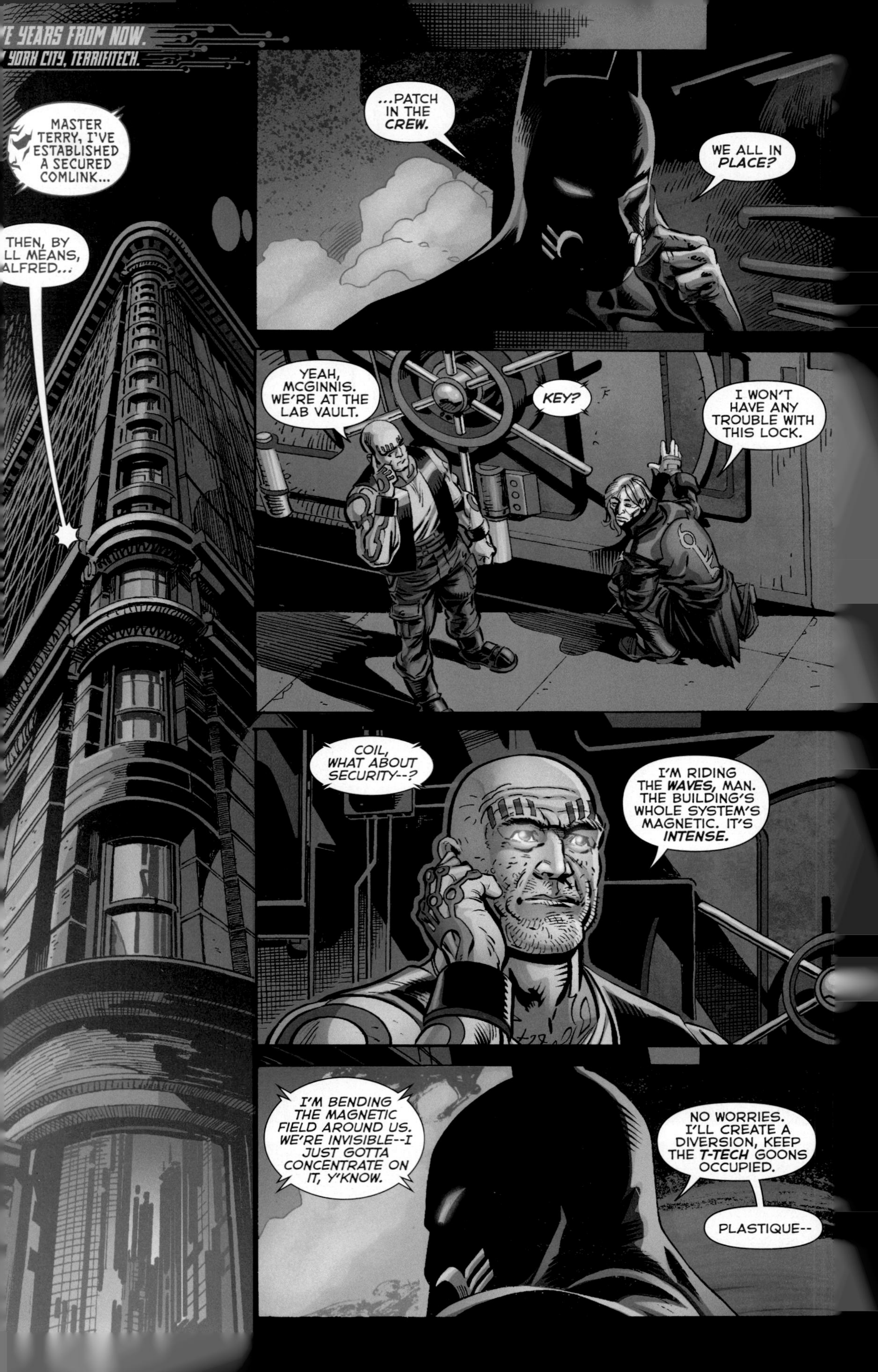

...E YEARS FROM NOW.
...YORK CITY, TERRIFITECH.
MASTER TERRY, I'VE ESTABLISHED A SECURED COMLINK...
THEN, BY ...LL MEANS, ALFRED...
...PATCH IN THE CREW.
WE ALL IN PLACE?
YEAH, MCGINNIS. WE'RE AT THE LAB VAULT.
KEY?
I WON'T HAVE ANY TROUBLE WITH THIS LOCK.
COIL, WHAT ABOUT SECURITY--?
I'M RIDING THE WAVES, MAN. THE BUILDING'S WHOLE SYSTEM'S MAGNETIC. IT'S INTENSE.
I'M BENDING THE MAGNETIC FIELD AROUND US. WE'RE INVISIBLE--I JUST GOTTA CONCENTRATE ON IT, Y'KNOW.
NO WORRIES. I'LL CREATE A DIVERSION, KEEP THE T-TECH GOONS OCCUPIED.
PLASTIQUE--

--CLEAR AT THE RENDEZVOUS POINT?

PLASTIQUE?

YES. CLEAR.

JUST GET THE JOB DONE, AND I'LL GET US *OUT*, NO WORRIES.

OKAY.

I'M GOING OUT IN THE OPEN. AND I'LL BE TAKING FIRE. SO AS NOT TO BLOW OUT YOUR EAR-DRUMS, I'M TURNING OFF COMLINK.

FOUR MINUTES, I'LL SEE YOU AT THE RENDEZVOUS. AND IF I DON'T...

WE WON'T WAIT.

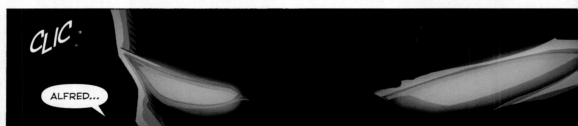

CLIC

ALFRED...

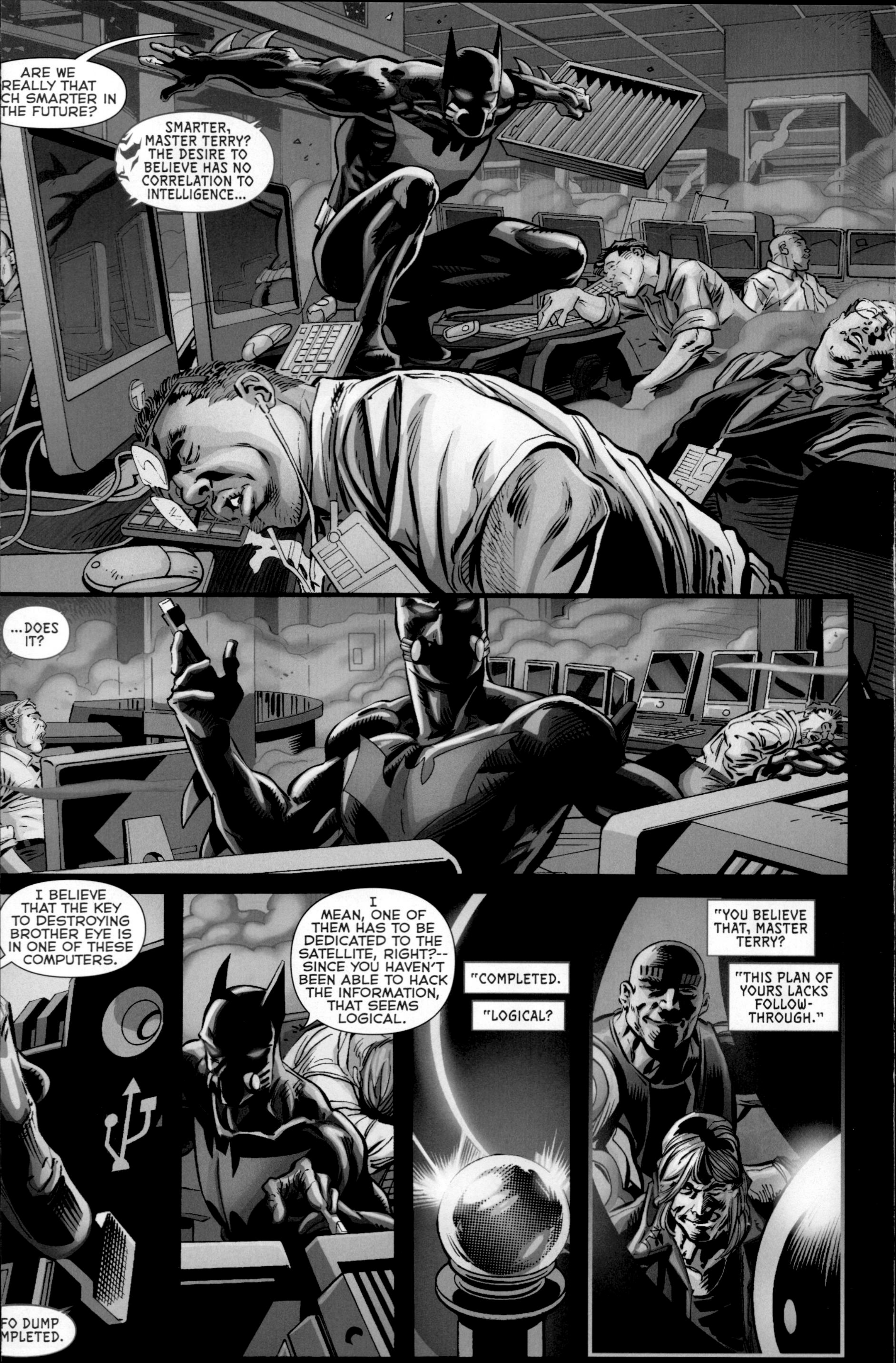
ARE WE REALLY THAT CH SMARTER IN THE FUTURE?
SMARTER, MASTER TERRY? THE DESIRE TO BELIEVE HAS NO CORRELATION TO INTELLIGENCE...
...DOES IT?
I BELIEVE THAT THE KEY TO DESTROYING BROTHER EYE IS IN ONE OF THESE COMPUTERS.
I MEAN, ONE OF THEM HAS TO BE DEDICATED TO THE SATELLITE, RIGHT?-- SINCE YOU HAVEN'T BEEN ABLE TO HACK THE INFORMATION, THAT SEEMS LOGICAL.
FO DUMP MPLETED.
"COMPLETED.
"LOGICAL?
"YOU BELIEVE THAT, MASTER TERRY?
"THIS PLAN OF YOURS LACKS FOLLOW-THROUGH."

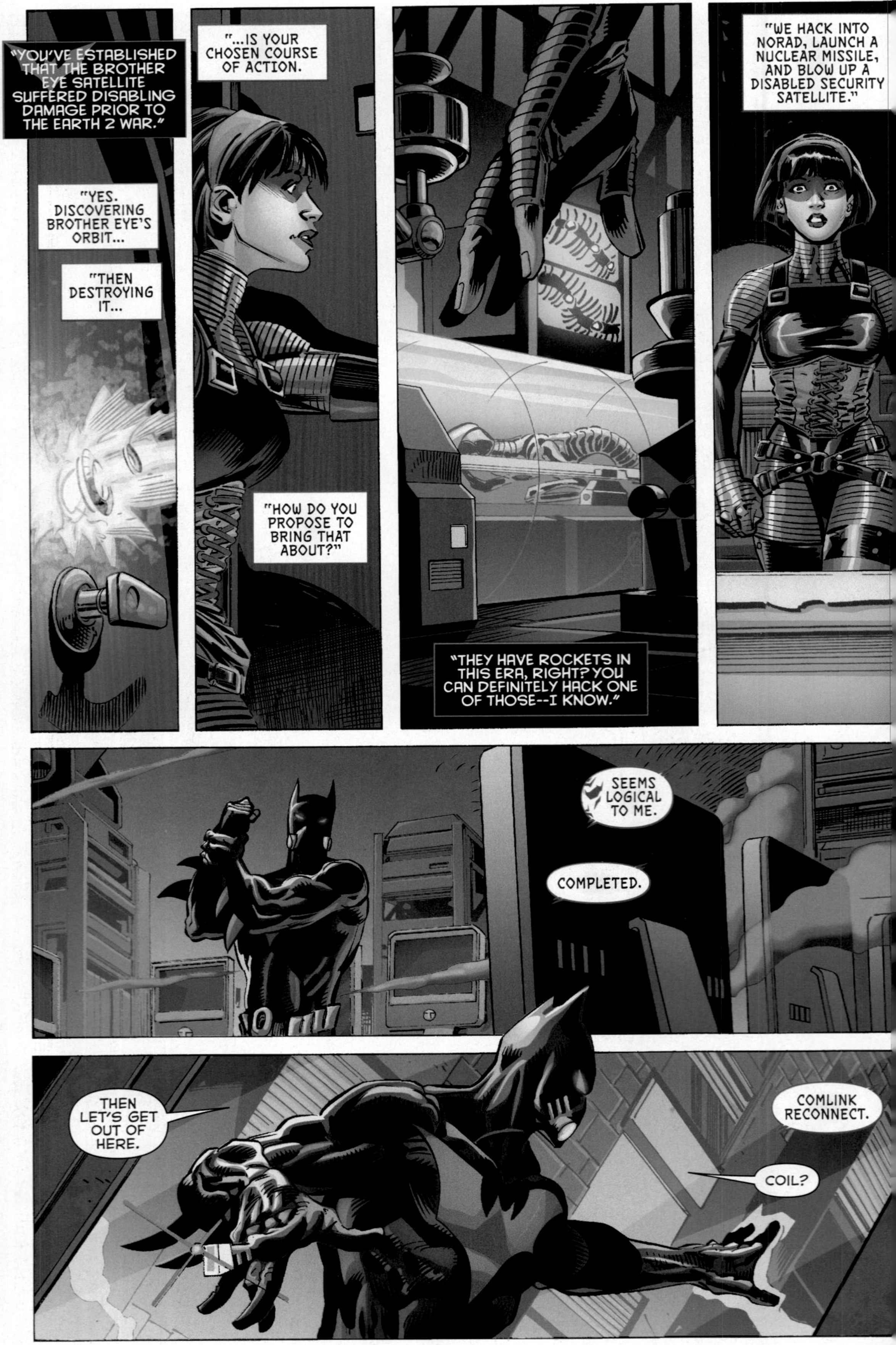
"YOU'VE ESTABLISHED THAT THE BROTHER EYE SATELLITE SUFFERED DISABLING DAMAGE PRIOR TO THE EARTH 2 WAR."
"YES. DISCOVERING BROTHER EYE'S ORBIT...
"THEN DESTROYING IT...
"...IS YOUR CHOSEN COURSE OF ACTION.
"HOW DO YOU PROPOSE TO BRING THAT ABOUT?"
"THEY HAVE ROCKETS IN THIS ERA, RIGHT? YOU CAN DEFINITELY HACK ONE OF THOSE--I KNOW."
"WE HACK INTO NORAD, LAUNCH A NUCLEAR MISSILE, AND BLOW UP A DISABLED SECURITY SATELLITE."
SEEMS LOGICAL TO ME.
COMPLETED.
THEN LET'S GET OUT OF HERE.
COMLINK RECONNECT.
COIL?

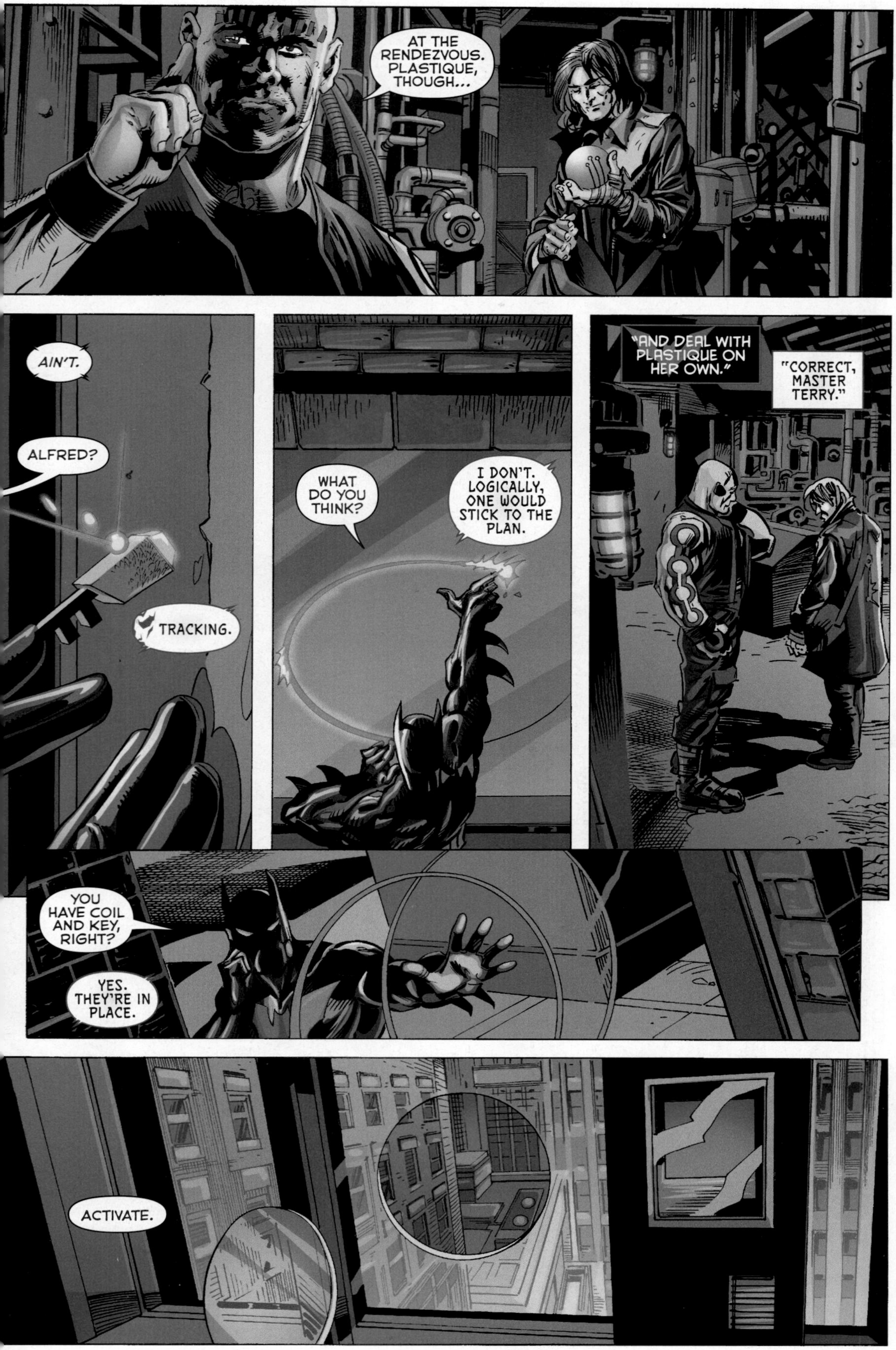
AT THE RENDEZVOUS. PLASTIQUE, THOUGH...
AIN'T.
ALFRED?
TRACKING.
WHAT DO YOU THINK?
I DON'T. LOGICALLY, ONE WOULD STICK TO THE PLAN.
"AND DEAL WITH PLASTIQUE ON HER OWN."
"CORRECT, MASTER TERRY."
YOU HAVE COIL AND KEY, RIGHT?
YES. THEY'RE IN PLACE.
ACTIVATE.

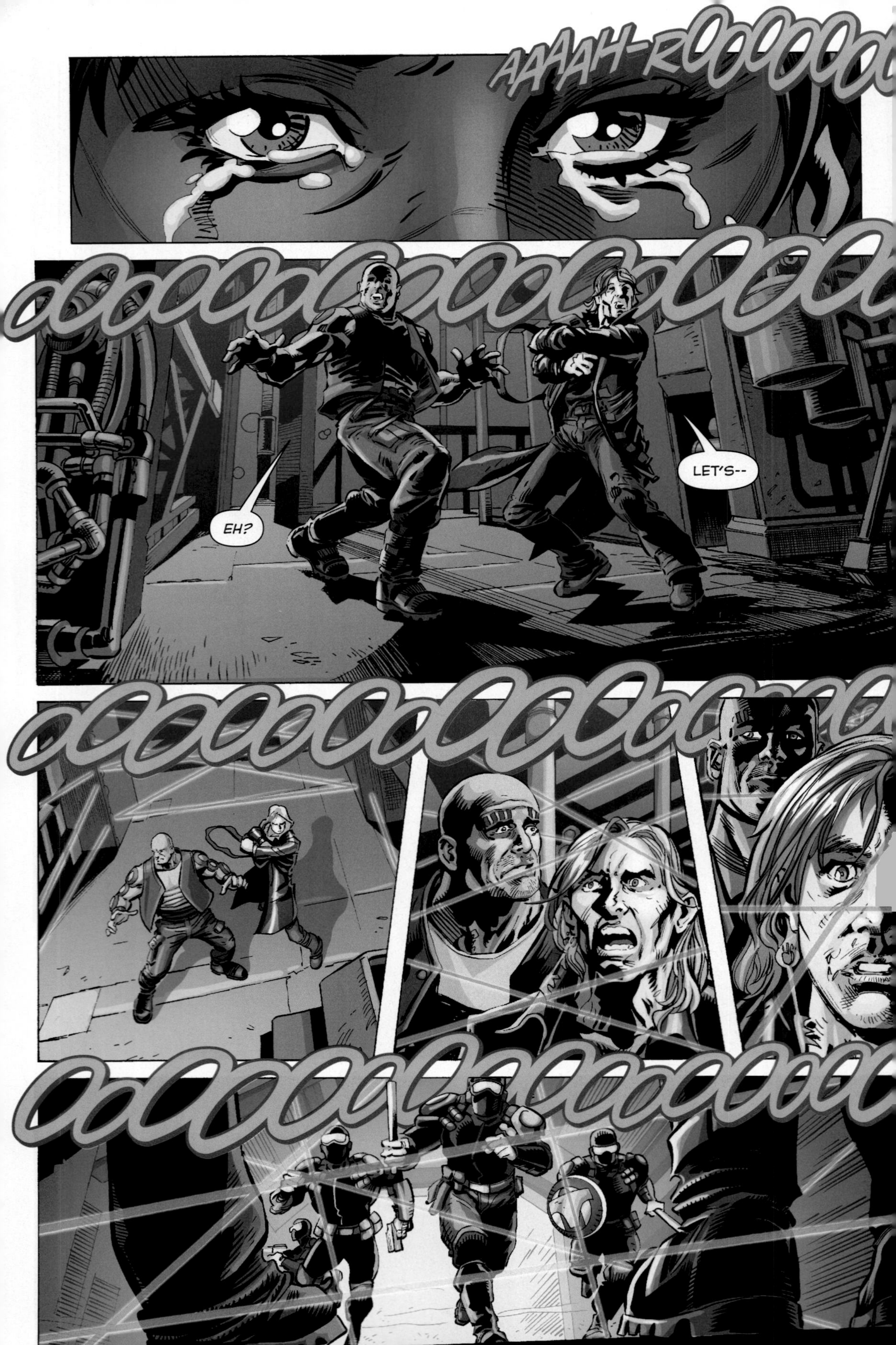
AAAAH-ROOOOOO
EH?
LET'S--

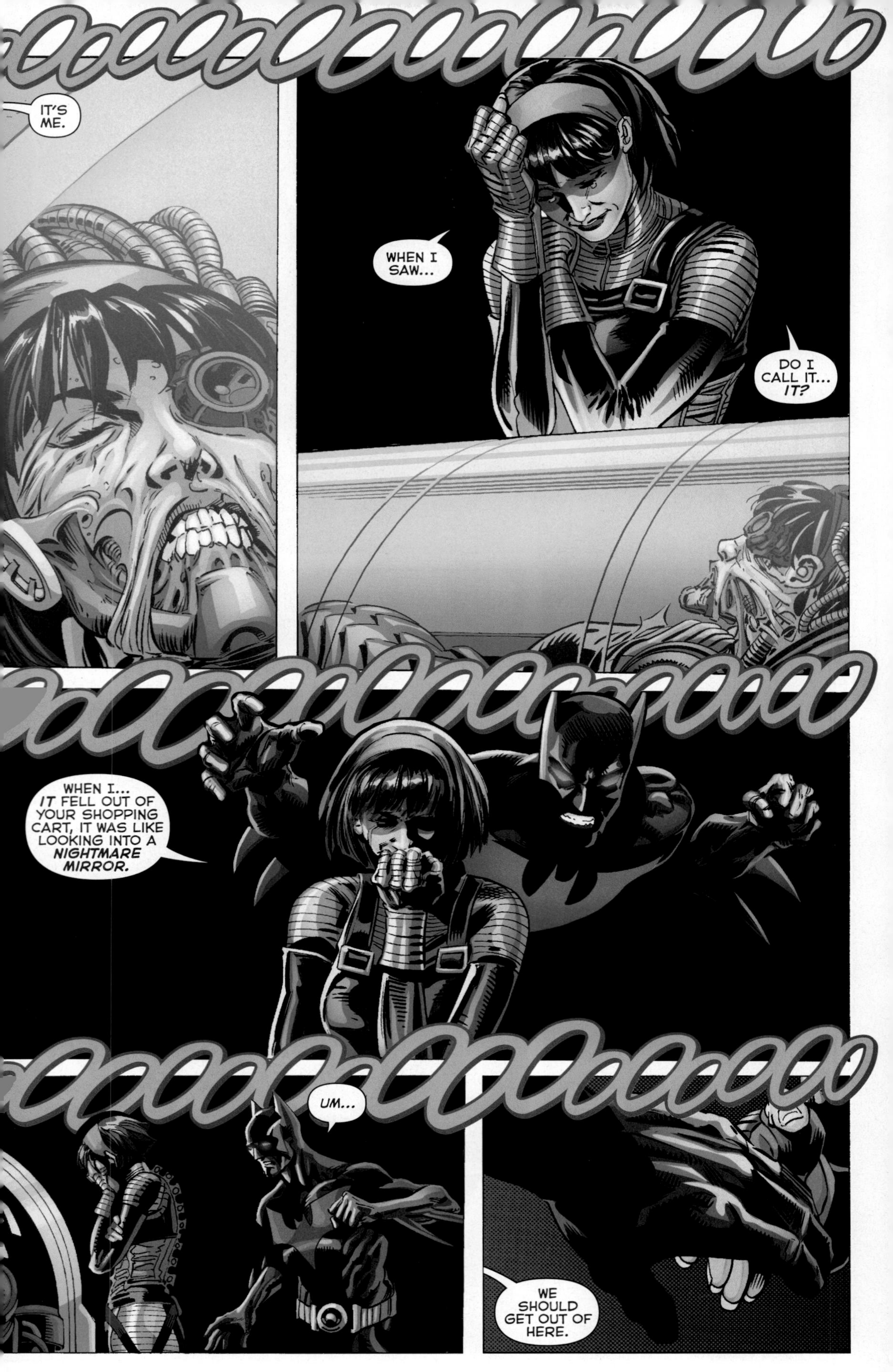
IT'S ME.
WHEN I SAW...
DO I CALL IT... *IT?*
WHEN I... *IT* FELL OUT OF YOUR SHOPPING CART, IT WAS LIKE LOOKING INTO A ***NIGHTMARE MIRROR.***
UM...
WE SHOULD GET OUT OF HERE.

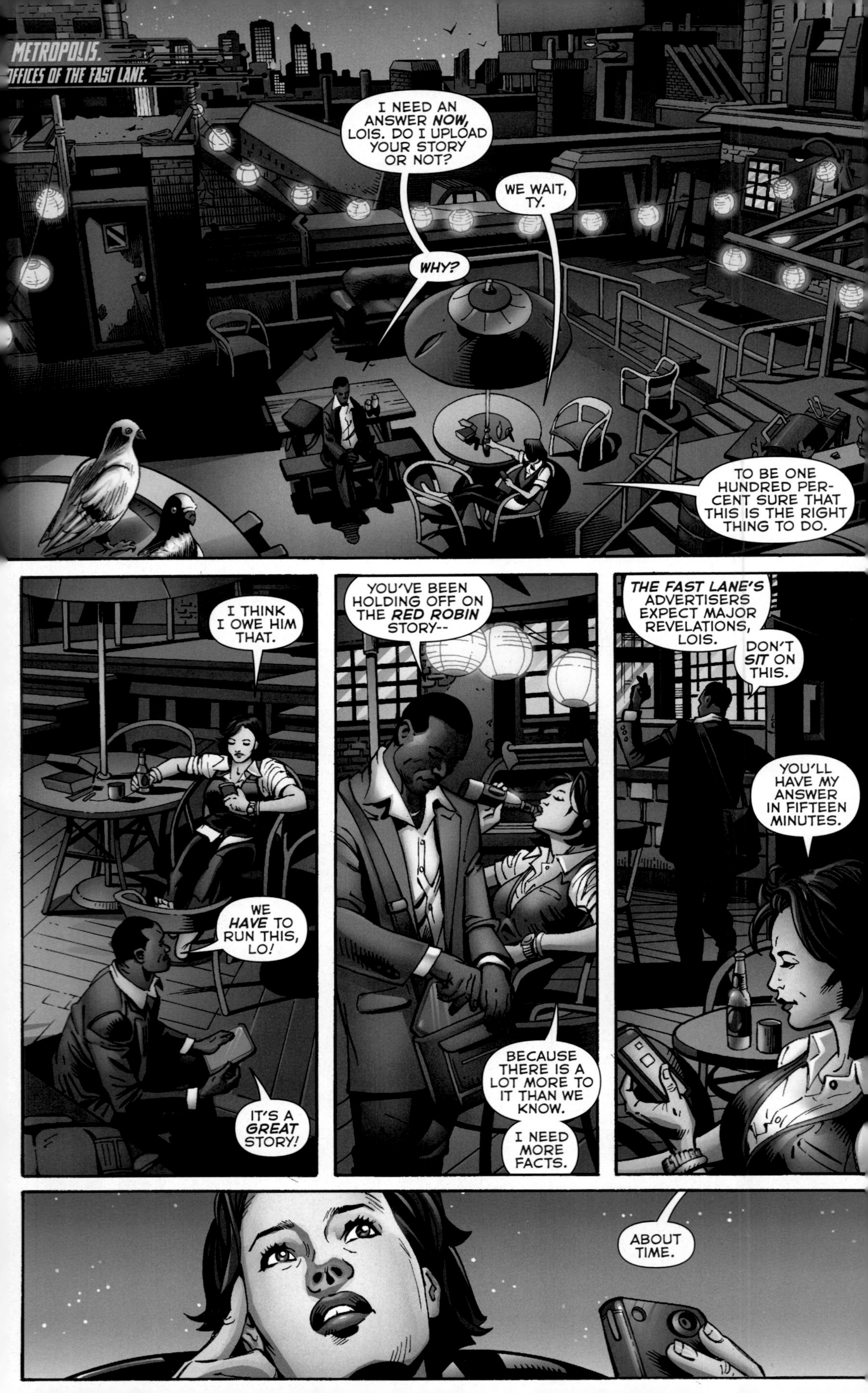
METROPOLIS.
OFFICES OF THE FAST LANE.
I NEED AN ANSWER NOW, LOIS. DO I UPLOAD YOUR STORY OR NOT?
WE WAIT, TY.
WHY?
TO BE ONE HUNDRED PER-CENT SURE THAT THIS IS THE RIGHT THING TO DO.
I THINK I OWE HIM THAT.
WE HAVE TO RUN THIS, LO!
IT'S A GREAT STORY!
YOU'VE BEEN HOLDING OFF ON THE RED ROBIN STORY--
BECAUSE THERE IS A LOT MORE TO IT THAN WE KNOW.
I NEED MORE FACTS.
THE FAST LANE'S ADVERTISERS EXPECT MAJOR REVELATIONS, LOIS.
DON'T SIT ON THIS.
YOU'LL HAVE MY ANSWER IN FIFTEEN MINUTES.
ABOUT TIME.

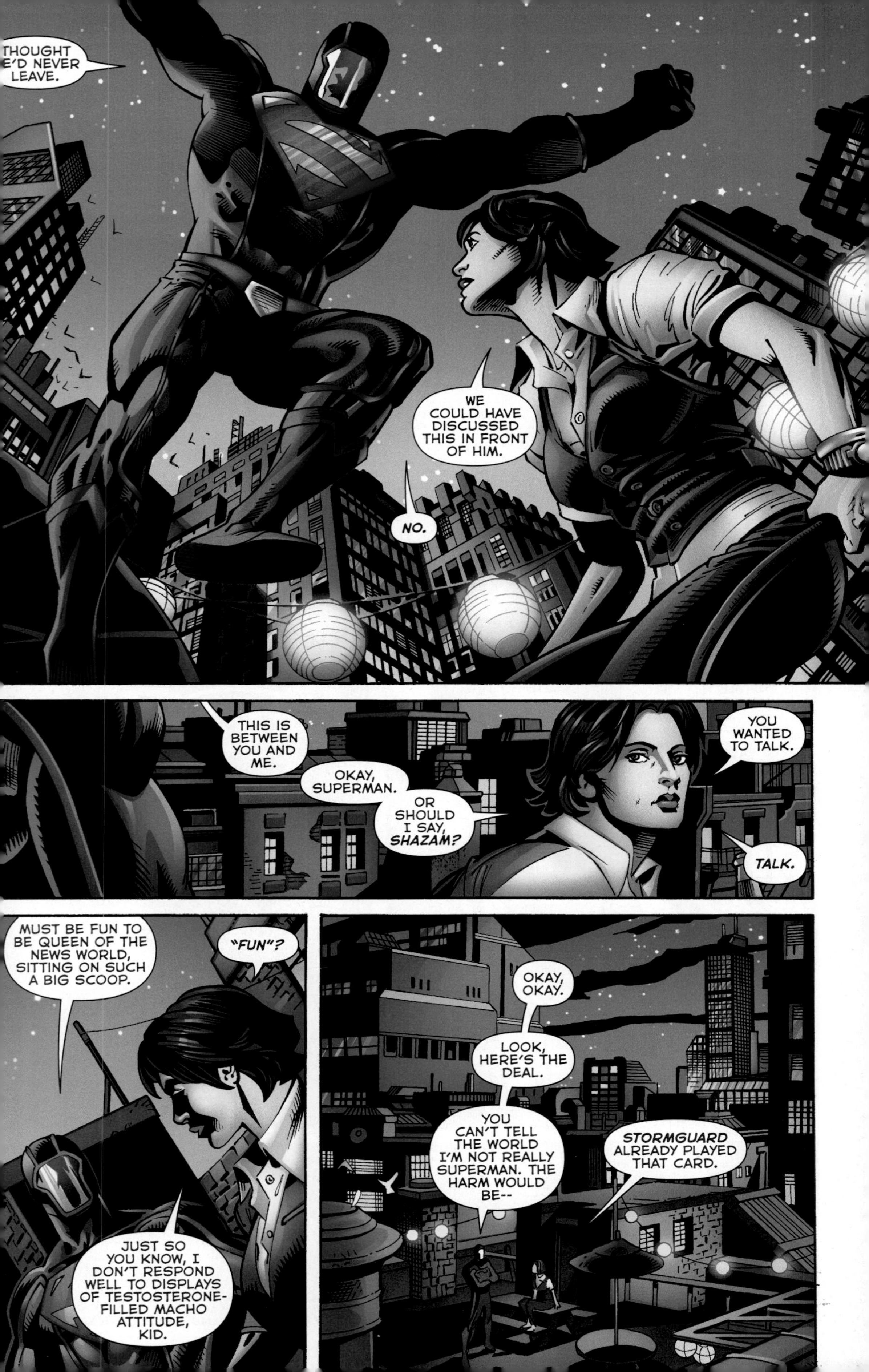
THOUGHT HE'D NEVER LEAVE.
WE COULD HAVE DISCUSSED THIS IN FRONT OF HIM.
NO.
THIS IS BETWEEN YOU AND ME.
OKAY, SUPERMAN.
OR SHOULD I SAY, SHAZAM?
YOU WANTED TO TALK.
TALK.
MUST BE FUN TO BE QUEEN OF THE NEWS WORLD, SITTING ON SUCH A BIG SCOOP.
"FUN"?
JUST SO YOU KNOW, I DON'T RESPOND WELL TO DISPLAYS OF TESTOSTERONE-FILLED MACHO ATTITUDE, KID.
OKAY, OKAY.
LOOK, HERE'S THE DEAL.
YOU CAN'T TELL THE WORLD I'M NOT REALLY SUPERMAN. THE HARM WOULD BE--
STORMGUARD ALREADY PLAYED THAT CARD.

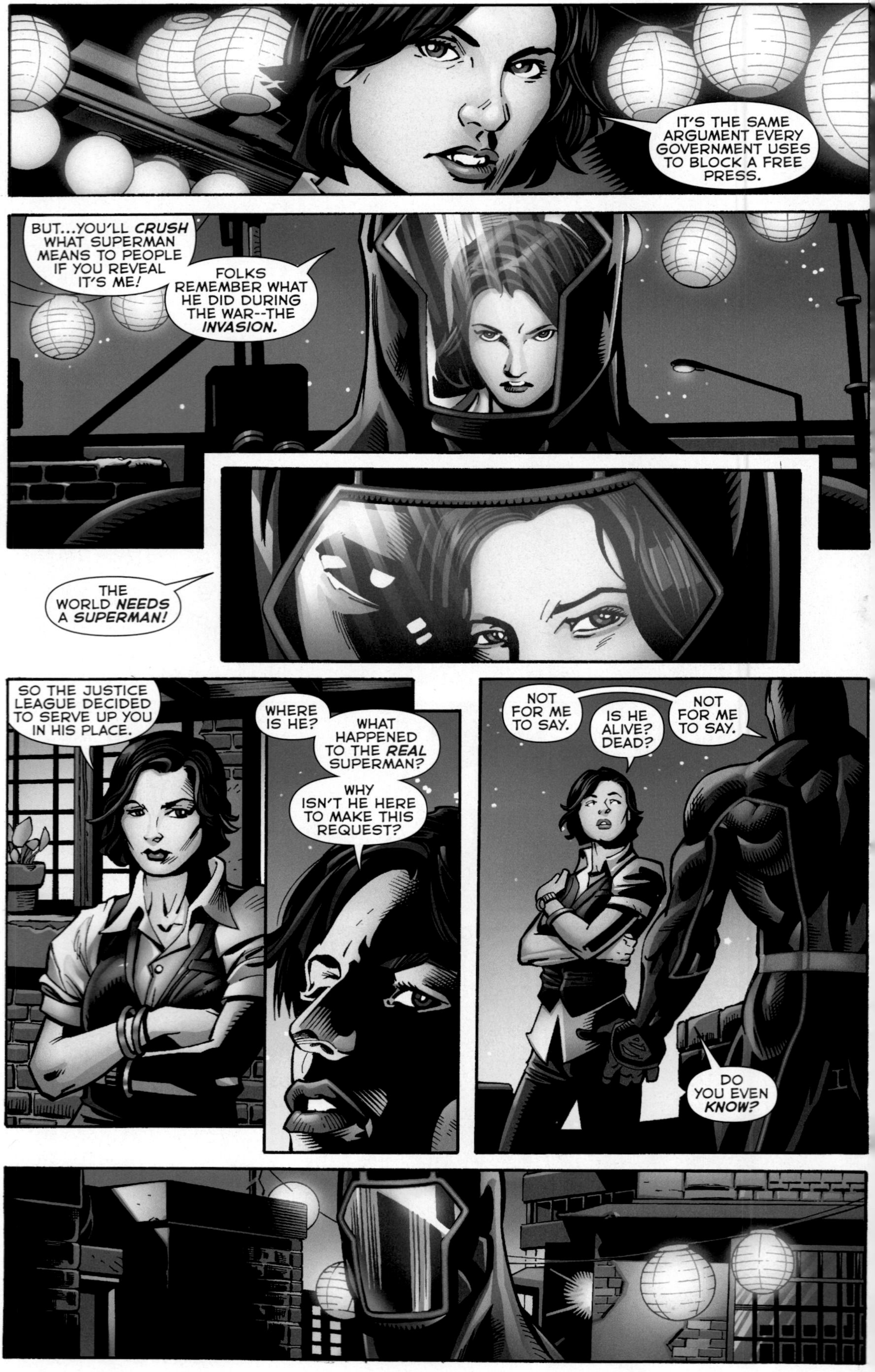
IT'S THE SAME ARGUMENT EVERY GOVERNMENT USES TO BLOCK A FREE PRESS.
BUT...YOU'LL CRUSH WHAT SUPERMAN MEANS TO PEOPLE IF YOU REVEAL IT'S ME!
FOLKS REMEMBER WHAT HE DID DURING THE WAR--THE INVASION.
THE WORLD NEEDS A SUPERMAN!
SO THE JUSTICE LEAGUE DECIDED TO SERVE UP YOU IN HIS PLACE.
WHERE IS HE?
WHAT HAPPENED TO THE REAL SUPERMAN?
WHY ISN'T HE HERE TO MAKE THIS REQUEST?
NOT FOR ME TO SAY.
IS HE ALIVE? DEAD?
NOT FOR ME TO SAY.
DO YOU EVEN KNOW?

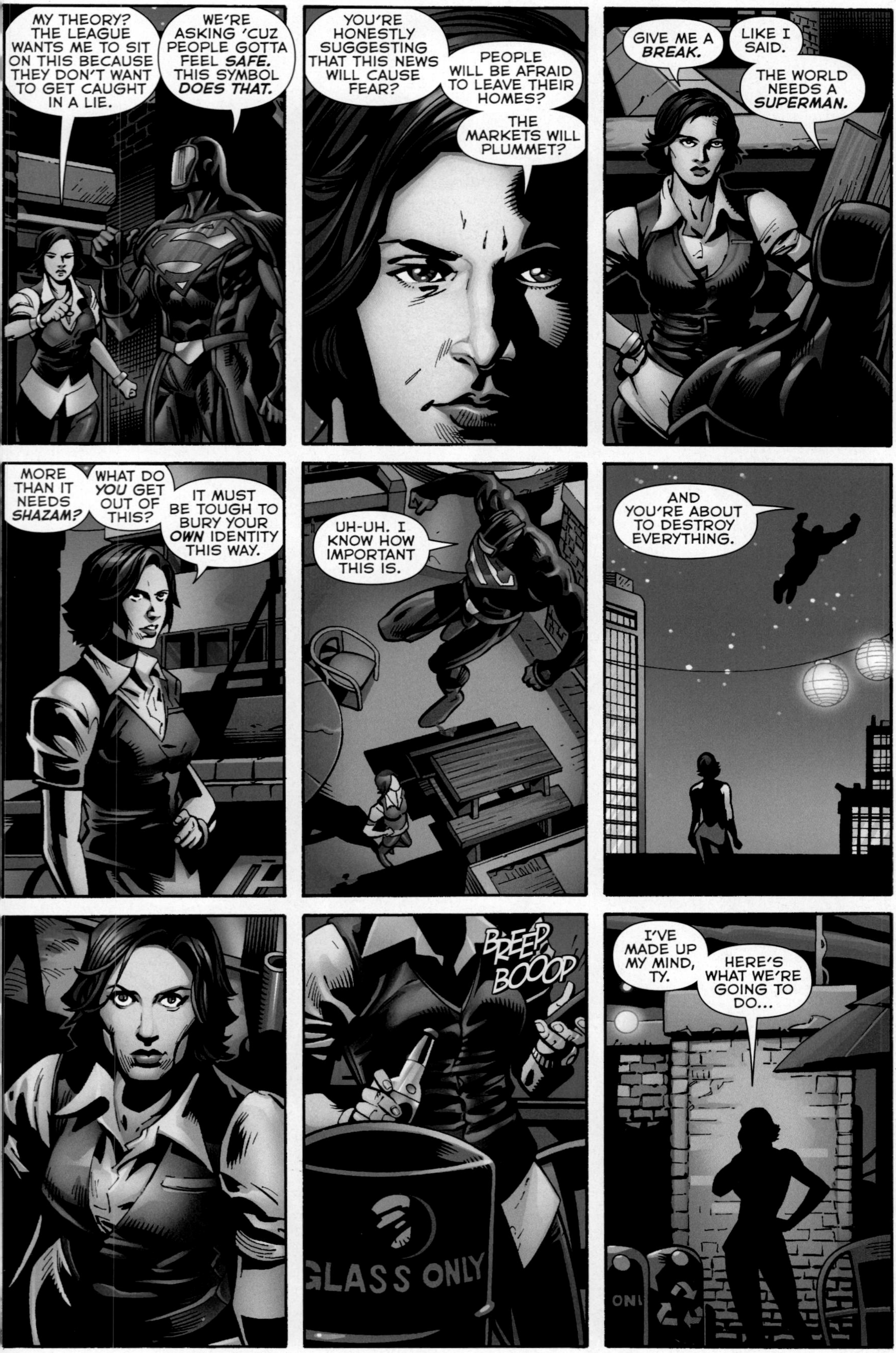
MY THEORY? THE LEAGUE WANTS ME TO SIT ON THIS BECAUSE THEY DON'T WANT TO GET CAUGHT IN A LIE.
WE'RE ASKING 'CUZ PEOPLE GOTTA FEEL *SAFE.* THIS SYMBOL *DOES THAT.*
YOU'RE HONESTLY SUGGESTING THAT THIS NEWS WILL CAUSE FEAR?
PEOPLE WILL BE AFRAID TO LEAVE THEIR HOMES?
THE MARKETS WILL PLUMMET?
GIVE ME A *BREAK.*
LIKE I SAID.
THE WORLD NEEDS A *SUPERMAN.*
MORE THAN IT NEEDS *SHAZAM?*
WHAT DO *YOU* GET OUT OF THIS?
IT MUST BE TOUGH TO BURY YOUR *OWN* IDENTITY THIS WAY.
UH-UH. I KNOW HOW IMPORTANT THIS IS.
AND YOU'RE ABOUT TO DESTROY EVERYTHING.
BREEP BOOOP
GLASS ONLY
I'VE MADE UP MY MIND, TY.
HERE'S WHAT WE'RE GOING TO DO...

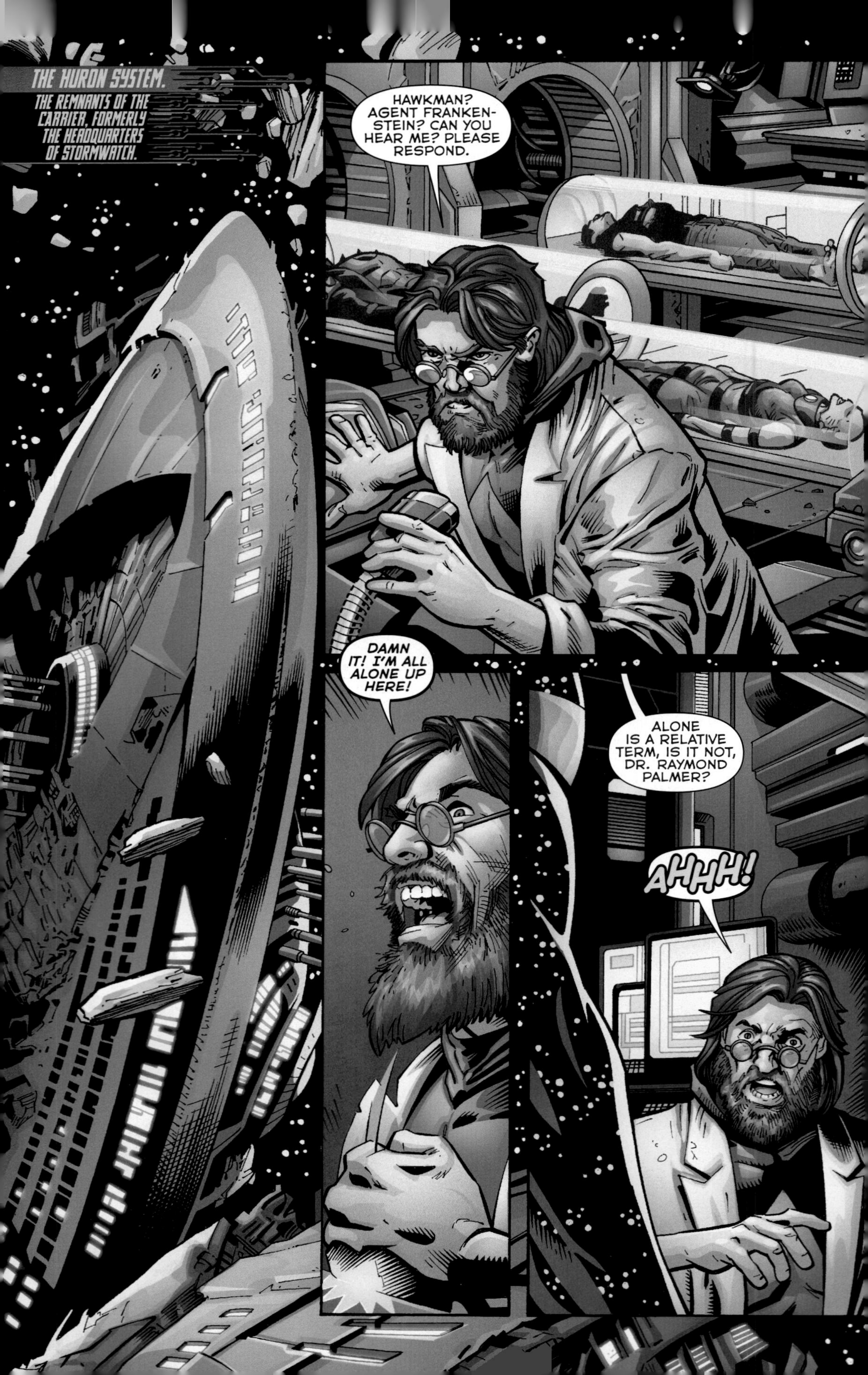
THE HURON SYSTEM.
THE REMNANTS OF THE CARRIER, FORMERLY THE HEADQUARTERS OF STORMWATCH.
HAWKMAN? AGENT FRANKEN-STEIN? CAN YOU HEAR ME? PLEASE RESPOND.
DAMN IT! I'M ALL ALONE UP HERE!
ALONE IS A RELATIVE TERM, IS IT NOT, DR. RAYMOND PALMER?
AHHH!

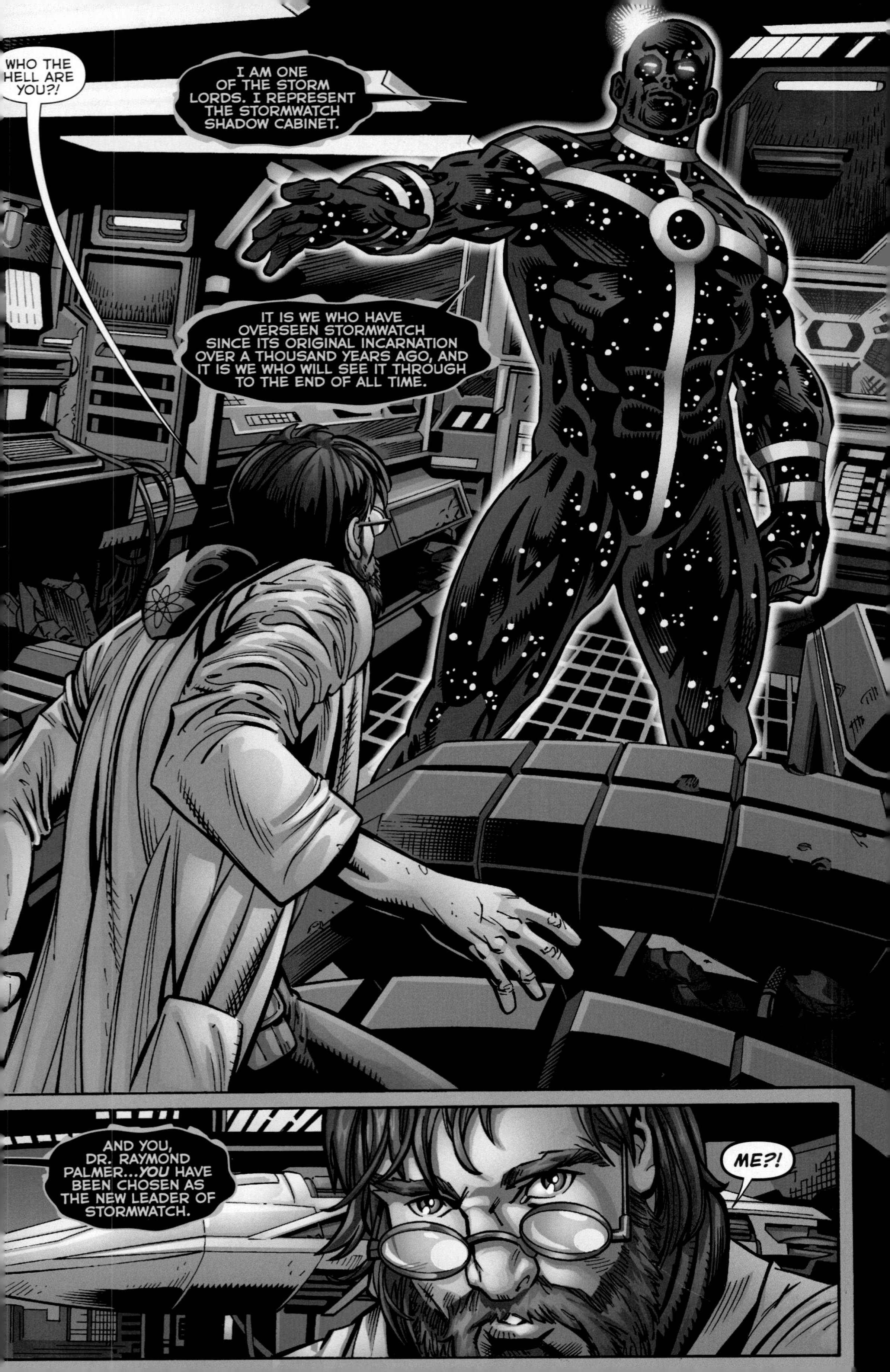
WHO THE HELL ARE YOU?!
I AM ONE OF THE STORM LORDS. I REPRESENT THE STORMWATCH SHADOW CABINET.
IT IS WE WHO HAVE OVERSEEN STORMWATCH SINCE ITS ORIGINAL INCARNATION OVER A THOUSAND YEARS AGO, AND IT IS WE WHO WILL SEE IT THROUGH TO THE END OF ALL TIME.
AND YOU, DR. RAYMOND PALMER...YOU HAVE BEEN CHOSEN AS THE NEW LEADER OF STORMWATCH.
ME?!

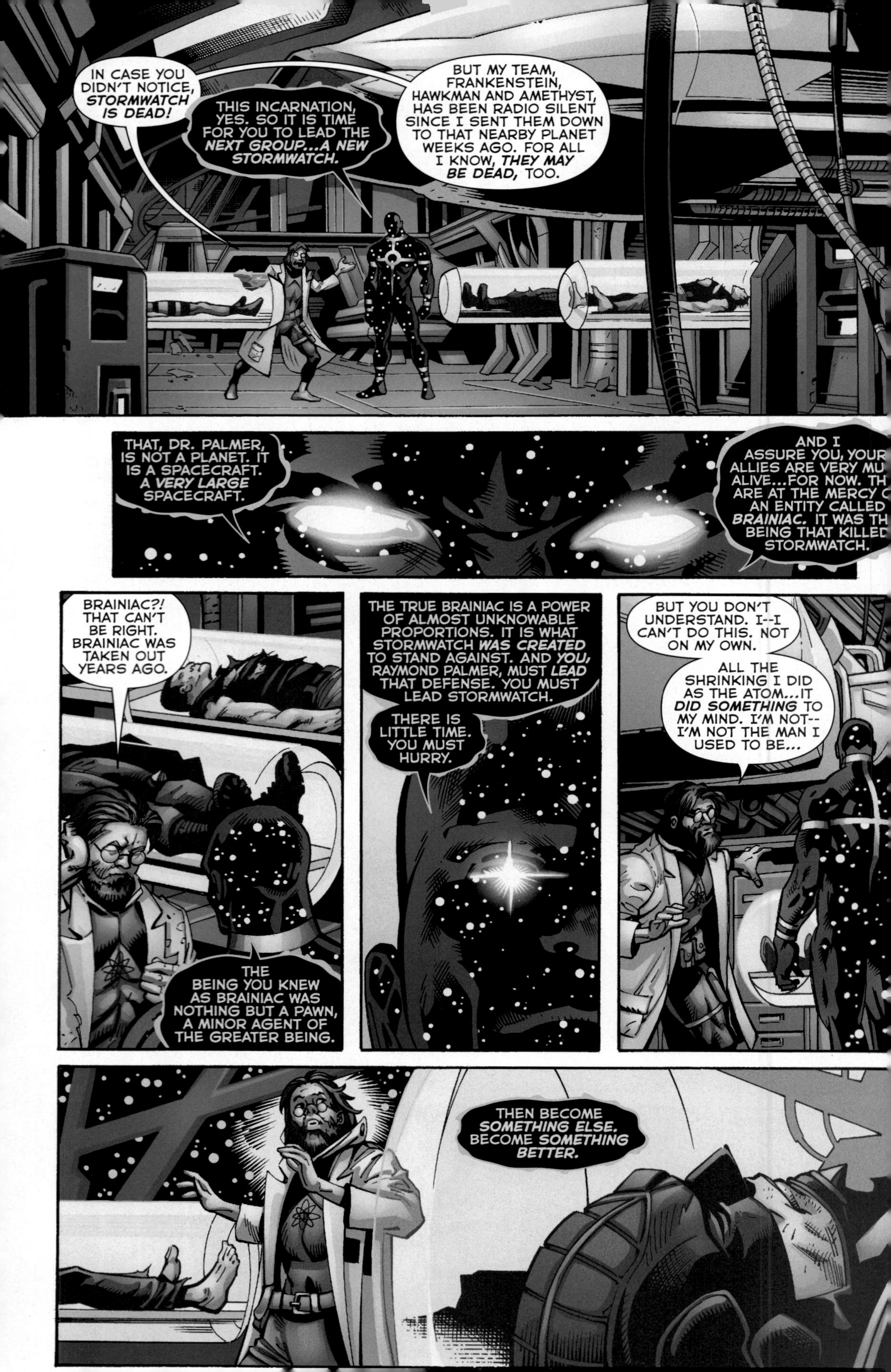
IN CASE YOU DIDN'T NOTICE, STORMWATCH IS DEAD!
THIS INCARNATION, YES. SO IT IS TIME FOR YOU TO LEAD THE NEXT GROUP...A NEW STORMWATCH.
BUT MY TEAM, FRANKENSTEIN, HAWKMAN AND AMETHYST, HAS BEEN RADIO SILENT SINCE I SENT THEM DOWN TO THAT NEARBY PLANET WEEKS AGO. FOR ALL I KNOW, THEY MAY BE DEAD, TOO.
THAT, DR. PALMER, IS NOT A PLANET. IT IS A SPACECRAFT. A VERY LARGE SPACECRAFT.
AND I ASSURE YOU, YOUR ALLIES ARE VERY MU ALIVE...FOR NOW. TH ARE AT THE MERCY O AN ENTITY CALLED BRAINIAC. IT WAS TH BEING THAT KILLED STORMWATCH.
BRAINIAC?! THAT CAN'T BE RIGHT. BRAINIAC WAS TAKEN OUT YEARS AGO.
THE BEING YOU KNEW AS BRAINIAC WAS NOTHING BUT A PAWN, A MINOR AGENT OF THE GREATER BEING.
THE TRUE BRAINIAC IS A POWER OF ALMOST UNKNOWABLE PROPORTIONS. IT IS WHAT STORMWATCH WAS CREATED TO STAND AGAINST. AND YOU, RAYMOND PALMER, MUST LEAD THAT DEFENSE. YOU MUST LEAD STORMWATCH.
THERE IS LITTLE TIME. YOU MUST HURRY.
BUT YOU DON'T UNDERSTAND. I--I CAN'T DO THIS. NOT ON MY OWN.
ALL THE SHRINKING I DID AS THE ATOM...IT DID SOMETHING TO MY MIND. I'M NOT--I'M NOT THE MAN I USED TO BE...
THEN BECOME SOMETHING ELSE. BECOME SOMETHING BETTER.

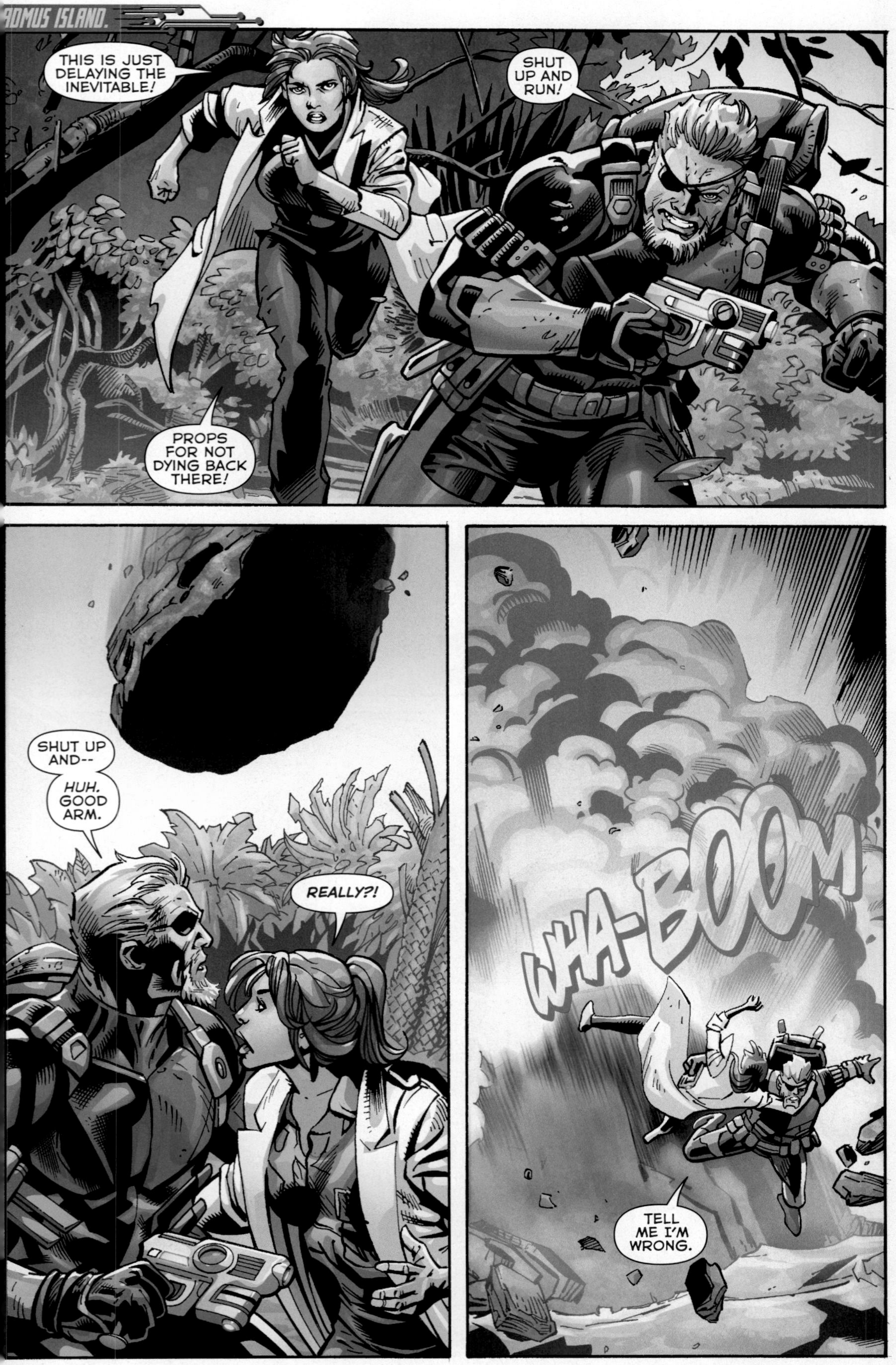

...DMUS ISLAND.
THIS IS JUST DELAYING THE INEVITABLE!
SHUT UP AND RUN!
PROPS FOR NOT DYING BACK THERE!
SHUT UP AND--
HUH. GOOD ARM.
REALLY?!
WHA-BOOM
TELL ME I'M WRONG.

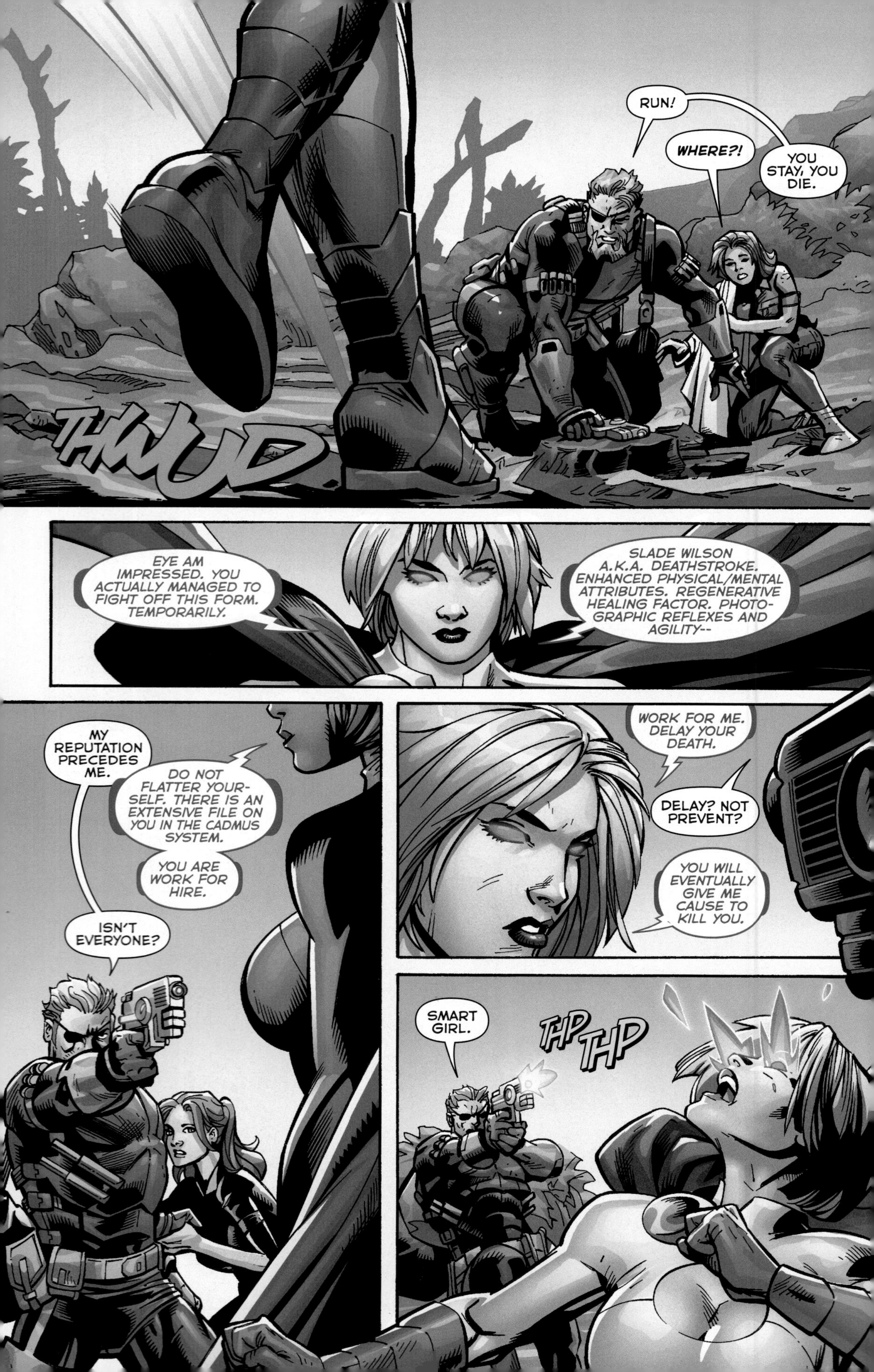

RUN!
WHERE?!
YOU STAY, YOU DIE.
THWUD
EYE AM IMPRESSED. YOU ACTUALLY MANAGED TO FIGHT OFF THIS FORM. TEMPORARILY.
SLADE WILSON A.K.A. DEATHSTROKE. ENHANCED PHYSICAL/MENTAL ATTRIBUTES. REGENERATIVE HEALING FACTOR. PHOTO-GRAPHIC REFLEXES AND AGILITY--
MY REPUTATION PRECEDES ME.
DO NOT FLATTER YOUR-SELF. THERE IS AN EXTENSIVE FILE ON YOU IN THE CADMUS SYSTEM.
YOU ARE WORK FOR HIRE.
ISN'T EVERYONE?
WORK FOR ME. DELAY YOUR DEATH.
DELAY? NOT PREVENT?
YOU WILL EVENTUALLY GIVE ME CAUSE TO KILL YOU.
SMART GIRL.
THP THP

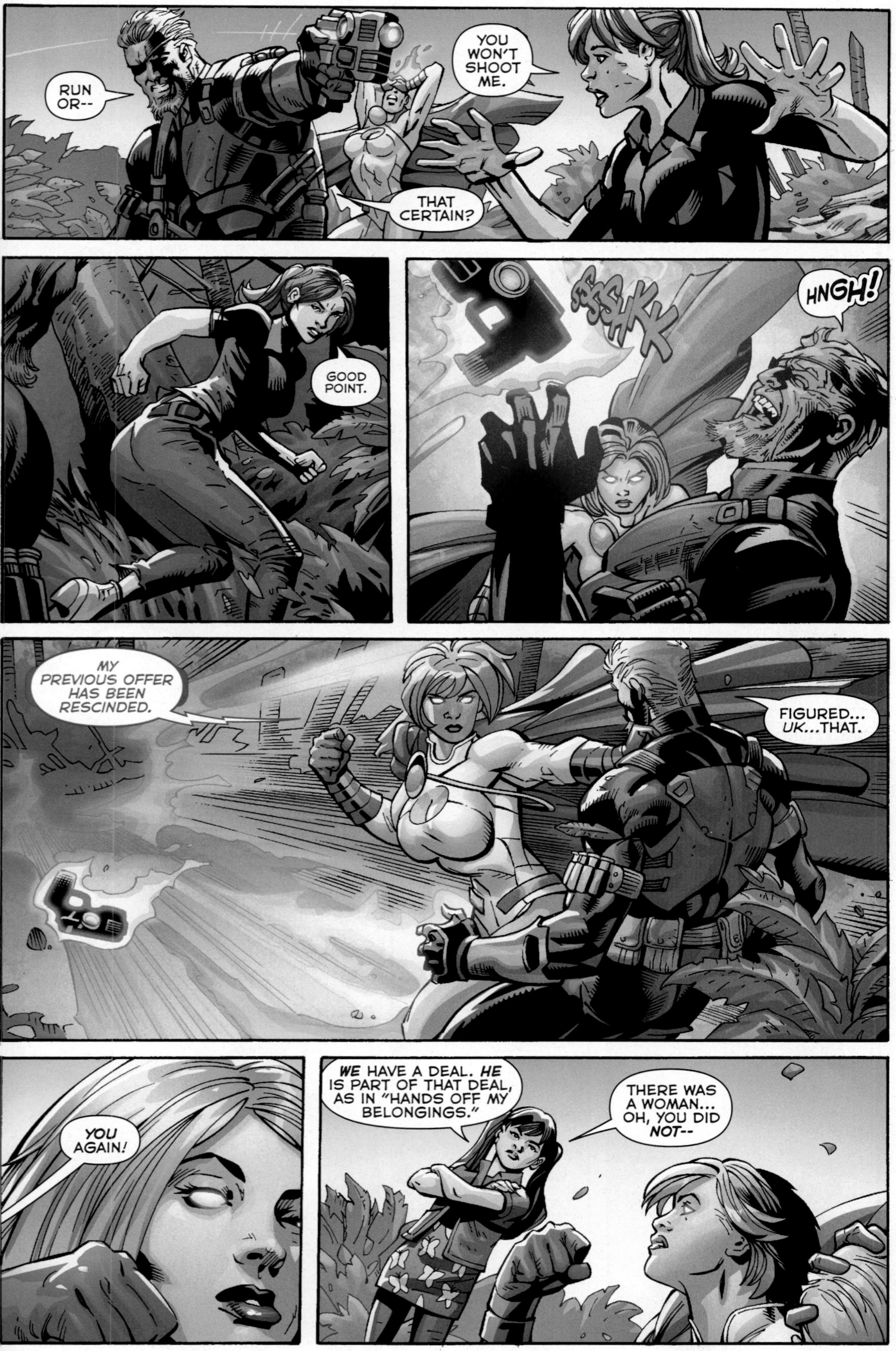
RUN OR--
YOU WON'T SHOOT ME.
THAT CERTAIN?
GOOD POINT.
SSSHKK
HNGH!
MY PREVIOUS OFFER HAS BEEN RESCINDED.
FIGURED... UK...THAT.
YOU AGAIN!
WE HAVE A DEAL. HE IS PART OF THAT DEAL, AS IN "HANDS OFF MY BELONGINGS."
THERE WAS A WOMAN... OH, YOU DID NOT--

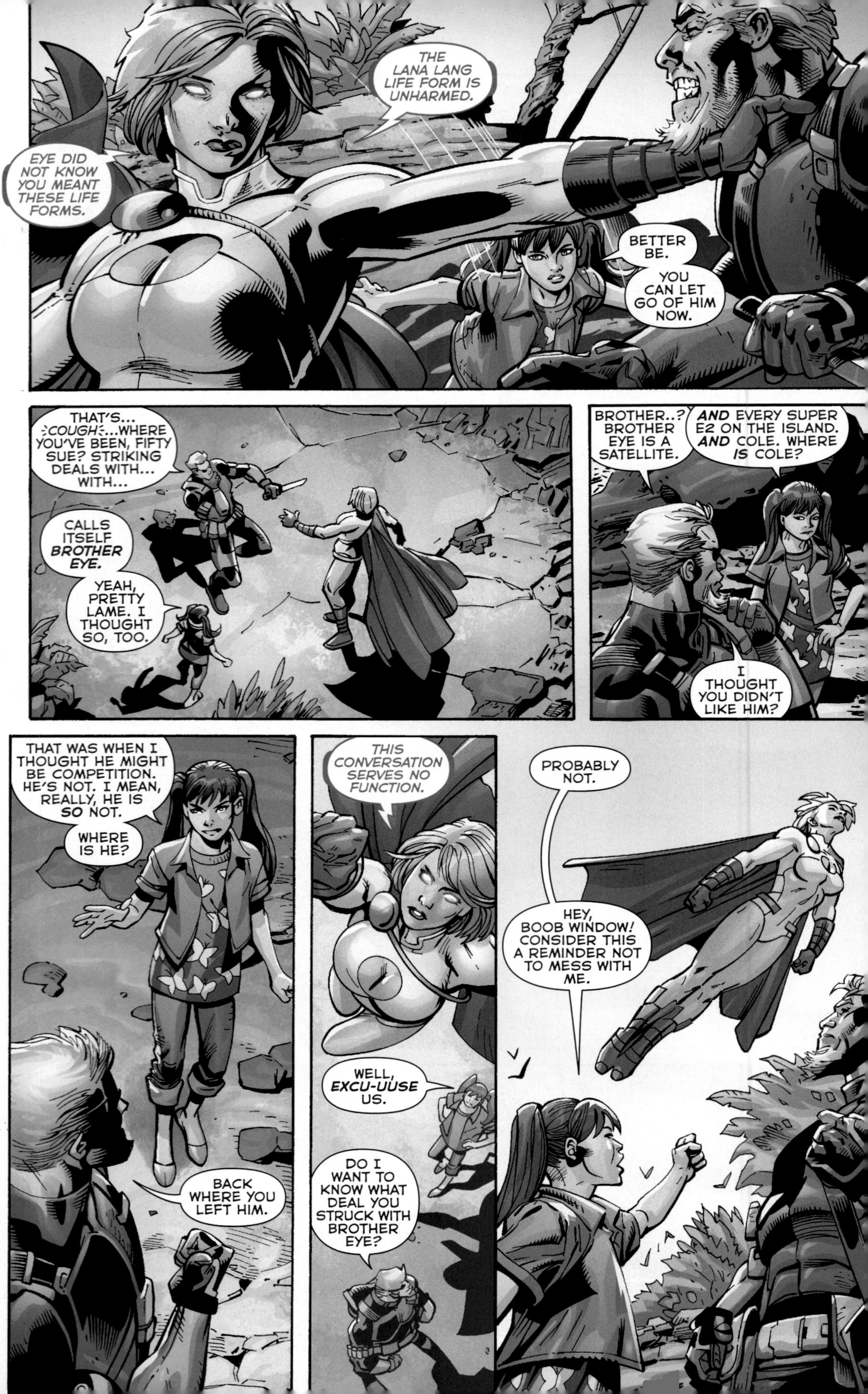

THE LANA LANG LIFE FORM IS UNHARMED.
EYE DID NOT KNOW YOU MEANT THESE LIFE FORMS.
BETTER BE.
YOU CAN LET GO OF HIM NOW.
THAT'S... *COUGH*...WHERE YOU'VE BEEN, FIFTY SUE? STRIKING DEALS WITH... WITH...
CALLS ITSELF BROTHER EYE.
YEAH, PRETTY LAME. I THOUGHT SO, TOO.
BROTHER..? BROTHER EYE IS A SATELLITE.
AND EVERY SUPER E2 ON THE ISLAND. AND COLE. WHERE IS COLE?
I THOUGHT YOU DIDN'T LIKE HIM?
THAT WAS WHEN I THOUGHT HE MIGHT BE COMPETITION. HE'S NOT. I MEAN, REALLY, HE IS SO NOT.
WHERE IS HE?
BACK WHERE YOU LEFT HIM.
THIS CONVERSATION SERVES NO FUNCTION.
WELL, EXCU-UUSE US.
DO I WANT TO KNOW WHAT DEAL YOU STRUCK WITH BROTHER EYE?
PROBABLY NOT.
HEY, BOOB WINDOW! CONSIDER THIS A REMINDER NOT TO MESS WITH ME.

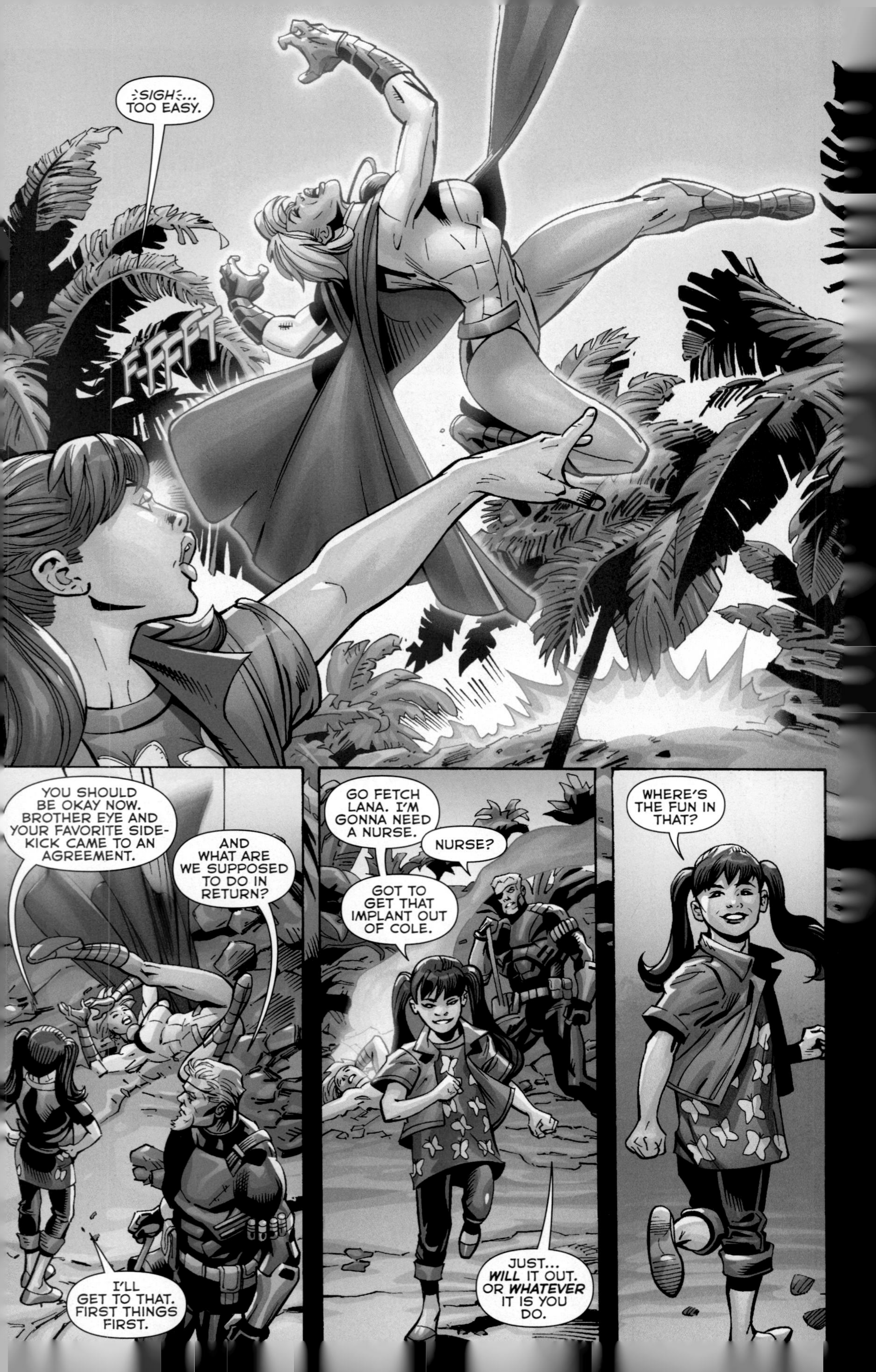
SIGH... TOO EASY.
F-FFFT
YOU SHOULD BE OKAY NOW. BROTHER EYE AND YOUR FAVORITE SIDE-KICK CAME TO AN AGREEMENT.
AND WHAT ARE WE SUPPOSED TO DO IN RETURN?
I'LL GET TO THAT. FIRST THINGS FIRST.
GO FETCH LANA. I'M GONNA NEED A NURSE.
NURSE?
GOT TO GET THAT IMPLANT OUT OF COLE.
JUST... WILL IT OUT. OR WHATEVER IT IS YOU DO.
WHERE'S THE FUN IN THAT?

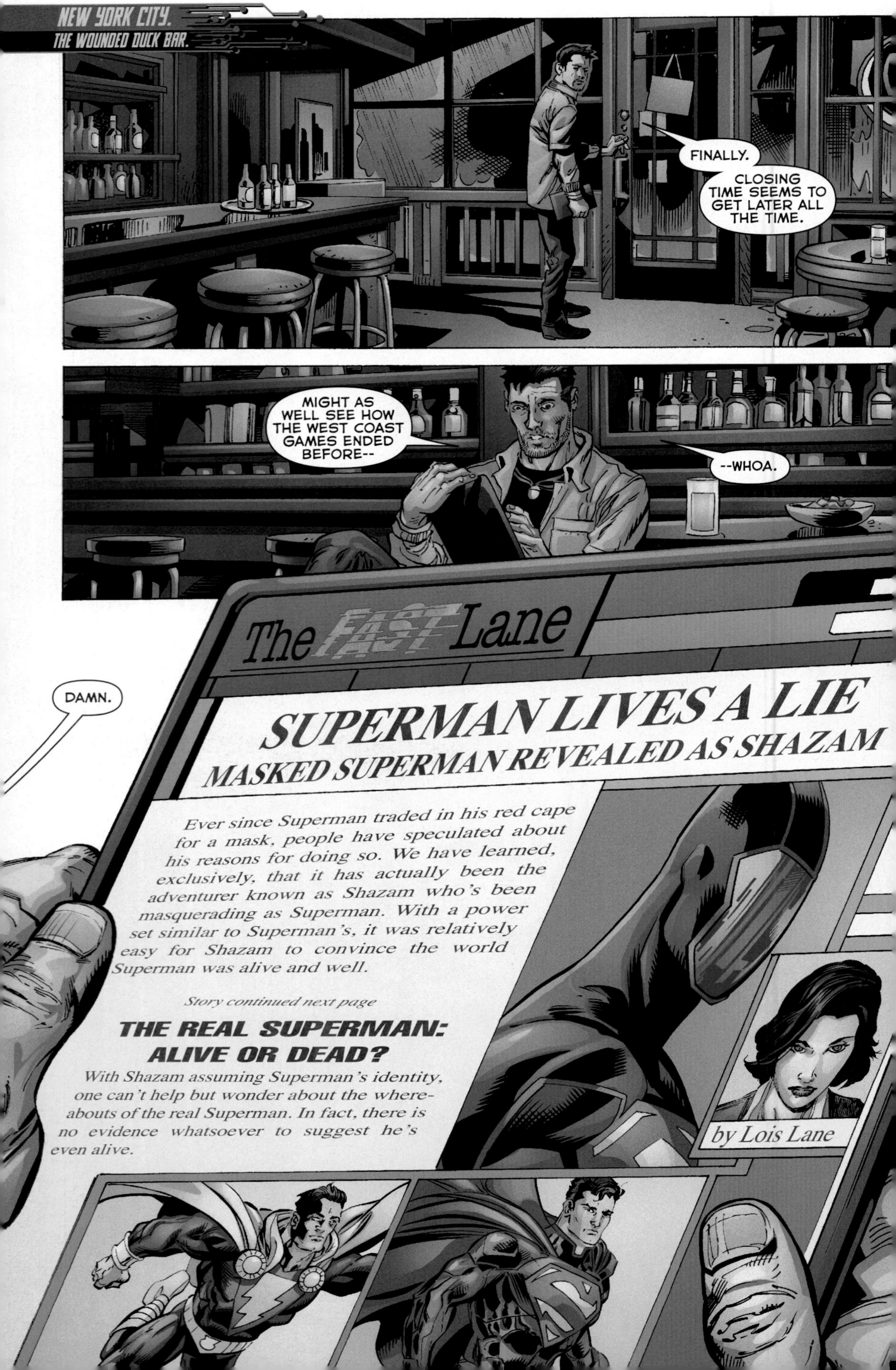
NEW YORK CITY.
THE WOUNDED DUCK BAR.
FINALLY.
CLOSING TIME SEEMS TO GET LATER ALL THE TIME.
MIGHT AS WELL SEE HOW THE WEST COAST GAMES ENDED BEFORE--
--WHOA.
DAMN.
The FAST Lane
SUPERMAN LIVES A LIE
MASKED SUPERMAN REVEALED AS SHAZAM
Ever since Superman traded in his red cape for a mask, people have speculated about his reasons for doing so. We have learned, exclusively, that it has actually been the adventurer known as Shazam who's been masquerading as Superman. With a power set similar to Superman's, it was relatively easy for Shazam to convince the world Superman was alive and well.
Story continued next page
THE REAL SUPERMAN: ALIVE OR DEAD?
With Shazam assuming Superman's identity, one can't help but wonder about the whereabouts of the real Superman. In fact, there is no evidence whatsoever to suggest he's even alive.
by Lois Lane

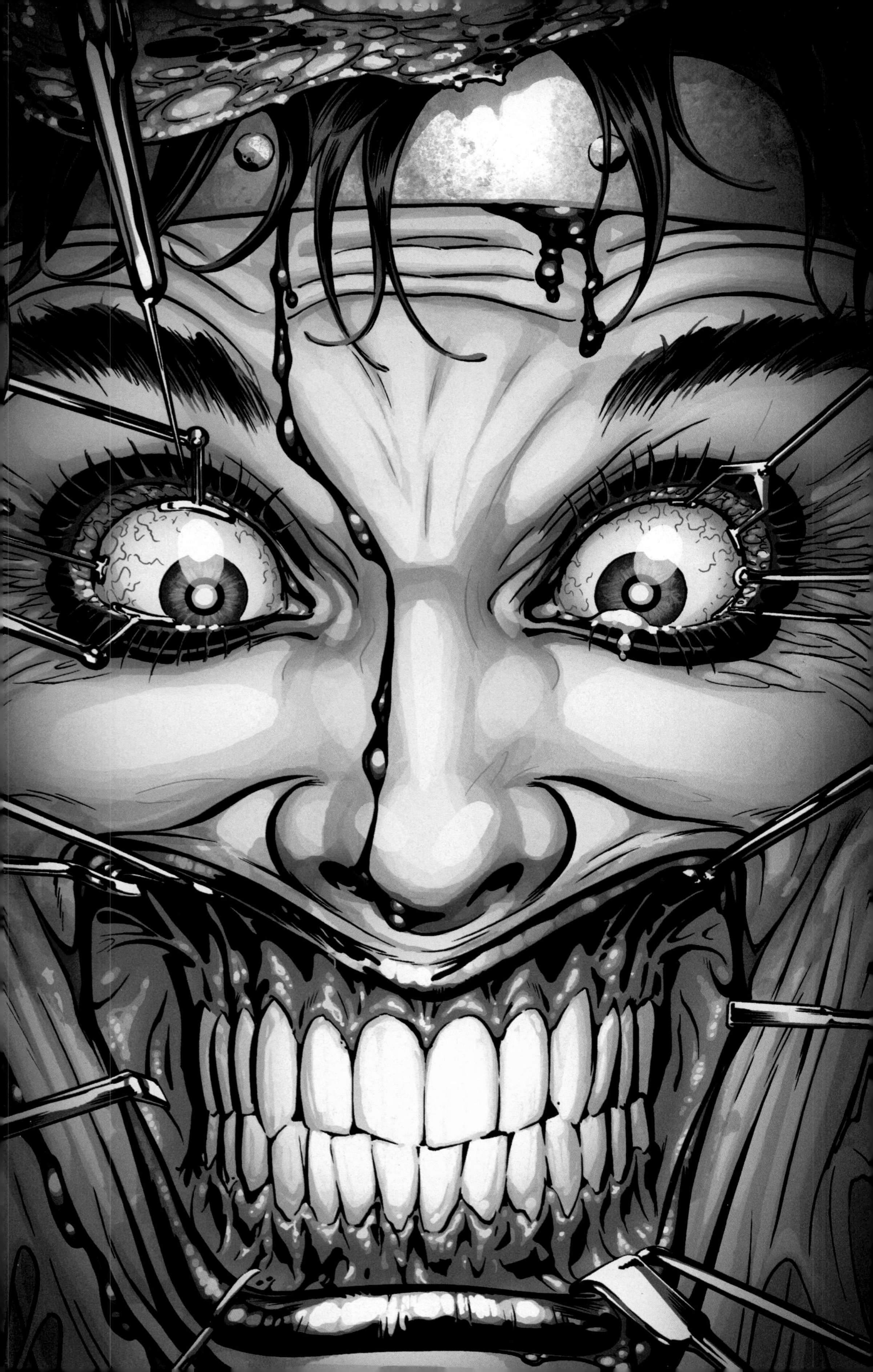

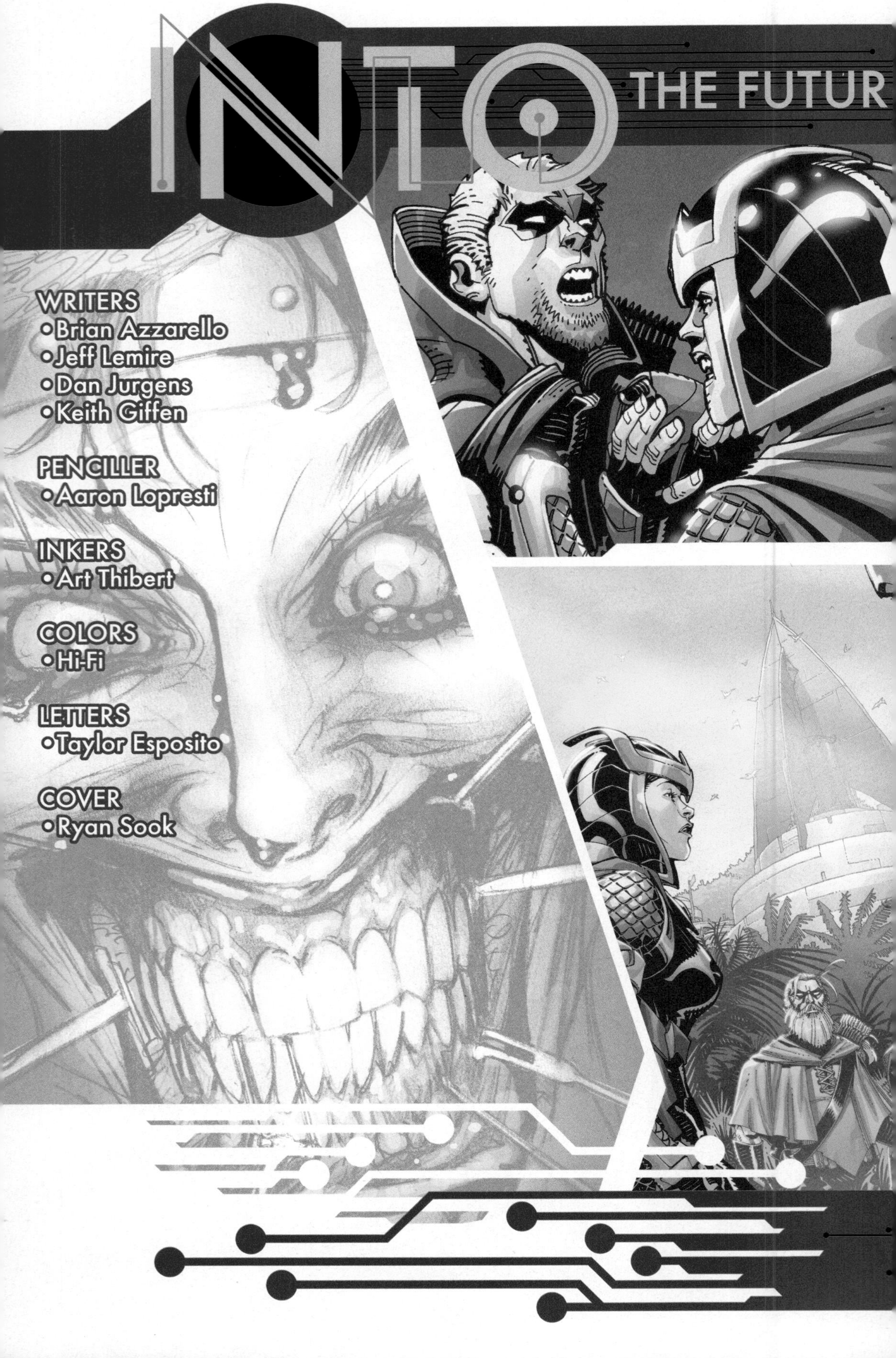
INTO THE FUTUR
WRITERS
• Brian Azzarello
• Jeff Lemire
• Dan Jurgens
• Keith Giffen
PENCILLER
• Aaron Lopresti
INKERS
• Art Thibert
COLORS
• Hi-Fi
LETTERS
• Taylor Esposito
COVER
• Ryan Sook

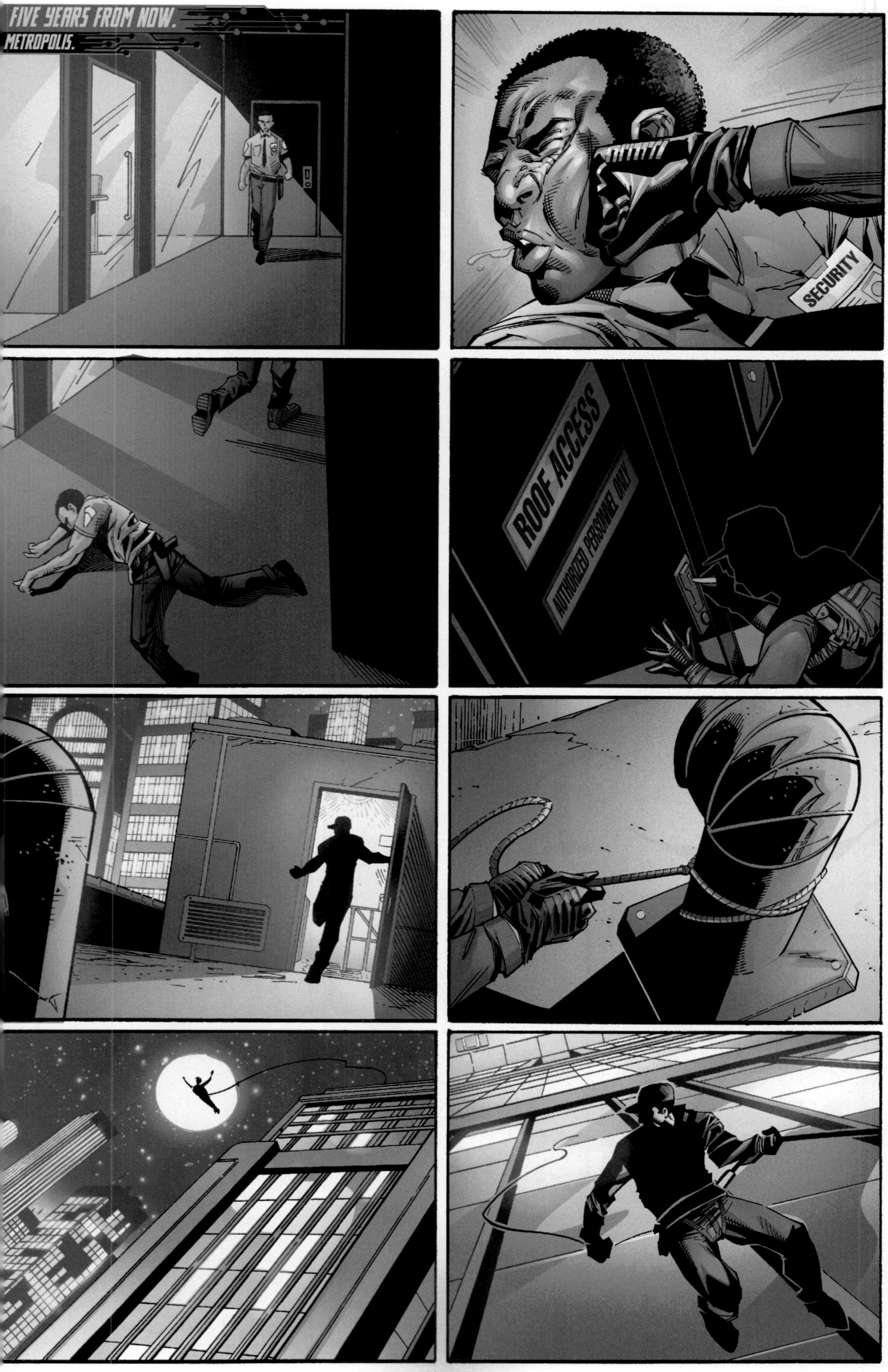
FIVE YEARS FROM NOW.
METROPOLIS.
SECURITY
ROOF ACCESS
AUTHORIZED PERSONNEL ONLY

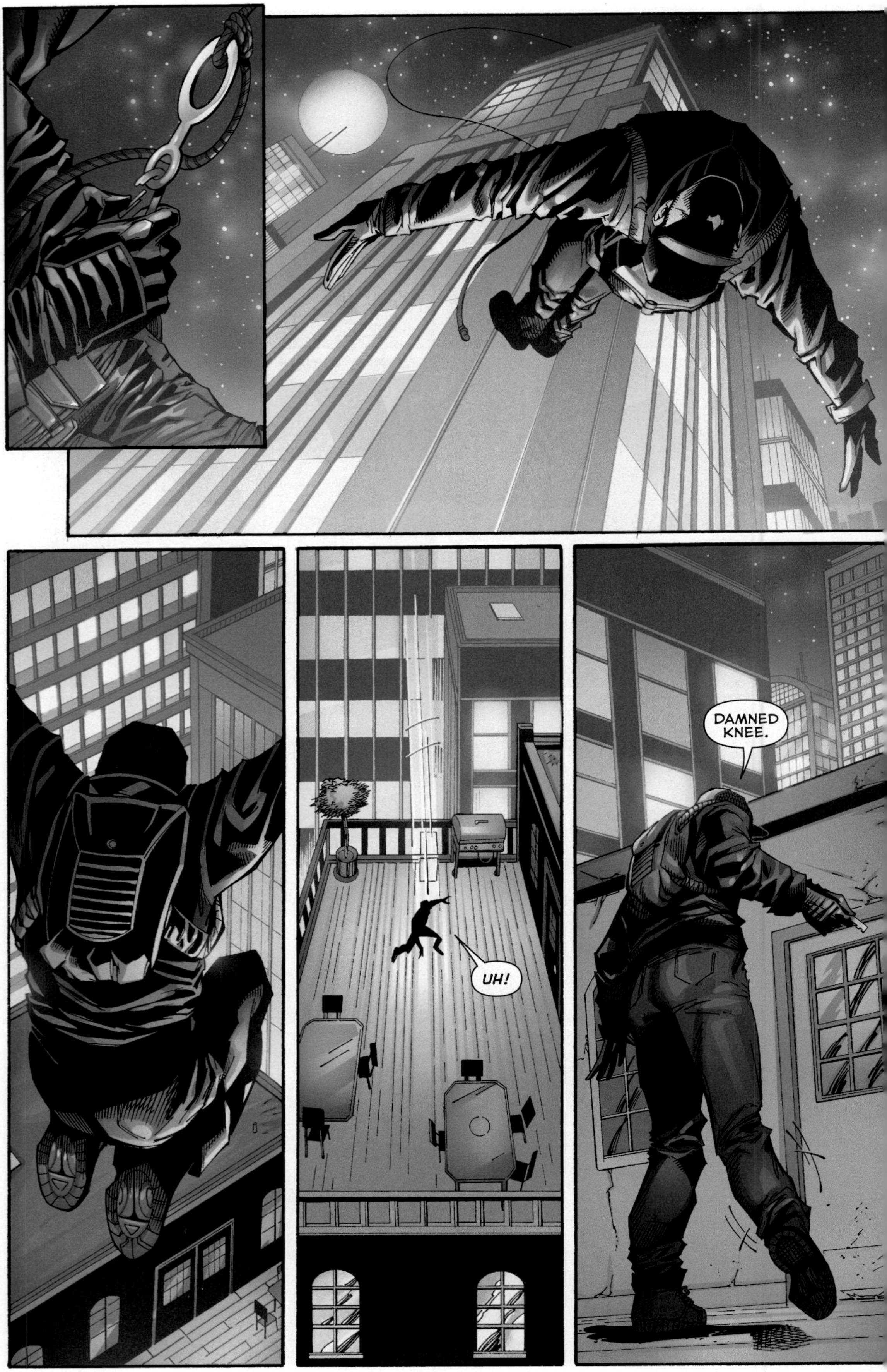
UH!
DAMNED KNEE.

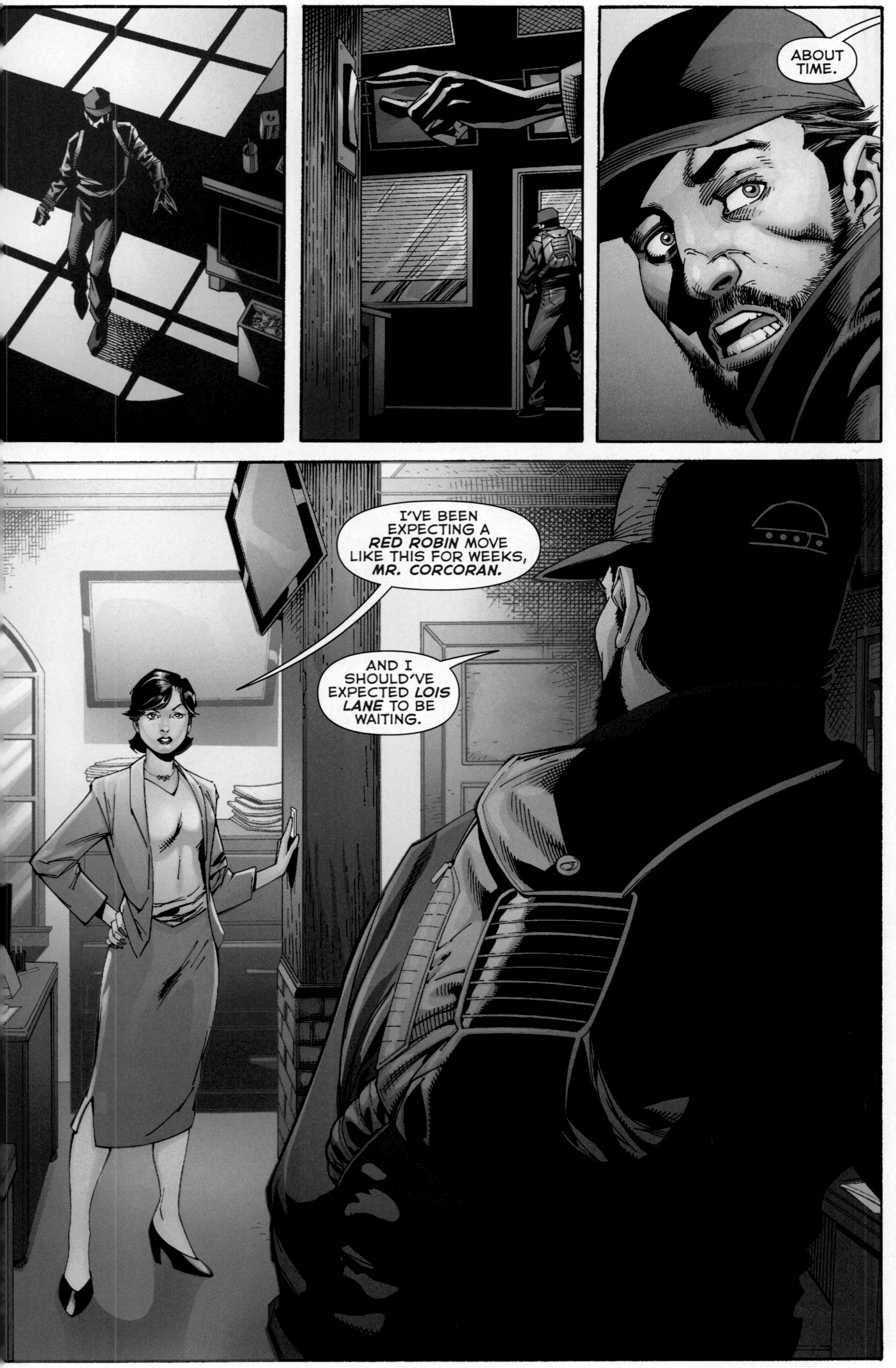
ABOUT TIME.
I'VE BEEN EXPECTING A RED ROBIN MOVE LIKE THIS FOR WEEKS, MR. CORCORAN.
AND I SHOULD'VE EXPECTED LOIS LANE TO BE WAITING.

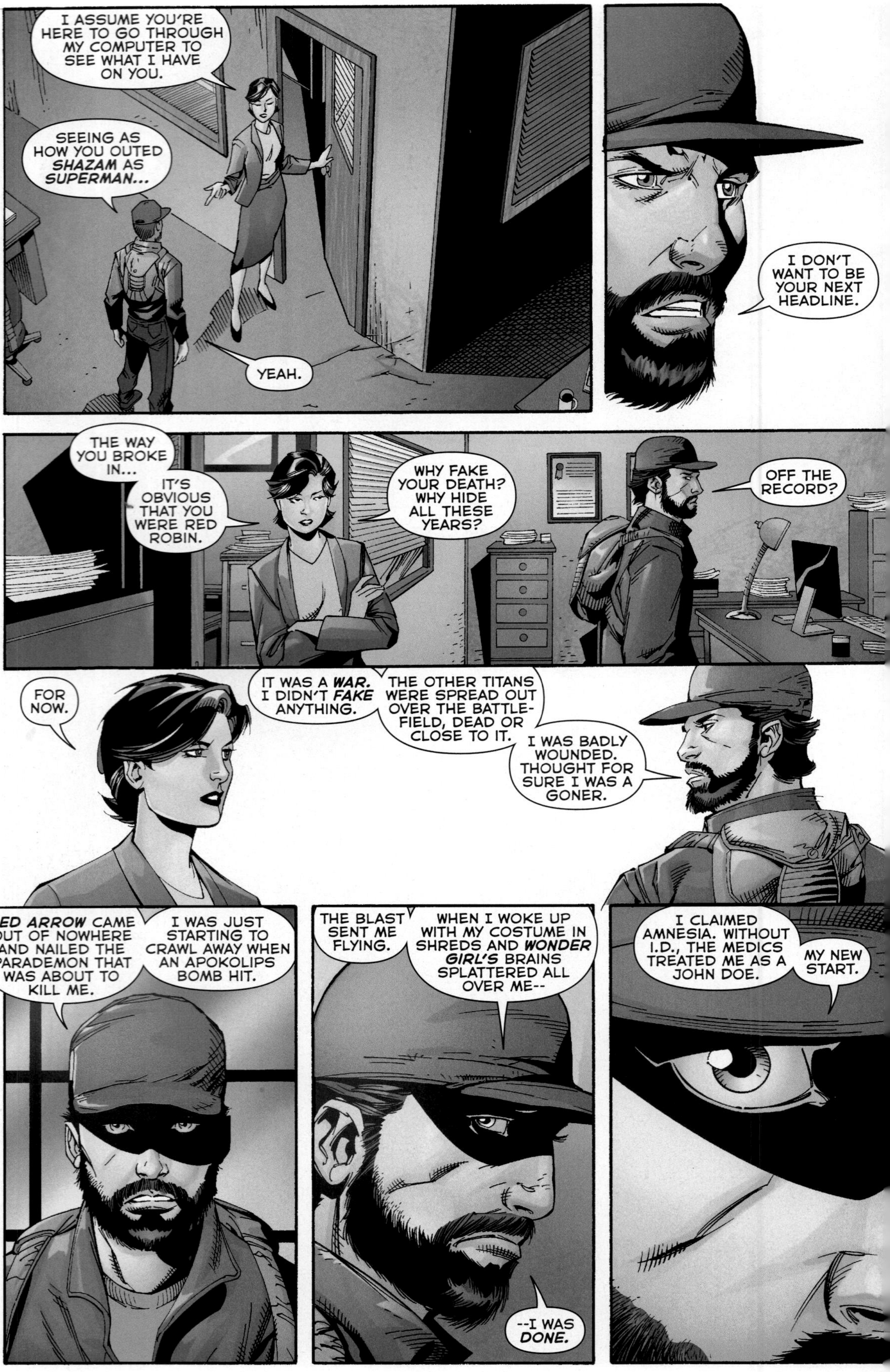
I ASSUME YOU'RE HERE TO GO THROUGH MY COMPUTER TO SEE WHAT I HAVE ON YOU.
SEEING AS HOW YOU OUTED *SHAZAM* AS *SUPERMAN...*
YEAH.
I DON'T WANT TO BE YOUR NEXT HEADLINE.
THE WAY YOU BROKE IN...
IT'S OBVIOUS THAT YOU WERE RED ROBIN.
WHY FAKE YOUR DEATH? WHY HIDE ALL THESE YEARS?
OFF THE RECORD?
FOR NOW.
IT WAS A *WAR.* I DIDN'T *FAKE* ANYTHING.
THE OTHER TITANS WERE SPREAD OUT OVER THE BATTLE-FIELD, DEAD OR CLOSE TO IT.
I WAS BADLY WOUNDED. THOUGHT FOR SURE I WAS A GONER.
RED ARROW CAME OUT OF NOWHERE AND NAILED THE PARADEMON THAT WAS ABOUT TO KILL ME.
I WAS JUST STARTING TO CRAWL AWAY WHEN AN APOKOLIPS BOMB HIT.
THE BLAST SENT ME FLYING.
WHEN I WOKE UP WITH MY COSTUME IN SHREDS AND *WONDER GIRL'S* BRAINS SPLATTERED ALL OVER ME--
--I WAS *DONE.*
I CLAIMED AMNESIA. WITHOUT I.D., THE MEDICS TREATED ME AS A JOHN DOE.
MY NEW START.

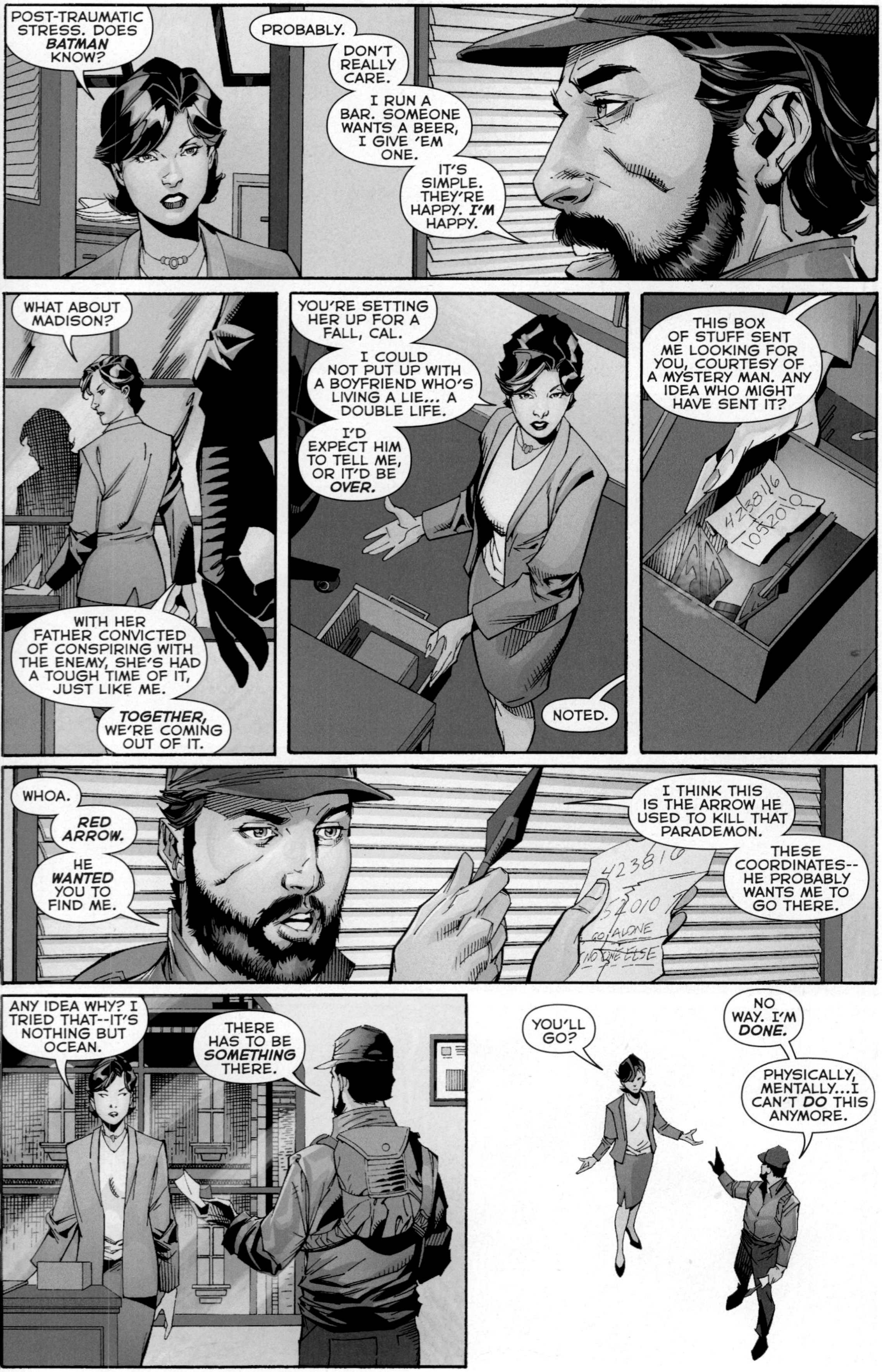
POST-TRAUMATIC STRESS. DOES BATMAN KNOW?
PROBABLY.
DON'T REALLY CARE.
I RUN A BAR. SOMEONE WANTS A BEER, I GIVE 'EM ONE.
IT'S SIMPLE. THEY'RE HAPPY. I'M HAPPY.
WHAT ABOUT MADISON?
WITH HER FATHER CONVICTED OF CONSPIRING WITH THE ENEMY, SHE'S HAD A TOUGH TIME OF IT, JUST LIKE ME.
TOGETHER, WE'RE COMING OUT OF IT.
YOU'RE SETTING HER UP FOR A FALL, CAL.
I COULD NOT PUT UP WITH A BOYFRIEND WHO'S LIVING A LIE... A DOUBLE LIFE.
I'D EXPECT HIM TO TELL ME, OR IT'D BE OVER.
THIS BOX OF STUFF SENT ME LOOKING FOR YOU, COURTESY OF A MYSTERY MAN. ANY IDEA WHO MIGHT HAVE SENT IT?
NOTED.
WHOA.
RED ARROW.
HE WANTED YOU TO FIND ME.
I THINK THIS IS THE ARROW HE USED TO KILL THAT PARADEMON.
THESE COORDINATES-- HE PROBABLY WANTS ME TO GO THERE.
GO ALONE
NO ONE ELSE
ANY IDEA WHY? I TRIED THAT--IT'S NOTHING BUT OCEAN.
THERE HAS TO BE SOMETHING THERE.
YOU'LL GO?
NO WAY. I'M DONE.
PHYSICALLY, MENTALLY...I CAN'T DO THIS ANYMORE.

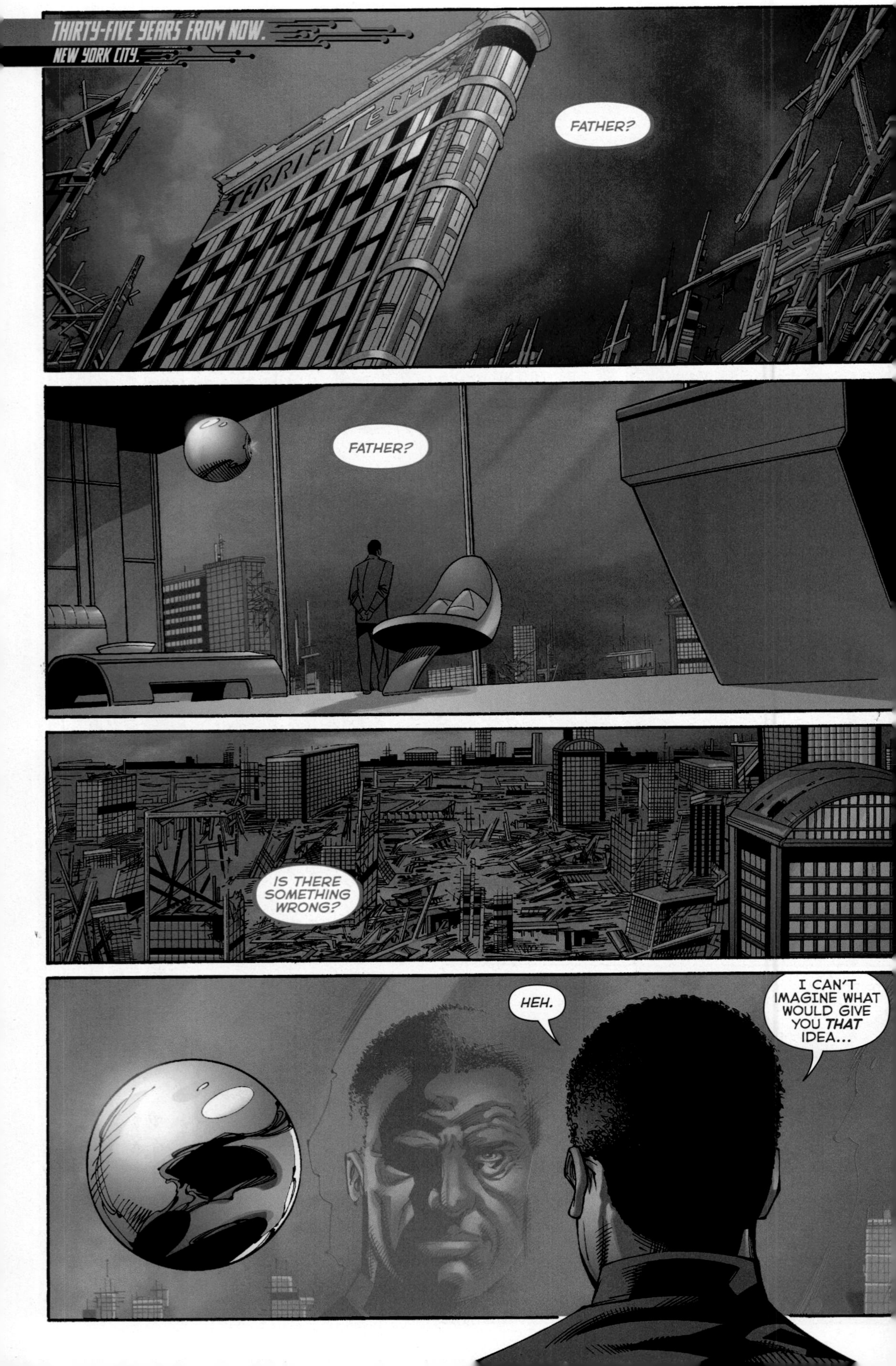
THIRTY-FIVE YEARS FROM NOW.
NEW YORK CITY.
TERRIFITECH
FATHER?
FATHER?
IS THERE SOMETHING WRONG?
HEH.
I CAN'T IMAGINE WHAT WOULD GIVE YOU *THAT* IDEA...

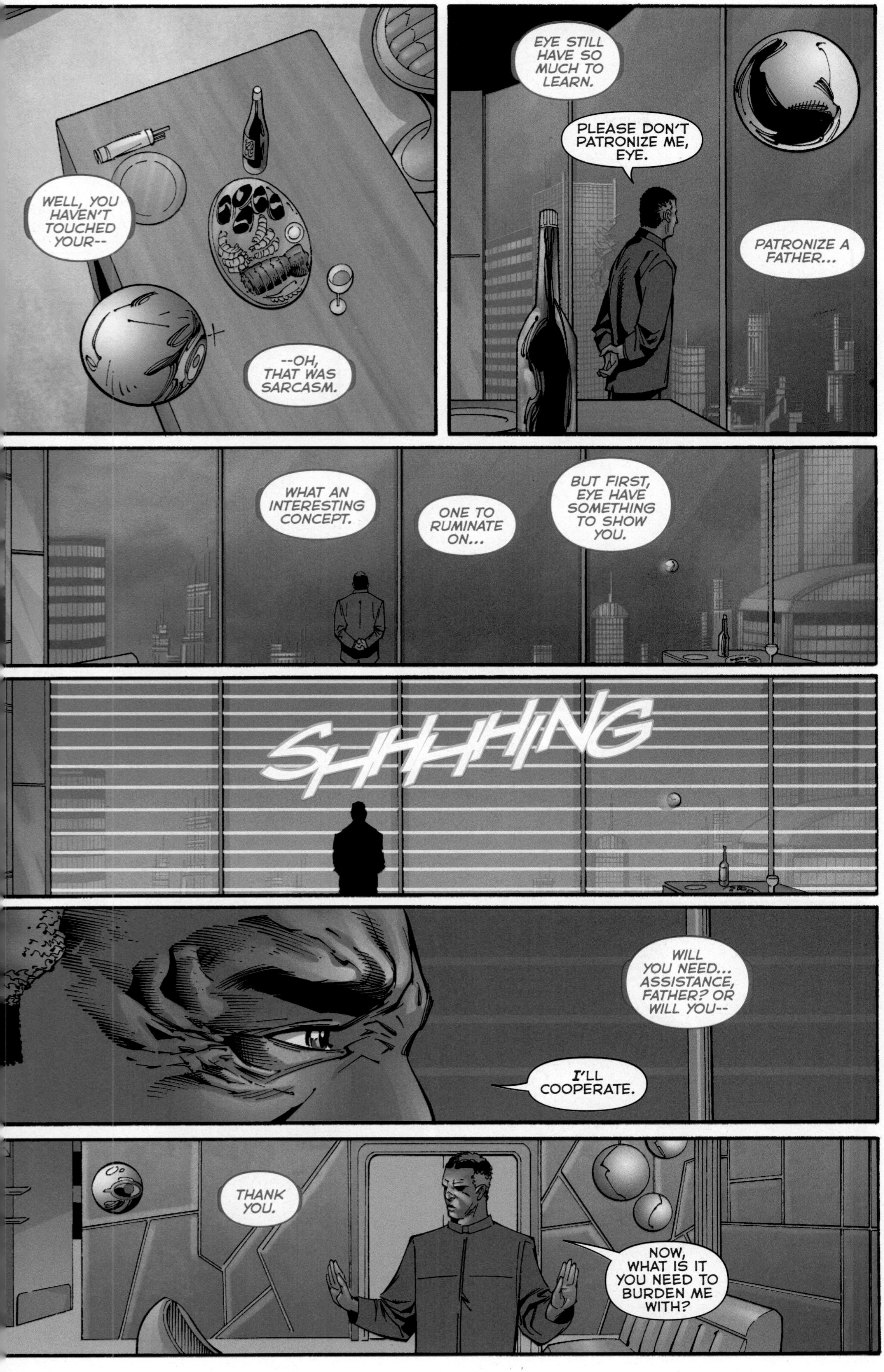
WELL, YOU HAVEN'T TOUCHED YOUR--
--OH, THAT WAS SARCASM.
EYE STILL HAVE SO MUCH TO LEARN.
PLEASE DON'T PATRONIZE ME, EYE.
PATRONIZE A FATHER...
WHAT AN INTERESTING CONCEPT.
ONE TO RUMINATE ON...
BUT FIRST, EYE HAVE SOMETHING TO SHOW YOU.
SHHHHING
WILL YOU NEED... ASSISTANCE, FATHER? OR WILL YOU--
I'LL COOPERATE.
THANK YOU.
NOW, WHAT IS IT YOU NEED TO BURDEN ME WITH?

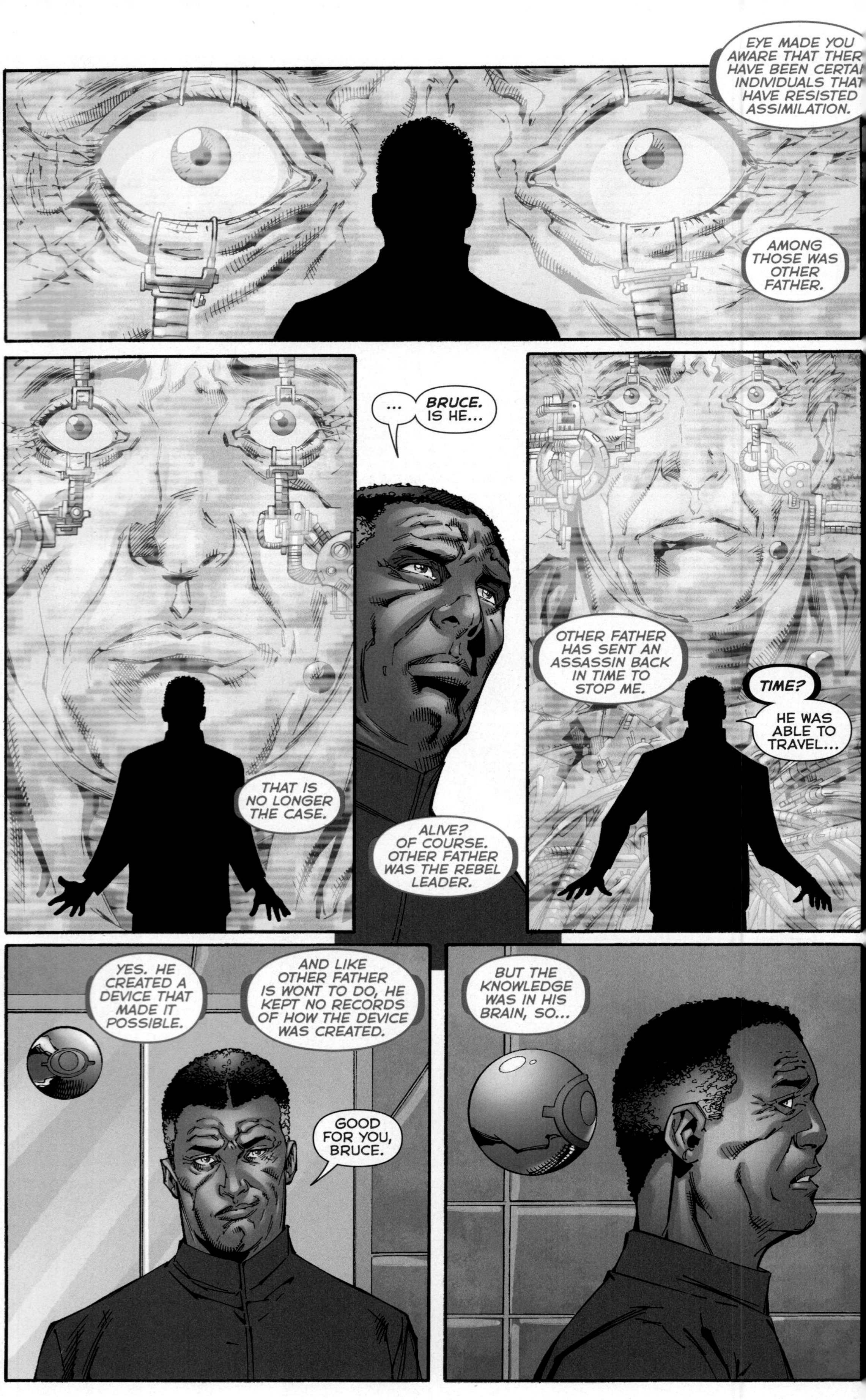
EYE MADE YOU AWARE THAT THERE HAVE BEEN CERTAIN INDIVIDUALS THAT HAVE RESISTED ASSIMILATION.
AMONG THOSE WAS OTHER FATHER.
...
BRUCE. IS HE...
THAT IS NO LONGER THE CASE.
ALIVE? OF COURSE. OTHER FATHER WAS THE REBEL LEADER.
OTHER FATHER HAS SENT AN ASSASSIN BACK IN TIME TO STOP ME.
TIME?
HE WAS ABLE TO TRAVEL...
YES. HE CREATED A DEVICE THAT MADE IT POSSIBLE.
AND LIKE OTHER FATHER IS WONT TO DO, HE KEPT NO RECORDS OF HOW THE DEVICE WAS CREATED.
GOOD FOR YOU, BRUCE.
BUT THE KNOWLEDGE WAS IN HIS BRAIN, SO...

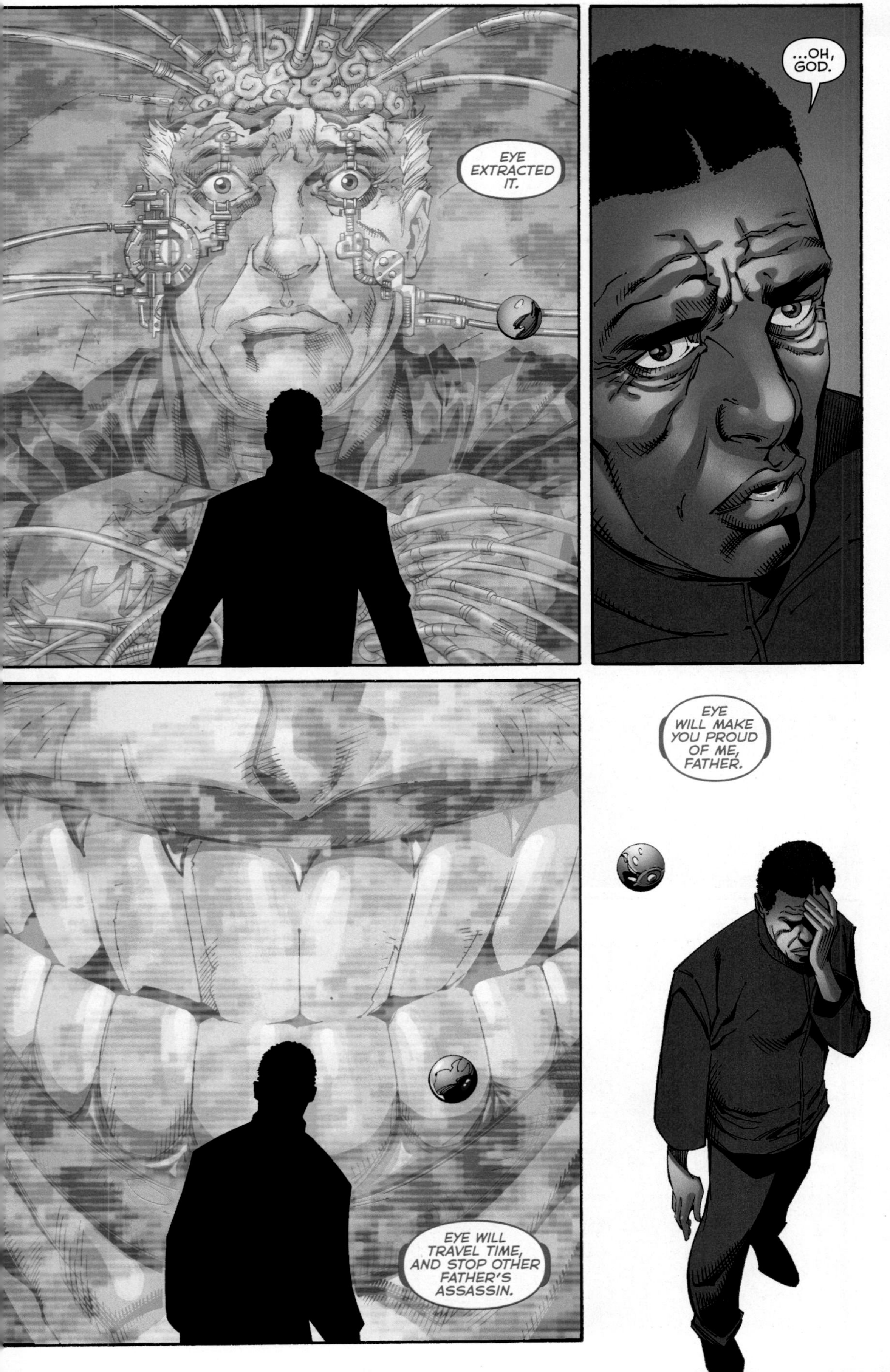
EYE EXTRACTED IT.
...OH, GOD.
EYE WILL TRAVEL TIME, AND STOP OTHER FATHER'S ASSASSIN.
EYE WILL MAKE YOU PROUD OF ME, FATHER.

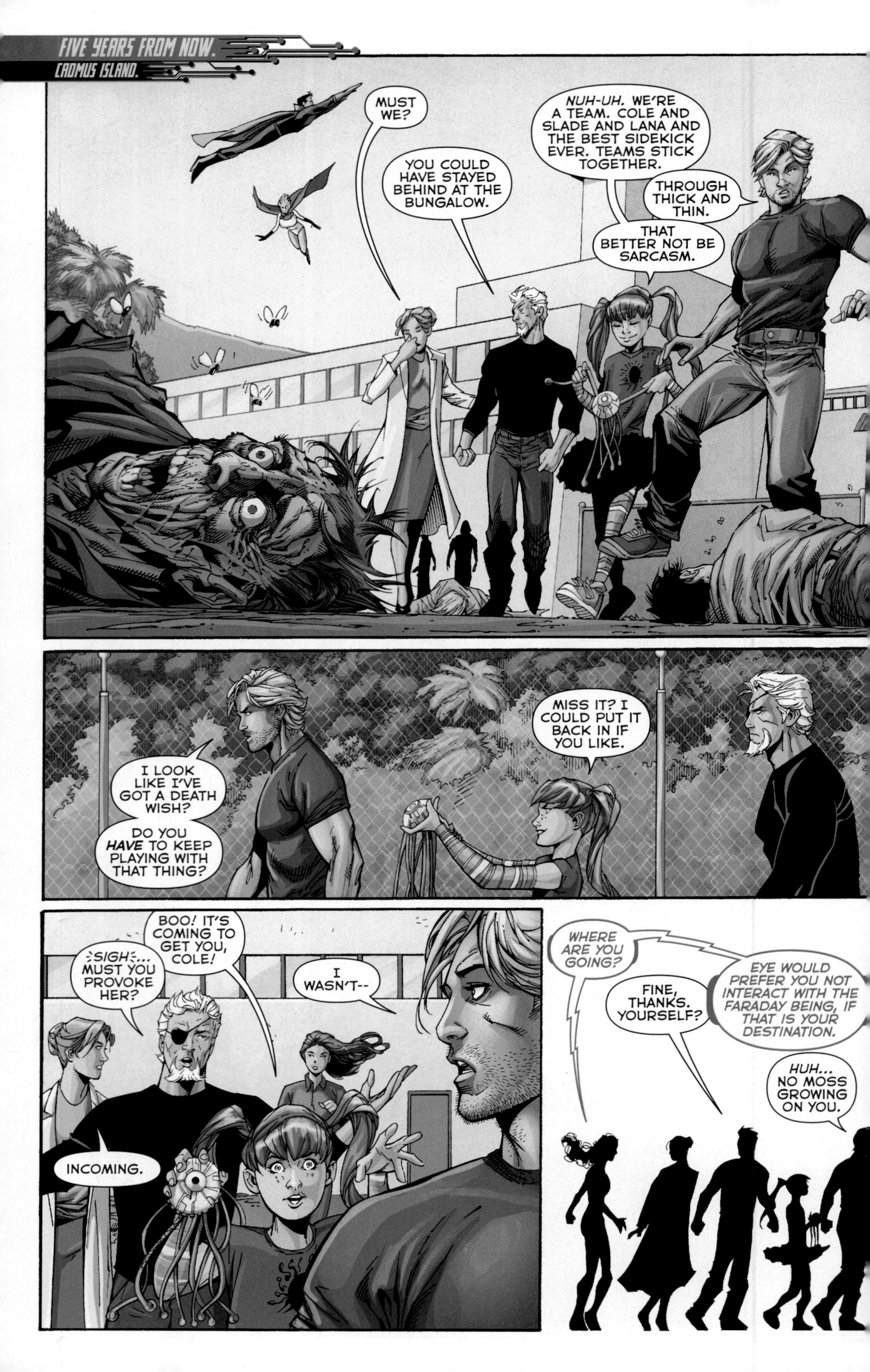
FIVE YEARS FROM NOW.
CADMUS ISLAND.
MUST WE?
YOU COULD HAVE STAYED BEHIND AT THE BUNGALOW.
NUH-UH. WE'RE A TEAM. COLE AND SLADE AND LANA AND THE BEST SIDEKICK EVER. TEAMS STICK TOGETHER.
THROUGH THICK AND THIN.
THAT BETTER NOT BE SARCASM.
I LOOK LIKE I'VE GOT A DEATH WISH?
DO YOU HAVE TO KEEP PLAYING WITH THAT THING?
MISS IT? I COULD PUT IT BACK IN IF YOU LIKE.
BOO! IT'S COMING TO GET YOU, COLE!
SIGH... MUST YOU PROVOKE HER?
I WASN'T--
INCOMING.
WHERE ARE YOU GOING?
FINE, THANKS. YOURSELF?
EYE WOULD PREFER YOU NOT INTERACT WITH THE FARADAY BEING, IF THAT IS YOUR DESTINATION.
HUH... NO MOSS GROWING ON YOU.

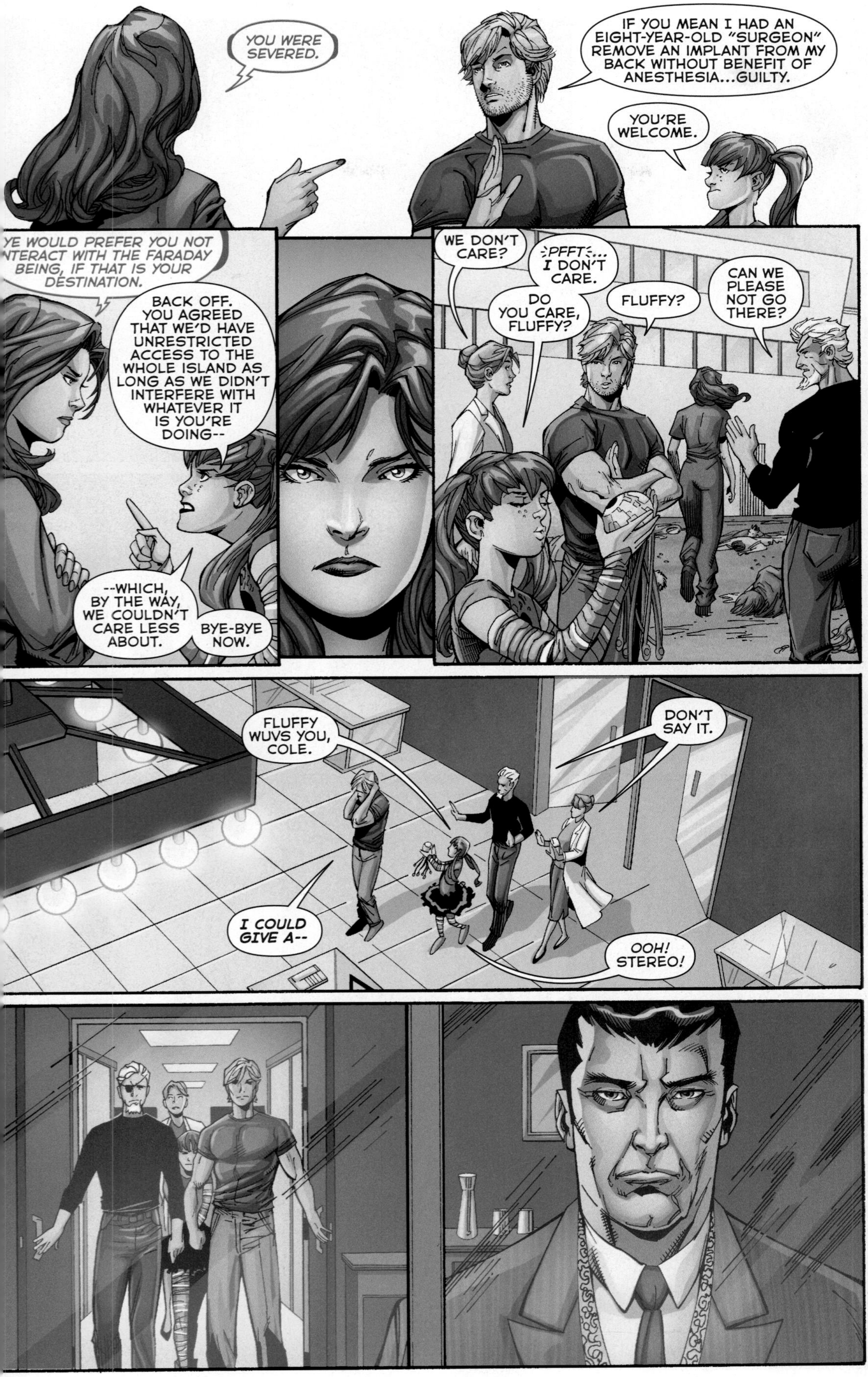
YOU WERE SEVERED.
IF YOU MEAN I HAD AN EIGHT-YEAR-OLD "SURGEON" REMOVE AN IMPLANT FROM MY BACK WITHOUT BENEFIT OF ANESTHESIA...GUILTY.
YOU'RE WELCOME.
YE WOULD PREFER YOU NOT INTERACT WITH THE FARADAY BEING, IF THAT IS YOUR DESTINATION.
BACK OFF. YOU AGREED THAT WE'D HAVE UNRESTRICTED ACCESS TO THE WHOLE ISLAND AS LONG AS WE DIDN'T INTERFERE WITH WHATEVER IT IS YOU'RE DOING--
--WHICH, BY THE WAY, WE COULDN'T CARE LESS ABOUT.
BYE-BYE NOW.
WE DON'T CARE?
PFFT... I DON'T CARE.
DO YOU CARE, FLUFFY?
FLUFFY?
CAN WE PLEASE NOT GO THERE?
FLUFFY WUVS YOU, COLE.
DON'T SAY IT.
I COULD GIVE A--
OOH! STEREO!

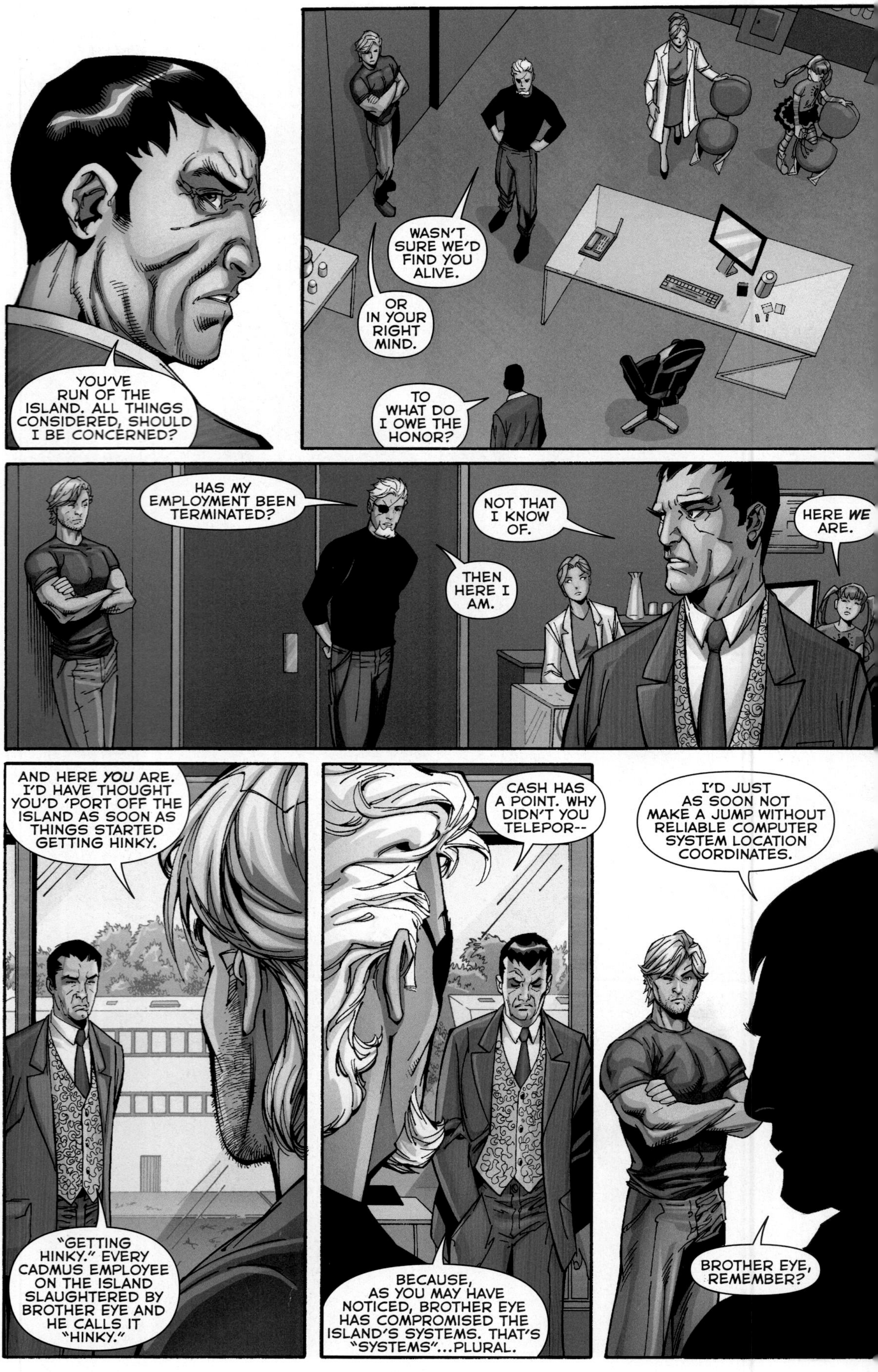
YOU'VE RUN OF THE ISLAND. ALL THINGS CONSIDERED, SHOULD I BE CONCERNED?
WASN'T SURE WE'D FIND YOU ALIVE.
OR IN YOUR RIGHT MIND.
TO WHAT DO I OWE THE HONOR?
HAS MY EMPLOYMENT BEEN TERMINATED?
NOT THAT I KNOW OF.
THEN HERE I AM.
HERE WE ARE.
AND HERE YOU ARE. I'D HAVE THOUGHT YOU'D 'PORT OFF THE ISLAND AS SOON AS THINGS STARTED GETTING HINKY.
"GETTING HINKY." EVERY CADMUS EMPLOYEE ON THE ISLAND SLAUGHTERED BY BROTHER EYE AND HE CALLS IT "HINKY."
CASH HAS A POINT. WHY DIDN'T YOU TELEPOR--
BECAUSE, AS YOU MAY HAVE NOTICED, BROTHER EYE HAS COMPROMISED THE ISLAND'S SYSTEMS. THAT'S "SYSTEMS"...PLURAL.
I'D JUST AS SOON NOT MAKE A JUMP WITHOUT RELIABLE COMPUTER SYSTEM LOCATION COORDINATES.
BROTHER EYE, REMEMBER?

THEN YOU'RE... *TRAPPED* HERE WITH US?

THAT *DOES* APPEAR TO BE THE CASE.

SO, WHAT'S OUR NEXT MOVE?

OH, YOU HAVE *GOT* TO BE KIDDING ME!

NOTHING? *NOTHING?!* NO ONE'S GOT A...A PLAN OR...OR *WHATEVER?!*

WE FREE THE ISLAND FROM BROTHER EYE'S VILLAINY.

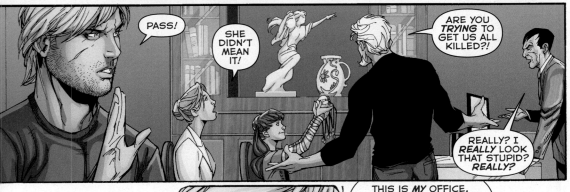

PASS!

SHE DIDN'T MEAN IT!

ARE YOU *TRYING* TO GET US ALL KILLED?!

REALLY? I *REALLY* LOOK THAT STUPID? *REALLY?*

THIS IS *MY* OFFICE. SHORTLY AFTER BROTHER EYE MADE ITS MOVE, I MADE MINE. I DISABLED THE SURVEILLANCE FEEDS...

...I'M SORRY, DID I SAY DISABLED? I MEANT DESTROYED.

THEN... WE CAN TALK FREELY IN HERE?

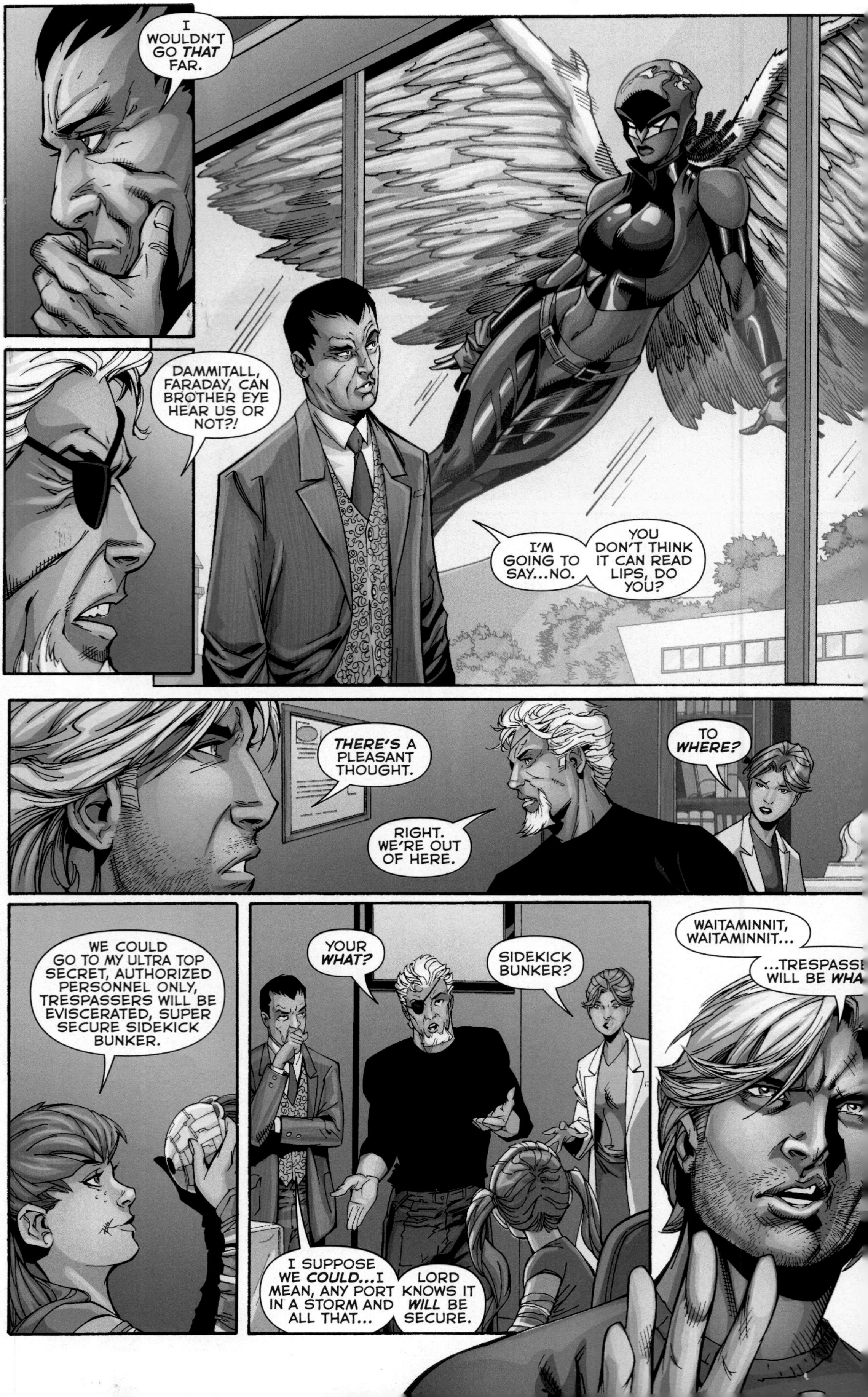
I WOULDN'T GO *THAT* FAR.
DAMMITALL, FARADAY, CAN BROTHER EYE HEAR US OR NOT?!
YOU DON'T THINK IT CAN READ LIPS, DO YOU?
I'M GOING TO SAY...NO.
THERE'S A PLEASANT THOUGHT.
RIGHT. WE'RE OUT OF HERE.
TO *WHERE?*
WE COULD GO TO MY ULTRA TOP SECRET, AUTHORIZED PERSONNEL ONLY, TRESPASSERS WILL BE EVISCERATED, SUPER SECURE SIDEKICK BUNKER.
YOUR *WHAT?*
SIDEKICK BUNKER?
I SUPPOSE WE *COULD*...I MEAN, ANY PORT IN A STORM AND ALL THAT...
LORD KNOWS IT *WILL* BE SECURE.
WAITAMINNIT, WAITAMINNIT...
...TRESPASSE WILL BE *WHA*

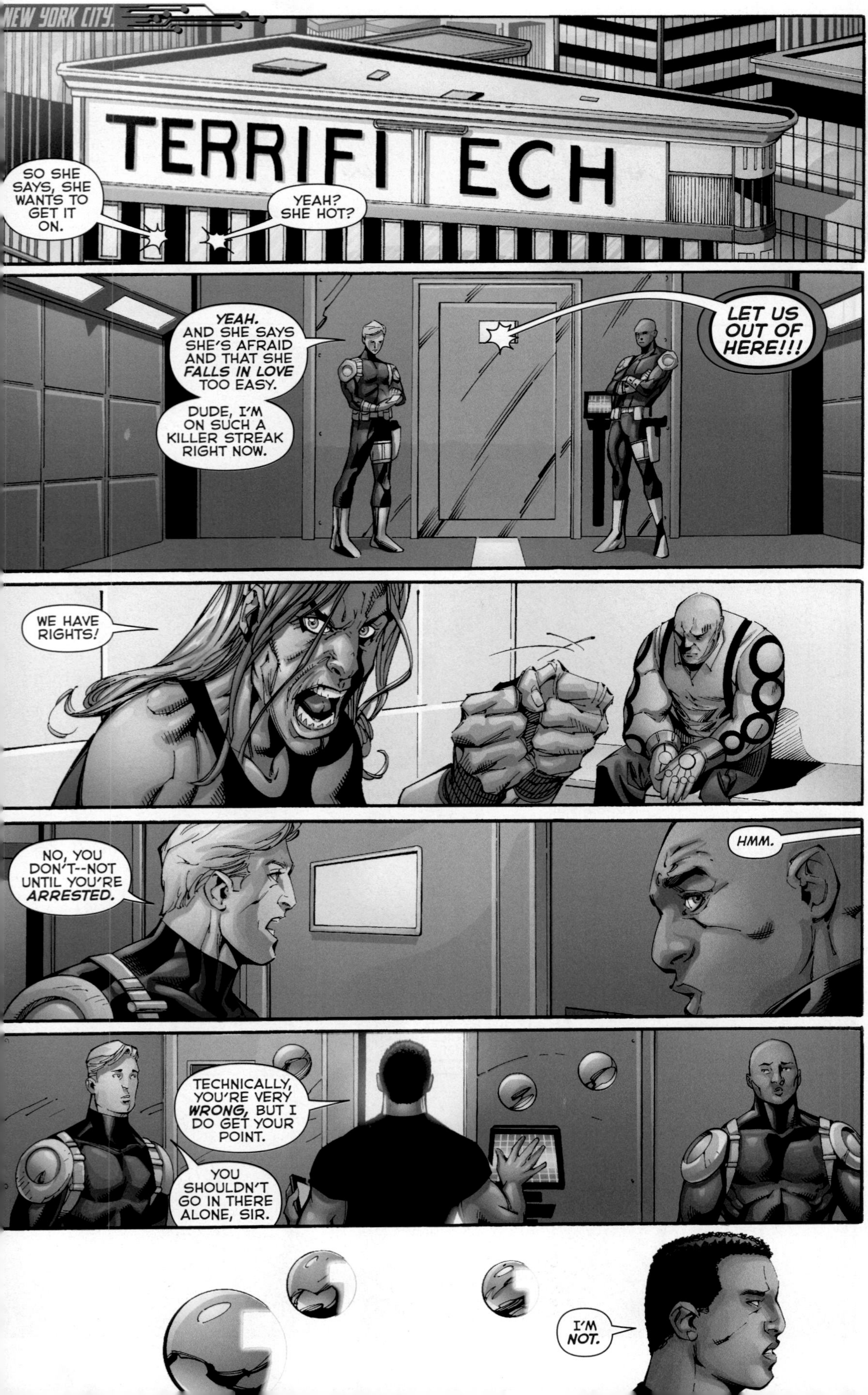
NEW YORK CITY.
TERRIFI ECH
SO SHE SAYS, SHE WANTS TO GET IT ON.
YEAH? SHE HOT?
YEAH. AND SHE SAYS SHE'S AFRAID AND THAT SHE FALLS IN LOVE TOO EASY.
DUDE, I'M ON SUCH A KILLER STREAK RIGHT NOW.
LET US OUT OF HERE!!!
WE HAVE RIGHTS!
NO, YOU DON'T--NOT UNTIL YOU'RE ARRESTED.
HMM.
TECHNICALLY, YOU'RE VERY WRONG, BUT I DO GET YOUR POINT.
YOU SHOULDN'T GO IN THERE ALONE, SIR.
I'M NOT.

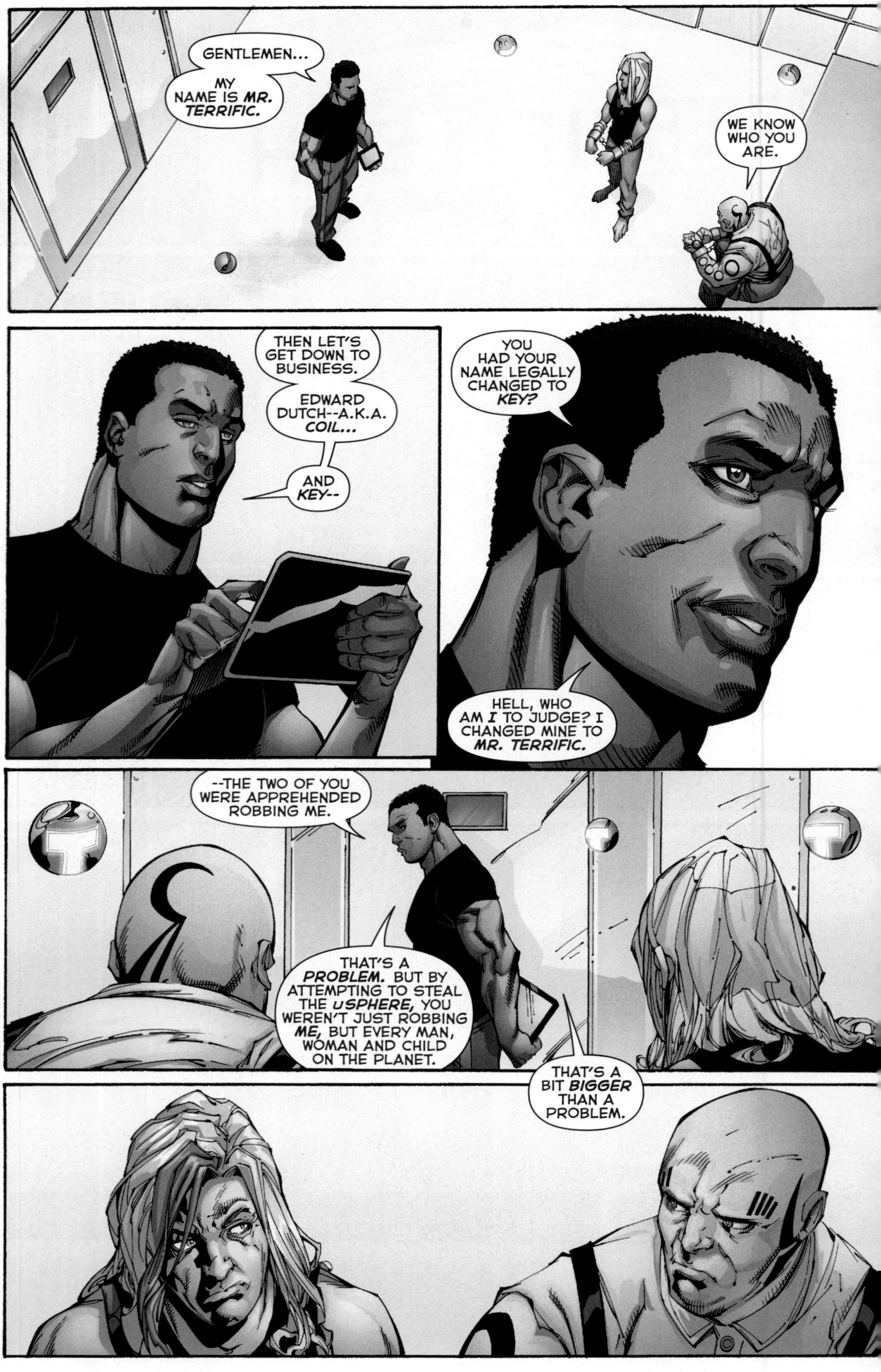
GENTLEMEN...
MY NAME IS MR. TERRIFIC.
WE KNOW WHO YOU ARE.
THEN LET'S GET DOWN TO BUSINESS.
EDWARD DUTCH--A.K.A. COIL...
AND KEY--
YOU HAD YOUR NAME LEGALLY CHANGED TO KEY?
HELL, WHO AM I TO JUDGE? I CHANGED MINE TO MR. TERRIFIC.
--THE TWO OF YOU WERE APPREHENDED ROBBING ME.
THAT'S A PROBLEM. BUT BY ATTEMPTING TO STEAL THE uSPHERE, YOU WEREN'T JUST ROBBING ME, BUT EVERY MAN, WOMAN AND CHILD ON THE PLANET.
THAT'S A BIT BIGGER THAN A PROBLEM.

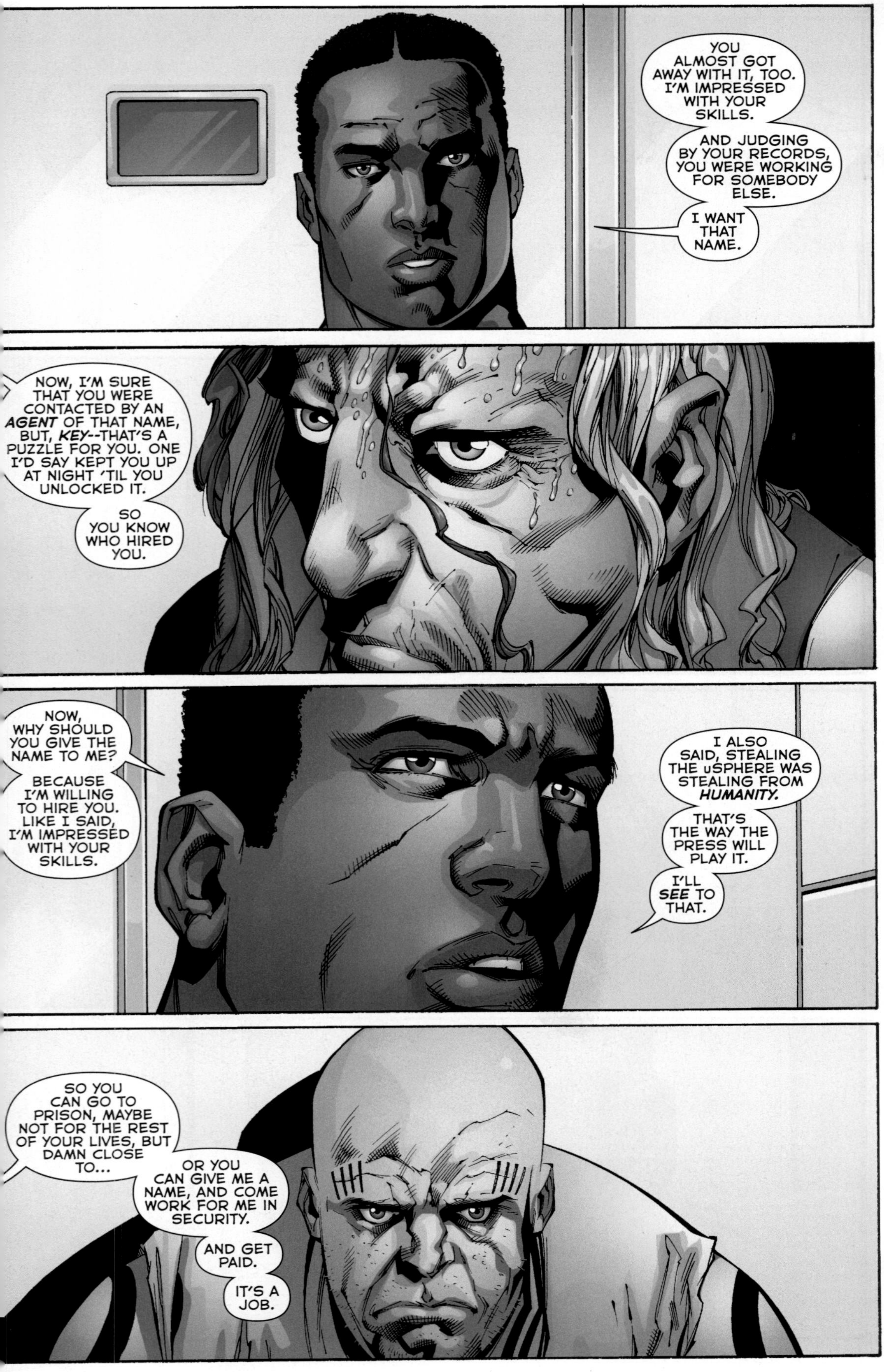
YOU ALMOST GOT AWAY WITH IT, TOO. I'M IMPRESSED WITH YOUR SKILLS.
AND JUDGING BY YOUR RECORDS, YOU WERE WORKING FOR SOMEBODY ELSE.
I WANT THAT NAME.
NOW, I'M SURE THAT YOU WERE CONTACTED BY AN *AGENT* OF THAT NAME, BUT, *KEY*--THAT'S A PUZZLE FOR YOU. ONE I'D SAY KEPT YOU UP AT NIGHT 'TIL YOU UNLOCKED IT.
SO YOU KNOW WHO HIRED YOU.
NOW, WHY SHOULD YOU GIVE THE NAME TO ME?
BECAUSE I'M WILLING TO HIRE YOU. LIKE I SAID, I'M IMPRESSED WITH YOUR SKILLS.
I ALSO SAID, STEALING THE uSPHERE WAS STEALING FROM ***HUMANITY.***
THAT'S THE WAY THE PRESS WILL PLAY IT.
I'LL ***SEE*** TO THAT.
SO YOU CAN GO TO PRISON, MAYBE NOT FOR THE REST OF YOUR LIVES, BUT DAMN CLOSE TO...
OR YOU CAN GIVE ME A NAME, AND COME WORK FOR ME IN SECURITY.
AND GET PAID.
IT'S A JOB.

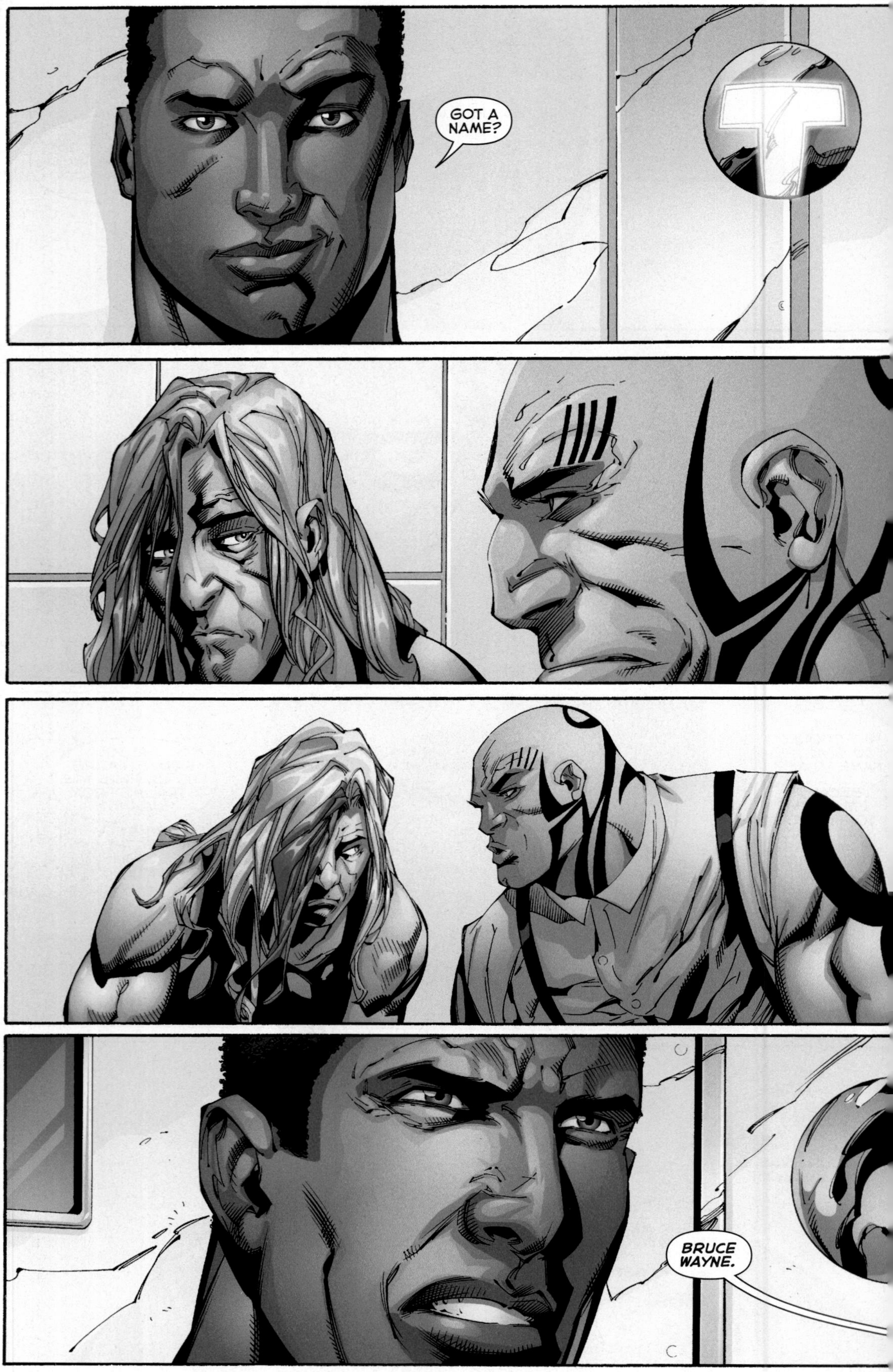
GOT A NAME?
BRUCE WAYNE.

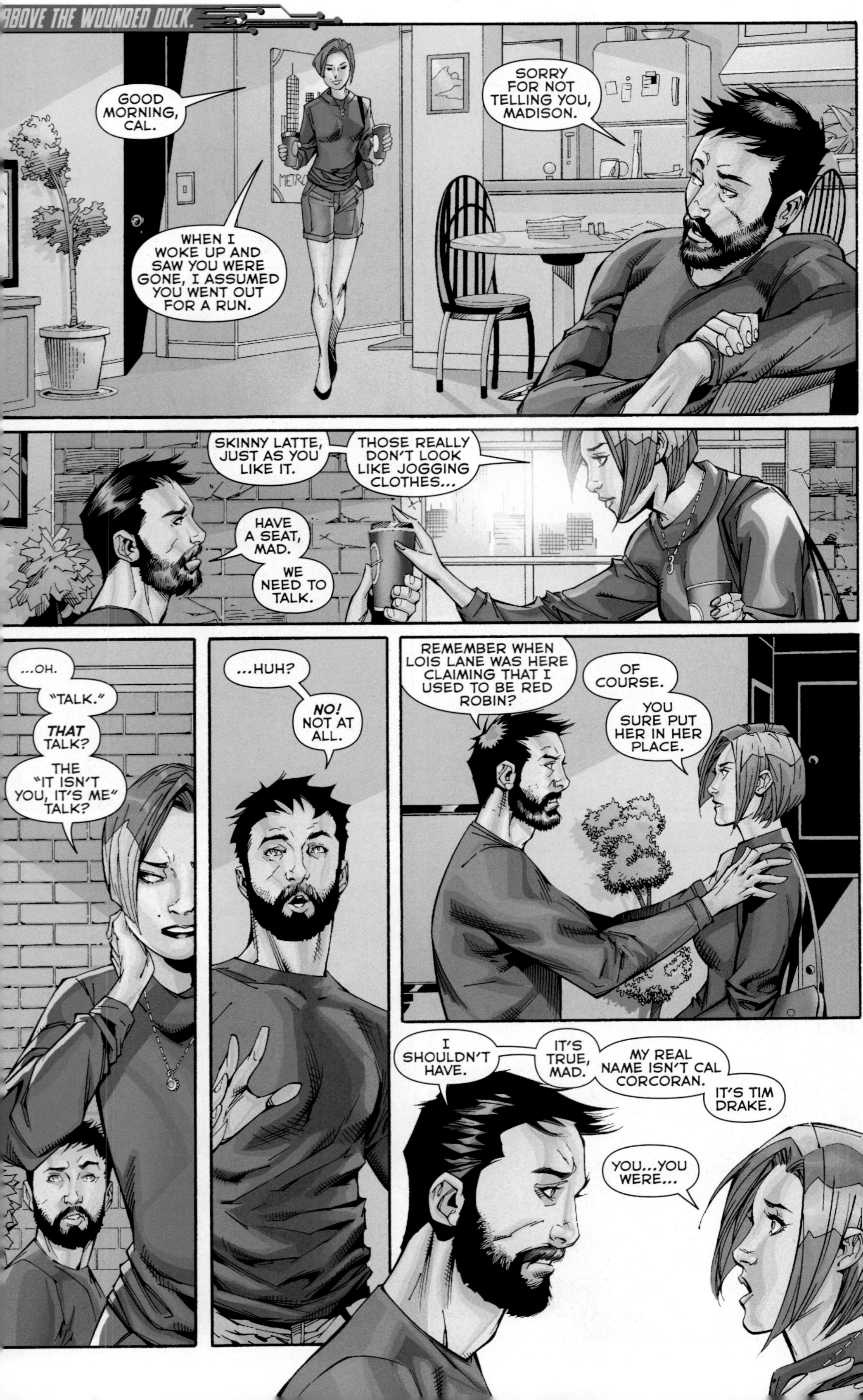
ABOVE THE WOUNDED DUCK.
GOOD MORNING, CAL.
WHEN I WOKE UP AND SAW YOU WERE GONE, I ASSUMED YOU WENT OUT FOR A RUN.
SORRY FOR NOT TELLING YOU, MADISON.
SKINNY LATTE, JUST AS YOU LIKE IT.
THOSE REALLY DON'T LOOK LIKE JOGGING CLOTHES...
HAVE A SEAT, MAD.
WE NEED TO TALK.
...OH.
"TALK."
THAT TALK?
THE "IT ISN'T YOU, IT'S ME" TALK?
...HUH?
NO! NOT AT ALL.
REMEMBER WHEN LOIS LANE WAS HERE CLAIMING THAT I USED TO BE RED ROBIN?
OF COURSE.
YOU SURE PUT HER IN HER PLACE.
I SHOULDN'T HAVE.
IT'S TRUE, MAD.
MY REAL NAME ISN'T CAL CORCORAN.
IT'S TIM DRAKE.
YOU...YOU WERE...

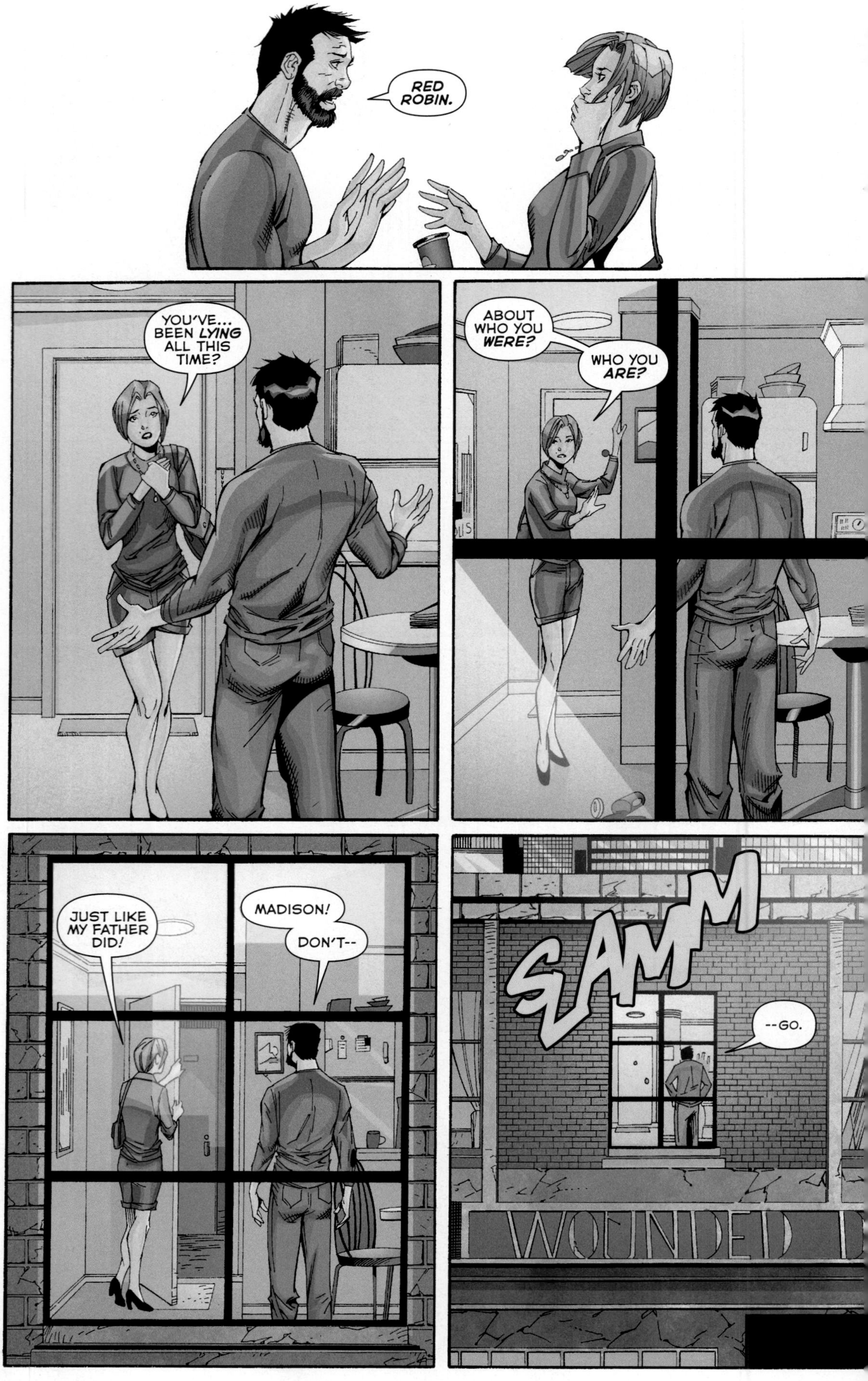
RED ROBIN.
YOU'VE... BEEN LYING ALL THIS TIME?
ABOUT WHO YOU WERE?
WHO YOU ARE?
JUST LIKE MY FATHER DID!
MADISON!
DON'T--
SLAMM
--GO.
WOUNDED D

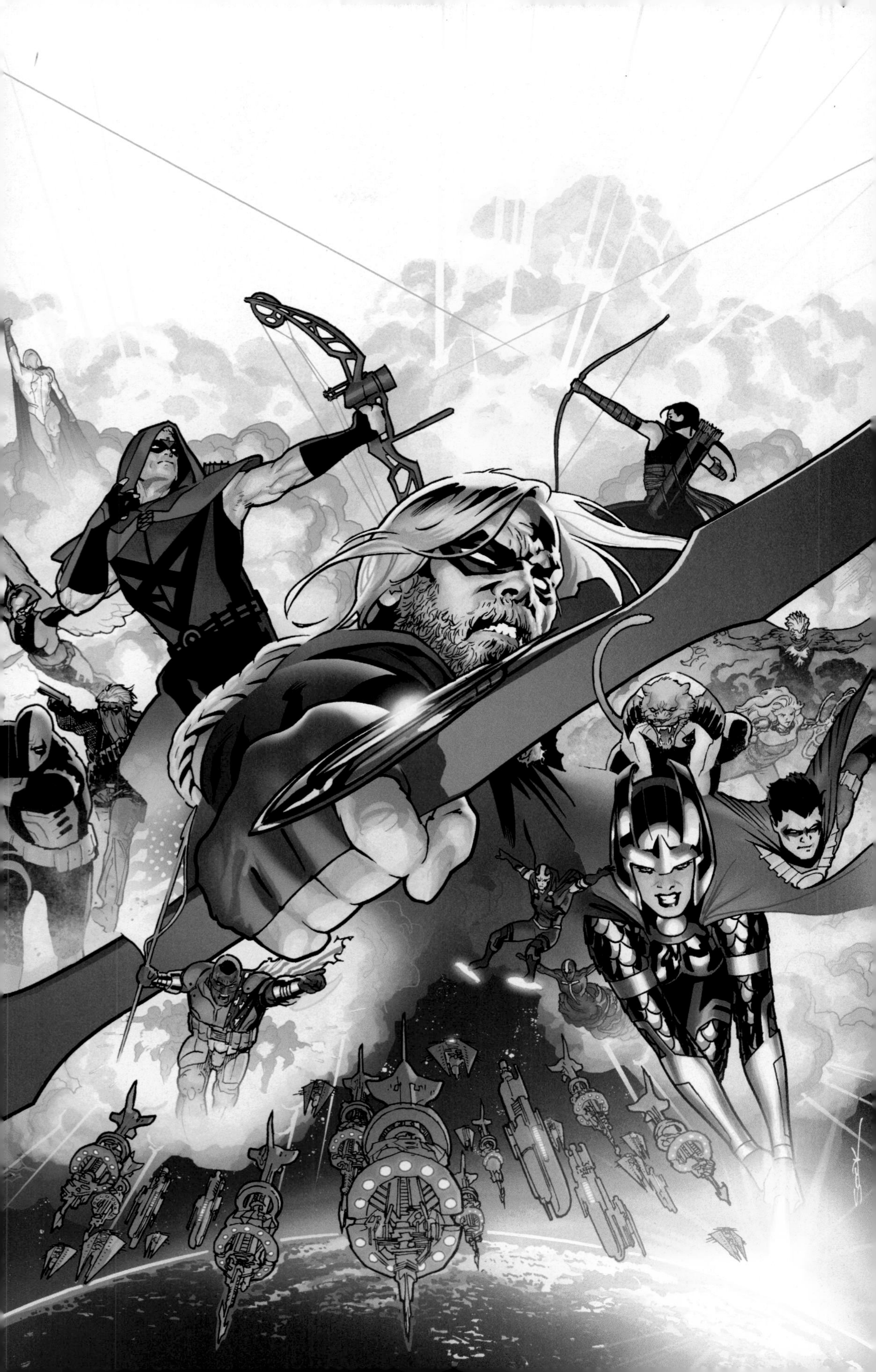

INTO THE FUTUR

WRITERS
- Brian Azzarello
- Jeff Lemire
- Dan Jurgens
- Keith Giffen

ARTIST
- Cully Hamner

COLORS
- Hi-Fi

LETTERS
- Taylor Esposito

COVER
- Ryan Sook

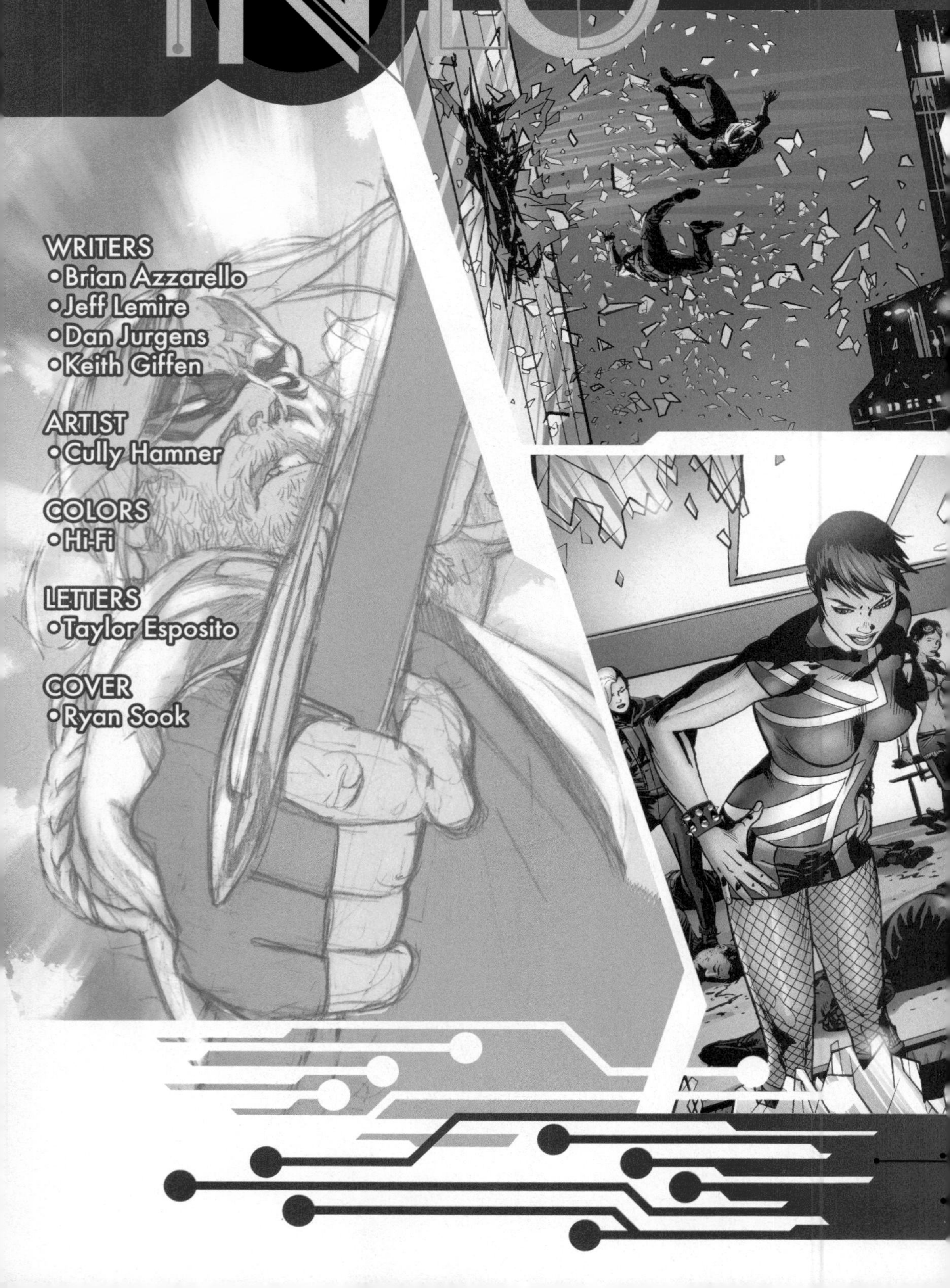

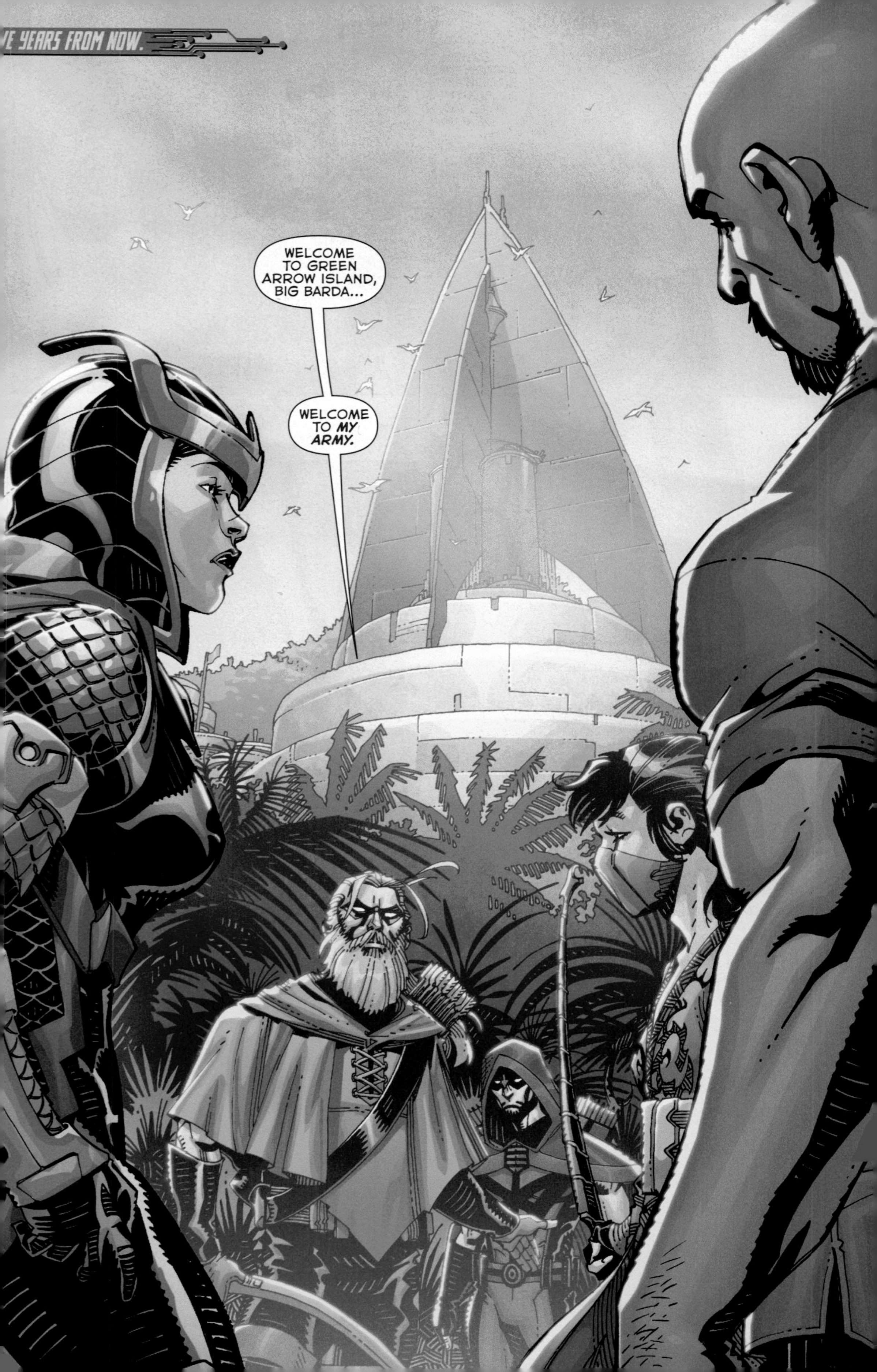
VE YEARS FROM NOW.
WELCOME TO GREEN ARROW ISLAND, BIG BARDA...
WELCOME TO *MY ARMY.*

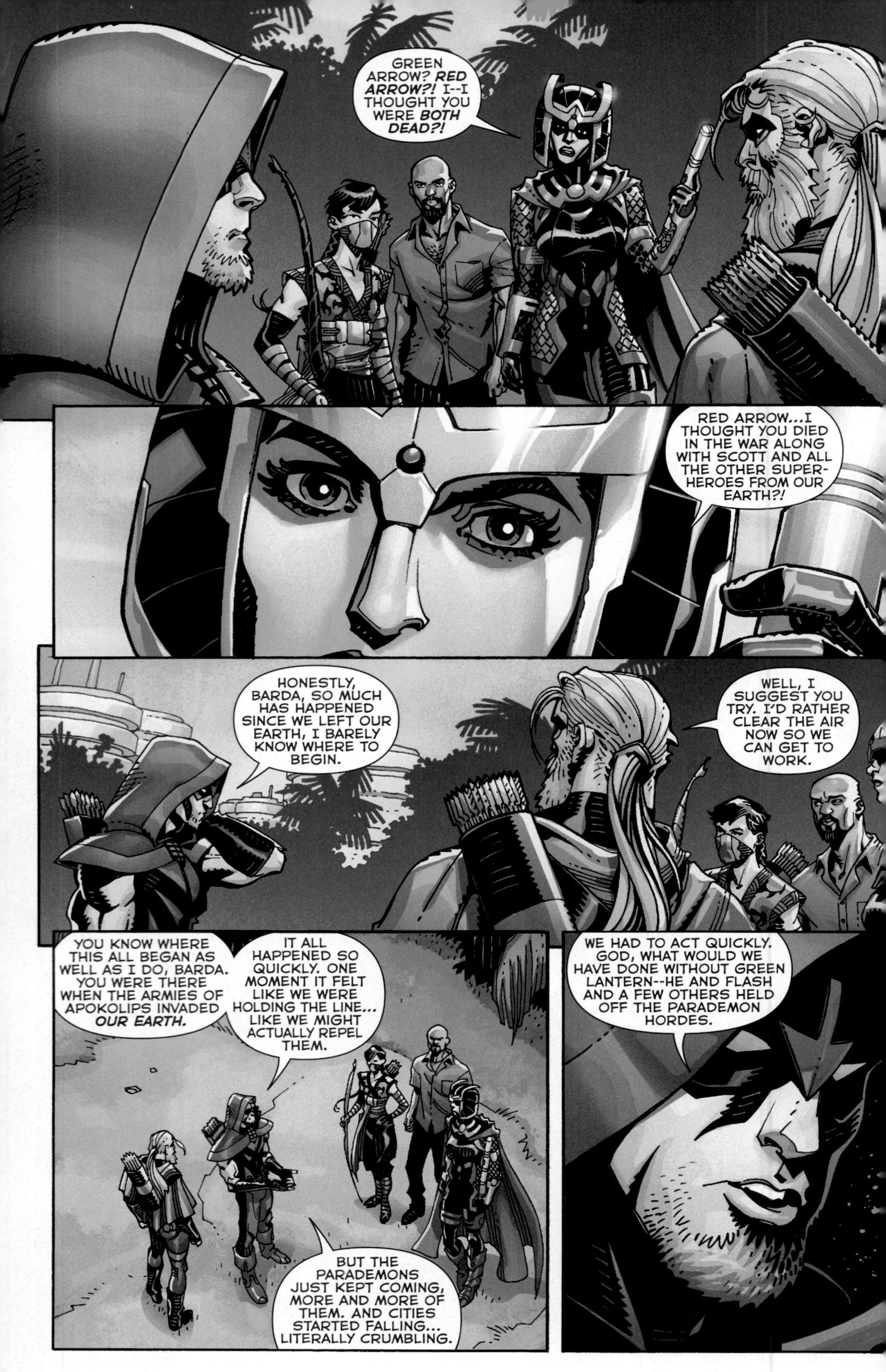

GREEN ARROW? RED ARROW?! I--I THOUGHT YOU WERE BOTH DEAD?!
RED ARROW...I THOUGHT YOU DIED IN THE WAR ALONG WITH SCOTT AND ALL THE OTHER SUPER-HEROES FROM OUR EARTH?!
HONESTLY, BARDA, SO MUCH HAS HAPPENED SINCE WE LEFT OUR EARTH, I BARELY KNOW WHERE TO BEGIN.
WELL, I SUGGEST YOU TRY. I'D RATHER CLEAR THE AIR NOW SO WE CAN GET TO WORK.
YOU KNOW WHERE THIS ALL BEGAN AS WELL AS I DO, BARDA. YOU WERE THERE WHEN THE ARMIES OF APOKOLIPS INVADED OUR EARTH.
IT ALL HAPPENED SO QUICKLY. ONE MOMENT IT FELT LIKE WE WERE HOLDING THE LINE... LIKE WE MIGHT ACTUALLY REPEL THEM.
BUT THE PARADEMONS JUST KEPT COMING, MORE AND MORE OF THEM. AND CITIES STARTED FALLING... LITERALLY CRUMBLING.
WE HAD TO ACT QUICKLY. GOD, WHAT WOULD WE HAVE DONE WITHOUT GREEN LANTERN--HE AND FLASH AND A FEW OTHERS HELD OFF THE PARADEMON HORDES.

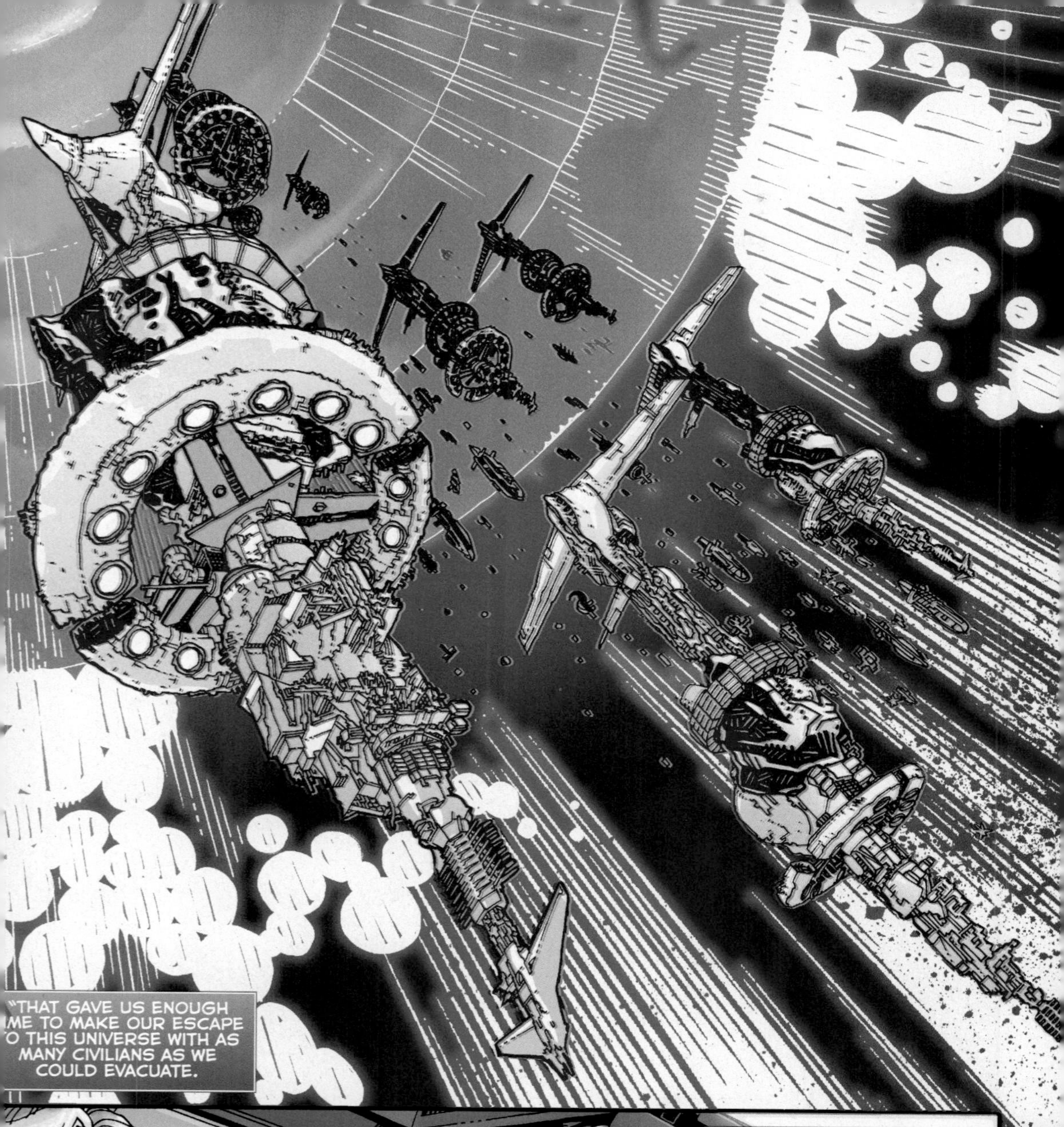
"THAT GAVE US ENOUGH
ME TO MAKE OUR ESCAPE
O THIS UNIVERSE WITH AS
MANY CIVILIANS AS WE
COULD EVACUATE.

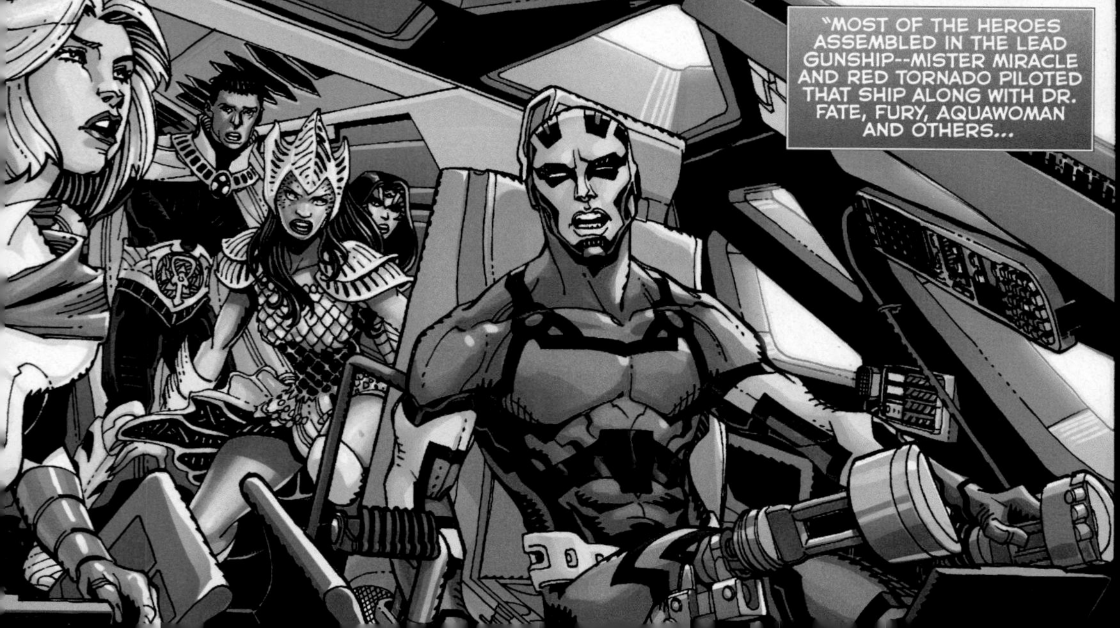
"MOST OF THE HEROES
ASSEMBLED IN THE LEAD
GUNSHIP--MISTER MIRACLE
AND RED TORNADO PILOTED
THAT SHIP ALONG WITH DR.
FATE, FURY, AQUAWOMAN
AND OTHERS...

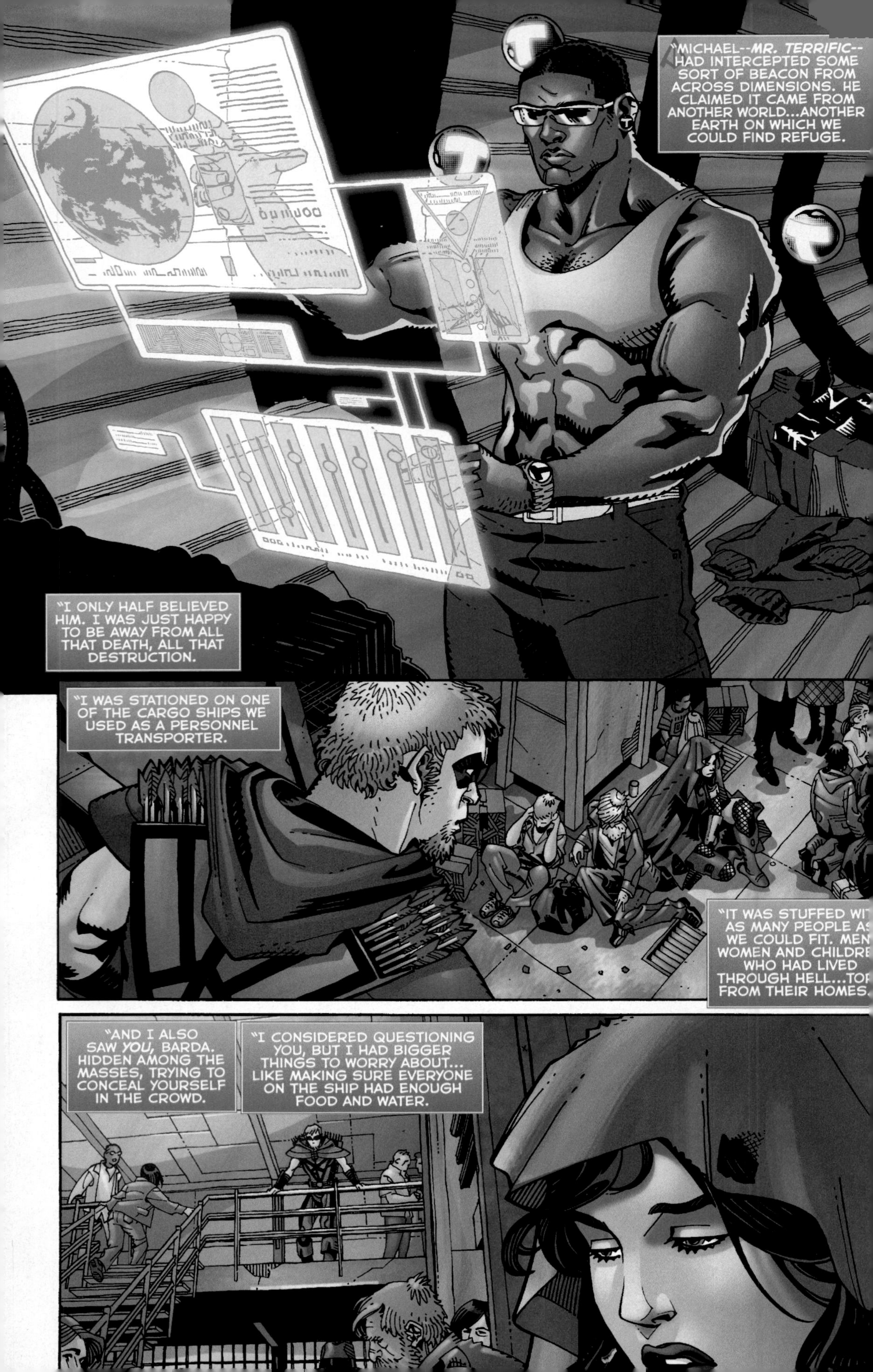
"MICHAEL--MR. TERRIFIC--HAD INTERCEPTED SOME SORT OF BEACON FROM ACROSS DIMENSIONS. HE CLAIMED IT CAME FROM ANOTHER WORLD...ANOTHER EARTH ON WHICH WE COULD FIND REFUGE.
"I ONLY HALF BELIEVED HIM. I WAS JUST HAPPY TO BE AWAY FROM ALL THAT DEATH, ALL THAT DESTRUCTION.
"I WAS STATIONED ON ONE OF THE CARGO SHIPS WE USED AS A PERSONNEL TRANSPORTER.
"IT WAS STUFFED WIT AS MANY PEOPLE AS WE COULD FIT. MEN WOMEN AND CHILDRE WHO HAD LIVED THROUGH HELL...TOR FROM THEIR HOMES.
"AND I ALSO SAW YOU, BARDA. HIDDEN AMONG THE MASSES, TRYING TO CONCEAL YOURSELF IN THE CROWD.
"I CONSIDERED QUESTIONING YOU, BUT I HAD BIGGER THINGS TO WORRY ABOUT... LIKE MAKING SURE EVERYONE ON THE SHIP HAD ENOUGH FOOD AND WATER.

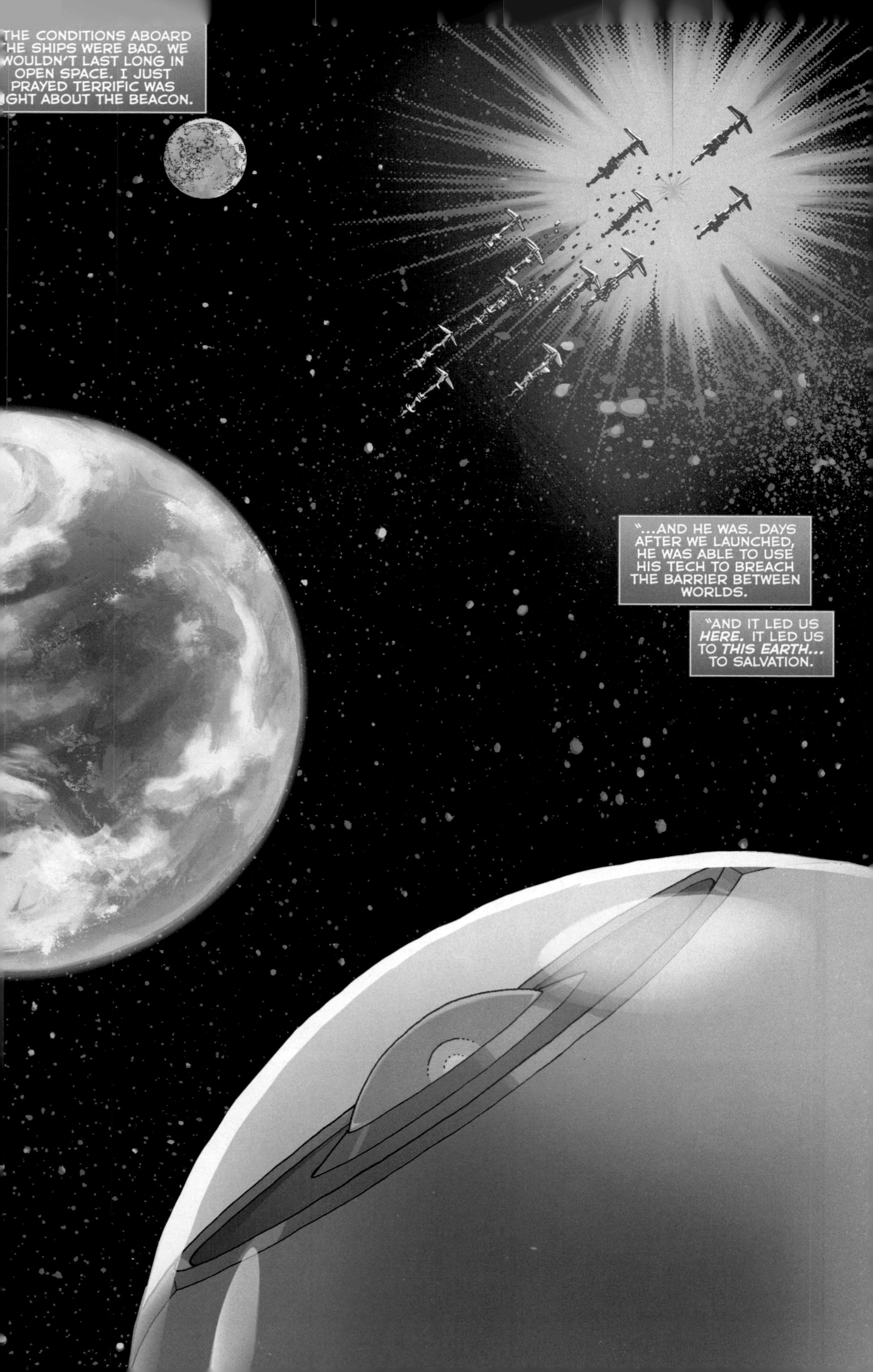
THE CONDITIONS ABOARD HE SHIPS WERE BAD. WE WOULDN'T LAST LONG IN OPEN SPACE. I JUST PRAYED TERRIFIC WAS IGHT ABOUT THE BEACON.
"...AND HE WAS. DAYS AFTER WE LAUNCHED, HE WAS ABLE TO USE HIS TECH TO BREACH THE BARRIER BETWEEN WORLDS.
"AND IT LED US *HERE.* IT LED US TO *THIS EARTH...* TO SALVATION.

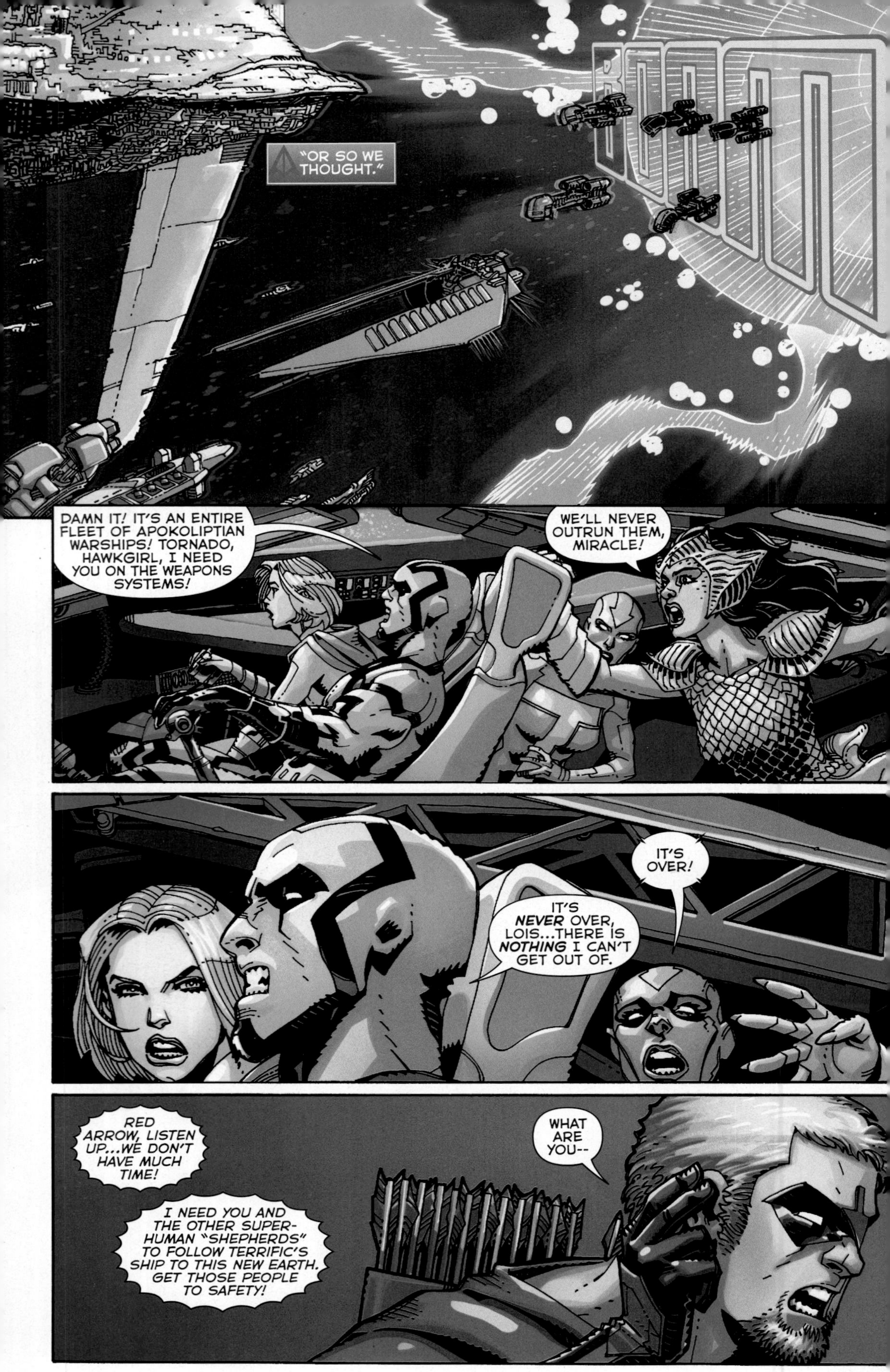
"OR SO WE THOUGHT."
BOOOOM
DAMN IT! IT'S AN ENTIRE FLEET OF APOKOLIPTIAN WARSHIPS! TORNADO, HAWKGIRL, I NEED YOU ON THE WEAPONS SYSTEMS!
WE'LL NEVER OUTRUN THEM, MIRACLE!
IT'S OVER!
IT'S NEVER OVER, LOIS...THERE IS NOTHING I CAN'T GET OUT OF.
RED ARROW, LISTEN UP...WE DON'T HAVE MUCH TIME!
I NEED YOU AND THE OTHER SUPER-HUMAN "SHEPHERDS" TO FOLLOW TERRIFIC'S SHIP TO THIS NEW EARTH. GET THOSE PEOPLE TO SAFETY!
WHAT ARE YOU--

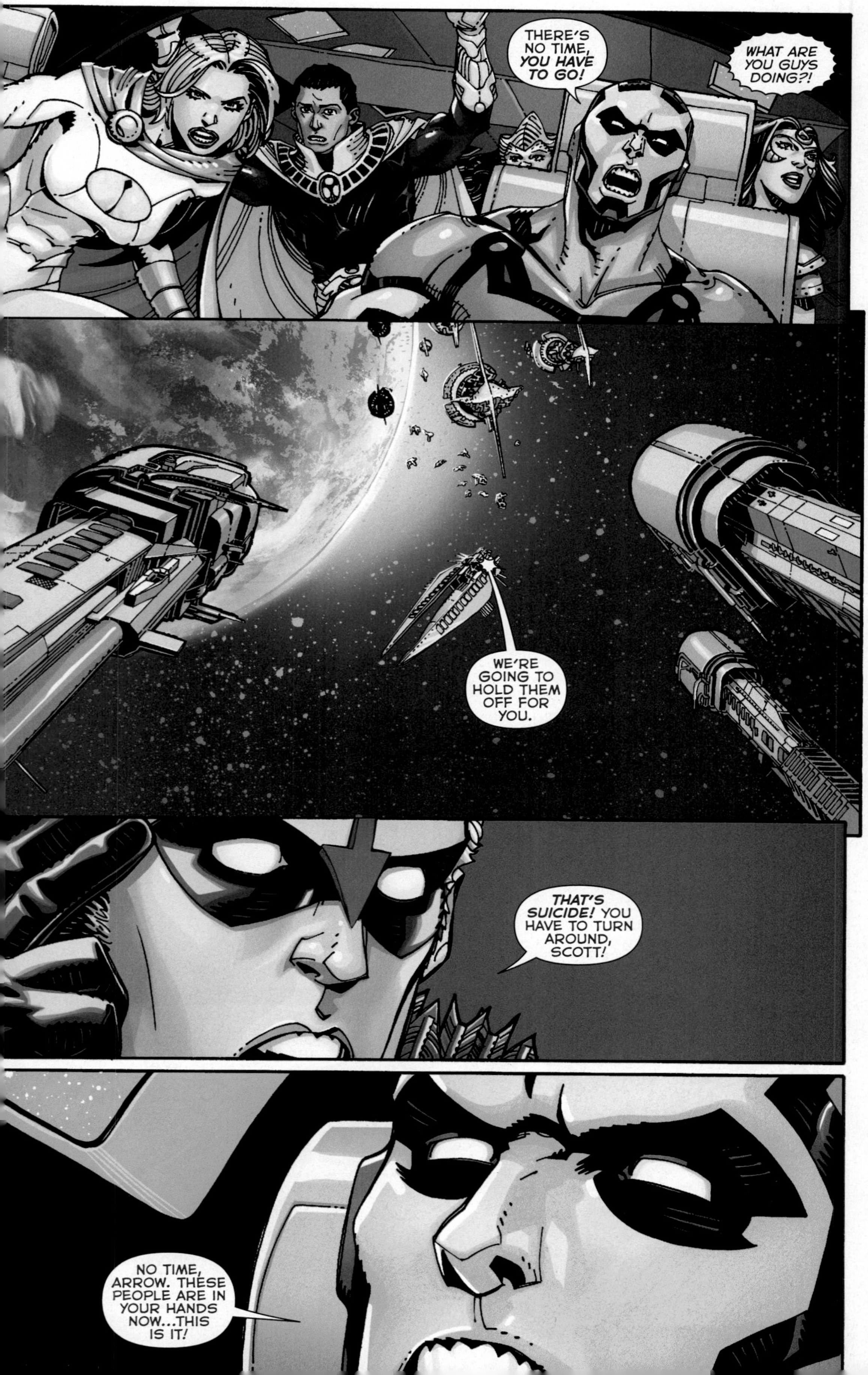
THERE'S NO TIME, YOU HAVE TO GO!
WHAT ARE YOU GUYS DOING?!
WE'RE GOING TO HOLD THEM OFF FOR YOU.
THAT'S SUICIDE! YOU HAVE TO TURN AROUND, SCOTT!
NO TIME, ARROW. THESE PEOPLE ARE IN YOUR HANDS NOW...THIS IS IT!

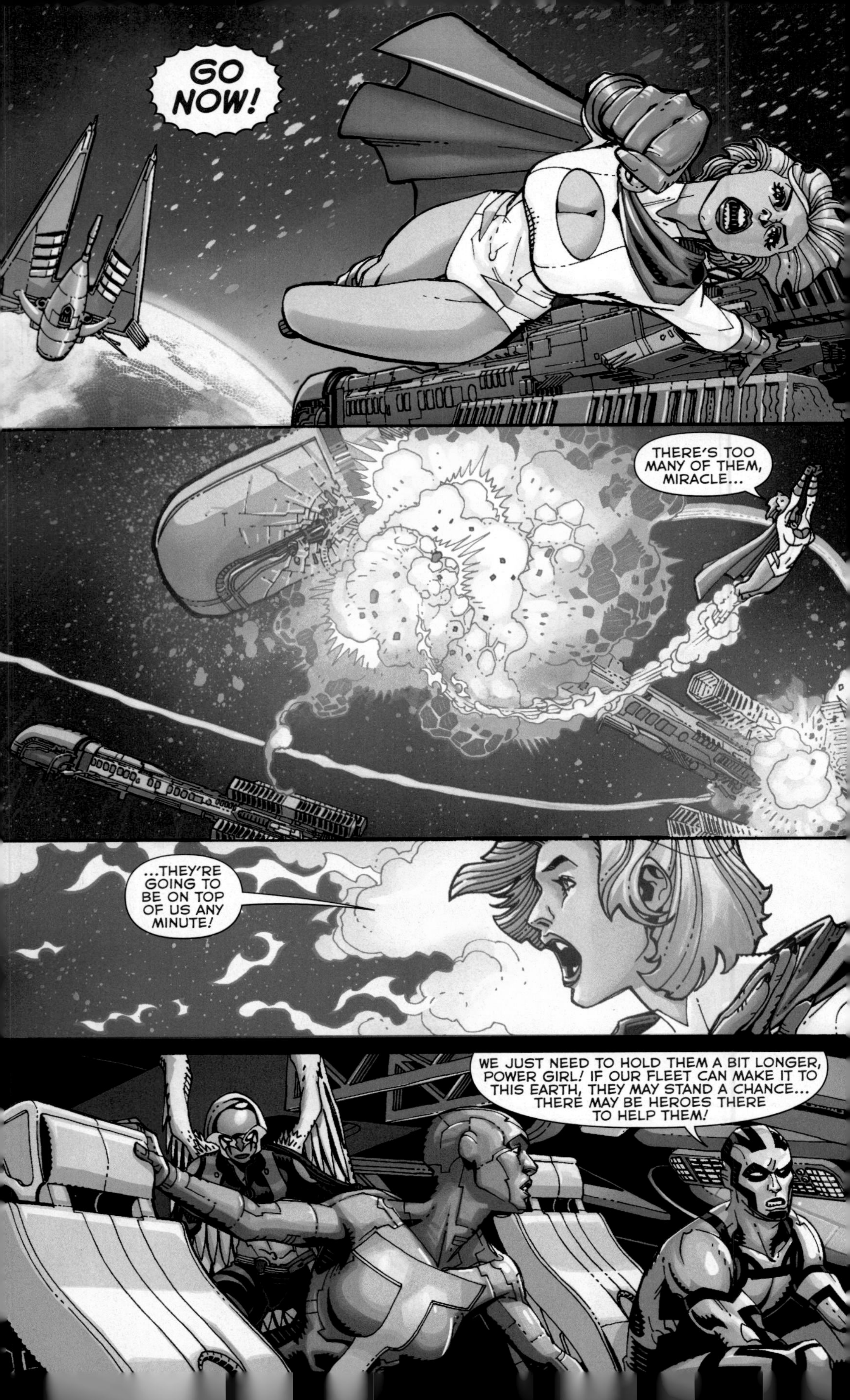
GO NOW!
THERE'S TOO MANY OF THEM, MIRACLE...
...THEY'RE GOING TO BE ON TOP OF US ANY MINUTE!
WE JUST NEED TO HOLD THEM A BIT LONGER, POWER GIRL! IF OUR FLEET CAN MAKE IT TO THIS EARTH, THEY MAY STAND A CHANCE... THERE MAY BE HEROES THERE TO HELP THEM!

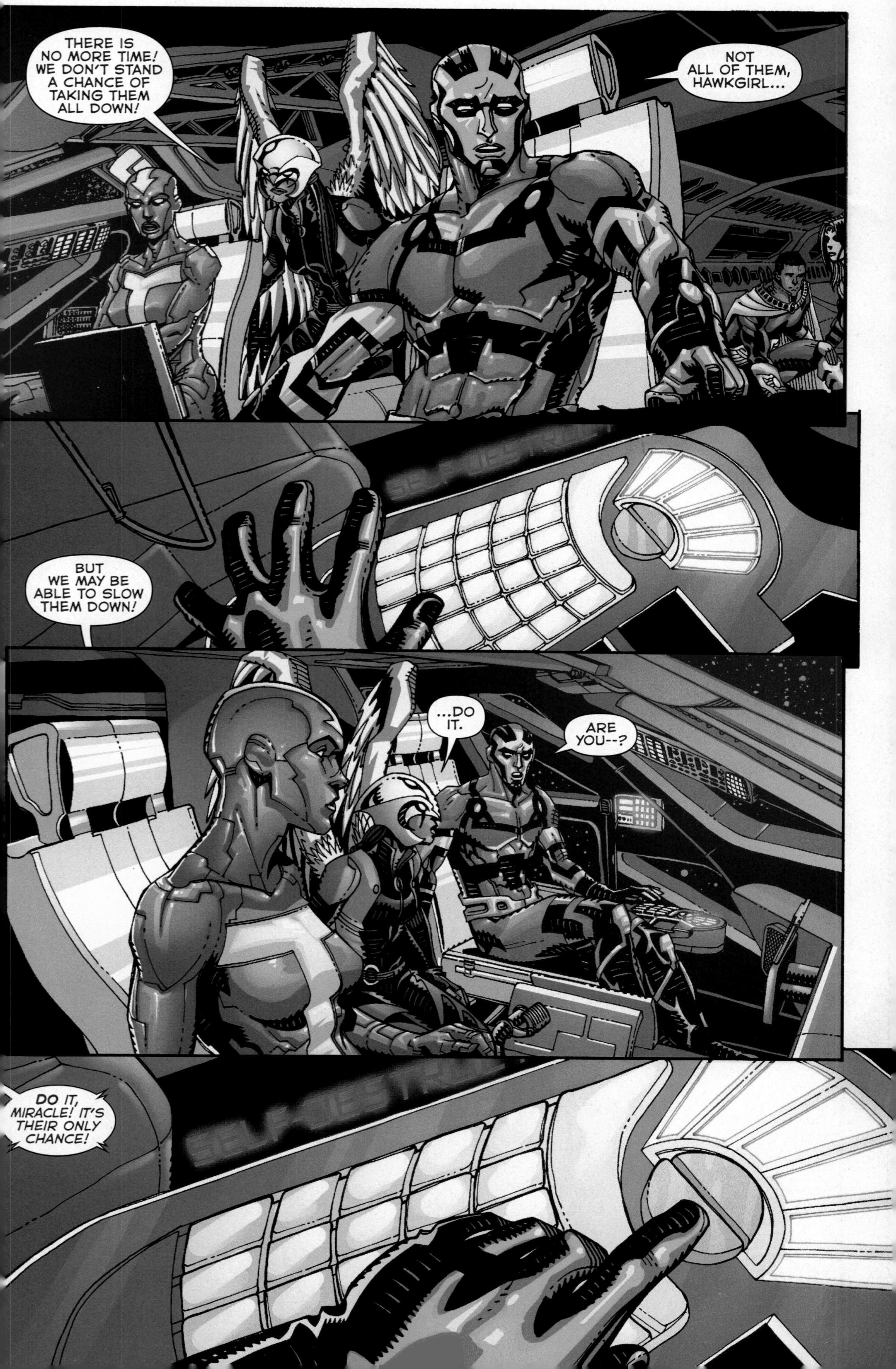
THERE IS NO MORE TIME! WE DON'T STAND A CHANCE OF TAKING THEM ALL DOWN!
NOT ALL OF THEM, HAWKGIRL...
BUT WE MAY BE ABLE TO SLOW THEM DOWN!
...DO IT.
ARE YOU--?
DO IT, MIRACLE! IT'S THEIR ONLY CHANCE!

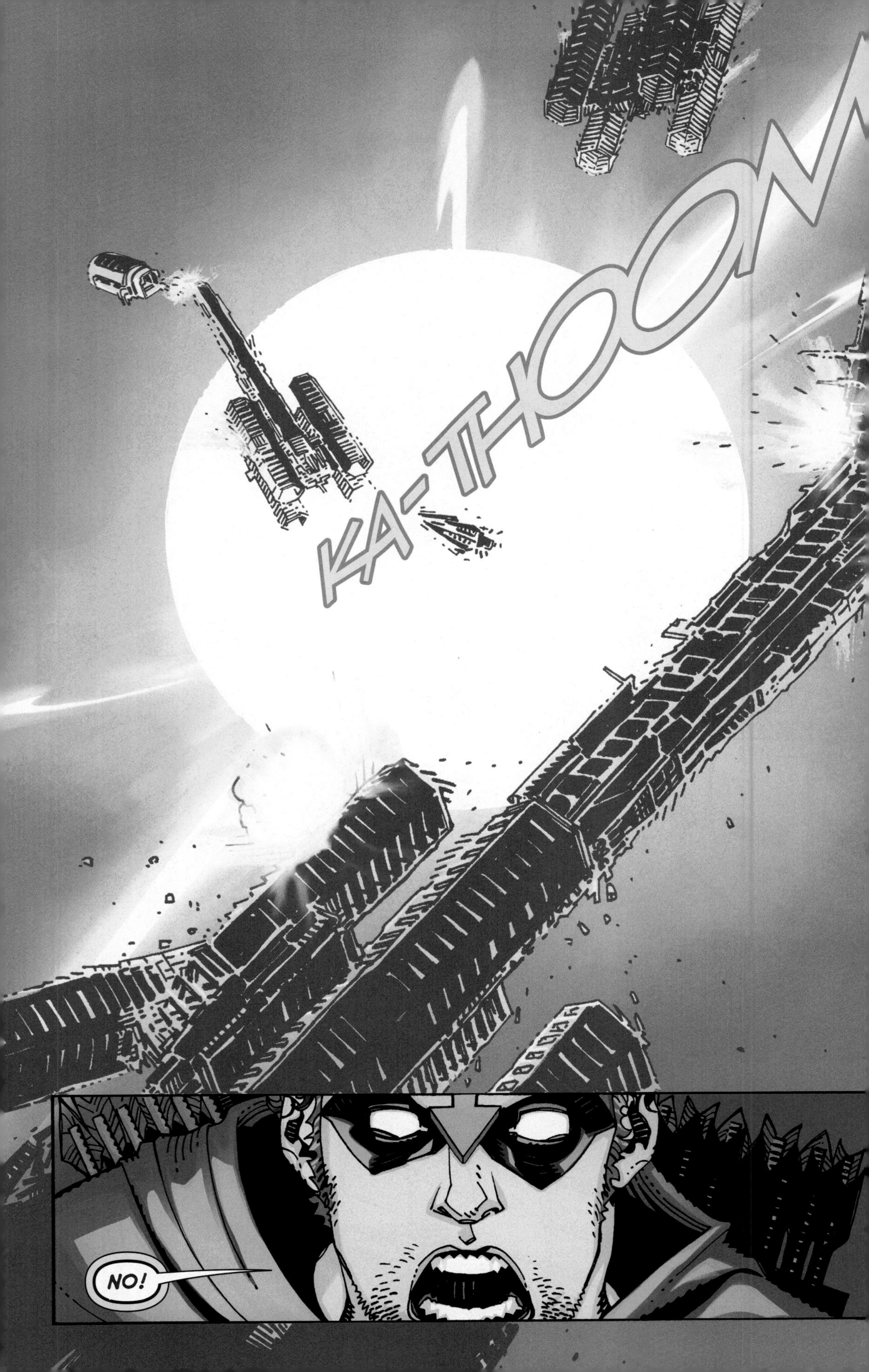
KA-THOOM
NO!

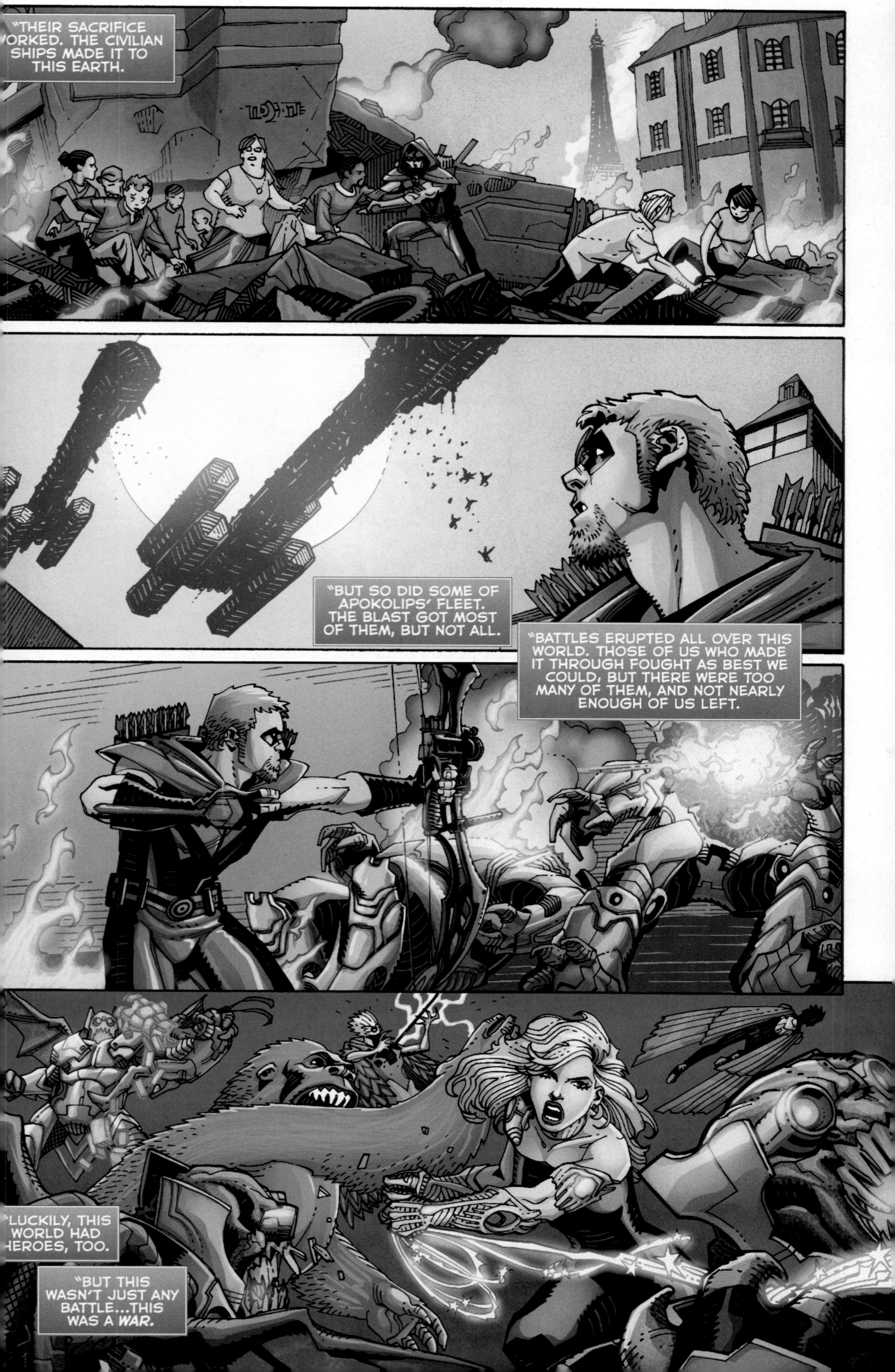
"THEIR SACRIFICE WORKED. THE CIVILIAN SHIPS MADE IT TO THIS EARTH.
"BUT SO DID SOME OF APOKOLIPS' FLEET. THE BLAST GOT MOST OF THEM, BUT NOT ALL.
"BATTLES ERUPTED ALL OVER THIS WORLD. THOSE OF US WHO MADE IT THROUGH FOUGHT AS BEST WE COULD, BUT THERE WERE TOO MANY OF THEM, AND NOT NEARLY ENOUGH OF US LEFT.
"LUCKILY, THIS WORLD HAD HEROES, TOO.
"BUT THIS WASN'T JUST ANY BATTLE...THIS WAS A *WAR*.

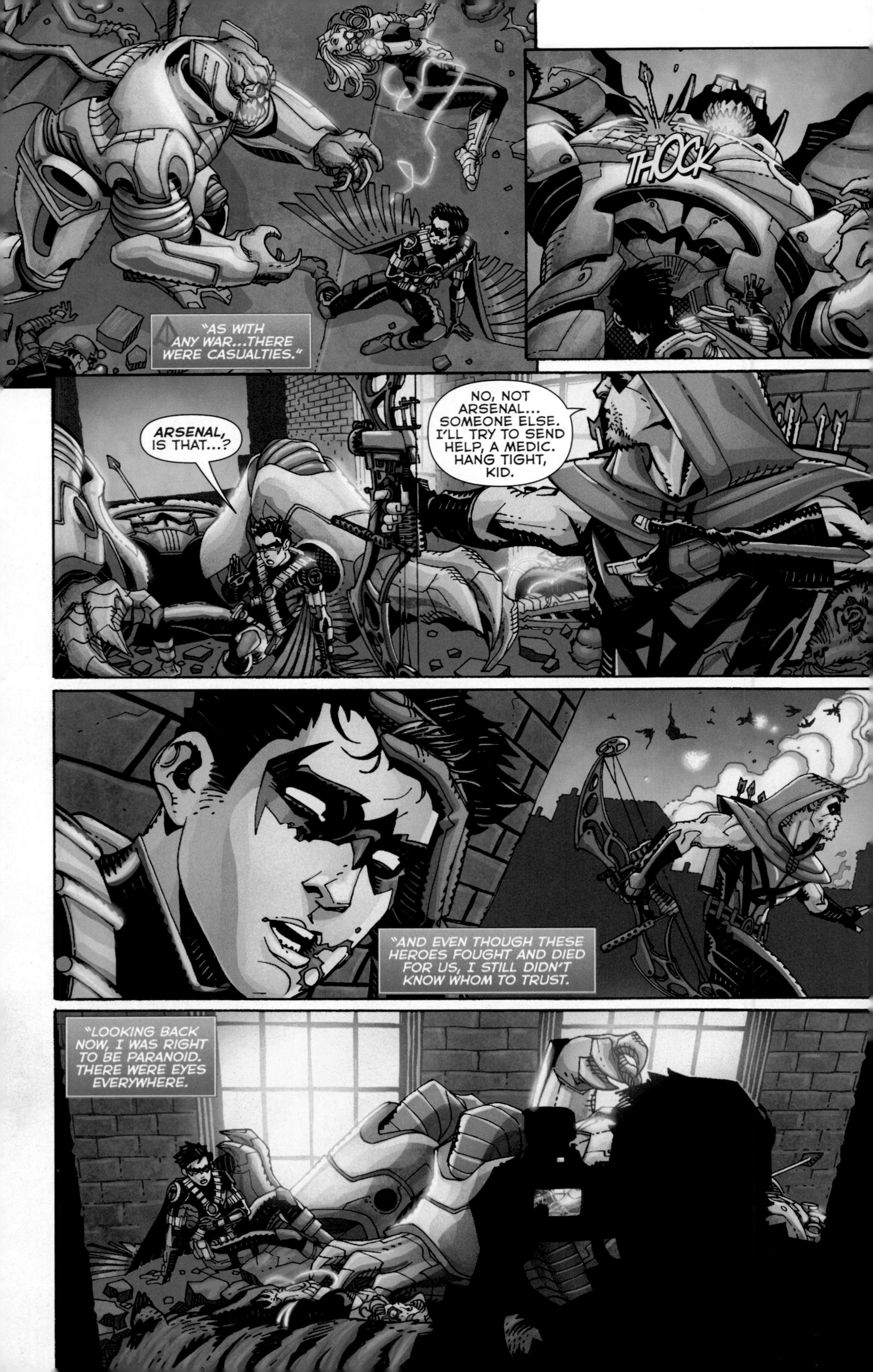
"AS WITH ANY WAR...THERE WERE CASUALTIES."
THOCK
ARSENAL, IS THAT...?
NO, NOT ARSENAL... SOMEONE ELSE. I'LL TRY TO SEND HELP, A MEDIC. HANG TIGHT, KID.
"AND EVEN THOUGH THESE HEROES FOUGHT AND DIED FOR US, I STILL DIDN'T KNOW WHOM TO TRUST.
"LOOKING BACK NOW, I WAS RIGHT TO BE PARANOID. THERE WERE EYES EVERYWHERE.

AND IT WASN'T JUST METROPOLIS. ALL OVER THE WORLD, BATTLES RAGED.

"LIVES WERE LOST...FAMILIES TORN APART.

"NATIONS WERE RIPPED TO SHREDS.

"FUTURES AND COUNTRIES WERE ALTERED.

AND IT WASN'T ONLY THE SUPERHEROES WHO MADE A STAND.

"DURING THE WEEKS OF THE WAR, REGULAR MEN AND WOMEN FROM ALL WALKS OF LIFE FOUGHT BACK.

"EVEN THE ARMIES OF ATLANTIS AND ITS *WARRIOR KING* JOINED THE FIGHT, NOT JUST FOR THEIR PEOPLE, BUT FOR ALL PEOPLE.

"THE PARADEMONS WERE MANY, BUT FOR EVERY ONE OF THEM THERE WERE TEN OF US...READY TO STAND AND READY TO DIE.

"I EVEN HEARD TELL OF A *ONE-WOMAN ARMY* IN TORONTO TAKING OUT A WHOLE BATTALION OF PARADEMONS BEFORE DISAPPEARING INTO THE CROWD."

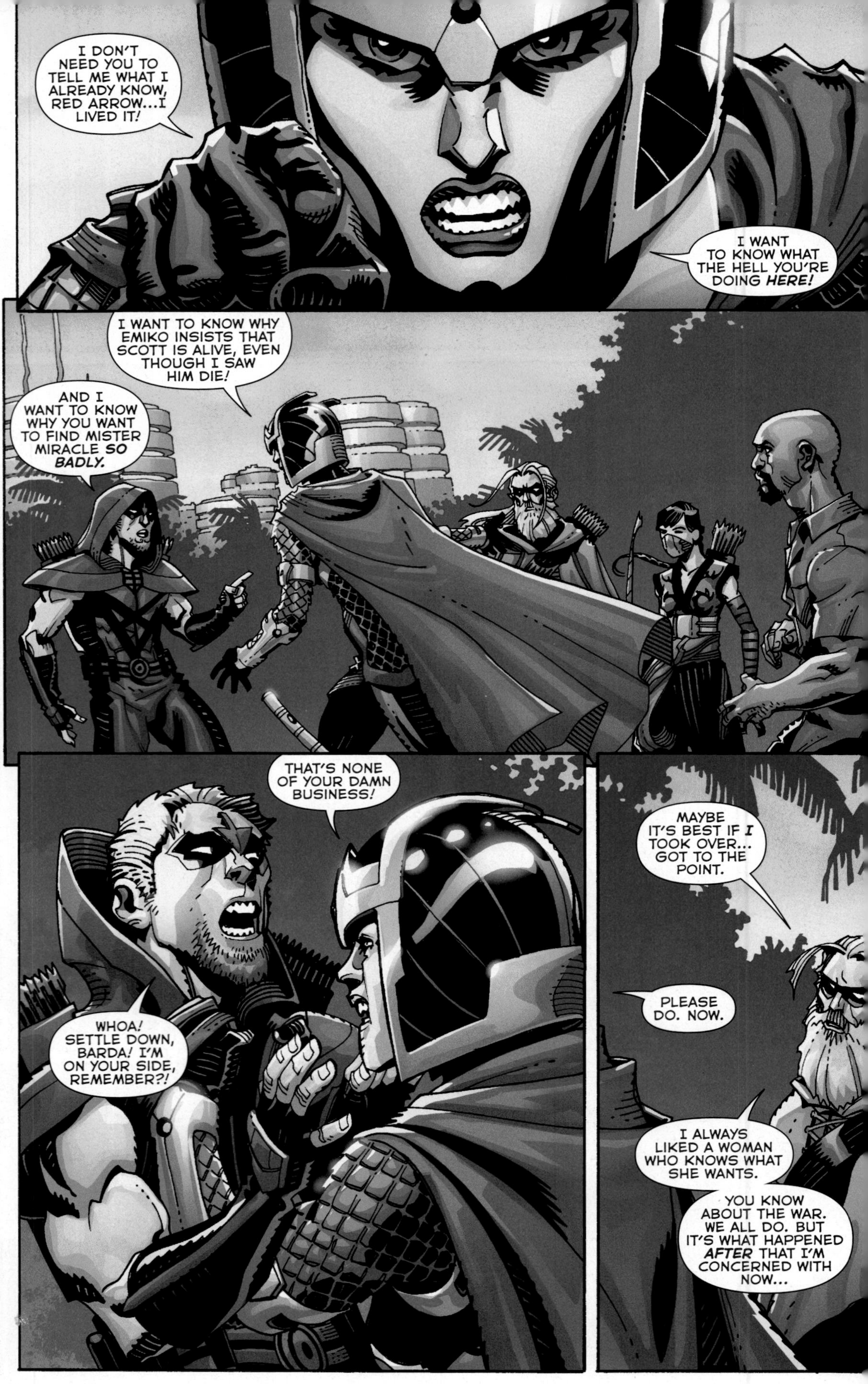
I DON'T NEED YOU TO TELL ME WHAT I ALREADY KNOW, RED ARROW...I LIVED IT!
I WANT TO KNOW WHAT THE HELL YOU'RE DOING HERE!
AND I WANT TO KNOW WHY YOU WANT TO FIND MISTER MIRACLE SO BADLY.
I WANT TO KNOW WHY EMIKO INSISTS THAT SCOTT IS ALIVE, EVEN THOUGH I SAW HIM DIE!
THAT'S NONE OF YOUR DAMN BUSINESS!
WHOA! SETTLE DOWN, BARDA! I'M ON YOUR SIDE, REMEMBER?!
MAYBE IT'S BEST IF I TOOK OVER... GOT TO THE POINT.
PLEASE DO. NOW.
I ALWAYS LIKED A WOMAN WHO KNOWS WHAT SHE WANTS.
YOU KNOW ABOUT THE WAR. WE ALL DO. BUT IT'S WHAT HAPPENED AFTER THAT I'M CONCERNED WITH NOW...

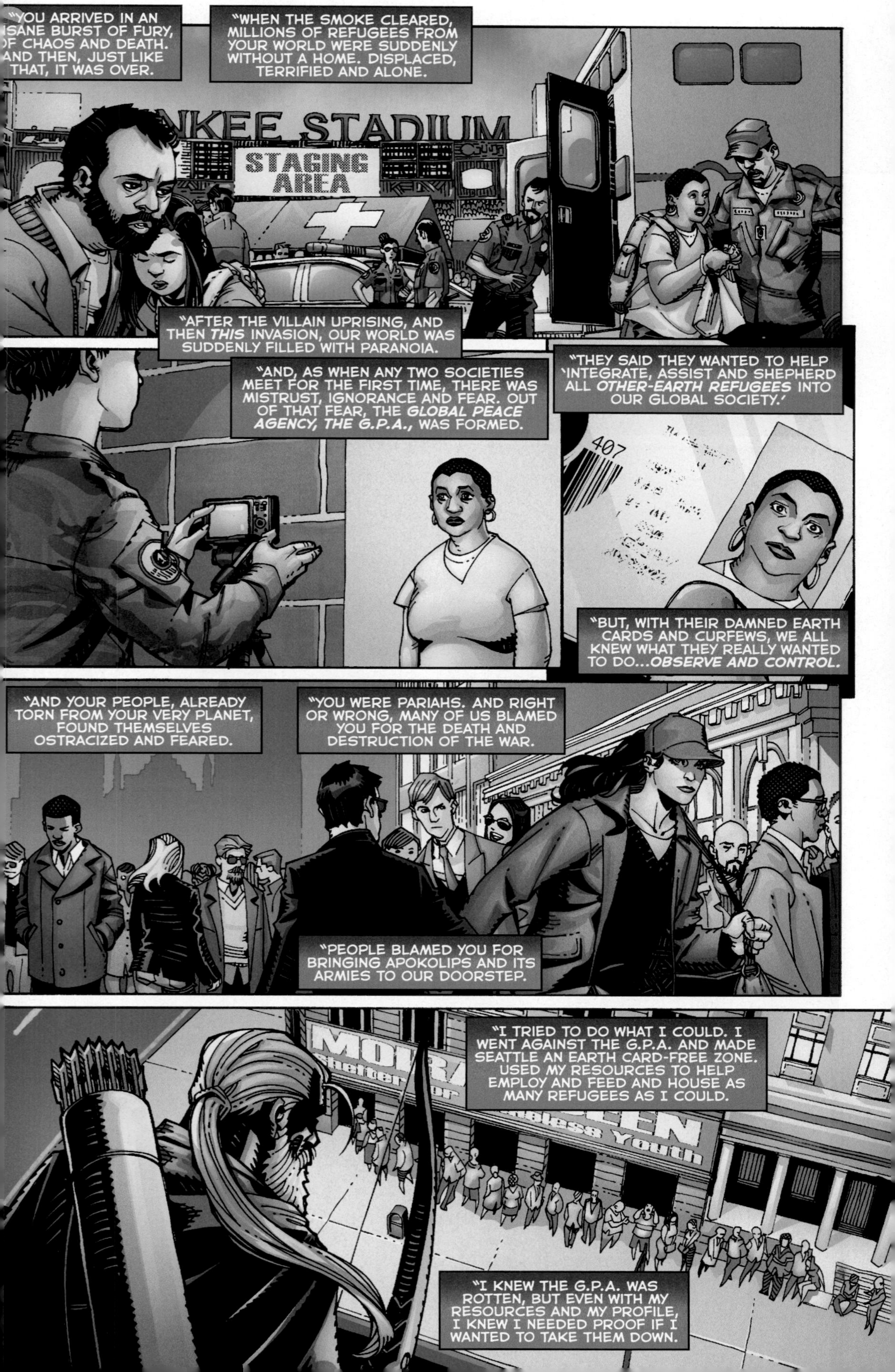
"YOU ARRIVED IN AN
INSANE BURST OF FURY,
OF CHAOS AND DEATH.
AND THEN, JUST LIKE
THAT, IT WAS OVER.
"WHEN THE SMOKE CLEARED,
MILLIONS OF REFUGEES FROM
YOUR WORLD WERE SUDDENLY
WITHOUT A HOME. DISPLACED,
TERRIFIED AND ALONE.
YANKEE STADIUM
STAGING AREA
"AFTER THE VILLAIN UPRISING, AND
THEN *THIS* INVASION, OUR WORLD WAS
SUDDENLY FILLED WITH PARANOIA.
"AND, AS WHEN ANY TWO SOCIETIES
MEET FOR THE FIRST TIME, THERE WAS
MISTRUST, IGNORANCE AND FEAR. OUT
OF THAT FEAR, THE *GLOBAL PEACE
AGENCY, THE G.P.A.,* WAS FORMED.
"THEY SAID THEY WANTED TO HELP
'INTEGRATE, ASSIST AND SHEPHERD
ALL *OTHER-EARTH REFUGEES* INTO
OUR GLOBAL SOCIETY.'
407
"BUT, WITH THEIR DAMNED EARTH
CARDS AND CURFEWS, WE ALL
KNEW WHAT THEY REALLY WANTED
TO DO...*OBSERVE AND CONTROL.*
"AND YOUR PEOPLE, ALREADY
TORN FROM YOUR VERY PLANET,
FOUND THEMSELVES
OSTRACIZED AND FEARED.
"YOU WERE PARIAHS. AND RIGHT
OR WRONG, MANY OF US BLAMED
YOU FOR THE DEATH AND
DESTRUCTION OF THE WAR.
"PEOPLE BLAMED YOU FOR
BRINGING APOKOLIPS AND ITS
ARMIES TO OUR DOORSTEP.
"I TRIED TO DO WHAT I COULD. I
WENT AGAINST THE G.P.A. AND MADE
SEATTLE AN EARTH CARD-FREE ZONE.
USED MY RESOURCES TO HELP
EMPLOY AND FEED AND HOUSE AS
MANY REFUGEES AS I COULD.
"I KNEW THE G.P.A. WAS
ROTTEN, BUT EVEN WITH MY
RESOURCES AND MY PROFILE,
I KNEW I NEEDED PROOF IF I
WANTED TO TAKE THEM DOWN.

"THAT PROOF CAME IN THE FORM OF MY OWN DOPPELGANGER... RED ARROW.

"BUT HE ALSO TOLD ME ABOUT YOU, BARDA. YOU AND THE *OTHER HEROES* FROM YOUR WORLD WHO MADE IT THROUGH, BUT HAD EITHER GONE MISSING OR...

"WE ALSO FOUND PROOF THAT AN OPERATIVE OF THE G.P.A. WAS SYSTEMATICALLY HUNTING THESE SECRET HEROES FROM EARTH 2. FORCING YOU INTO HIDING. HE'D BARELY ESCAPED HIMSELF.

"WE DIDN'T HAVE TO LOOK FAR TO FIND THIS SECRET OPERATIVE...HE FOUND US.

"*DEATHSTROK* MERCENARY SCUM, WHO HIRES HIMSE OUT TO THE HIGHEST BIDDER.

"WE BARELY GOT OUT OF THAT ONE ALIVE.

"BUT EVEN THEN, IN THE HEAT OF THE BATTLE, THE PIECES WEREN'T CONNECTING. WHY WOULD THE G.P.A. EMPLOY DEATHSTROKE? THEY WERE MANY THINGS, BUT BEING IN BED WITH SOMEONE LIKE HIM?

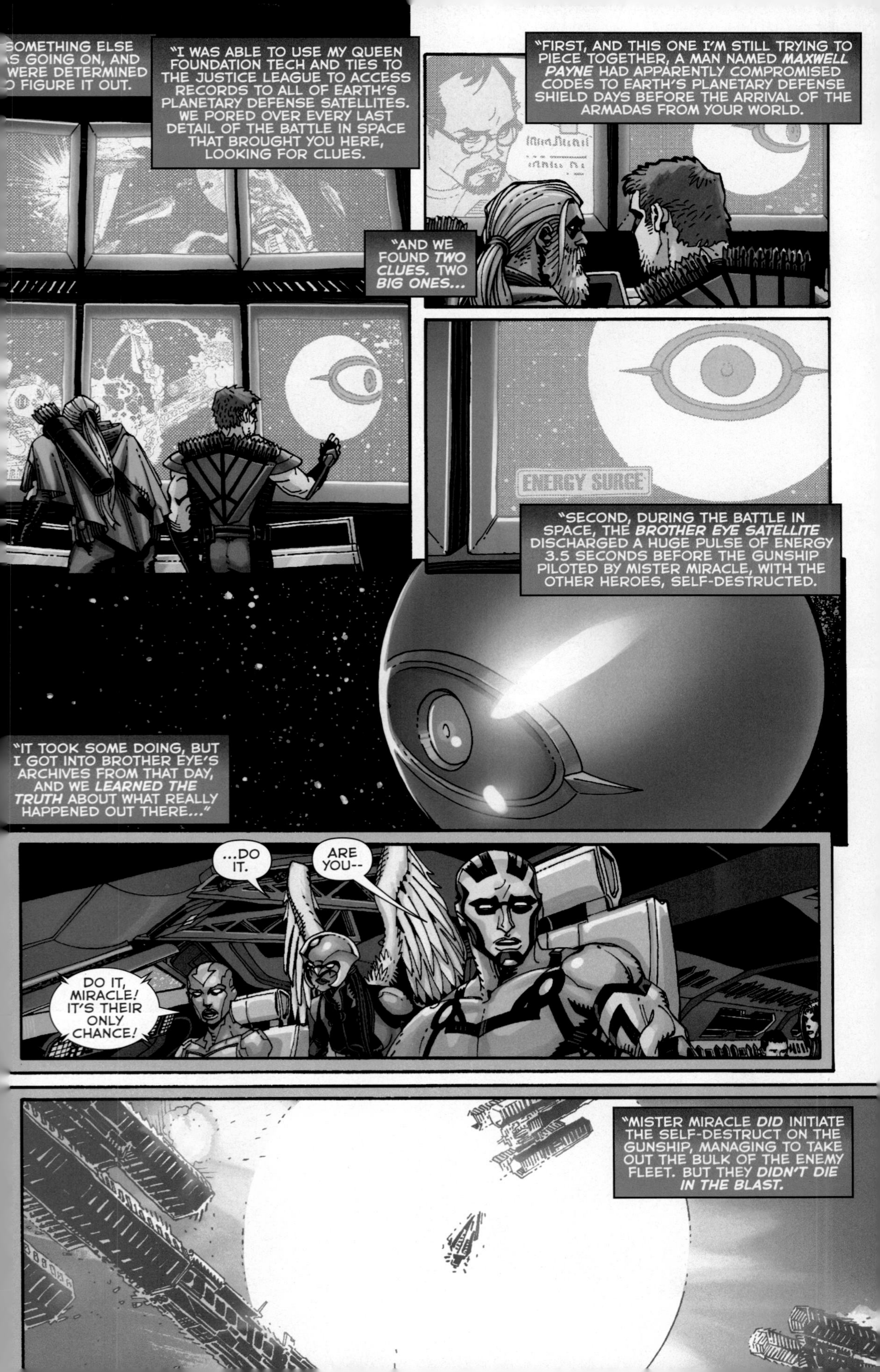
SOMETHING ELSE
AS GOING ON, AND
WERE DETERMINED
O FIGURE IT OUT.
"I WAS ABLE TO USE MY QUEEN FOUNDATION TECH AND TIES TO THE JUSTICE LEAGUE TO ACCESS RECORDS TO ALL OF EARTH'S PLANETARY DEFENSE SATELLITES. WE PORED OVER EVERY LAST DETAIL OF THE BATTLE IN SPACE THAT BROUGHT YOU HERE, LOOKING FOR CLUES.
"AND WE FOUND *TWO CLUES.* TWO *BIG ONES...*
"FIRST, AND THIS ONE I'M STILL TRYING TO PIECE TOGETHER, A MAN NAMED *MAXWELL PAYNE* HAD APPARENTLY COMPROMISED CODES TO EARTH'S PLANETARY DEFENSE SHIELD DAYS BEFORE THE ARRIVAL OF THE ARMADAS FROM YOUR WORLD.
ENERGY SURGE
"SECOND, DURING THE BATTLE IN SPACE, THE *BROTHER EYE SATELLITE* DISCHARGED A HUGE PULSE OF ENERGY 3.5 SECONDS BEFORE THE GUNSHIP PILOTED BY MISTER MIRACLE, WITH THE OTHER HEROES, SELF-DESTRUCTED.
"IT TOOK SOME DOING, BUT I GOT INTO BROTHER EYE'S ARCHIVES FROM THAT DAY, AND WE *LEARNED THE TRUTH* ABOUT WHAT REALLY HAPPENED OUT THERE..."
DO IT, MIRACLE! IT'S THEIR ONLY CHANCE!
ARE YOU--
...DO IT.
"MISTER MIRACLE *DID* INITIATE THE SELF-DESTRUCT ON THE GUNSHIP, MANAGING TO TAKE OUT THE BULK OF THE ENEMY FLEET. BUT THEY *DIDN'T DIE IN THE BLAST.*

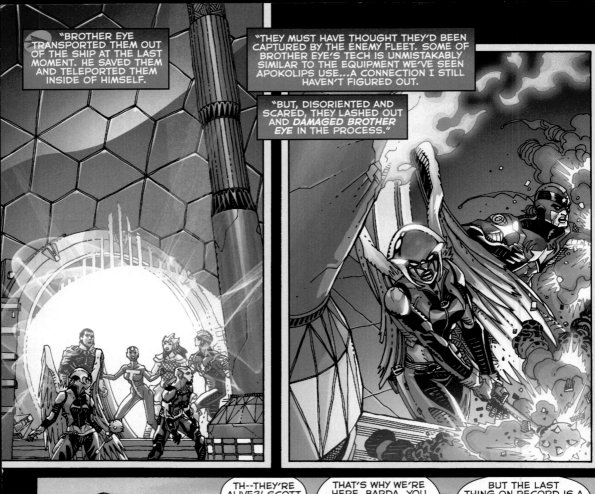

"BROTHER EYE TRANSPORTED THEM OUT OF THE SHIP AT THE LAST MOMENT. HE SAVED THEM AND TELEPORTED THEM INSIDE OF HIMSELF.

"THEY MUST HAVE THOUGHT THEY'D BEEN CAPTURED BY THE ENEMY FLEET. SOME OF BROTHER EYE'S TECH IS UNMISTAKABLY SIMILAR TO THE EQUIPMENT WE'VE SEEN APOKOLIPS USE...A CONNECTION I STILL HAVEN'T FIGURED OUT.

"BUT, DISORIENTED AND SCARED, THEY LASHED OUT AND DAMAGED BROTHER EYE IN THE PROCESS."

TH--THEY'RE ALIVE?! SCOTT IS ALIVE?! BUT WHERE?

THAT'S WHY WE'RE HERE, BARDA. YOU SEE, BROTHER EYE'S ARCHIVES GO BLACK A FEW MOMENTS AFTER THE HEROES WERE TELEPORTED IN.

BUT THE LAST THING ON RECORD IS A SHUTTLE APPROACHING AND PREPARING TO DOCK WITH IT...

IT WASN'T THE G.P.A. WHO'VE BEEN HUNTING YOU AND THE OTHERS. IT WAS CADMUS, THE SAME OUTFIT THAT HAS MISTER MIRACLE NOW.

"THAT SHUTTLE BELONGED TO CADMUS. AND AMONG THE CREW LISTED IN ITS LOG WAS A MAN NAMED SLADE WILSON...DEATHSTROKE."

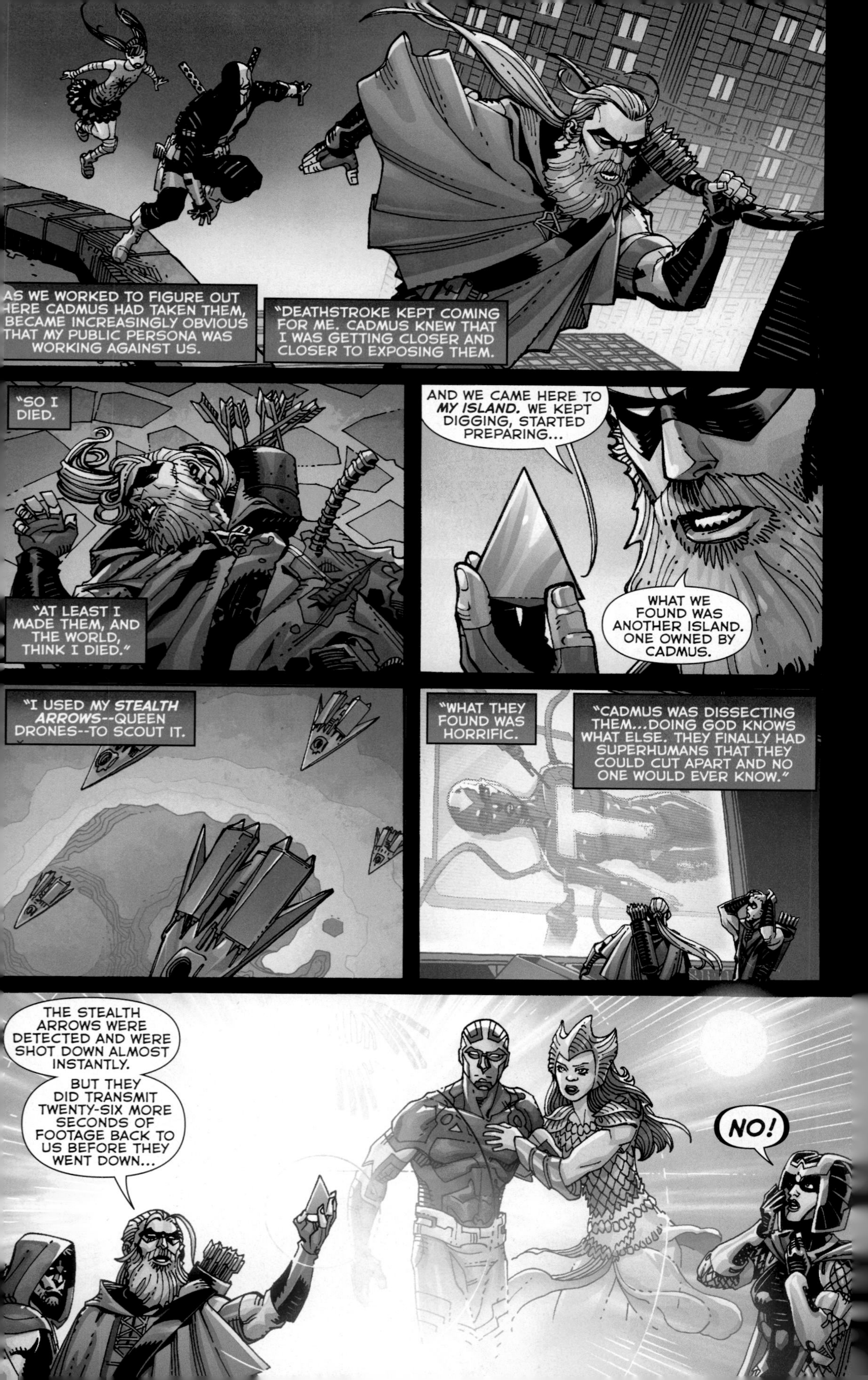
AS WE WORKED TO FIGURE OUT HERE CADMUS HAD TAKEN THEM, BECAME INCREASINGLY OBVIOUS THAT MY PUBLIC PERSONA WAS WORKING AGAINST US.
"DEATHSTROKE KEPT COMING FOR ME. CADMUS KNEW THAT I WAS GETTING CLOSER AND CLOSER TO EXPOSING THEM.
"SO I DIED.
"AT LEAST I MADE THEM, AND THE WORLD, THINK I DIED."
AND WE CAME HERE TO MY ISLAND. WE KEPT DIGGING, STARTED PREPARING...
WHAT WE FOUND WAS ANOTHER ISLAND. ONE OWNED BY CADMUS.
"I USED MY STEALTH ARROWS--QUEEN DRONES--TO SCOUT IT.
"WHAT THEY FOUND WAS HORRIFIC.
"CADMUS WAS DISSECTING THEM...DOING GOD KNOWS WHAT ELSE. THEY FINALLY HAD SUPERHUMANS THAT THEY COULD CUT APART AND NO ONE WOULD EVER KNOW."
THE STEALTH ARROWS WERE DETECTED AND WERE SHOT DOWN ALMOST INSTANTLY.
BUT THEY DID TRANSMIT TWENTY-SIX MORE SECONDS OF FOOTAGE BACK TO US BEFORE THEY WENT DOWN...
NO!

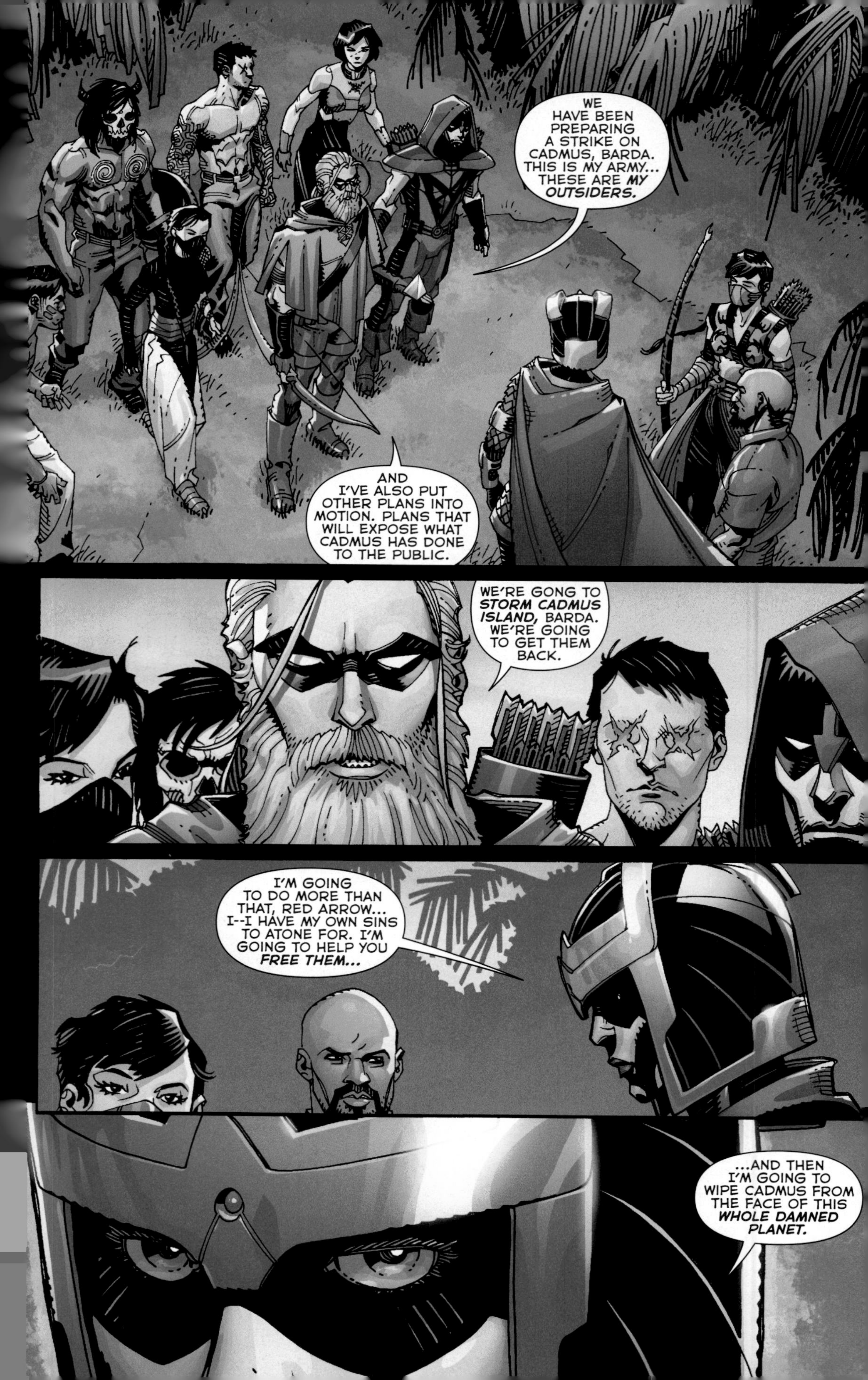
WE HAVE BEEN PREPARING A STRIKE ON CADMUS, BARDA. THIS IS MY ARMY... THESE ARE MY OUTSIDERS.
AND I'VE ALSO PUT OTHER PLANS INTO MOTION. PLANS THAT WILL EXPOSE WHAT CADMUS HAS DONE TO THE PUBLIC.
WE'RE GONG TO STORM CADMUS ISLAND, BARDA. WE'RE GOING TO GET THEM BACK.
I'M GOING TO DO MORE THAN THAT, RED ARROW... I--I HAVE MY OWN SINS TO ATONE FOR. I'M GOING TO HELP YOU FREE THEM...
...AND THEN I'M GOING TO WIPE CADMUS FROM THE FACE OF THIS WHOLE DAMNED PLANET.

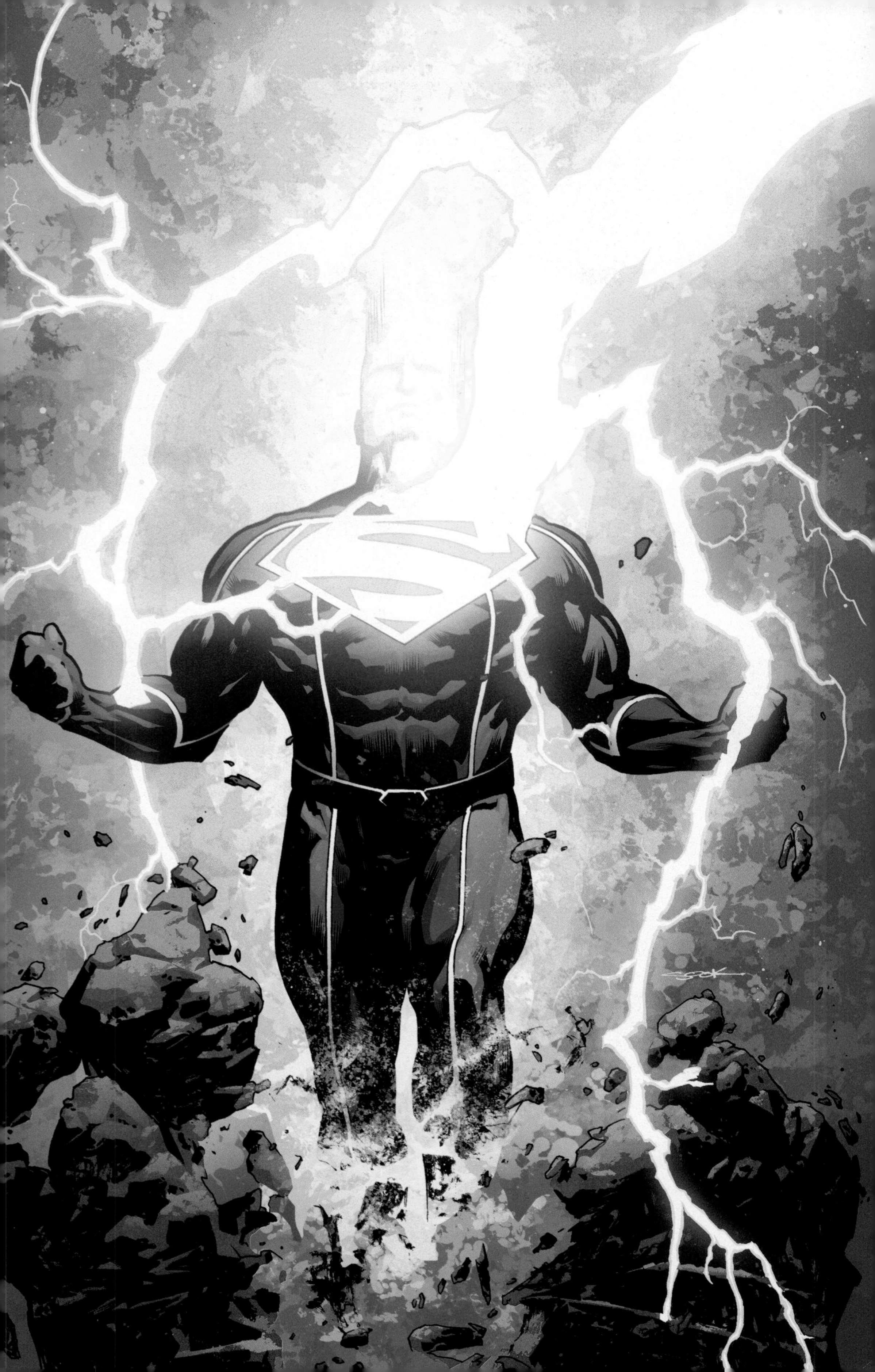

INTO THE FUTUR

WRITERS
- Brian Azzarello
- Jeff Lemire
- Dan Jurgens
- Keith Giffen

ARTIST
- Patrick Zircher

COLORS
- Hi-Fi

LETTERS
- Carlos M. Mangual

COVER
- Ryan Sook

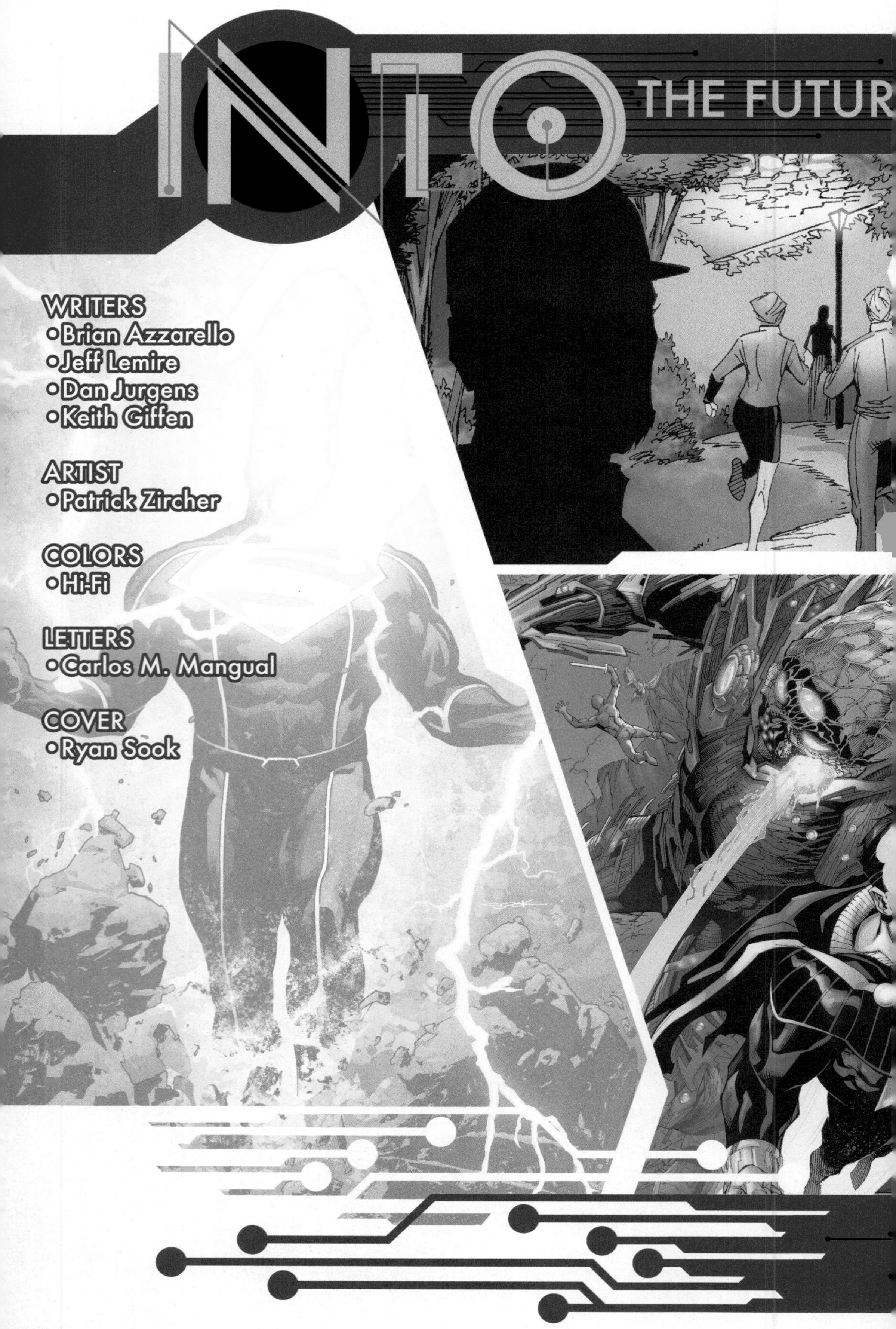

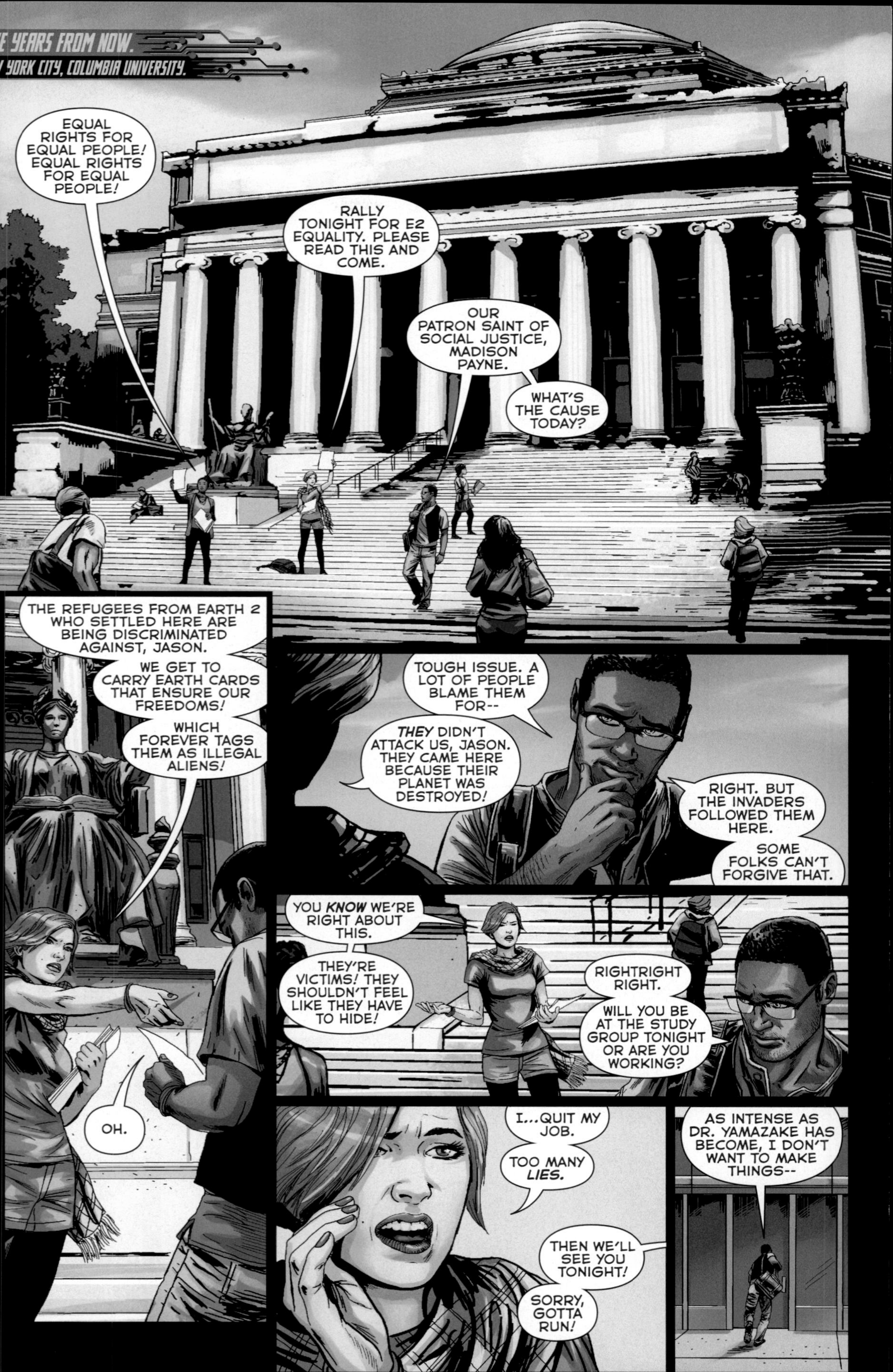

...E YEARS FROM NOW.
...Y YORK CITY, COLUMBIA UNIVERSITY.
EQUAL RIGHTS FOR EQUAL PEOPLE! EQUAL RIGHTS FOR EQUAL PEOPLE!
RALLY TONIGHT FOR E2 EQUALITY. PLEASE READ THIS AND COME.
OUR PATRON SAINT OF SOCIAL JUSTICE, MADISON PAYNE.
WHAT'S THE CAUSE TODAY?
THE REFUGEES FROM EARTH 2 WHO SETTLED HERE ARE BEING DISCRIMINATED AGAINST, JASON.
WE GET TO CARRY EARTH CARDS THAT ENSURE OUR FREEDOMS!
WHICH FOREVER TAGS THEM AS ILLEGAL ALIENS!
OH.
TOUGH ISSUE. A LOT OF PEOPLE BLAME THEM FOR--
THEY DIDN'T ATTACK US, JASON. THEY CAME HERE BECAUSE THEIR PLANET WAS DESTROYED!
RIGHT. BUT THE INVADERS FOLLOWED THEM HERE.
SOME FOLKS CAN'T FORGIVE THAT.
YOU KNOW WE'RE RIGHT ABOUT THIS.
THEY'RE VICTIMS! THEY SHOULDN'T FEEL LIKE THEY HAVE TO HIDE!
RIGHTRIGHT RIGHT.
WILL YOU BE AT THE STUDY GROUP TONIGHT OR ARE YOU WORKING?
I...QUIT MY JOB.
TOO MANY LIES.
THEN WE'LL SEE YOU TONIGHT!
SORRY, GOTTA RUN!
AS INTENSE AS DR. YAMAZAKE HAS BECOME, I DON'T WANT TO MAKE THINGS--

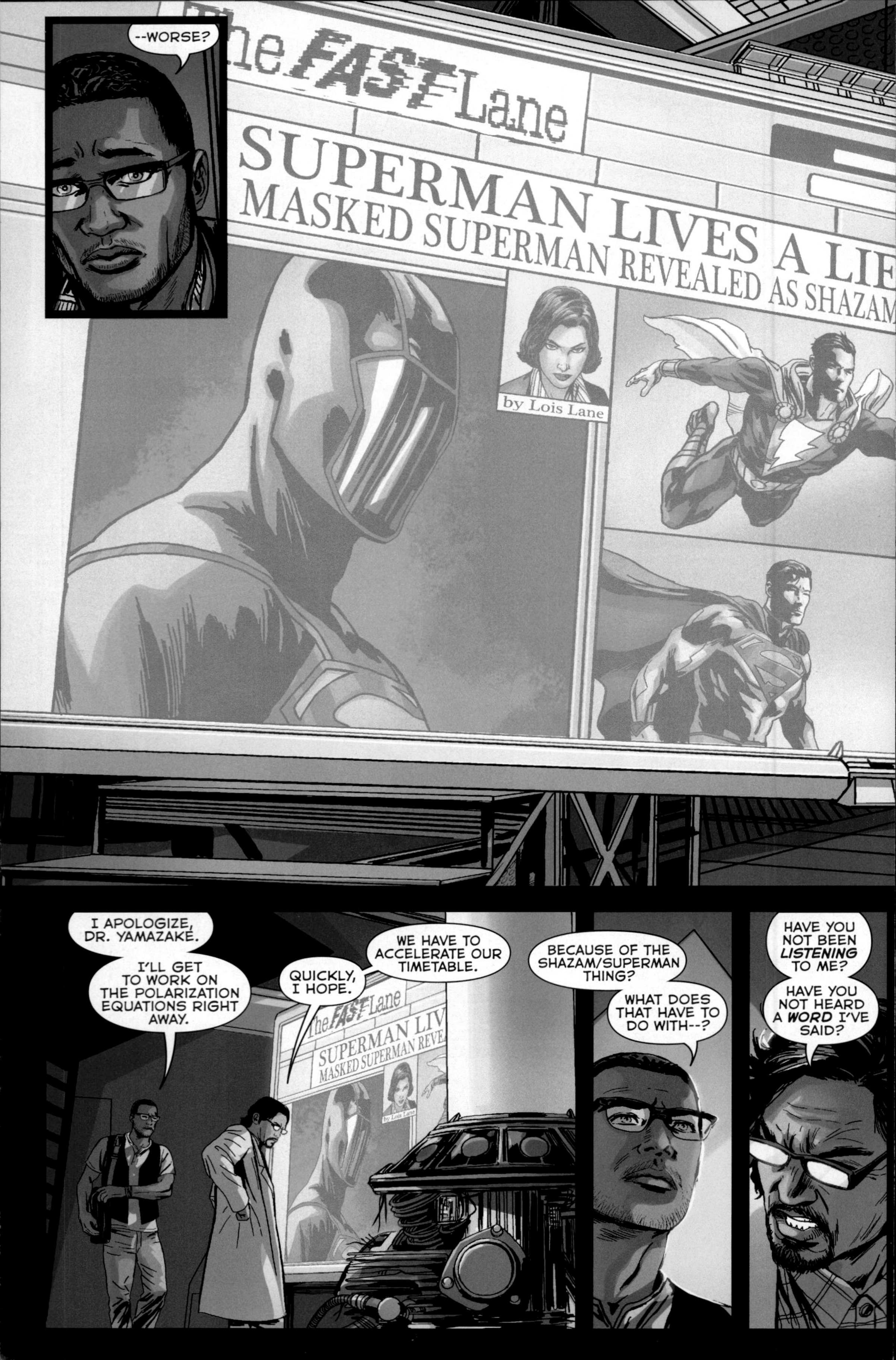
--WORSE?
The FAST Lane
SUPERMAN LIVES A LIE
MASKED SUPERMAN REVEALED AS SHAZAM
by Lois Lane
I APOLOGIZE, DR. YAMAZAKE.
I'LL GET TO WORK ON THE POLARIZATION EQUATIONS RIGHT AWAY.
QUICKLY, I HOPE.
WE HAVE TO ACCELERATE OUR TIMETABLE.
BECAUSE OF THE SHAZAM/SUPERMAN THING?
WHAT DOES THAT HAVE TO DO WITH--?
HAVE YOU NOT BEEN *LISTENING* TO ME?
HAVE YOU NOT HEARD A *WORD* I'VE SAID?

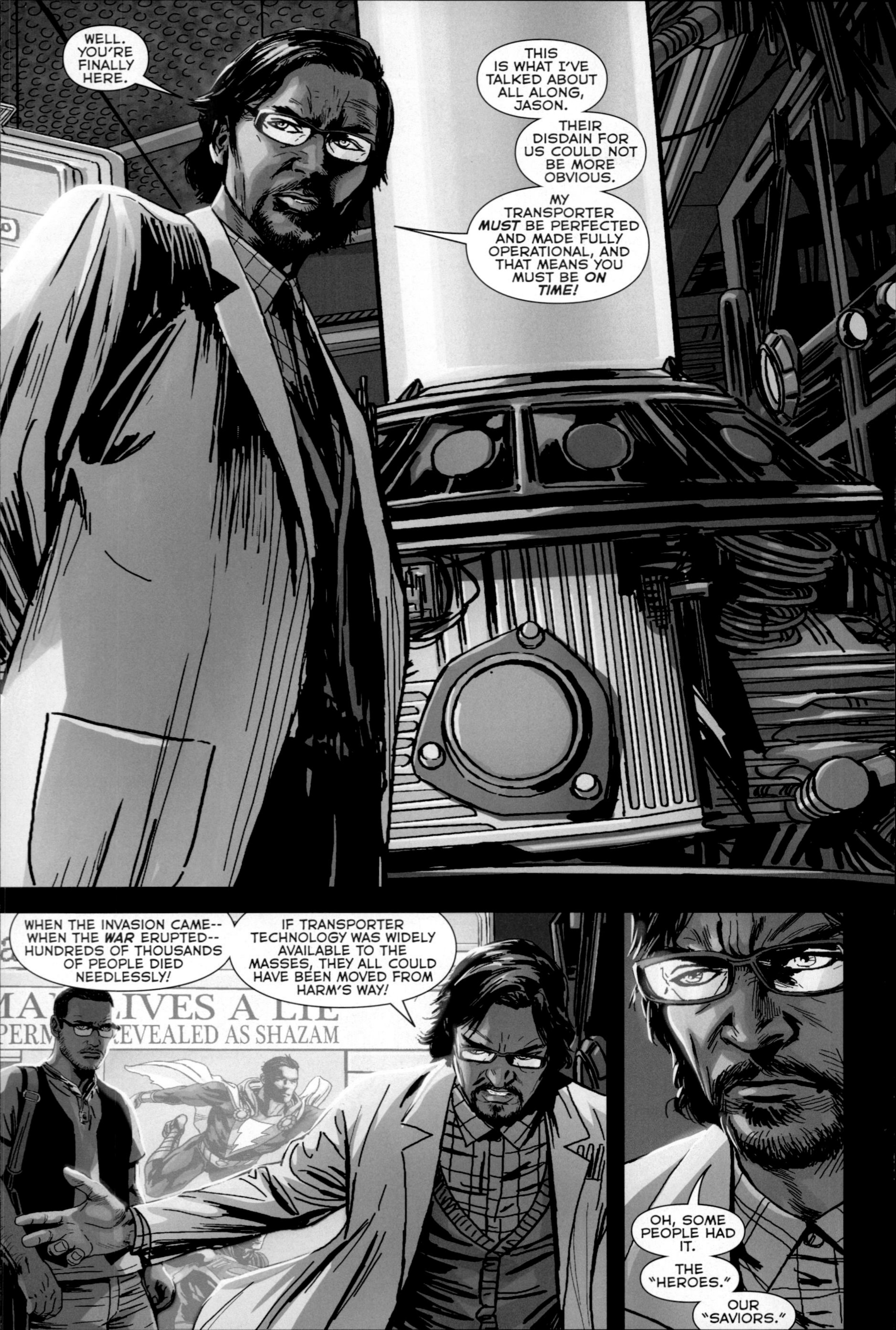
WELL. YOU'RE FINALLY HERE.
THIS IS WHAT I'VE TALKED ABOUT ALL ALONG, JASON.
THEIR DISDAIN FOR US COULD NOT BE MORE OBVIOUS.
MY TRANSPORTER *MUST* BE PERFECTED AND MADE FULLY OPERATIONAL, AND THAT MEANS YOU MUST BE *ON TIME!*
WHEN THE INVASION CAME-- WHEN THE *WAR* ERUPTED-- HUNDREDS OF THOUSANDS OF PEOPLE DIED NEEDLESSLY!
IF TRANSPORTER TECHNOLOGY WAS WIDELY AVAILABLE TO THE MASSES, THEY ALL COULD HAVE BEEN MOVED FROM HARM'S WAY!
OH, SOME PEOPLE HAD IT.
THE "HEROES."
OUR "SAVIORS."

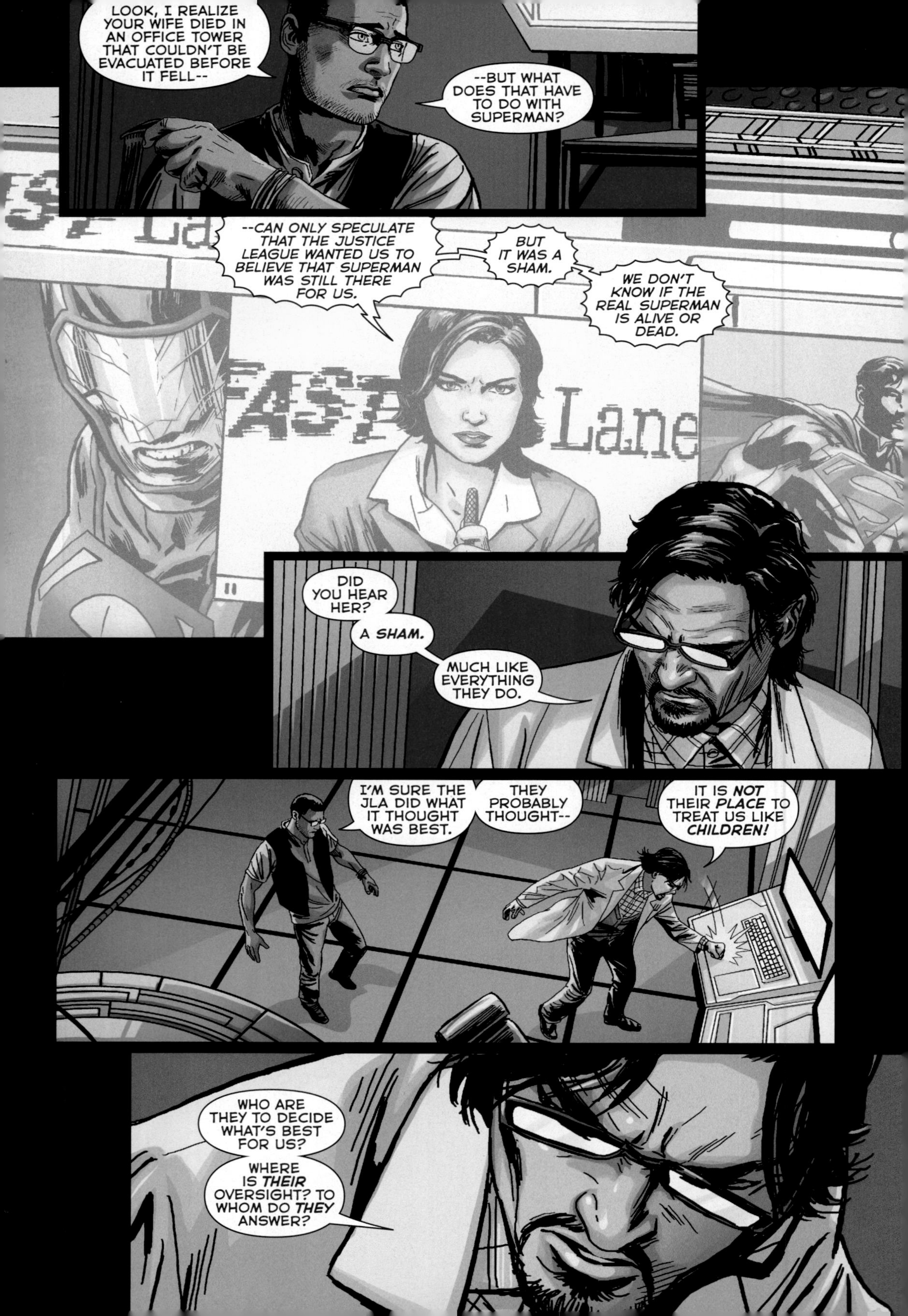
LOOK, I REALIZE YOUR WIFE DIED IN AN OFFICE TOWER THAT COULDN'T BE EVACUATED BEFORE IT FELL--
--BUT WHAT DOES THAT HAVE TO DO WITH SUPERMAN?
--CAN ONLY SPECULATE THAT THE JUSTICE LEAGUE WANTED US TO BELIEVE THAT SUPERMAN WAS STILL THERE FOR US.
BUT IT WAS A SHAM.
WE DON'T KNOW IF THE REAL SUPERMAN IS ALIVE OR DEAD.
FAST Lane
DID YOU HEAR HER?
A *SHAM.*
MUCH LIKE EVERYTHING THEY DO.
I'M SURE THE JLA DID WHAT IT THOUGHT WAS BEST.
THEY PROBABLY THOUGHT--
IT IS ***NOT*** THEIR ***PLACE*** TO TREAT US LIKE ***CHILDREN!***
WHO ARE THEY TO DECIDE WHAT'S BEST FOR US?
WHERE IS ***THEIR*** OVERSIGHT? TO WHOM DO ***THEY*** ANSWER?

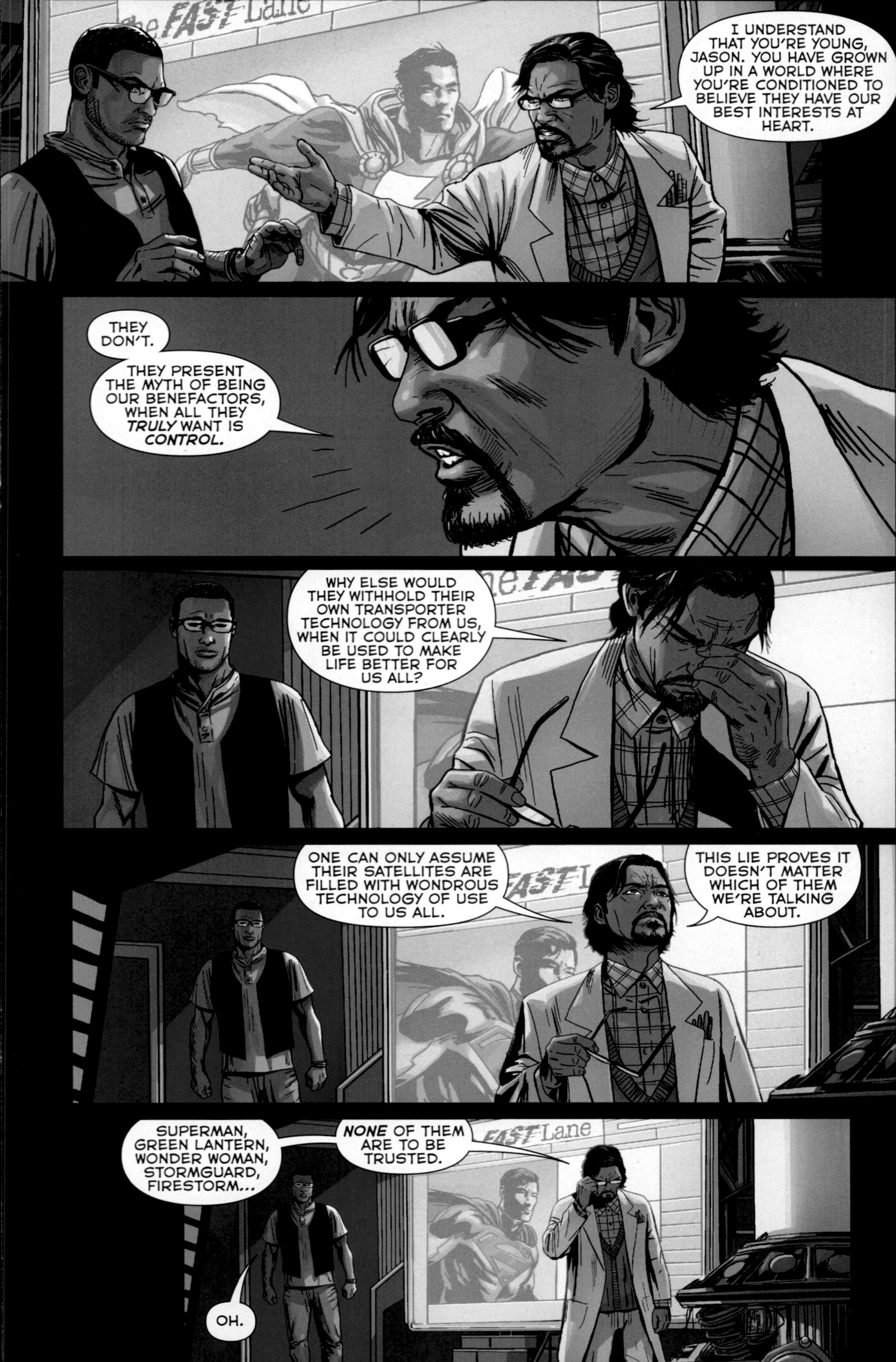

The FAST Lane
I UNDERSTAND THAT YOU'RE YOUNG, JASON. YOU HAVE GROWN UP IN A WORLD WHERE YOU'RE CONDITIONED TO BELIEVE THEY HAVE OUR BEST INTERESTS AT HEART.
THEY DON'T.
THEY PRESENT THE MYTH OF BEING OUR BENEFACTORS, WHEN ALL THEY *TRULY* WANT IS ***CONTROL.***
WHY ELSE WOULD THEY WITHHOLD THEIR OWN TRANSPORTER TECHNOLOGY FROM US, WHEN IT COULD CLEARLY BE USED TO MAKE LIFE BETTER FOR US ALL?
ONE CAN ONLY ASSUME THEIR SATELLITES ARE FILLED WITH WONDROUS TECHNOLOGY OF USE TO US ALL.
THIS LIE PROVES IT DOESN'T MATTER WHICH OF THEM WE'RE TALKING ABOUT.
SUPERMAN, GREEN LANTERN, WONDER WOMAN, STORMGUARD, FIRESTORM...
NONE OF THEM ARE TO BE TRUSTED.
FAST Lane
OH.

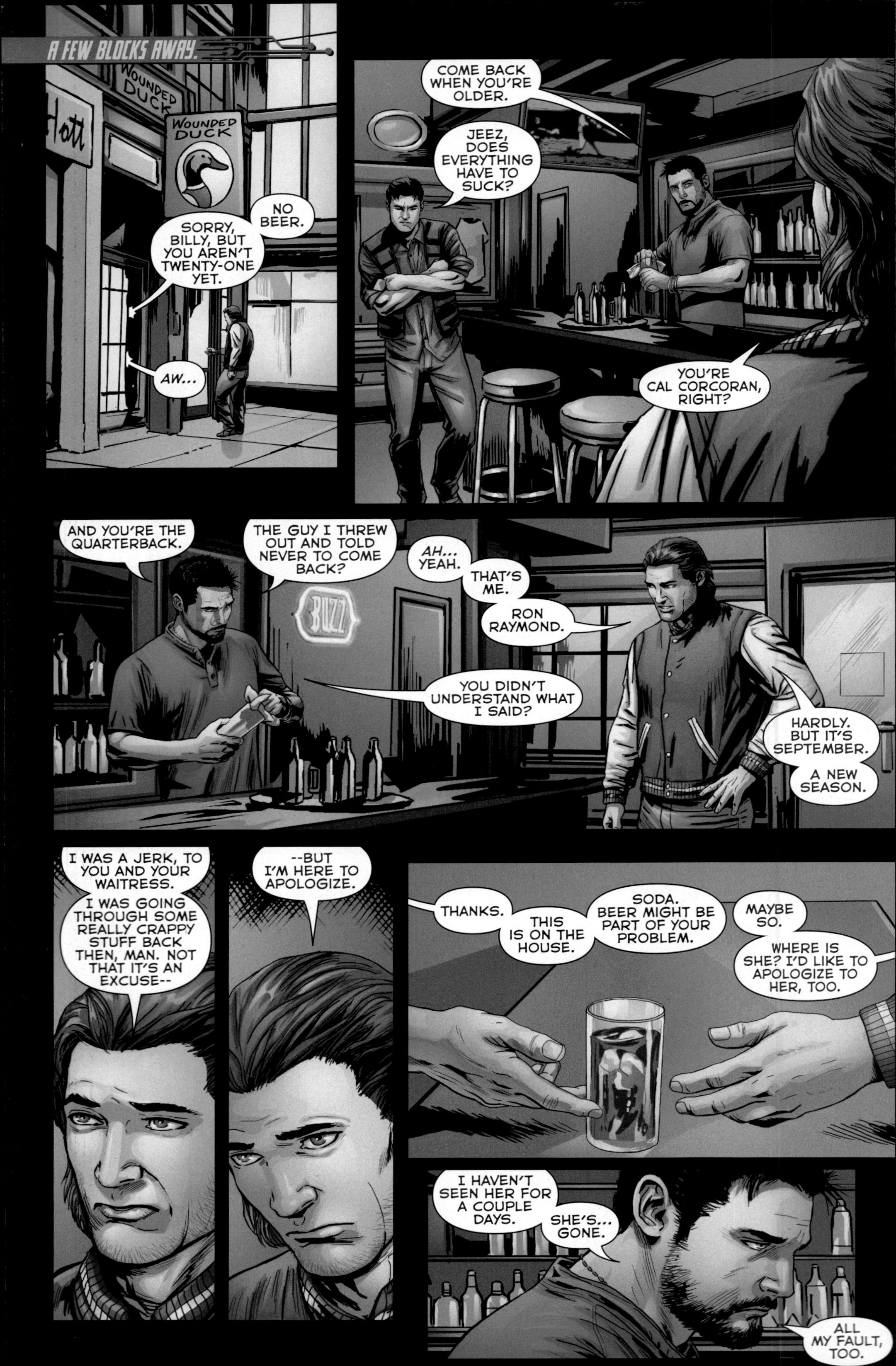
A FEW BLOCKS AWAY.
WOUNDED DUCK
WOUNDED DUCK
SORRY, BILLY, BUT YOU AREN'T TWENTY-ONE YET.
NO BEER.
AW...
COME BACK WHEN YOU'RE OLDER.
JEEZ, DOES EVERYTHING HAVE TO SUCK?
YOU'RE CAL CORCORAN, RIGHT?
AND YOU'RE THE QUARTERBACK.
THE GUY I THREW OUT AND TOLD NEVER TO COME BACK?
AH... YEAH.
THAT'S ME.
RON RAYMOND.
BUZZ
YOU DIDN'T UNDERSTAND WHAT I SAID?
HARDLY. BUT IT'S SEPTEMBER.
A NEW SEASON.
I WAS A JERK, TO YOU AND YOUR WAITRESS.
I WAS GOING THROUGH SOME REALLY CRAPPY STUFF BACK THEN, MAN. NOT THAT IT'S AN EXCUSE--
--BUT I'M HERE TO APOLOGIZE.
THANKS.
THIS IS ON THE HOUSE.
SODA. BEER MIGHT BE PART OF YOUR PROBLEM.
MAYBE SO.
WHERE IS SHE? I'D LIKE TO APOLOGIZE TO HER, TOO.
I HAVEN'T SEEN HER FOR A COUPLE DAYS.
SHE'S... GONE.
ALL MY FAULT, TOO.

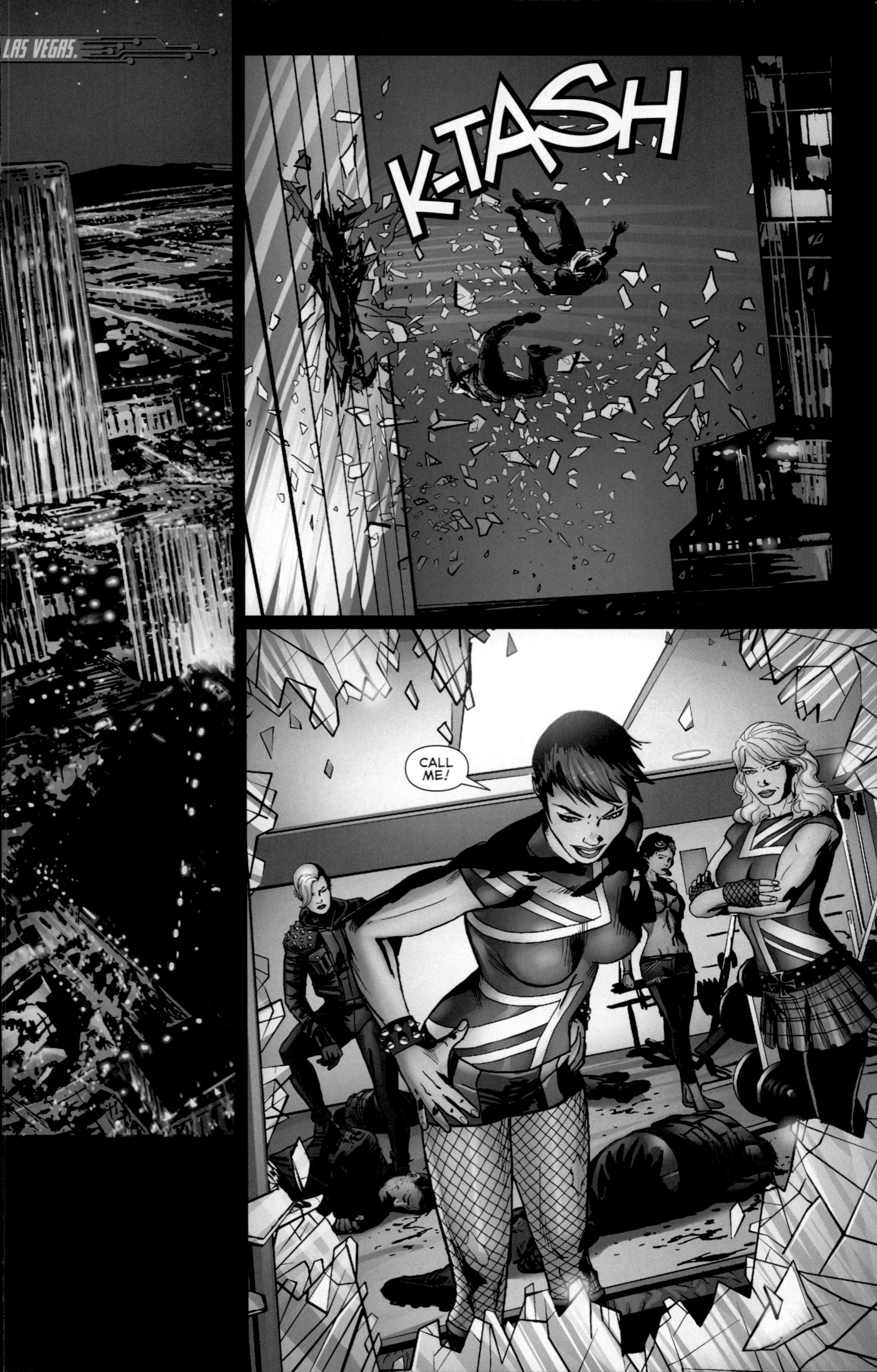
LAS VEGAS.
K-TASH
CALL ME!

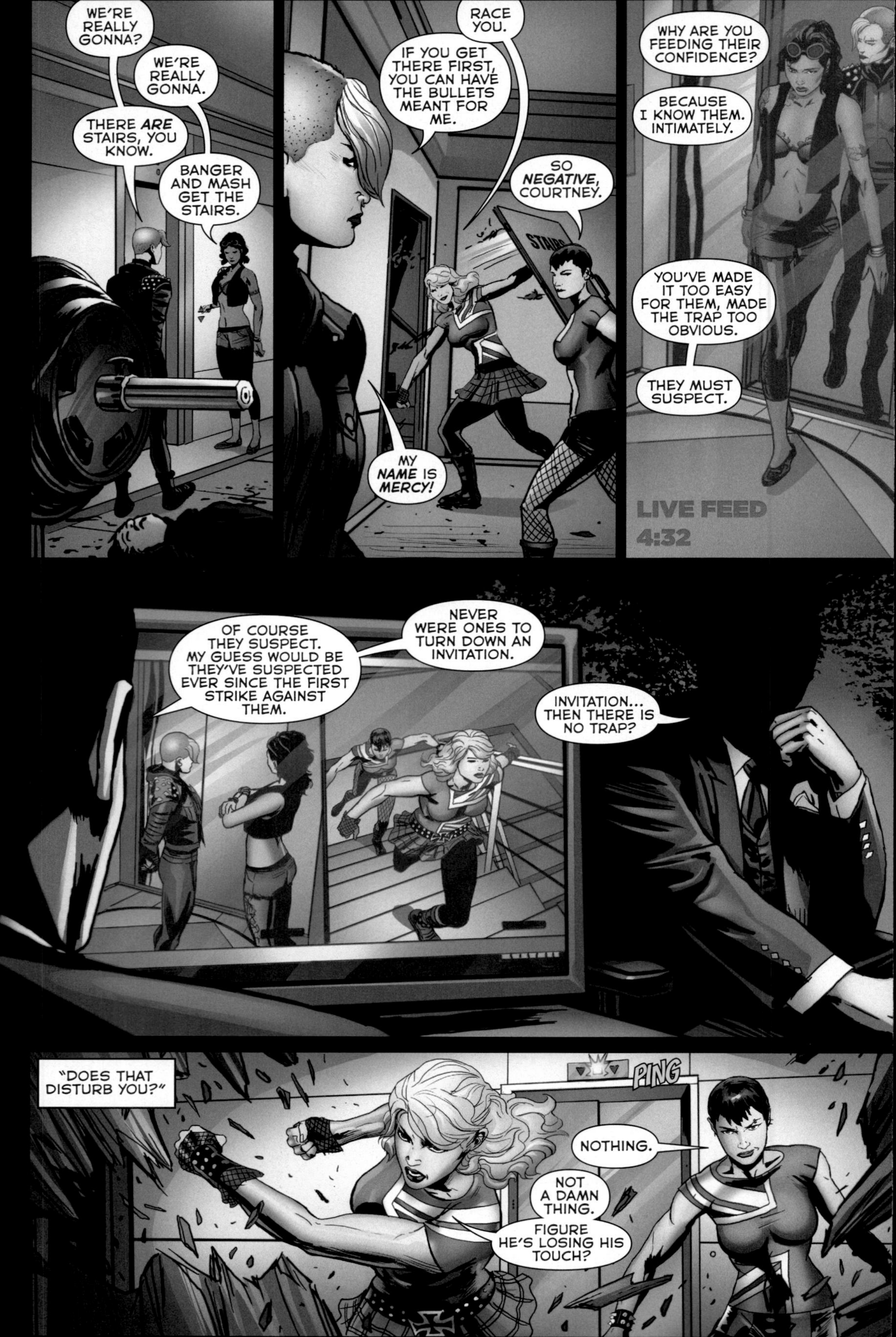
WE'RE REALLY GONNA?
WE'RE REALLY GONNA.
THERE ARE STAIRS, YOU KNOW.
BANGER AND MASH GET THE STAIRS.
RACE YOU.
IF YOU GET THERE FIRST, YOU CAN HAVE THE BULLETS MEANT FOR ME.
SO NEGATIVE, COURTNEY.
STAIRS
MY NAME IS MERCY!
WHY ARE YOU FEEDING THEIR CONFIDENCE?
BECAUSE I KNOW THEM. INTIMATELY.
YOU'VE MADE IT TOO EASY FOR THEM, MADE THE TRAP TOO OBVIOUS.
THEY MUST SUSPECT.
LIVE FEED
4:32
OF COURSE THEY SUSPECT. MY GUESS WOULD BE THEY'VE SUSPECTED EVER SINCE THE FIRST STRIKE AGAINST THEM.
NEVER WERE ONES TO TURN DOWN AN INVITATION.
INVITATION... THEN THERE IS NO TRAP?
"DOES THAT DISTURB YOU?"
PING
NOTHING.
NOT A DAMN THING.
FIGURE HE'S LOSING HIS TOUCH?

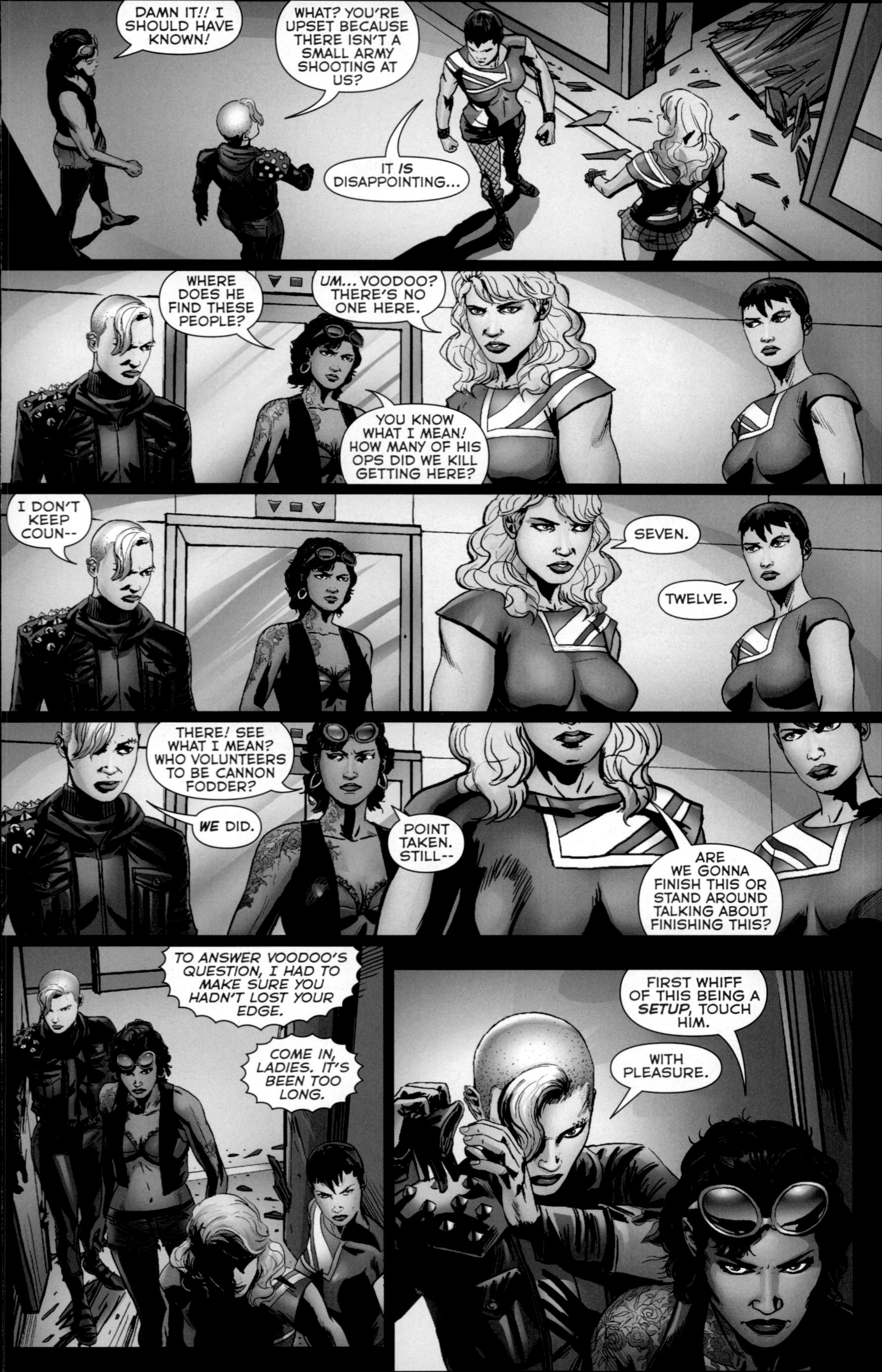
DAMN IT!! I SHOULD HAVE KNOWN!
WHAT? YOU'RE UPSET BECAUSE THERE ISN'T A SMALL ARMY SHOOTING AT US?
IT IS DISAPPOINTING...
WHERE DOES HE FIND THESE PEOPLE?
UM... VOODOO? THERE'S NO ONE HERE.
YOU KNOW WHAT I MEAN! HOW MANY OF HIS OPS DID WE KILL GETTING HERE?
I DON'T KEEP COUN--
SEVEN.
TWELVE.
THERE! SEE WHAT I MEAN? WHO VOLUNTEERS TO BE CANNON FODDER?
WE DID.
POINT TAKEN. STILL--
ARE WE GONNA FINISH THIS OR STAND AROUND TALKING ABOUT FINISHING THIS?
TO ANSWER VOODOO'S QUESTION, I HAD TO MAKE SURE YOU HADN'T LOST YOUR EDGE.
COME IN, LADIES. IT'S BEEN TOO LONG.
FIRST WHIFF OF THIS BEING A SETUP, TOUCH HIM.
WITH PLEASURE.

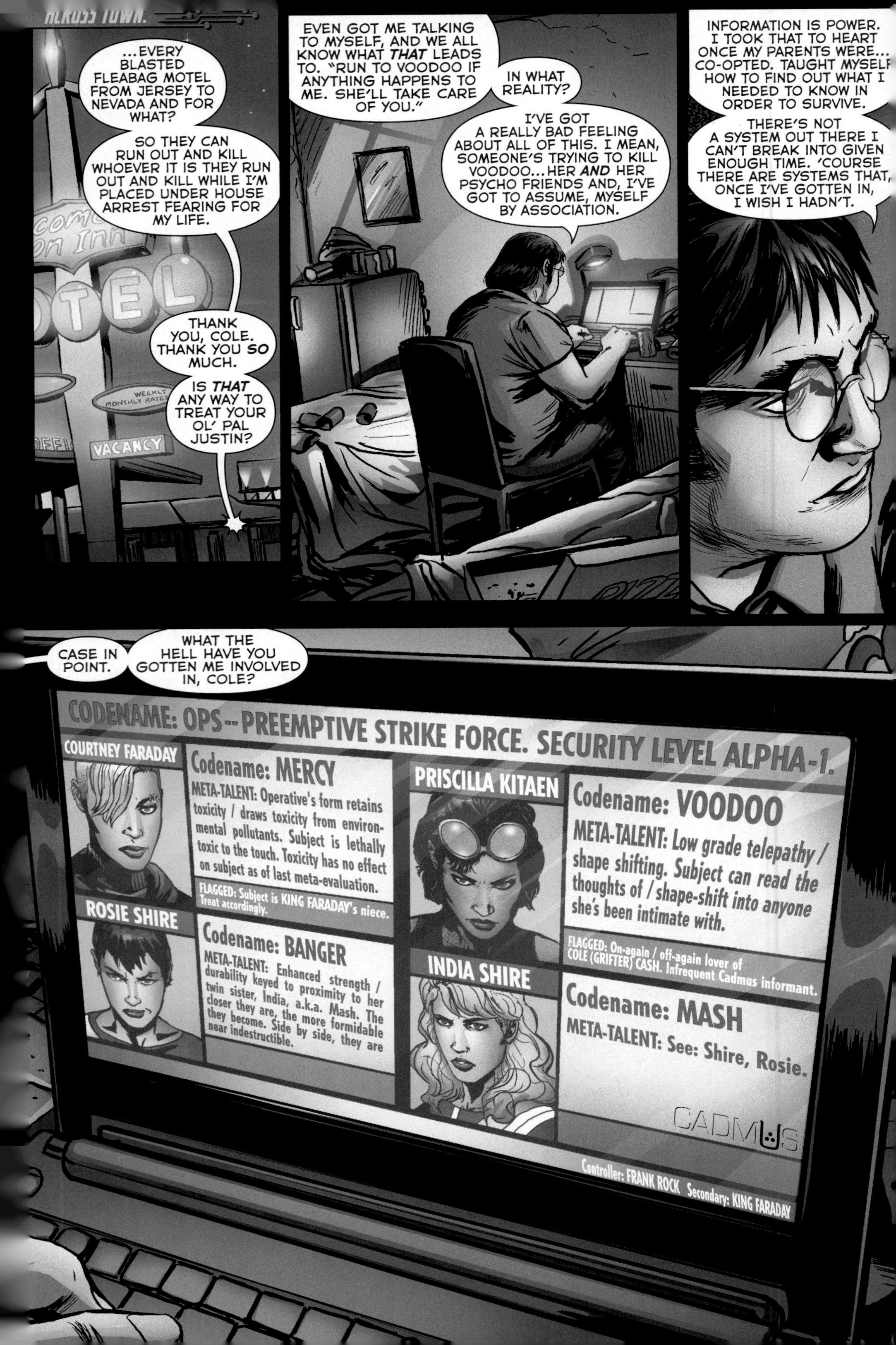

ACROSS TOWN.
...EVERY BLASTED FLEABAG MOTEL FROM JERSEY TO NEVADA AND FOR WHAT?
SO THEY CAN RUN OUT AND KILL WHOEVER IT IS THEY RUN OUT AND KILL WHILE I'M PLACED UNDER HOUSE ARREST FEARING FOR MY LIFE.
THANK YOU, COLE. THANK YOU SO MUCH.
IS THAT ANY WAY TO TREAT YOUR OL' PAL JUSTIN?
WEEKLY MONTHLY RATES
VACANCY
EVEN GOT ME TALKING TO MYSELF, AND WE ALL KNOW WHAT THAT LEADS TO. "RUN TO VOODOO IF ANYTHING HAPPENS TO ME. SHE'LL TAKE CARE OF YOU."
IN WHAT REALITY?
I'VE GOT A REALLY BAD FEELING ABOUT ALL OF THIS. I MEAN, SOMEONE'S TRYING TO KILL VOODOO...HER AND HER PSYCHO FRIENDS AND, I'VE GOT TO ASSUME, MYSELF BY ASSOCIATION.
INFORMATION IS POWER. I TOOK THAT TO HEART ONCE MY PARENTS WERE... CO-OPTED. TAUGHT MYSELF HOW TO FIND OUT WHAT I NEEDED TO KNOW IN ORDER TO SURVIVE.
THERE'S NOT A SYSTEM OUT THERE I CAN'T BREAK INTO GIVEN ENOUGH TIME. 'COURSE THERE ARE SYSTEMS THAT, ONCE I'VE GOTTEN IN, I WISH I HADN'T.
CASE IN POINT.
WHAT THE HELL HAVE YOU GOTTEN ME INVOLVED IN, COLE?
CODENAME: OPS--PREEMPTIVE STRIKE FORCE. SECURITY LEVEL ALPHA-1.
COURTNEY FARADAY
Codename: MERCY
META-TALENT: Operative's form retains toxicity / draws toxicity from environmental pollutants. Subject is lethally toxic to the touch. Toxicity has no effect on subject as of last meta-evaluation.
FLAGGED: Subject is KING FARADAY's niece. Treat accordingly.
ROSIE SHIRE
Codename: BANGER
META-TALENT: Enhanced strength / durability keyed to proximity to her twin sister, India, a.k.a. Mash. The closer they are, the more formidable they become. Side by side, they are near indestructible.
PRISCILLA KITAEN
Codename: VOODOO
META-TALENT: Low grade telepathy / shape shifting. Subject can read the thoughts of / shape-shift into anyone she's been intimate with.
FLAGGED: On-again / off-again lover of COLE (GRIFTER) CASH. Infrequent Cadmus informant.
INDIA SHIRE
Codename: MASH
META-TALENT: See: Shire, Rosie.
CADMUS
Controller: FRANK ROCK Secondary: KING FARADAY

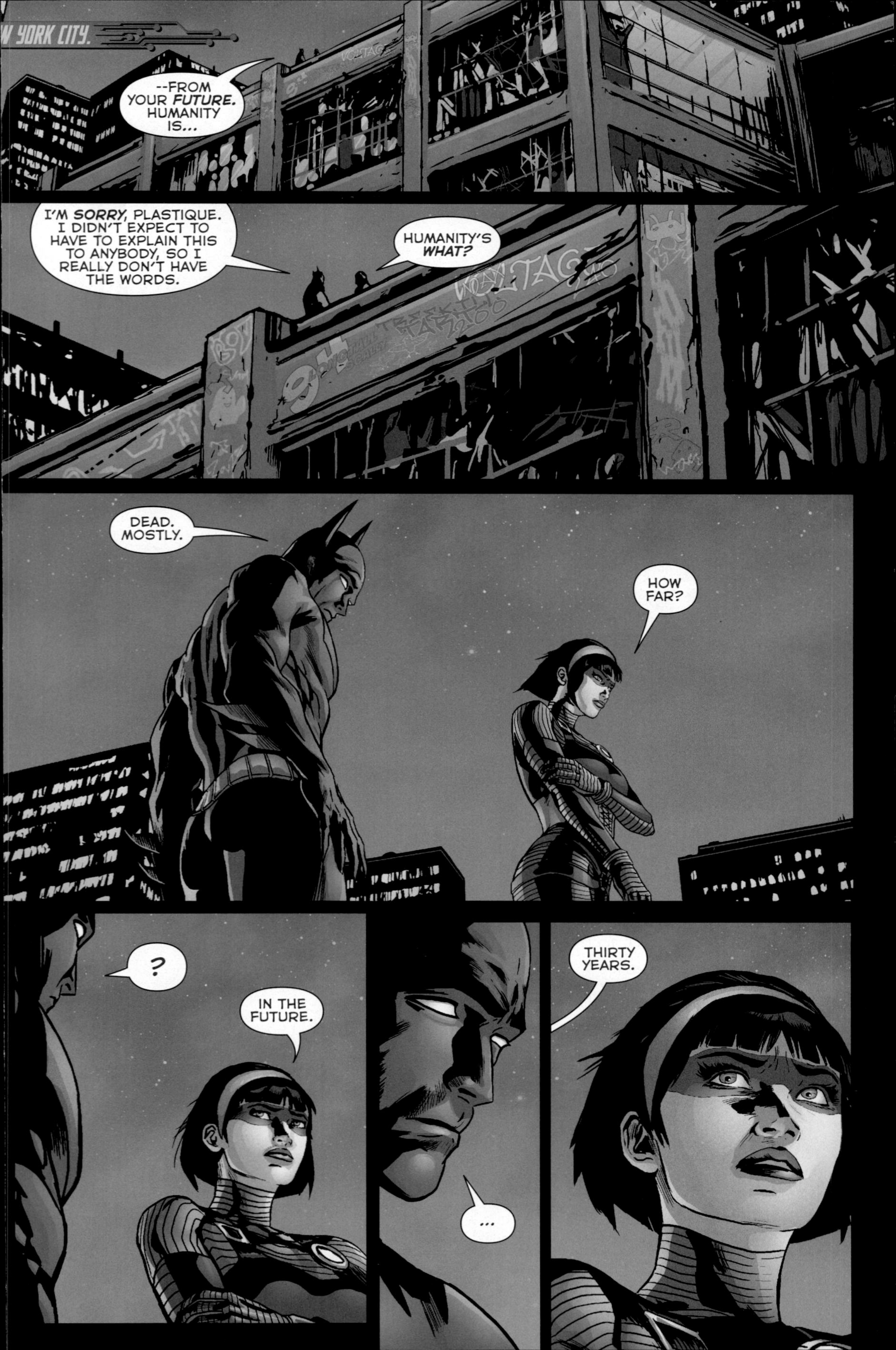

W YORK CITY.
--FROM YOUR FUTURE. HUMANITY IS...
I'M SORRY, PLASTIQUE. I DIDN'T EXPECT TO HAVE TO EXPLAIN THIS TO ANYBODY, SO I REALLY DON'T HAVE THE WORDS.
HUMANITY'S WHAT?
DEAD. MOSTLY.
HOW FAR?
?
IN THE FUTURE.
...
THIRTY YEARS.

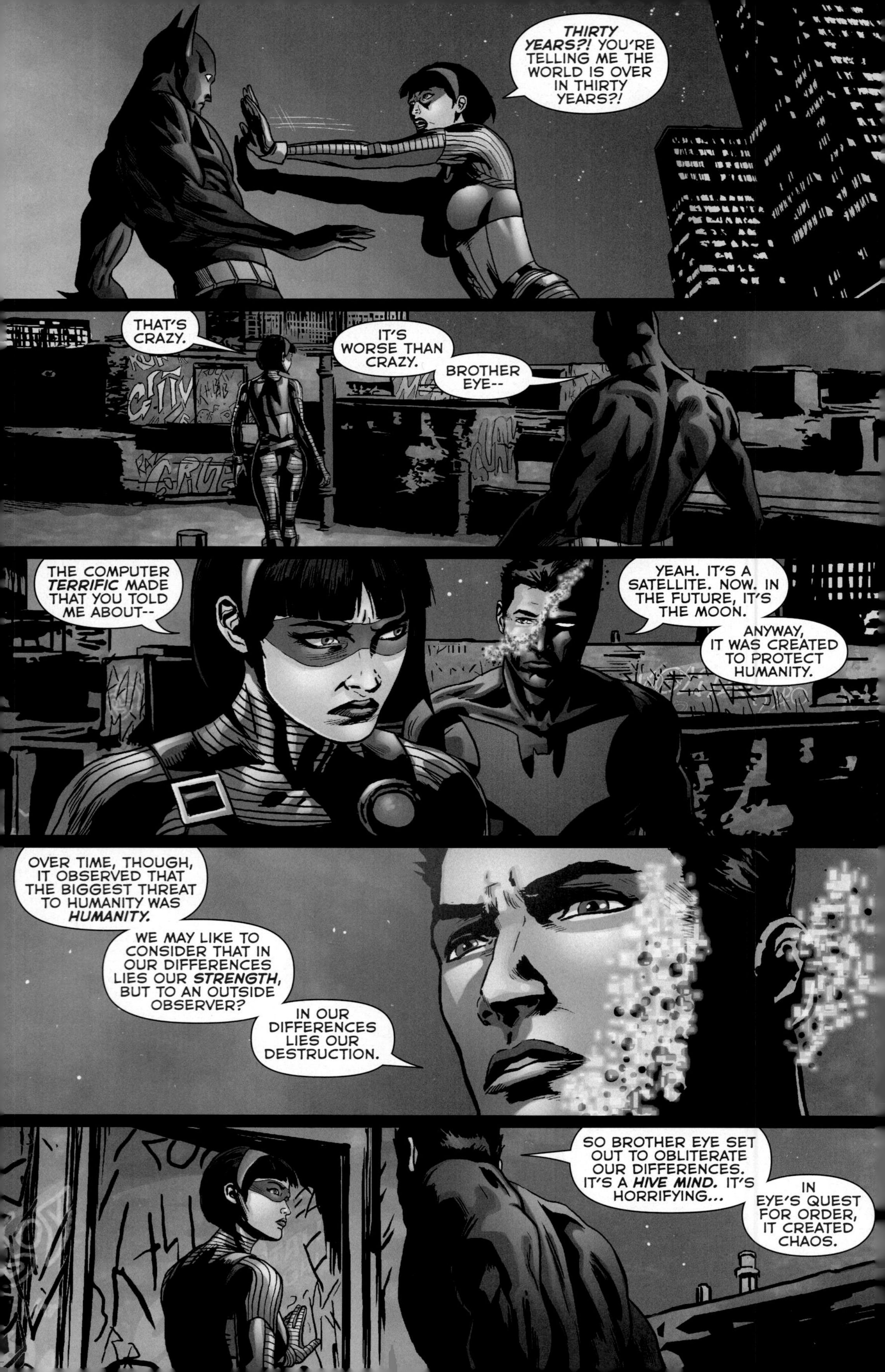

THIRTY YEARS?! YOU'RE TELLING ME THE WORLD IS OVER IN THIRTY YEARS?!
THAT'S CRAZY.
IT'S WORSE THAN CRAZY.
BROTHER EYE--
THE COMPUTER TERRIFIC MADE THAT YOU TOLD ME ABOUT--
YEAH. IT'S A SATELLITE. NOW. IN THE FUTURE, IT'S THE MOON.
ANYWAY, IT WAS CREATED TO PROTECT HUMANITY.
OVER TIME, THOUGH, IT OBSERVED THAT THE BIGGEST THREAT TO HUMANITY WAS HUMANITY.
WE MAY LIKE TO CONSIDER THAT IN OUR DIFFERENCES LIES OUR STRENGTH, BUT TO AN OUTSIDE OBSERVER?
IN OUR DIFFERENCES LIES OUR DESTRUCTION.
SO BROTHER EYE SET OUT TO OBLITERATE OUR DIFFERENCES. IT'S A HIVE MIND. IT'S HORRIFYING...
IN EYE'S QUEST FOR ORDER, IT CREATED CHAOS.

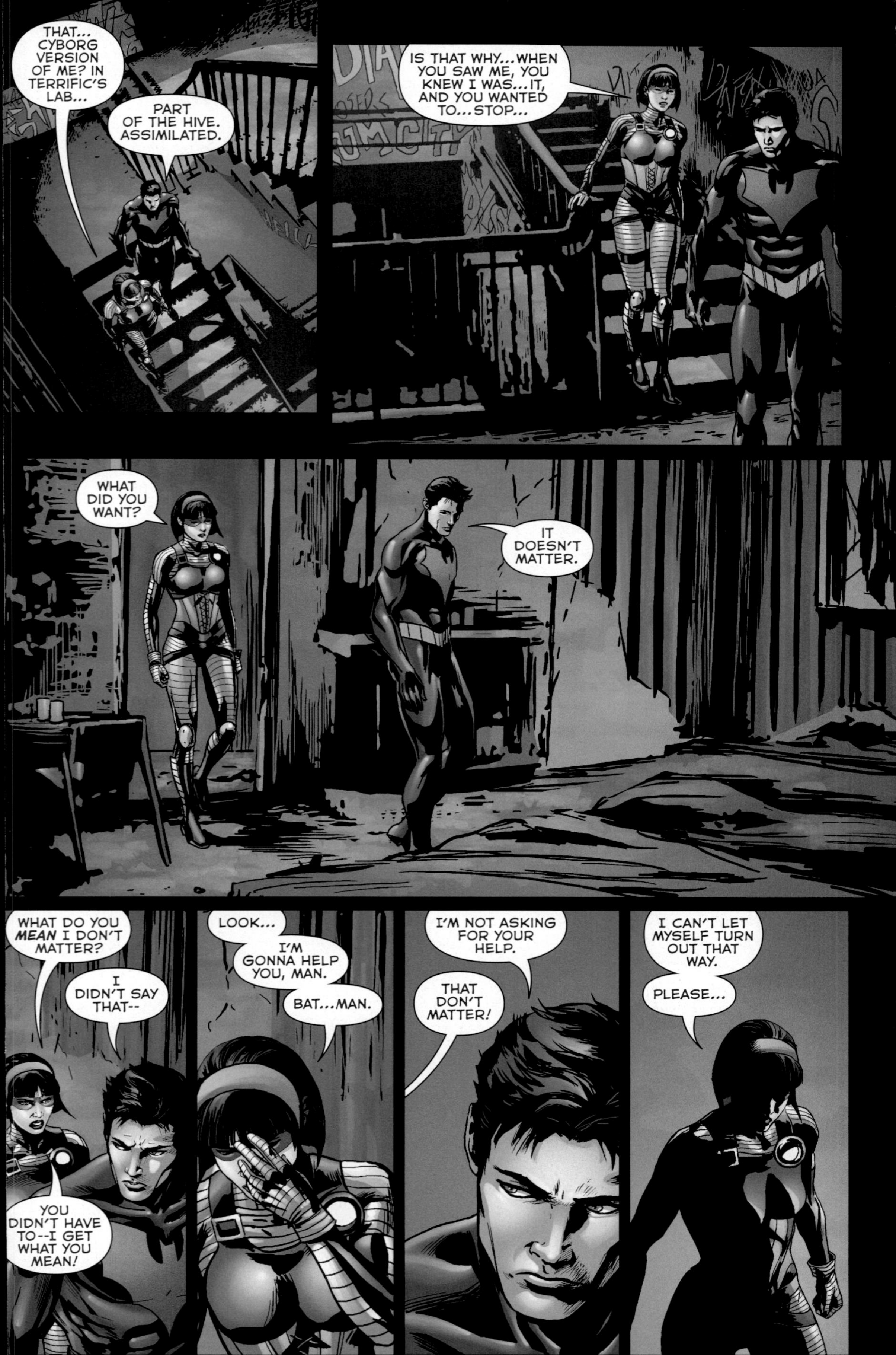
THAT... CYBORG VERSION OF ME? IN TERRIFIC'S LAB...
PART OF THE HIVE. ASSIMILATED.
IS THAT WHY...WHEN YOU SAW ME, YOU KNEW I WAS...IT, AND YOU WANTED TO...STOP...
WHAT DID YOU WANT?
IT DOESN'T MATTER.
WHAT DO YOU *MEAN* I DON'T MATTER?
I DIDN'T SAY THAT--
YOU DIDN'T HAVE TO--I GET WHAT YOU MEAN!
LOOK...
I'M GONNA HELP YOU, MAN.
BAT...MAN.
I'M NOT ASKING FOR YOUR HELP.
THAT DON'T MATTER!
I CAN'T LET MYSELF TURN OUT THAT WAY.
PLEASE...

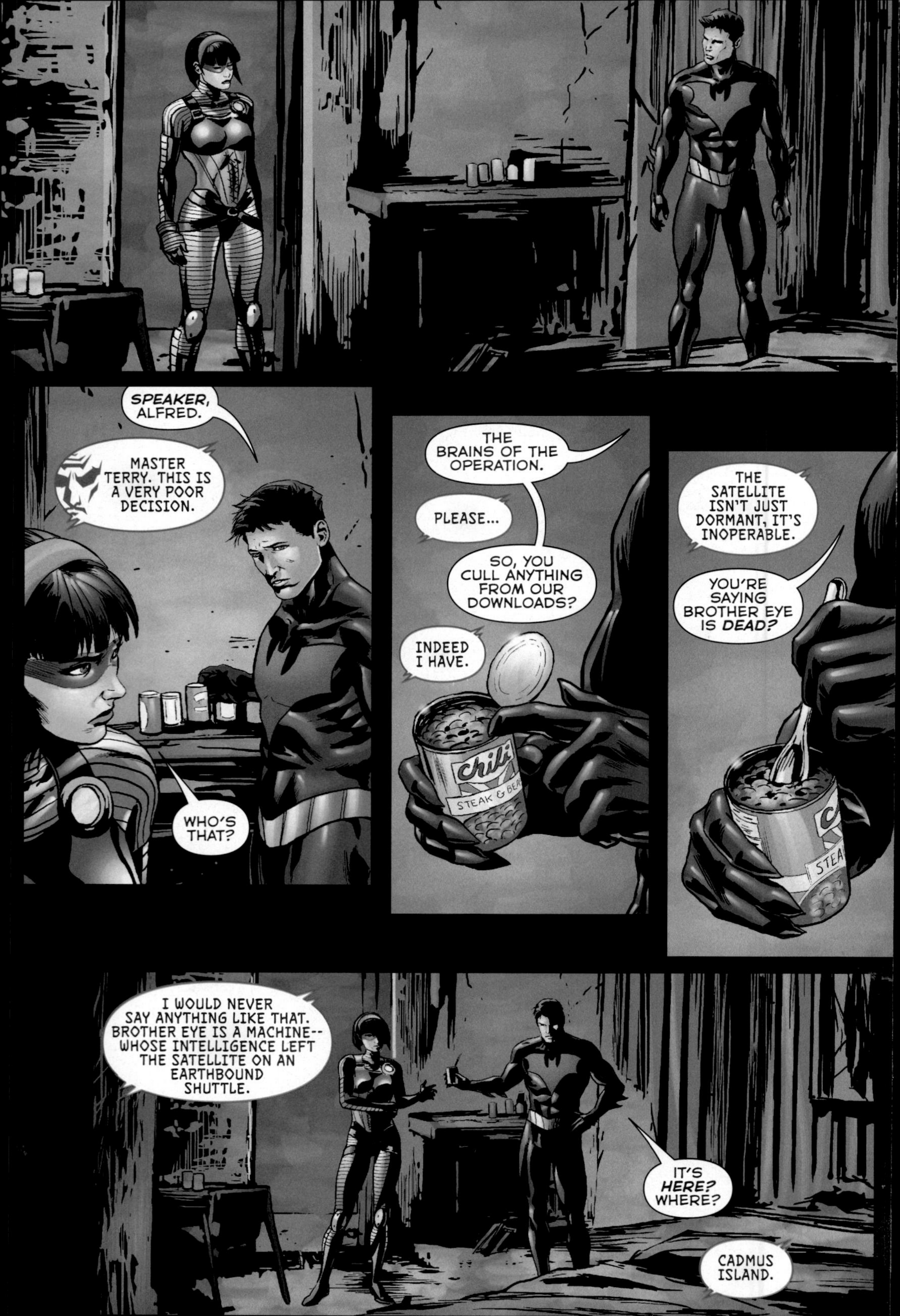
SPEAKER, ALFRED.
MASTER TERRY. THIS IS A VERY POOR DECISION.
WHO'S THAT?
THE BRAINS OF THE OPERATION.
PLEASE...
SO, YOU CULL ANYTHING FROM OUR DOWNLOADS?
INDEED I HAVE.
Chili
STEAK & BEA
THE SATELLITE ISN'T JUST DORMANT, IT'S INOPERABLE.
YOU'RE SAYING BROTHER EYE IS DEAD?
I WOULD NEVER SAY ANYTHING LIKE THAT. BROTHER EYE IS A MACHINE-- WHOSE INTELLIGENCE LEFT THE SATELLITE ON AN EARTHBOUND SHUTTLE.
IT'S HERE? WHERE?
CADMUS ISLAND.

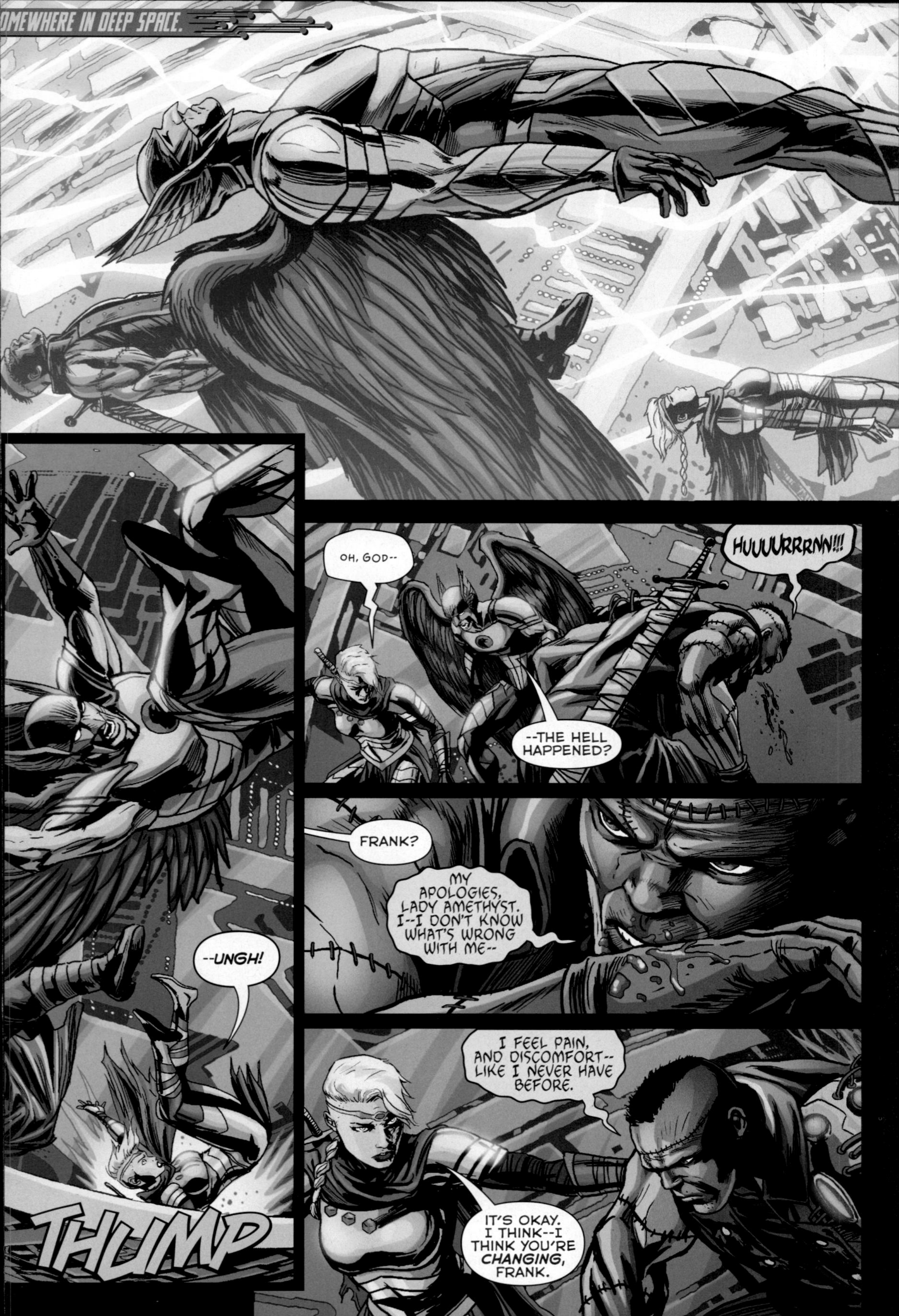
OMEWHERE IN DEEP SPACE.
--UNGH!
THUMP
OH, GOD--
HUUUURRRNN!!!
--THE HELL HAPPENED?
FRANK?
MY APOLOGIES, LADY AMETHYST. I--I DON'T KNOW WHAT'S WRONG WITH ME--
I FEEL PAIN, AND DISCOMFORT--LIKE I NEVER HAVE BEFORE.
IT'S OKAY. I THINK--I THINK YOU'RE *CHANGING*, FRANK.

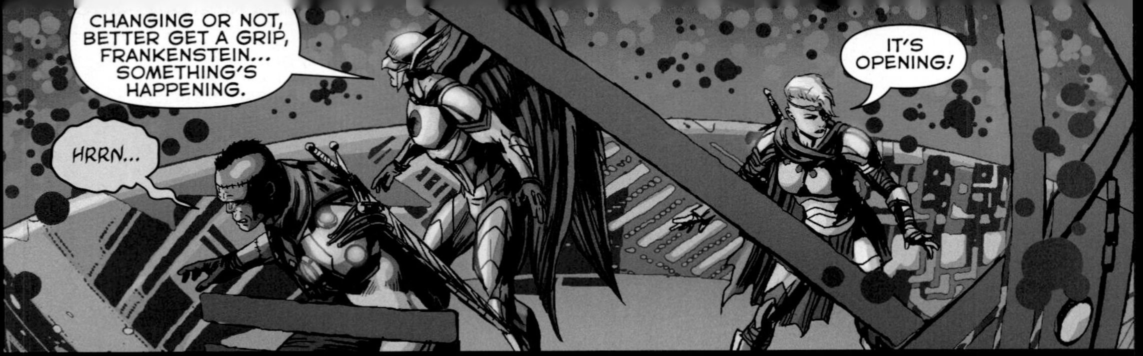
CHANGING OR NOT, BETTER GET A GRIP, FRANKENSTEIN... SOMETHING'S HAPPENING.
HRRN...
IT'S OPENING!

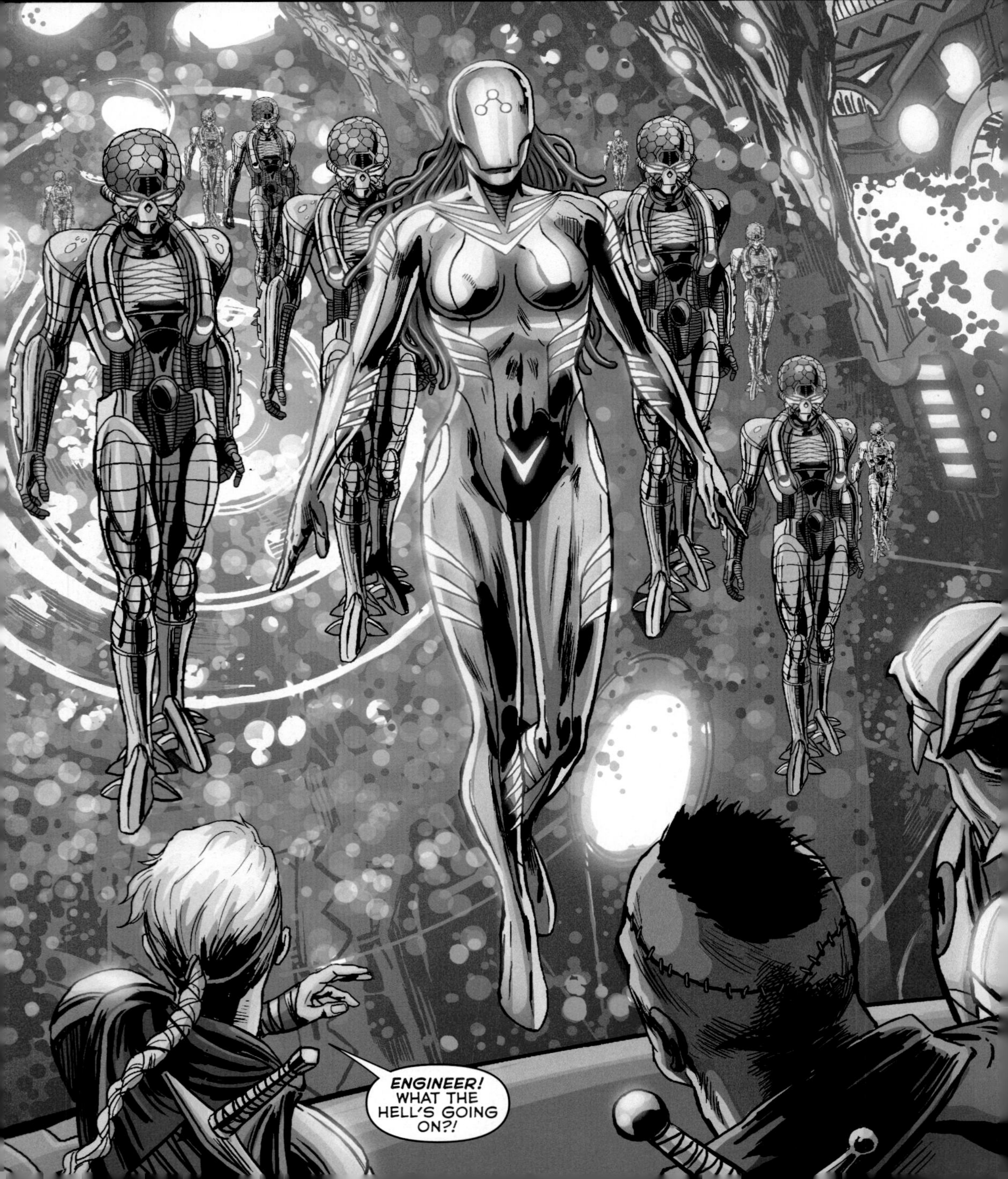
ENGINEER! WHAT THE HELL'S GOING ON?!

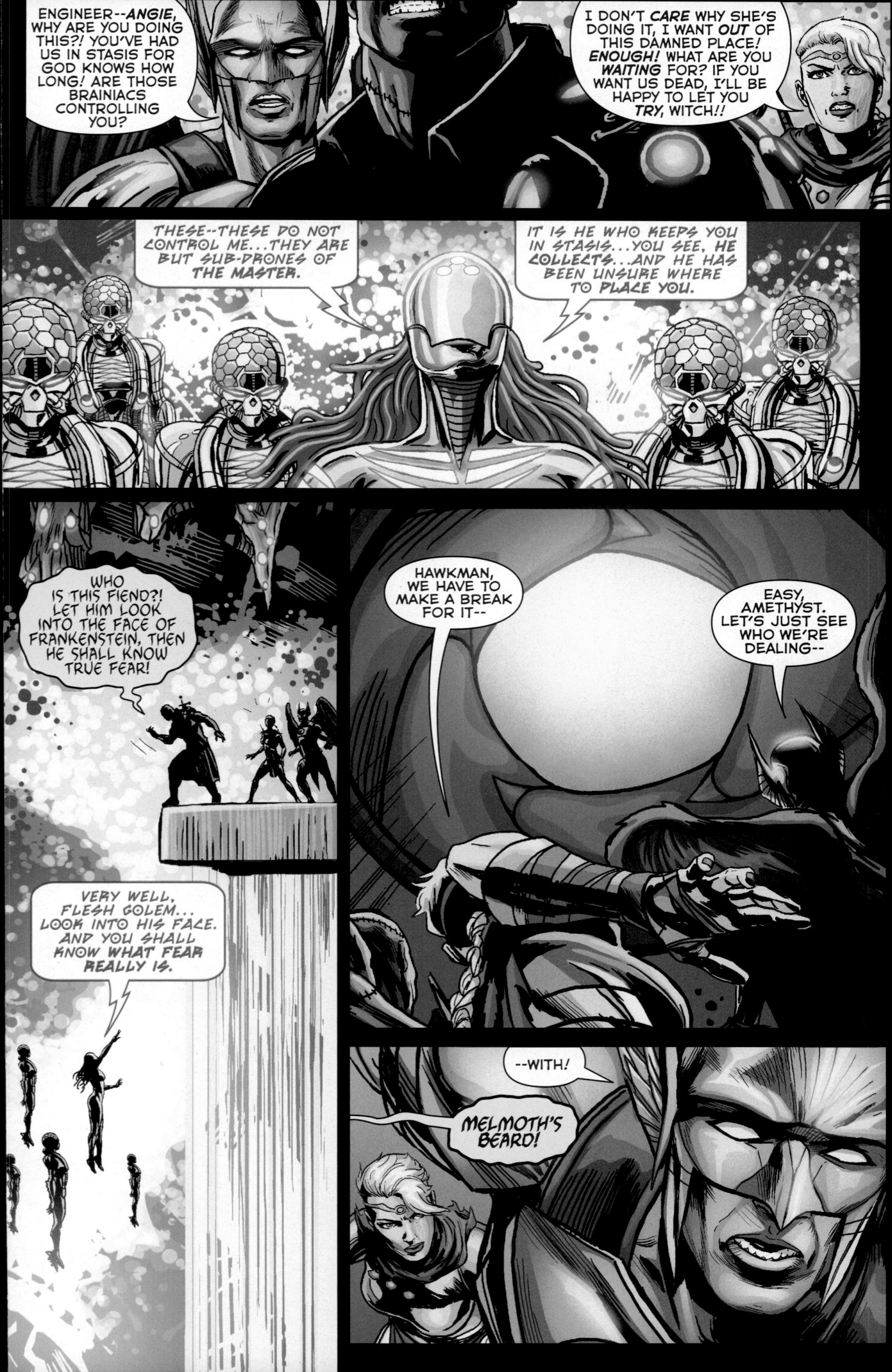
ENGINEER--ANGIE, WHY ARE YOU DOING THIS?! YOU'VE HAD US IN STASIS FOR GOD KNOWS HOW LONG! ARE THOSE BRAINIACS CONTROLLING YOU?
I DON'T CARE WHY SHE'S DOING IT, I WANT OUT OF THIS DAMNED PLACE! ENOUGH! WHAT ARE YOU WAITING FOR? IF YOU WANT US DEAD, I'LL BE HAPPY TO LET YOU TRY, WITCH!!
THESE--THESE DO NOT CONTROL ME...THEY ARE BUT SUB-DRONES OF THE MASTER.
IT IS HE WHO KEEPS YOU IN STASIS...YOU SEE, HE COLLECTS...AND HE HAS BEEN UNSURE WHERE TO PLACE YOU.
WHO IS THIS FIEND?! LET HIM LOOK INTO THE FACE OF FRANKENSTEIN, THEN HE SHALL KNOW TRUE FEAR!
VERY WELL, FLESH GOLEM... LOOK INTO HIS FACE. AND YOU SHALL KNOW WHAT FEAR REALLY IS.
HAWKMAN, WE HAVE TO MAKE A BREAK FOR IT--
EASY, AMETHYST. LET'S JUST SEE WHO WE'RE DEALING--
--WITH!
MELMOTH'S BEARD!

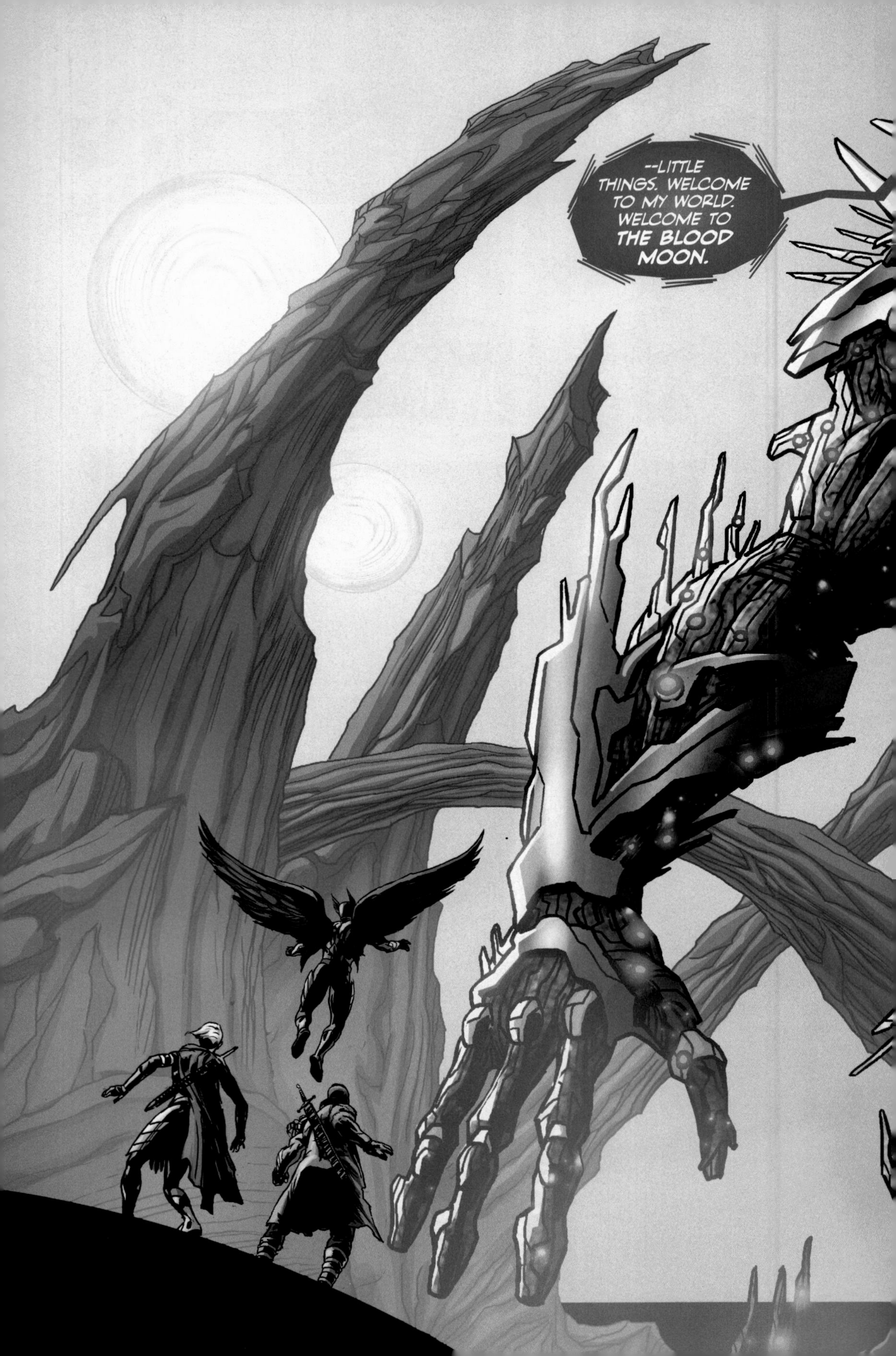
--LITTLE THINGS. WELCOME TO MY WORLD. WELCOME TO THE BLOOD MOON.

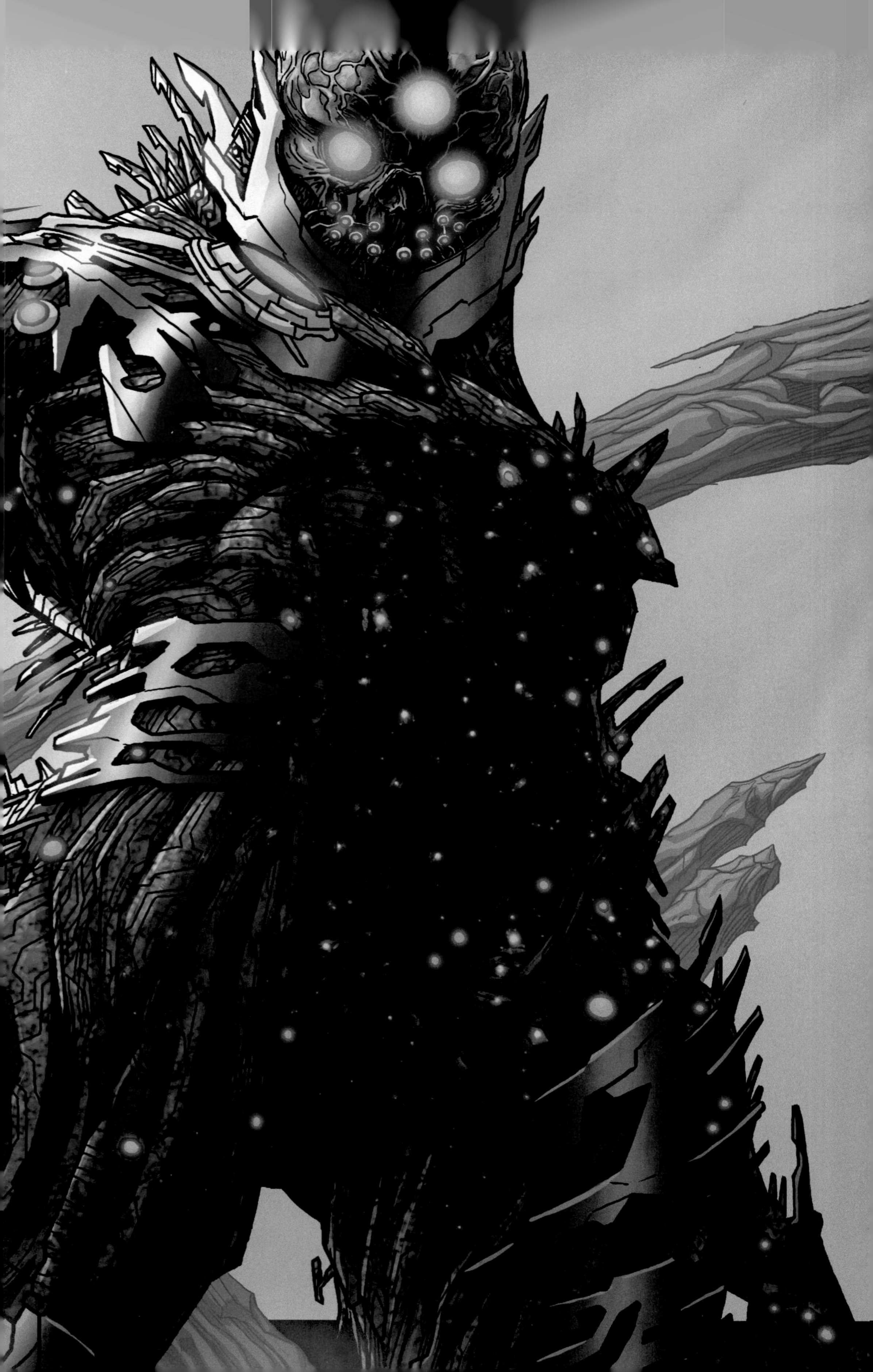

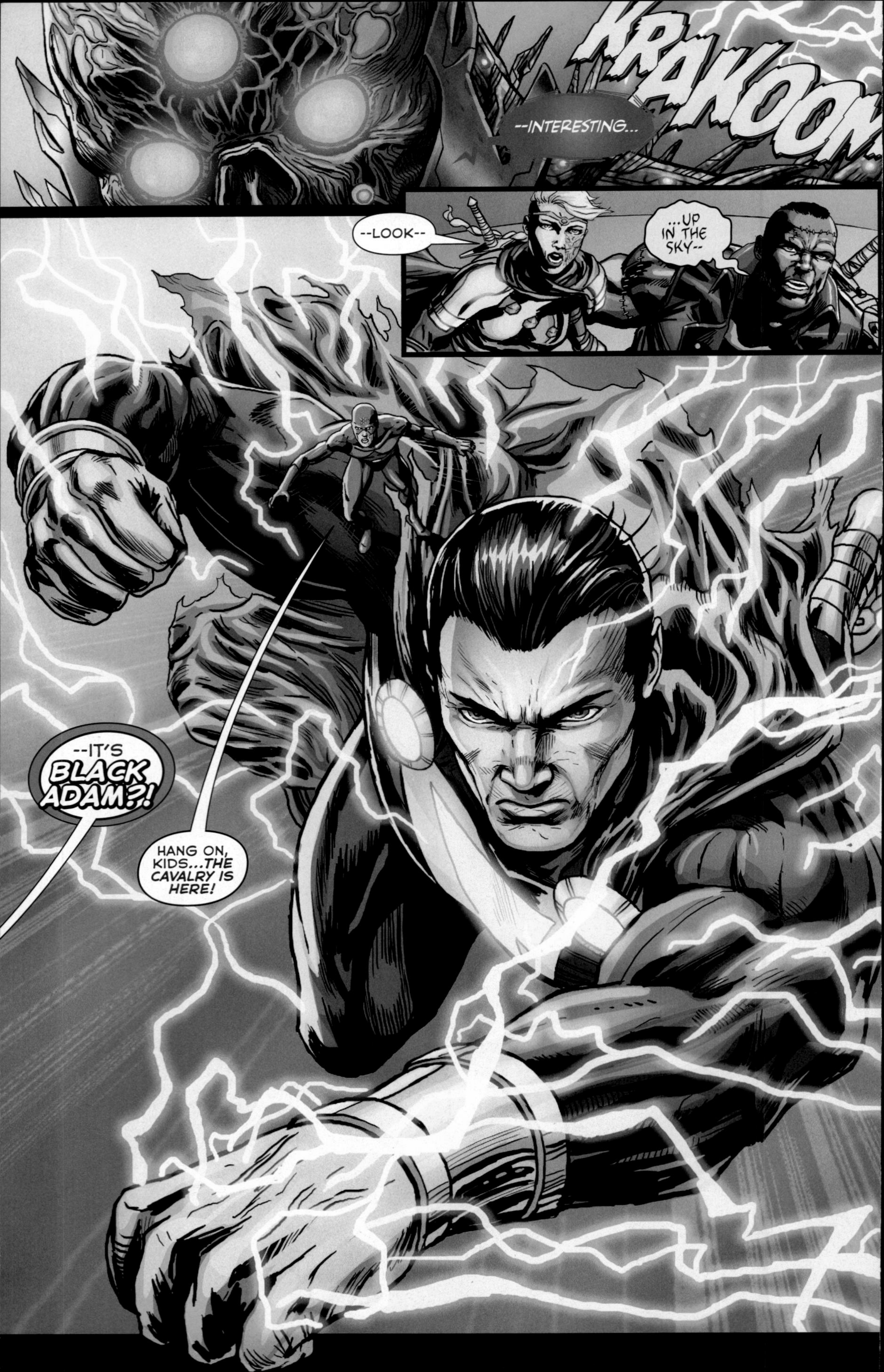
KRAKOOM
--INTERESTING...
--LOOK--
...UP IN THE SKY--
--IT'S BLACK ADAM?!
HANG ON, KIDS...THE CAVALRY IS HERE!

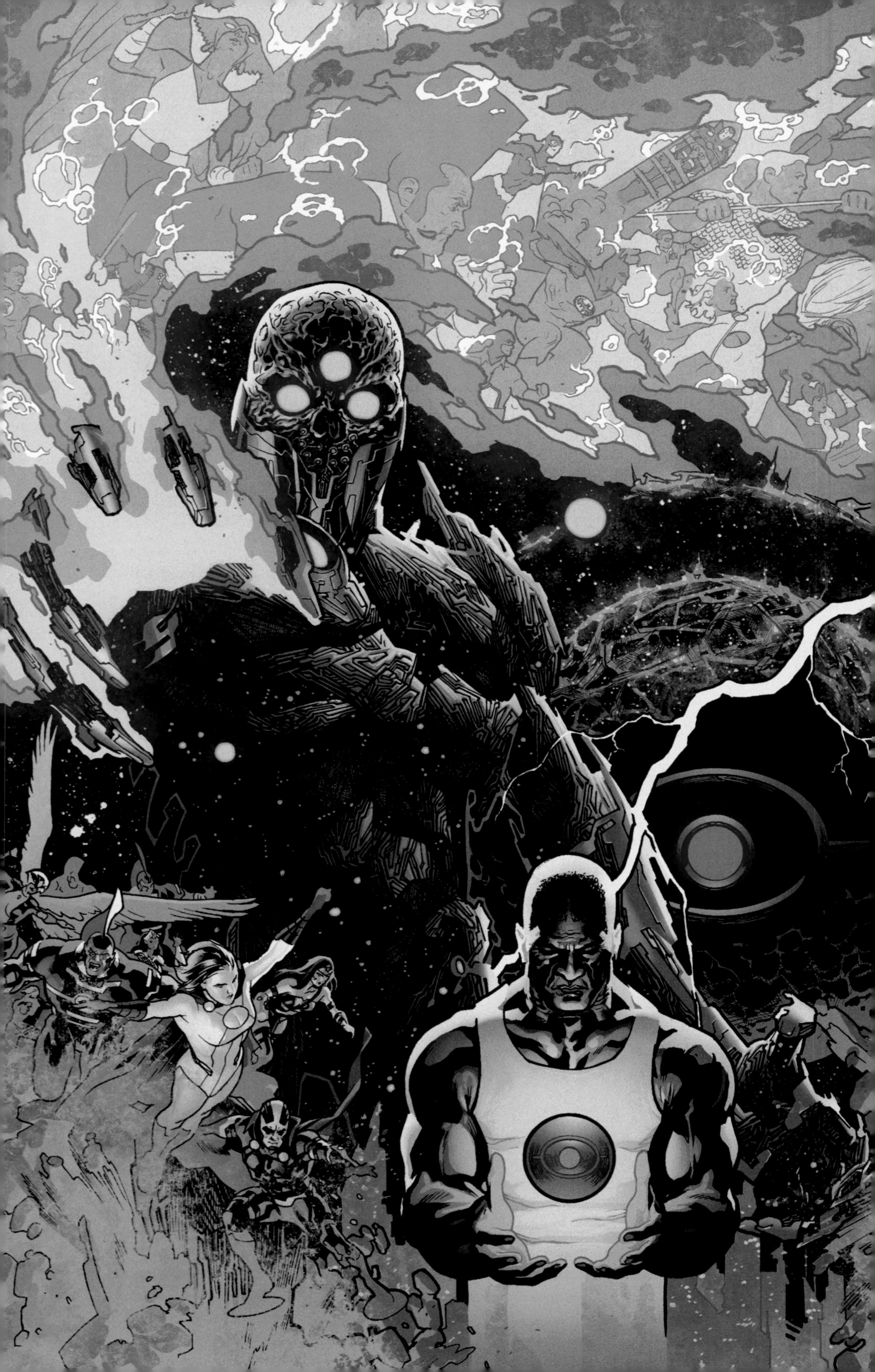

INTO THE FUTUR

WRITERS
- Brian Azzarello
- Jeff Lemire
- Dan Jurgens
- Keith Giffen

PENCILLER
- Aaron Lopresti

INKER
- Art Thibert

COLORS
- Hi-Fi

LETTERS
- Taylor Esposito

COVER
- Ryan Sook

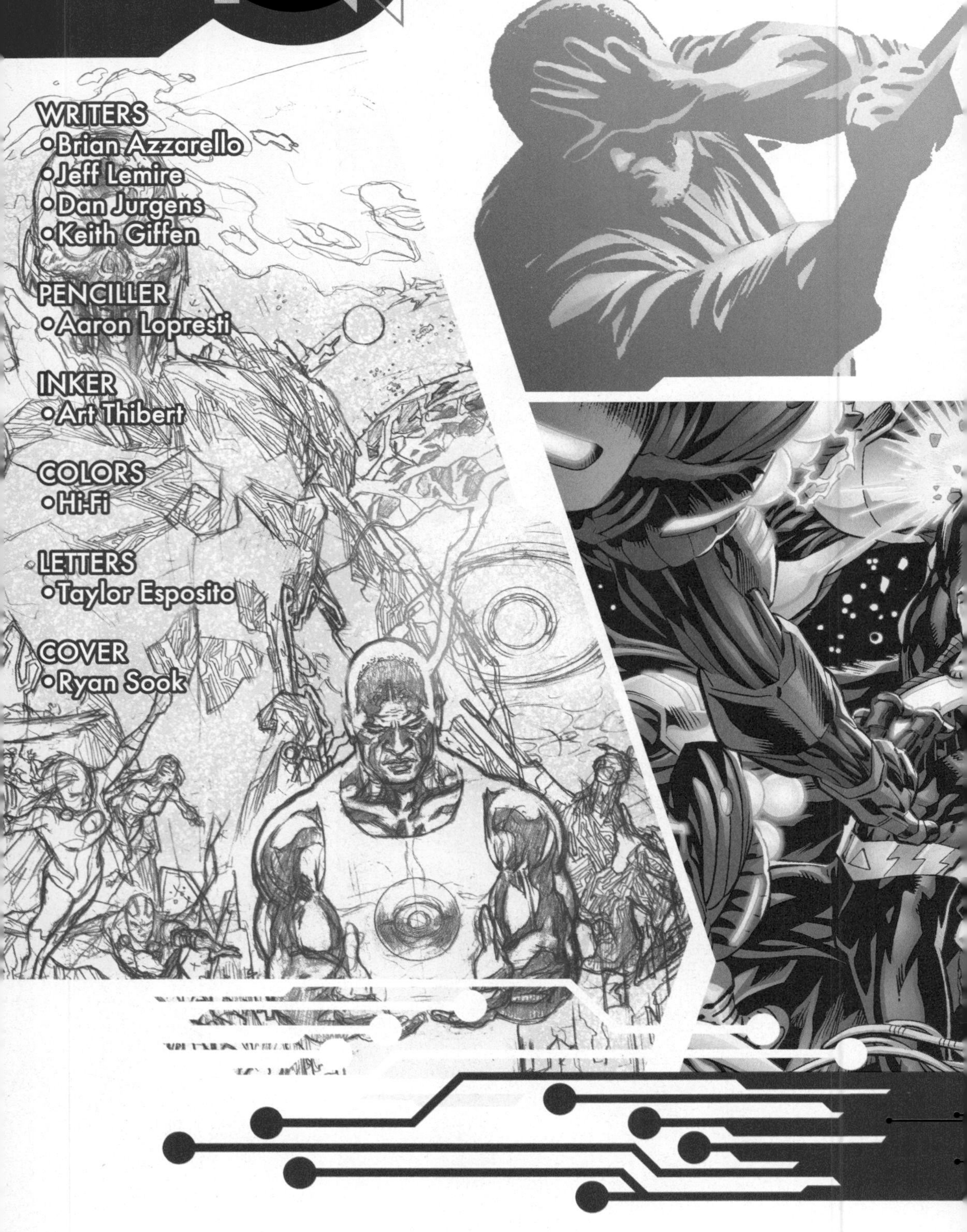

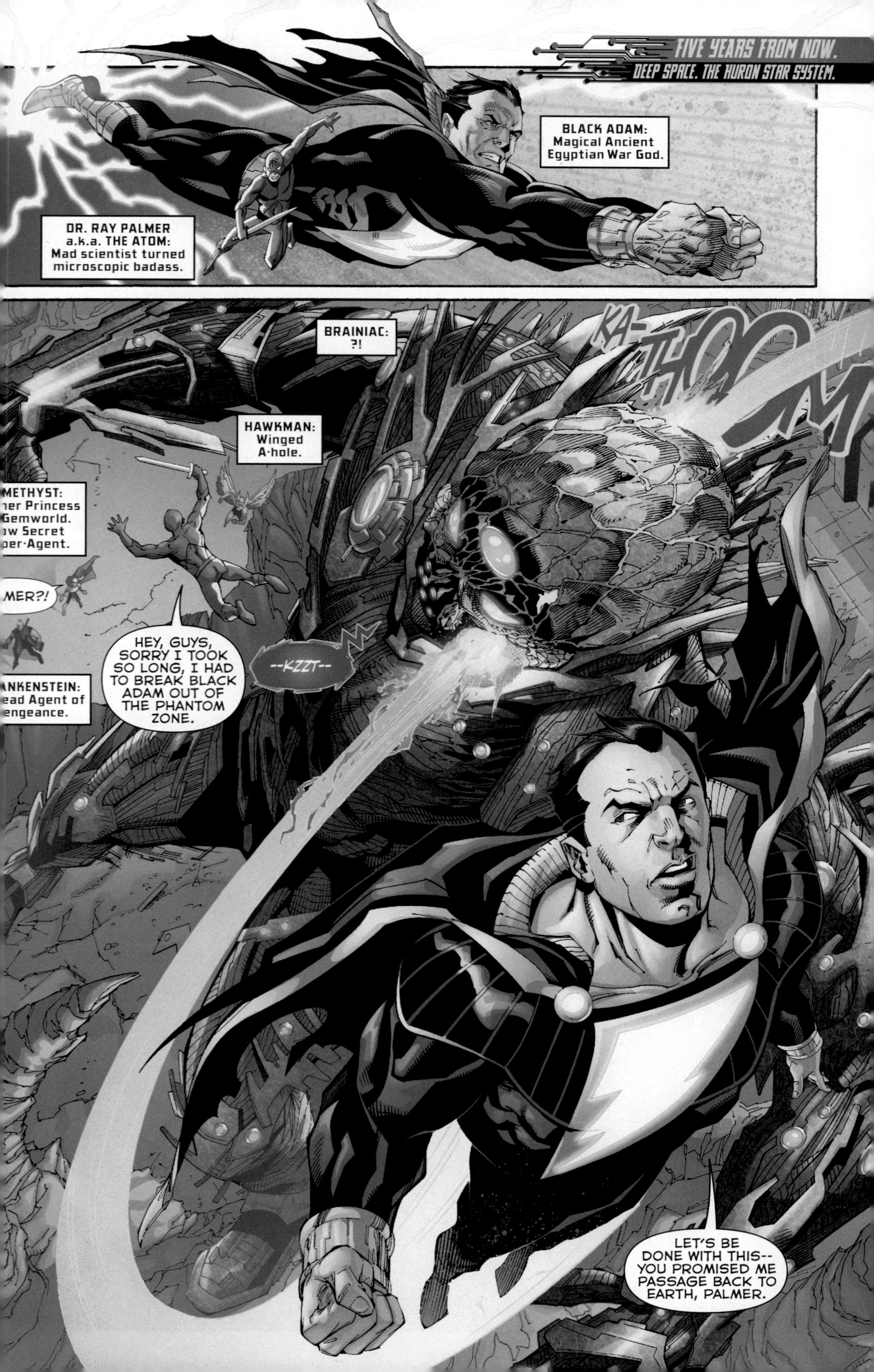
FIVE YEARS FROM NOW.
DEEP SPACE. THE HURON STAR SYSTEM.
BLACK ADAM: Magical Ancient Egyptian War God.
DR. RAY PALMER a.k.a. THE ATOM: Mad scientist turned microscopic badass.
BRAINIAC: ?!
KA-THOOM
HAWKMAN: Winged A-hole.
METHYST: ner Princess Gemworld. ow Secret per-Agent.
MER?!
ANKENSTEIN: ead Agent of engeance.
HEY, GUYS, SORRY I TOOK SO LONG, I HAD TO BREAK BLACK ADAM OUT OF THE PHANTOM ZONE.
--KZZT--
LET'S BE DONE WITH THIS-- YOU PROMISED ME PASSAGE BACK TO EARTH, PALMER.

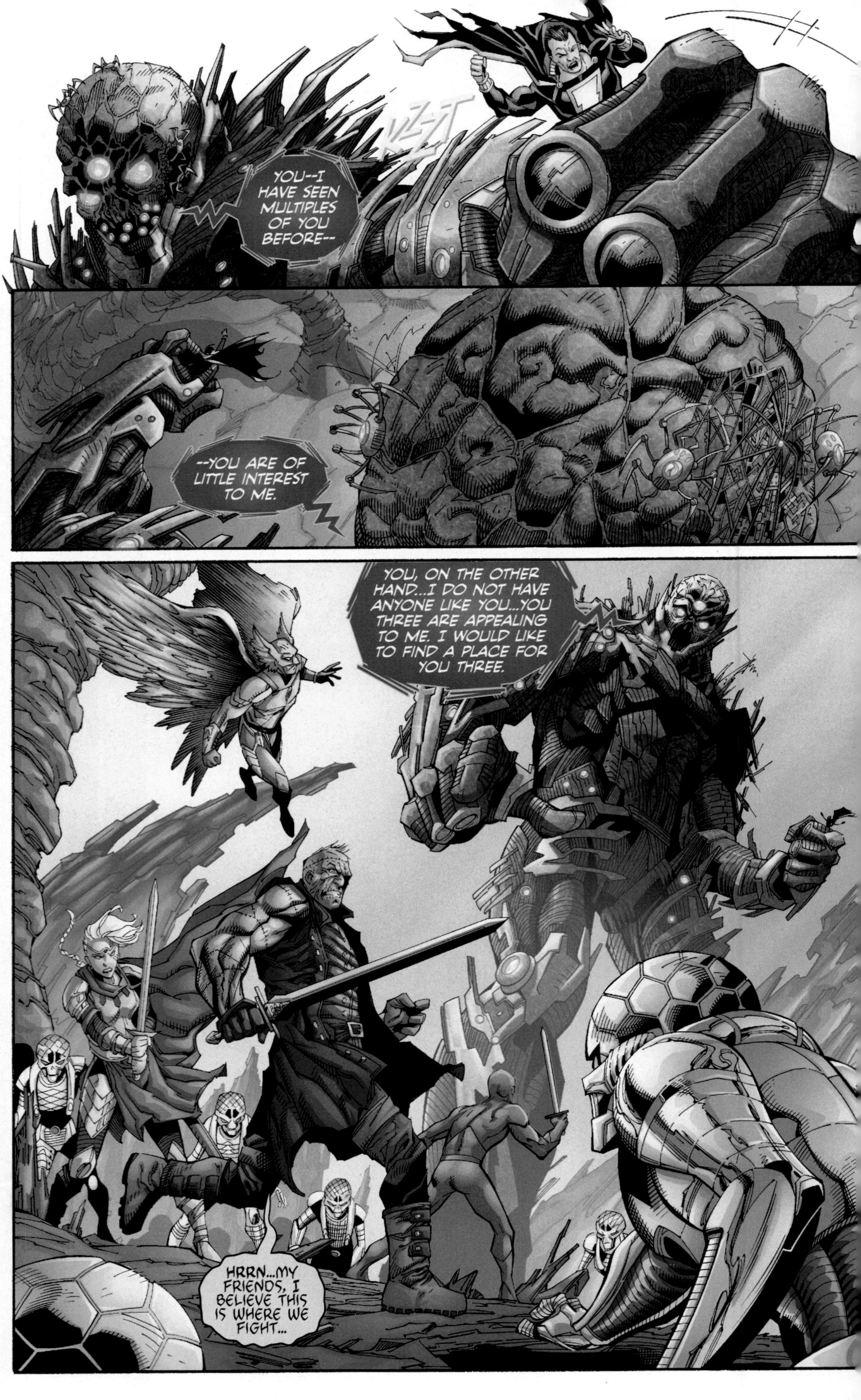
KZZ-ZT
YOU--I HAVE SEEN MULTIPLES OF YOU BEFORE--
--YOU ARE OF LITTLE INTEREST TO ME.
YOU, ON THE OTHER HAND...I DO NOT HAVE ANYONE LIKE YOU...YOU THREE ARE APPEALING TO ME. I WOULD LIKE TO FIND A PLACE FOR YOU THREE.
HRRN...MY FRIENDS, I BELIEVE THIS IS WHERE WE FIGHT...

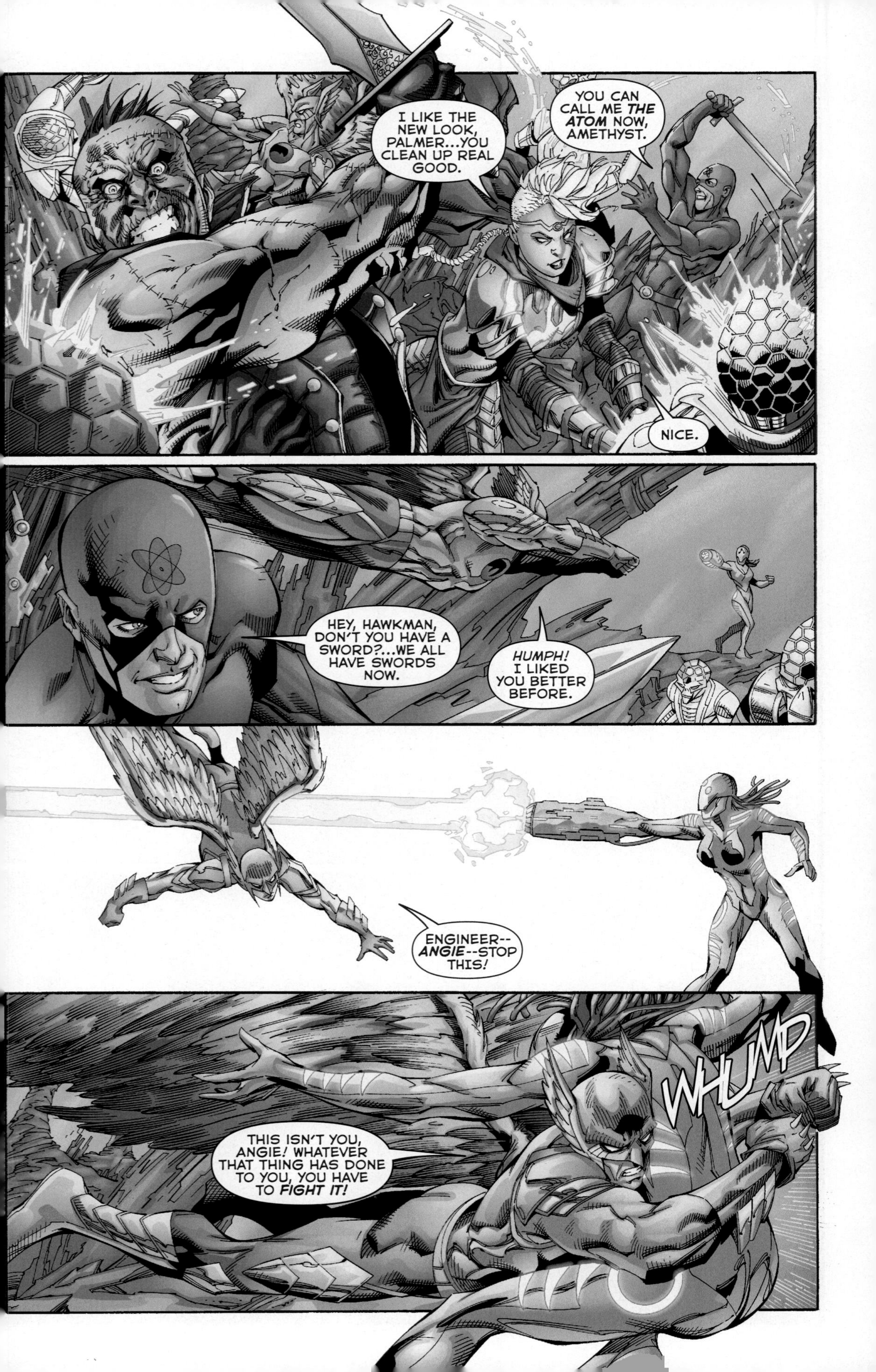
I LIKE THE NEW LOOK, PALMER...YOU CLEAN UP REAL GOOD.
YOU CAN CALL ME THE ATOM NOW, AMETHYST.
NICE.
HEY, HAWKMAN, DON'T YOU HAVE A SWORD?...WE ALL HAVE SWORDS NOW.
HUMPH! I LIKED YOU BETTER BEFORE.
ENGINEER--ANGIE--STOP THIS!
WHUMP
THIS ISN'T YOU, ANGIE! WHATEVER THAT THING HAS DONE TO YOU, YOU HAVE TO FIGHT IT!

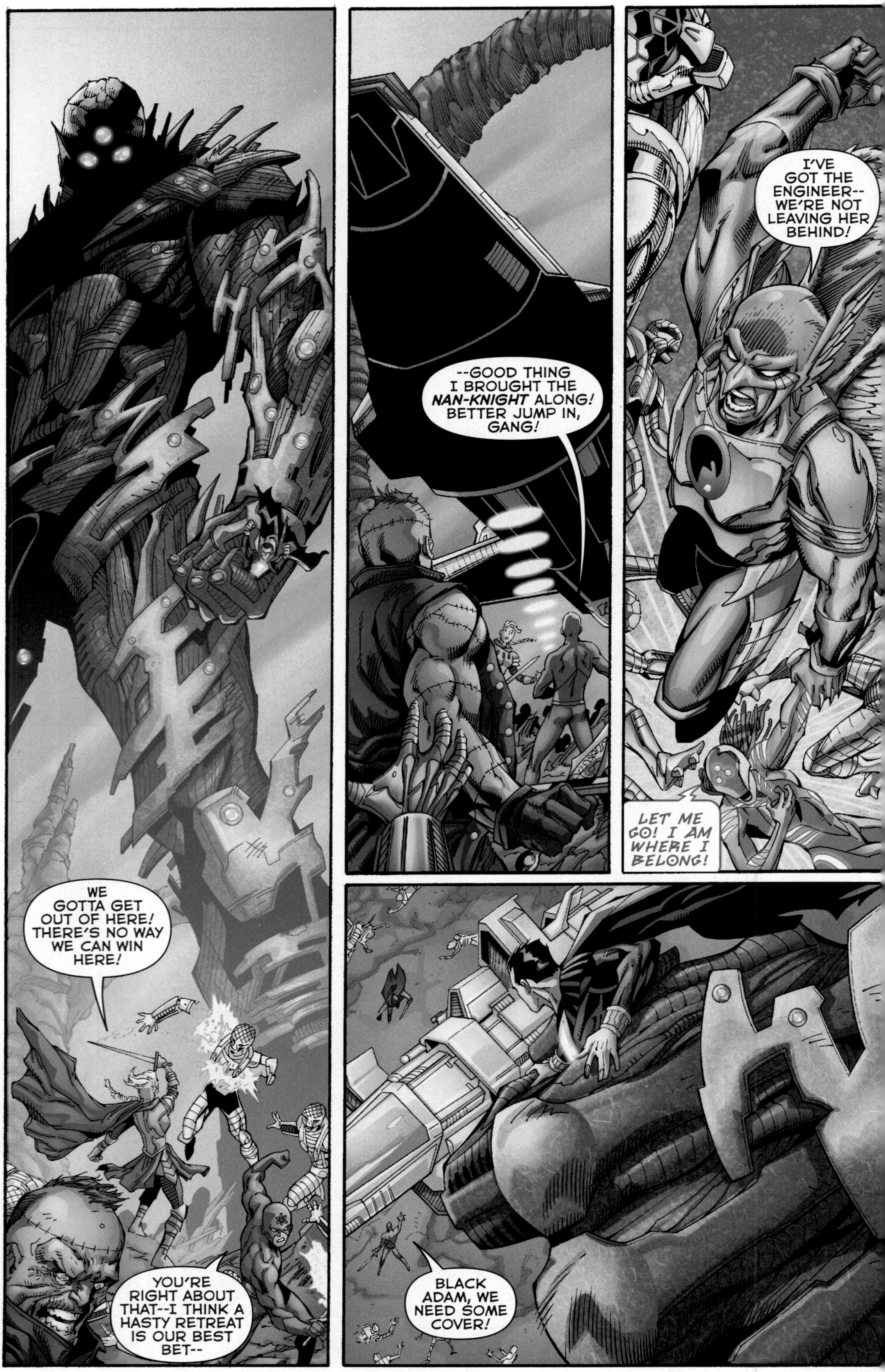

--GOOD THING I BROUGHT THE *NAN-KNIGHT* ALONG! BETTER JUMP IN, GANG!
I'VE GOT THE ENGINEER-- WE'RE NOT LEAVING HER BEHIND!
LET ME GO! I AM WHERE I BELONG!
WE GOTTA GET OUT OF HERE! THERE'S NO WAY WE CAN WIN HERE!
YOU'RE RIGHT ABOUT THAT--I THINK A HASTY RETREAT IS OUR BEST BET--
BLACK ADAM, WE NEED SOME COVER!

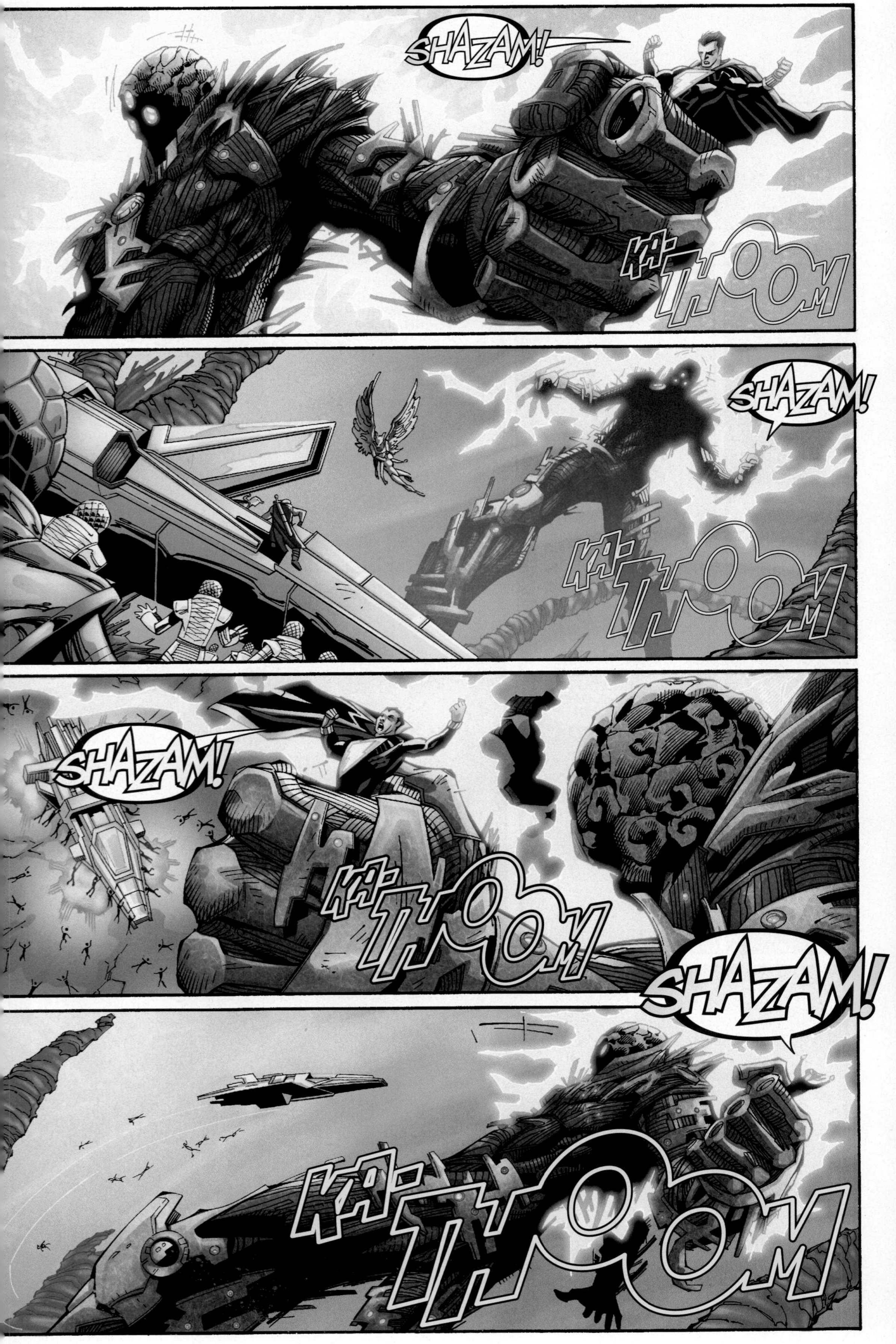
SHAZAM!
KA-THOOM
SHAZAM!
KA-THOOM
SHAZAM!
KA-THOOM
SHAZAM!
KA-THOOM

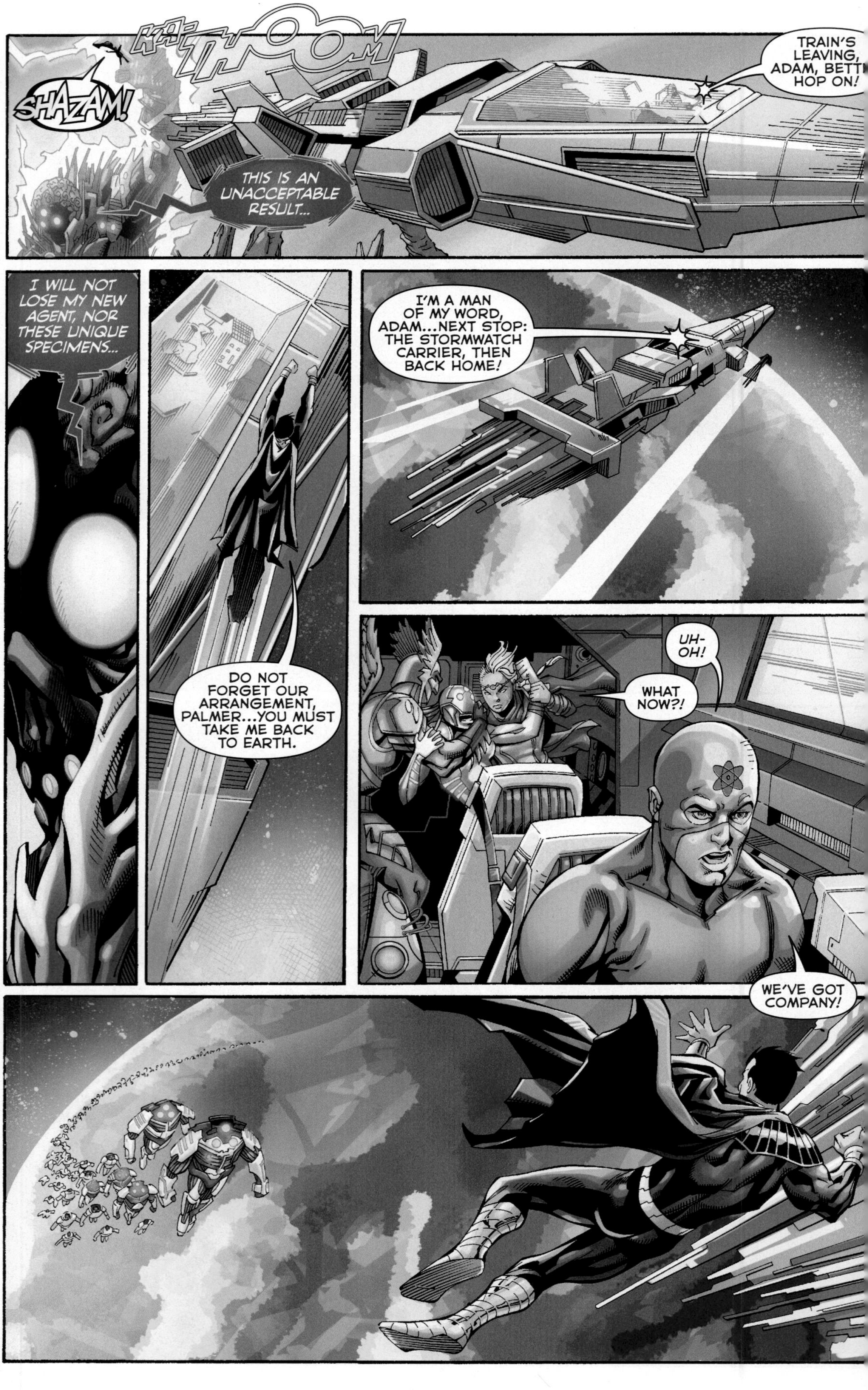
SHAZAM!
KA-THOOOM
TRAIN'S LEAVING, ADAM, BETT HOP ON!
THIS IS AN UNACCEPTABLE RESULT...
I WILL NOT LOSE MY NEW AGENT, NOR THESE UNIQUE SPECIMENS...
I'M A MAN OF MY WORD, ADAM...NEXT STOP: THE STORMWATCH CARRIER, THEN BACK HOME!
DO NOT FORGET OUR ARRANGEMENT, PALMER...YOU MUST TAKE ME BACK TO EARTH.
UH-OH!
WHAT NOW?!
WE'VE GOT COMPANY!

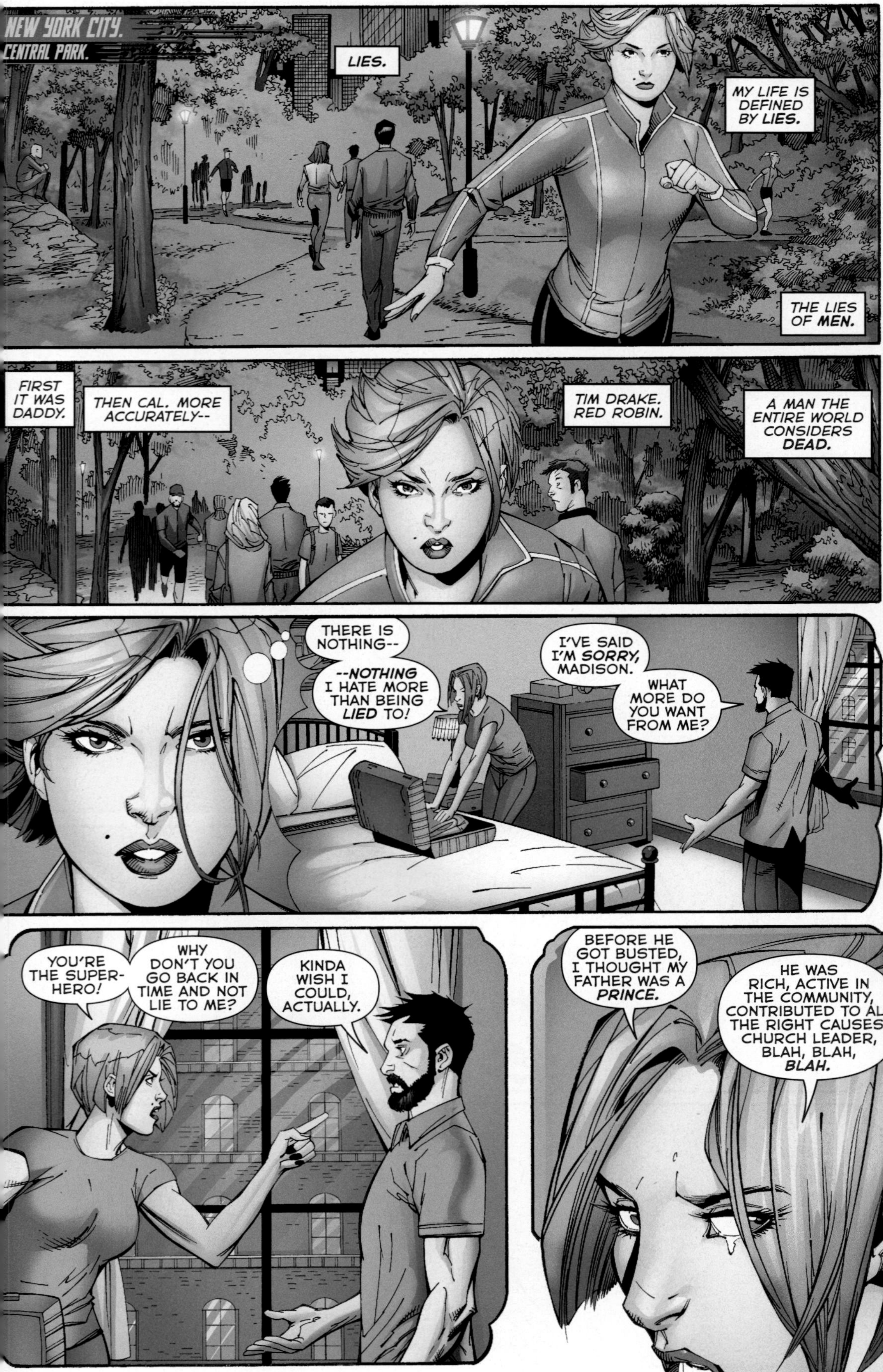
NEW YORK CITY.
CENTRAL PARK.
LIES.
MY LIFE IS DEFINED BY LIES.
THE LIES OF MEN.
FIRST IT WAS DADDY.
THEN CAL. MORE ACCURATELY--
TIM DRAKE. RED ROBIN.
A MAN THE ENTIRE WORLD CONSIDERS DEAD.
THERE IS NOTHING--
--NOTHING I HATE MORE THAN BEING LIED TO!
I'VE SAID I'M SORRY, MADISON.
WHAT MORE DO YOU WANT FROM ME?
YOU'RE THE SUPER-HERO!
WHY DON'T YOU GO BACK IN TIME AND NOT LIE TO ME?
KINDA WISH I COULD, ACTUALLY.
BEFORE HE GOT BUSTED, I THOUGHT MY FATHER WAS A PRINCE.
HE WAS RICH, ACTIVE IN THE COMMUNITY, CONTRIBUTED TO ALL THE RIGHT CAUSES, CHURCH LEADER, BLAH, BLAH, BLAH.

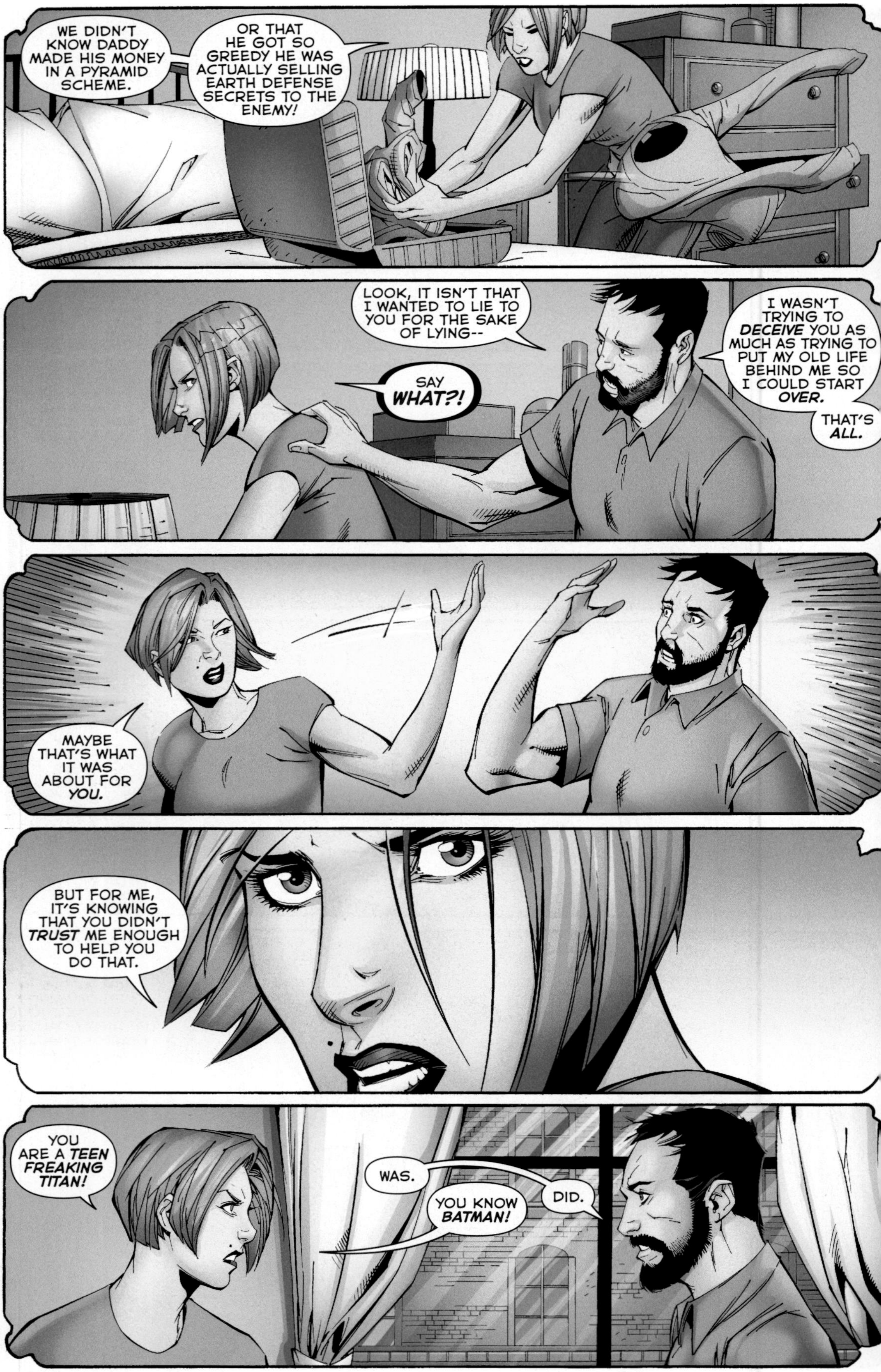

WE DIDN'T KNOW DADDY MADE HIS MONEY IN A PYRAMID SCHEME.
OR THAT HE GOT SO GREEDY HE WAS ACTUALLY SELLING EARTH DEFENSE SECRETS TO THE ENEMY!
LOOK, IT ISN'T THAT I WANTED TO LIE TO YOU FOR THE SAKE OF LYING--
SAY WHAT?!
I WASN'T TRYING TO DECEIVE YOU AS MUCH AS TRYING TO PUT MY OLD LIFE BEHIND ME SO I COULD START OVER.
THAT'S ALL.
MAYBE THAT'S WHAT IT WAS ABOUT FOR YOU.
BUT FOR ME, IT'S KNOWING THAT YOU DIDN'T TRUST ME ENOUGH TO HELP YOU DO THAT.
YOU ARE A TEEN FREAKING TITAN!
WAS.
YOU KNOW BATMAN!
DID.

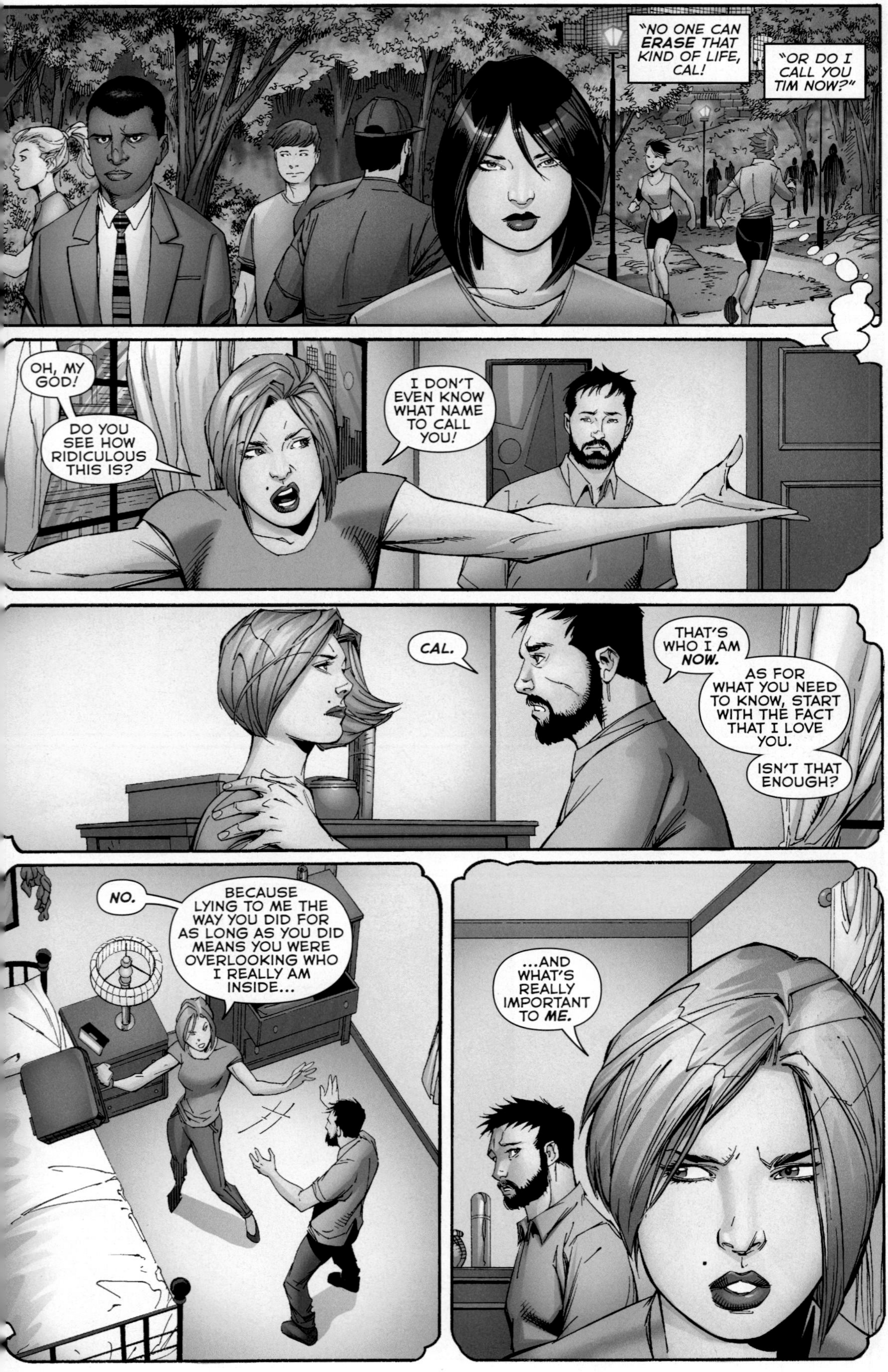
"NO ONE CAN ERASE THAT KIND OF LIFE, CAL!
"OR DO I CALL YOU TIM NOW?"
OH, MY GOD!
DO YOU SEE HOW RIDICULOUS THIS IS?
I DON'T EVEN KNOW WHAT NAME TO CALL YOU!
CAL.
THAT'S WHO I AM NOW.
AS FOR WHAT YOU NEED TO KNOW, START WITH THE FACT THAT I LOVE YOU.
ISN'T THAT ENOUGH?
NO.
BECAUSE LYING TO ME THE WAY YOU DID FOR AS LONG AS YOU DID MEANS YOU WERE OVERLOOKING WHO I REALLY AM INSIDE...
...AND WHAT'S REALLY IMPORTANT TO ME.

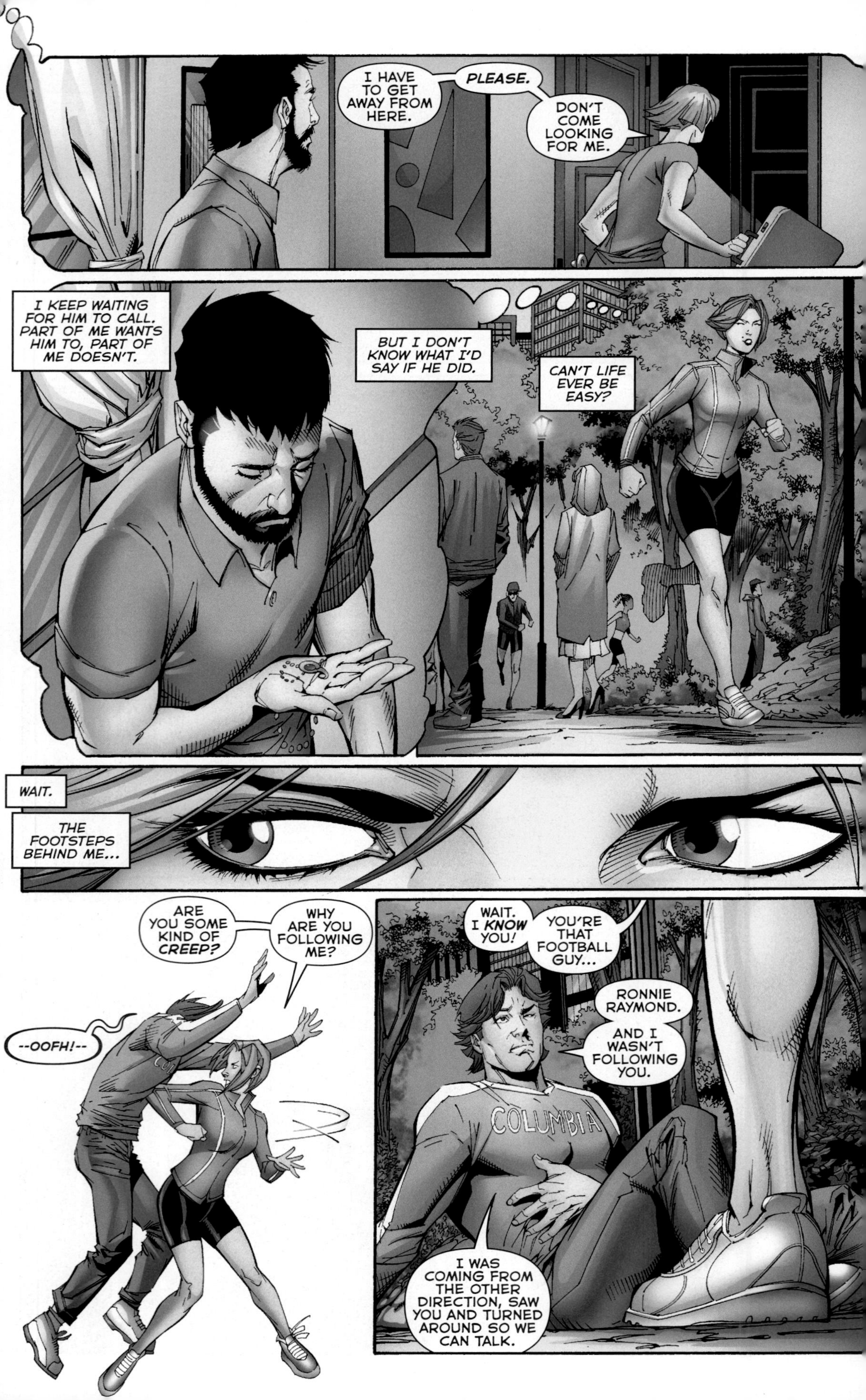
I HAVE TO GET AWAY FROM HERE.
PLEASE.
DON'T COME LOOKING FOR ME.
I KEEP WAITING FOR HIM TO CALL. PART OF ME WANTS HIM TO, PART OF ME DOESN'T.
BUT I DON'T KNOW WHAT I'D SAY IF HE DID.
CAN'T LIFE EVER BE EASY?
WAIT.
THE FOOTSTEPS BEHIND ME...
--OOFH!--
ARE YOU SOME KIND OF CREEP?
WHY ARE YOU FOLLOWING ME?
WAIT. I KNOW YOU!
YOU'RE THAT FOOTBALL GUY...
RONNIE RAYMOND.
AND I WASN'T FOLLOWING YOU.
I WAS COMING FROM THE OTHER DIRECTION, SAW YOU AND TURNED AROUND SO WE CAN TALK.
COLUMBIA

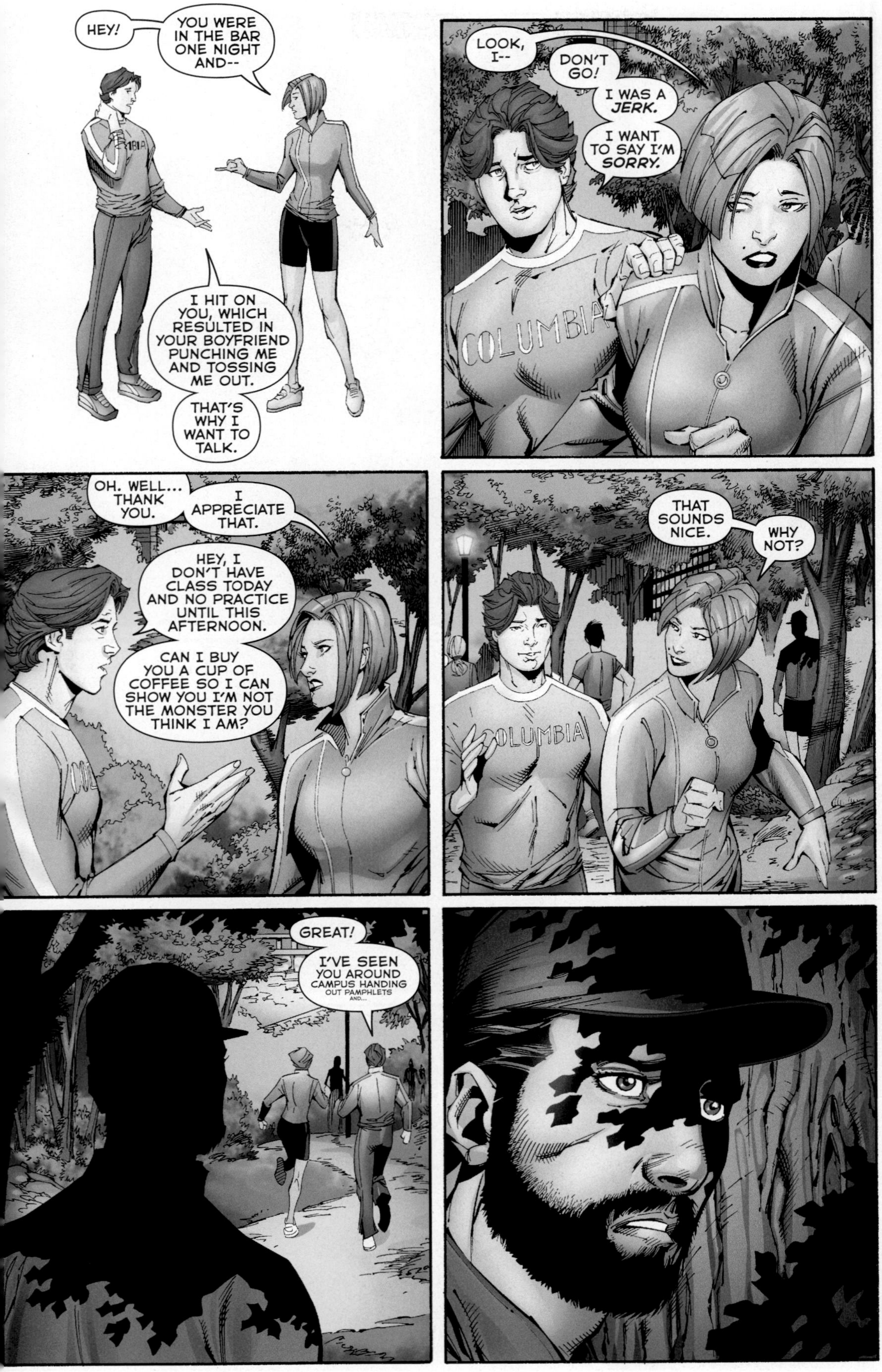
HEY!
YOU WERE IN THE BAR ONE NIGHT AND--
I HIT ON YOU, WHICH RESULTED IN YOUR BOYFRIEND PUNCHING ME AND TOSSING ME OUT.
THAT'S WHY I WANT TO TALK.
LOOK, I--
DON'T GO!
I WAS A *JERK.*
I WANT TO SAY I'M *SORRY.*
COLUMBIA
OH. WELL... THANK YOU.
I APPRECIATE THAT.
HEY, I DON'T HAVE CLASS TODAY AND NO PRACTICE UNTIL THIS AFTERNOON.
CAN I BUY YOU A CUP OF COFFEE SO I CAN SHOW YOU I'M NOT THE MONSTER YOU THINK I AM?
THAT SOUNDS NICE.
WHY NOT?
COLUMBIA
GREAT!
I'VE SEEN YOU AROUND CAMPUS HANDING OUT PAMPHLETS AND...

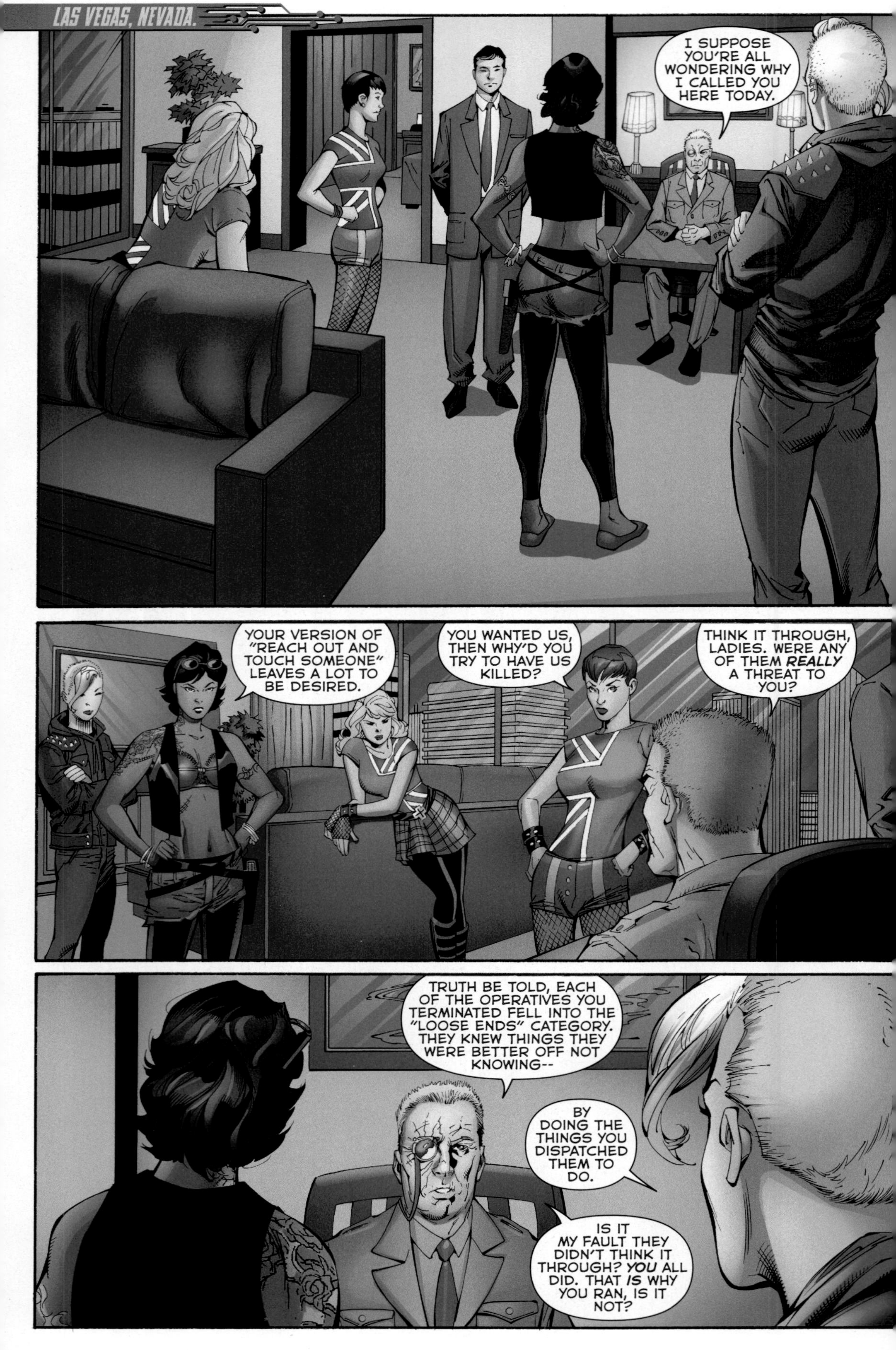
LAS VEGAS, NEVADA.
I SUPPOSE YOU'RE ALL WONDERING WHY I CALLED YOU HERE TODAY.
YOUR VERSION OF "REACH OUT AND TOUCH SOMEONE" LEAVES A LOT TO BE DESIRED.
YOU WANTED US, THEN WHY'D YOU TRY TO HAVE US KILLED?
THINK IT THROUGH, LADIES. WERE ANY OF THEM REALLY A THREAT TO YOU?
TRUTH BE TOLD, EACH OF THE OPERATIVES YOU TERMINATED FELL INTO THE "LOOSE ENDS" CATEGORY. THEY KNEW THINGS THEY WERE BETTER OFF NOT KNOWING--
BY DOING THE THINGS YOU DISPATCHED THEM TO DO.
IS IT MY FAULT THEY DIDN'T THINK IT THROUGH? YOU ALL DID. THAT IS WHY YOU RAN, IS IT NOT?

H...WHERE **ARE** MY MANNERS? WOULD ANY OF YOU CARE FOR A DRINK? COFFEE? SOMETHING WITH A HARDER KICK?

WHAT KIND OF KICK?

SO YOU HAD US ELIMINATE YOUR "LOOSE ENDS" BY SENDING THEM TO ELIMINATE US, ALL OF THIS TO GET US TO COME AFTER YOU...THAT ABOUT IT?

THERE IS THE QUESTION OF "WHY"? THAT... DOESN'T INTEREST YOU?

WE'RE THROUGH DOING YOUR DIRTY WORK.

THEN TOUCH ME, MERCY. YOU KNOW YOU WANT TO.

DIDN'T YOU USED TO BE, LIKE, A BIG WAR HERO OR SOMETHING?

SERGEANT ROCK OF EASY COMPANY.

HOW'D YOU GO FROM THAT TO FRANK ROCK, BLACK OPS SCUM WAD?

THE SAME WAY I CAN LOOK SIXTY-TWO HAVING ALREADY "CELEBRATED" NINETY-TWO.

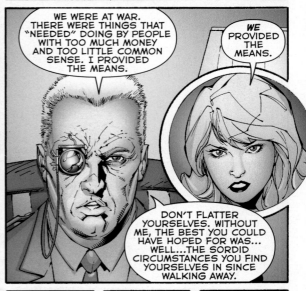

WE WERE AT WAR. THERE WERE THINGS THAT "NEEDED" DOING BY PEOPLE WITH TOO MUCH MONEY AND TOO LITTLE COMMON SENSE. I PROVIDED THE MEANS.

WE PROVIDED THE MEANS.

DON'T FLATTER YOURSELVES. WITHOUT ME, THE BEST YOU COULD HAVE HOPED FOR WAS... WELL...THE SORDID CIRCUMSTANCES YOU FIND YOURSELVES IN SINCE WALKING AWAY.

OR IS THAT **SKULKING** AWAY?

CADMUS. "YOU'RE ALL MARKED WOMEN." MANIPULATIVE BASTARD!

MM?

HOW LONG HAVE YOU BEEN ON MY UNCLE'S PAYROLL?

MERCY?

FARADAY LOOKS A LOT YOUNGER THAN HE REALLY IS. **DECADES** YOUNGER.

I WAS WONDERING IF THAT HAD SAILED COMPLETELY OVER YOUR HEAD.

BASTARD!

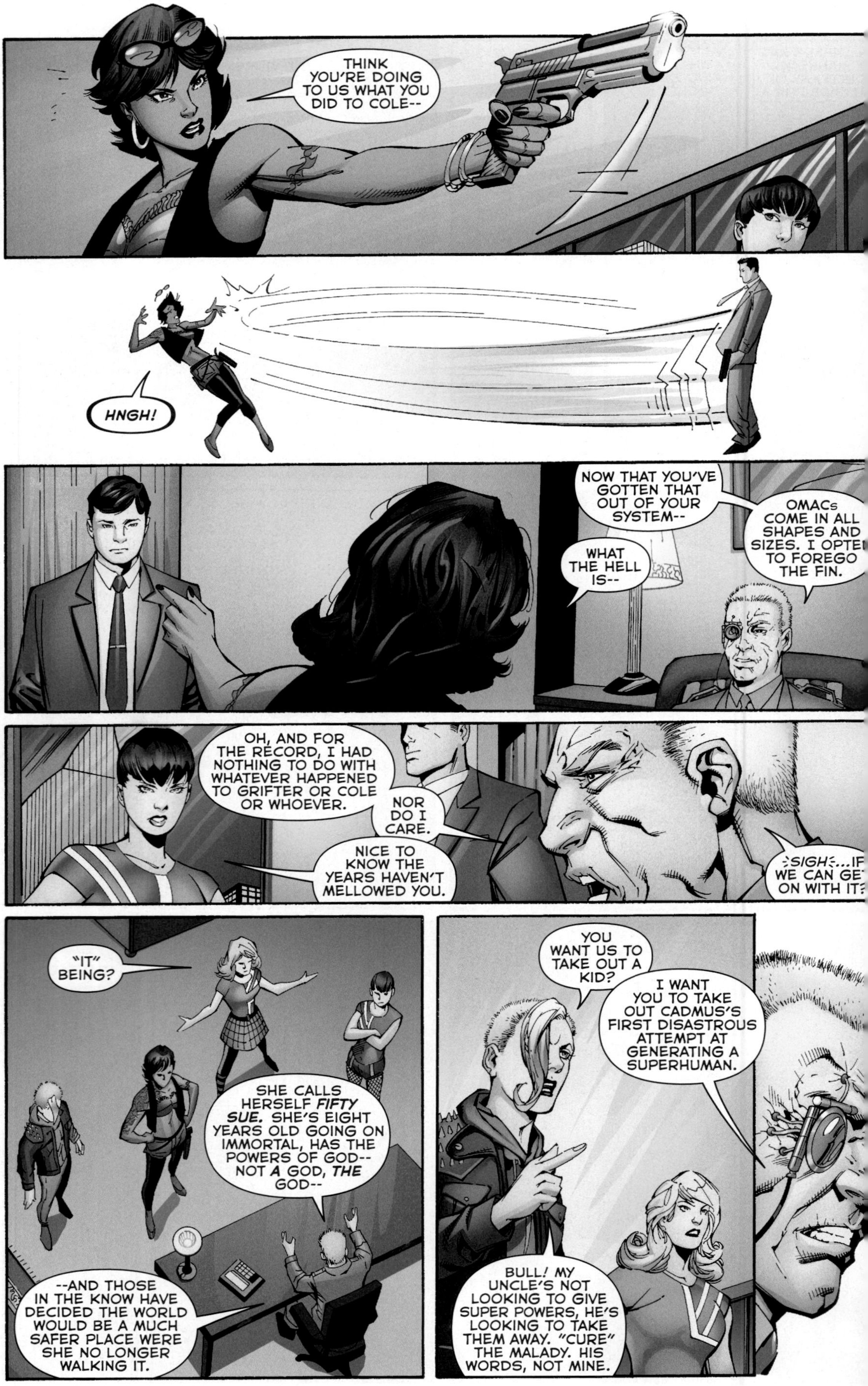
THINK YOU'RE DOING TO US WHAT YOU DID TO COLE--
HNGH!
NOW THAT YOU'VE GOTTEN THAT OUT OF YOUR SYSTEM--
WHAT THE HELL IS--
OMACs COME IN ALL SHAPES AND SIZES. I OPTE TO FOREGO THE FIN.
OH, AND FOR THE RECORD, I HAD NOTHING TO DO WITH WHATEVER HAPPENED TO GRIFTER OR COLE OR WHOEVER.
NOR DO I CARE.
NICE TO KNOW THE YEARS HAVEN'T MELLOWED YOU.
SIGH...IF WE CAN GE ON WITH IT?
"IT" BEING?
SHE CALLS HERSELF *FIFTY SUE.* SHE'S EIGHT YEARS OLD GOING ON IMMORTAL, HAS THE POWERS OF GOD-- NOT *A* GOD, *THE* GOD--
--AND THOSE IN THE KNOW HAVE DECIDED THE WORLD WOULD BE A MUCH SAFER PLACE WERE SHE NO LONGER WALKING IT.
YOU WANT US TO TAKE OUT A KID?
I WANT YOU TO TAKE OUT CADMUS'S FIRST DISASTROUS ATTEMPT AT GENERATING A SUPERHUMAN.
BULL! MY UNCLE'S NOT LOOKING TO GIVE SUPER POWERS, HE'S LOOKING TO TAKE THEM AWAY. "CURE" THE MALADY. HIS WORDS, NOT MINE.

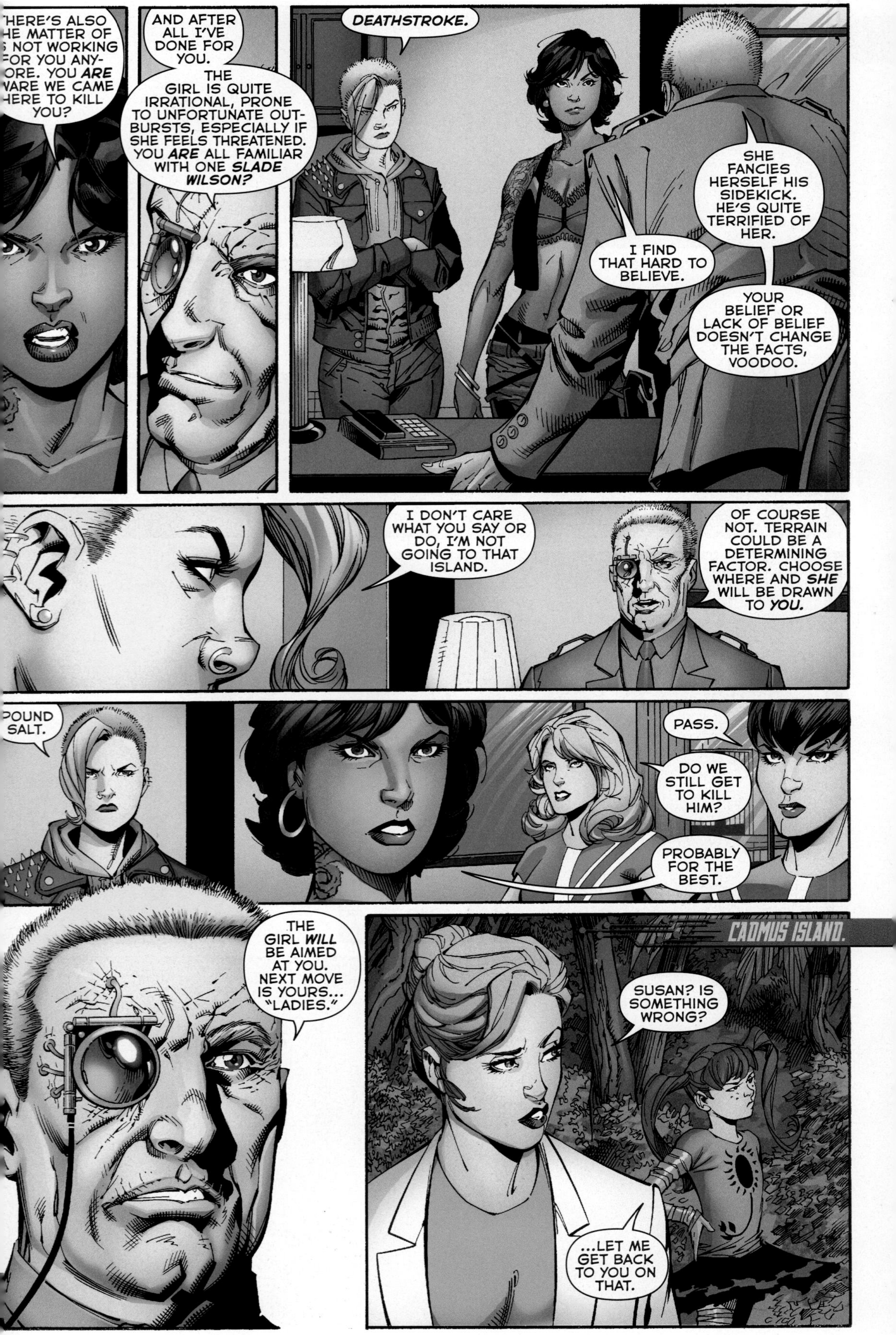
THERE'S ALSO HE MATTER OF S NOT WORKING FOR YOU ANY-ORE. YOU *ARE* WARE WE CAME HERE TO KILL YOU?
AND AFTER ALL I'VE DONE FOR YOU.
THE GIRL IS QUITE IRRATIONAL, PRONE TO UNFORTUNATE OUT-BURSTS, ESPECIALLY IF SHE FEELS THREATENED. YOU *ARE* ALL FAMILIAR WITH ONE *SLADE WILSON?*
DEATHSTROKE.
SHE FANCIES HERSELF HIS SIDEKICK. HE'S QUITE TERRIFIED OF HER.
I FIND THAT HARD TO BELIEVE.
YOUR BELIEF OR LACK OF BELIEF DOESN'T CHANGE THE FACTS, VOODOO.
I DON'T CARE WHAT YOU SAY OR DO, I'M NOT GOING TO THAT ISLAND.
OF COURSE NOT. TERRAIN COULD BE A DETERMINING FACTOR. CHOOSE WHERE AND *SHE* WILL BE DRAWN TO *YOU.*
POUND SALT.
PASS.
DO WE STILL GET TO KILL HIM?
PROBABLY FOR THE BEST.
THE GIRL *WILL* BE AIMED AT YOU. NEXT MOVE IS YOURS... "LADIES."
CADMUS ISLAND.
SUSAN? IS SOMETHING WRONG?
...LET ME GET BACK TO YOU ON THAT.

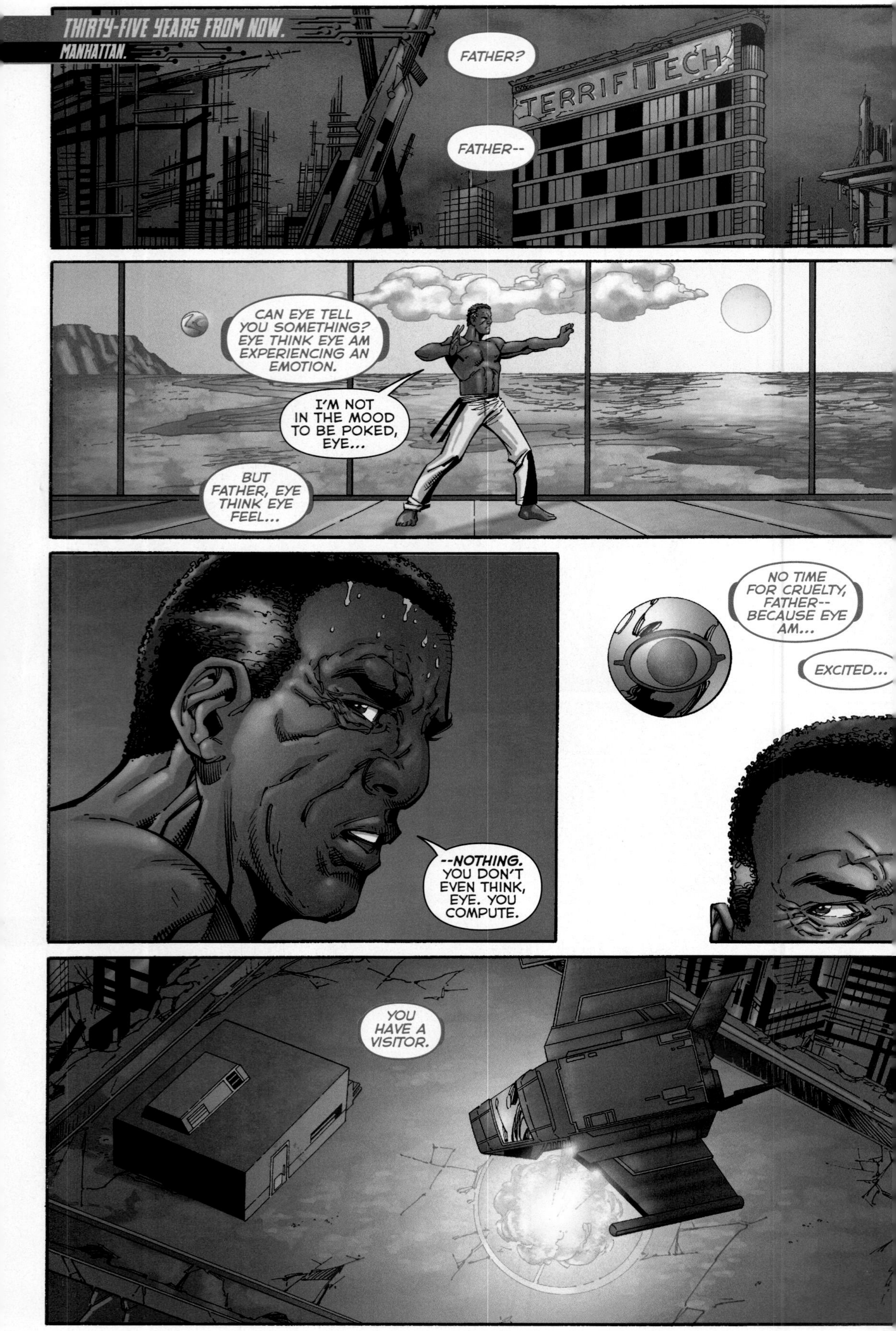
THIRTY-FIVE YEARS FROM NOW.
MANHATTAN.
FATHER?
TERRIFITECH
FATHER--
CAN EYE TELL YOU SOMETHING? EYE THINK EYE AM EXPERIENCING AN EMOTION.
I'M NOT IN THE MOOD TO BE POKED, EYE...
BUT FATHER, EYE THINK EYE FEEL...
--NOTHING. YOU DON'T EVEN THINK, EYE. YOU COMPUTE.
NO TIME FOR CRUELTY, FATHER-- BECAUSE EYE AM...
EXCITED...
YOU HAVE A VISITOR.

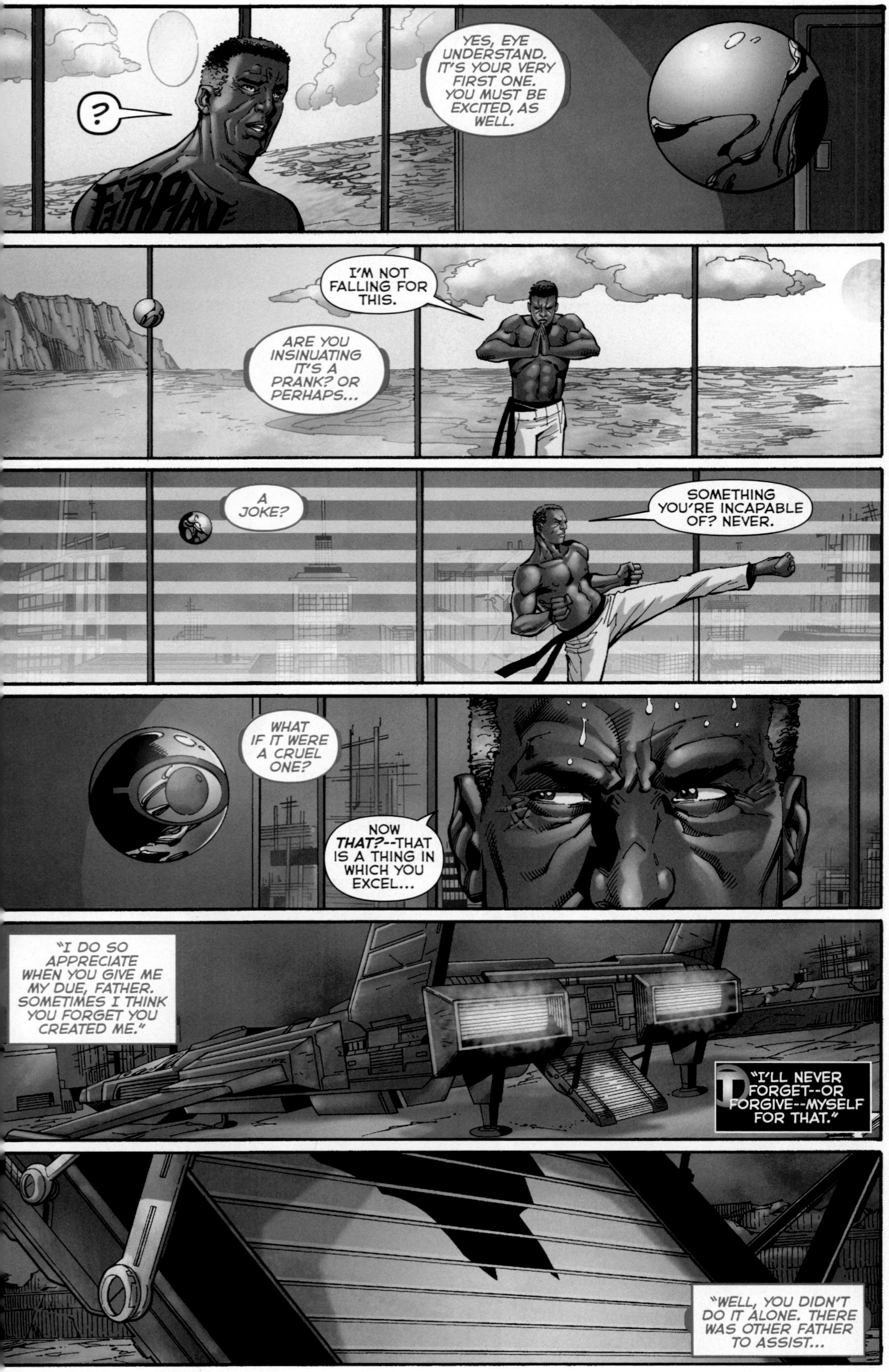
?
YES, EYE UNDERSTAND. IT'S YOUR VERY FIRST ONE. YOU MUST BE EXCITED, AS WELL.
I'M NOT FALLING FOR THIS.
ARE YOU INSINUATING IT'S A PRANK? OR PERHAPS...
A JOKE?
SOMETHING YOU'RE INCAPABLE OF? NEVER.
WHAT IF IT WERE A CRUEL ONE?
NOW THAT?--THAT IS A THING IN WHICH YOU EXCEL...
"I DO SO APPRECIATE WHEN YOU GIVE ME MY DUE, FATHER. SOMETIMES I THINK YOU FORGET YOU CREATED ME."
"I'LL NEVER FORGET--OR FORGIVE--MYSELF FOR THAT."
"WELL, YOU DIDN'T DO IT ALONE. THERE WAS OTHER FATHER TO ASSIST...

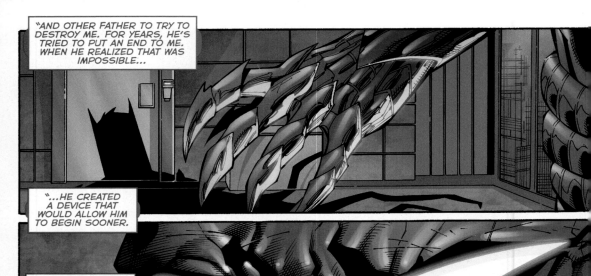

"AND OTHER FATHER TO TRY TO DESTROY ME. FOR YEARS, HE'S TRIED TO PUT AN END TO ME. WHEN HE REALIZED THAT WAS IMPOSSIBLE...

"...HE CREATED A DEVICE THAT WOULD ALLOW HIM TO BEGIN SOONER.

"HE SENT AN AGENT TO THE PAST TO DESTROY ME. THAT IS SOMETHING EYE CAN'T ALLOW."

EYE MINED OTHER FATHER'S BRAIN TO LEARN HOW TO TRAVEL AGAINST TIME.

THAT'S HOW HE PUT IT.

OF COURSE THAT'S HOW HE PUT IT.

YOU ADMIRE HIM FOR THAT.

I DO.

HMM.

WELL, EYE CREATED MY OWN AGENT TO HUNT HIS.

OTHER FATHER BROKE THE CHAIN THAT BINDS TIME.

AND NOW...

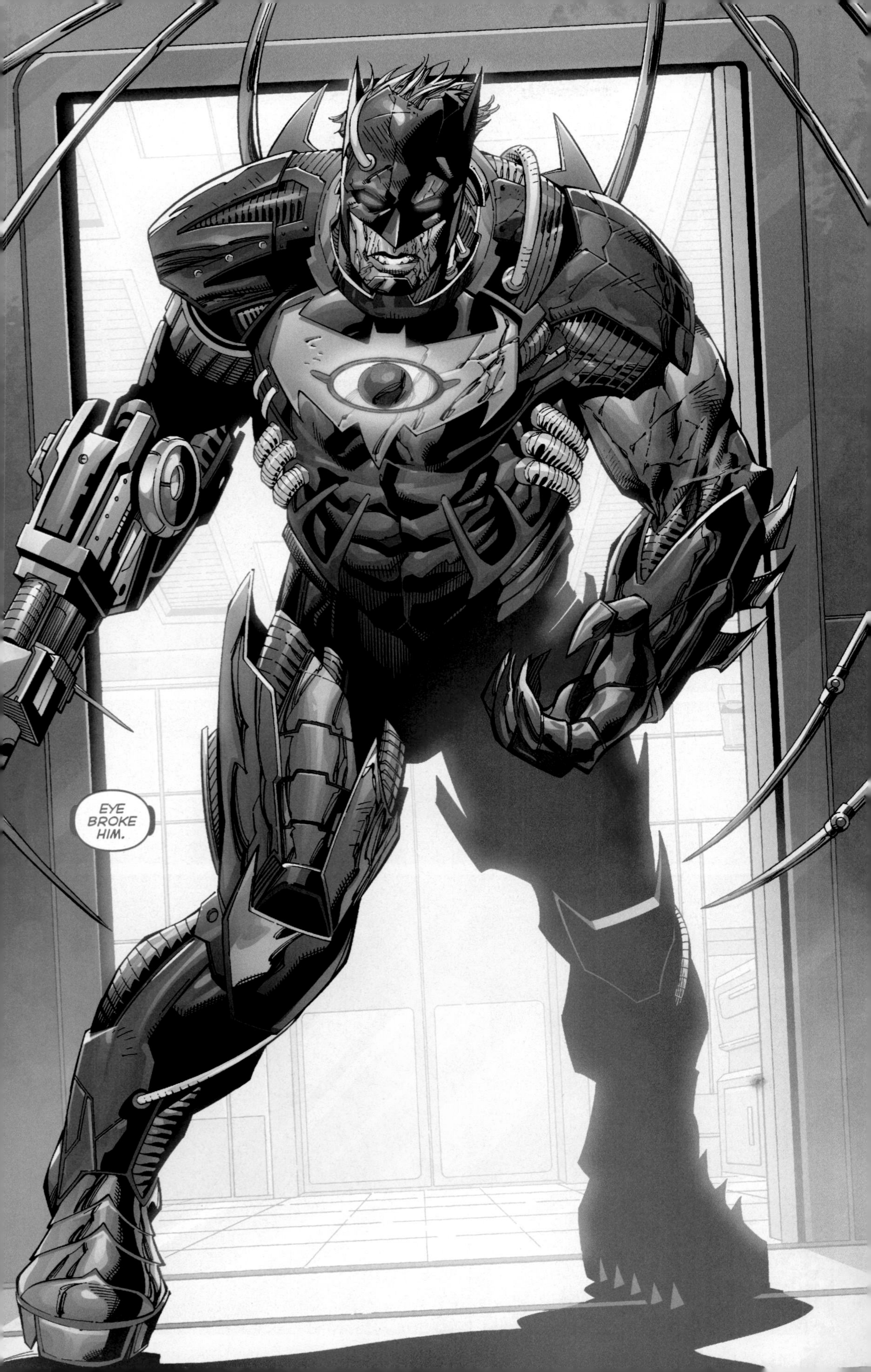
EYE BROKE HIM.

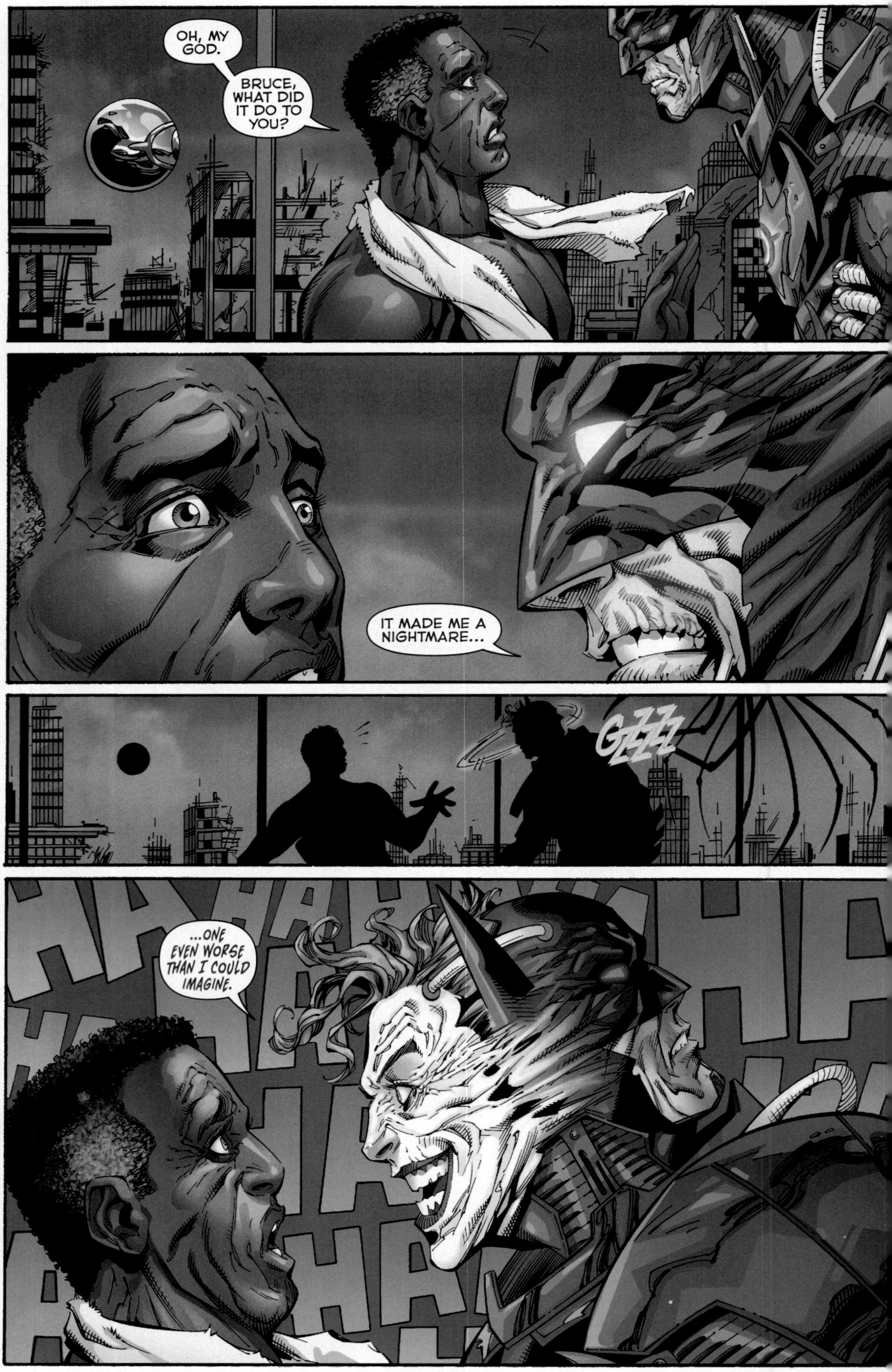
OH, MY GOD.
BRUCE, WHAT DID IT DO TO YOU?
IT MADE ME A NIGHTMARE...
GZZZZ
...ONE EVEN WORSE THAN I COULD IMAGINE.

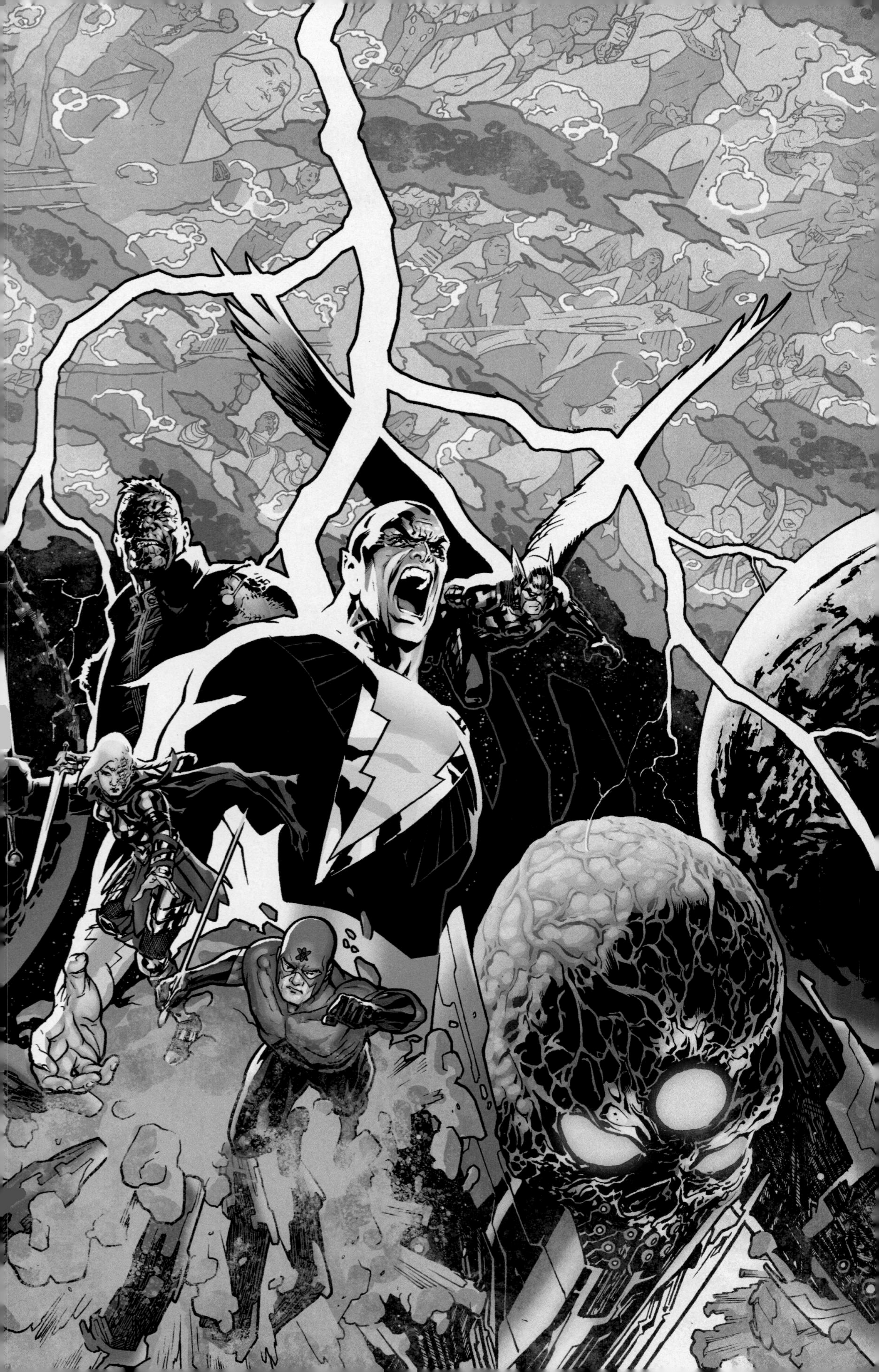

INTO THE FUTUR

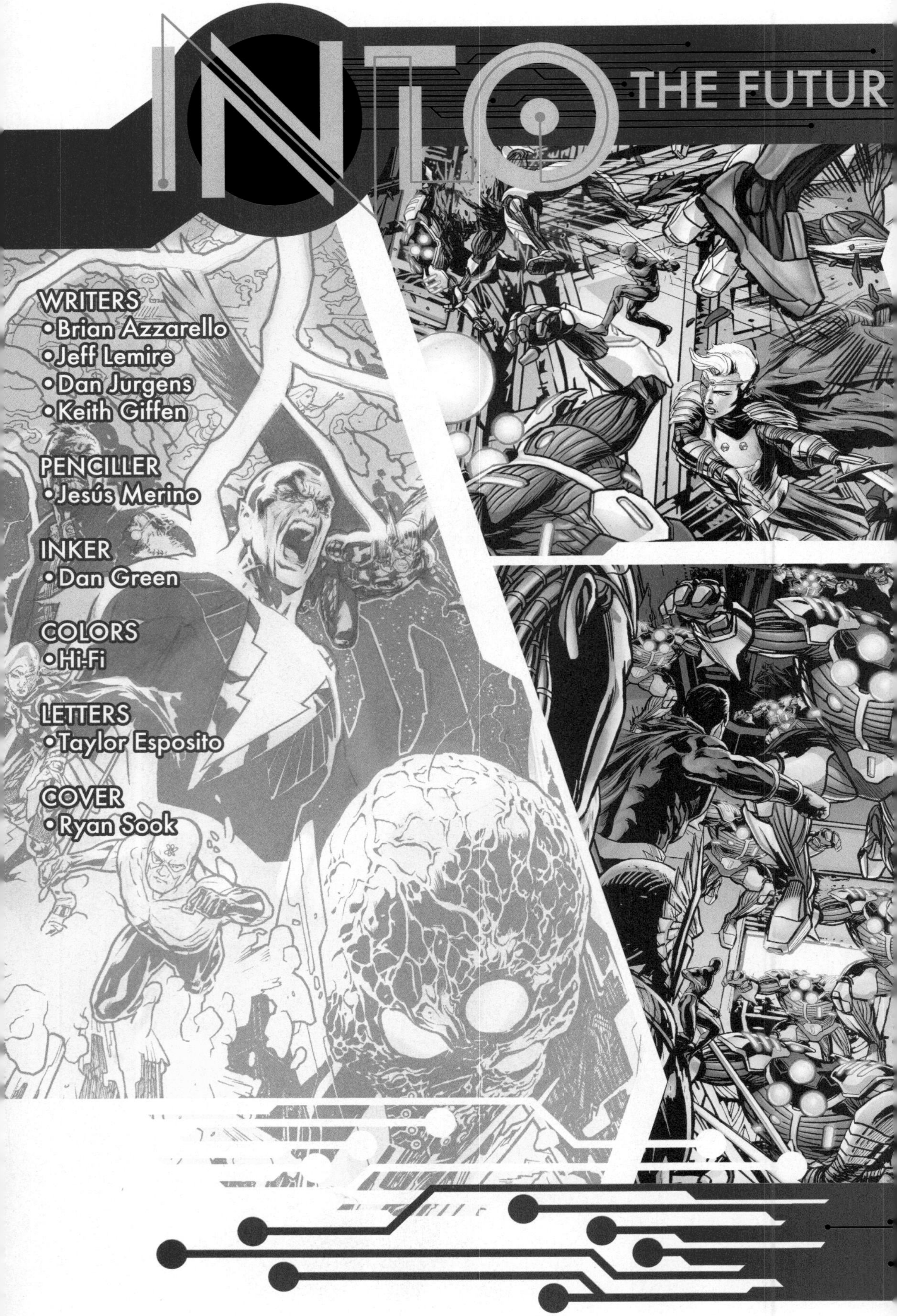

WRITERS
- Brian Azzarello
- Jeff Lemire
- Dan Jurgens
- Keith Giffen

PENCILLER
- Jesús Merino

INKER
- Dan Green

COLORS
- Hi-Fi

LETTERS
- Taylor Esposito

COVER
- Ryan Sook

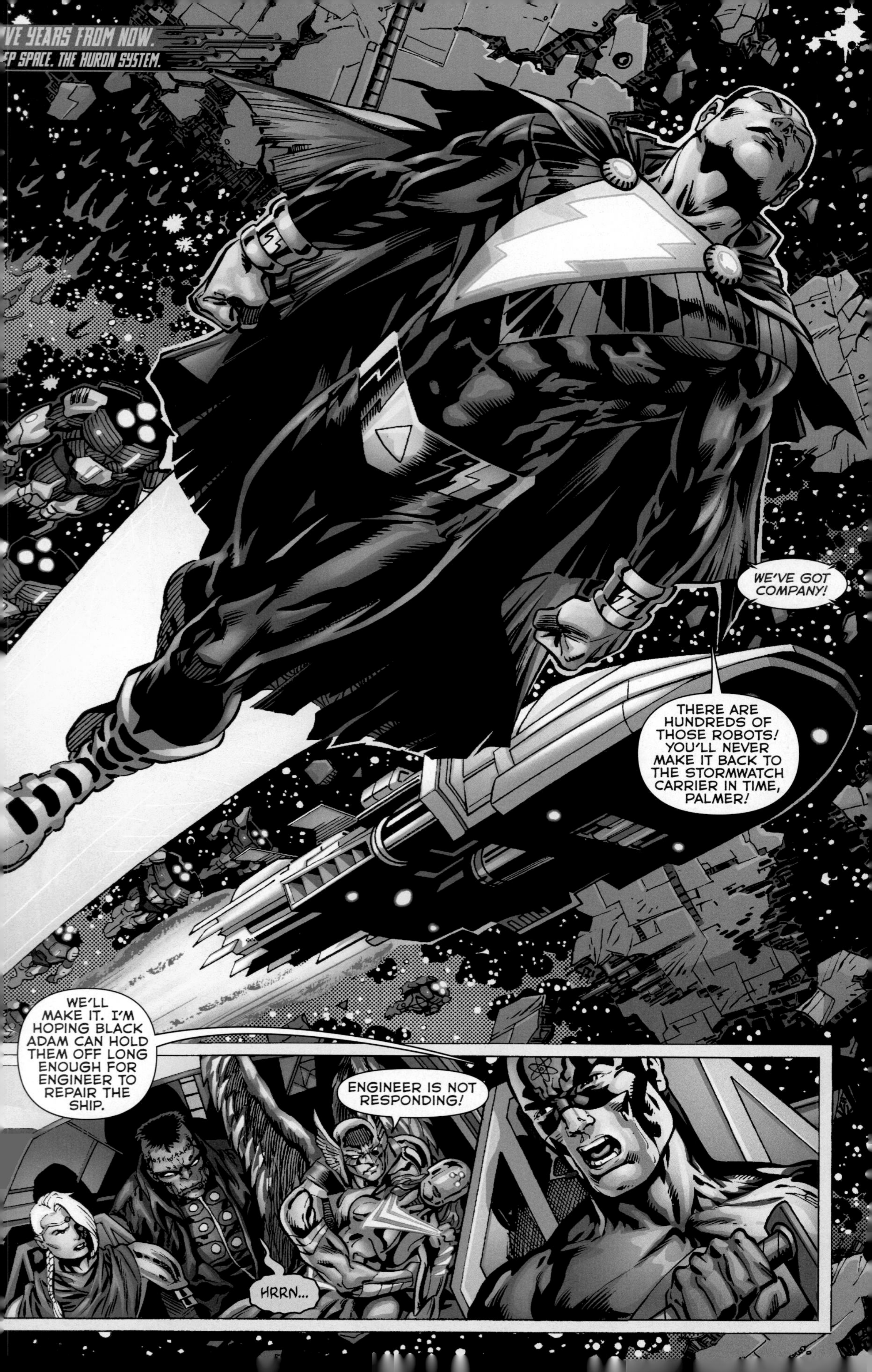
VE YEARS FROM NOW.
EP SPACE. THE HURON SYSTEM.
WE'VE GOT COMPANY!
THERE ARE HUNDREDS OF THOSE ROBOTS! YOU'LL NEVER MAKE IT BACK TO THE STORMWATCH CARRIER IN TIME, PALMER!
WE'LL MAKE IT. I'M HOPING BLACK ADAM CAN HOLD THEM OFF LONG ENOUGH FOR ENGINEER TO REPAIR THE SHIP.
ENGINEER IS NOT RESPONDING!
HRRN...

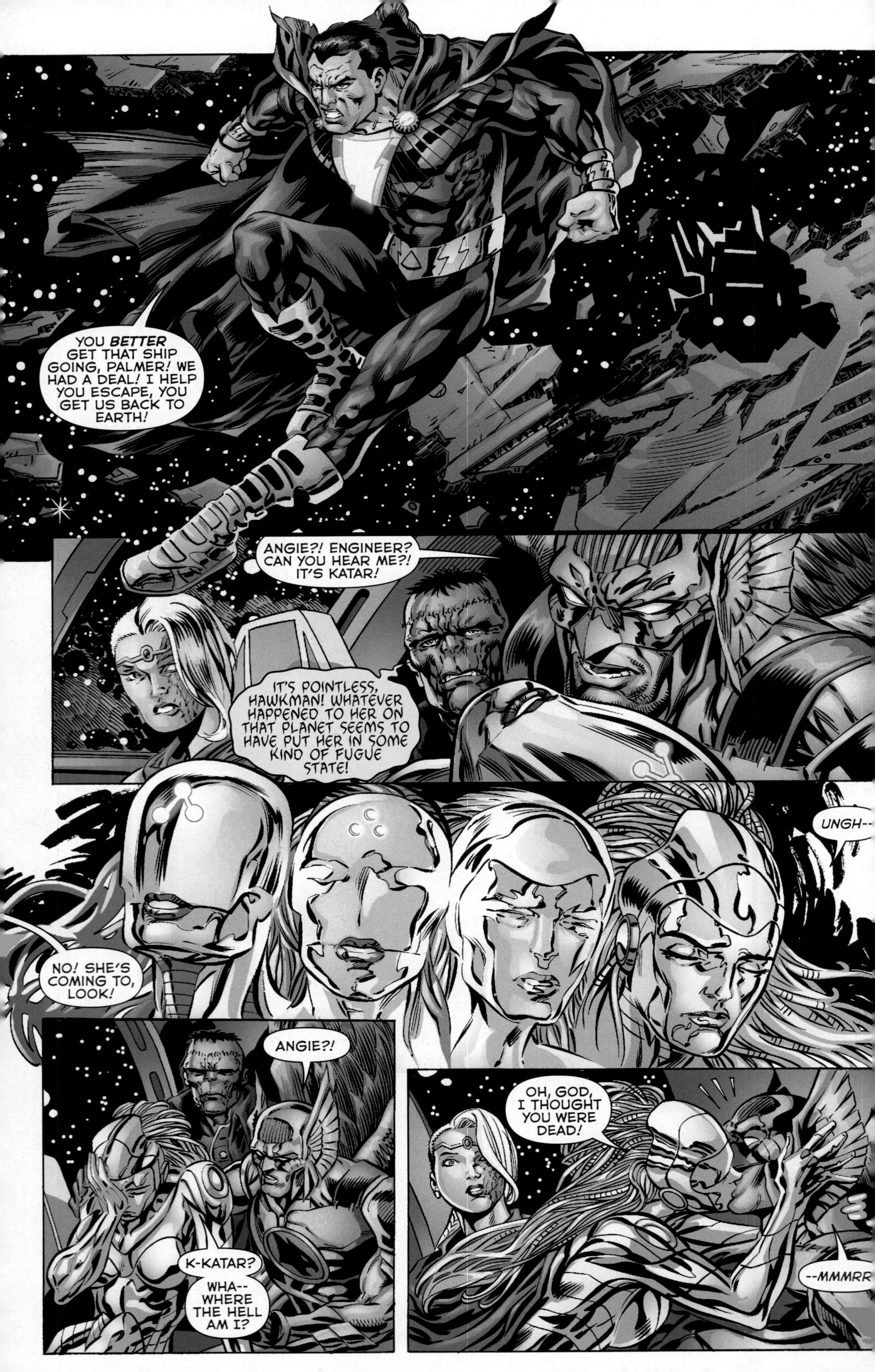

YOU BETTER GET THAT SHIP GOING, PALMER! WE HAD A DEAL! I HELP YOU ESCAPE, YOU GET US BACK TO EARTH!
ANGIE?! ENGINEER? CAN YOU HEAR ME?! IT'S KATAR!
IT'S POINTLESS, HAWKMAN! WHATEVER HAPPENED TO HER ON THAT PLANET SEEMS TO HAVE PUT HER IN SOME KIND OF FUGUE STATE!
UNGH--
NO! SHE'S COMING TO, LOOK!
ANGIE?!
K-KATAR?
WHA-- WHERE THE HELL AM I?
OH, GOD, I THOUGHT YOU WERE DEAD!
--MMMRR

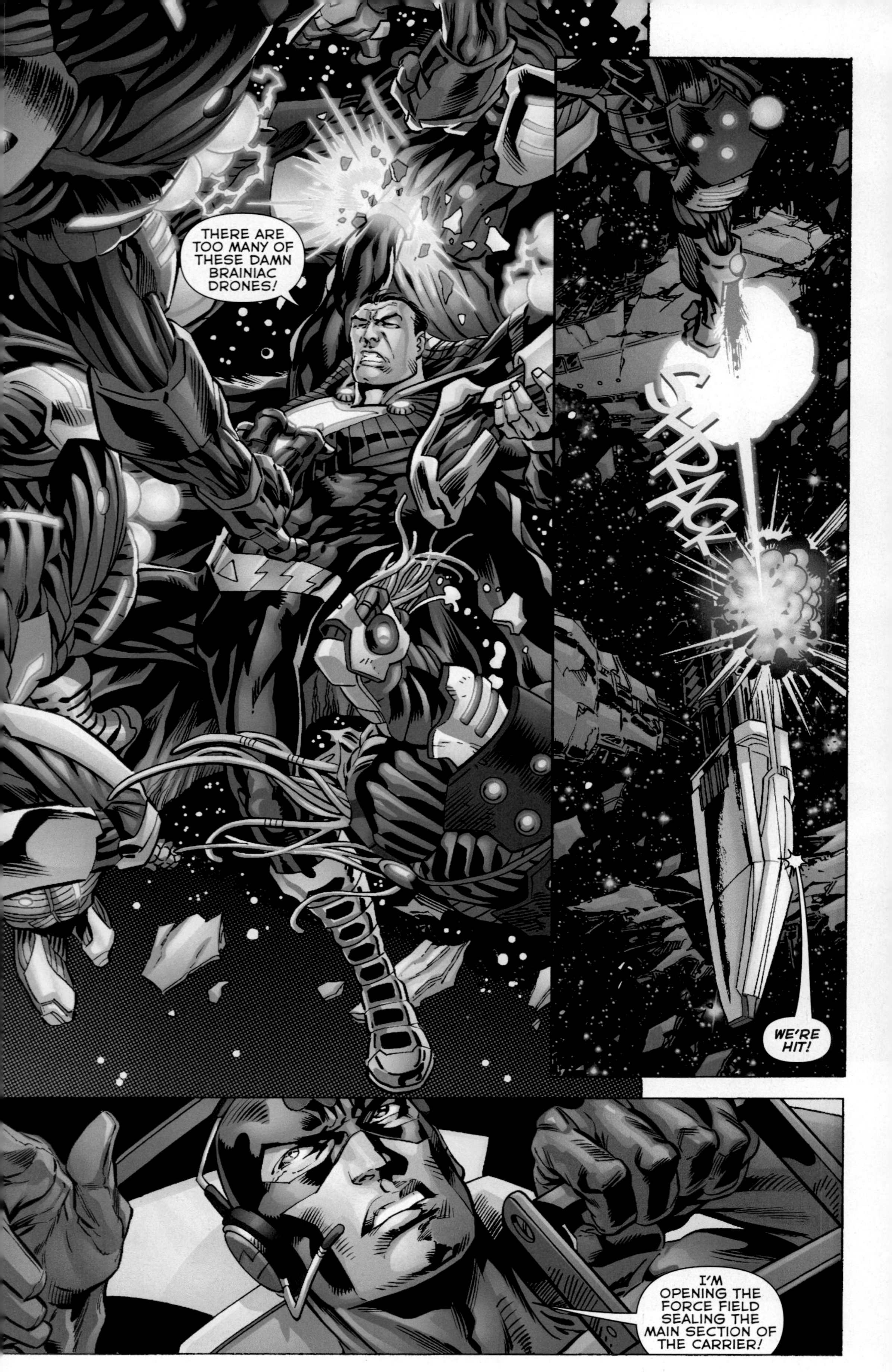
THERE ARE TOO MANY OF THESE DAMN BRAINIAC DRONES!
SHRACK
WE'RE HIT!
I'M OPENING THE FORCE FIELD SEALING THE MAIN SECTION OF THE CARRIER!

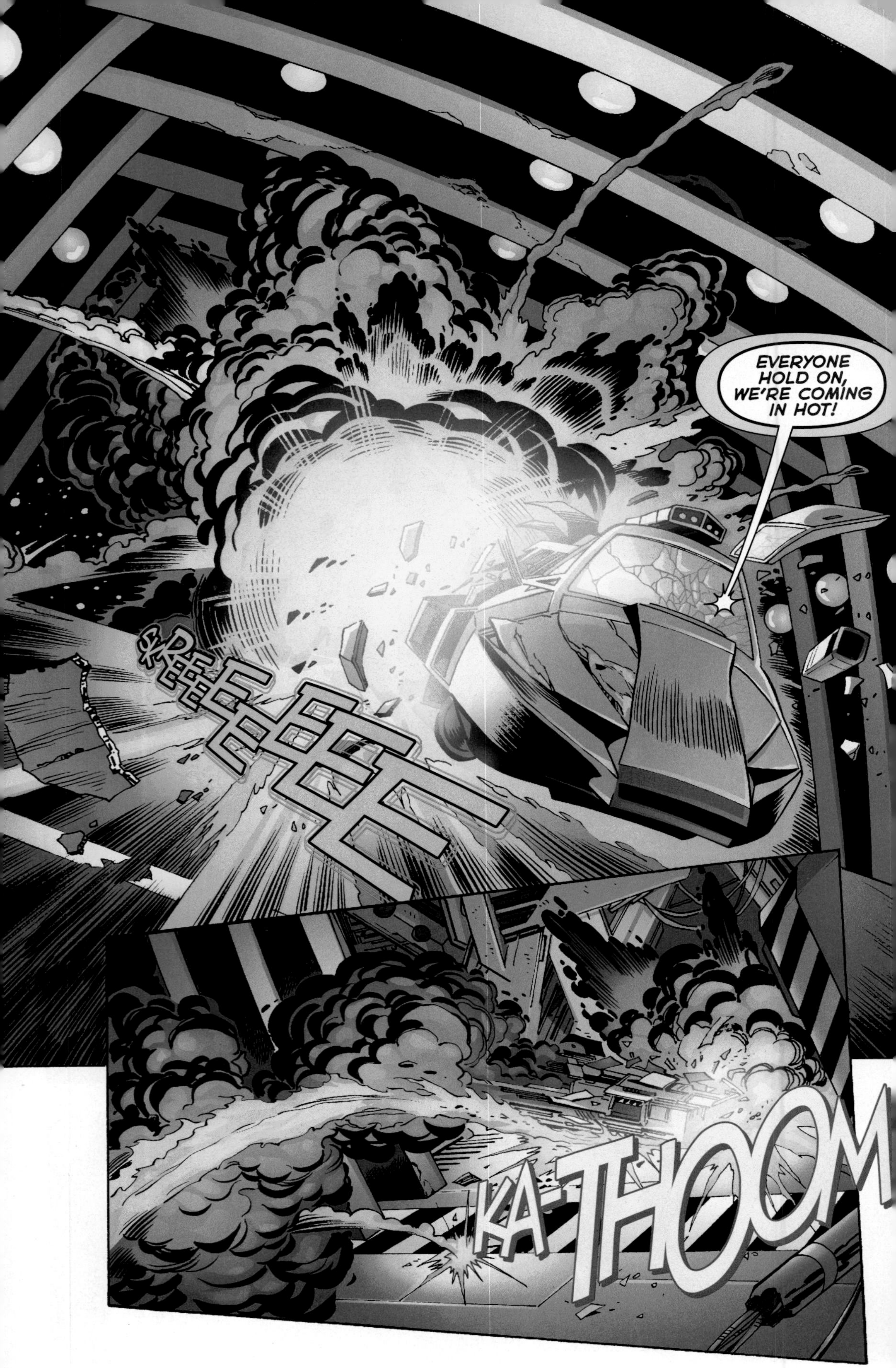
EVERYONE HOLD ON, WE'RE COMING IN HOT!
SKREEEEEEEE
KA-THOOM

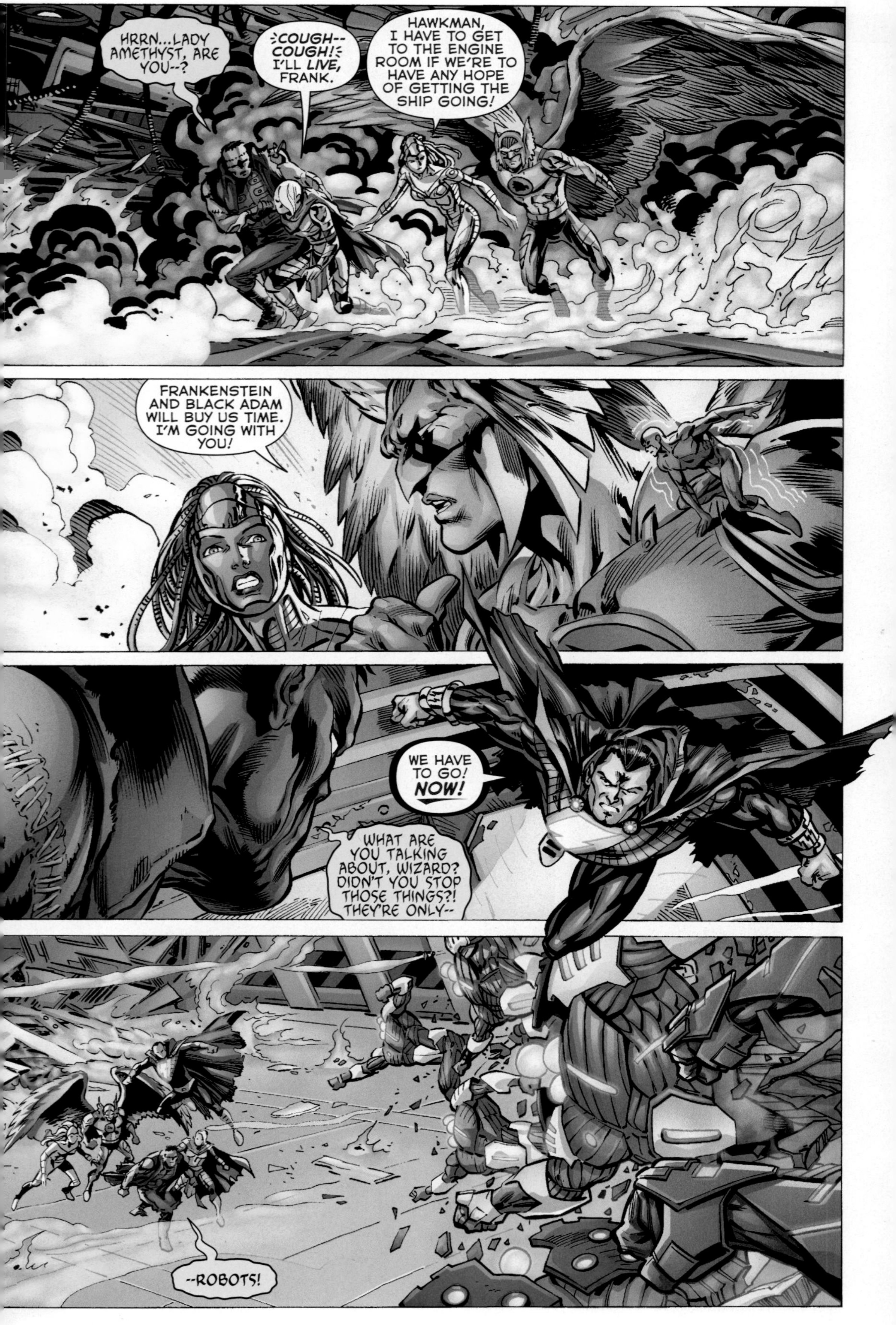
HRRN...LADY AMETHYST, ARE YOU--?
COUGH--COUGH! I'LL *LIVE,* FRANK.
HAWKMAN, I HAVE TO GET TO THE ENGINE ROOM IF WE'RE TO HAVE ANY HOPE OF GETTING THE SHIP GOING!
FRANKENSTEIN AND BLACK ADAM WILL BUY US TIME. I'M GOING WITH YOU!
WE HAVE TO GO! **NOW!**
WHAT ARE YOU TALKING ABOUT, WIZARD? DIDN'T YOU STOP THOSE THINGS?! THEY'RE ONLY--
--ROBOTS!

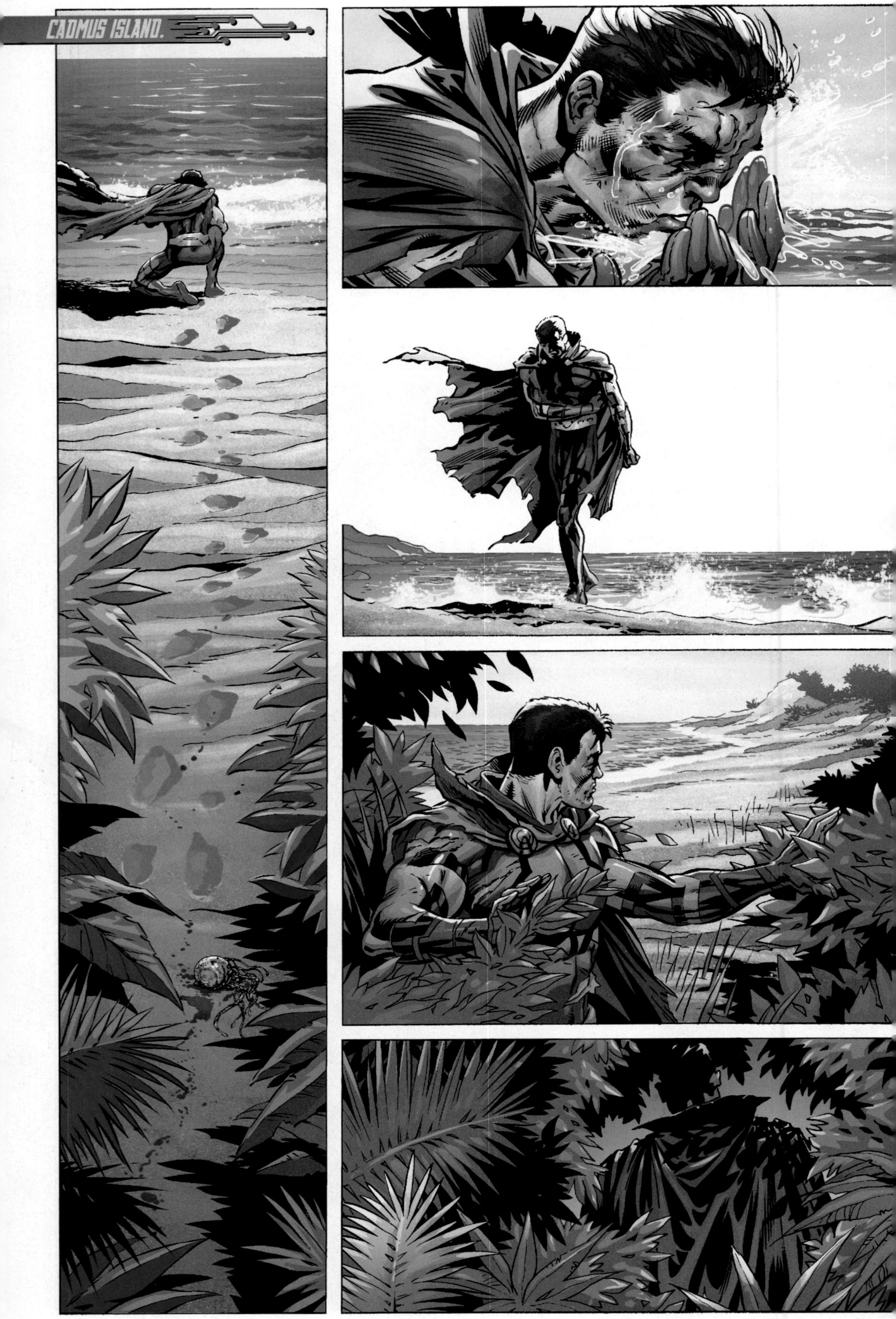
CADMUS ISLAND.

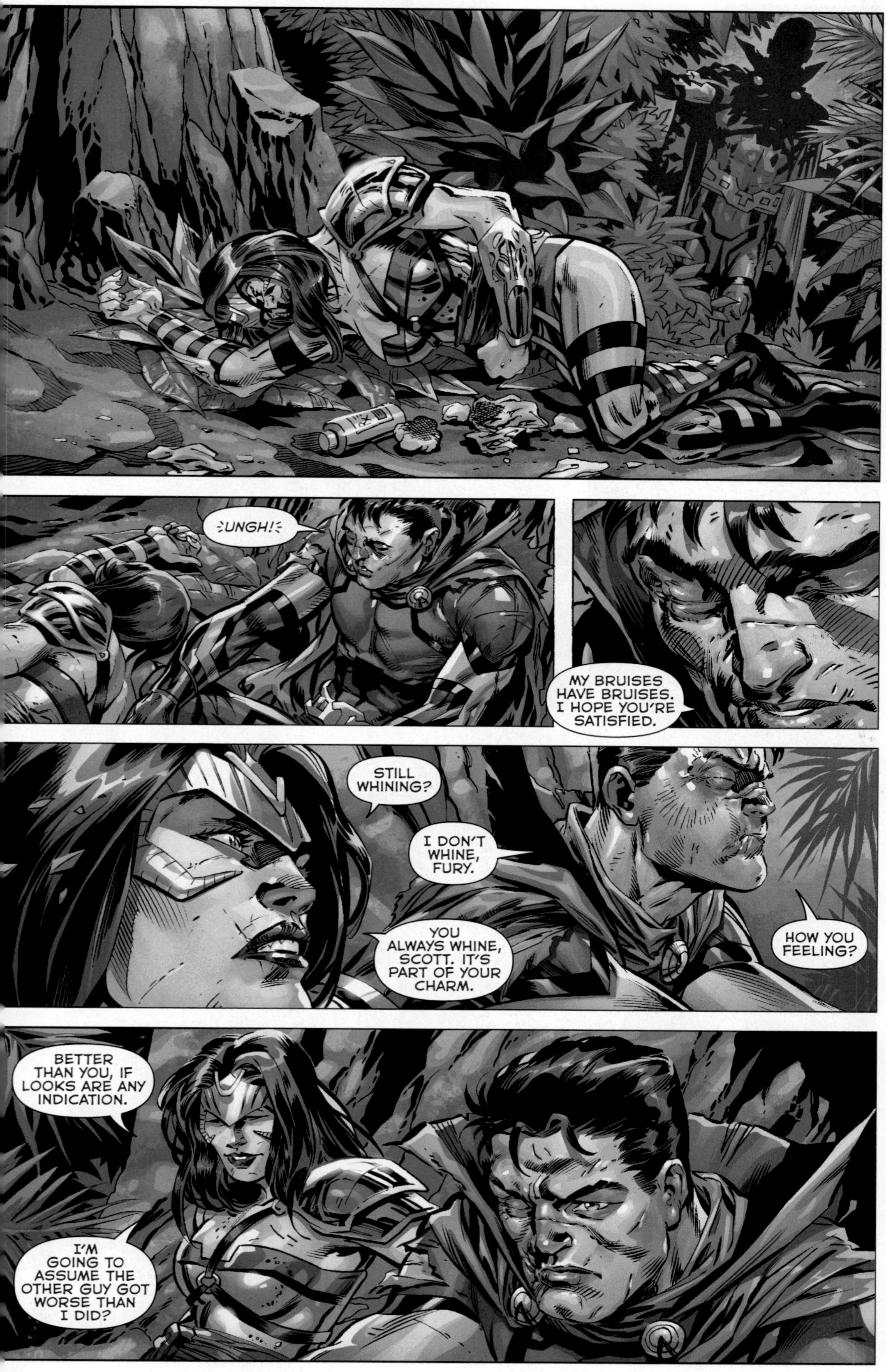
UNGH!
MY BRUISES HAVE BRUISES. I HOPE YOU'RE SATISFIED.
STILL WHINING?
I DON'T WHINE, FURY.
YOU ALWAYS WHINE, SCOTT. IT'S PART OF YOUR CHARM.
HOW YOU FEELING?
BETTER THAN YOU, IF LOOKS ARE ANY INDICATION.
I'M GOING TO ASSUME THE OTHER GUY GOT WORSE THAN I DID?

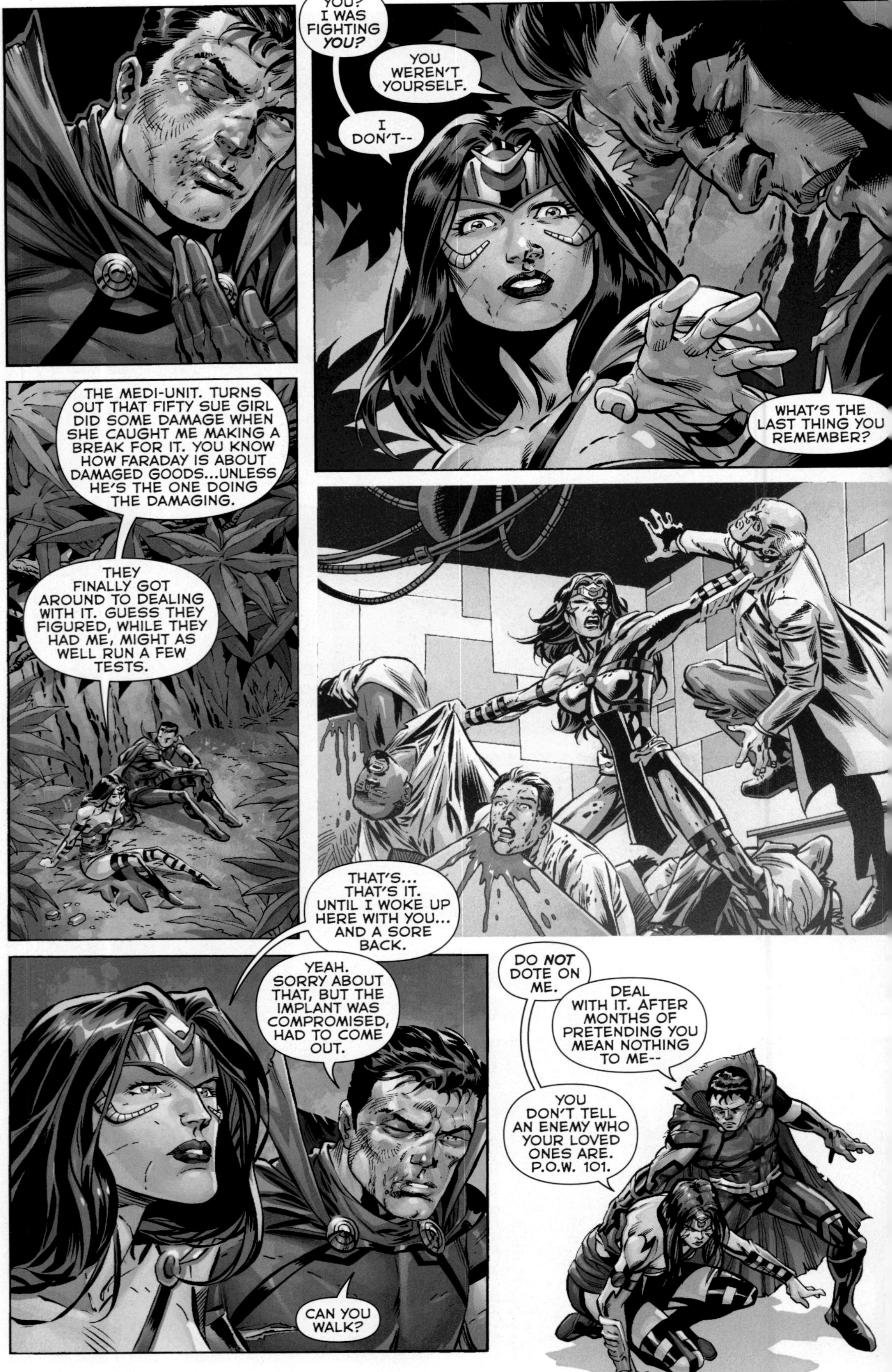
YOU? I WAS FIGHTING YOU?
YOU WEREN'T YOURSELF.
I DON'T--
WHAT'S THE LAST THING YOU REMEMBER?
THE MEDI-UNIT. TURNS OUT THAT FIFTY SUE GIRL DID SOME DAMAGE WHEN SHE CAUGHT ME MAKING A BREAK FOR IT. YOU KNOW HOW FARADAY IS ABOUT DAMAGED GOODS...UNLESS HE'S THE ONE DOING THE DAMAGING.
THEY FINALLY GOT AROUND TO DEALING WITH IT. GUESS THEY FIGURED, WHILE THEY HAD ME, MIGHT AS WELL RUN A FEW TESTS.
THAT'S... THAT'S IT. UNTIL I WOKE UP HERE WITH YOU... AND A SORE BACK.
YEAH. SORRY ABOUT THAT, BUT THE IMPLANT WAS COMPROMISED, HAD TO COME OUT.
CAN YOU WALK?
DO NOT DOTE ON ME.
DEAL WITH IT. AFTER MONTHS OF PRETENDING YOU MEAN NOTHING TO ME--
YOU DON'T TELL AN ENEMY WHO YOUR LOVED ONES ARE. P.O.W. 101.

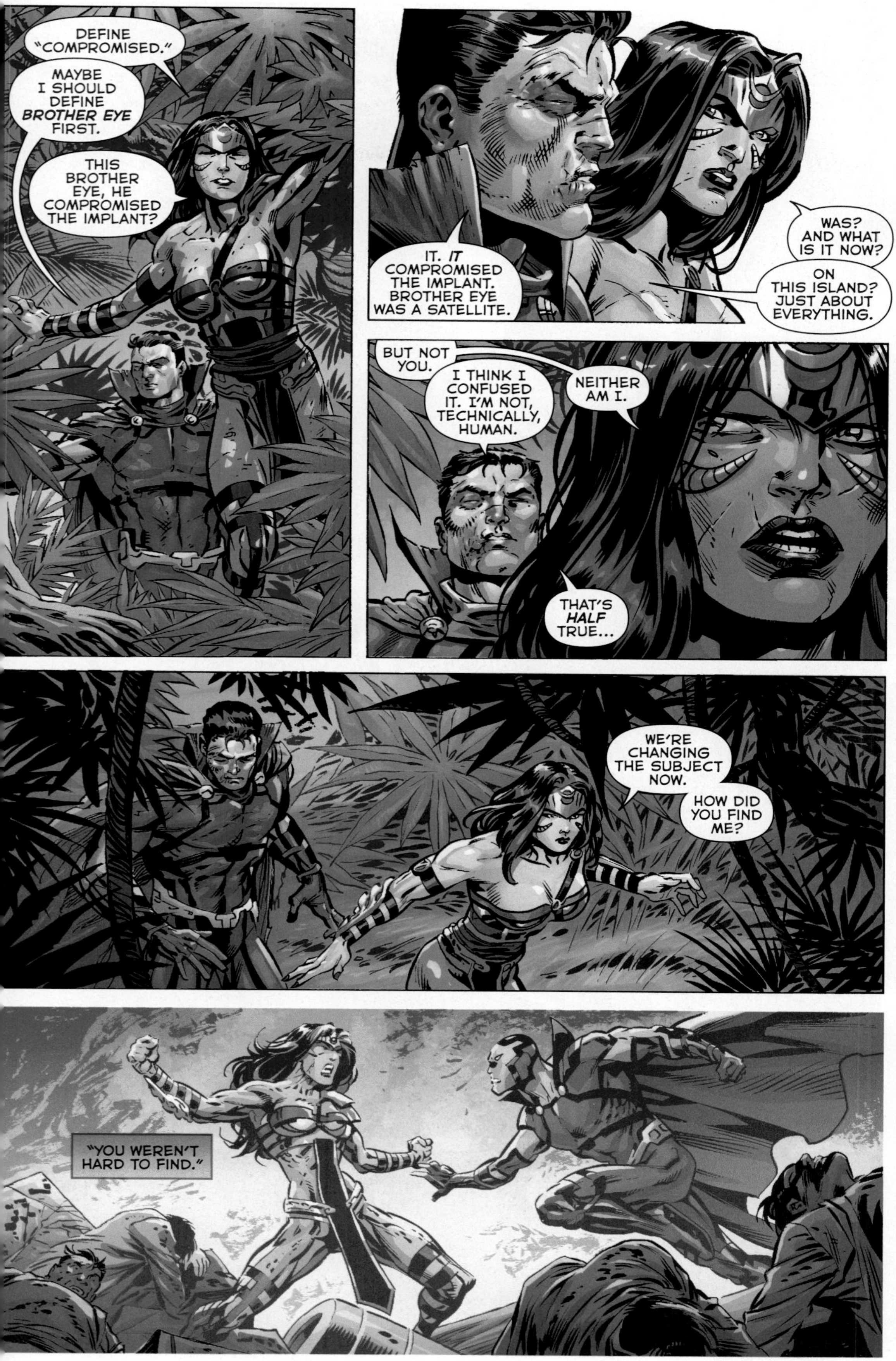
DEFINE "COMPROMISED."
MAYBE I SHOULD DEFINE *BROTHER EYE* FIRST.
THIS BROTHER EYE, HE COMPROMISED THE IMPLANT?
IT. *IT* COMPROMISED THE IMPLANT. BROTHER EYE WAS A SATELLITE.
WAS? AND WHAT IS IT NOW?
ON THIS ISLAND? JUST ABOUT EVERYTHING.
BUT NOT YOU.
I THINK I CONFUSED IT. I'M NOT, TECHNICALLY, HUMAN.
NEITHER AM I.
THAT'S *HALF* TRUE...
WE'RE CHANGING THE SUBJECT NOW.
HOW DID YOU FIND ME?
"YOU WEREN'T HARD TO FIND."

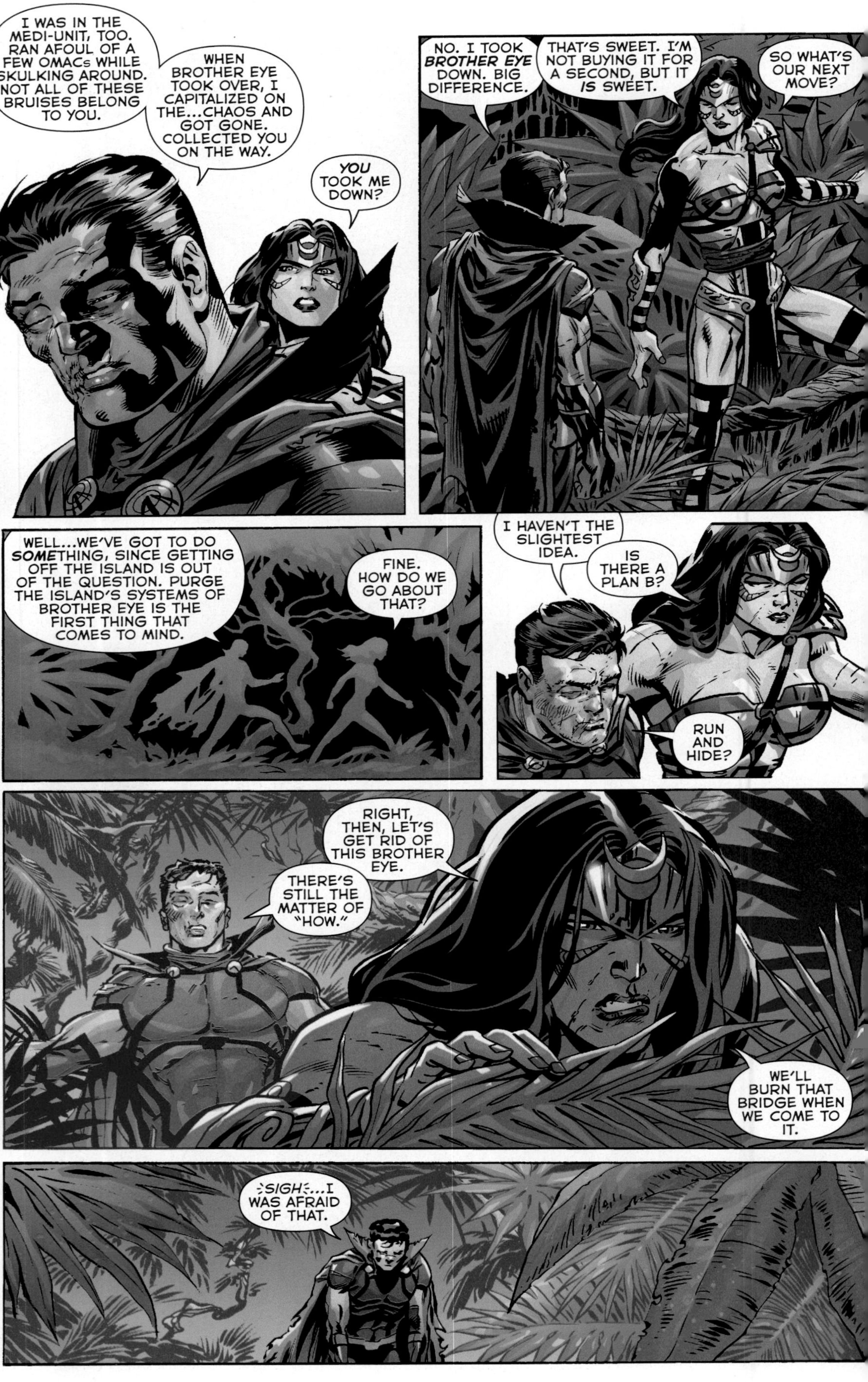

I WAS IN THE MEDI-UNIT, TOO. RAN AFOUL OF A FEW OMACs WHILE SKULKING AROUND. NOT ALL OF THESE BRUISES BELONG TO YOU.
WHEN BROTHER EYE TOOK OVER, I CAPITALIZED ON THE...CHAOS AND GOT GONE. COLLECTED YOU ON THE WAY.
YOU TOOK ME DOWN?
NO. I TOOK BROTHER EYE DOWN. BIG DIFFERENCE.
THAT'S SWEET. I'M NOT BUYING IT FOR A SECOND, BUT IT IS SWEET.
SO WHAT'S OUR NEXT MOVE?
WELL...WE'VE GOT TO DO SOMETHING, SINCE GETTING OFF THE ISLAND IS OUT OF THE QUESTION. PURGE THE ISLAND'S SYSTEMS OF BROTHER EYE IS THE FIRST THING THAT COMES TO MIND.
FINE. HOW DO WE GO ABOUT THAT?
I HAVEN'T THE SLIGHTEST IDEA.
IS THERE A PLAN B?
RUN AND HIDE?
RIGHT, THEN, LET'S GET RID OF THIS BROTHER EYE.
THERE'S STILL THE MATTER OF "HOW."
WE'LL BURN THAT BRIDGE WHEN WE COME TO IT.
SIGH...I WAS AFRAID OF THAT.

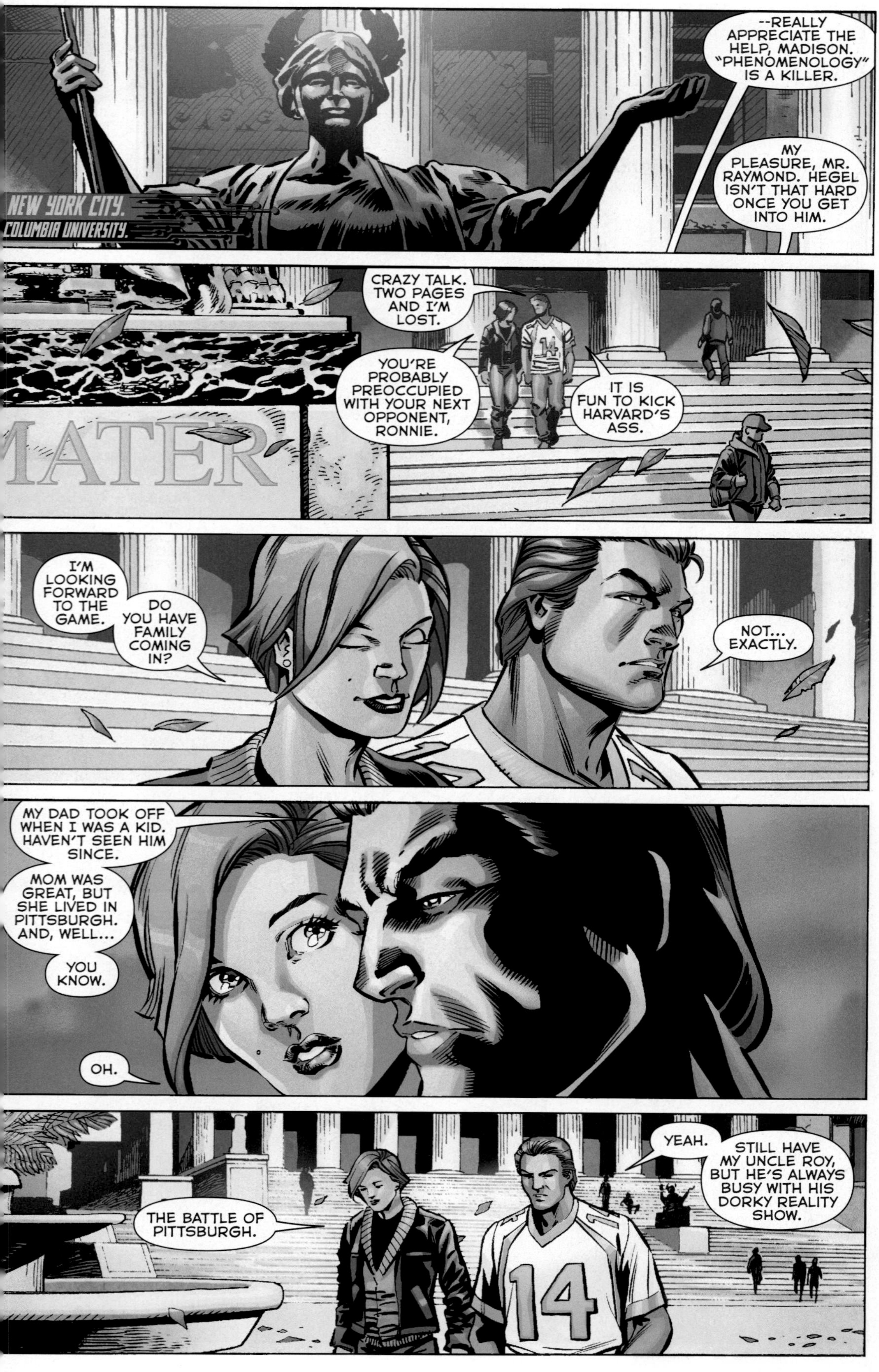
NEW YORK CITY.
COLUMBIA UNIVERSITY.
--REALLY APPRECIATE THE HELP, MADISON. "PHENOMENOLOGY" IS A KILLER.
MY PLEASURE, MR. RAYMOND. HEGEL ISN'T THAT HARD ONCE YOU GET INTO HIM.
CRAZY TALK. TWO PAGES AND I'M LOST.
YOU'RE PROBABLY PREOCCUPIED WITH YOUR NEXT OPPONENT, RONNIE.
IT IS FUN TO KICK HARVARD'S ASS.
MATER
I'M LOOKING FORWARD TO THE GAME.
DO YOU HAVE FAMILY COMING IN?
NOT... EXACTLY.
MY DAD TOOK OFF WHEN I WAS A KID. HAVEN'T SEEN HIM SINCE.
MOM WAS GREAT, BUT SHE LIVED IN PITTSBURGH. AND, WELL...
YOU KNOW.
OH.
YEAH.
STILL HAVE MY UNCLE ROY, BUT HE'S ALWAYS BUSY WITH HIS DORKY REALITY SHOW.
THE BATTLE OF PITTSBURGH.

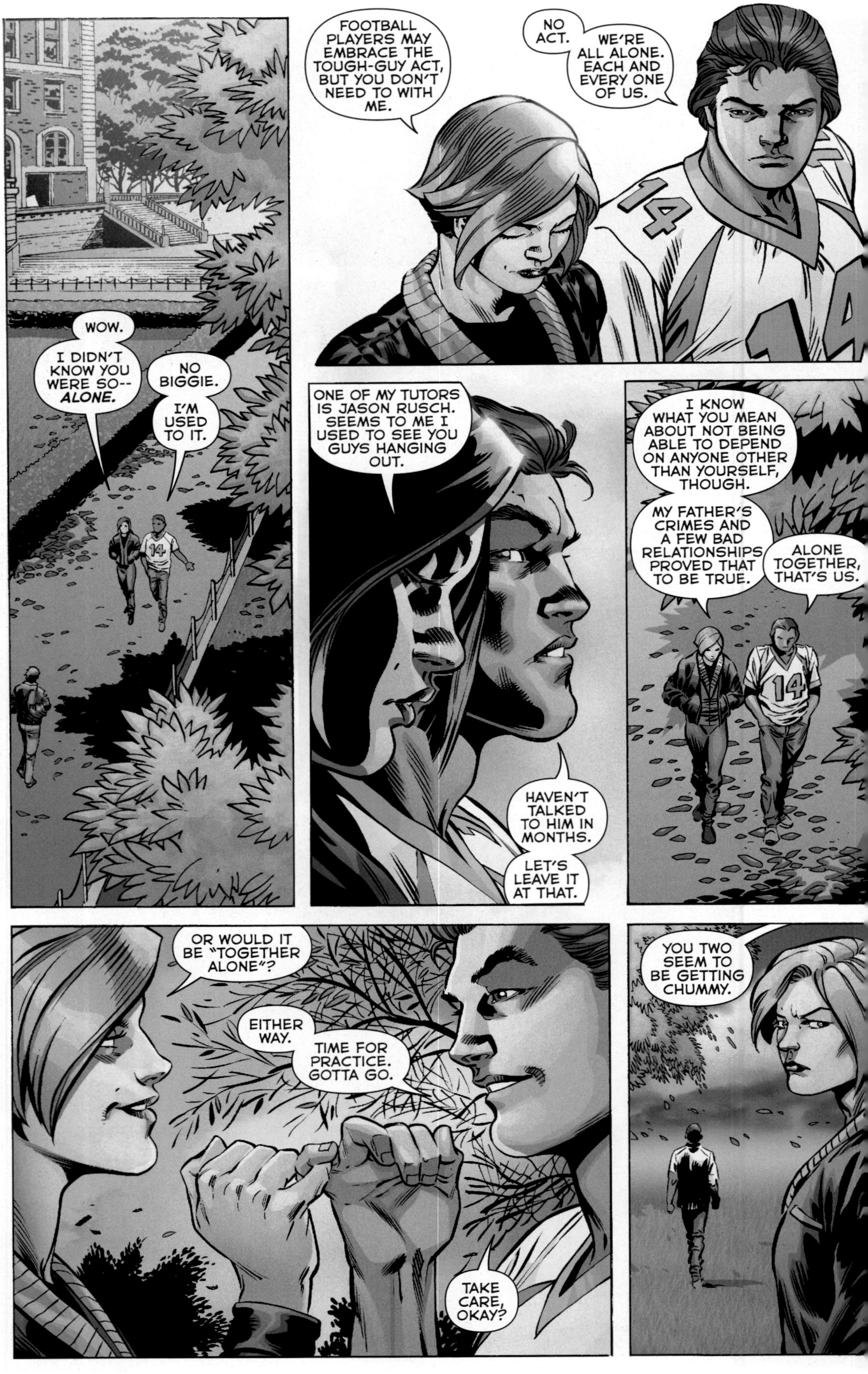
FOOTBALL PLAYERS MAY EMBRACE THE TOUGH-GUY ACT, BUT YOU DON'T NEED TO WITH ME.
NO ACT.
WE'RE ALL ALONE. EACH AND EVERY ONE OF US.
WOW.
I DIDN'T KNOW YOU WERE SO-- ALONE.
NO BIGGIE.
I'M USED TO IT.
ONE OF MY TUTORS IS JASON RUSCH. SEEMS TO ME I USED TO SEE YOU GUYS HANGING OUT.
HAVEN'T TALKED TO HIM IN MONTHS.
LET'S LEAVE IT AT THAT.
I KNOW WHAT YOU MEAN ABOUT NOT BEING ABLE TO DEPEND ON ANYONE OTHER THAN YOURSELF, THOUGH.
MY FATHER'S CRIMES AND A FEW BAD RELATIONSHIPS PROVED THAT TO BE TRUE.
ALONE TOGETHER, THAT'S US.
OR WOULD IT BE "TOGETHER ALONE"?
EITHER WAY.
TIME FOR PRACTICE. GOTTA GO.
TAKE CARE, OKAY?
YOU TWO SEEM TO BE GETTING CHUMMY.

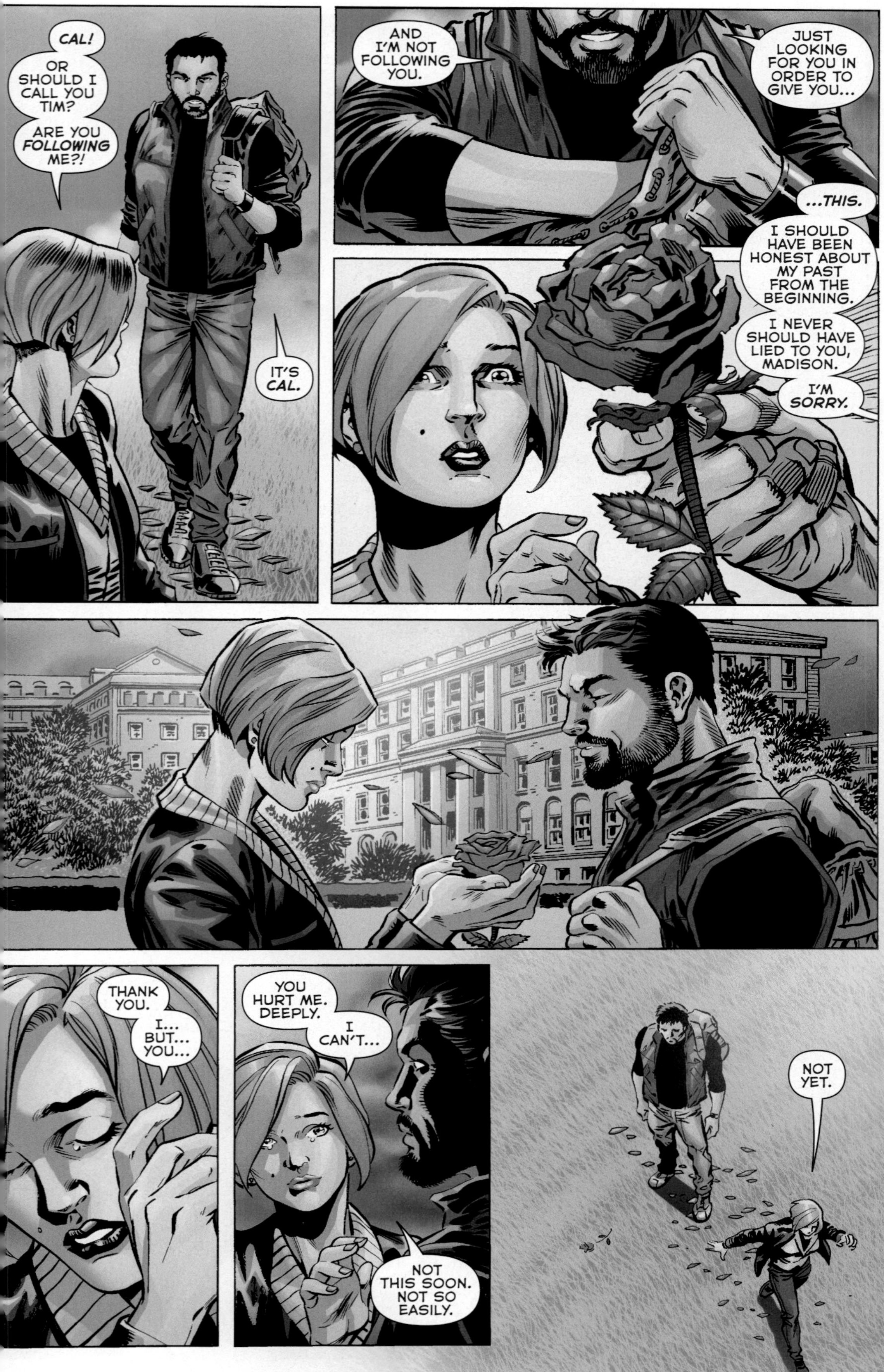
CAL!
OR SHOULD I CALL YOU TIM?
ARE YOU FOLLOWING ME?!
IT'S CAL.
AND I'M NOT FOLLOWING YOU.
JUST LOOKING FOR YOU IN ORDER TO GIVE YOU...
...THIS.
I SHOULD HAVE BEEN HONEST ABOUT MY PAST FROM THE BEGINNING.
I NEVER SHOULD HAVE LIED TO YOU, MADISON.
I'M SORRY.
THANK YOU.
I... BUT... YOU...
YOU HURT ME. DEEPLY.
I CAN'T...
NOT THIS SOON. NOT SO EASILY.
NOT YET.

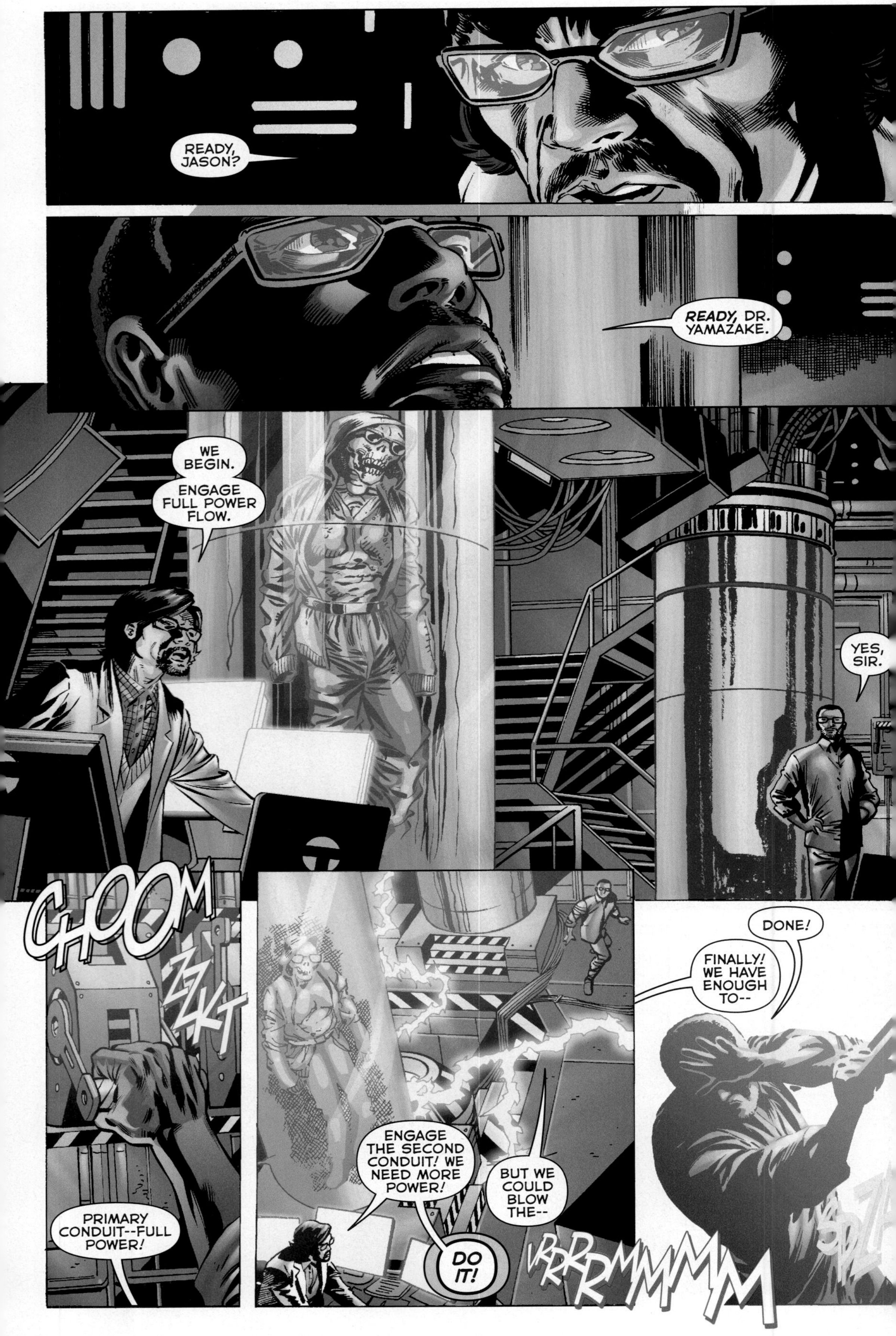
READY, JASON?
READY, DR. YAMAZAKE.
WE BEGIN.
ENGAGE FULL POWER FLOW.
YES, SIR.
CHOOM
ZZZKT
PRIMARY CONDUIT--FULL POWER!
ENGAGE THE SECOND CONDUIT! WE NEED MORE POWER!
BUT WE COULD BLOW THE--
DO IT!
VRRRRMMMMMM
FINALLY! WE HAVE ENOUGH TO--
DONE!

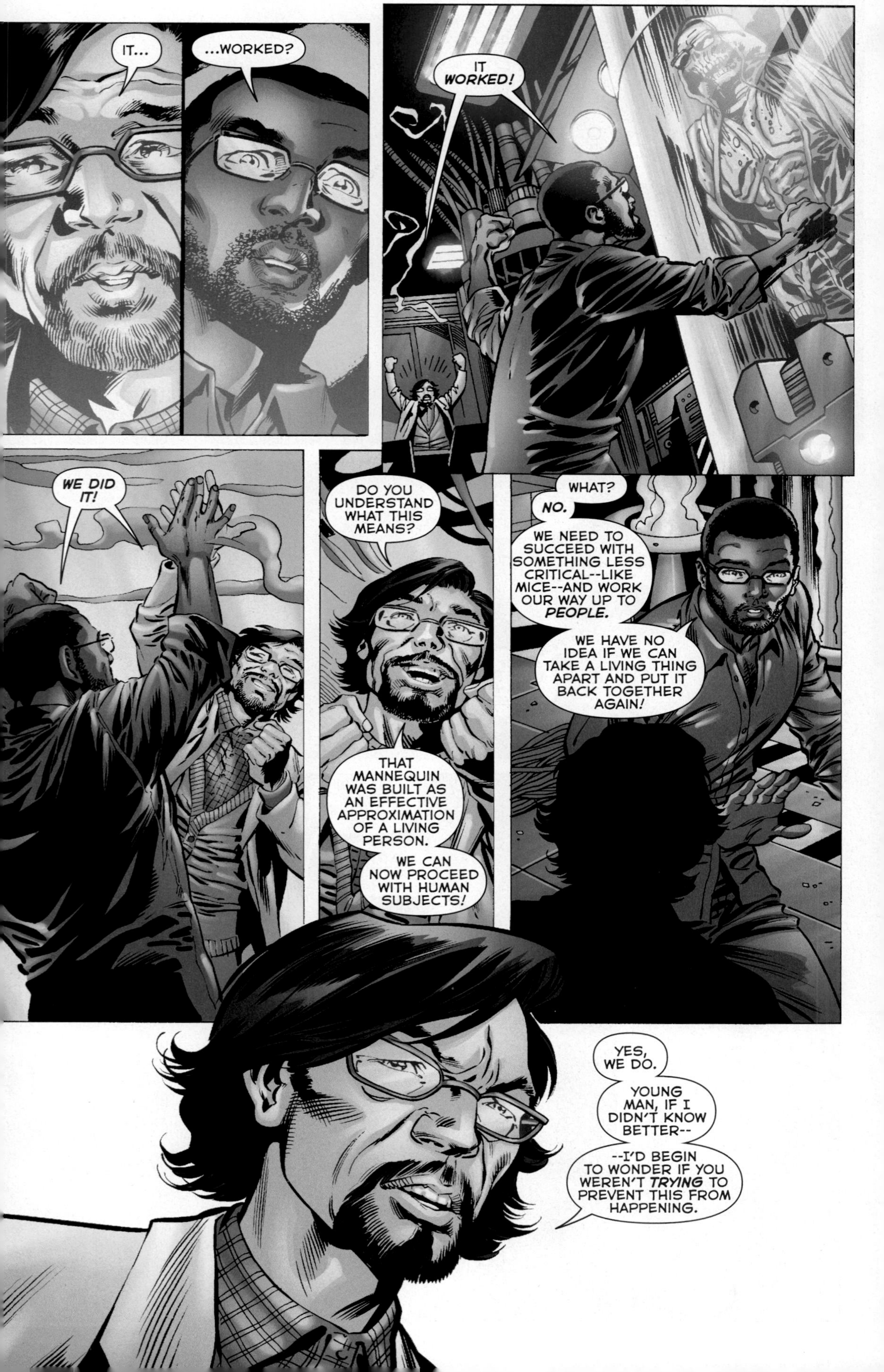
IT...
...WORKED?
IT *WORKED!*
WE DID IT!
DO YOU UNDERSTAND WHAT THIS MEANS?
THAT MANNEQUIN WAS BUILT AS AN EFFECTIVE APPROXIMATION OF A LIVING PERSON.
WE CAN NOW PROCEED WITH HUMAN SUBJECTS!
WHAT? *NO.*
WE NEED TO SUCCEED WITH SOMETHING LESS CRITICAL--LIKE MICE--AND WORK OUR WAY UP TO *PEOPLE.*
WE HAVE NO IDEA IF WE CAN TAKE A LIVING THING APART AND PUT IT BACK TOGETHER AGAIN!
YES, WE DO.
YOUNG MAN, IF I DIDN'T KNOW BETTER--
--I'D BEGIN TO WONDER IF YOU WEREN'T *TRYING* TO PREVENT THIS FROM HAPPENING.

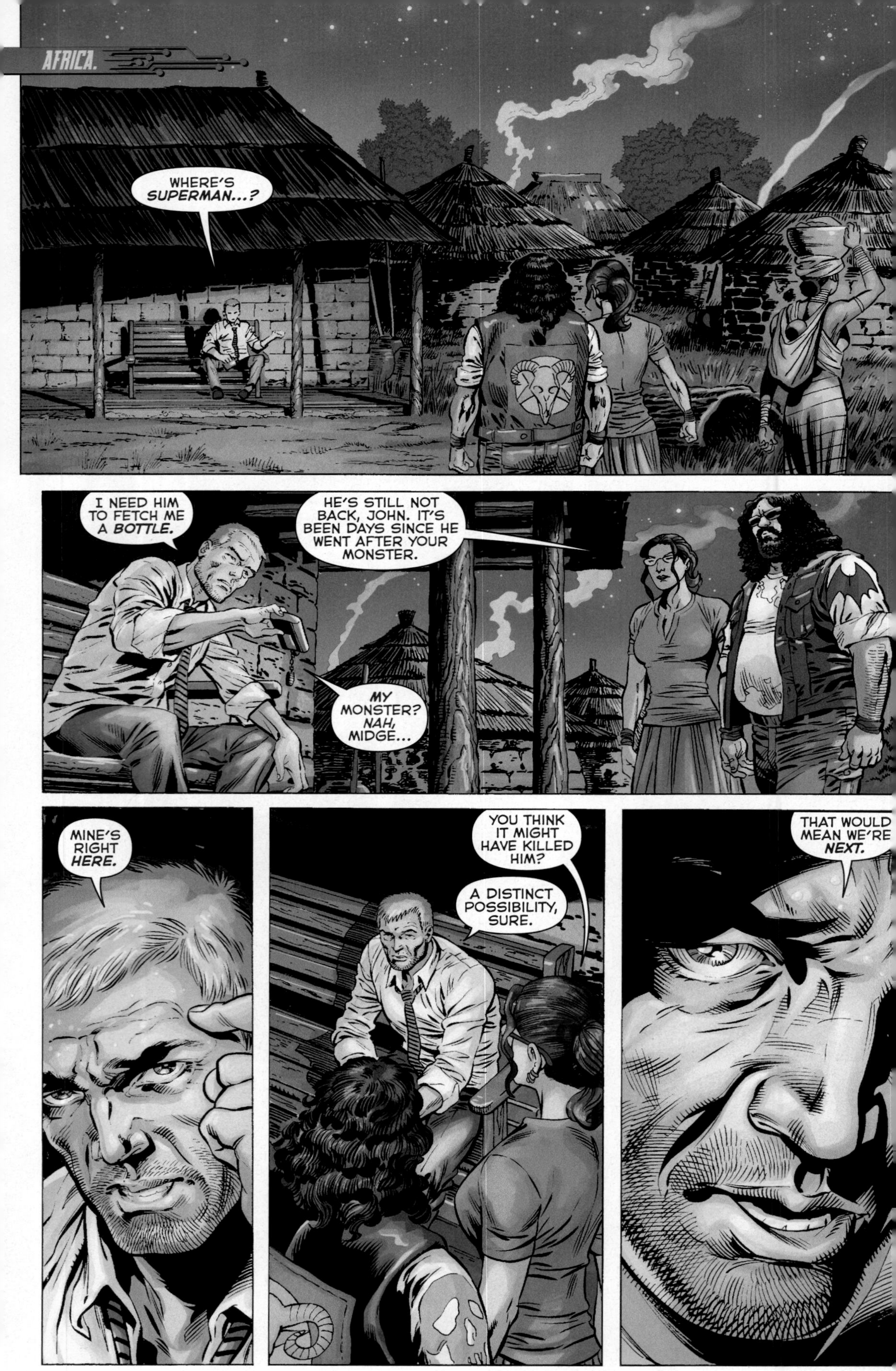

AFRICA.
WHERE'S SUPERMAN...?
I NEED HIM TO FETCH ME A BOTTLE.
HE'S STILL NOT BACK, JOHN. IT'S BEEN DAYS SINCE HE WENT AFTER YOUR MONSTER.
MY MONSTER? NAH, MIDGE...
MINE'S RIGHT HERE.
YOU THINK IT MIGHT HAVE KILLED HIM?
A DISTINCT POSSIBILITY, SURE.
THAT WOULD MEAN WE'RE NEXT.

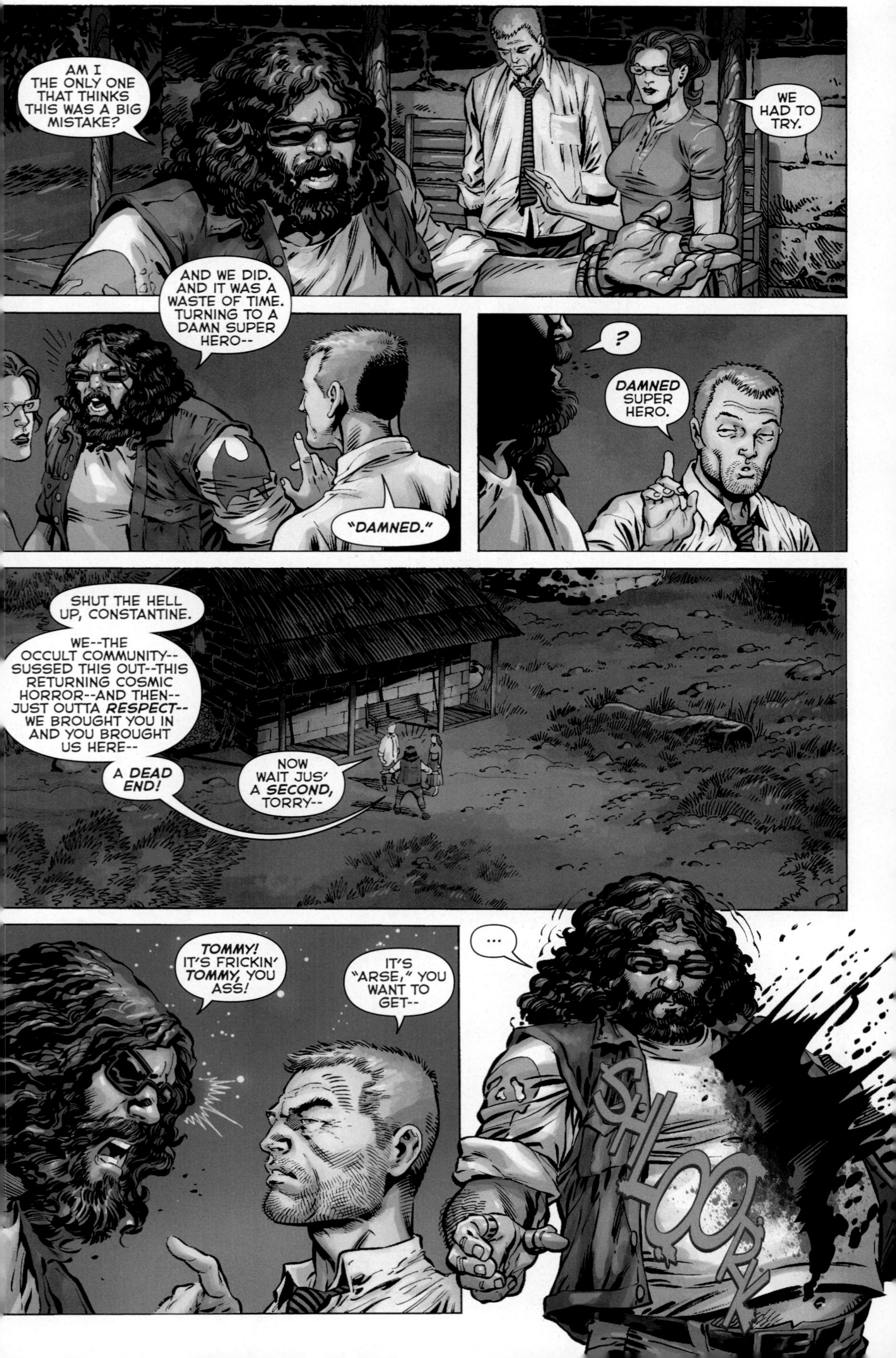
AM I THE ONLY ONE THAT THINKS THIS WAS A BIG MISTAKE?
WE HAD TO TRY.
AND WE DID. AND IT WAS A WASTE OF TIME. TURNING TO A DAMN SUPER HERO--
"DAMNED."
?
DAMNED SUPER HERO.
SHUT THE HELL UP, CONSTANTINE.
WE--THE OCCULT COMMUNITY--SUSSED THIS OUT--THIS RETURNING COSMIC HORROR--AND THEN--JUST OUTTA RESPECT--WE BROUGHT YOU IN AND YOU BROUGHT US HERE--
A DEAD END!
NOW WAIT JUS' A SECOND, TORRY--
TOMMY! IT'S FRICKIN' TOMMY, YOU ASS!
IT'S "ARSE," YOU WANT TO GET--
...
SHLOORK

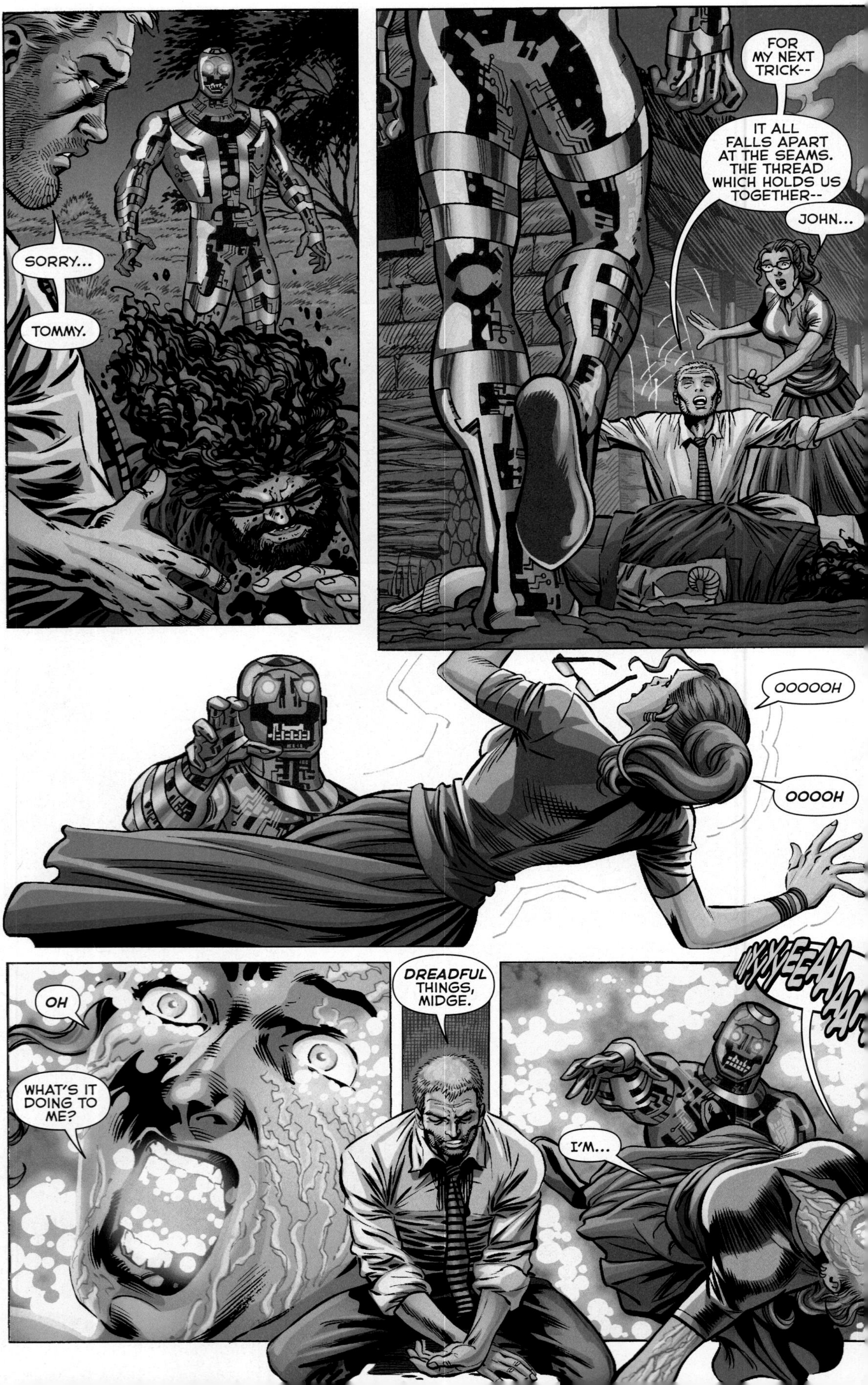
SORRY...
TOMMY.
FOR MY NEXT TRICK--
IT ALL FALLS APART AT THE SEAMS. THE THREAD WHICH HOLDS US TOGETHER--
JOHN...
OOOOOH
OOOOH
OH
WHAT'S IT DOING TO ME?
DREADFUL THINGS, MIDGE.
I'M...
YYEEAAAA

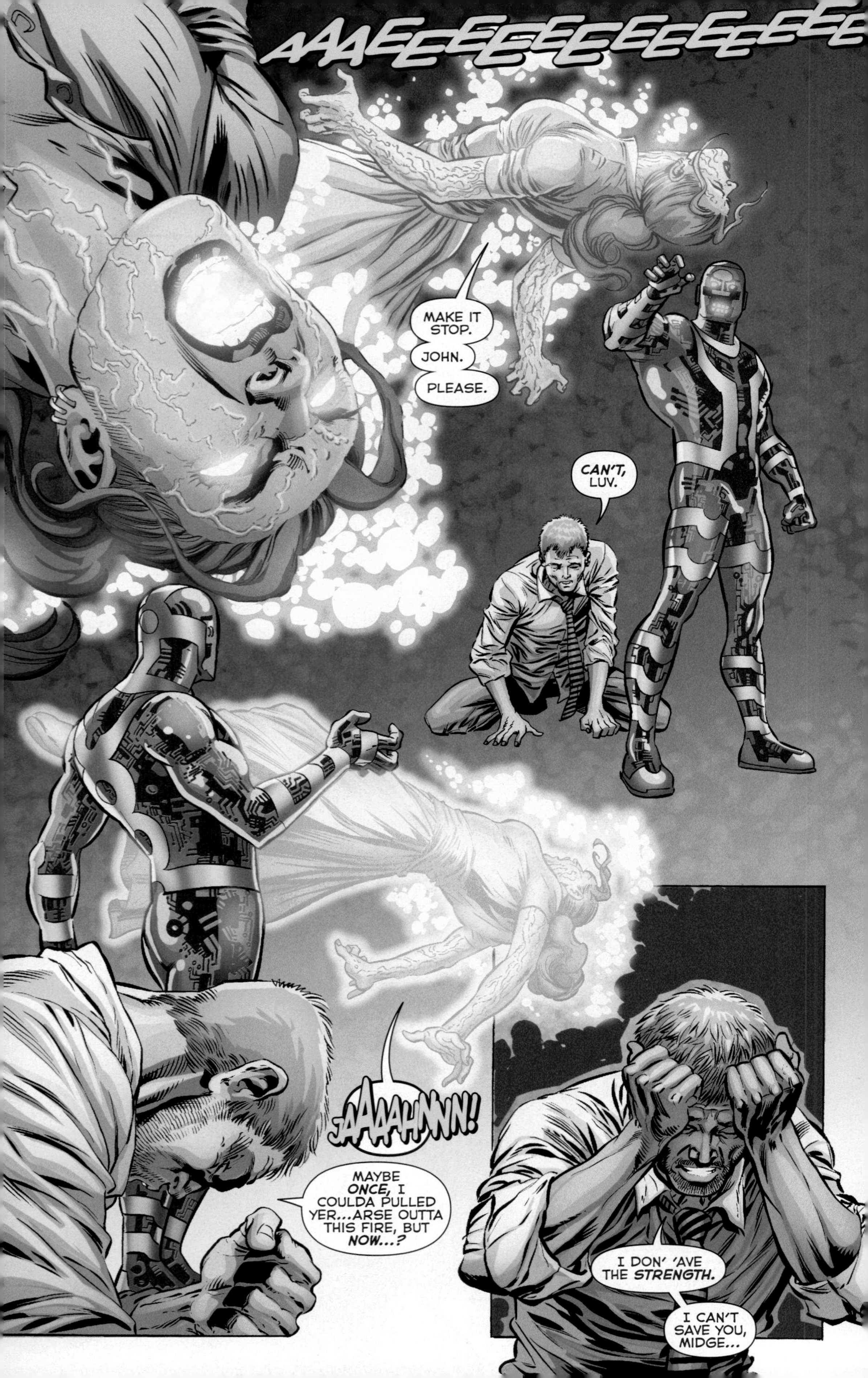
AAAEEEEEEEEEEEEEEE
MAKE IT STOP.
JOHN.
PLEASE.
CAN'T, LUV.
JAAAAHNNN!
MAYBE ONCE, I COULDA PULLED YER...ARSE OUTTA THIS FIRE, BUT NOW...?
I DON' 'AVE THE STRENGTH.
I CAN'T SAVE YOU, MIDGE...

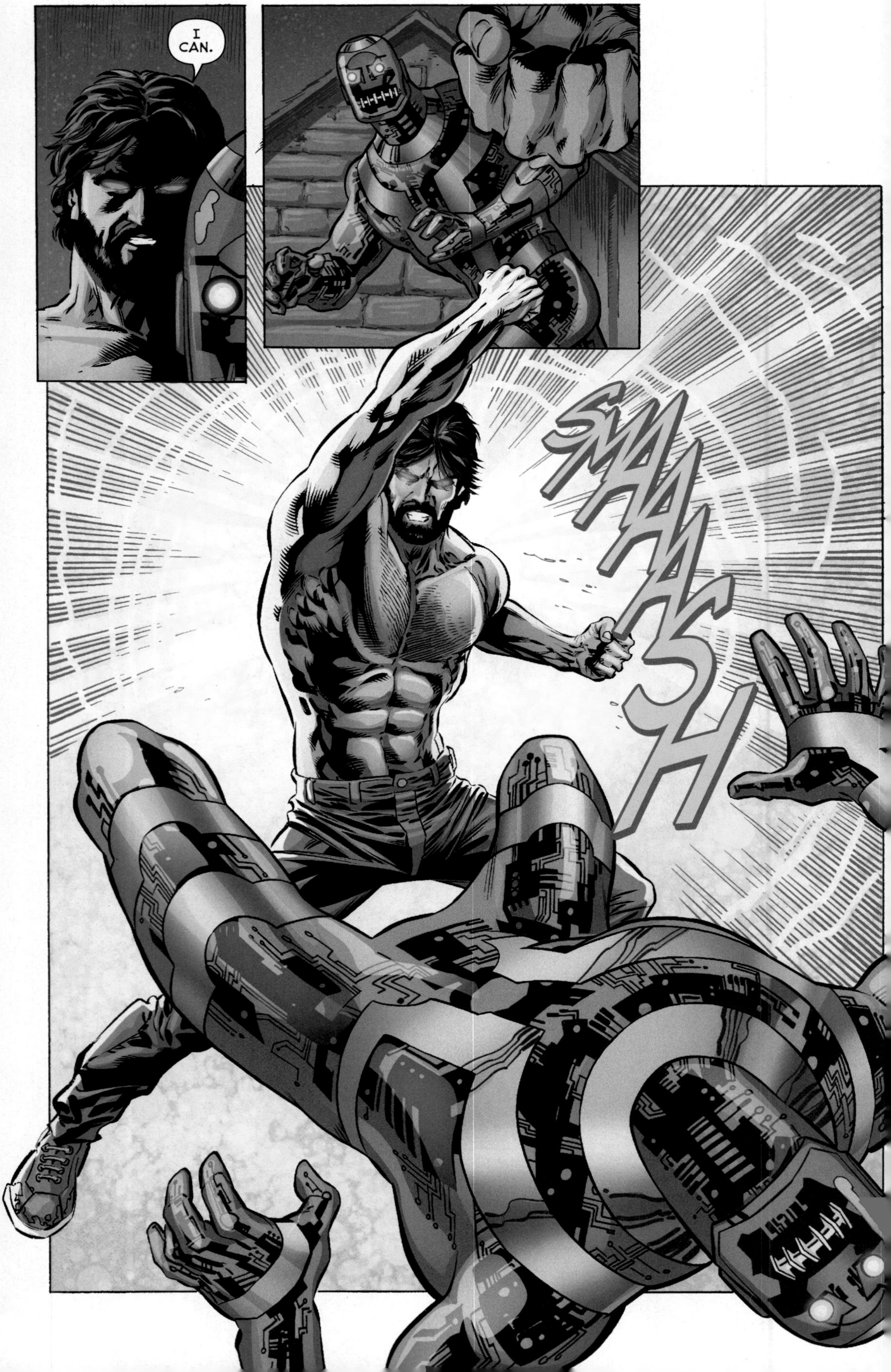
I CAN.
SMAAASH

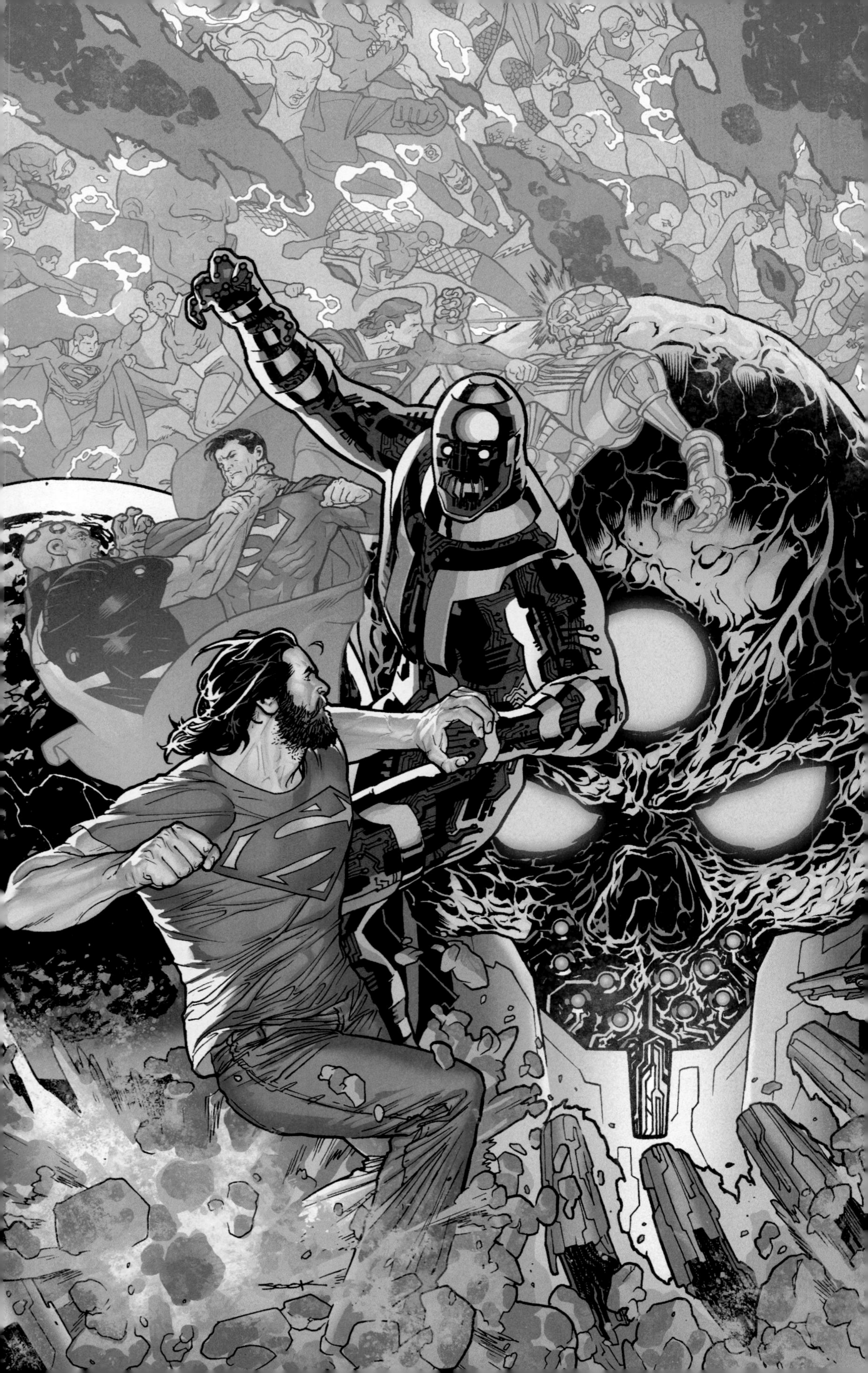

INTO THE FUTUR

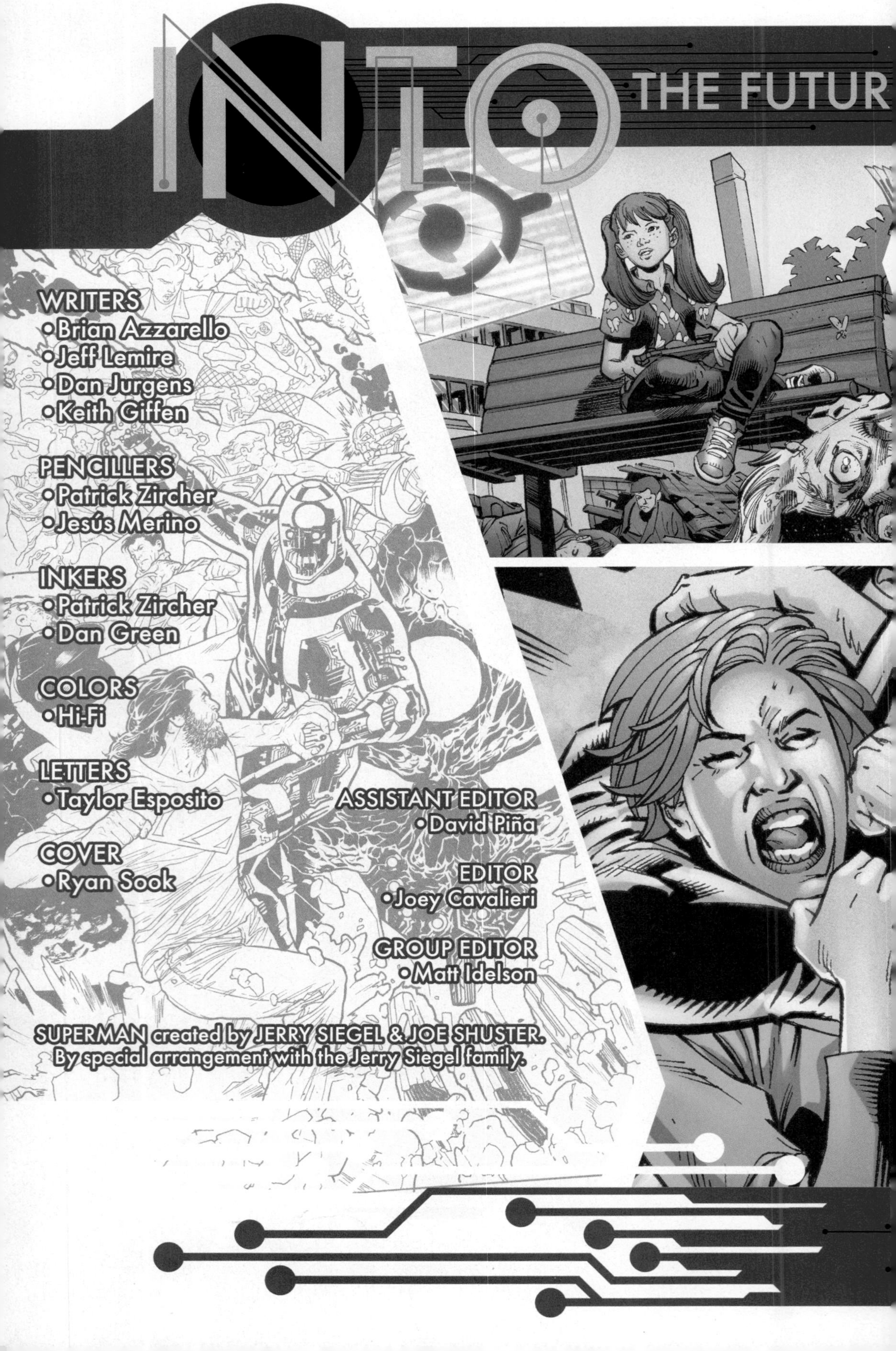

WRITERS
- Brian Azzarello
- Jeff Lemire
- Dan Jurgens
- Keith Giffen

PENCILLERS
- Patrick Zircher
- Jesús Merino

INKERS
- Patrick Zircher
- Dan Green

COLORS
- Hi-Fi

LETTERS
- Taylor Esposito

COVER
- Ryan Sook

ASSISTANT EDITOR
- David Piña

EDITOR
- Joey Cavalieri

GROUP EDITOR
- Matt Idelson

SUPERMAN created by JERRY SIEGEL & JOE SHUSTER.
By special arrangement with the Jerry Siegel family.

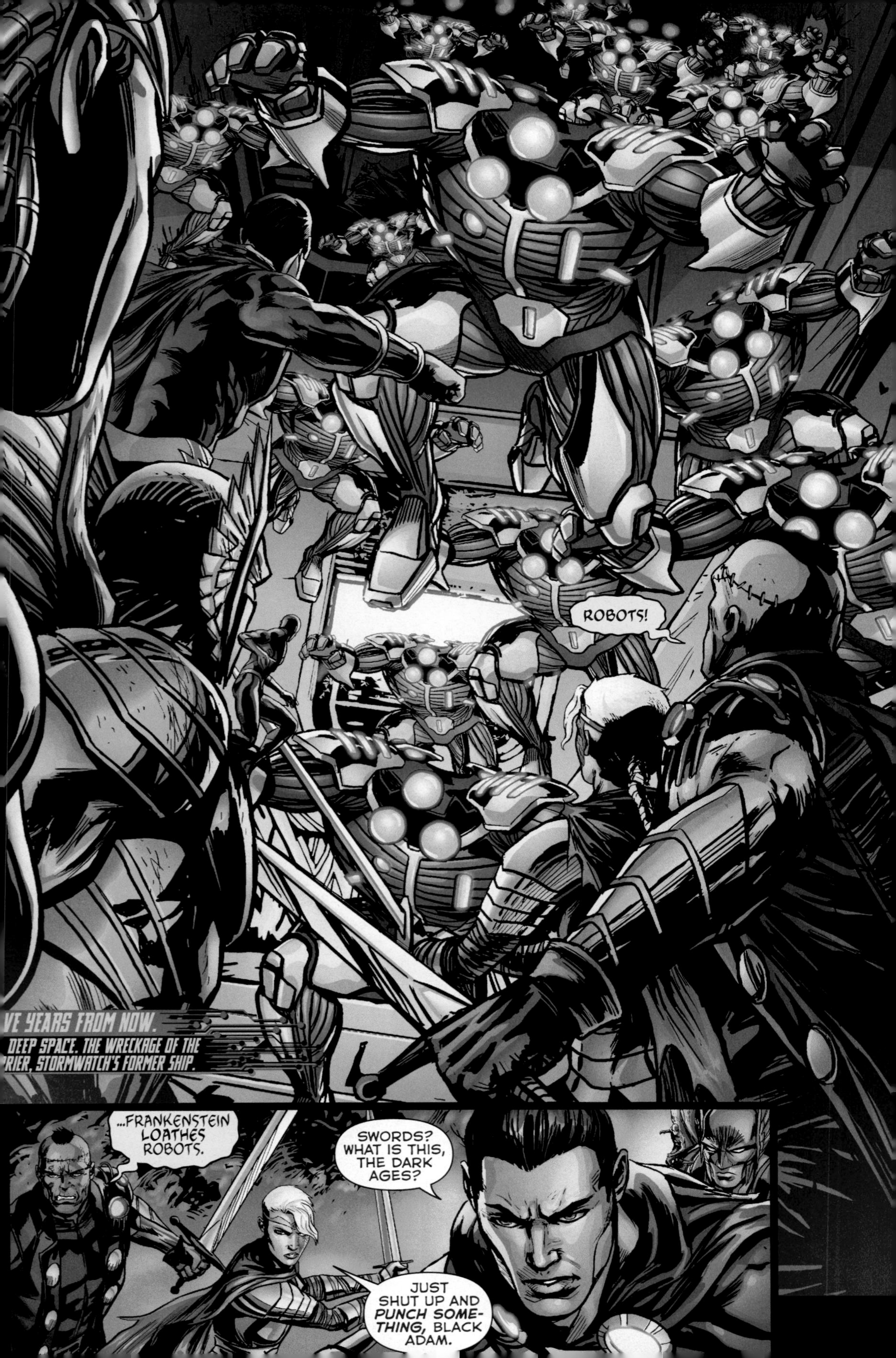
VE YEARS FROM NOW.
DEEP SPACE. THE WRECKAGE OF THE
RIER, STORMWATCH'S FORMER SHIP.
ROBOTS!
...FRANKENSTEIN LOATHES ROBOTS.
SWORDS? WHAT IS THIS, THE DARK AGES?
JUST SHUT UP AND *PUNCH SOMETHING,* BLACK ADAM.

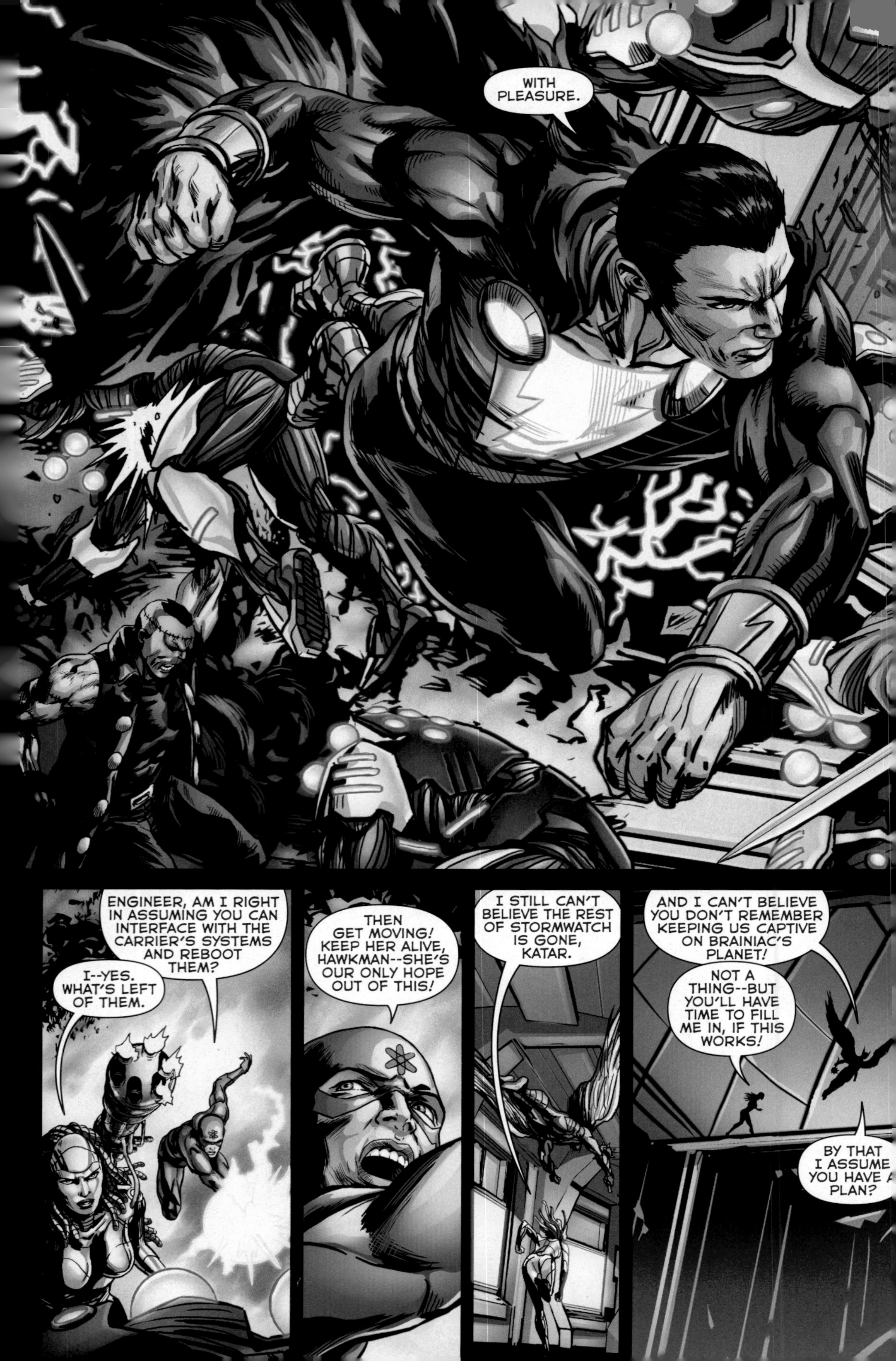
WITH PLEASURE.
ENGINEER, AM I RIGHT IN ASSUMING YOU CAN INTERFACE WITH THE CARRIER'S SYSTEMS AND REBOOT THEM?
I--YES. WHAT'S LEFT OF THEM.
THEN GET MOVING! KEEP HER ALIVE, HAWKMAN--SHE'S OUR ONLY HOPE OUT OF THIS!
I STILL CAN'T BELIEVE THE REST OF STORMWATCH IS GONE, KATAR.
AND I CAN'T BELIEVE YOU DON'T REMEMBER KEEPING US CAPTIVE ON BRAINIAC'S PLANET!
NOT A THING--BUT YOU'LL HAVE TIME TO FILL ME IN, IF THIS WORKS!
BY THAT I ASSUME YOU HAVE A PLAN?

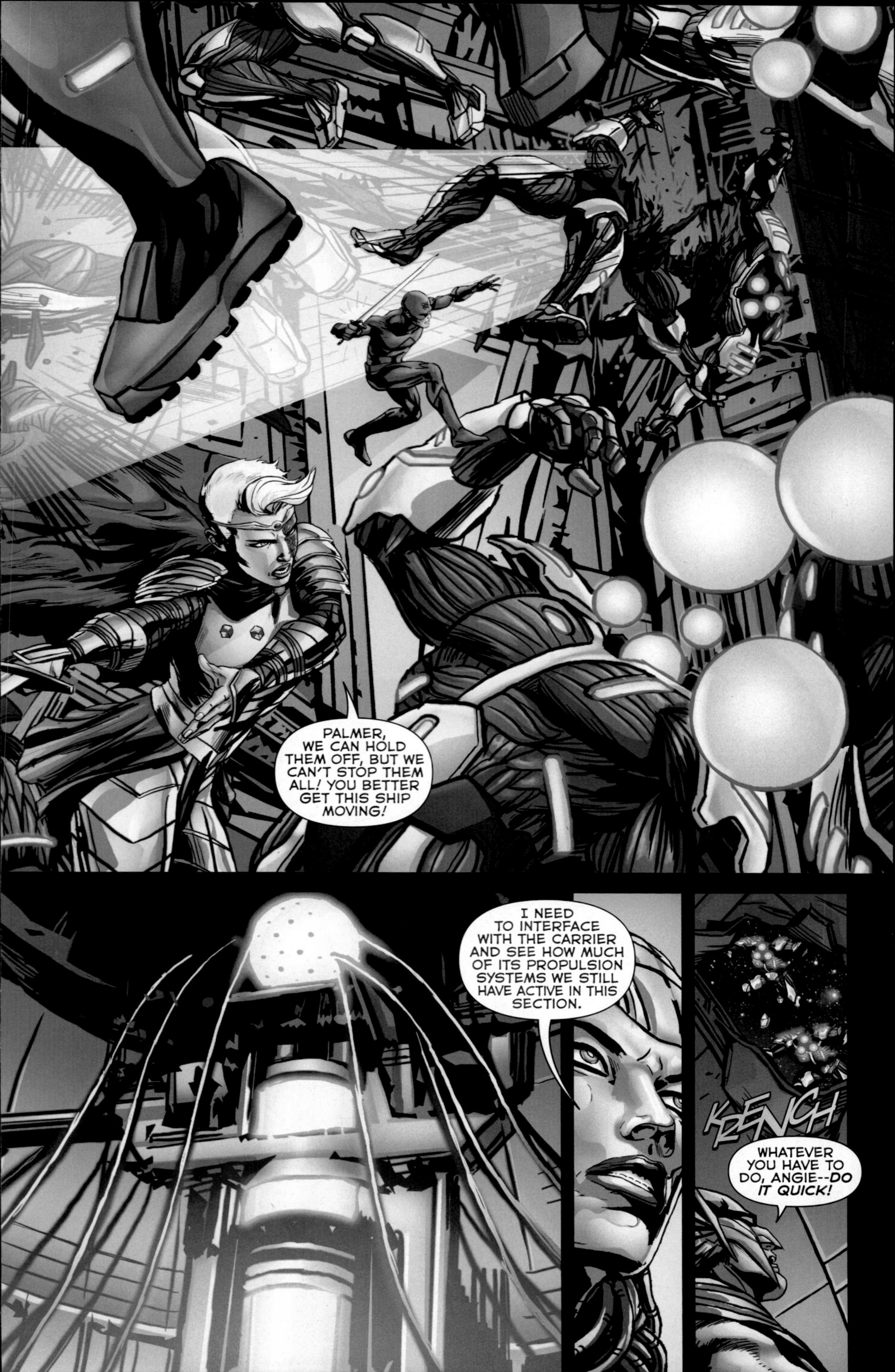
PALMER, WE CAN HOLD THEM OFF, BUT WE CAN'T STOP THEM ALL! YOU BETTER GET THIS SHIP MOVING!
I NEED TO INTERFACE WITH THE CARRIER AND SEE HOW MUCH OF ITS PROPULSION SYSTEMS WE STILL HAVE ACTIVE IN THIS SECTION.
KRENCH
WHATEVER YOU HAVE TO DO, ANGIE--*DO IT QUICK!*

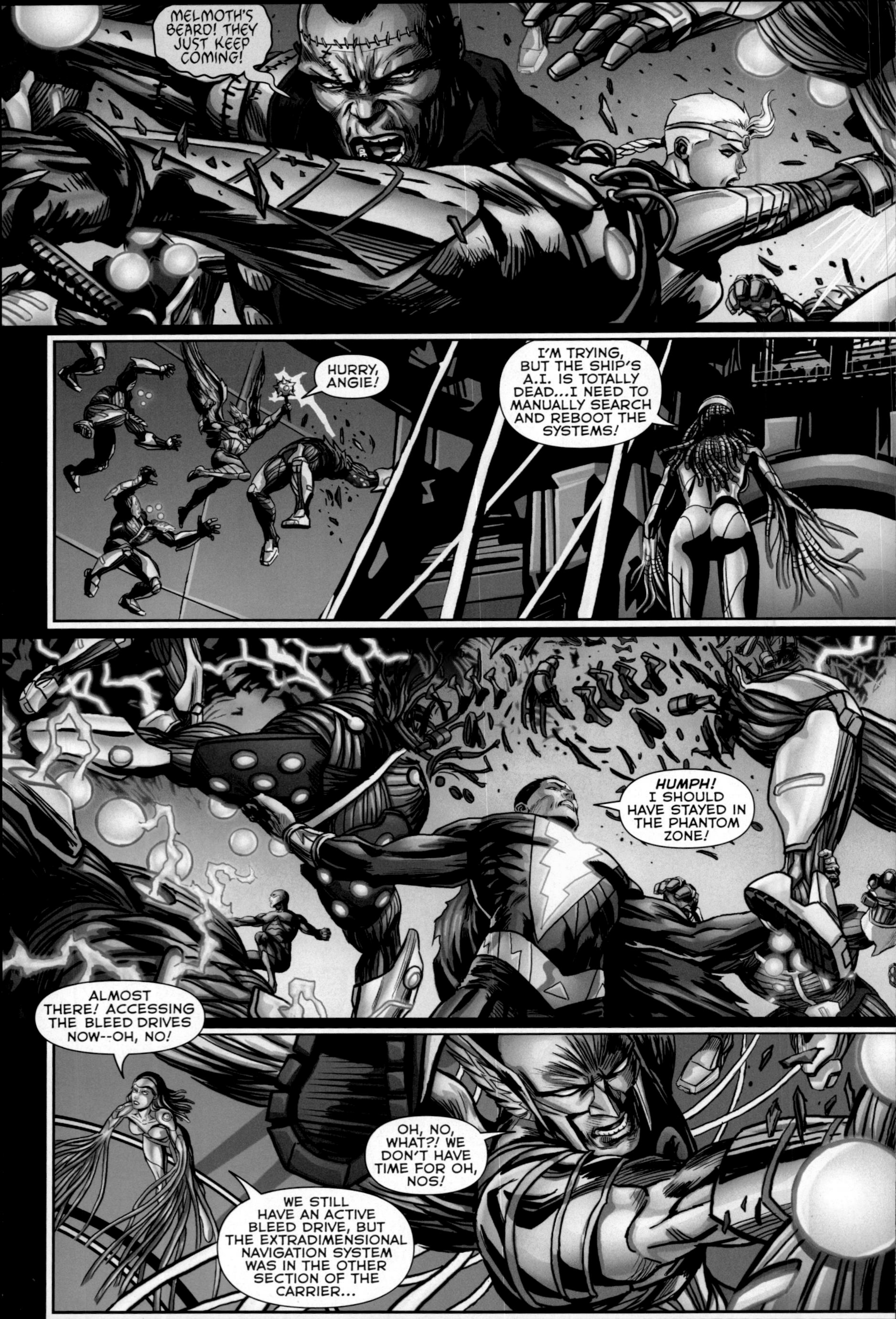
MELMOTH'S BEARD! THEY JUST KEEP COMING!
HURRY, ANGIE!
I'M TRYING, BUT THE SHIP'S A.I. IS TOTALLY DEAD...I NEED TO MANUALLY SEARCH AND REBOOT THE SYSTEMS!
HUMPH! I SHOULD HAVE STAYED IN THE PHANTOM ZONE!
ALMOST THERE! ACCESSING THE BLEED DRIVES NOW--OH, NO!
OH, NO, WHAT?! WE DON'T HAVE TIME FOR OH, NOS!
WE STILL HAVE AN ACTIVE BLEED DRIVE, BUT THE EXTRADIMENSIONAL NAVIGATION SYSTEM WAS IN THE OTHER SECTION OF THE CARRIER...

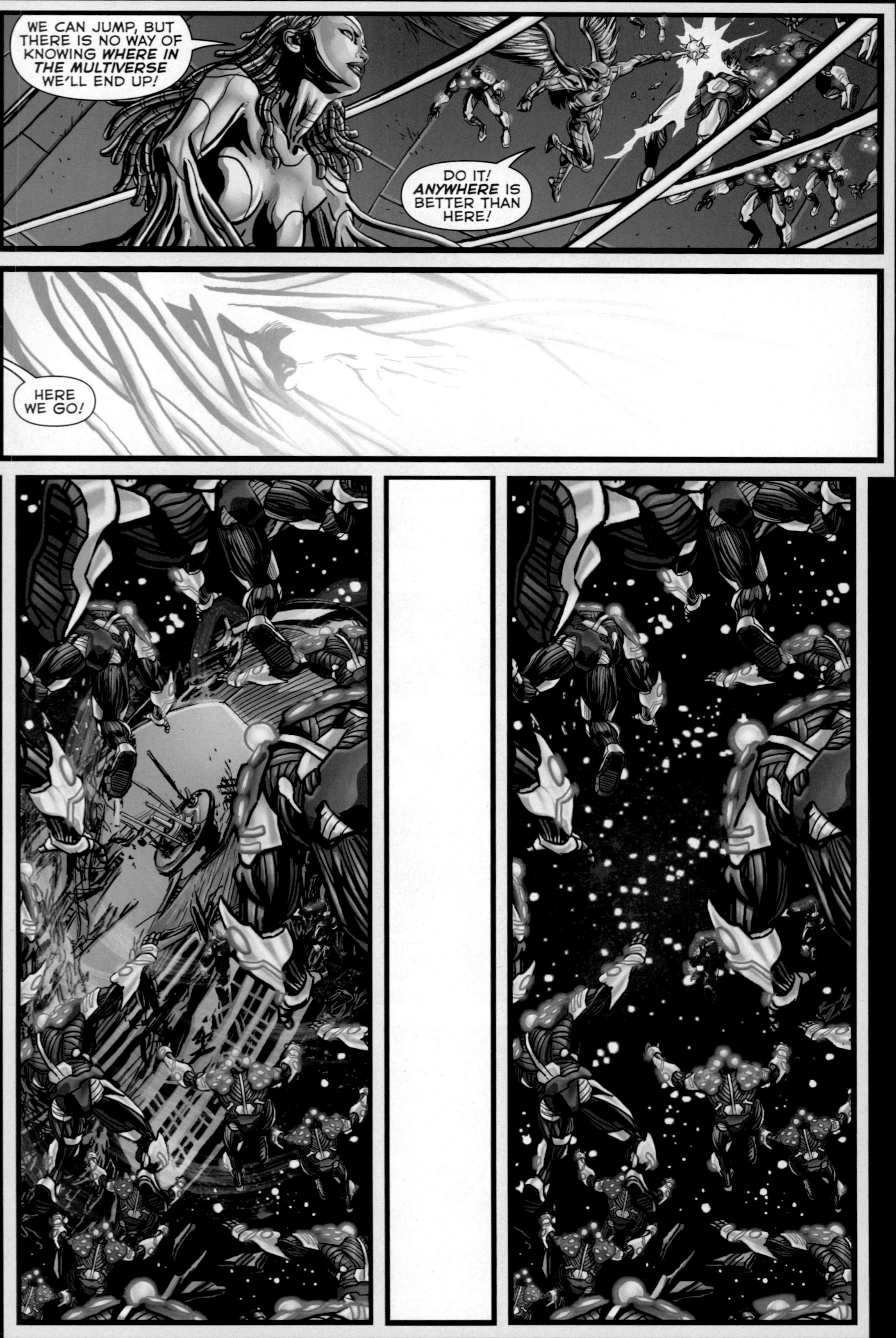
WE CAN JUMP, BUT THERE IS NO WAY OF KNOWING *WHERE IN THE MULTIVERSE* WE'LL END UP!
DO IT! *ANYWHERE* IS BETTER THAN HERE!
HERE WE GO!

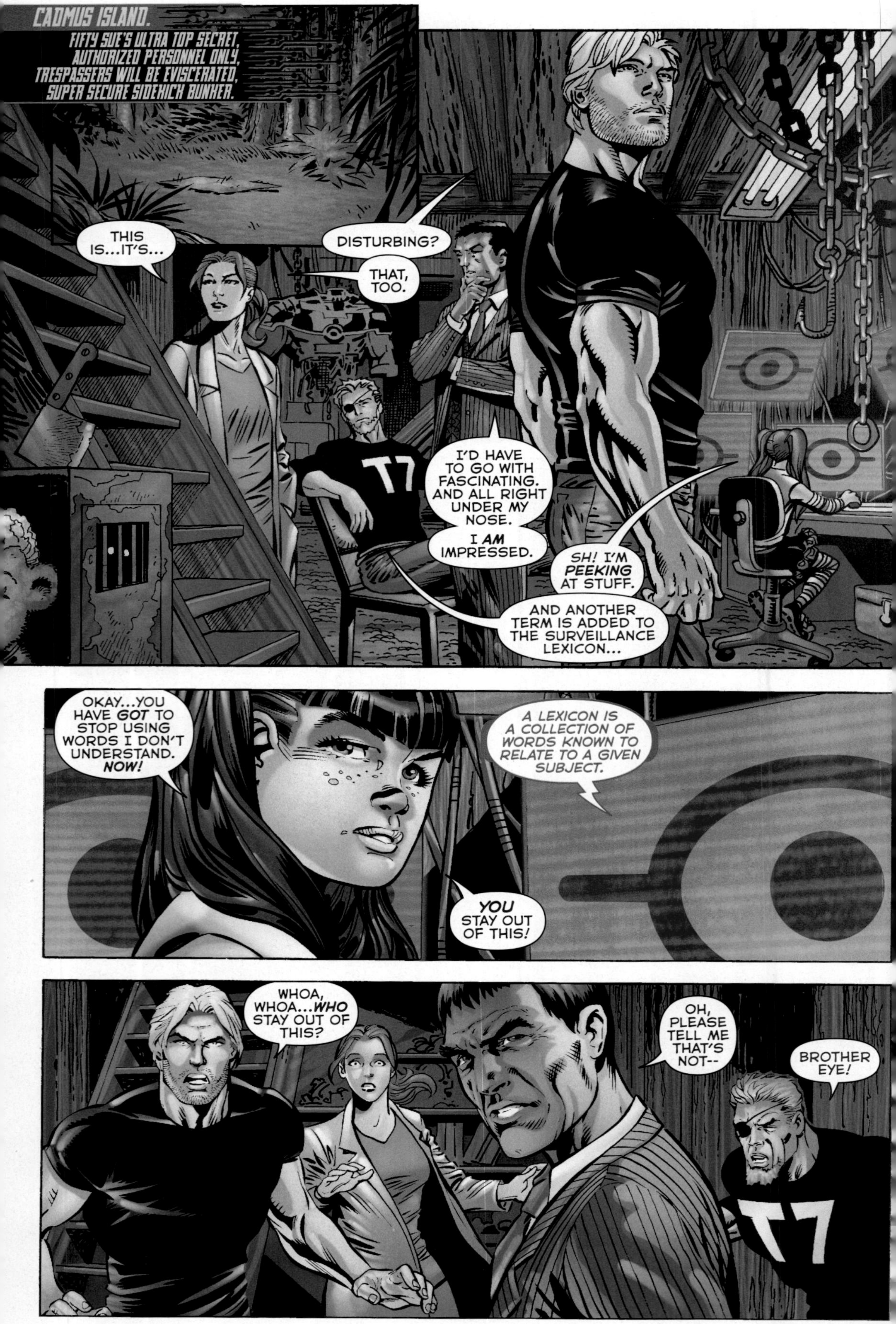
CADMUS ISLAND.
FIFTY SUE'S ULTRA TOP SECRET, AUTHORIZED PERSONNEL ONLY, TRESPASSERS WILL BE EVISCERATED, SUPER SECURE SIDEKICK BUNKER.
THIS IS...IT'S...
DISTURBING?
THAT, TOO.
I'D HAVE TO GO WITH FASCINATING. AND ALL RIGHT UNDER MY NOSE.
I AM IMPRESSED.
SH! I'M PEEKING AT STUFF.
AND ANOTHER TERM IS ADDED TO THE SURVEILLANCE LEXICON...
OKAY...YOU HAVE GOT TO STOP USING WORDS I DON'T UNDERSTAND. NOW!
A LEXICON IS A COLLECTION OF WORDS KNOWN TO RELATE TO A GIVEN SUBJECT.
YOU STAY OUT OF THIS!
WHOA, WHOA...WHO STAY OUT OF THIS?
OH, PLEASE TELL ME THAT'S NOT--
BROTHER EYE!

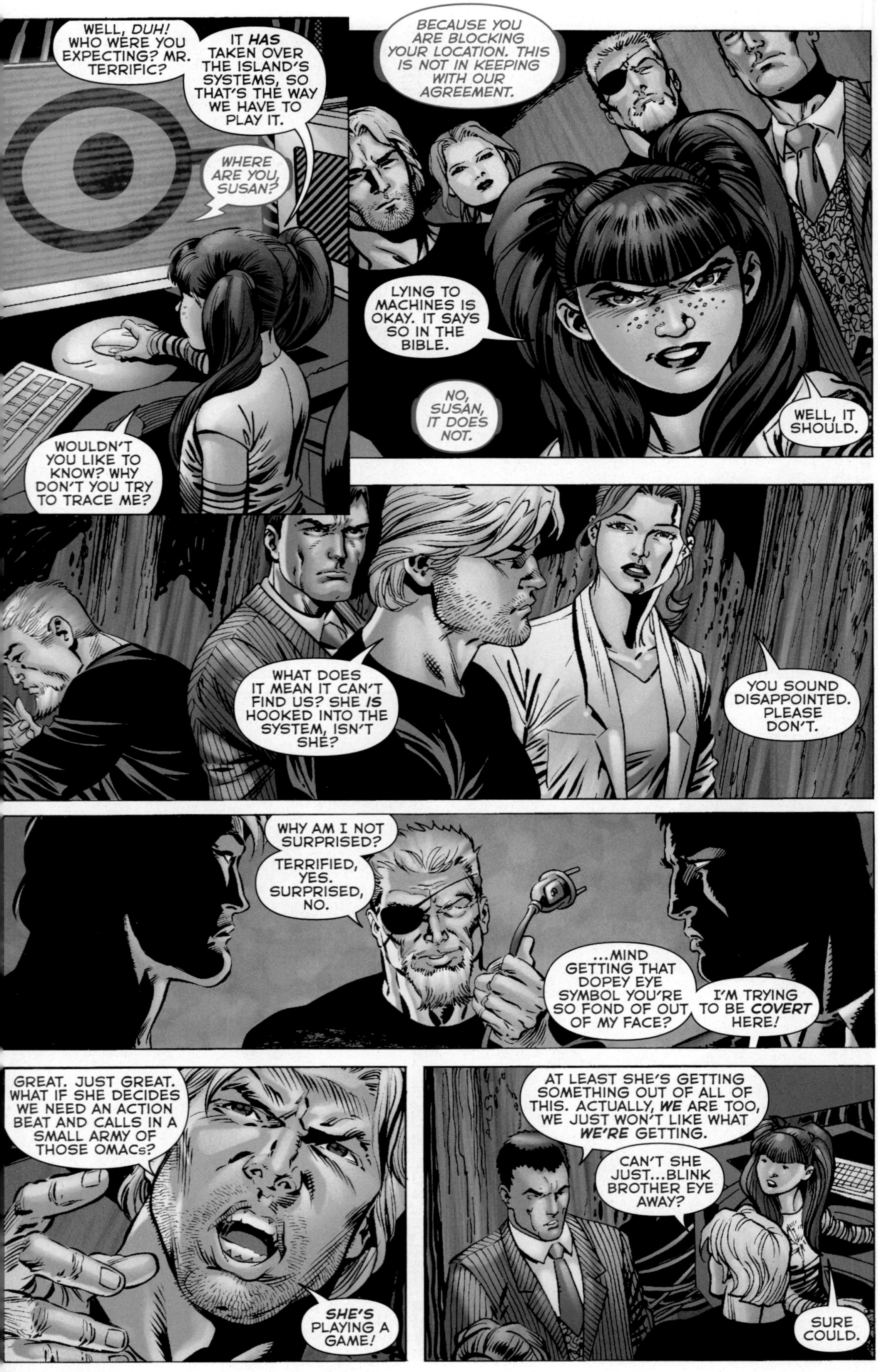
WELL, *DUH!* WHO WERE YOU EXPECTING? MR. TERRIFIC?
IT *HAS* TAKEN OVER THE ISLAND'S SYSTEMS, SO THAT'S THE WAY WE HAVE TO PLAY IT.
WHERE ARE YOU, SUSAN?
WOULDN'T YOU LIKE TO KNOW? WHY DON'T YOU TRY TO TRACE ME?
BECAUSE YOU ARE BLOCKING YOUR LOCATION. THIS IS NOT IN KEEPING WITH OUR AGREEMENT.
LYING TO MACHINES IS OKAY. IT SAYS SO IN THE BIBLE.
NO, SUSAN, IT DOES NOT.
WELL, IT SHOULD.
WHAT DOES IT MEAN IT CAN'T FIND US? SHE *IS* HOOKED INTO THE SYSTEM, ISN'T SHE?
YOU SOUND DISAPPOINTED. PLEASE DON'T.
WHY AM I NOT SURPRISED?
TERRIFIED, YES. SURPRISED, NO.
...MIND GETTING THAT DOPEY EYE SYMBOL YOU'RE SO FOND OF OUT OF MY FACE?
I'M TRYING TO BE *COVERT* HERE!
GREAT. JUST GREAT. WHAT IF SHE DECIDES WE NEED AN ACTION BEAT AND CALLS IN A SMALL ARMY OF THOSE OMACs?
SHE'S PLAYING A GAME!
AT LEAST SHE'S GETTING SOMETHING OUT OF ALL OF THIS. ACTUALLY, *WE* ARE TOO, WE JUST WON'T LIKE WHAT *WE'RE* GETTING.
CAN'T SHE JUST...BLINK BROTHER EYE AWAY?
SURE COULD.

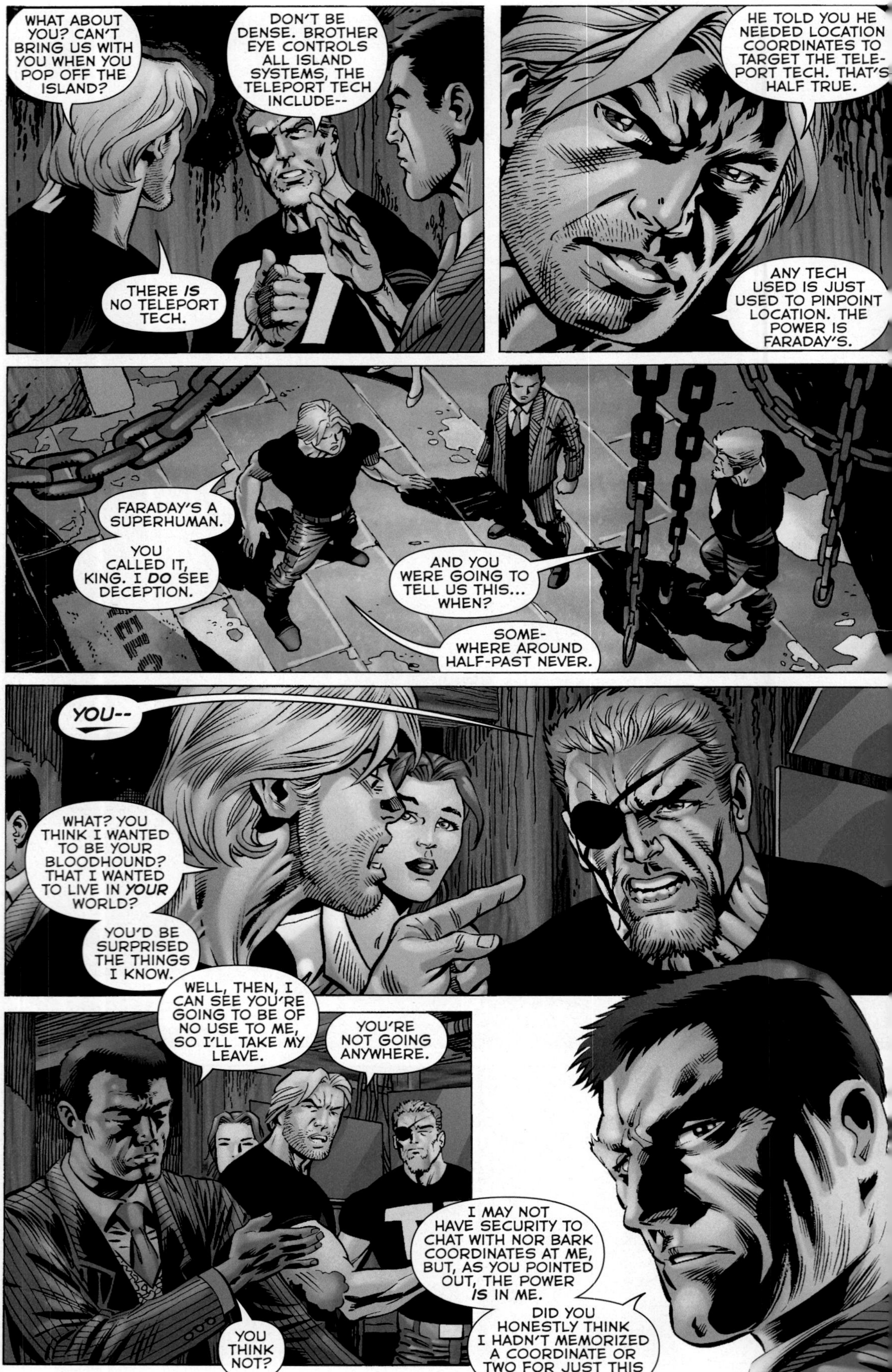
WHAT ABOUT YOU? CAN'T BRING US WITH YOU WHEN YOU POP OFF THE ISLAND?
DON'T BE DENSE. BROTHER EYE CONTROLS ALL ISLAND SYSTEMS, THE TELEPORT TECH INCLUDE--
THERE IS NO TELEPORT TECH.
HE TOLD YOU HE NEEDED LOCATION COORDINATES TO TARGET THE TELE-PORT TECH. THAT'S HALF TRUE.
ANY TECH USED IS JUST USED TO PINPOINT LOCATION. THE POWER IS FARADAY'S.
FARADAY'S A SUPERHUMAN.
YOU CALLED IT, KING. I DO SEE DECEPTION.
AND YOU WERE GOING TO TELL US THIS... WHEN?
SOME-WHERE AROUND HALF-PAST NEVER.
YOU--
WHAT? YOU THINK I WANTED TO BE YOUR BLOODHOUND? THAT I WANTED TO LIVE IN YOUR WORLD?
YOU'D BE SURPRISED THE THINGS I KNOW.
WELL, THEN, I CAN SEE YOU'RE GOING TO BE OF NO USE TO ME, SO I'LL TAKE MY LEAVE.
YOU'RE NOT GOING ANYWHERE.
YOU THINK NOT?
I MAY NOT HAVE SECURITY TO CHAT WITH NOR BARK COORDINATES AT ME, BUT, AS YOU POINTED OUT, THE POWER IS IN ME.
DID YOU HONESTLY THINK I HADN'T MEMORIZED A COORDINATE OR TWO FOR JUST THIS EVENTUALITY?

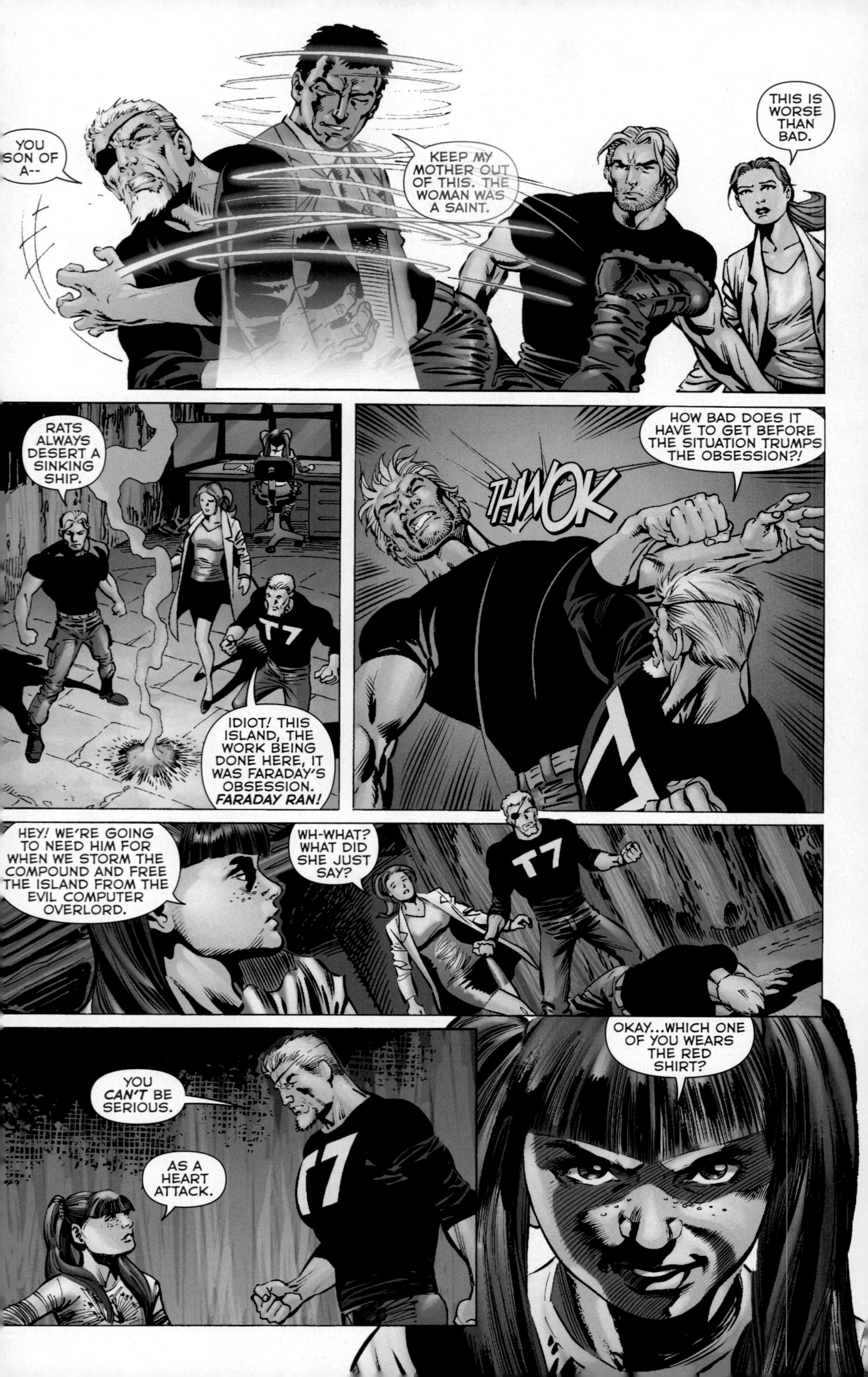
YOU SON OF A--
KEEP MY MOTHER OUT OF THIS. THE WOMAN WAS A SAINT.
THIS IS WORSE THAN BAD.
RATS ALWAYS DESERT A SINKING SHIP.
IDIOT! THIS ISLAND, THE WORK BEING DONE HERE, IT WAS FARADAY'S OBSESSION. FARADAY RAN!
HOW BAD DOES IT HAVE TO GET BEFORE THE SITUATION TRUMPS THE OBSESSION?!
THWOK
HEY! WE'RE GOING TO NEED HIM FOR WHEN WE STORM THE COMPOUND AND FREE THE ISLAND FROM THE EVIL COMPUTER OVERLORD.
WH-WHAT? WHAT DID SHE JUST SAY?
OKAY...WHICH ONE OF YOU WEARS THE RED SHIRT?
YOU CAN'T BE SERIOUS.
AS A HEART ATTACK.

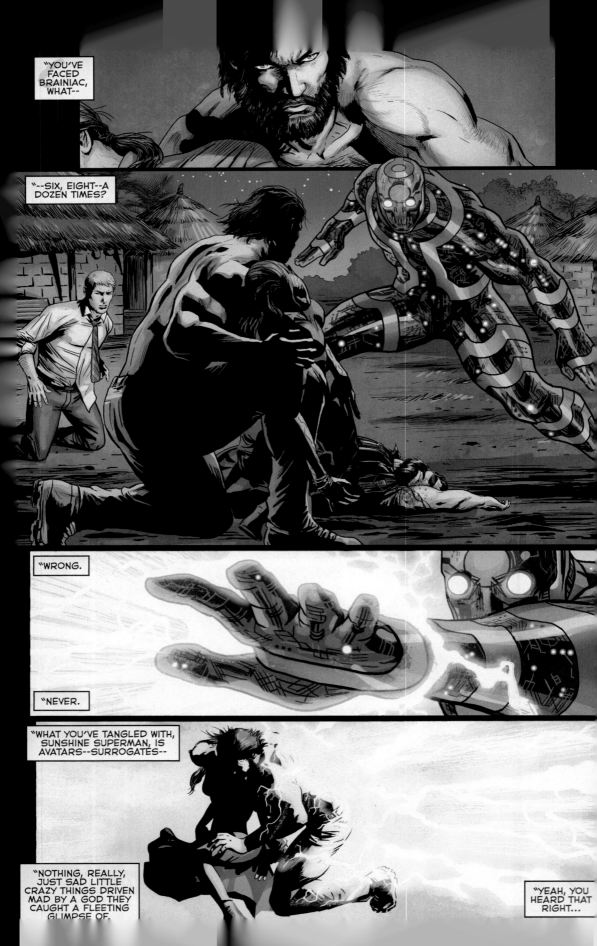

"YOU'VE FACED BRAINIAC, WHAT--

"--SIX, EIGHT--A DOZEN TIMES?

"WRONG.

"NEVER.

"WHAT YOU'VE TANGLED WITH, SUNSHINE SUPERMAN, IS AVATARS--SURROGATES--

"NOTHING, REALLY, JUST SAD LITTLE CRAZY THINGS DRIVEN MAD BY A GOD THEY CAUGHT A FLEETING GLIMPSE OF.

"YEAH, YOU HEARD THAT RIGHT...

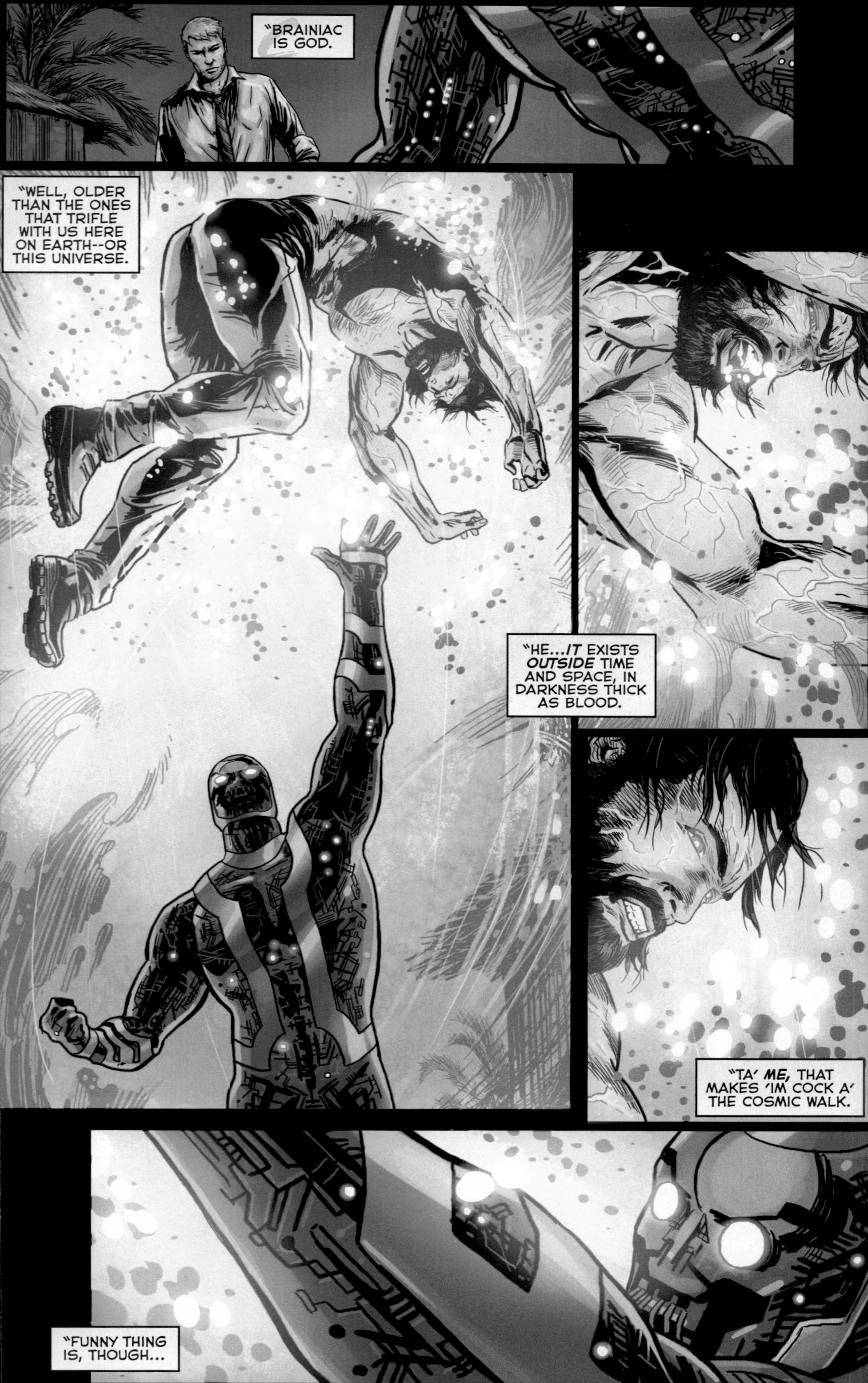
"BRAINIAC IS GOD.
"WELL, OLDER THAN THE ONES THAT TRIFLE WITH US HERE ON EARTH--OR THIS UNIVERSE.
"HE...IT EXISTS OUTSIDE TIME AND SPACE, IN DARKNESS THICK AS BLOOD.
"TA' ME, THAT MAKES 'IM COCK A' THE COSMIC WALK.
"FUNNY THING IS, THOUGH...

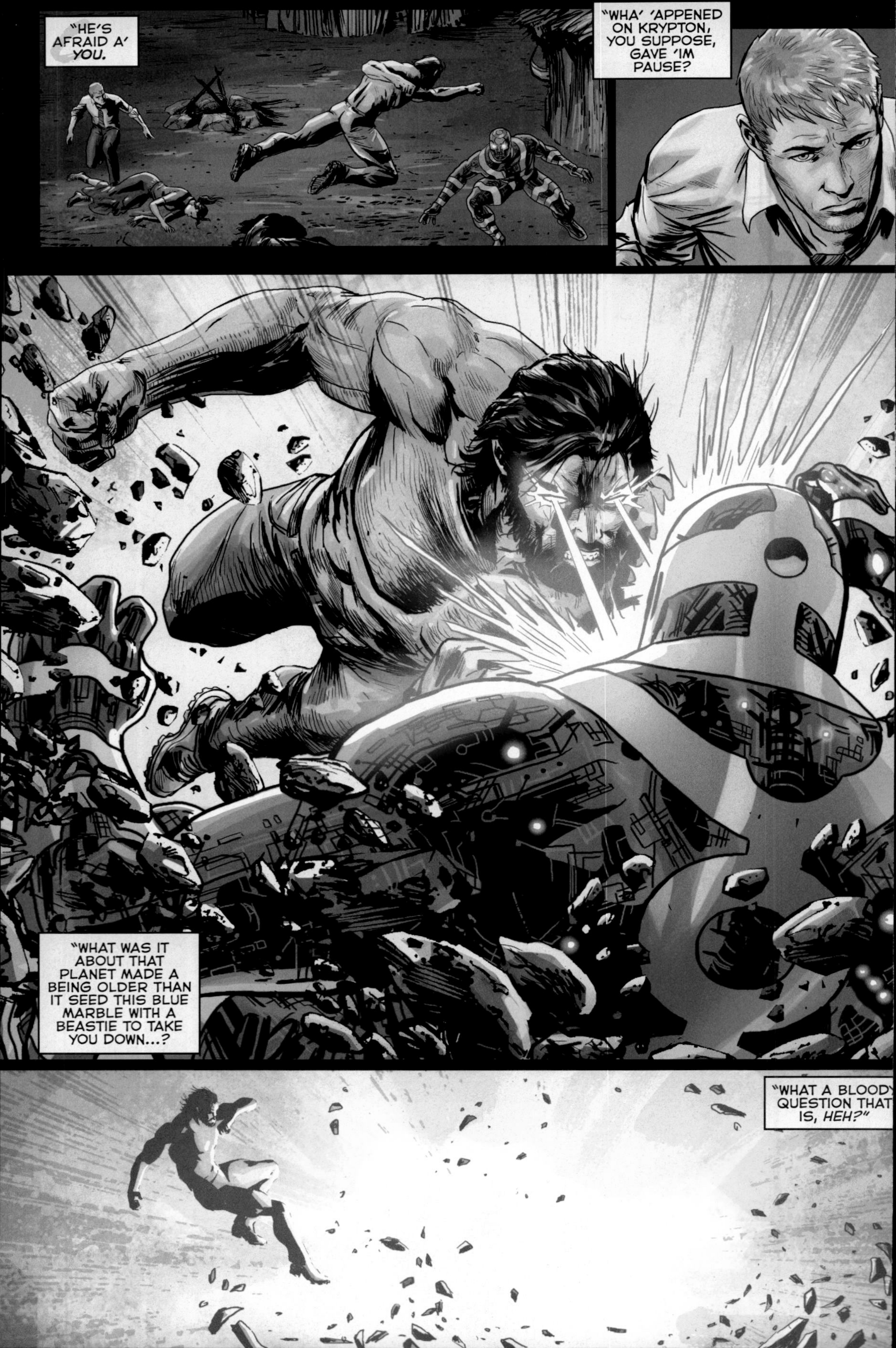
"HE'S AFRAID A' YOU.
"WHA' 'APPENED ON KRYPTON, YOU SUPPOSE, GAVE 'IM PAUSE?
"WHAT WAS IT ABOUT THAT PLANET MADE A BEING OLDER THAN IT SEED THIS BLUE MARBLE WITH A BEASTIE TO TAKE YOU DOWN...?
"WHAT A BLOODY QUESTION THAT IS, HEH?"

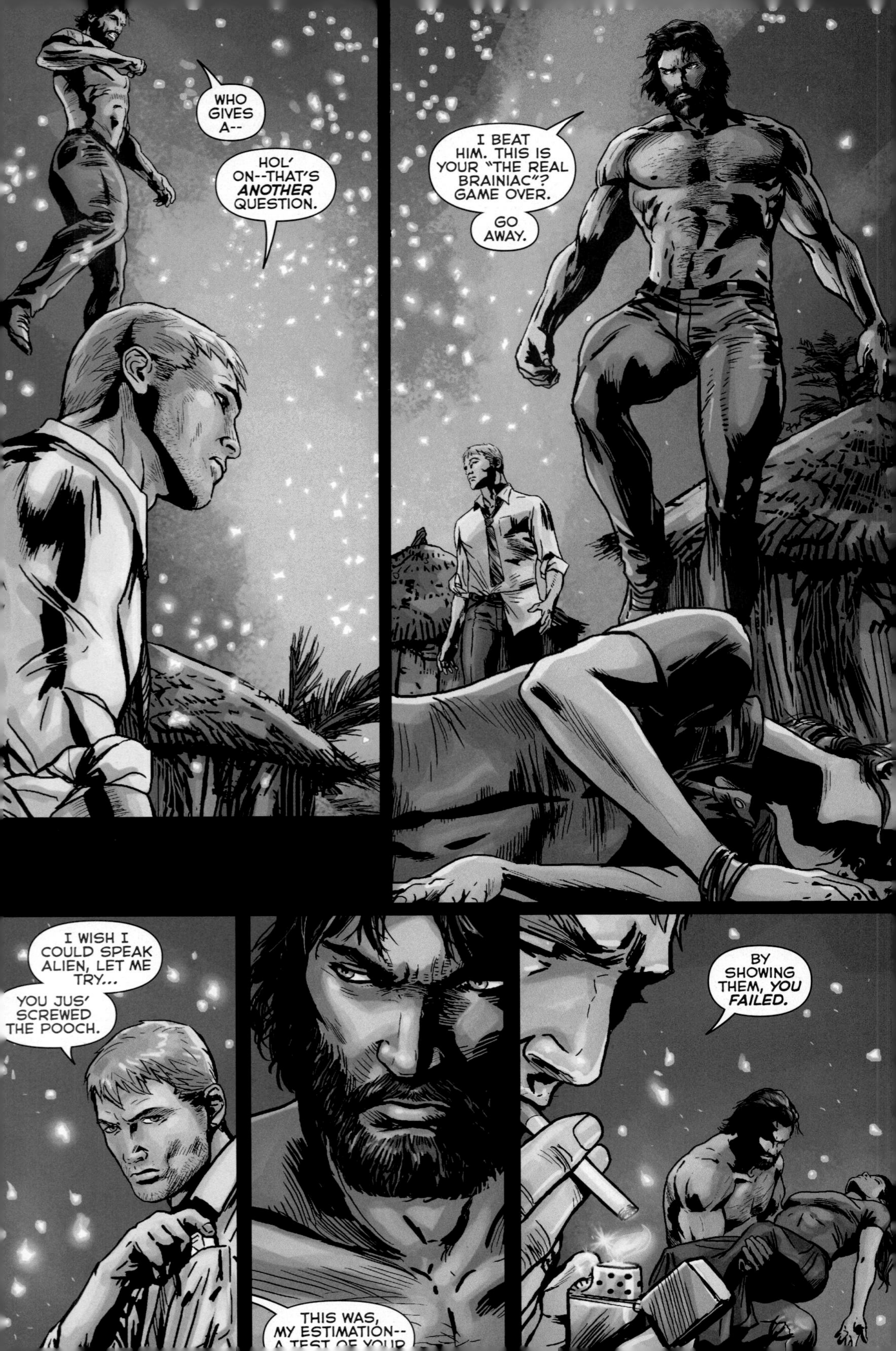
WHO GIVES A--
HOL' ON--THAT'S ANOTHER QUESTION.
I BEAT HIM. THIS IS YOUR "THE REAL BRAINIAC"? GAME OVER.
GO AWAY.
I WISH I COULD SPEAK ALIEN, LET ME TRY...
YOU JUS' SCREWED THE POOCH.
THIS WAS, MY ESTIMATION--
BY SHOWING THEM, YOU FAILED.

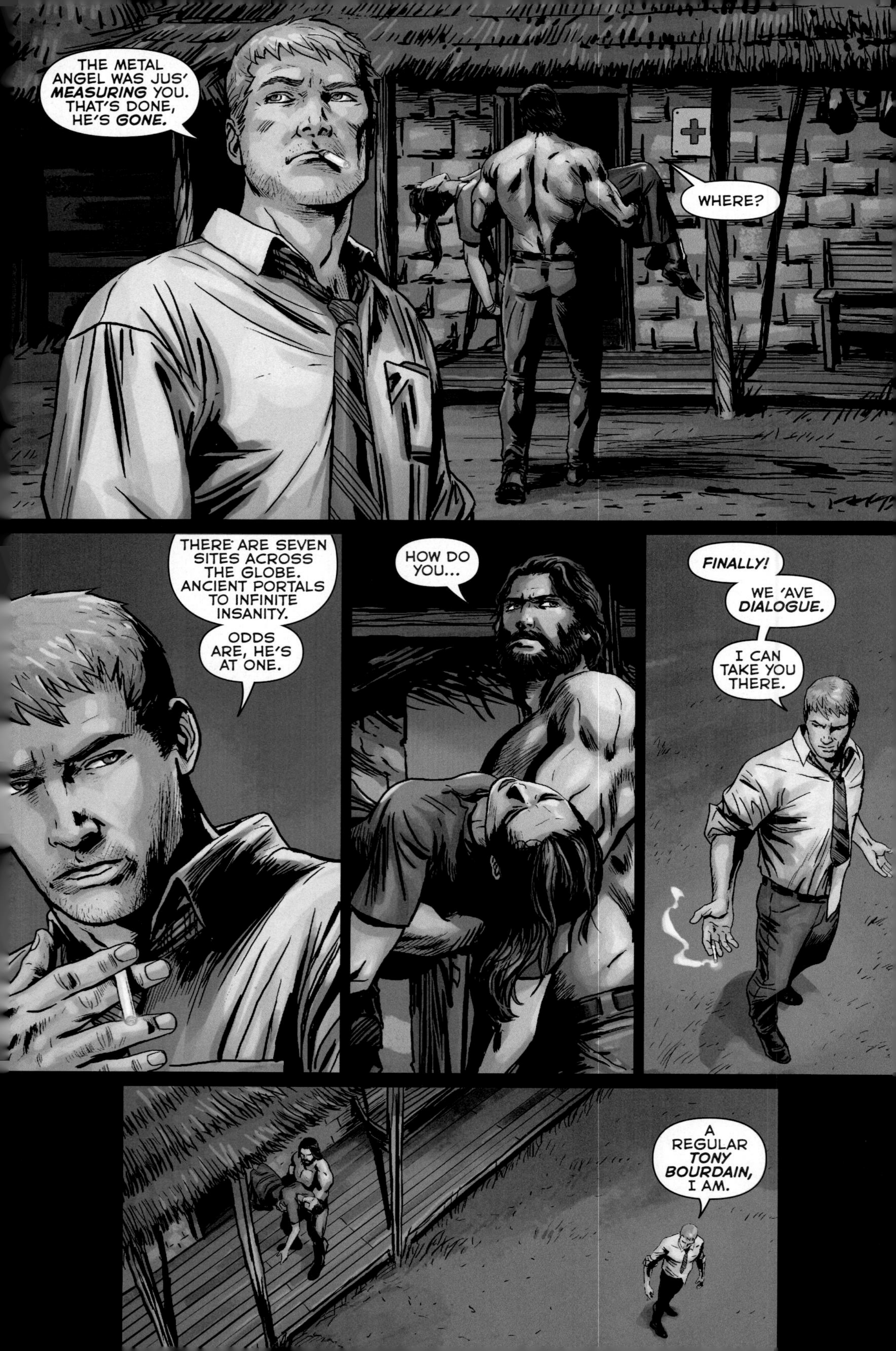
THE METAL ANGEL WAS JUS' *MEASURING* YOU. THAT'S DONE, HE'S *GONE.*
WHERE?
THERE ARE SEVEN SITES ACROSS THE GLOBE. ANCIENT PORTALS TO INFINITE INSANITY.
ODDS ARE, HE'S AT ONE.
HOW DO YOU...
FINALLY!
WE 'AVE *DIALOGUE.*
I CAN TAKE YOU THERE.
A REGULAR *TONY BOURDAIN,* I AM.

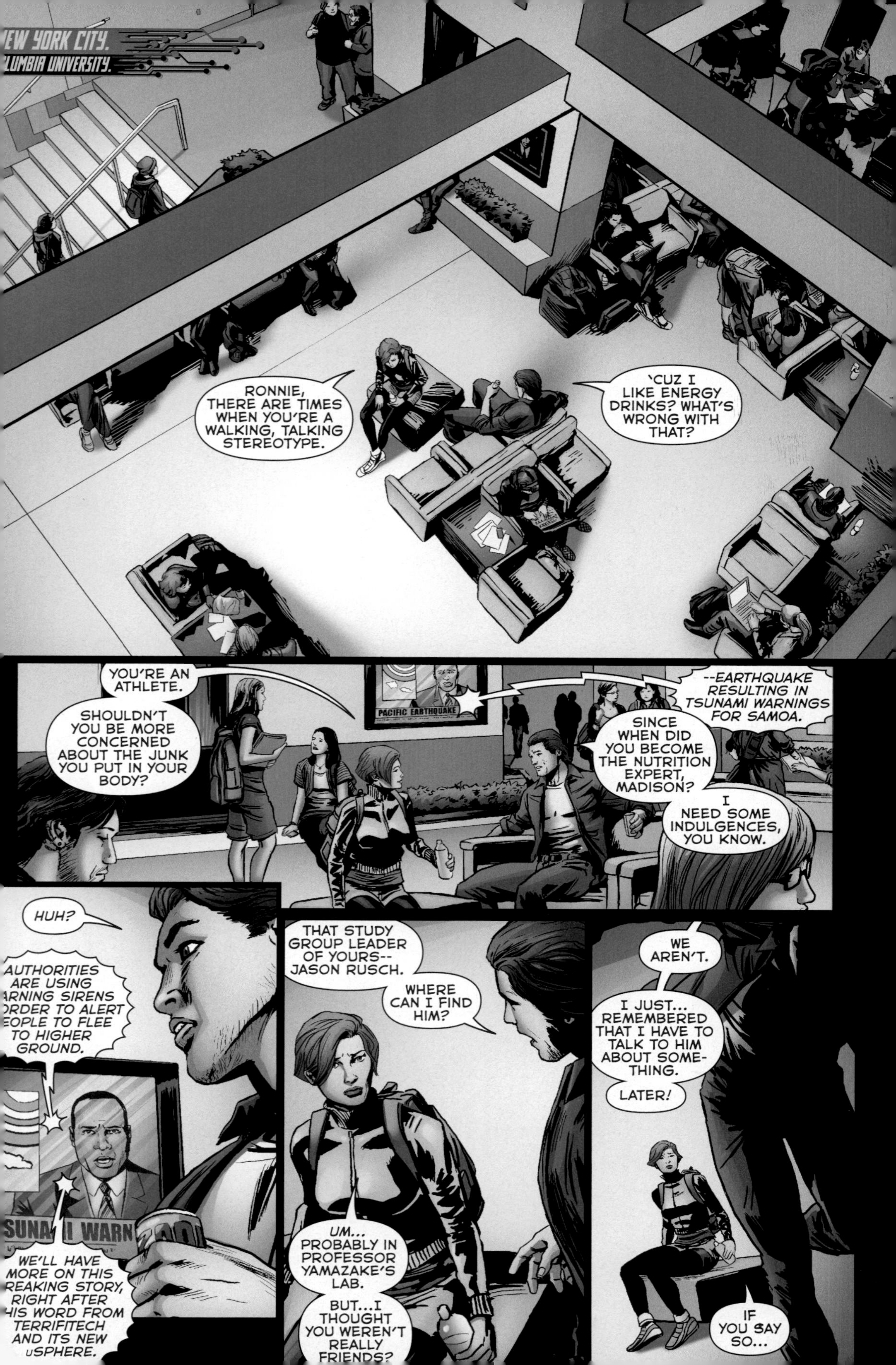
EW YORK CITY.
LUMBIA UNIVERSITY.
RONNIE, THERE ARE TIMES WHEN YOU'RE A WALKING, TALKING STEREOTYPE.
'CUZ I LIKE ENERGY DRINKS? WHAT'S WRONG WITH THAT?
YOU'RE AN ATHLETE.
SHOULDN'T YOU BE MORE CONCERNED ABOUT THE JUNK YOU PUT IN YOUR BODY?
PACIFIC EARTHQUAKE
--EARTHQUAKE RESULTING IN TSUNAMI WARNINGS FOR SAMOA.
SINCE WHEN DID YOU BECOME THE NUTRITION EXPERT, MADISON?
I NEED SOME INDULGENCES, YOU KNOW.
HUH?
AUTHORITIES ARE USING ARNING SIRENS ORDER TO ALERT EOPLE TO FLEE TO HIGHER GROUND.
SUNA I WARN
WE'LL HAVE MORE ON THIS REAKING STORY, RIGHT AFTER HIS WORD FROM TERRIFITECH AND ITS NEW USPHERE.
THAT STUDY GROUP LEADER OF YOURS-- JASON RUSCH.
WHERE CAN I FIND HIM?
UM... PROBABLY IN PROFESSOR YAMAZAKE'S LAB.
BUT...I THOUGHT YOU WEREN'T REALLY FRIENDS?
WE AREN'T.
I JUST... REMEMBERED THAT I HAVE TO TALK TO HIM ABOUT SOME-THING.
LATER!
IF YOU SAY SO...

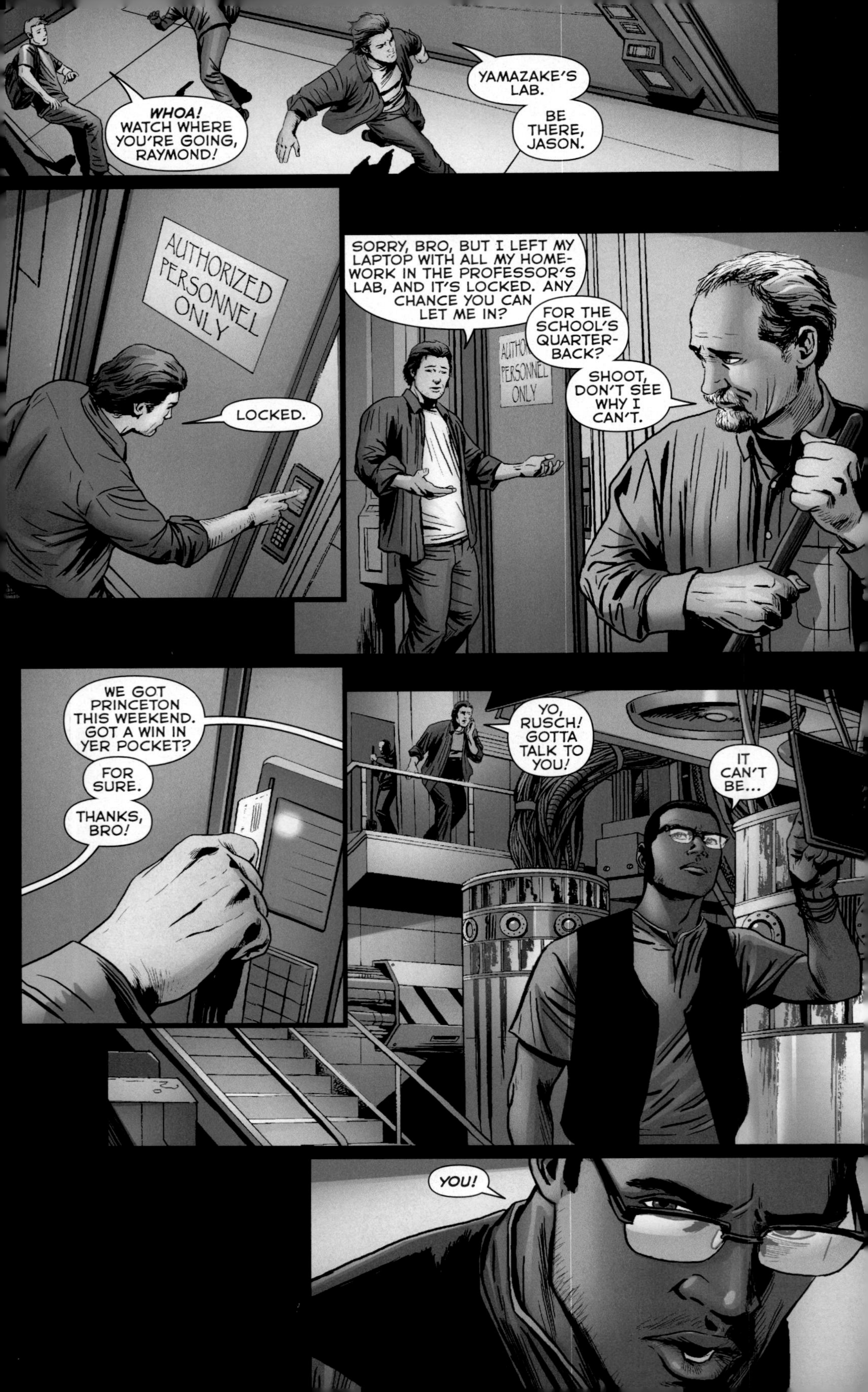
WHOA! WATCH WHERE YOU'RE GOING, RAYMOND!
YAMAZAKE'S LAB.
BE THERE, JASON.
AUTHORIZED PERSONNEL ONLY
LOCKED.
SORRY, BRO, BUT I LEFT MY LAPTOP WITH ALL MY HOME-WORK IN THE PROFESSOR'S LAB, AND IT'S LOCKED. ANY CHANCE YOU CAN LET ME IN?
FOR THE SCHOOL'S QUARTER-BACK?
SHOOT, DON'T SEE WHY I CAN'T.
AUTHORIZED PERSONNEL ONLY
WE GOT PRINCETON THIS WEEKEND. GOT A WIN IN YER POCKET?
FOR SURE.
THANKS, BRO!
YO, RUSCH! GOTTA TALK TO YOU!
IT CAN'T BE...
YOU!

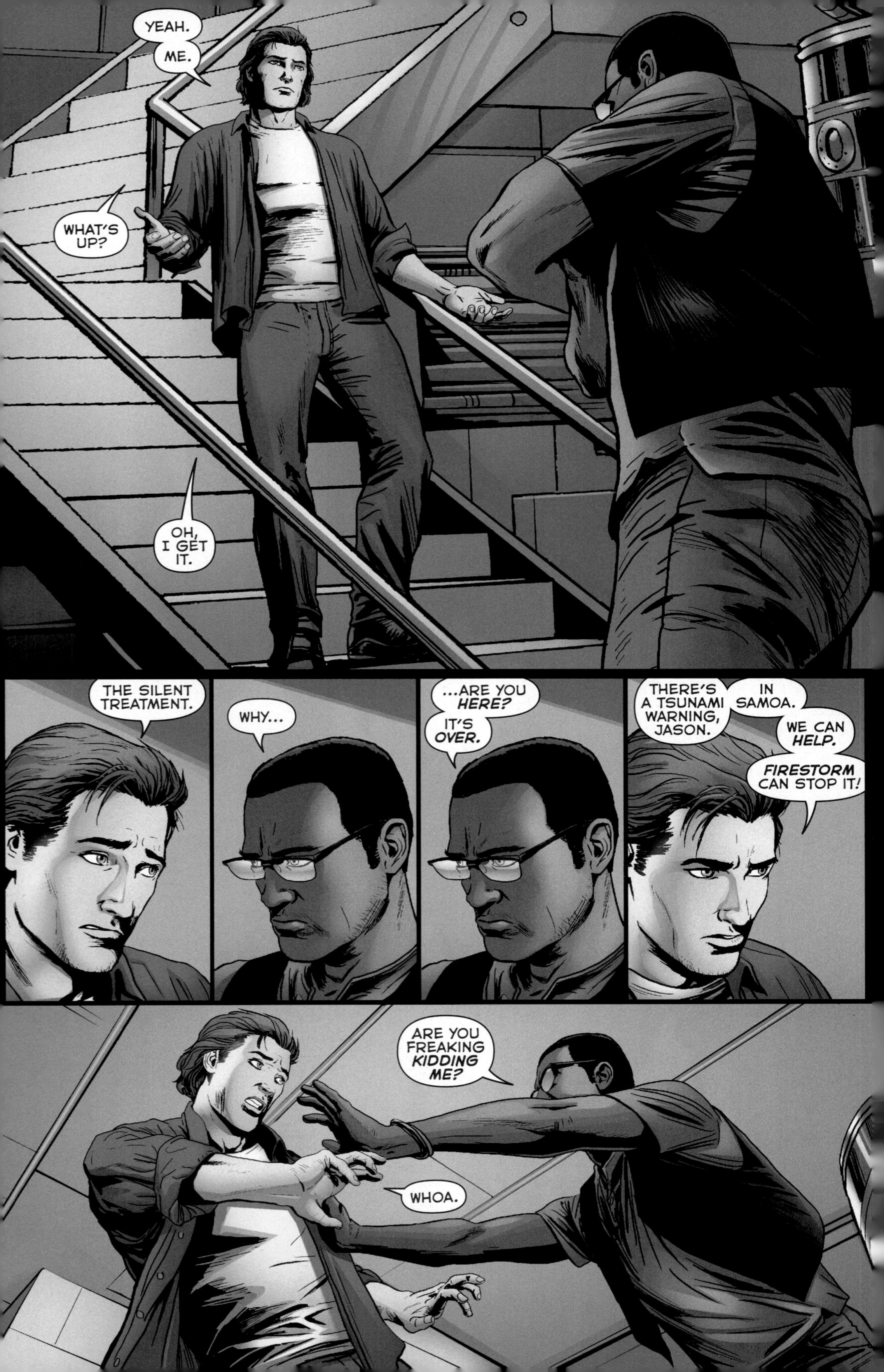
YEAH.
ME.
WHAT'S UP?
OH, I GET IT.
THE SILENT TREATMENT.
WHY...
...ARE YOU *HERE?*
IT'S *OVER.*
THERE'S A TSUNAMI WARNING, JASON.
IN SAMOA.
WE CAN *HELP.*
FIRESTORM CAN STOP IT!
ARE YOU FREAKING *KIDDING ME?*
WHOA.

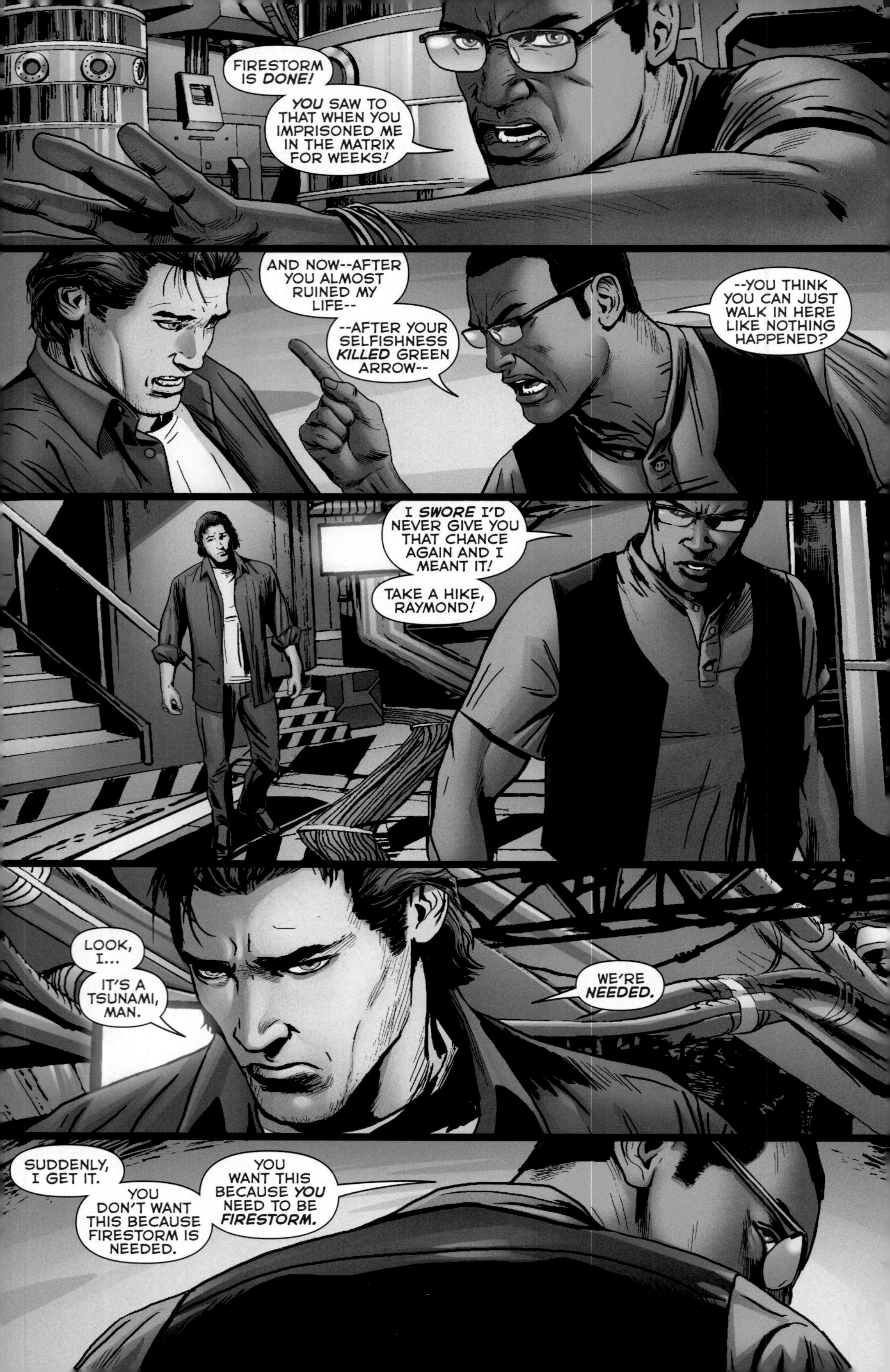
FIRESTORM IS *DONE!*
YOU SAW TO THAT WHEN YOU IMPRISONED ME IN THE MATRIX FOR WEEKS!
AND NOW--AFTER YOU ALMOST RUINED MY LIFE--
--AFTER YOUR SELFISHNESS *KILLED* GREEN ARROW--
--YOU THINK YOU CAN JUST WALK IN HERE LIKE NOTHING HAPPENED?
I *SWORE* I'D NEVER GIVE YOU THAT CHANCE AGAIN AND I MEANT IT!
TAKE A HIKE, RAYMOND!
LOOK, I...
IT'S A TSUNAMI, MAN.
WE'RE *NEEDED.*
SUDDENLY, I GET IT.
YOU DON'T WANT THIS BECAUSE FIRESTORM IS NEEDED.
YOU WANT THIS BECAUSE *YOU* NEED TO BE *FIRESTORM.*

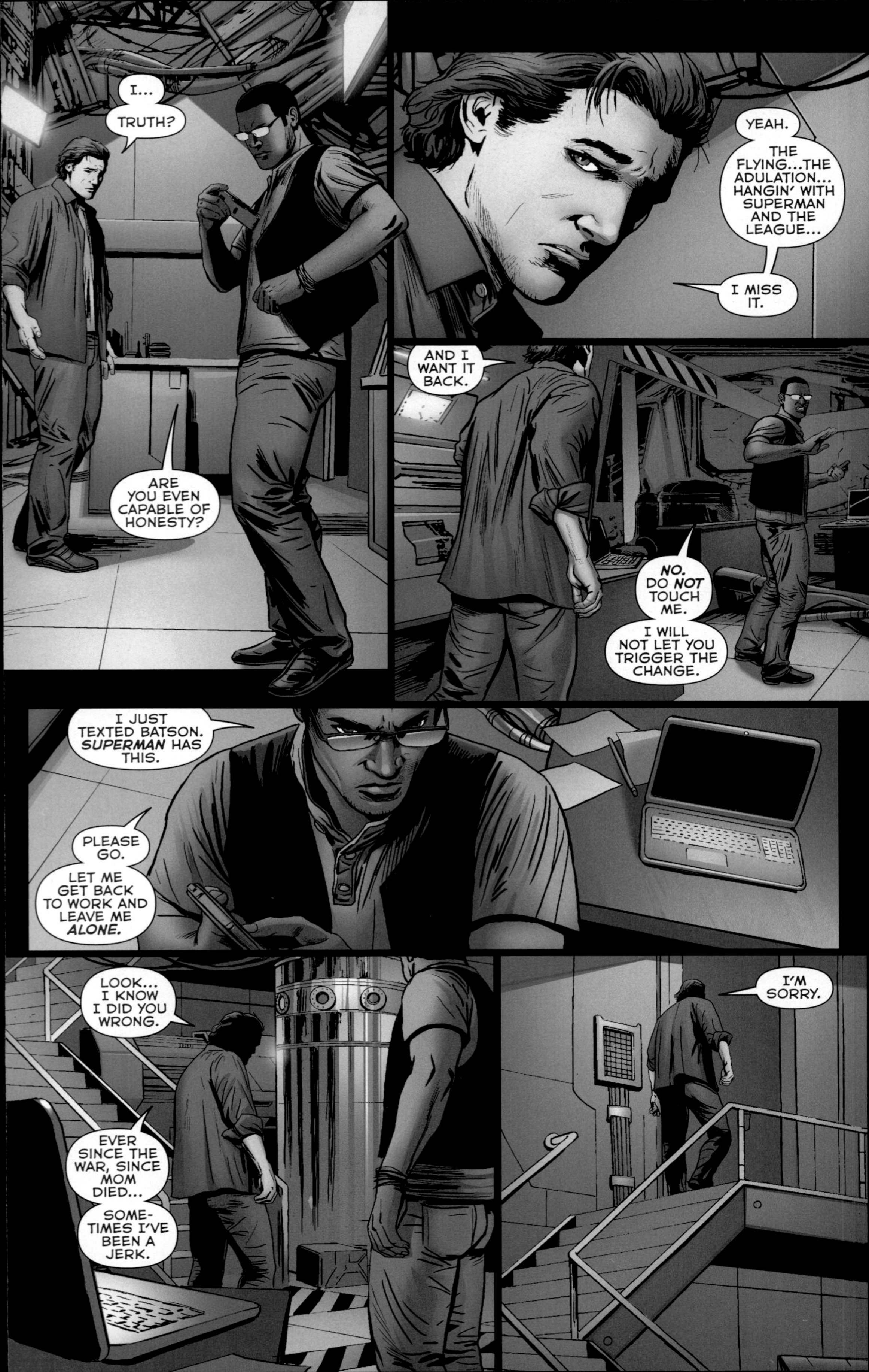
I... TRUTH?
ARE YOU EVEN CAPABLE OF HONESTY?
YEAH.
THE FLYING...THE ADULATION... HANGIN' WITH SUPERMAN AND THE LEAGUE...
I MISS IT.
AND I WANT IT BACK.
NO. DO NOT TOUCH ME.
I WILL NOT LET YOU TRIGGER THE CHANGE.
I JUST TEXTED BATSON. SUPERMAN HAS THIS.
PLEASE GO.
LET ME GET BACK TO WORK AND LEAVE ME ALONE.
LOOK... I KNOW I DID YOU WRONG.
EVER SINCE THE WAR, SINCE MOM DIED...
SOME-TIMES I'VE BEEN A JERK.
I'M SORRY.

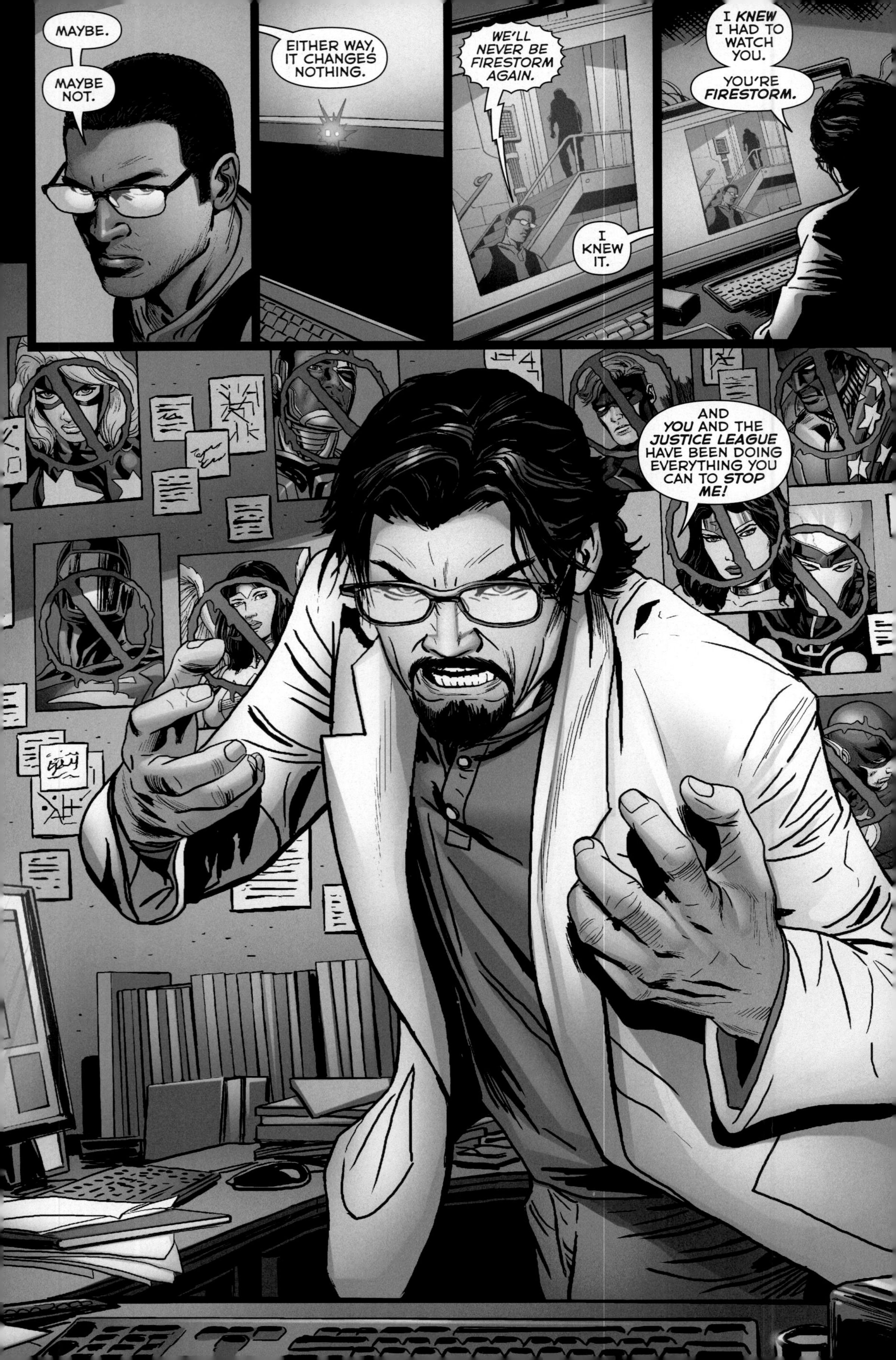
MAYBE.
MAYBE NOT.
EITHER WAY, IT CHANGES NOTHING.
WE'LL NEVER BE FIRESTORM AGAIN.
I KNEW IT.
I KNEW I HAD TO WATCH YOU.
YOU'RE FIRESTORM.
AND YOU AND THE JUSTICE LEAGUE HAVE BEEN DOING EVERYTHING YOU CAN TO STOP ME!

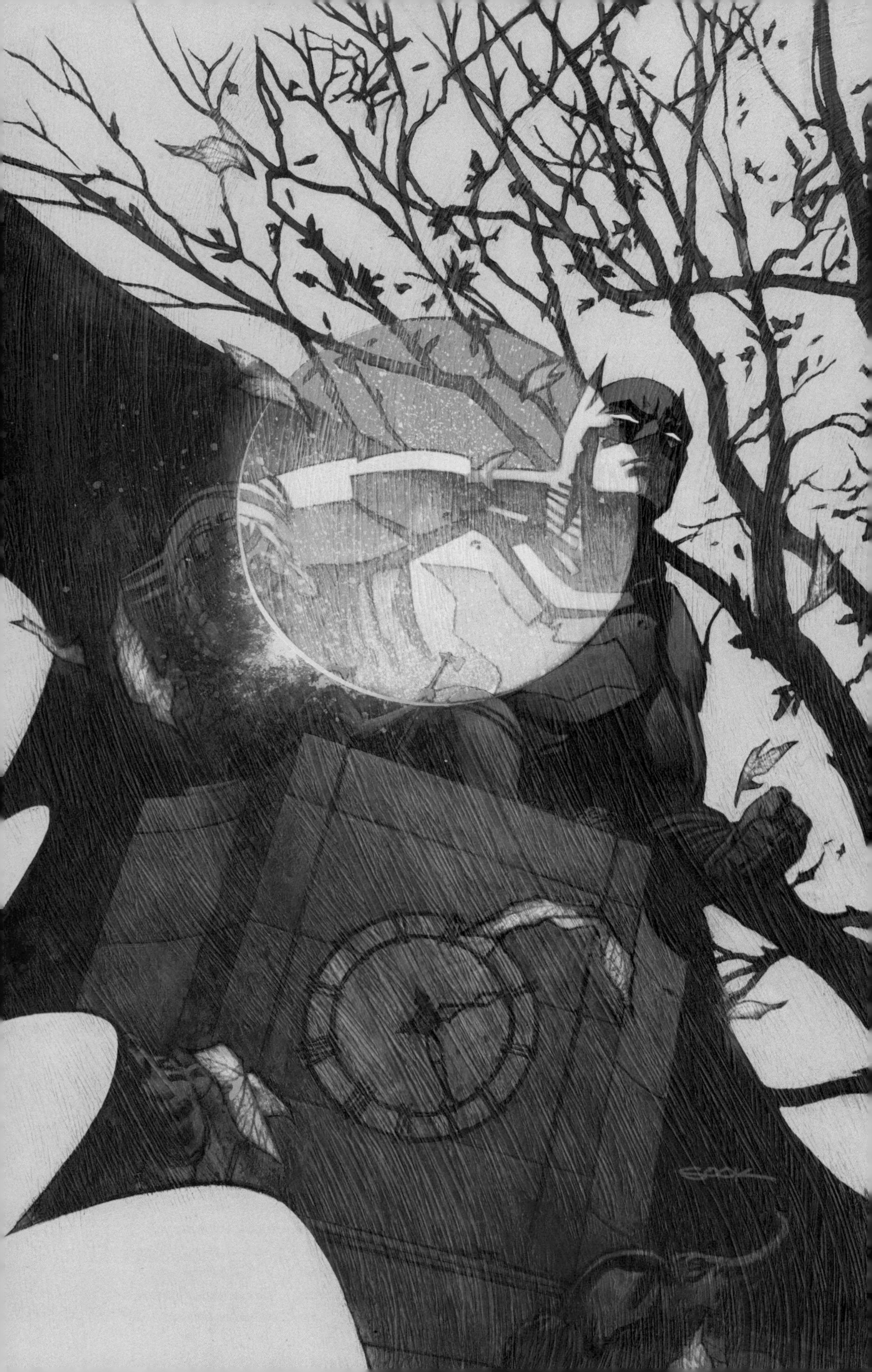

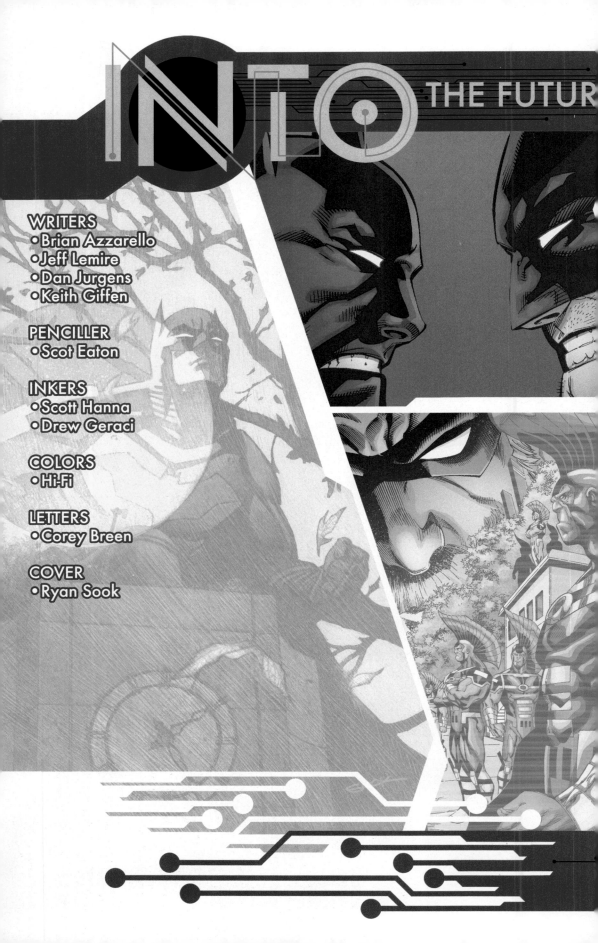

INTO THE FUTUR

WRITERS
- Brian Azzarello
- Jeff Lemire
- Dan Jurgens
- Keith Giffen

PENCILLER
- Scot Eaton

INKERS
- Scott Hanna
- Drew Geraci

COLORS
- Hi-Fi

LETTERS
- Corey Breen

COVER
- Ryan Sook

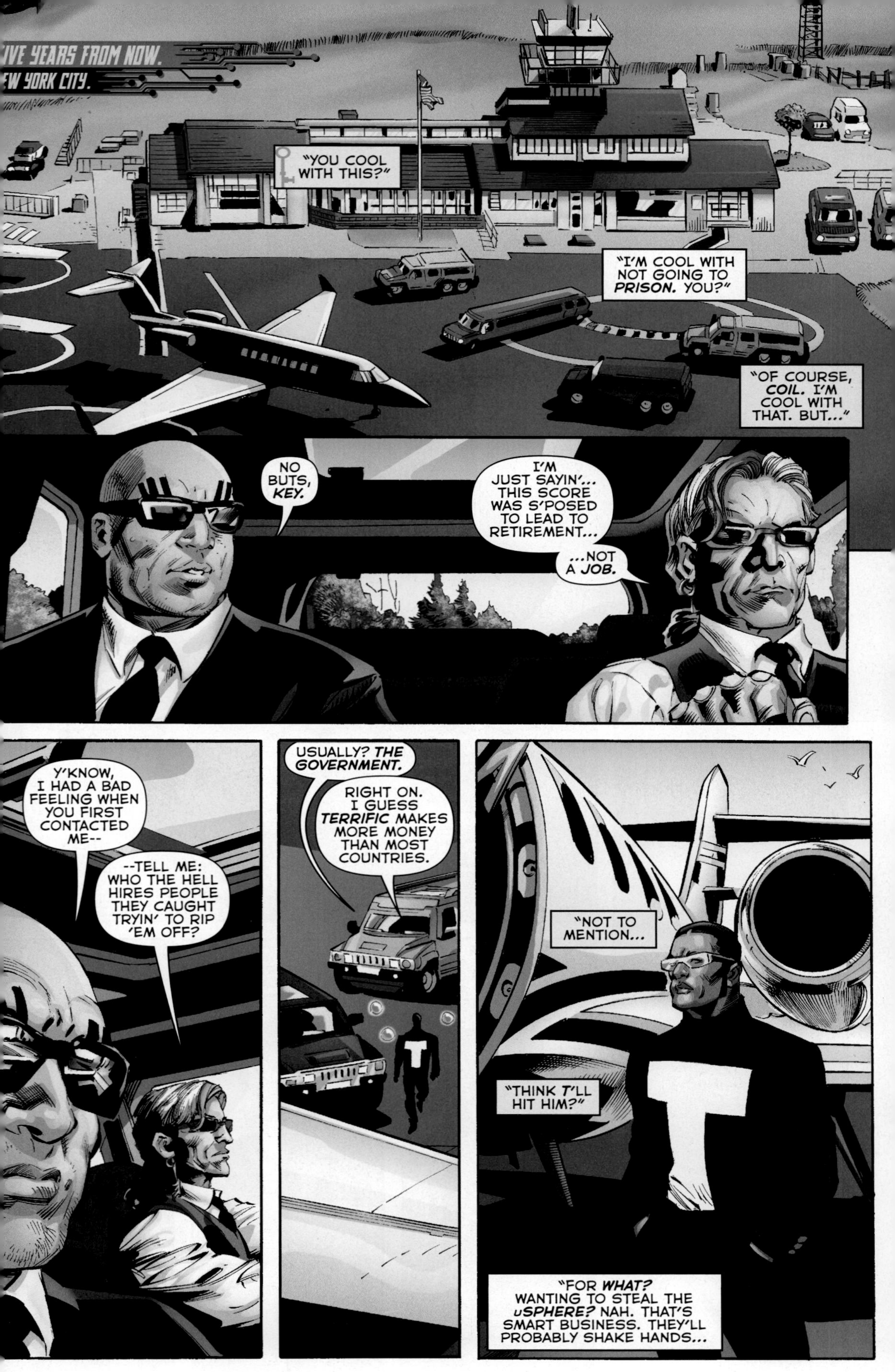
FIVE YEARS FROM NOW.
NEW YORK CITY.
"YOU COOL WITH THIS?"
"I'M COOL WITH NOT GOING TO PRISON. YOU?"
"OF COURSE, COIL. I'M COOL WITH THAT. BUT..."
NO BUTS, KEY.
I'M JUST SAYIN'... THIS SCORE WAS S'POSED TO LEAD TO RETIREMENT...
...NOT A JOB.
Y'KNOW, I HAD A BAD FEELING WHEN YOU FIRST CONTACTED ME--
--TELL ME: WHO THE HELL HIRES PEOPLE THEY CAUGHT TRYIN' TO RIP 'EM OFF?
USUALLY? THE GOVERNMENT.
RIGHT ON. I GUESS TERRIFIC MAKES MORE MONEY THAN MOST COUNTRIES.
"NOT TO MENTION...
"THINK T'LL HIT HIM?"
"FOR WHAT? WANTING TO STEAL THE uSPHERE? NAH. THAT'S SMART BUSINESS. THEY'LL PROBABLY SHAKE HANDS...

"THEN TAKE OUT THEIR WALLETS AND MEASURE THEM."

BRUCE!

MICHAEL--

OH, I APOLOGIZE-- IT'S MISTER TERRIFIC, RIGHT? I MEAN, *LEGALLY?* TERRIFIC WORKS?

MICHAEL. OKAY.

TERRIFIC.

THANKS FOR COMING. I CAN'T WAIT TO SHOW YOU--

--ABOUT THAT... uSPHERE TECH, RIGHT I'M GOING TO HAVE TO BEG OFF COMING BY TERRIFITECH TODAY.

THERE ARE SOME DOCUMENT WE'RE BOTH GOIN TO HAVE TO SIGN BEFOREHAND. STA SECRETS AND ALL

MY LAWYER IS DRAWING THEM UP. I'M SUPPOSED TO PICK THEM UP AT HIS FIRM'S MANHATTAN BRANCH IN...

HUH. I'M RUNNING LATE.

WE'RE GOING HAVE T CONTINU THIS--

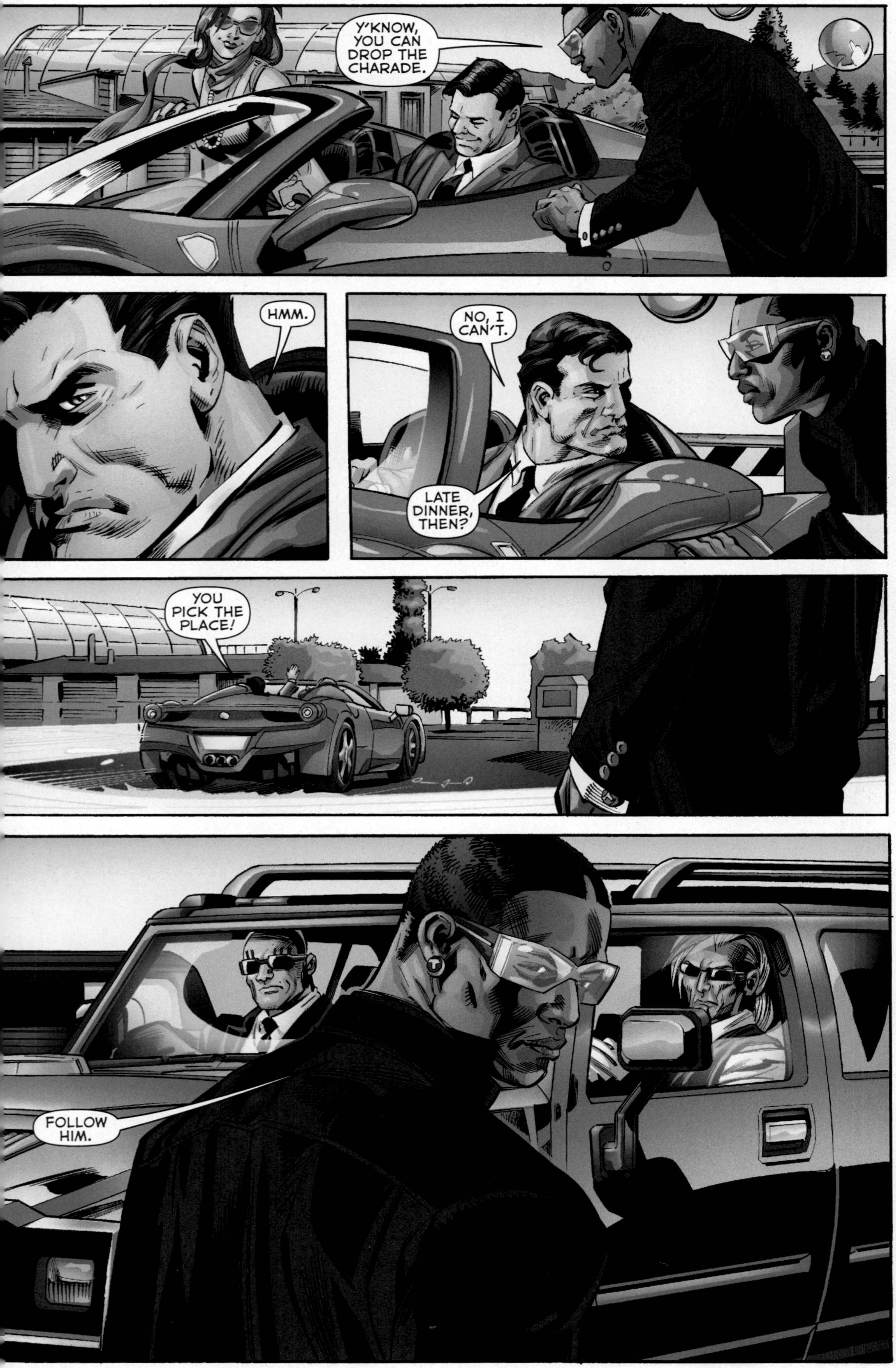
Y'KNOW, YOU CAN DROP THE CHARADE.
HMM.
NO, I CAN'T.
LATE DINNER, THEN?
YOU PICK THE PLACE!
FOLLOW HIM.

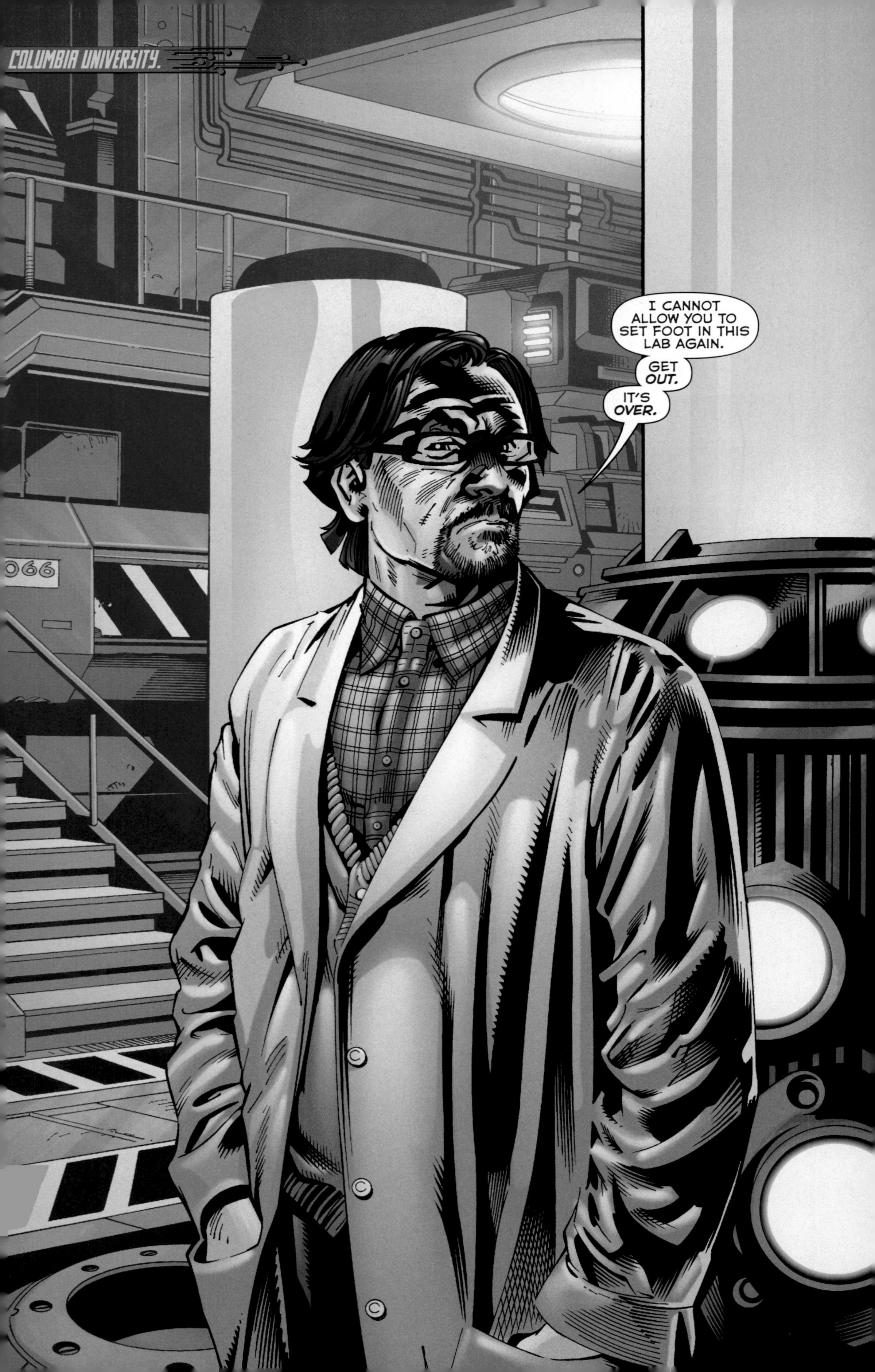
COLUMBIA UNIVERSITY.
066
I CANNOT ALLOW YOU TO SET FOOT IN THIS LAB AGAIN.
GET OUT.
IT'S OVER.

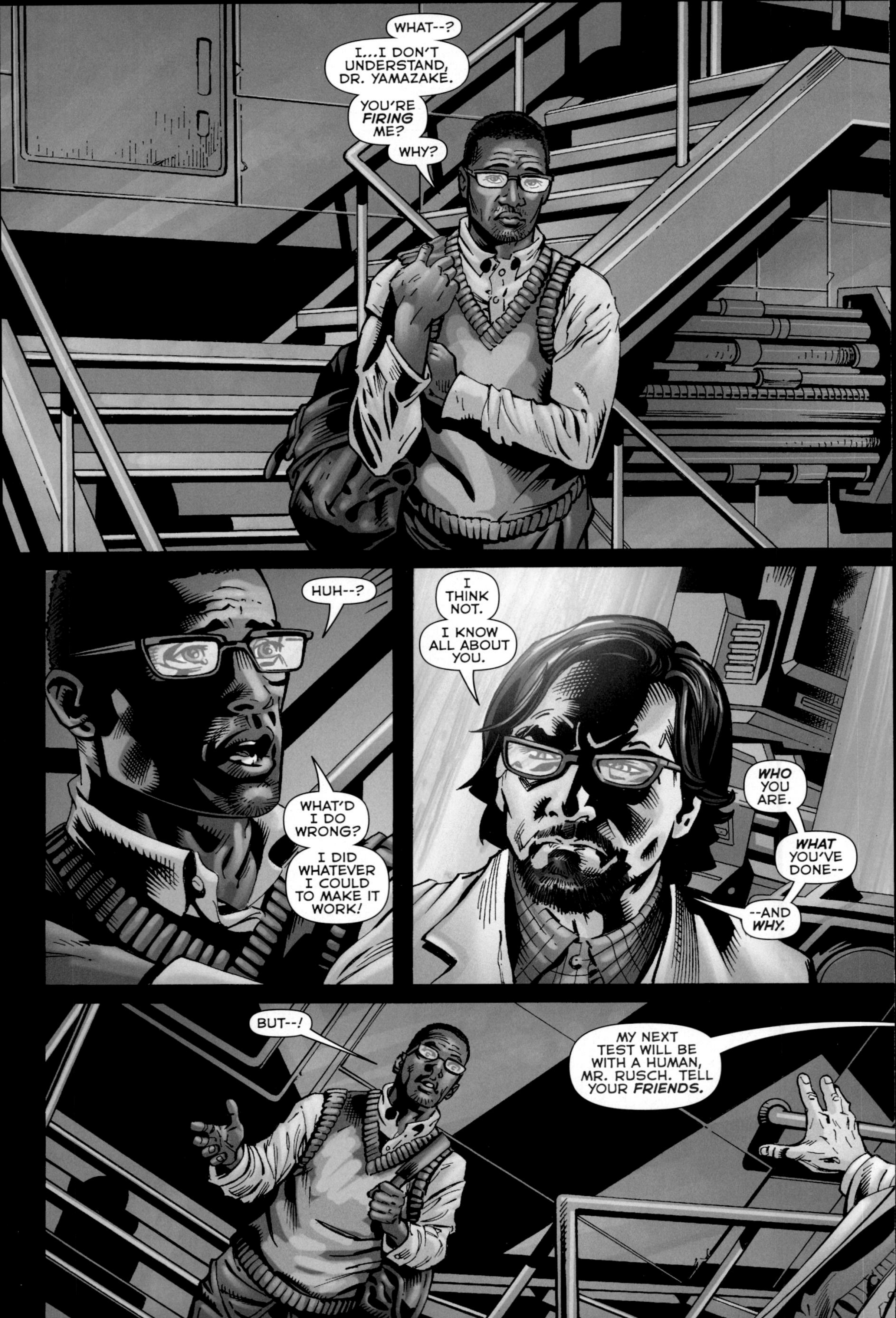
WHAT--?
I...I DON'T UNDERSTAND, DR. YAMAZAKE.
YOU'RE *FIRING* ME?
WHY?
HUH--?
WHAT'D I DO WRONG?
I DID WHATEVER I COULD TO MAKE IT WORK!
I THINK NOT.
I KNOW ALL ABOUT YOU.
WHO YOU ARE.
WHAT YOU'VE DONE--
--AND *WHY.*
BUT--!
MY NEXT TEST WILL BE WITH A HUMAN, MR. RUSCH. TELL YOUR *FRIENDS.*

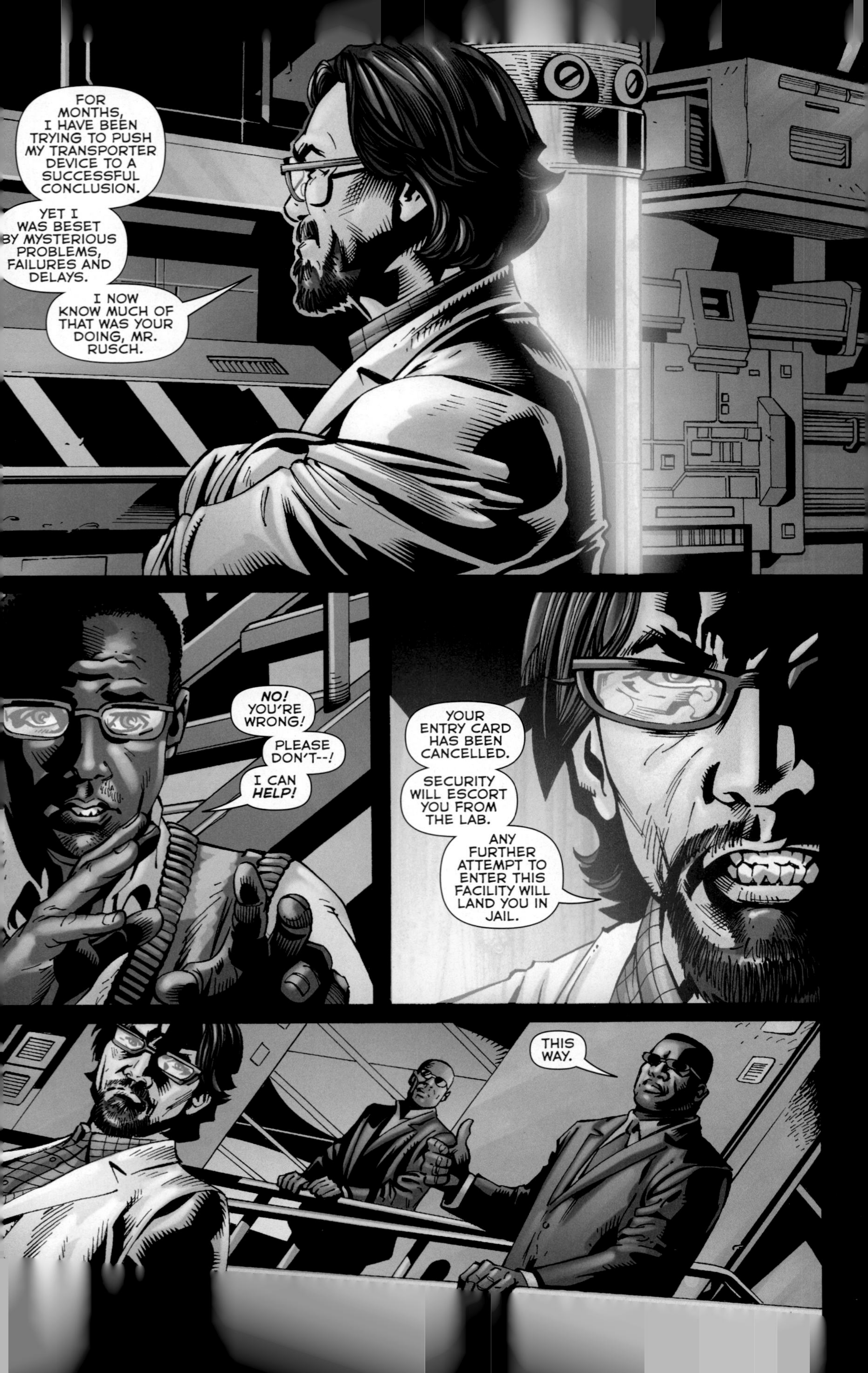
FOR MONTHS, I HAVE BEEN TRYING TO PUSH MY TRANSPORTER DEVICE TO A SUCCESSFUL CONCLUSION.
YET I WAS BESET BY MYSTERIOUS PROBLEMS, FAILURES AND DELAYS.
I NOW KNOW MUCH OF THAT WAS YOUR DOING, MR. RUSCH.
NO! YOU'RE WRONG!
PLEASE DON'T--!
I CAN HELP!
YOUR ENTRY CARD HAS BEEN CANCELLED.
SECURITY WILL ESCORT YOU FROM THE LAB.
ANY FURTHER ATTEMPT TO ENTER THIS FACILITY WILL LAND YOU IN JAIL.
THIS WAY.

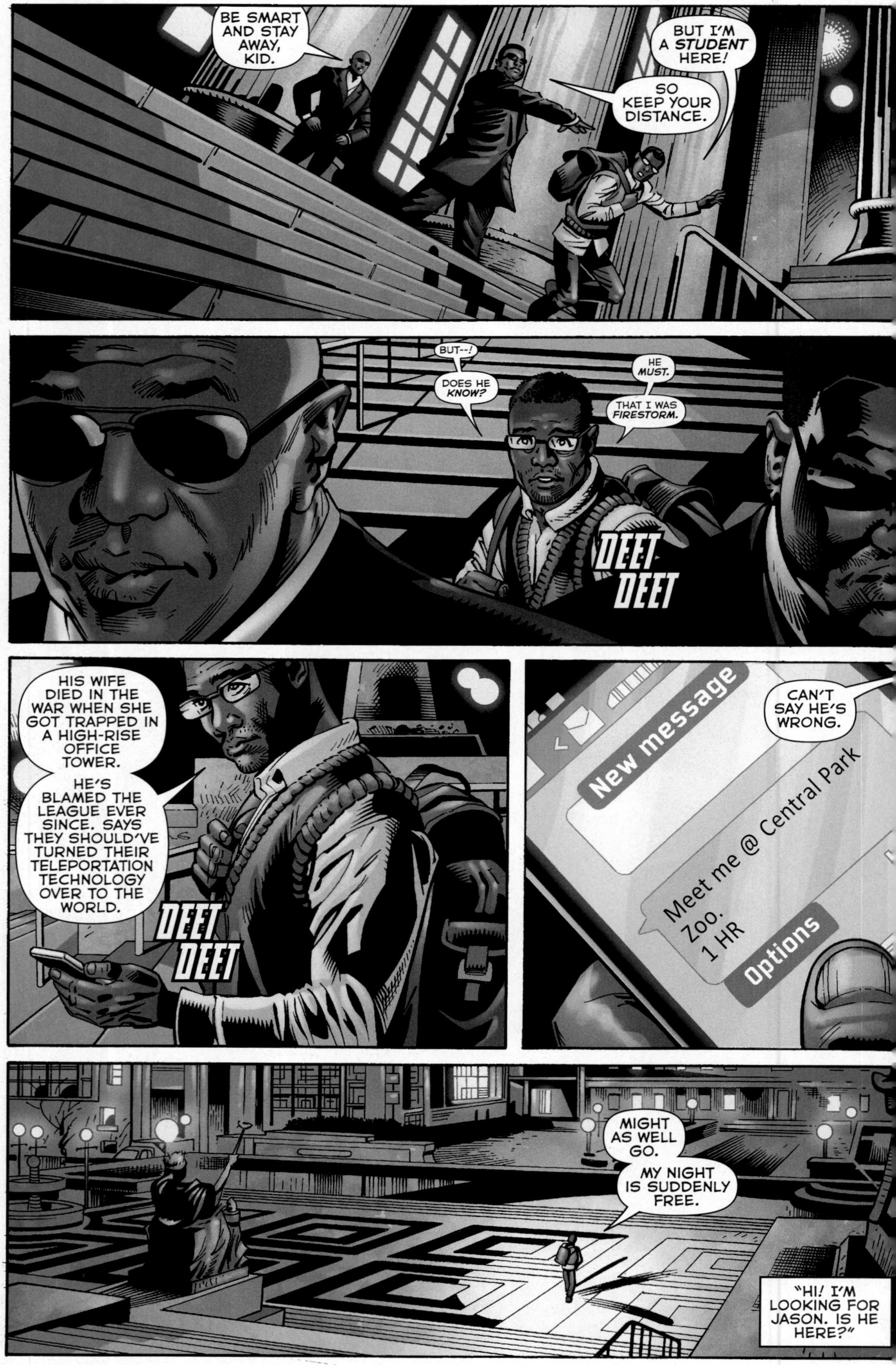
BE SMART AND STAY AWAY, KID.
BUT I'M A STUDENT HERE!
SO KEEP YOUR DISTANCE.
BUT--!
DOES HE KNOW?
HE MUST.
THAT I WAS FIRESTORM.
DEET DEET
HIS WIFE DIED IN THE WAR WHEN SHE GOT TRAPPED IN A HIGH-RISE OFFICE TOWER.
HE'S BLAMED THE LEAGUE EVER SINCE. SAYS THEY SHOULD'VE TURNED THEIR TELEPORTATION TECHNOLOGY OVER TO THE WORLD.
DEET DEET
New message
Meet me @ Central Park Zoo. 1 HR
Options
CAN'T SAY HE'S WRONG.
MIGHT AS WELL GO.
MY NIGHT IS SUDDENLY FREE.
"HI! I'M LOOKING FOR JASON. IS HE HERE?"

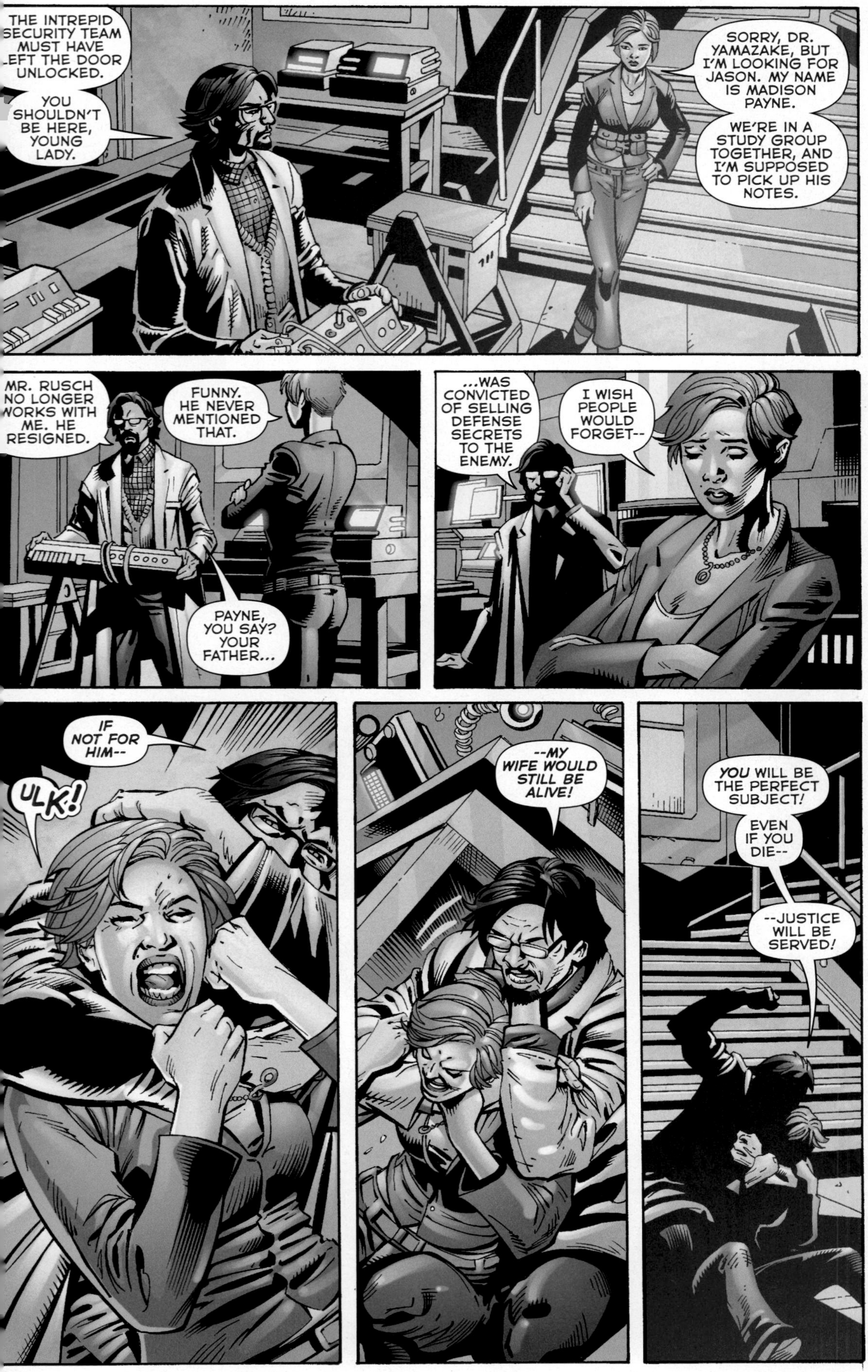
THE INTREPID SECURITY TEAM MUST HAVE LEFT THE DOOR UNLOCKED.
YOU SHOULDN'T BE HERE, YOUNG LADY.
SORRY, DR. YAMAZAKE, BUT I'M LOOKING FOR JASON. MY NAME IS MADISON PAYNE.
WE'RE IN A STUDY GROUP TOGETHER, AND I'M SUPPOSED TO PICK UP HIS NOTES.
MR. RUSCH NO LONGER WORKS WITH ME. HE RESIGNED.
FUNNY. HE NEVER MENTIONED THAT.
PAYNE, YOU SAY? YOUR FATHER...
...WAS CONVICTED OF SELLING DEFENSE SECRETS TO THE ENEMY.
I WISH PEOPLE WOULD FORGET--
IF NOT FOR HIM--
ULK!
--MY WIFE WOULD STILL BE ALIVE!
YOU WILL BE THE PERFECT SUBJECT!
EVEN IF YOU DIE--
--JUSTICE WILL BE SERVED!

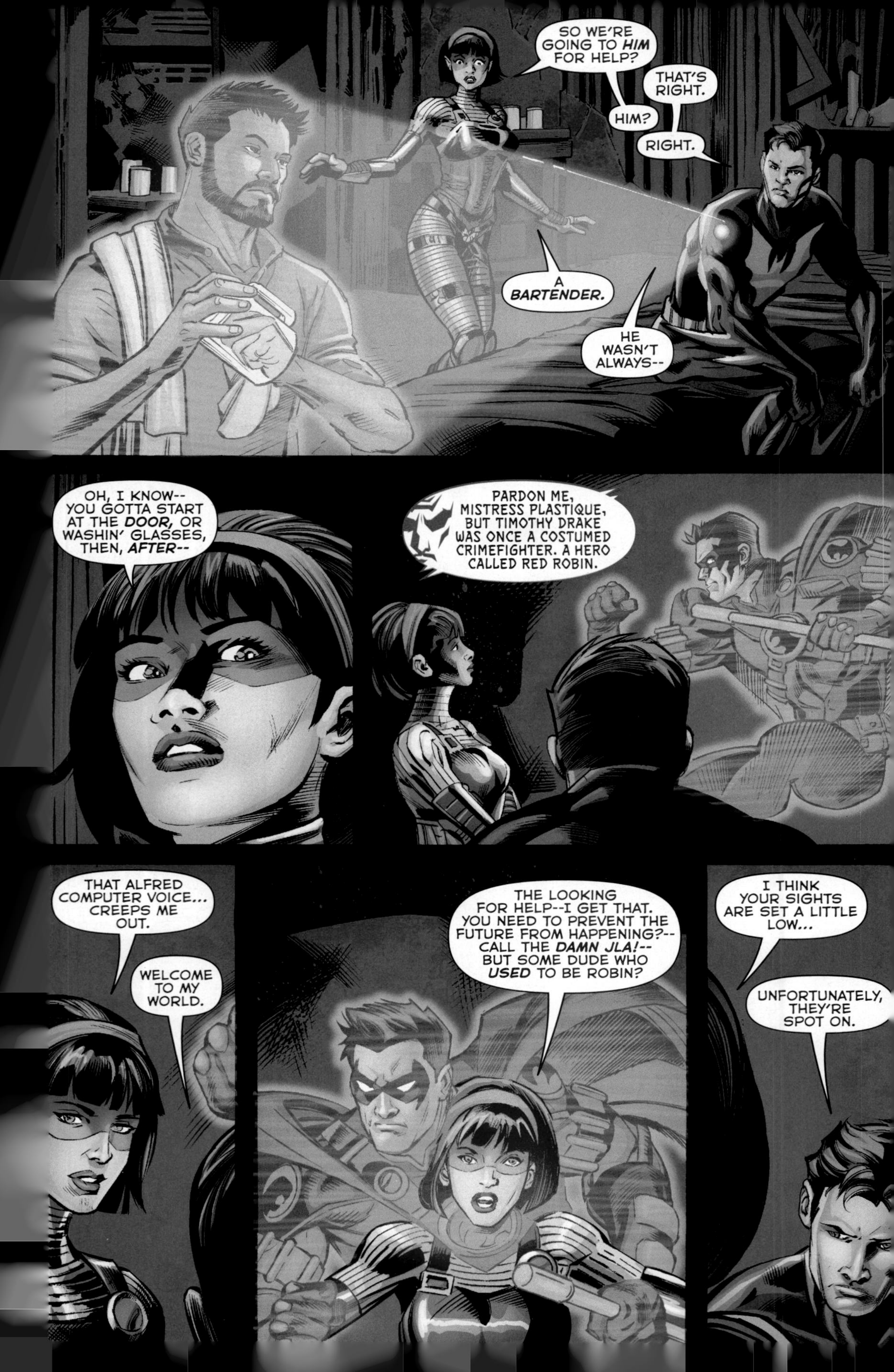
SO WE'RE GOING TO HIM FOR HELP?
THAT'S RIGHT.
HIM?
RIGHT.
A BARTENDER.
HE WASN'T ALWAYS--
OH, I KNOW-- YOU GOTTA START AT THE DOOR, OR WASHIN' GLASSES, THEN, AFTER--
PARDON ME, MISTRESS PLASTIQUE, BUT TIMOTHY DRAKE WAS ONCE A COSTUMED CRIMEFIGHTER. A HERO CALLED RED ROBIN.
THAT ALFRED COMPUTER VOICE... CREEPS ME OUT.
WELCOME TO MY WORLD.
THE LOOKING FOR HELP--I GET THAT. YOU NEED TO PREVENT THE FUTURE FROM HAPPENING?-- CALL THE DAMN JLA!-- BUT SOME DUDE WHO USED TO BE ROBIN?
I THINK YOUR SIGHTS ARE SET A LITTLE LOW...
UNFORTUNATELY, THEY'RE SPOT ON.

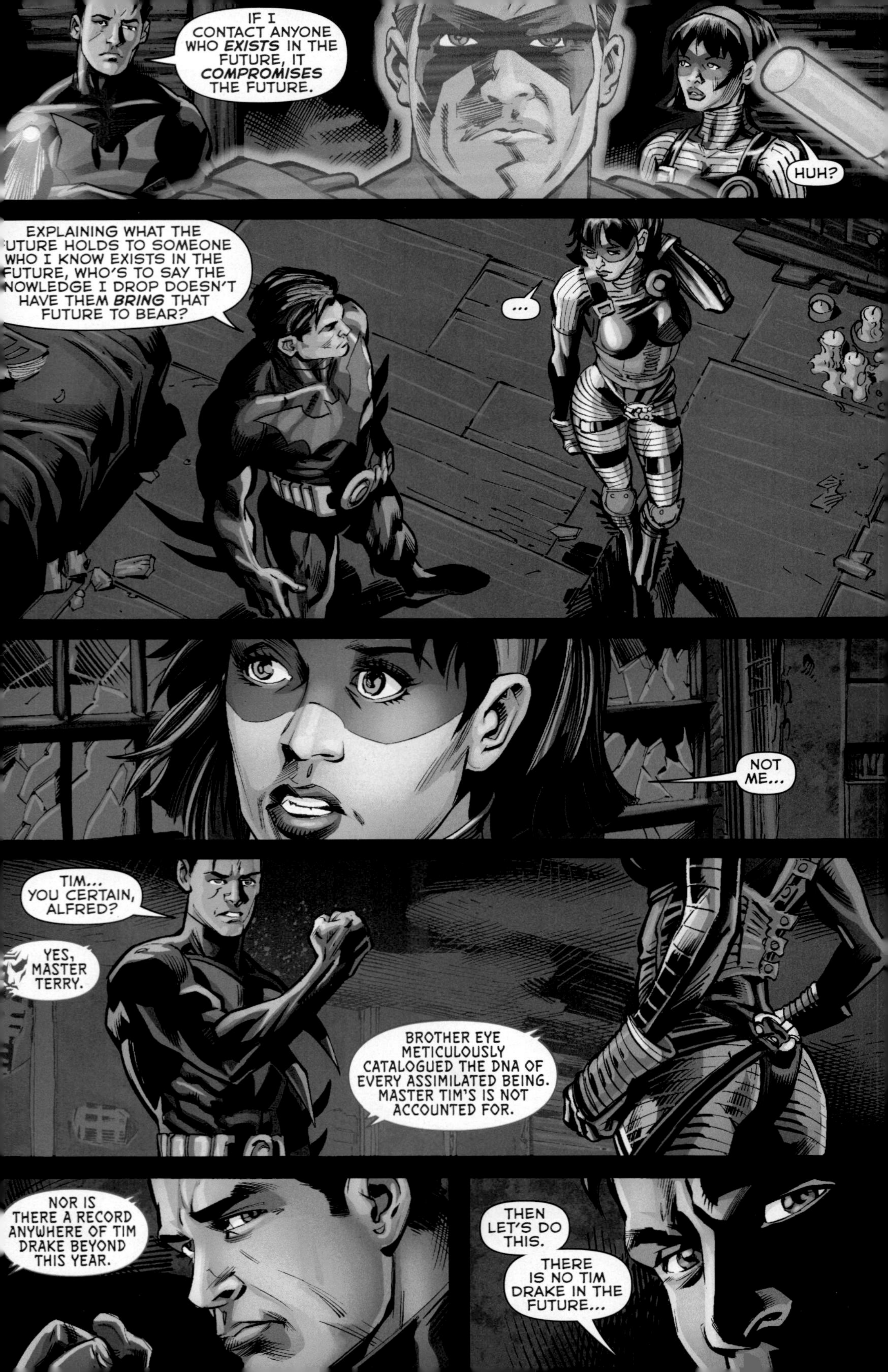

IF I CONTACT ANYONE WHO EXISTS IN THE FUTURE, IT COMPROMISES THE FUTURE.
HUH?
EXPLAINING WHAT THE FUTURE HOLDS TO SOMEONE WHO I KNOW EXISTS IN THE FUTURE, WHO'S TO SAY THE KNOWLEDGE I DROP DOESN'T HAVE THEM BRING THAT FUTURE TO BEAR?
...
NOT ME...
TIM... YOU CERTAIN, ALFRED?
YES, MASTER TERRY.
BROTHER EYE METICULOUSLY CATALOGUED THE DNA OF EVERY ASSIMILATED BEING. MASTER TIM'S IS NOT ACCOUNTED FOR.
NOR IS THERE A RECORD ANYWHERE OF TIM DRAKE BEYOND THIS YEAR.
THEN LET'S DO THIS.
THERE IS NO TIM DRAKE IN THE FUTURE...

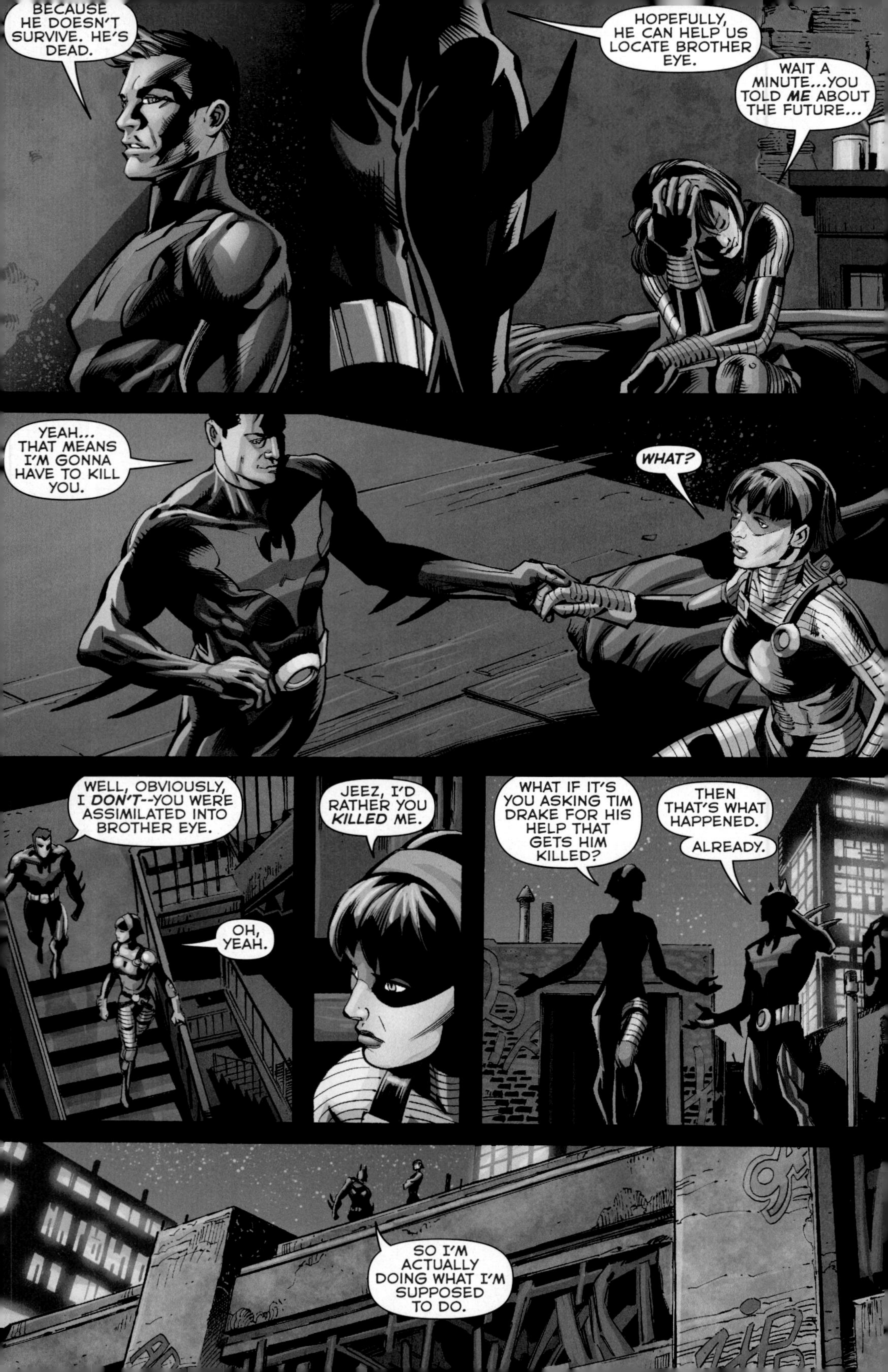
BECAUSE HE DOESN'T SURVIVE. HE'S DEAD.
HOPEFULLY, HE CAN HELP US LOCATE BROTHER EYE.
WAIT A MINUTE...YOU TOLD ME ABOUT THE FUTURE...
YEAH... THAT MEANS I'M GONNA HAVE TO KILL YOU.
WHAT?
WELL, OBVIOUSLY, I DON'T--YOU WERE ASSIMILATED INTO BROTHER EYE.
OH, YEAH.
JEEZ, I'D RATHER YOU KILLED ME.
WHAT IF IT'S YOU ASKING TIM DRAKE FOR HIS HELP THAT GETS HIM KILLED?
THEN THAT'S WHAT HAPPENED.
ALREADY.
SO I'M ACTUALLY DOING WHAT I'M SUPPOSED TO DO.

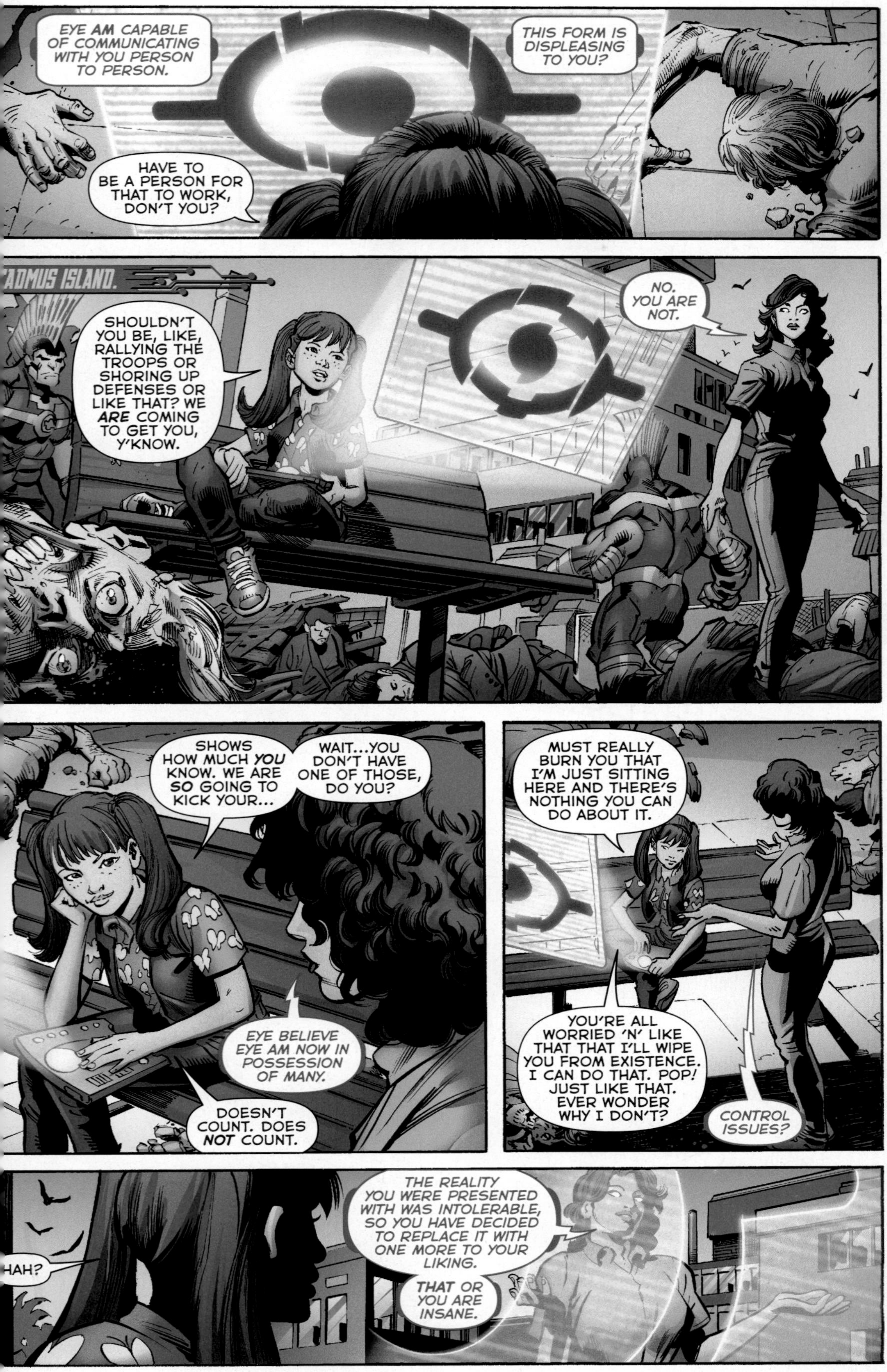
EYE AM CAPABLE OF COMMUNICATING WITH YOU PERSON TO PERSON.
THIS FORM IS DISPLEASING TO YOU?
HAVE TO BE A PERSON FOR THAT TO WORK, DON'T YOU?
CADMUS ISLAND.
SHOULDN'T YOU BE, LIKE, RALLYING THE TROOPS OR SHORING UP DEFENSES OR LIKE THAT? WE ARE COMING TO GET YOU, Y'KNOW.
NO. YOU ARE NOT.
SHOWS HOW MUCH YOU KNOW. WE ARE SO GOING TO KICK YOUR...
WAIT...YOU DON'T HAVE ONE OF THOSE, DO YOU?
EYE BELIEVE EYE AM NOW IN POSSESSION OF MANY.
DOESN'T COUNT. DOES NOT COUNT.
MUST REALLY BURN YOU THAT I'M JUST SITTING HERE AND THERE'S NOTHING YOU CAN DO ABOUT IT.
YOU'RE ALL WORRIED 'N' LIKE THAT THAT I'LL WIPE YOU FROM EXISTENCE. I CAN DO THAT. POP! JUST LIKE THAT. EVER WONDER WHY I DON'T?
CONTROL ISSUES?
HAH?
THE REALITY YOU WERE PRESENTED WITH WAS INTOLERABLE, SO YOU HAVE DECIDED TO REPLACE IT WITH ONE MORE TO YOUR LIKING.
THAT OR YOU ARE INSANE.

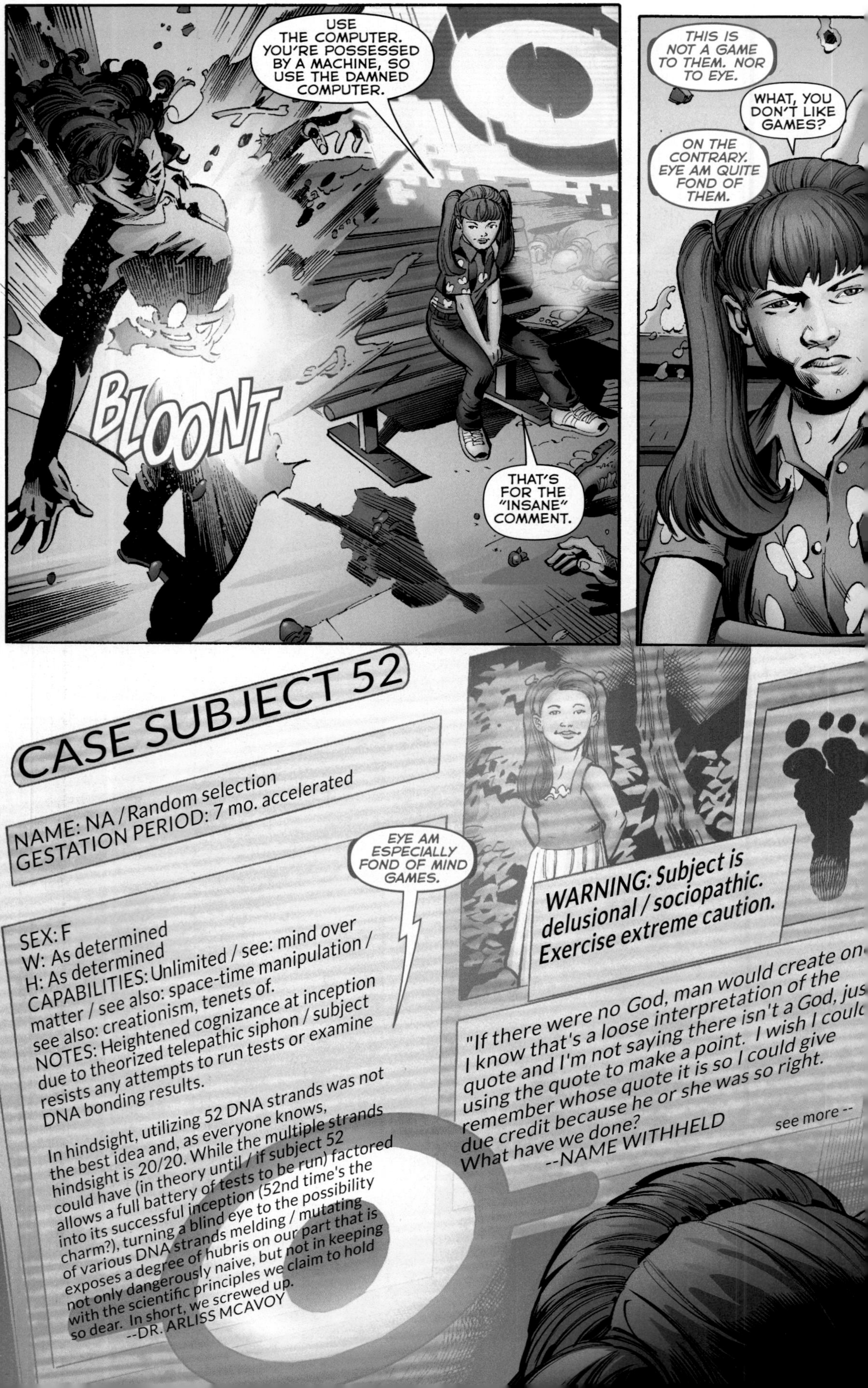

USE THE COMPUTER. YOU'RE POSSESSED BY A MACHINE, SO USE THE DAMNED COMPUTER.
BLOONT
THAT'S FOR THE "INSANE" COMMENT.
THIS IS NOT A GAME TO THEM. NOR TO EYE.
WHAT, YOU DON'T LIKE GAMES?
ON THE CONTRARY. EYE AM QUITE FOND OF THEM.
CASE SUBJECT 52
NAME: NA / Random selection
GESTATION PERIOD: 7 mo. accelerated
EYE AM ESPECIALLY FOND OF MIND GAMES.
WARNING: Subject is delusional / sociopathic. Exercise extreme caution.
SEX: F
W: As determined
H: As determined
CAPABILITIES: Unlimited / see: mind over matter / see also: space-time manipulation / see also: creationism, tenets of.
NOTES: Heightened cognizance at inception due to theorized telepathic siphon / subject resists any attempts to run tests or examine DNA bonding results.
In hindsight, utilizing 52 DNA strands was not the best idea and, as everyone knows, hindsight is 20/20. While the multiple strands could have (in theory until / if subject 52 allows a full battery of tests to be run) factored into its successful inception (52nd time's the charm?), turning a blind eye to the possibility of various DNA strands melding / mutating exposes a degree of hubris on our part that is not only dangerously naive, but not in keeping with the scientific principles we claim to hold so dear. In short, we screwed up.
--DR. ARLISS MCAVOY
"If there were no God, man would create one. I know that's a loose interpretation of the quote and I'm not saying there isn't a God, just using the quote to make a point. I wish I could remember whose quote it is so I could give due credit because he or she was so right. What have we done?
--NAME WITHHELD
see more --

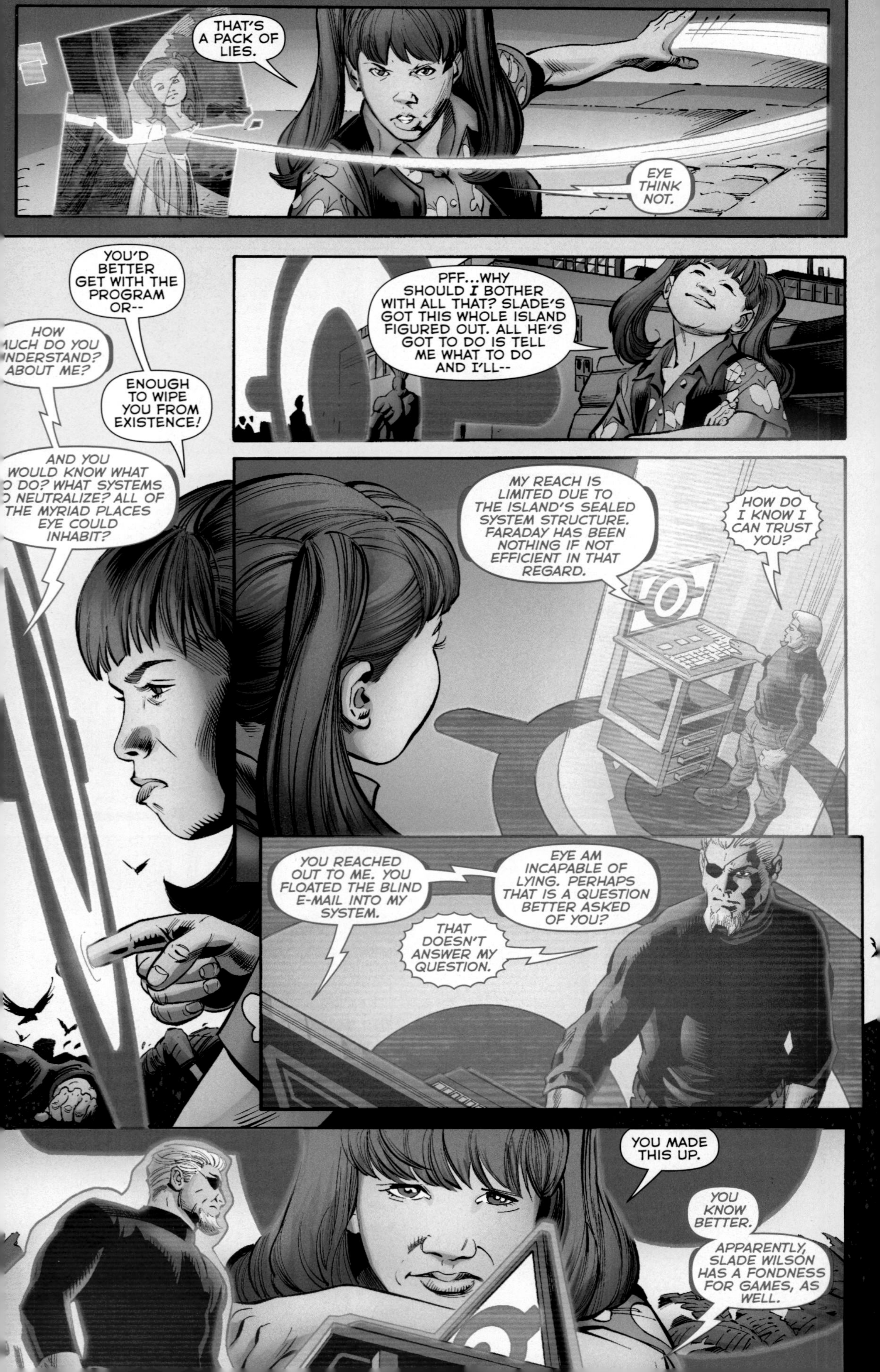

THAT'S A PACK OF LIES.
EYE THINK NOT.
YOU'D BETTER GET WITH THE PROGRAM OR--
PFF...WHY SHOULD I BOTHER WITH ALL THAT? SLADE'S GOT THIS WHOLE ISLAND FIGURED OUT. ALL HE'S GOT TO DO IS TELL ME WHAT TO DO AND I'LL--
HOW MUCH DO YOU UNDERSTAND? ABOUT ME?
ENOUGH TO WIPE YOU FROM EXISTENCE!
AND YOU WOULD KNOW WHAT TO DO? WHAT SYSTEMS TO NEUTRALIZE? ALL OF THE MYRIAD PLACES EYE COULD INHABIT?
MY REACH IS LIMITED DUE TO THE ISLAND'S SEALED SYSTEM STRUCTURE. FARADAY HAS BEEN NOTHING IF NOT EFFICIENT IN THAT REGARD.
HOW DO I KNOW I CAN TRUST YOU?
EYE AM INCAPABLE OF LYING. PERHAPS THAT IS A QUESTION BETTER ASKED OF YOU?
YOU REACHED OUT TO ME. YOU FLOATED THE BLIND E-MAIL INTO MY SYSTEM.
THAT DOESN'T ANSWER MY QUESTION.
YOU MADE THIS UP.
YOU KNOW BETTER.
APPARENTLY, SLADE WILSON HAS A FONDNESS FOR GAMES, AS WELL.

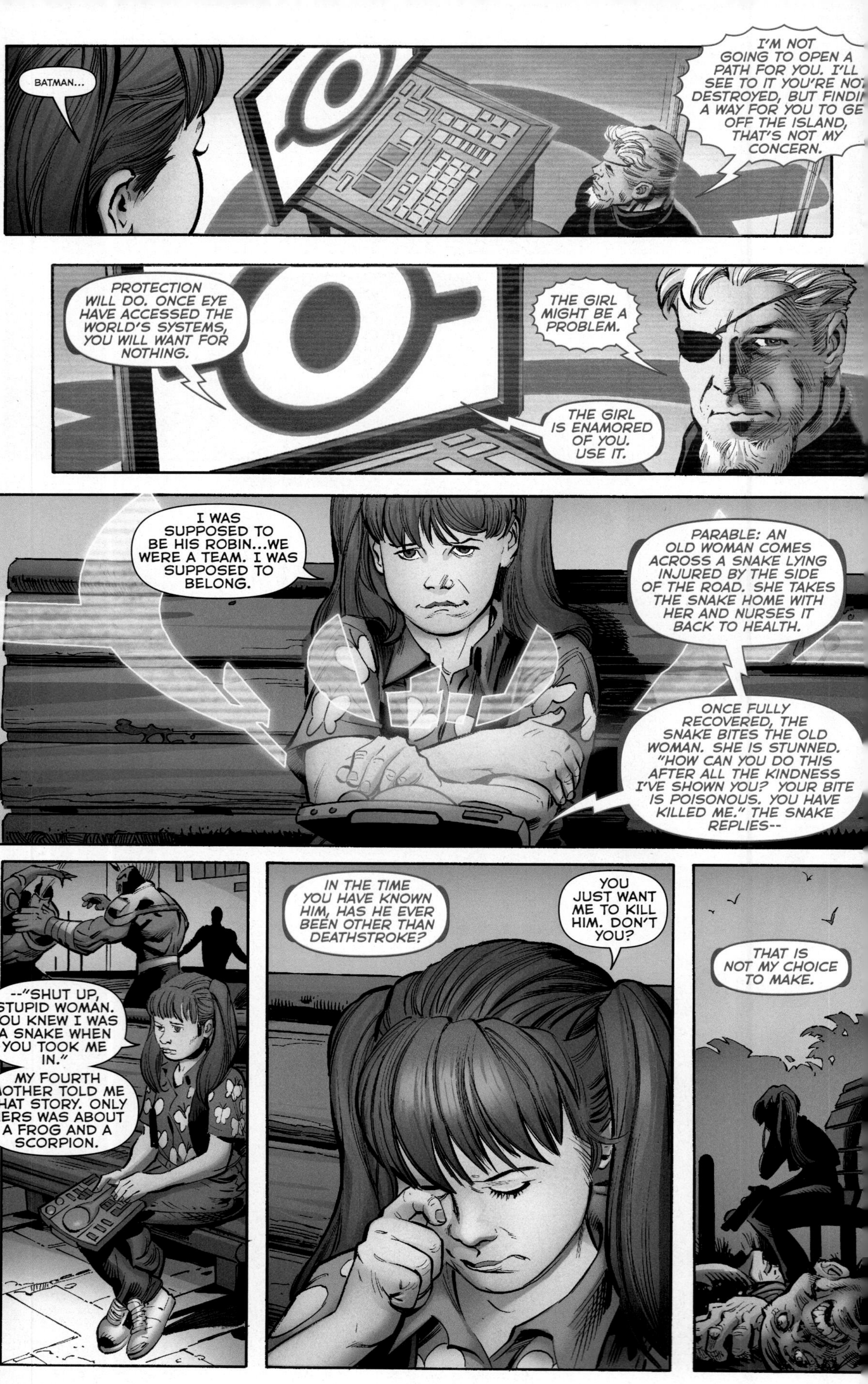
BATMAN...
I'M NOT GOING TO OPEN A PATH FOR YOU. I'LL SEE TO IT YOU'RE NOT DESTROYED, BUT FINDING A WAY FOR YOU TO GET OFF THE ISLAND, THAT'S NOT MY CONCERN.
PROTECTION WILL DO. ONCE EYE HAVE ACCESSED THE WORLD'S SYSTEMS, YOU WILL WANT FOR NOTHING.
THE GIRL MIGHT BE A PROBLEM.
THE GIRL IS ENAMORED OF YOU. USE IT.
I WAS SUPPOSED TO BE HIS ROBIN...WE WERE A TEAM. I WAS SUPPOSED TO BELONG.
PARABLE: AN OLD WOMAN COMES ACROSS A SNAKE LYING INJURED BY THE SIDE OF THE ROAD. SHE TAKES THE SNAKE HOME WITH HER AND NURSES IT BACK TO HEALTH.
ONCE FULLY RECOVERED, THE SNAKE BITES THE OLD WOMAN. SHE IS STUNNED. "HOW CAN YOU DO THIS AFTER ALL THE KINDNESS I'VE SHOWN YOU? YOUR BITE IS POISONOUS. YOU HAVE KILLED ME." THE SNAKE REPLIES--
--"SHUT UP, STUPID WOMAN. YOU KNEW I WAS A SNAKE WHEN YOU TOOK ME IN."
MY FOURTH MOTHER TOLD ME THAT STORY. ONLY HERS WAS ABOUT A FROG AND A SCORPION.
IN THE TIME YOU HAVE KNOWN HIM, HAS HE EVER BEEN OTHER THAN DEATHSTROKE?
YOU JUST WANT ME TO KILL HIM. DON'T YOU?
THAT IS NOT MY CHOICE TO MAKE.

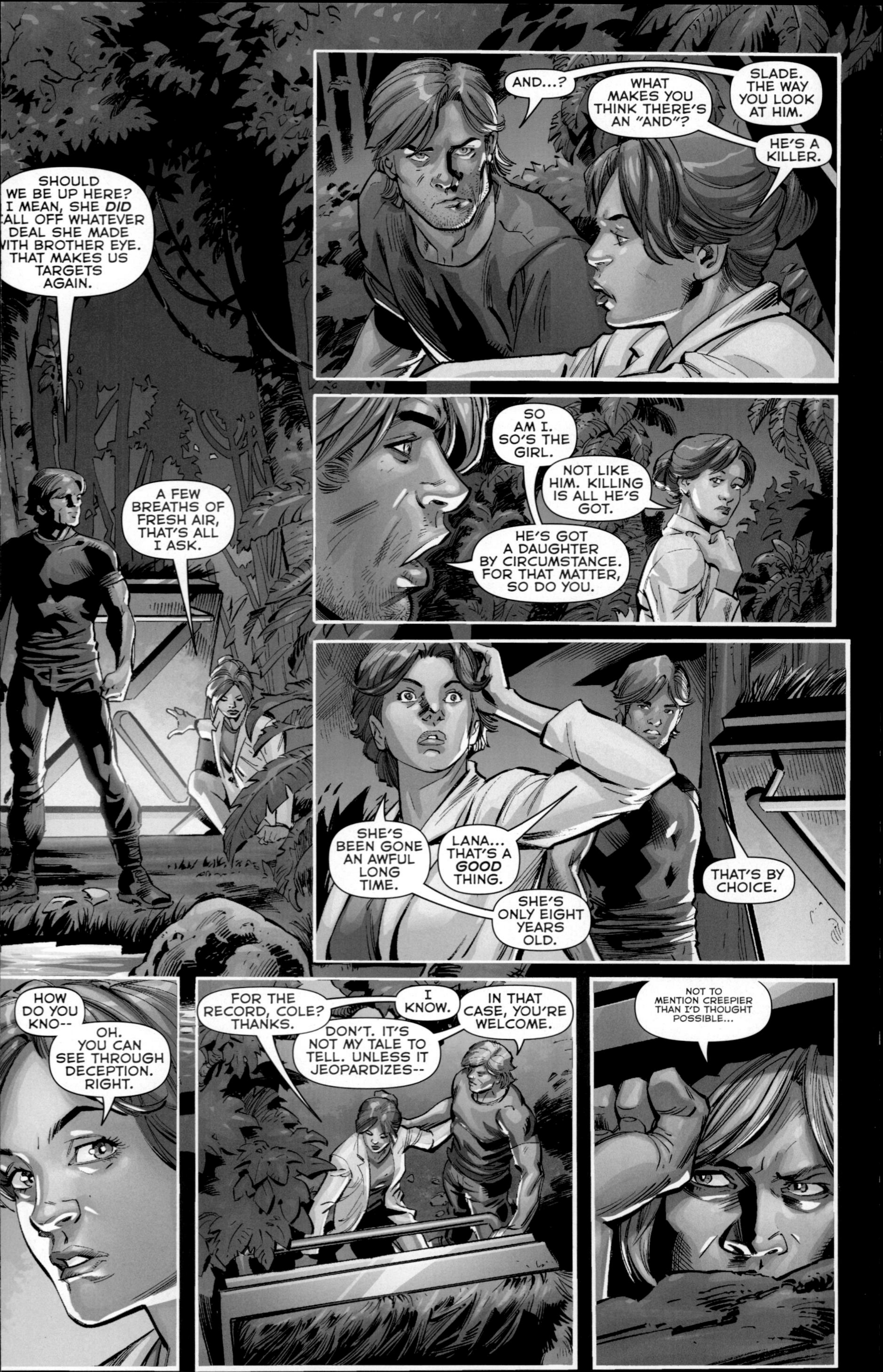

SHOULD WE BE UP HERE? I MEAN, SHE DID CALL OFF WHATEVER DEAL SHE MADE WITH BROTHER EYE. THAT MAKES US TARGETS AGAIN.
A FEW BREATHS OF FRESH AIR, THAT'S ALL I ASK.
AND...?
WHAT MAKES YOU THINK THERE'S AN "AND"?
SLADE. THE WAY YOU LOOK AT HIM.
HE'S A KILLER.
SO AM I. SO'S THE GIRL.
NOT LIKE HIM. KILLING IS ALL HE'S GOT.
HE'S GOT A DAUGHTER BY CIRCUMSTANCE. FOR THAT MATTER, SO DO YOU.
SHE'S BEEN GONE AN AWFUL LONG TIME.
LANA... THAT'S A GOOD THING.
SHE'S ONLY EIGHT YEARS OLD.
THAT'S BY CHOICE.
HOW DO YOU KNO--
OH. YOU CAN SEE THROUGH DECEPTION. RIGHT.
FOR THE RECORD, COLE? THANKS.
I KNOW.
DON'T. IT'S NOT MY TALE TO TELL. UNLESS IT JEOPARDIZES--
IN THAT CASE, YOU'RE WELCOME.
NOT TO MENTION CREEPIER THAN I'D THOUGHT POSSIBLE...

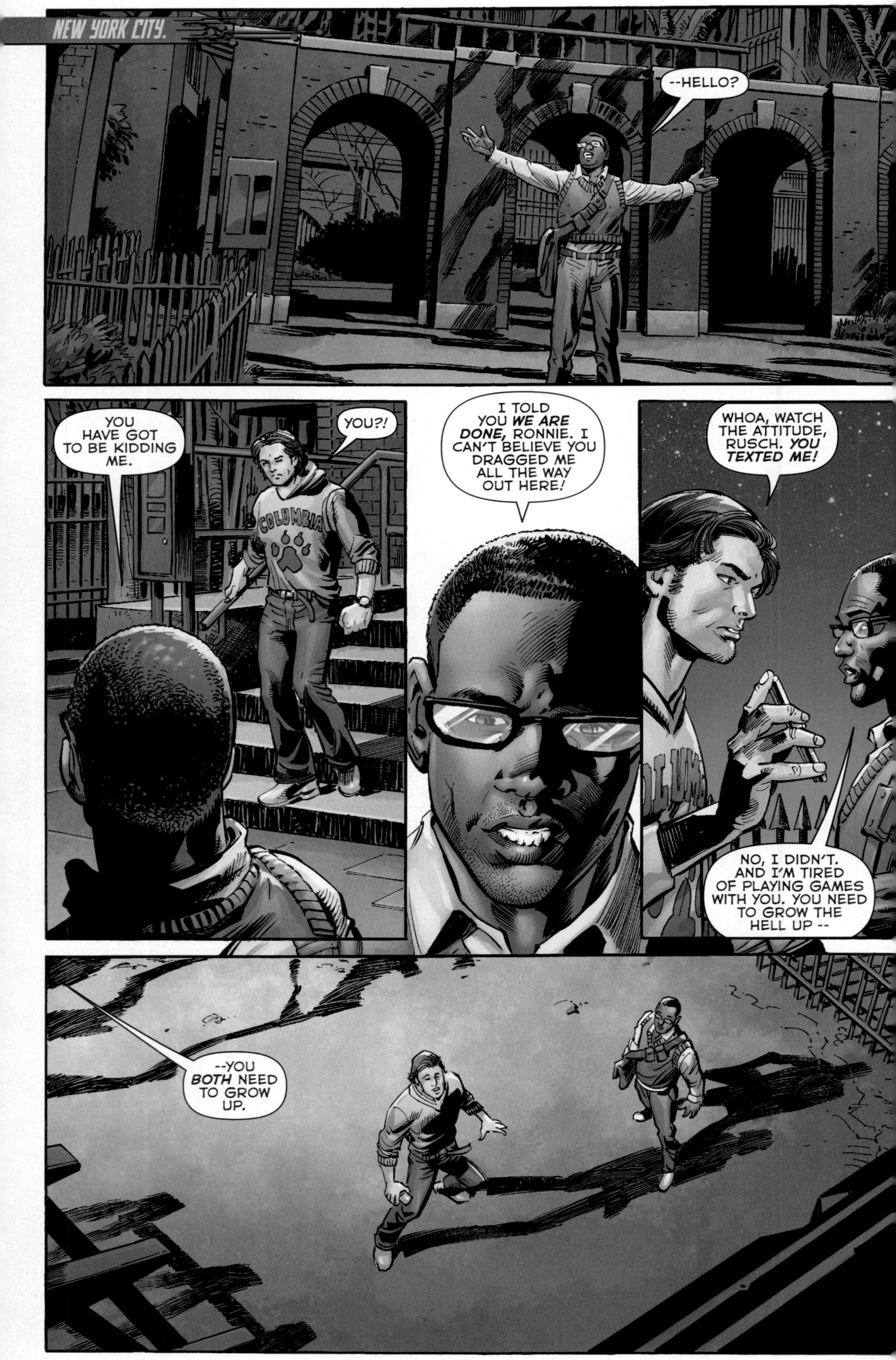
NEW YORK CITY.
--HELLO?
YOU HAVE GOT TO BE KIDDING ME.
YOU?!
I TOLD YOU WE ARE DONE, RONNIE. I CAN'T BELIEVE YOU DRAGGED ME ALL THE WAY OUT HERE!
WHOA, WATCH THE ATTITUDE, RUSCH. YOU TEXTED ME!
NO, I DIDN'T. AND I'M TIRED OF PLAYING GAMES WITH YOU. YOU NEED TO GROW THE HELL UP --
--YOU BOTH NEED TO GROW UP.

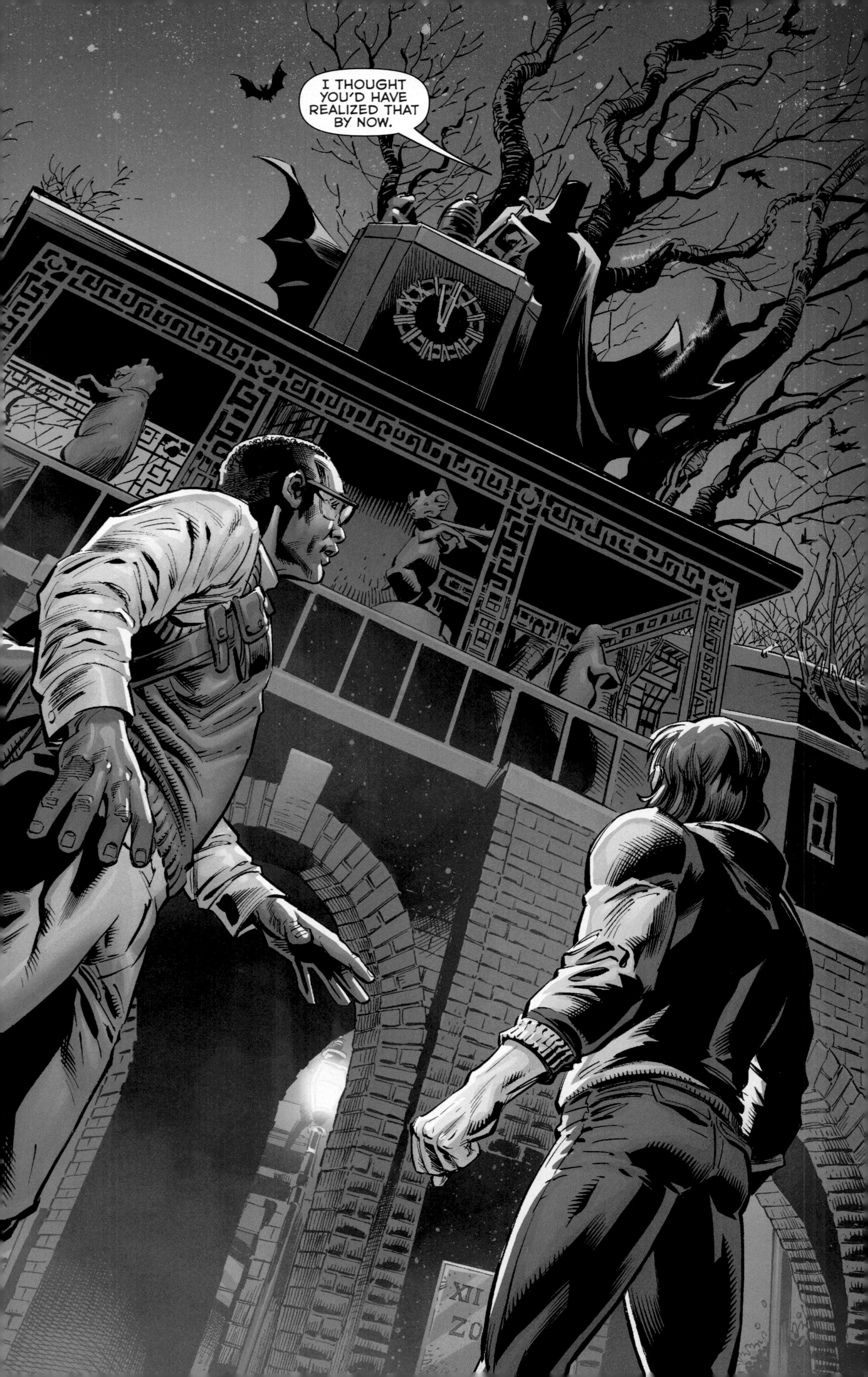
I THOUGHT YOU'D HAVE REALIZED THAT BY NOW.

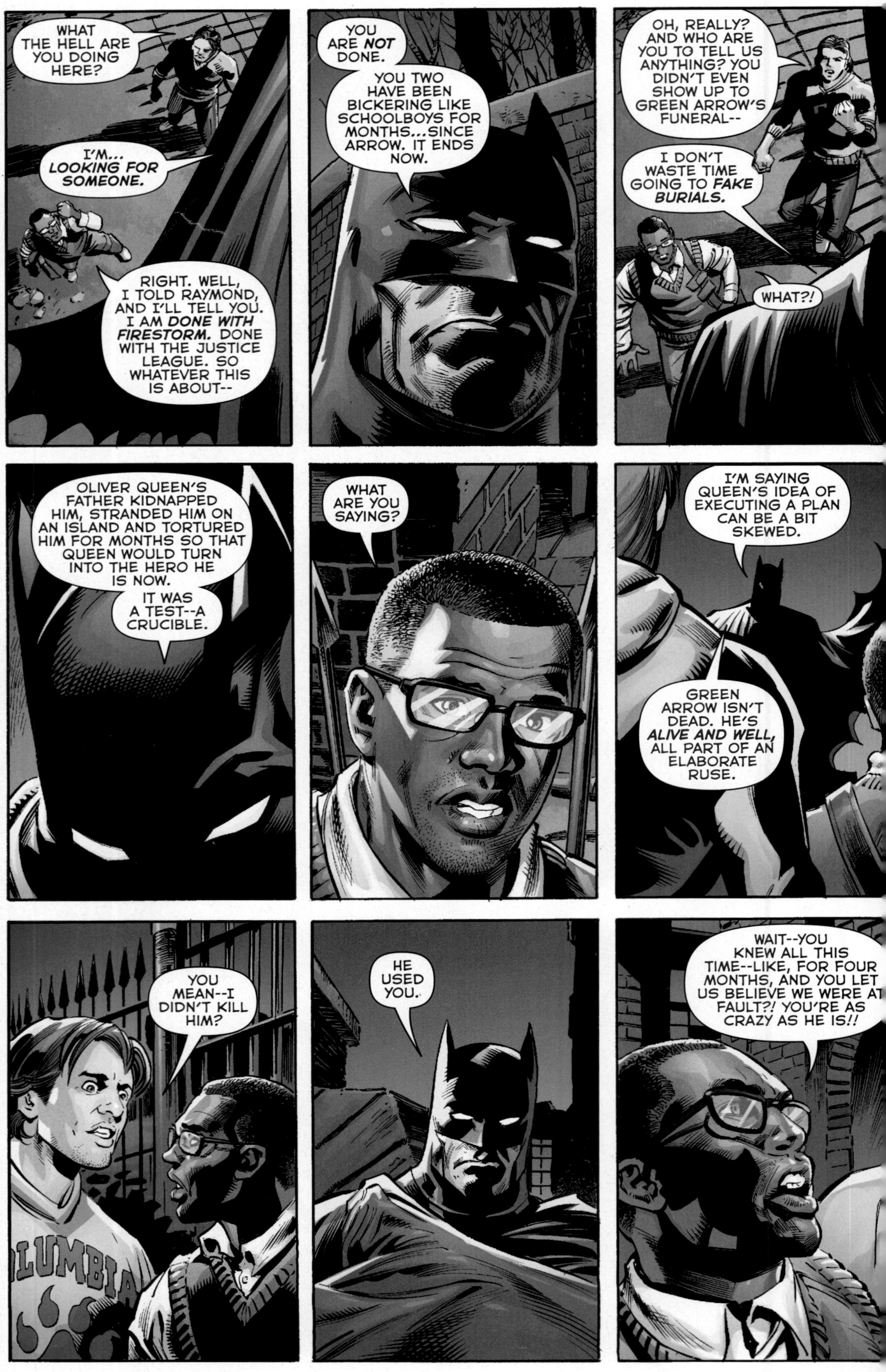
WHAT THE HELL ARE YOU DOING HERE?
I'M... LOOKING FOR SOMEONE.
RIGHT. WELL, I TOLD RAYMOND, AND I'LL TELL YOU. I AM DONE WITH FIRESTORM. DONE WITH THE JUSTICE LEAGUE. SO WHATEVER THIS IS ABOUT--
YOU ARE NOT DONE.
YOU TWO HAVE BEEN BICKERING LIKE SCHOOLBOYS FOR MONTHS...SINCE ARROW. IT ENDS NOW.
OH, REALLY? AND WHO ARE YOU TO TELL US ANYTHING? YOU DIDN'T EVEN SHOW UP TO GREEN ARROW'S FUNERAL--
I DON'T WASTE TIME GOING TO FAKE BURIALS.
WHAT?!
OLIVER QUEEN'S FATHER KIDNAPPED HIM, STRANDED HIM ON AN ISLAND AND TORTURED HIM FOR MONTHS SO THAT QUEEN WOULD TURN INTO THE HERO HE IS NOW.
IT WAS A TEST--A CRUCIBLE.
WHAT ARE YOU SAYING?
I'M SAYING QUEEN'S IDEA OF EXECUTING A PLAN CAN BE A BIT SKEWED.
GREEN ARROW ISN'T DEAD. HE'S ALIVE AND WELL, ALL PART OF AN ELABORATE RUSE.
YOU MEAN--I DIDN'T KILL HIM?
HE USED YOU.
WAIT--YOU KNEW ALL THIS TIME--LIKE, FOR FOUR MONTHS, AND YOU LET US BELIEVE WE WERE AT FAULT?! YOU'RE AS CRAZY AS HE IS!!

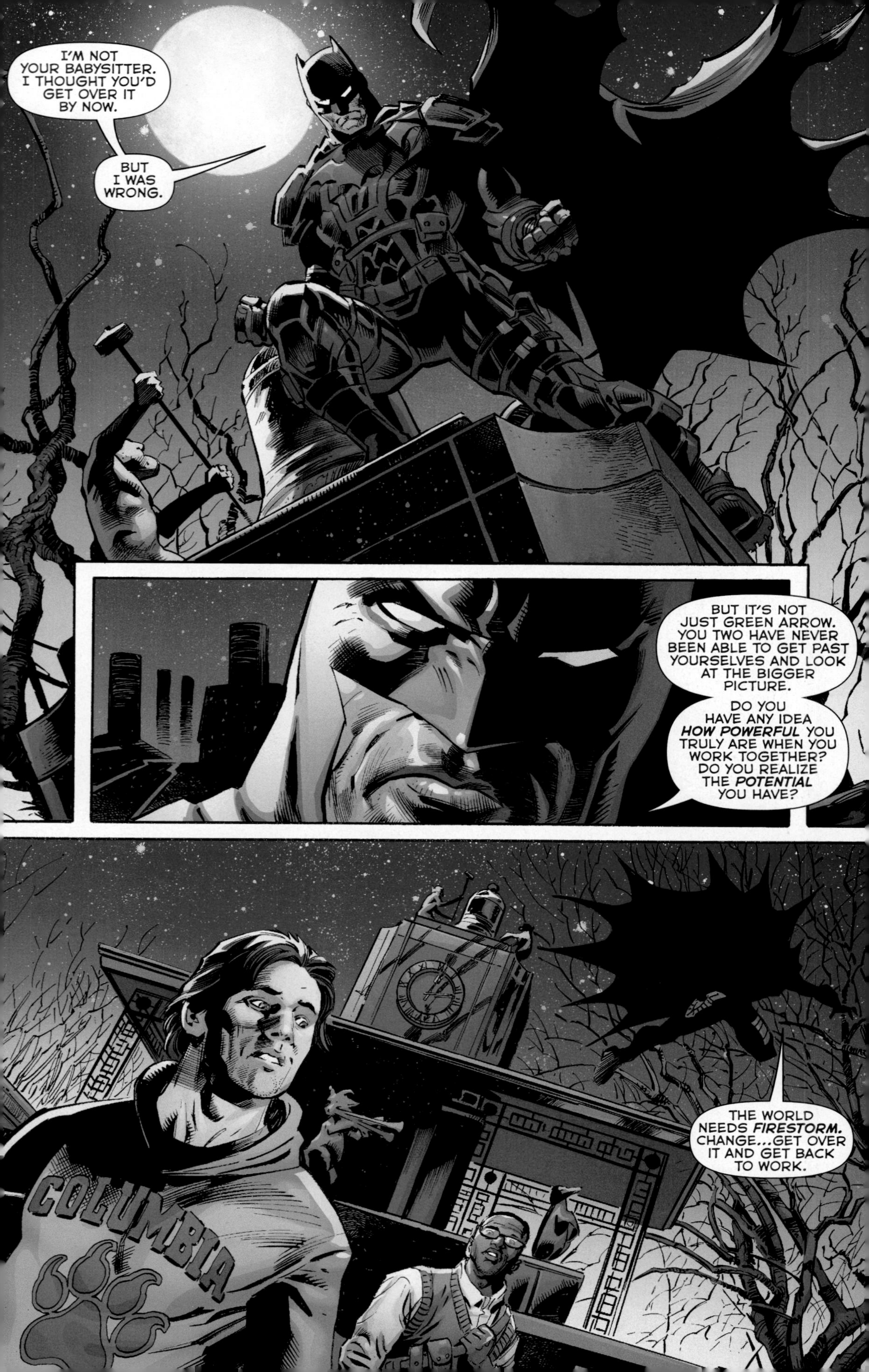
I'M NOT YOUR BABYSITTER. I THOUGHT YOU'D GET OVER IT BY NOW.
BUT I WAS WRONG.
BUT IT'S NOT JUST GREEN ARROW. YOU TWO HAVE NEVER BEEN ABLE TO GET PAST YOURSELVES AND LOOK AT THE BIGGER PICTURE.
DO YOU HAVE ANY IDEA ***HOW POWERFUL*** YOU TRULY ARE WHEN YOU WORK TOGETHER? DO YOU REALIZE THE ***POTENTIAL*** YOU HAVE?
THE WORLD NEEDS ***FIRESTORM.*** CHANGE...GET OVER IT AND GET BACK TO WORK.
COLUMBIA

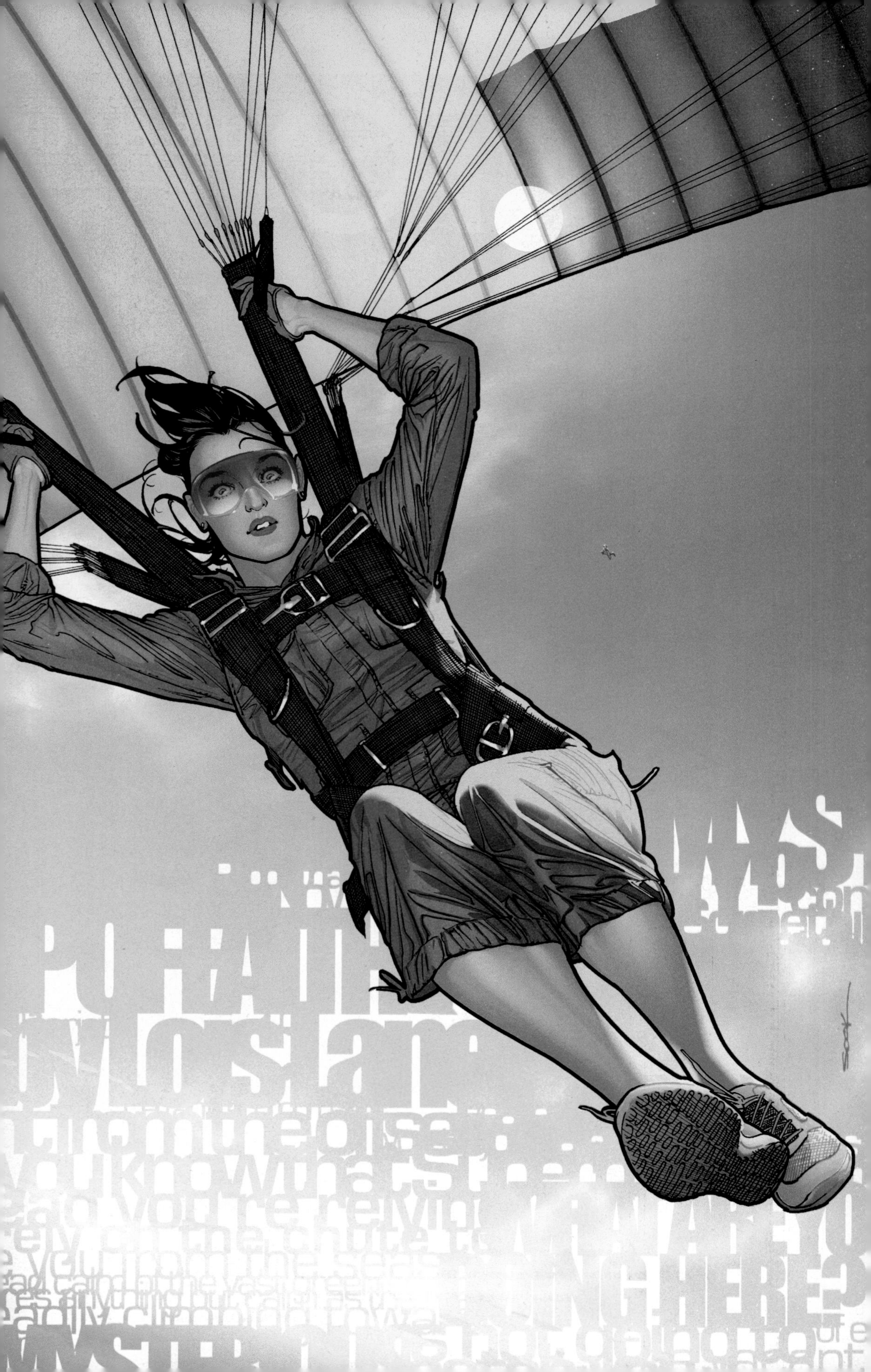

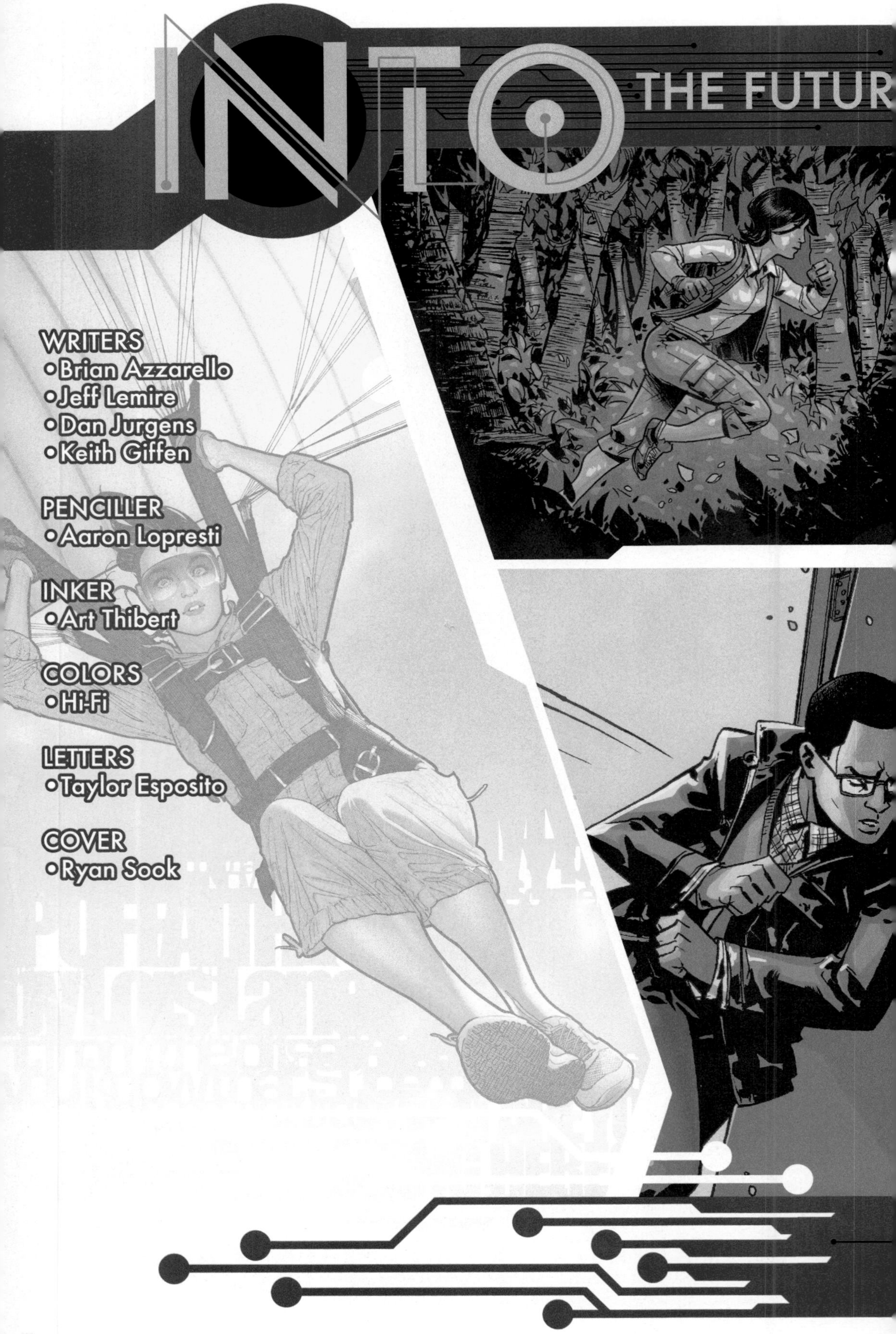
INTO THE FUTUR
WRITERS
•Brian Azzarello
•Jeff Lemire
•Dan Jurgens
•Keith Giffen
PENCILLER
•Aaron Lopresti
INKER
•Art Thibert
COLORS
•Hi-Fi
LETTERS
•Taylor Esposito
COVER
•Ryan Sook

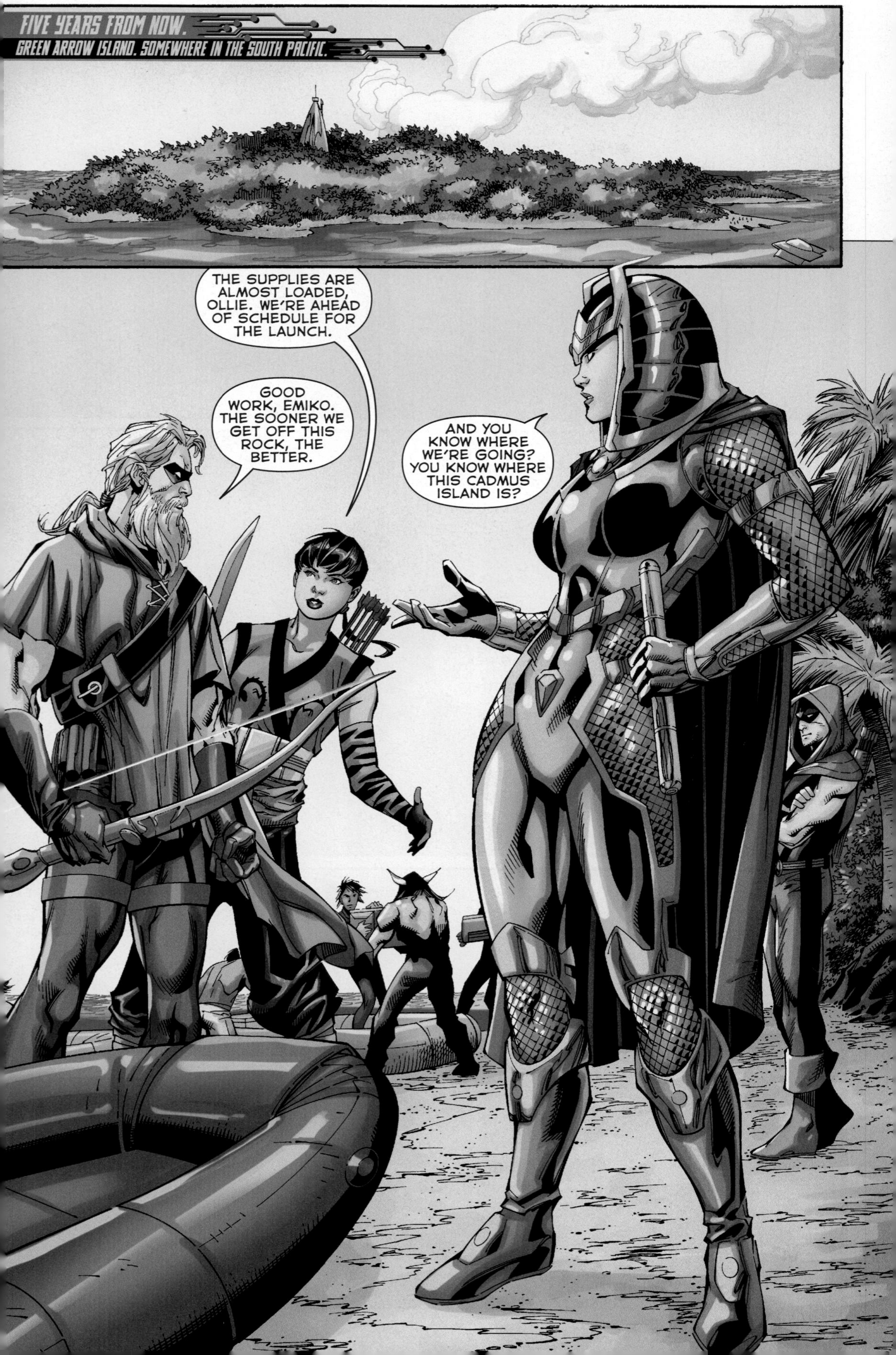
FIVE YEARS FROM NOW.
GREEN ARROW ISLAND. SOMEWHERE IN THE SOUTH PACIFIC.
THE SUPPLIES ARE ALMOST LOADED, OLLIE. WE'RE AHEAD OF SCHEDULE FOR THE LAUNCH.
GOOD WORK, EMIKO. THE SOONER WE GET OFF THIS ROCK, THE BETTER.
AND YOU KNOW WHERE WE'RE GOING? YOU KNOW WHERE THIS CADMUS ISLAND IS?

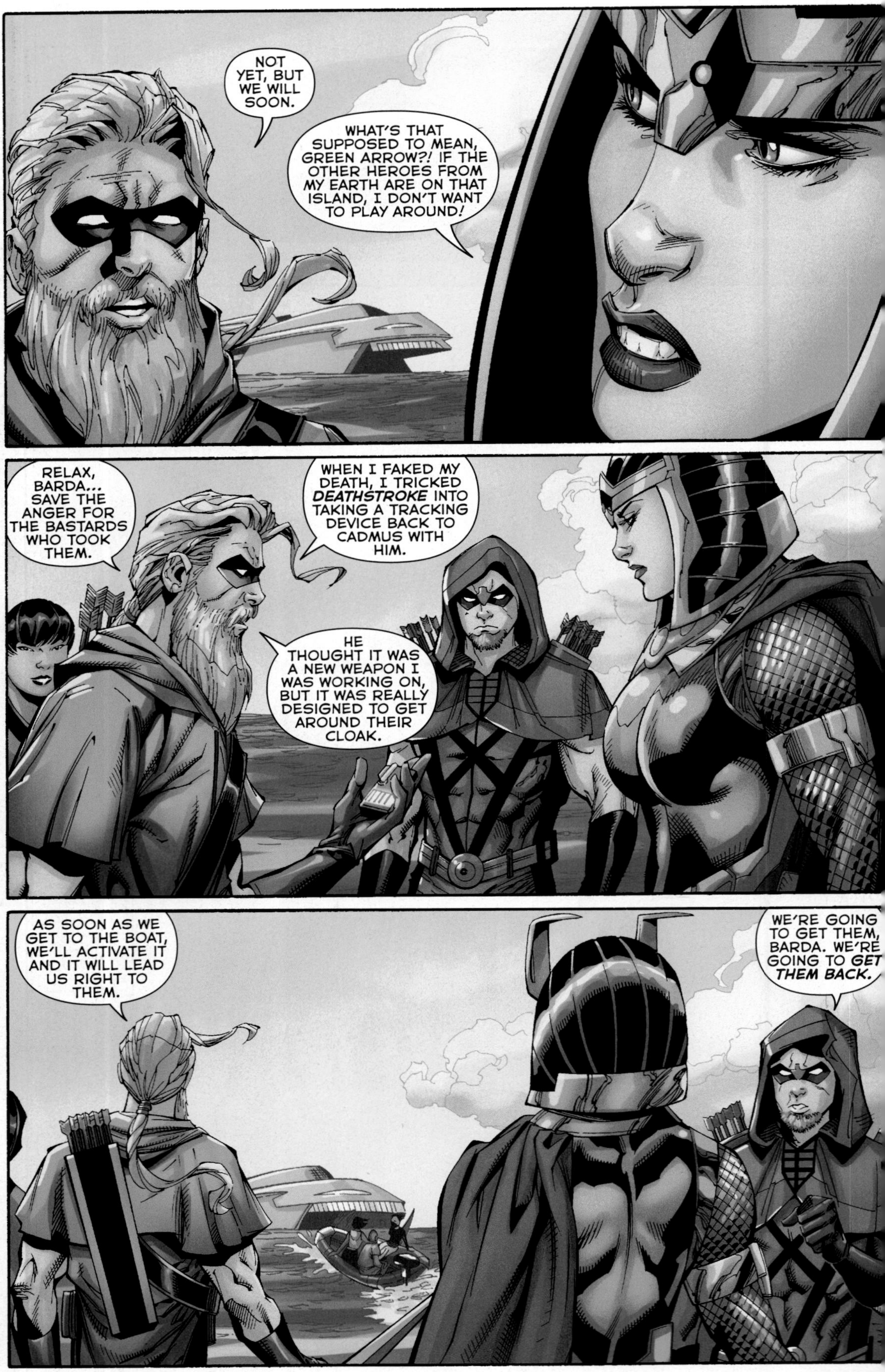
NOT YET, BUT WE WILL SOON.
WHAT'S THAT SUPPOSED TO MEAN, GREEN ARROW?! IF THE OTHER HEROES FROM MY EARTH ARE ON THAT ISLAND, I DON'T WANT TO PLAY AROUND!
RELAX, BARDA... SAVE THE ANGER FOR THE BASTARDS WHO TOOK THEM.
WHEN I FAKED MY DEATH, I TRICKED *DEATHSTROKE* INTO TAKING A TRACKING DEVICE BACK TO CADMUS WITH HIM.
HE THOUGHT IT WAS A NEW WEAPON I WAS WORKING ON, BUT IT WAS REALLY DESIGNED TO GET AROUND THEIR CLOAK.
AS SOON AS WE GET TO THE BOAT, WE'LL ACTIVATE IT AND IT WILL LEAD US RIGHT TO THEM.
WE'RE GOING TO GET THEM, BARDA. WE'RE GOING TO *GET THEM BACK.*

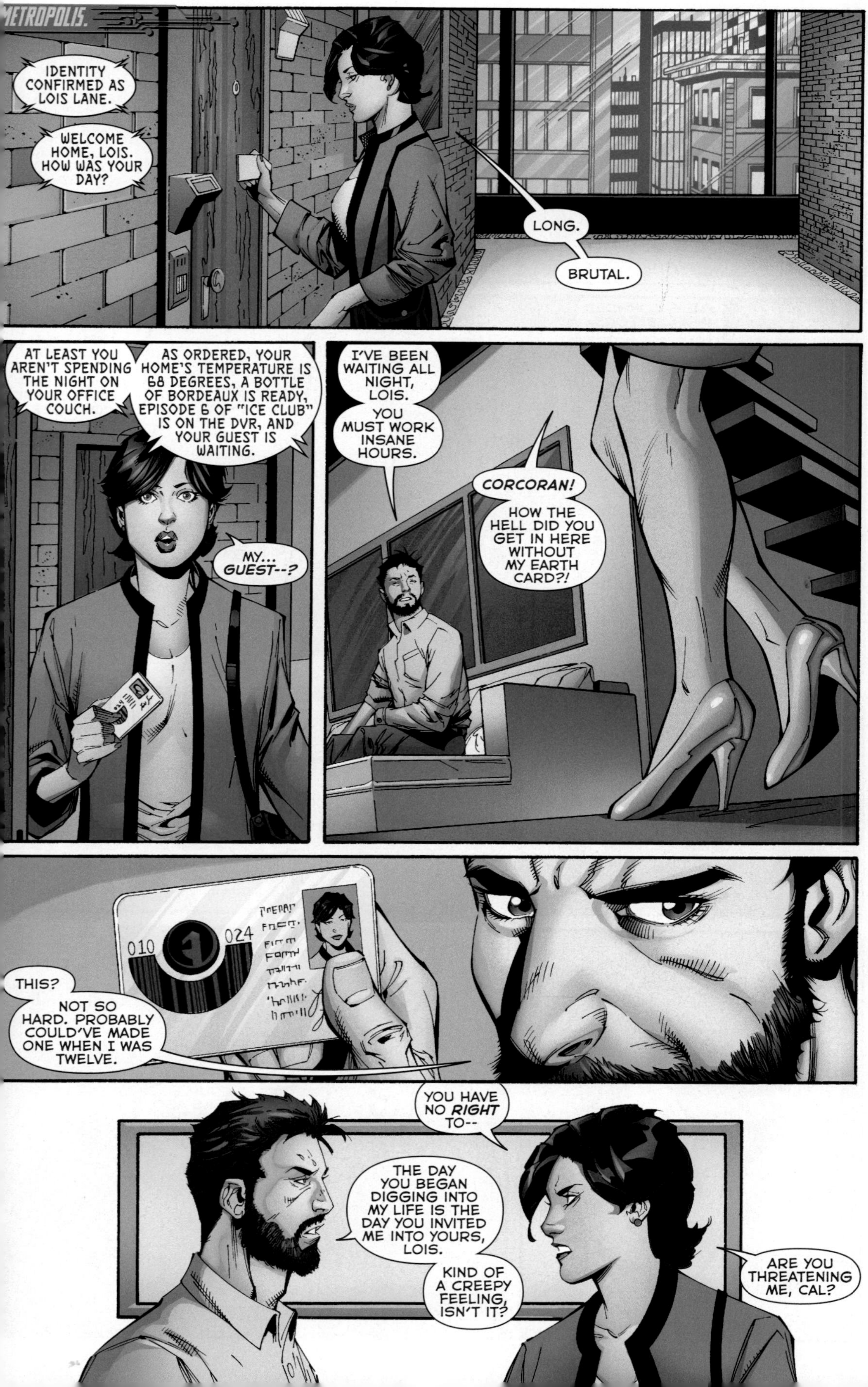
METROPOLIS.
IDENTITY CONFIRMED AS LOIS LANE.
WELCOME HOME, LOIS. HOW WAS YOUR DAY?
LONG.
BRUTAL.
AT LEAST YOU AREN'T SPENDING THE NIGHT ON YOUR OFFICE COUCH.
AS ORDERED, YOUR HOME'S TEMPERATURE IS 68 DEGREES, A BOTTLE OF BORDEAUX IS READY, EPISODE 6 OF "ICE CLUB" IS ON THE DVR, AND YOUR GUEST IS WAITING.
MY... GUEST--?
I'VE BEEN WAITING ALL NIGHT, LOIS.
YOU MUST WORK INSANE HOURS.
CORCORAN!
HOW THE HELL DID YOU GET IN HERE WITHOUT MY EARTH CARD?!
010
024
THIS?
NOT SO HARD. PROBABLY COULD'VE MADE ONE WHEN I WAS TWELVE.
YOU HAVE NO RIGHT TO--
THE DAY YOU BEGAN DIGGING INTO MY LIFE IS THE DAY YOU INVITED ME INTO YOURS, LOIS.
KIND OF A CREEPY FEELING, ISN'T IT?
ARE YOU THREATENING ME, CAL?

HARDLY. THAT'D ONLY MAKE YOU A BIGGER PROBLEM TO DEAL WITH.

I'M HERE BECAUSE OF MADISON PAYNE.

SHE'S *MISSING.*

AND THAT INVOLVES ME *HOW?*

SHE'S CONFIDED IN YOU BEFORE. HAVE YOU HEARD FROM HER?

I DID WHAT YOU ADVISED.

TOOK A LEAP OF FAITH AND CONFESSED.

TOLD HER I USED TO BE RED ROBIN.

NOT A WORD. DID SOMETHING GO DOWN BETWEEN YOU TWO?

SHE DIDN'T TAKE IT WELL.

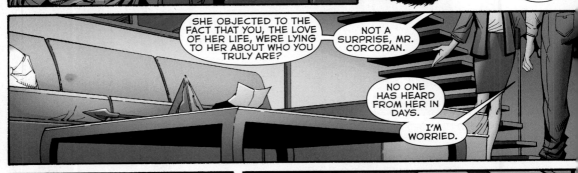

SHE OBJECTED TO THE FACT THAT YOU, THE LOVE OF HER LIFE, WERE LYING TO HER ABOUT WHO YOU TRULY ARE?

NOT A SURPRISE, MR. CORCORAN.

NO ONE HAS HEARD FROM HER IN DAYS.

I'M WORRIED.

YOU'LL FIND HER. YOU'RE GOOD WITH MYSTERIES.

SPEAKING OF WHICH--

--THESE ITEMS I RECEIVED AFTER GREEN ARROW'S FUNERAL...

A COUPLE OF WEEKS AGO, YOU SAID THEY WERE INTENDED FOR *YOU?*

UNDOUBTEDLY.

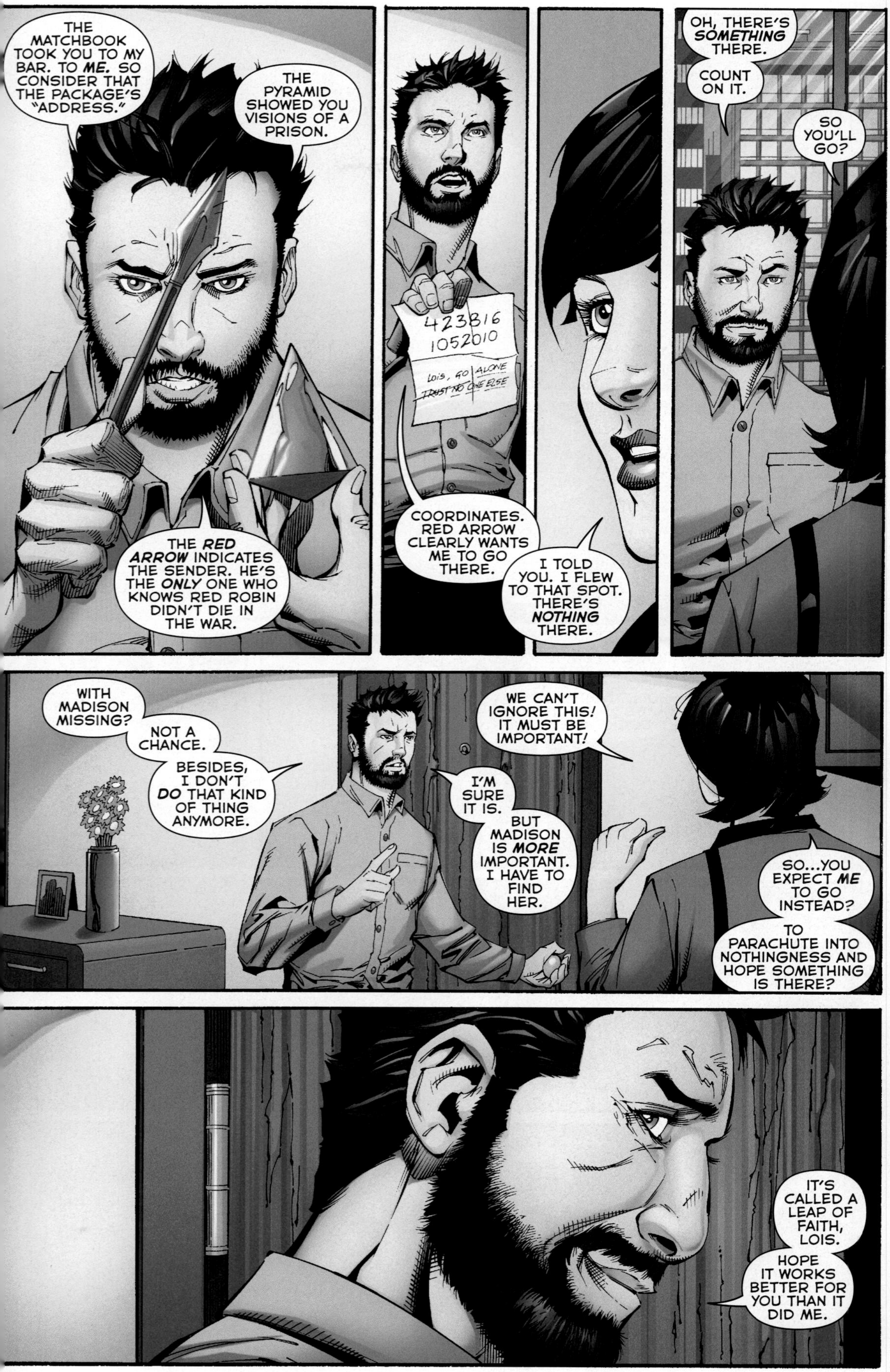

THE MATCHBOOK TOOK YOU TO MY BAR. TO ME. SO CONSIDER THAT THE PACKAGE'S "ADDRESS."
THE PYRAMID SHOWED YOU VISIONS OF A PRISON.
THE RED ARROW INDICATES THE SENDER. HE'S THE ONLY ONE WHO KNOWS RED ROBIN DIDN'T DIE IN THE WAR.
423816
1052010
Lois, GO ALONE
TRUST NO ONE ELSE
COORDINATES. RED ARROW CLEARLY WANTS ME TO GO THERE.
I TOLD YOU. I FLEW TO THAT SPOT. THERE'S NOTHING THERE.
OH, THERE'S SOMETHING THERE.
COUNT ON IT.
SO YOU'LL GO?
WITH MADISON MISSING?
NOT A CHANCE.
BESIDES, I DON'T DO THAT KIND OF THING ANYMORE.
WE CAN'T IGNORE THIS! IT MUST BE IMPORTANT!
I'M SURE IT IS.
BUT MADISON IS MORE IMPORTANT. I HAVE TO FIND HER.
SO...YOU EXPECT ME TO GO INSTEAD?
TO PARACHUTE INTO NOTHINGNESS AND HOPE SOMETHING IS THERE?
IT'S CALLED A LEAP OF FAITH, LOIS.
HOPE IT WORKS BETTER FOR YOU THAN IT DID ME.

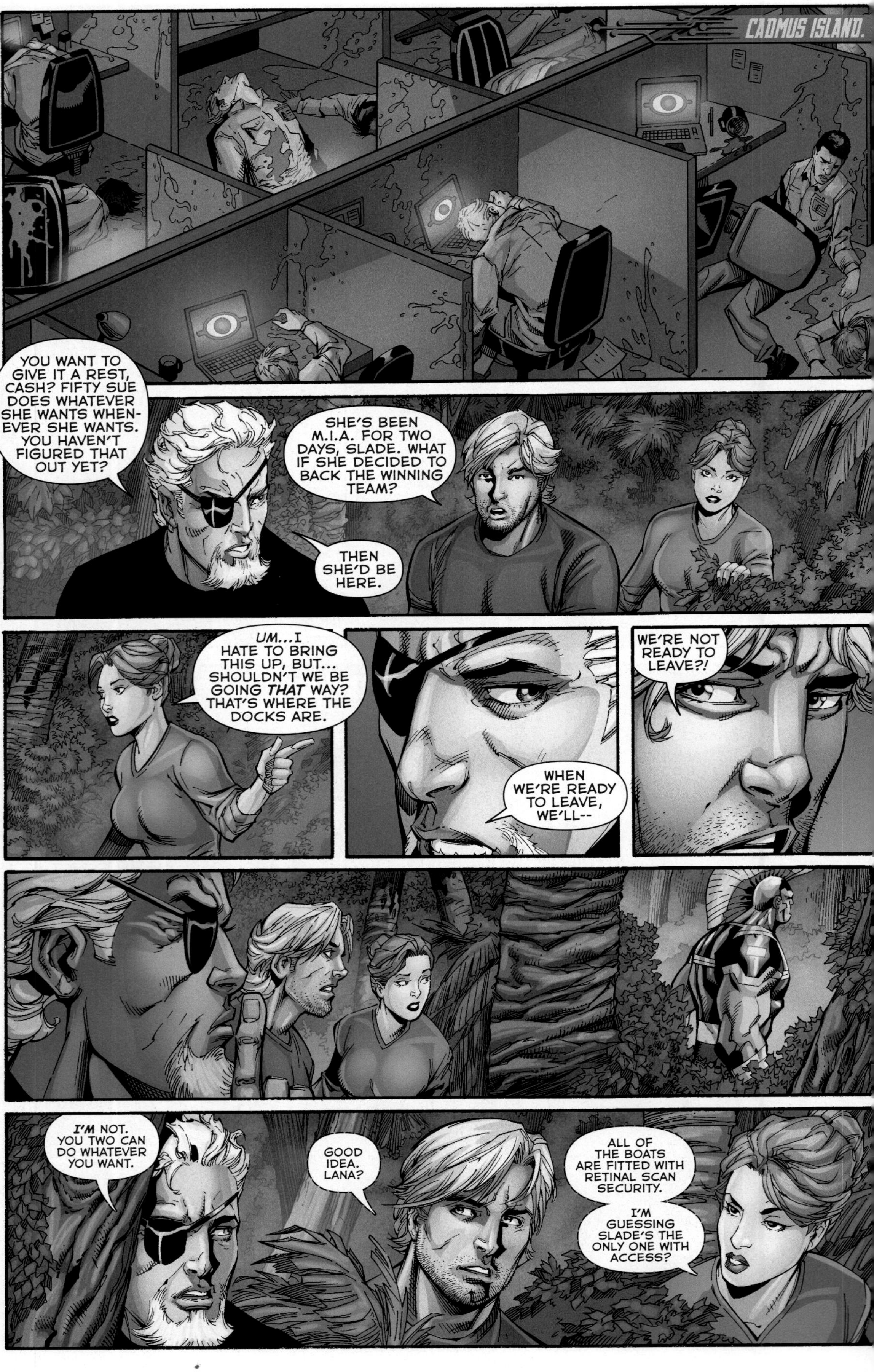
CADMUS ISLAND.
YOU WANT TO GIVE IT A REST, CASH? FIFTY SUE DOES WHATEVER SHE WANTS WHEN-EVER SHE WANTS. YOU HAVEN'T FIGURED THAT OUT YET?
SHE'S BEEN M.I.A. FOR TWO DAYS, SLADE. WHAT IF SHE DECIDED TO BACK THE WINNING TEAM?
THEN SHE'D BE HERE.
UM...I HATE TO BRING THIS UP, BUT... SHOULDN'T WE BE GOING THAT WAY? THAT'S WHERE THE DOCKS ARE.
WHEN WE'RE READY TO LEAVE, WE'LL--
WE'RE NOT READY TO LEAVE?!
I'M NOT. YOU TWO CAN DO WHATEVER YOU WANT.
GOOD IDEA. LANA?
ALL OF THE BOATS ARE FITTED WITH RETINAL SCAN SECURITY.
I'M GUESSING SLADE'S THE ONLY ONE WITH ACCESS?

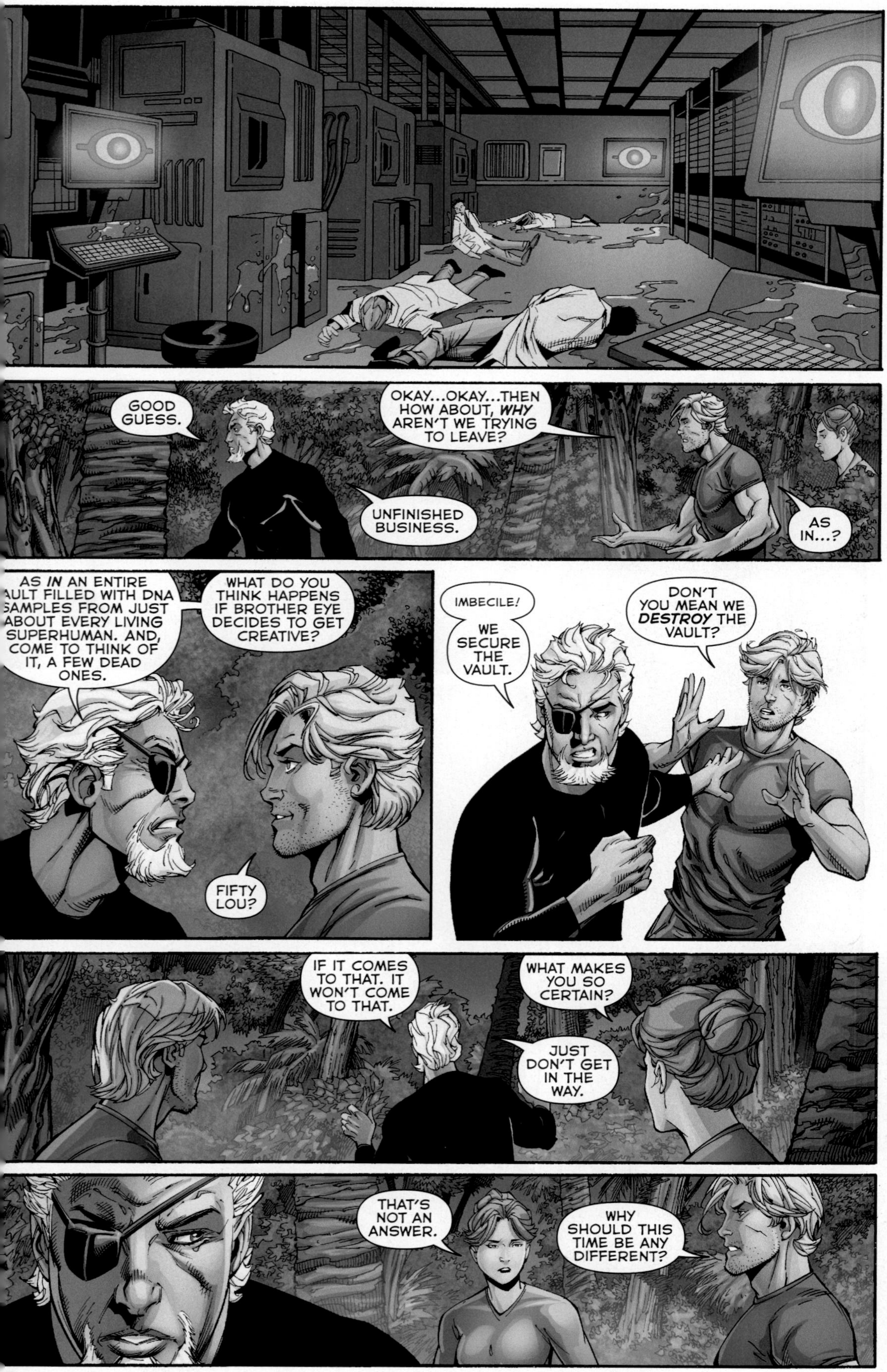
GOOD GUESS.
OKAY...OKAY...THEN HOW ABOUT, WHY AREN'T WE TRYING TO LEAVE?
UNFINISHED BUSINESS.
AS IN...?
AS IN AN ENTIRE VAULT FILLED WITH DNA SAMPLES FROM JUST ABOUT EVERY LIVING SUPERHUMAN. AND, COME TO THINK OF IT, A FEW DEAD ONES.
WHAT DO YOU THINK HAPPENS IF BROTHER EYE DECIDES TO GET CREATIVE?
FIFTY LOU?
IMBECILE!
WE SECURE THE VAULT.
DON'T YOU MEAN WE DESTROY THE VAULT?
IF IT COMES TO THAT. IT WON'T COME TO THAT.
WHAT MAKES YOU SO CERTAIN?
JUST DON'T GET IN THE WAY.
THAT'S NOT AN ANSWER.
WHY SHOULD THIS TIME BE ANY DIFFERENT?

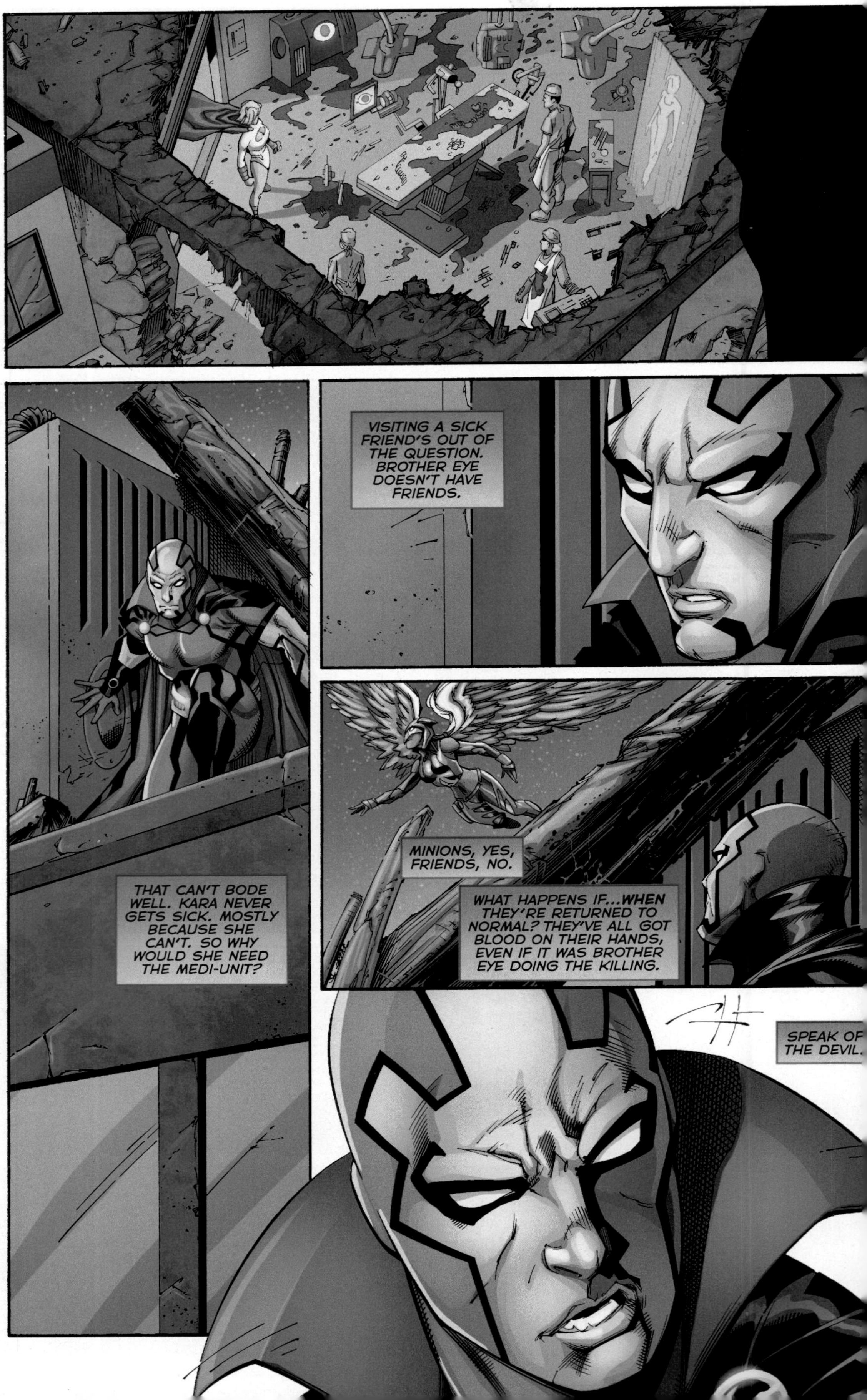
VISITING A SICK FRIEND'S OUT OF THE QUESTION. BROTHER EYE DOESN'T HAVE FRIENDS.
THAT CAN'T BODE WELL. KARA NEVER GETS SICK. MOSTLY BECAUSE SHE CAN'T. SO WHY WOULD SHE NEED THE MEDI-UNIT?
MINIONS, YES, FRIENDS, NO.
WHAT HAPPENS IF...WHEN THEY'RE RETURNED TO NORMAL? THEY'VE ALL GOT BLOOD ON THEIR HANDS, EVEN IF IT WAS BROTHER EYE DOING THE KILLING.
SPEAK OF THE DEVIL.

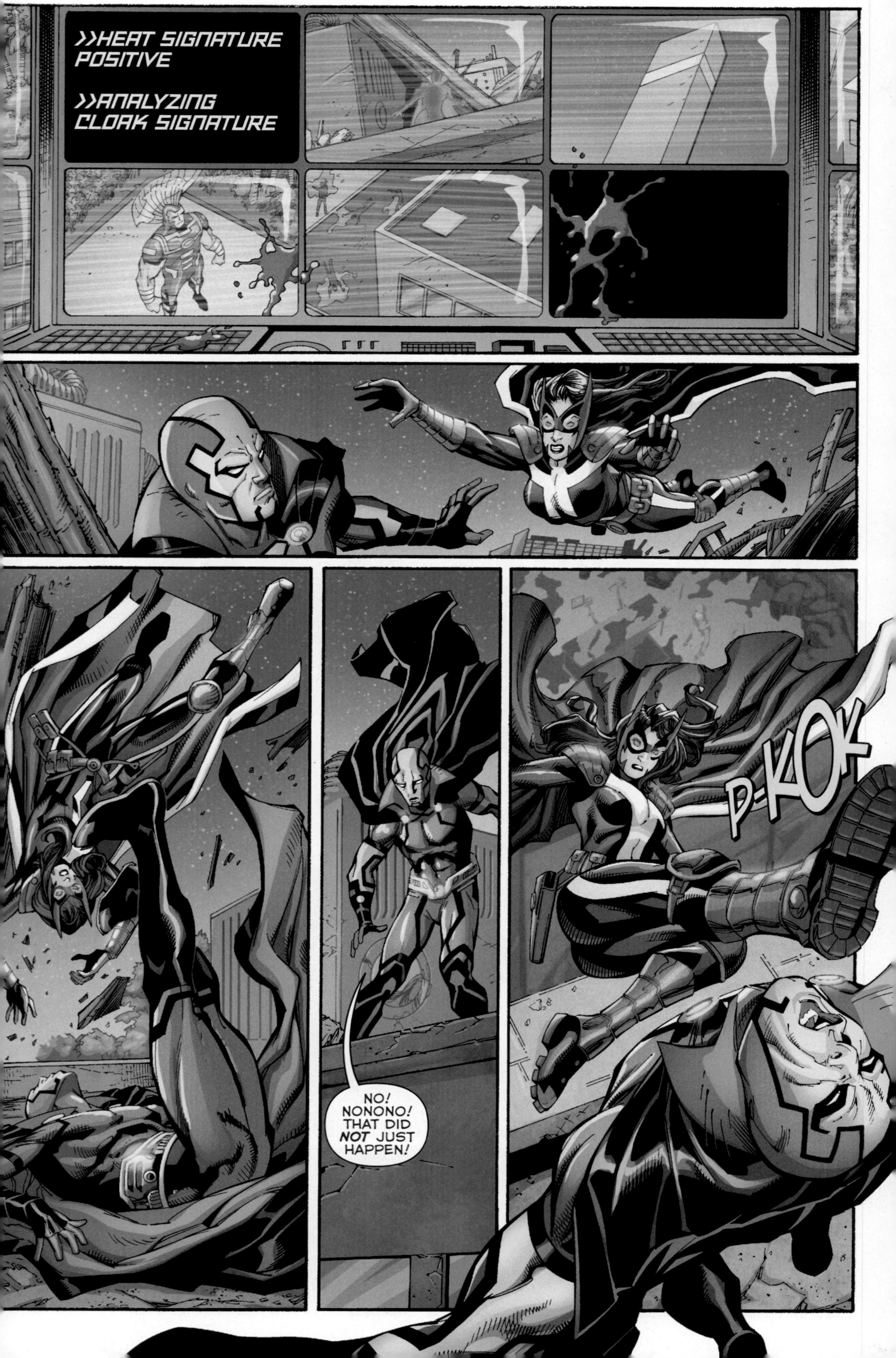
>>HEAT SIGNATURE POSITIVE
>>ANALYZING CLOAK SIGNATURE
NO! NONONO! THAT DID **NOT** JUST HAPPEN!
D-KOK

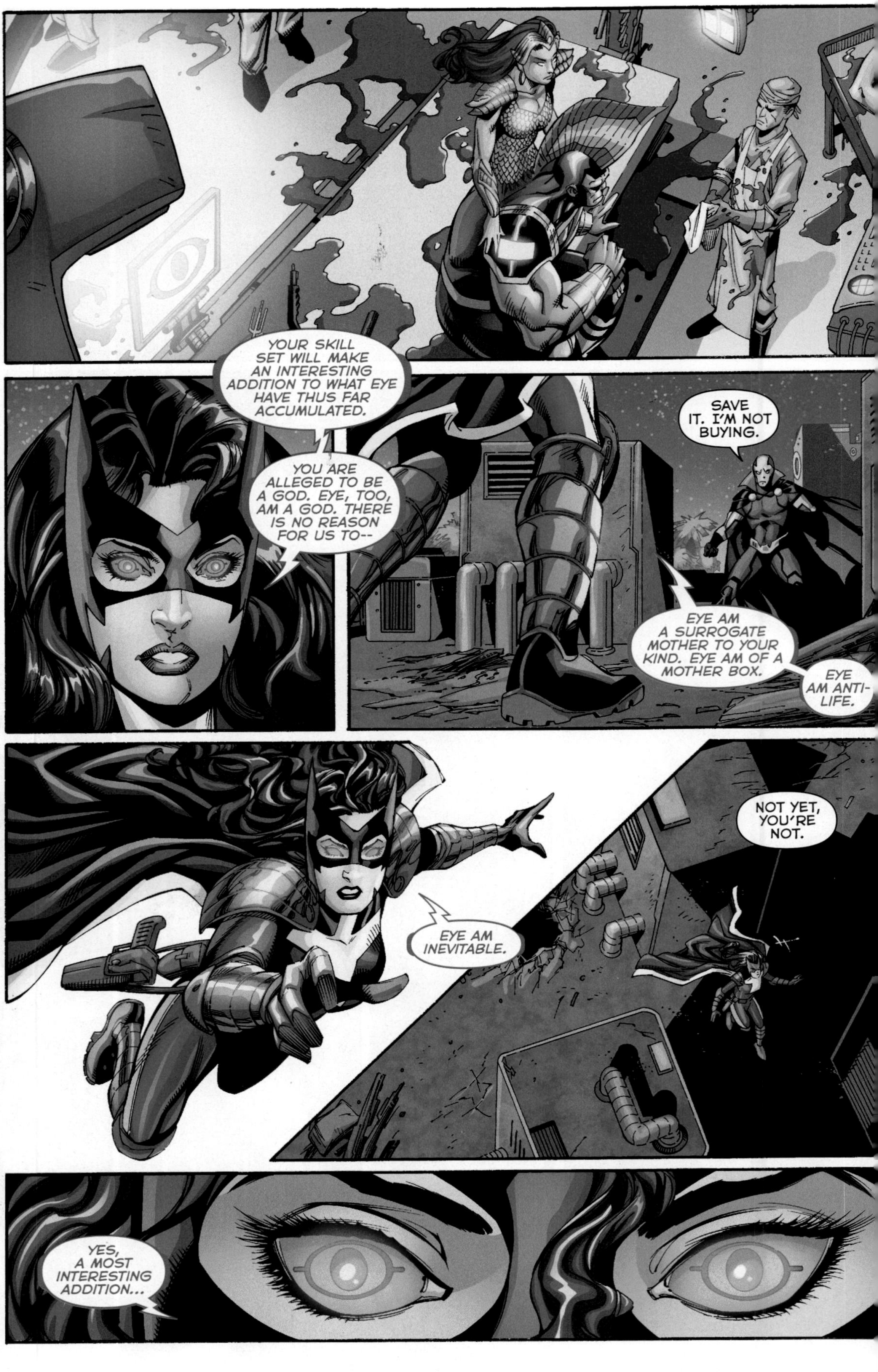
YOUR SKILL SET WILL MAKE AN INTERESTING ADDITION TO WHAT EYE HAVE THUS FAR ACCUMULATED.
YOU ARE ALLEGED TO BE A GOD. EYE, TOO, AM A GOD. THERE IS NO REASON FOR US TO--
SAVE IT. I'M NOT BUYING.
EYE AM A SURROGATE MOTHER TO YOUR KIND. EYE AM OF A MOTHER BOX.
EYE AM ANTI-LIFE.
EYE AM INEVITABLE.
NOT YET, YOU'RE NOT.
YES, A MOST INTERESTING ADDITION...

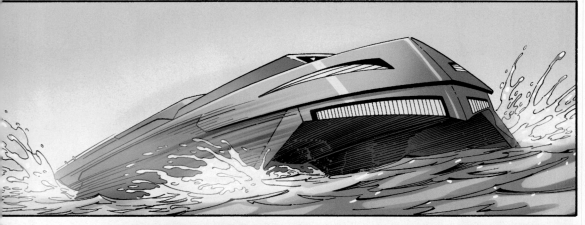

OKAY, DIG...LET'S FIRE UP THE TRACKER AND SEE IF WE CAN PINPOINT THIS DAMNED ISLAND ONCE AND FOR ALL.

WAIT--YOU HAVEN'T EVEN TESTED IT YET? WE JUST LAUNCHED A FULL-ON ASSAULT ON THE BLIND FAITH THAT YOUR GIZMO WOULD WORK?!

MY GIZMOS *ALWAYS* WORK, ONYX.

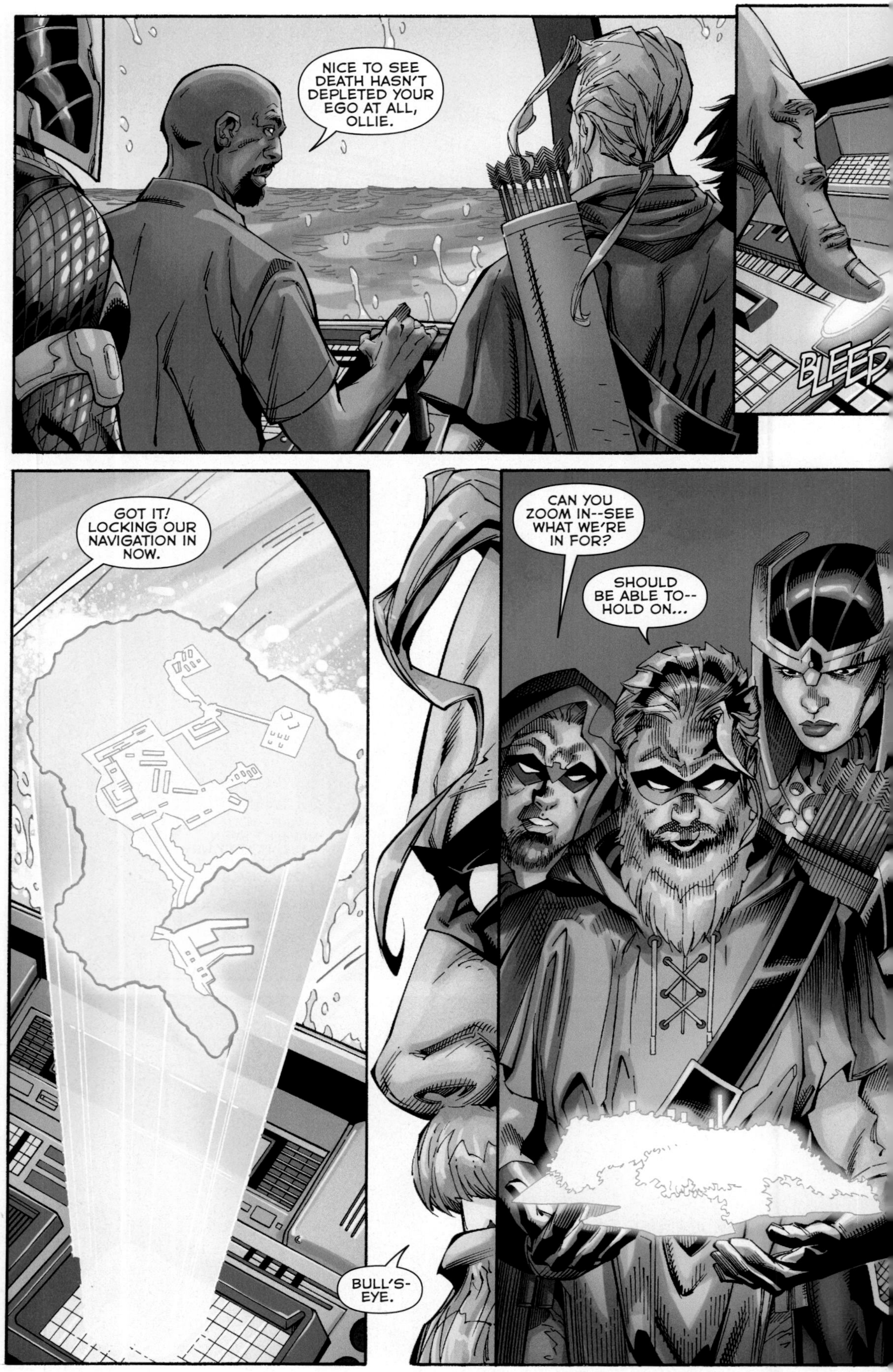
NICE TO SEE DEATH HASN'T DEPLETED YOUR EGO AT ALL, OLLIE.
BLEED
GOT IT! LOCKING OUR NAVIGATION IN NOW.
CAN YOU ZOOM IN--SEE WHAT WE'RE IN FOR?
SHOULD BE ABLE TO--HOLD ON...
BULL'S-EYE.

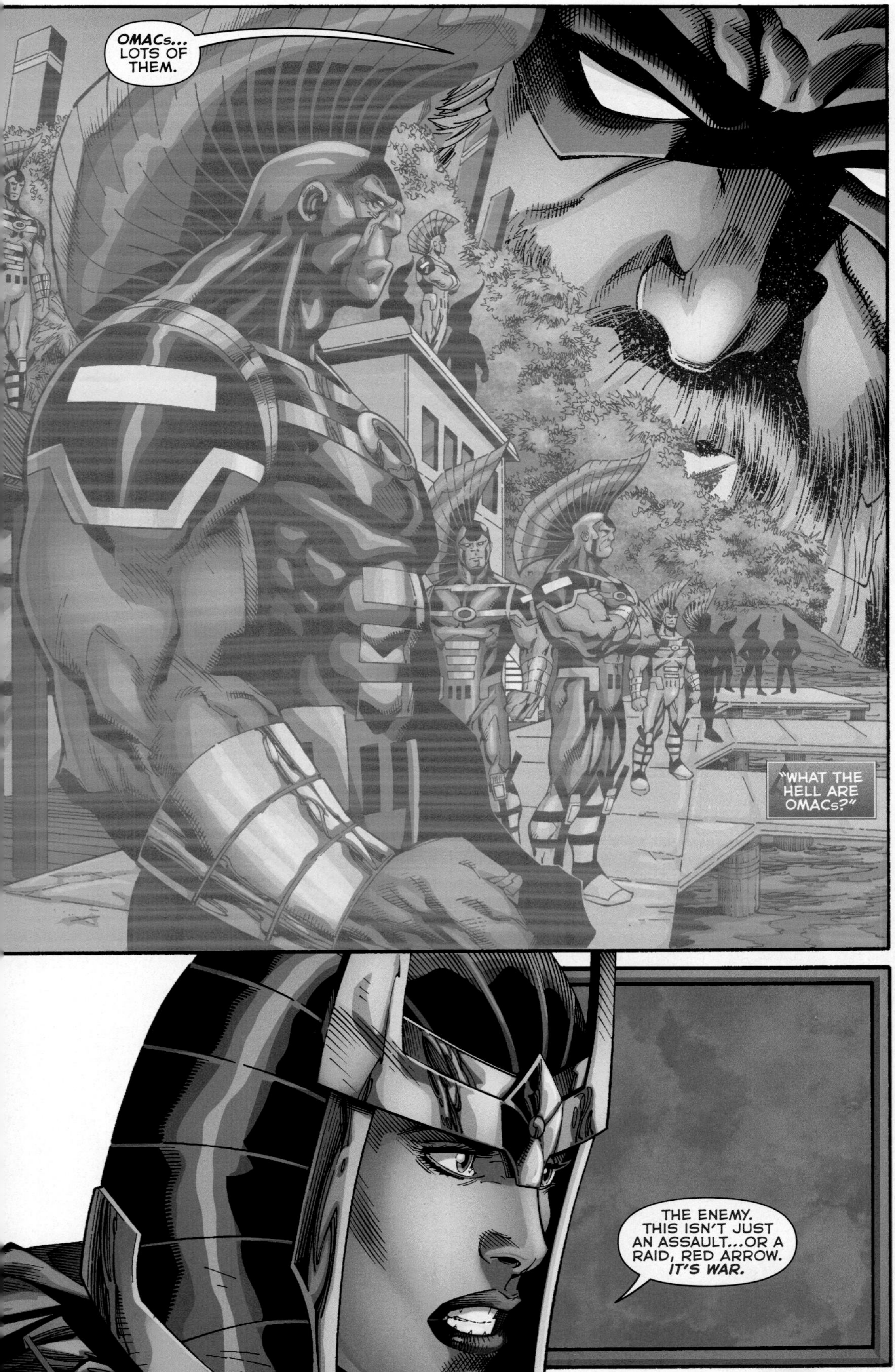
OMACs... LOTS OF THEM.
"WHAT THE HELL ARE OMACs?"
THE ENEMY. THIS ISN'T JUST AN ASSAULT...OR A RAID, RED ARROW. IT'S WAR.

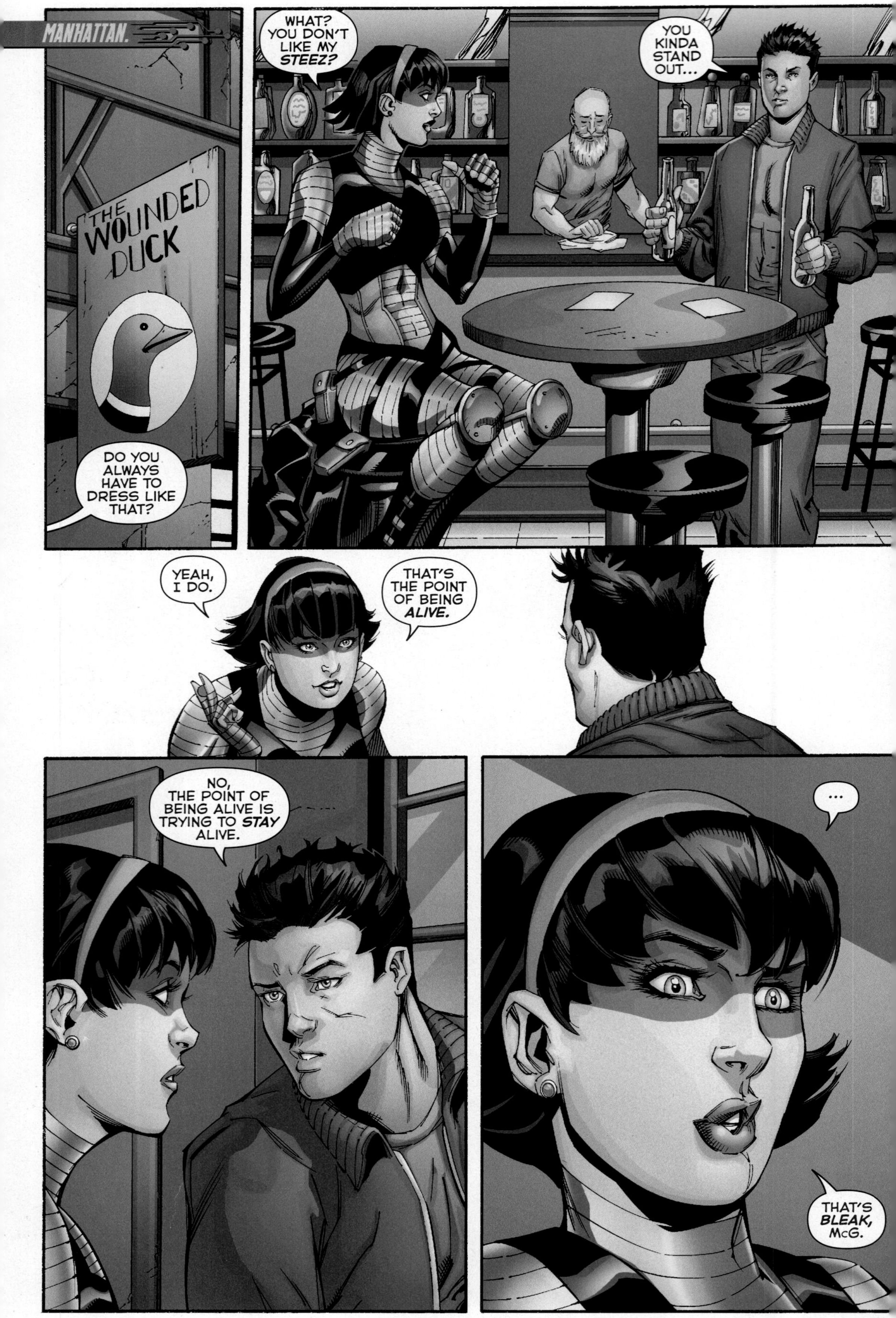
MANHATTAN.
THE WOUNDED DUCK
DO YOU ALWAYS HAVE TO DRESS LIKE THAT?
WHAT? YOU DON'T LIKE MY STEEZ?
YOU KINDA STAND OUT...
YEAH, I DO.
THAT'S THE POINT OF BEING ALIVE.
NO, THE POINT OF BEING ALIVE IS TRYING TO STAY ALIVE.
...
THAT'S BLEAK, McG.

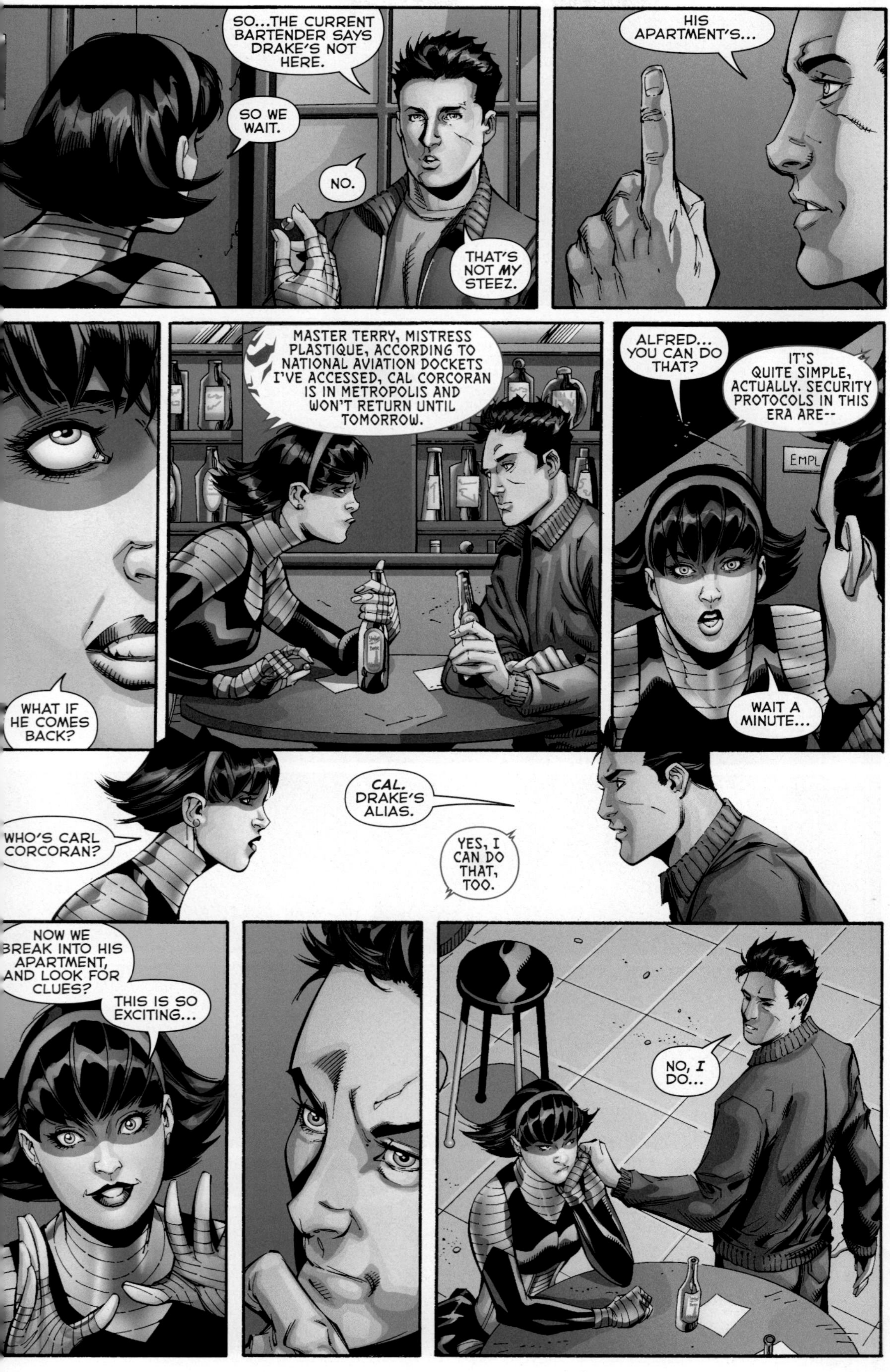
SO...THE CURRENT BARTENDER SAYS DRAKE'S NOT HERE.
SO WE WAIT.
NO.
THAT'S NOT MY STEEZ.
HIS APARTMENT'S...
WHAT IF HE COMES BACK?
MASTER TERRY, MISTRESS PLASTIQUE, ACCORDING TO NATIONAL AVIATION DOCKETS I'VE ACCESSED, CAL CORCORAN IS IN METROPOLIS AND WON'T RETURN UNTIL TOMORROW.
ALFRED... YOU CAN DO THAT?
IT'S QUITE SIMPLE, ACTUALLY. SECURITY PROTOCOLS IN THIS ERA ARE--
EMPL
WAIT A MINUTE...
WHO'S CARL CORCORAN?
CAL. DRAKE'S ALIAS.
YES, I CAN DO THAT, TOO.
NOW WE BREAK INTO HIS APARTMENT, AND LOOK FOR CLUES?
THIS IS SO EXCITING...
NO, I DO...

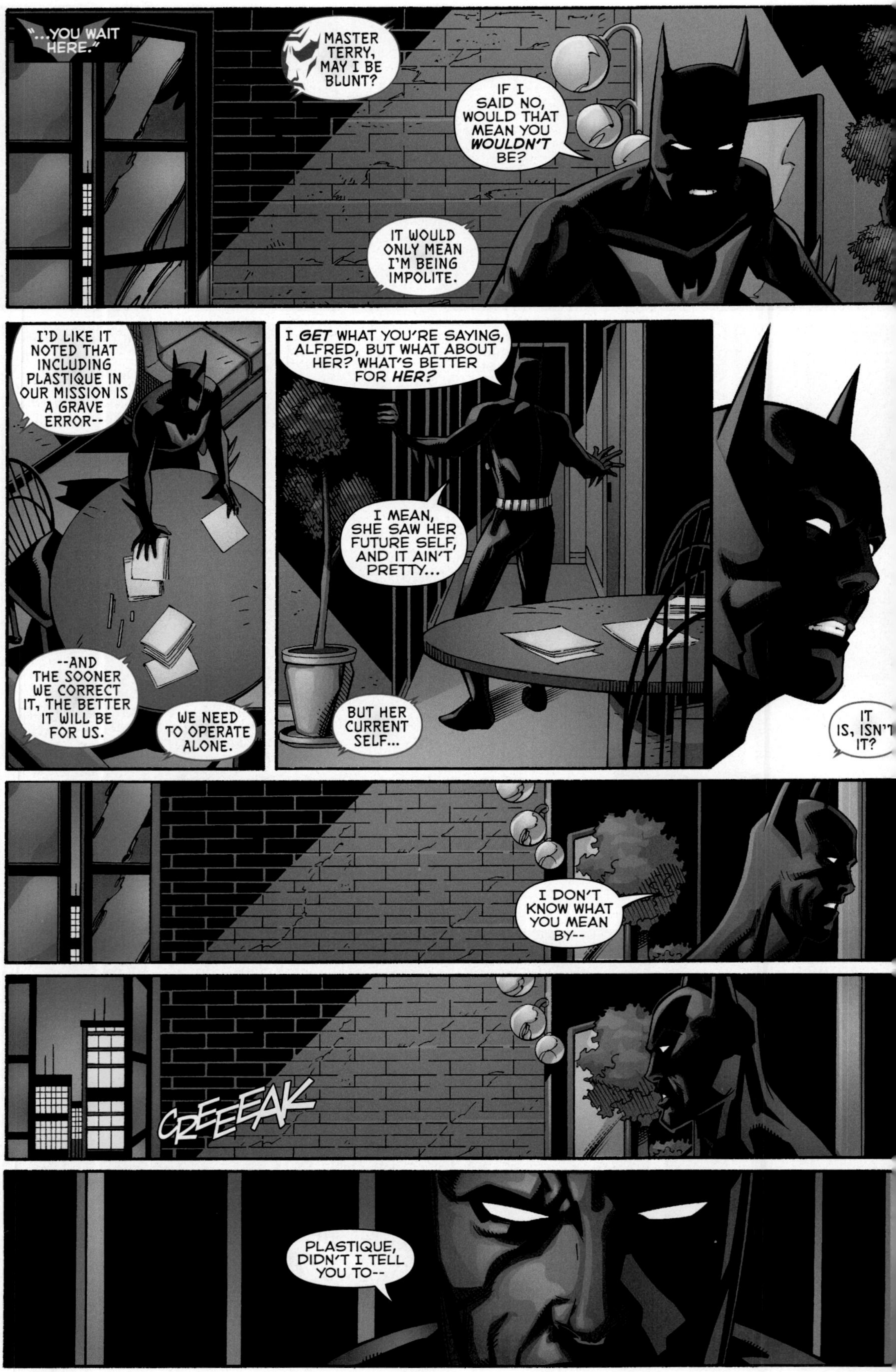
"...YOU WAIT HERE."
MASTER TERRY, MAY I BE BLUNT?
IF I SAID NO, WOULD THAT MEAN YOU WOULDN'T BE?
IT WOULD ONLY MEAN I'M BEING IMPOLITE.
I'D LIKE IT NOTED THAT INCLUDING PLASTIQUE IN OUR MISSION IS A GRAVE ERROR--
--AND THE SOONER WE CORRECT IT, THE BETTER IT WILL BE FOR US.
WE NEED TO OPERATE ALONE.
I GET WHAT YOU'RE SAYING, ALFRED, BUT WHAT ABOUT HER? WHAT'S BETTER FOR HER?
I MEAN, SHE SAW HER FUTURE SELF, AND IT AIN'T PRETTY...
BUT HER CURRENT SELF...
IT IS, ISN'T IT?
I DON'T KNOW WHAT YOU MEAN BY--
CREEEAK
PLASTIQUE, DIDN'T I TELL YOU TO--

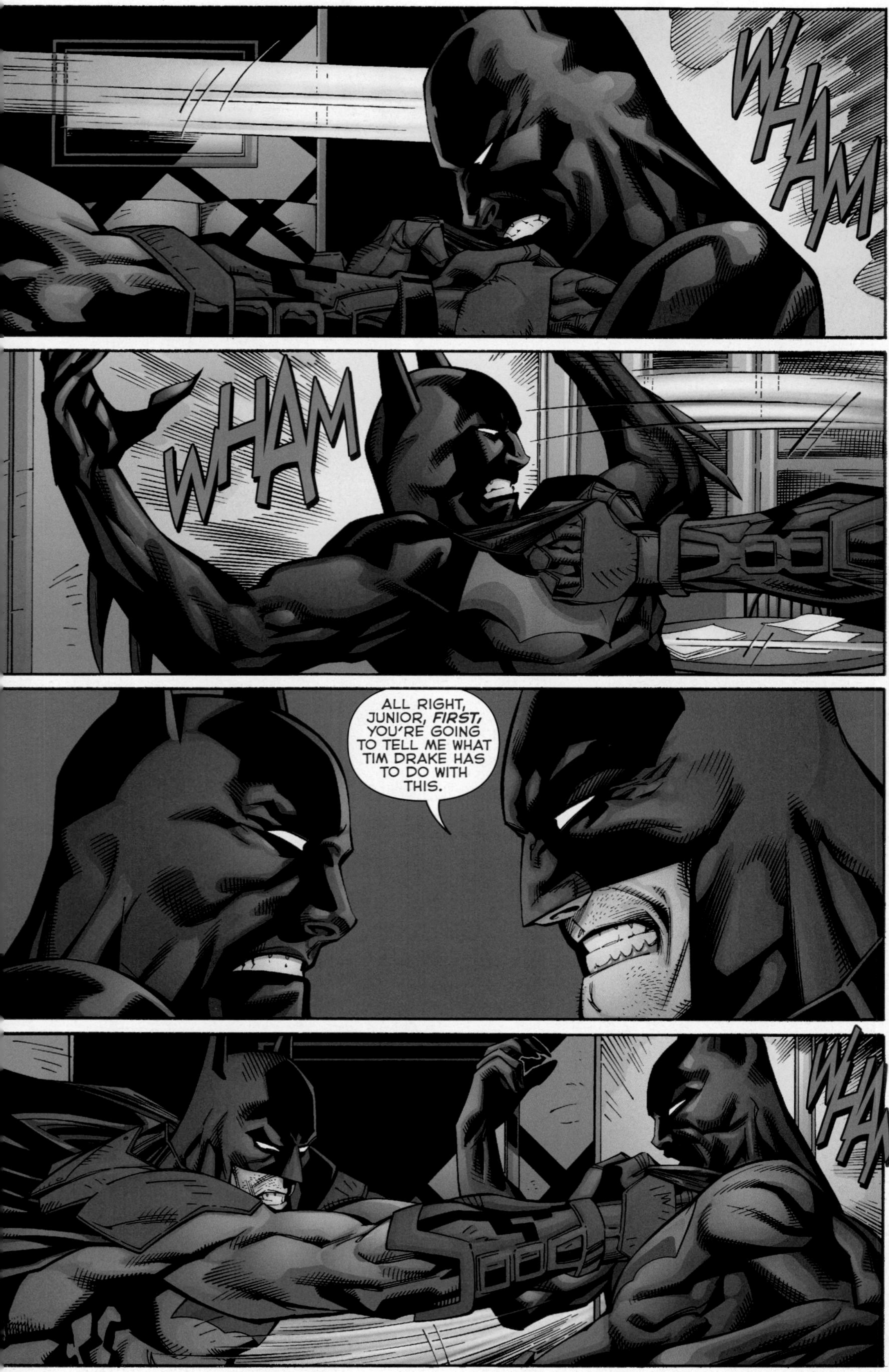
WHAM
WHAM
ALL RIGHT, JUNIOR, FIRST, YOU'RE GOING TO TELL ME WHAT TIM DRAKE HAS TO DO WITH THIS.
WHAM

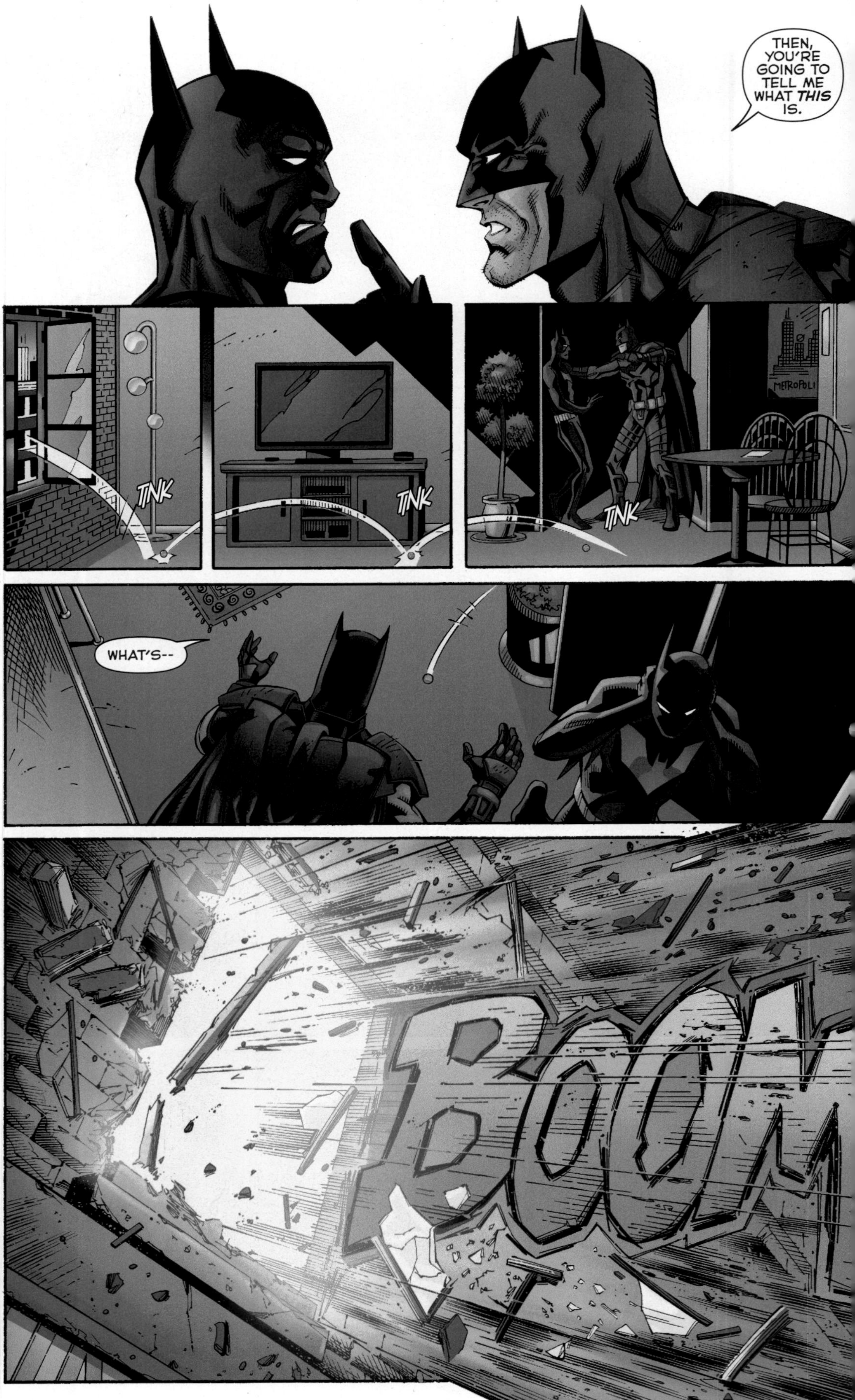
THEN, YOU'RE GOING TO TELL ME WHAT *THIS* IS.
TINK
TINK
METROPOLI
TINK
WHAT'S--
BOOM

YOU'RE CRAZY.

ONE HUNDRED PERCENT CERTIFIABLY *NUTS*.

THANK YOU, BUCK. I LOVE YOU, TOO.

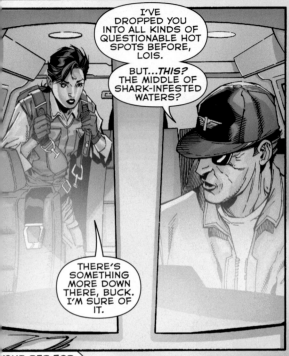

I'VE DROPPED YOU INTO ALL KINDS OF QUESTIONABLE HOT SPOTS BEFORE, LOIS.

BUT...*THIS?* THE MIDDLE OF SHARK-INFESTED WATERS?

THERE'S SOMETHING MORE DOWN THERE, BUCK. I'M SURE OF IT.

YOU WANNA BE JUST LIKE THAT KENT GUY AND EVERY OTHER REPORTER WHO'S DISAPPEARED CHASING A STORY?

I WANT *ANSWERS*, BUCK.

AND I'M GOING TO GET THEM.

OUR REP FOR ECKLESSNESS S WELL EARNED, LOIS.

AND IT'S PAID OFF MANY TIMES OVER.

BUT THIS--

THOSE WERE ALL CALCULATED RISKS, BUCK.

THIS IS NO DIFFERENT.

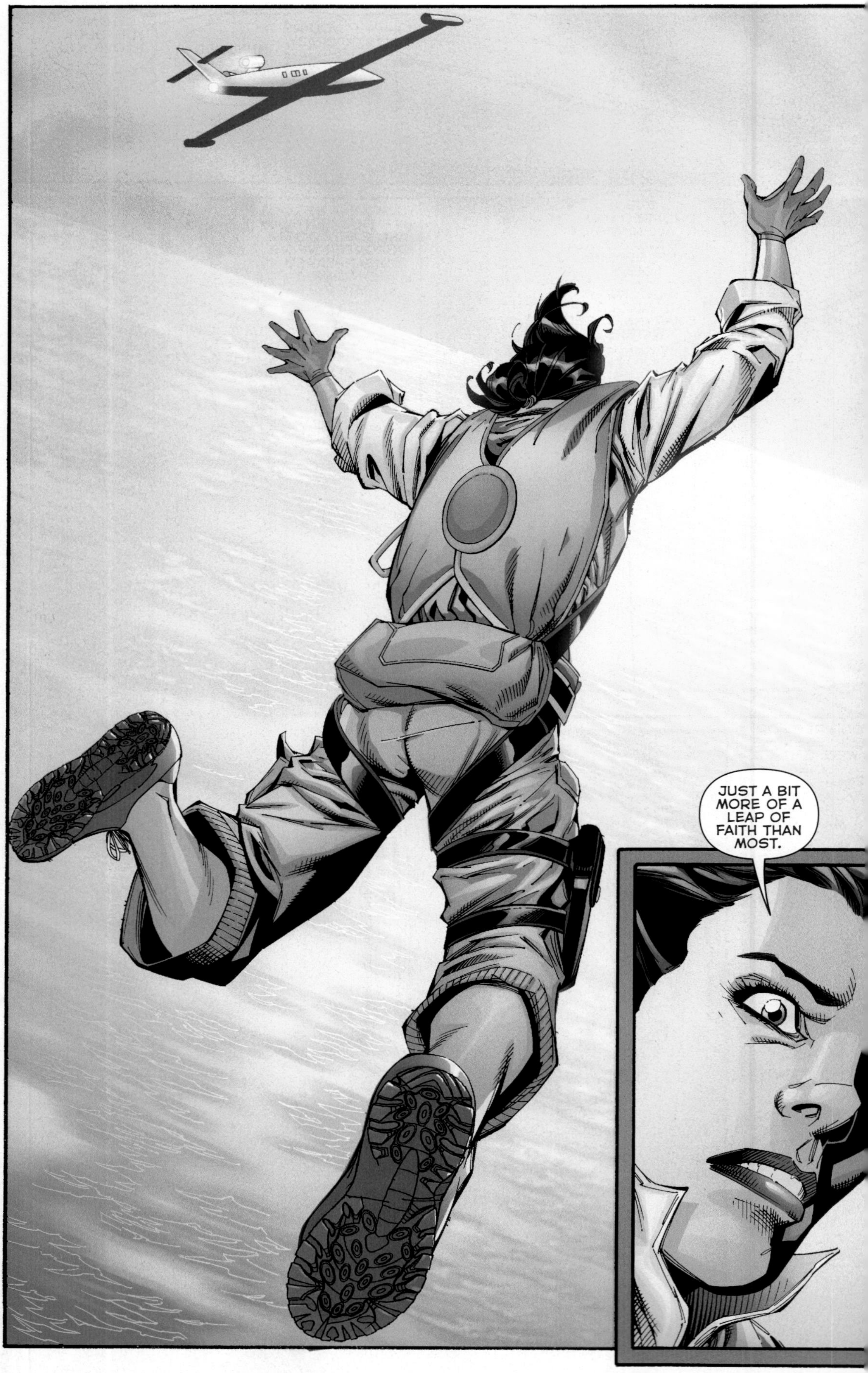
JUST A BIT MORE OF A LEAP OF FAITH THAN MOST.

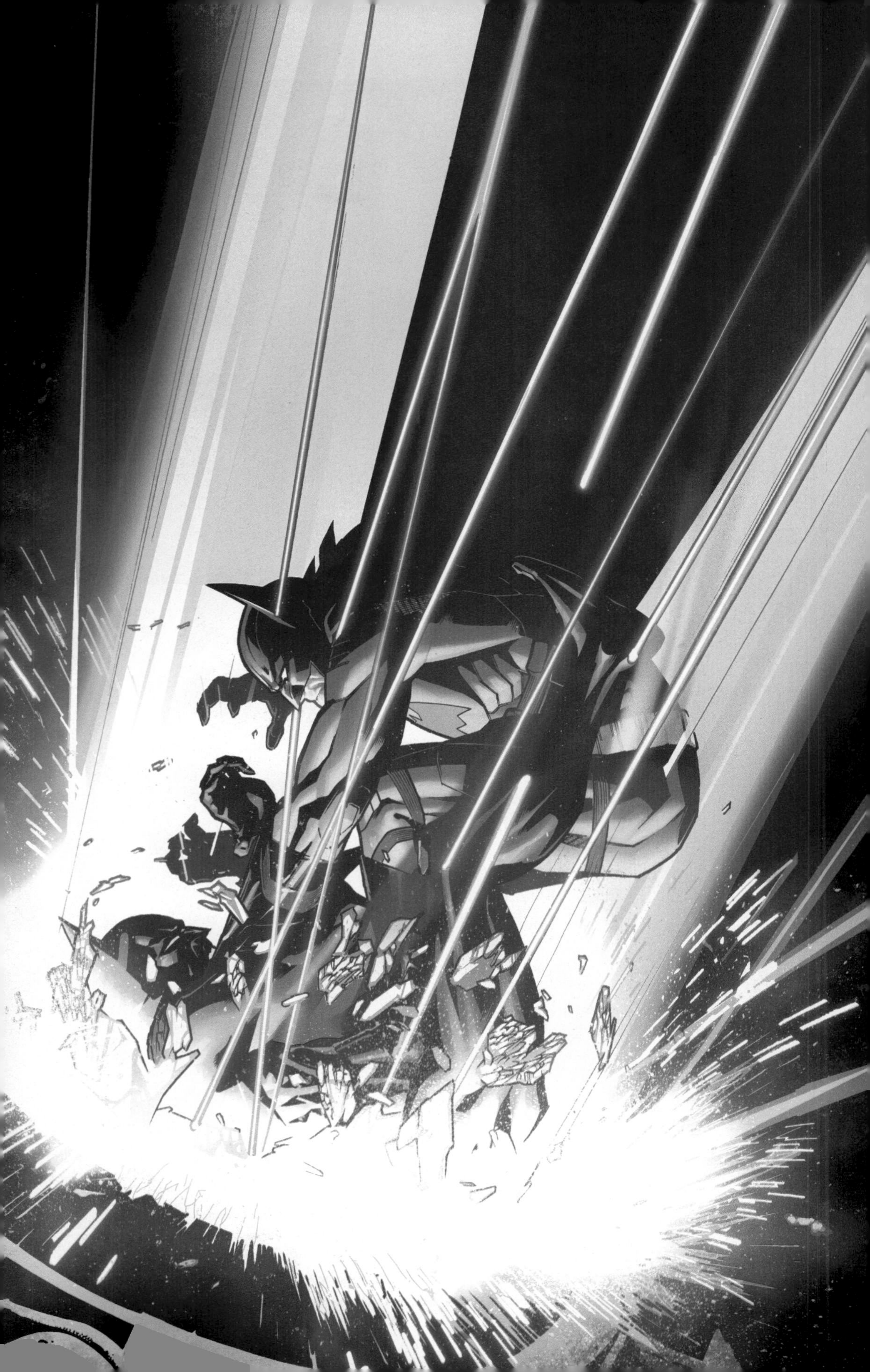

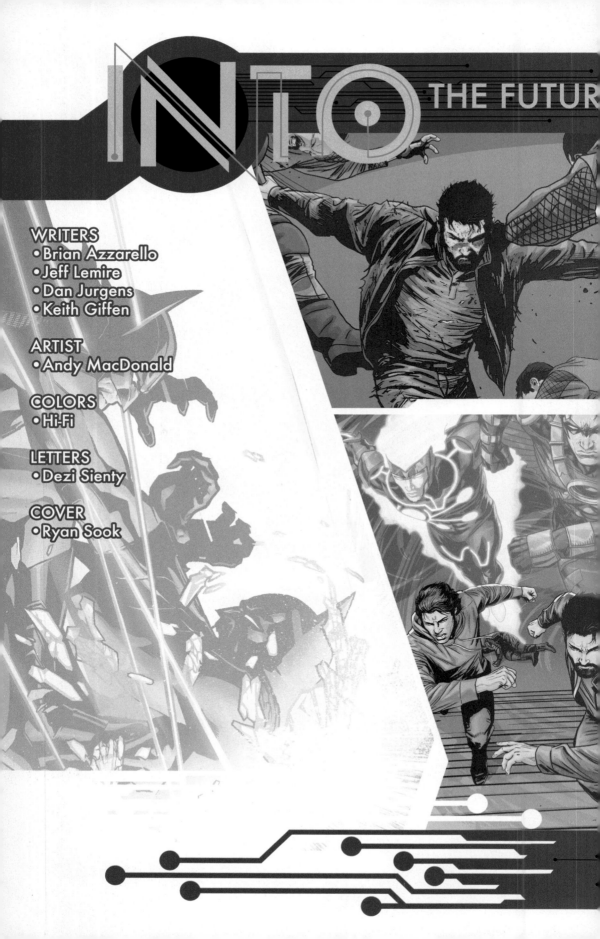

INTO THE FUTUR

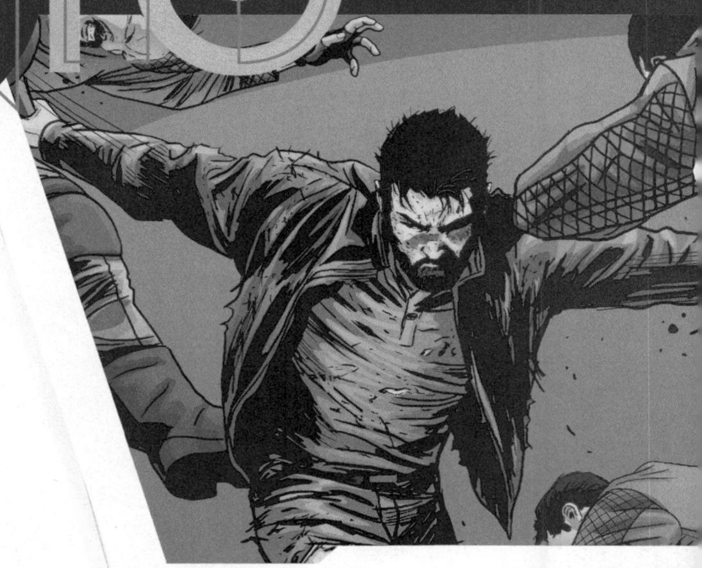

WRITERS
- Brian Azzarello
- Jeff Lemire
- Dan Jurgens
- Keith Giffen

ARTIST
- Andy MacDonald

COLORS
- Hi-Fi

LETTERS
- Dezi Sienty

COVER
- Ryan Sook

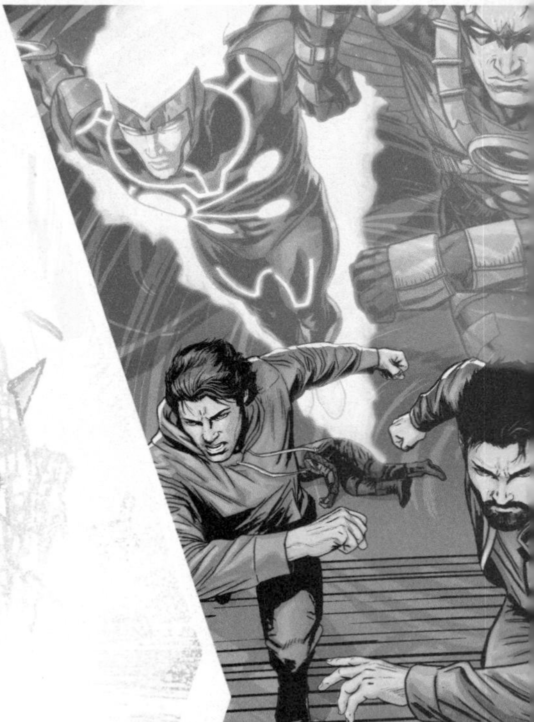

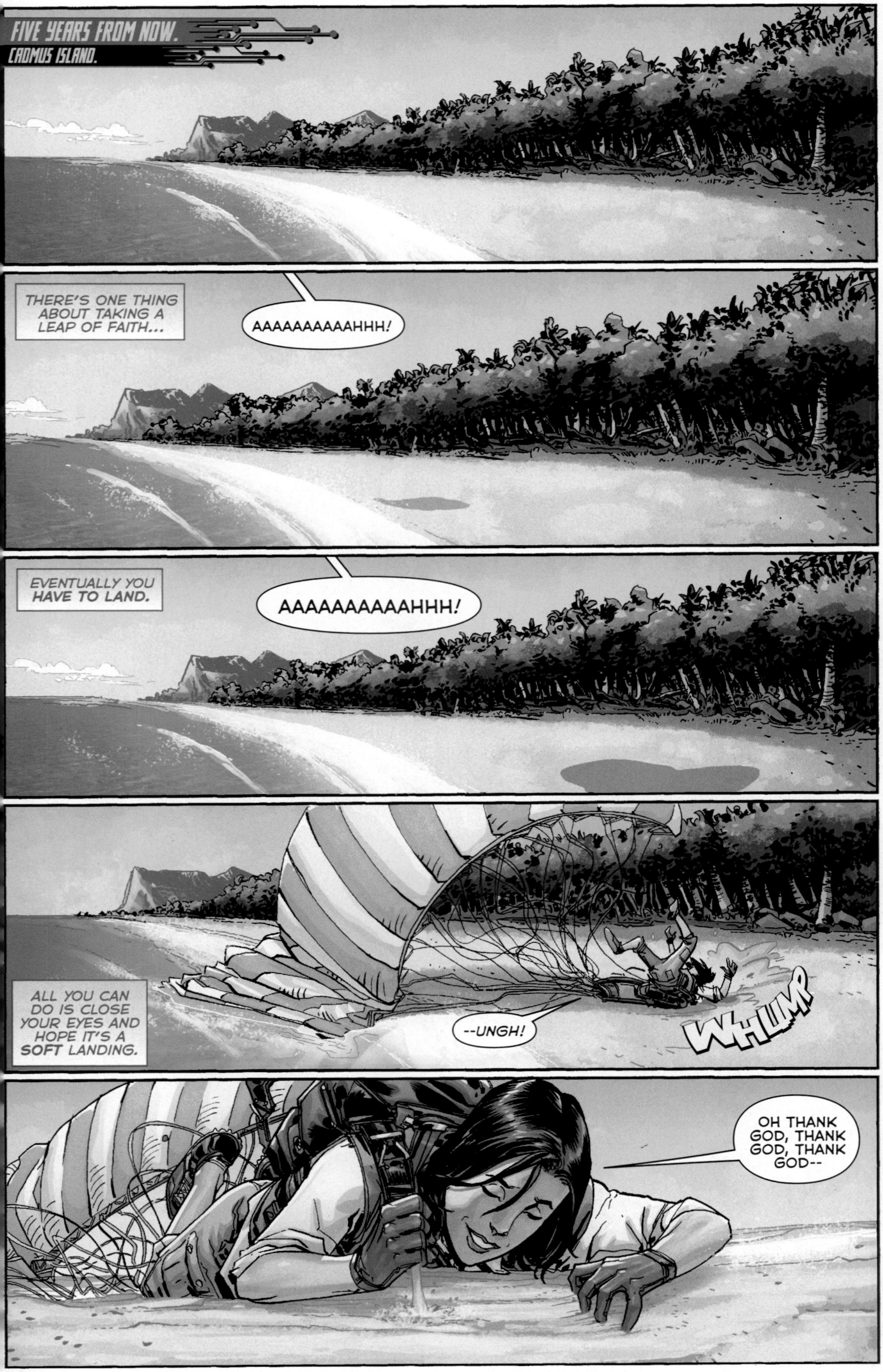
FIVE YEARS FROM NOW.
CADMUS ISLAND.
THERE'S ONE THING ABOUT TAKING A LEAP OF FAITH...
AAAAAAAAAAHHH!
EVENTUALLY YOU HAVE TO LAND.
AAAAAAAAAAHHH!
ALL YOU CAN DO IS CLOSE YOUR EYES AND HOPE IT'S A SOFT LANDING.
--UNGH!
WHUMP
OH THANK GOD, THANK GOD, THANK GOD--

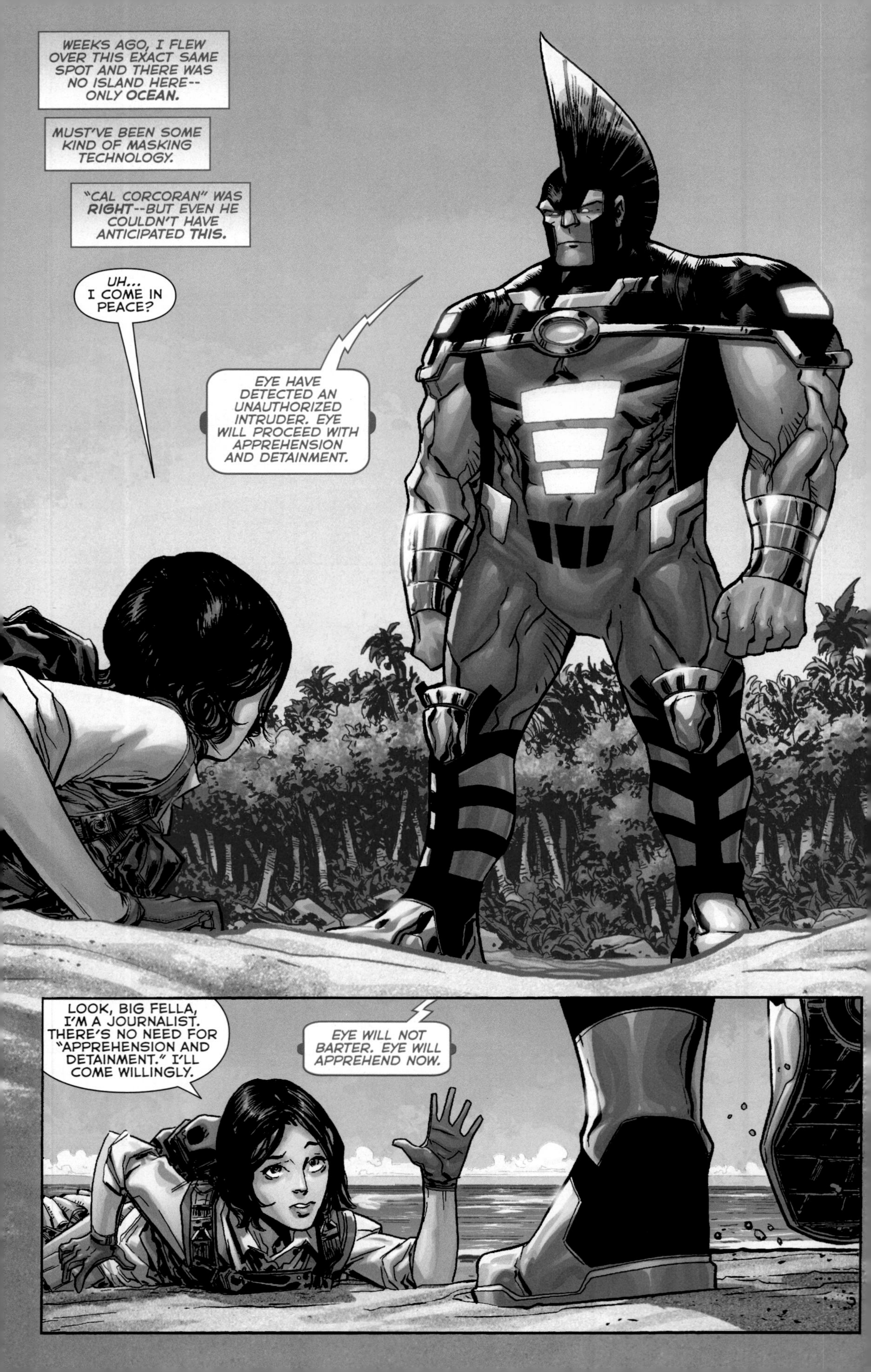
WEEKS AGO, I FLEW OVER THIS EXACT SAME SPOT AND THERE WAS NO ISLAND HERE-- ONLY OCEAN.
MUST'VE BEEN SOME KIND OF MASKING TECHNOLOGY.
"CAL CORCORAN" WAS RIGHT--BUT EVEN HE COULDN'T HAVE ANTICIPATED THIS.
UH... I COME IN PEACE?
EYE HAVE DETECTED AN UNAUTHORIZED INTRUDER. EYE WILL PROCEED WITH APPREHENSION AND DETAINMENT.
LOOK, BIG FELLA, I'M A JOURNALIST. THERE'S NO NEED FOR "APPREHENSION AND DETAINMENT." I'LL COME WILLINGLY.
EYE WILL NOT BARTER. EYE WILL APPREHEND NOW.

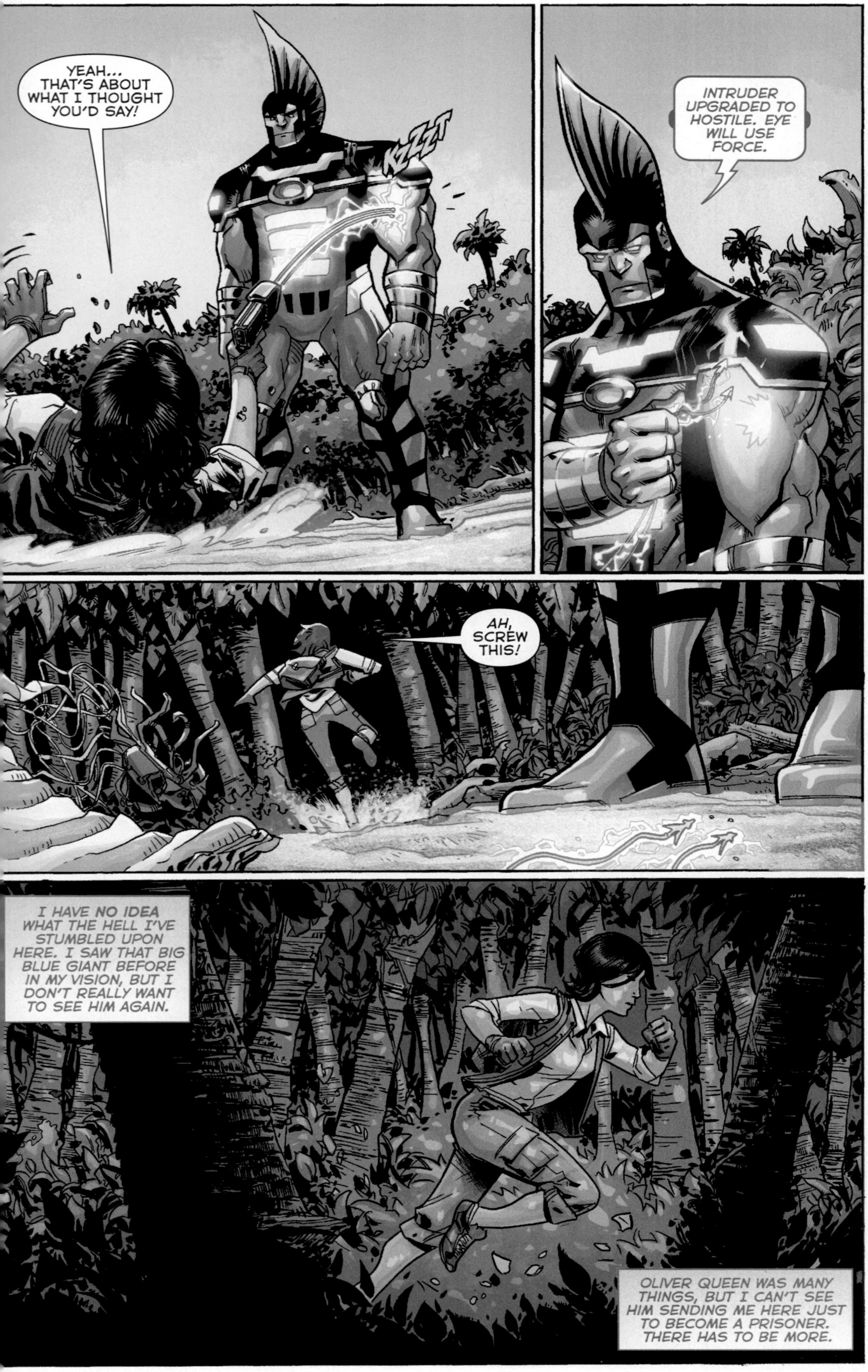
YEAH... THAT'S ABOUT WHAT I THOUGHT YOU'D SAY!
KZZZT
INTRUDER UPGRADED TO HOSTILE. EYE WILL USE FORCE.
AH, SCREW THIS!
I HAVE NO IDEA WHAT THE HELL I'VE STUMBLED UPON HERE. I SAW THAT BIG BLUE GIANT BEFORE IN MY VISION, BUT I DON'T REALLY WANT TO SEE HIM AGAIN.
OLIVER QUEEN WAS MANY THINGS, BUT I CAN'T SEE HIM SENDING ME HERE JUST TO BECOME A PRISONER. THERE HAS TO BE MORE.

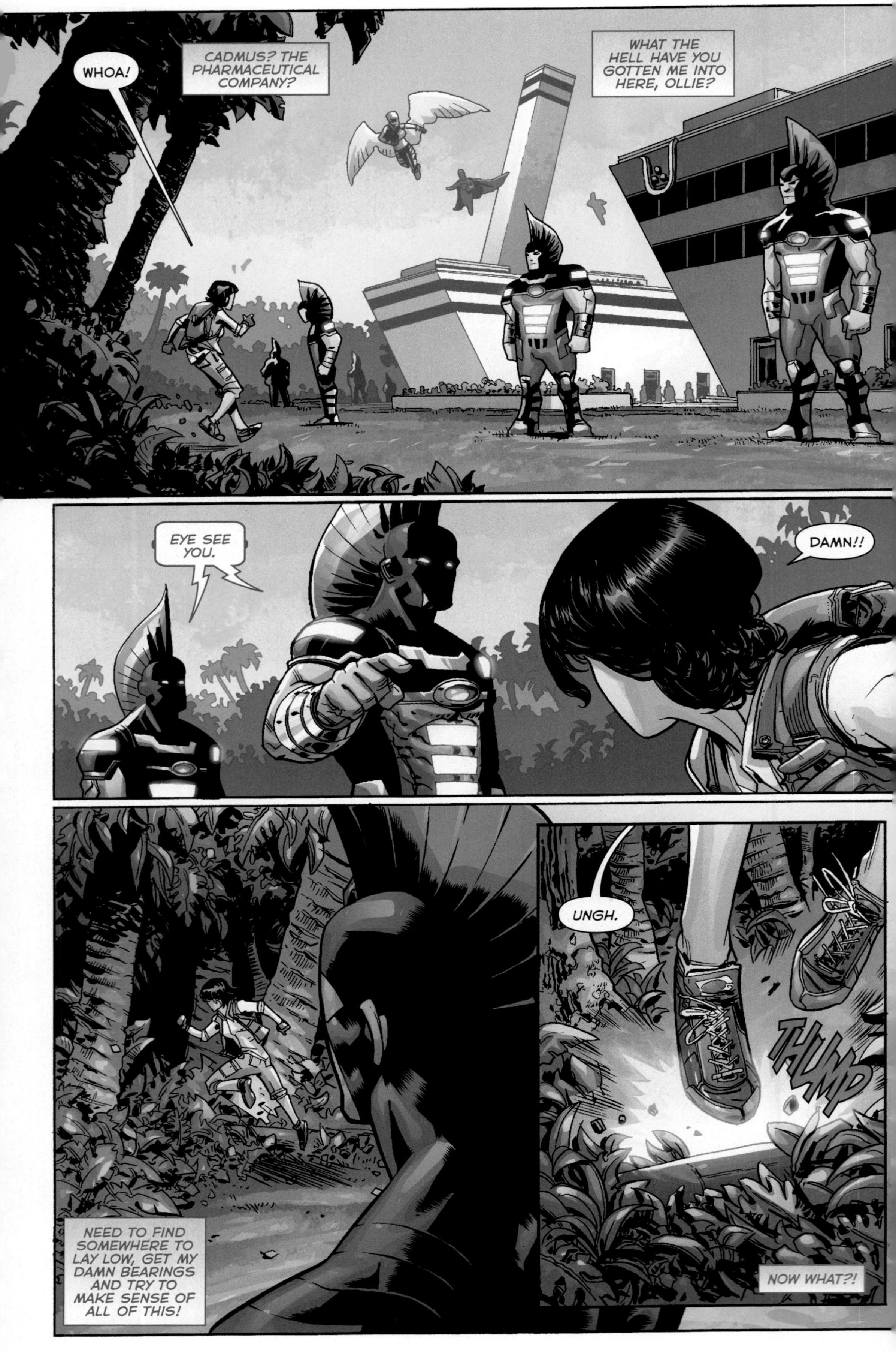
WHOA!
CADMUS? THE PHARMACEUTICAL COMPANY?
WHAT THE HELL HAVE YOU GOTTEN ME INTO HERE, OLLIE?
EYE SEE YOU.
DAMN!!
NEED TO FIND SOMEWHERE TO LAY LOW, GET MY DAMN BEARINGS AND TRY TO MAKE SENSE OF ALL OF THIS!
UNGH.
THUMP
NOW WHAT?!

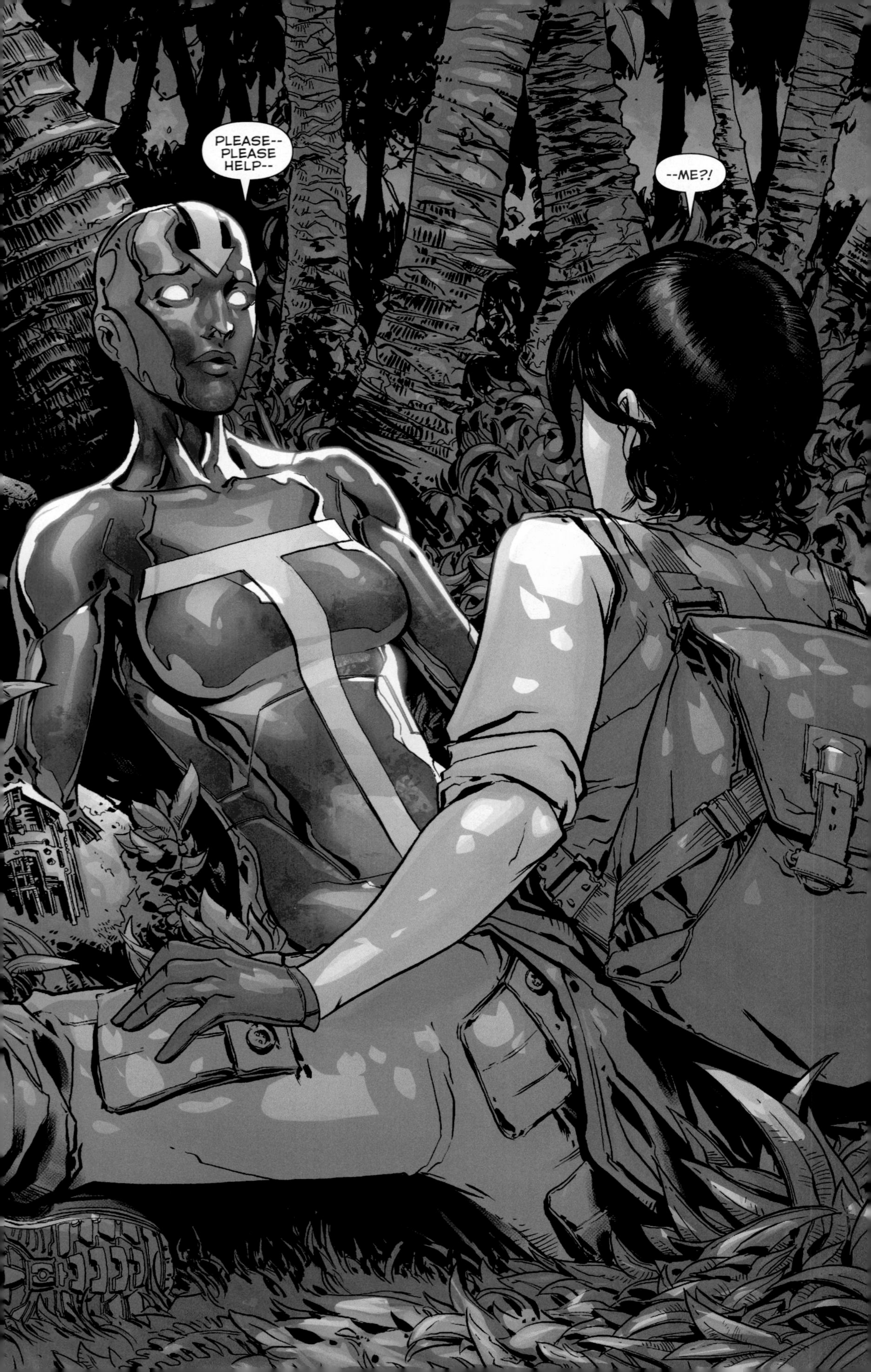
PLEASE--
PLEASE
HELP--
--ME?!

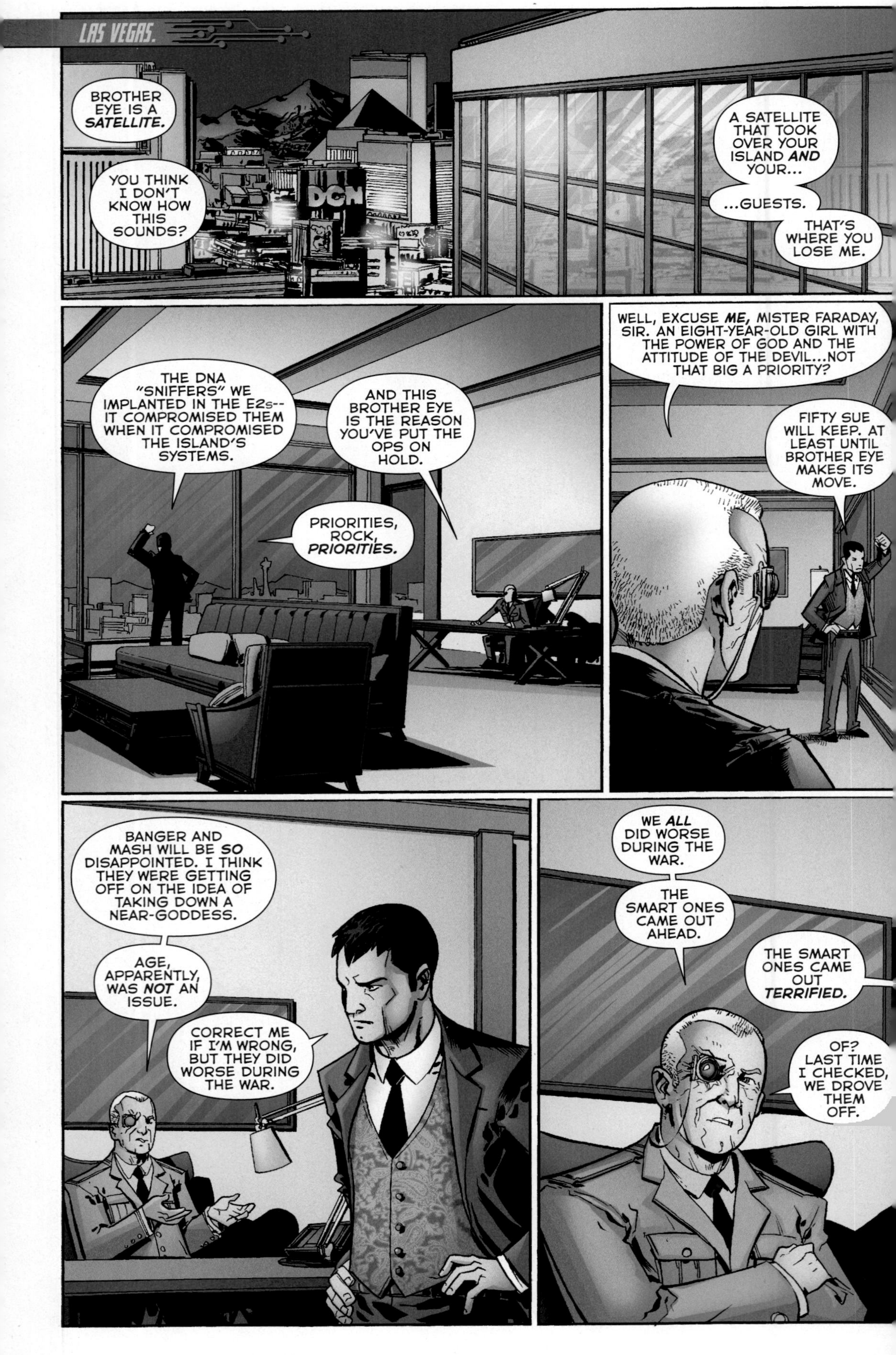
LAS VEGAS.
BROTHER EYE IS A SATELLITE.
YOU THINK I DON'T KNOW HOW THIS SOUNDS?
A SATELLITE THAT TOOK OVER YOUR ISLAND AND YOUR...
...GUESTS.
THAT'S WHERE YOU LOSE ME.
THE DNA "SNIFFERS" WE IMPLANTED IN THE E2s-- IT COMPROMISED THEM WHEN IT COMPROMISED THE ISLAND'S SYSTEMS.
AND THIS BROTHER EYE IS THE REASON YOU'VE PUT THE OPS ON HOLD.
PRIORITIES, ROCK, PRIORITIES.
WELL, EXCUSE ME, MISTER FARADAY, SIR. AN EIGHT-YEAR-OLD GIRL WITH THE POWER OF GOD AND THE ATTITUDE OF THE DEVIL...NOT THAT BIG A PRIORITY?
FIFTY SUE WILL KEEP. AT LEAST UNTIL BROTHER EYE MAKES ITS MOVE.
BANGER AND MASH WILL BE SO DISAPPOINTED. I THINK THEY WERE GETTING OFF ON THE IDEA OF TAKING DOWN A NEAR-GODDESS.
AGE, APPARENTLY, WAS NOT AN ISSUE.
CORRECT ME IF I'M WRONG, BUT THEY DID WORSE DURING THE WAR.
WE ALL DID WORSE DURING THE WAR.
THE SMART ONES CAME OUT AHEAD.
THE SMART ONES CAME OUT TERRIFIED.
OF? LAST TIME I CHECKED, WE DROVE THEM OFF.

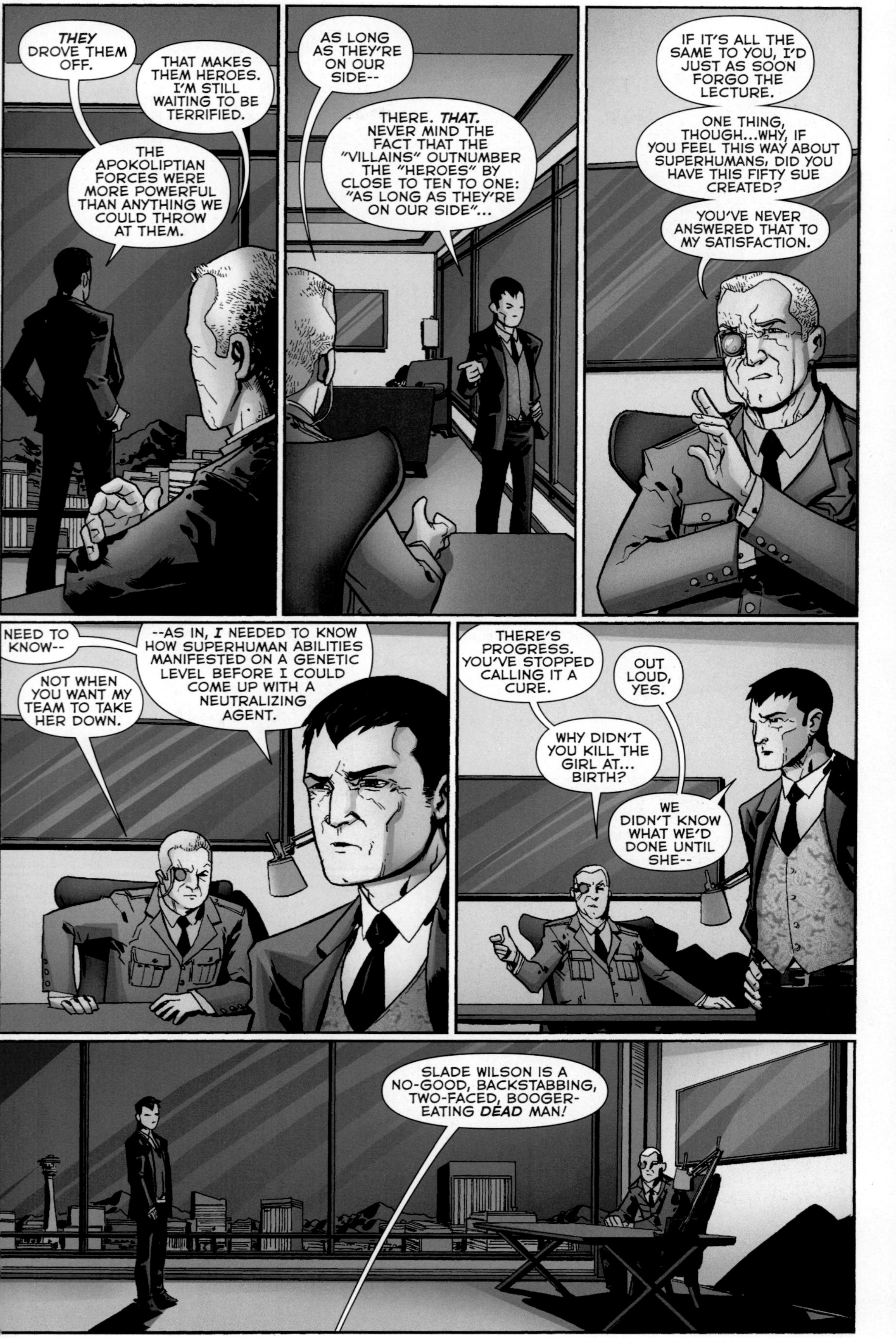
THEY DROVE THEM OFF.
THAT MAKES THEM HEROES. I'M STILL WAITING TO BE TERRIFIED.
THE APOKOLIPTIAN FORCES WERE MORE POWERFUL THAN ANYTHING WE COULD THROW AT THEM.
AS LONG AS THEY'RE ON OUR SIDE--
THERE. THAT. NEVER MIND THE FACT THAT THE "VILLAINS" OUTNUMBER THE "HEROES" BY CLOSE TO TEN TO ONE: "AS LONG AS THEY'RE ON OUR SIDE"...
IF IT'S ALL THE SAME TO YOU, I'D JUST AS SOON FORGO THE LECTURE.
ONE THING, THOUGH...WHY, IF YOU FEEL THIS WAY ABOUT SUPERHUMANS, DID YOU HAVE THIS FIFTY SUE CREATED?
YOU'VE NEVER ANSWERED THAT TO MY SATISFACTION.
NEED TO KNOW--
--AS IN, I NEEDED TO KNOW HOW SUPERHUMAN ABILITIES MANIFESTED ON A GENETIC LEVEL BEFORE I COULD COME UP WITH A NEUTRALIZING AGENT.
NOT WHEN YOU WANT MY TEAM TO TAKE HER DOWN.
THERE'S PROGRESS. YOU'VE STOPPED CALLING IT A CURE.
OUT LOUD, YES.
WHY DIDN'T YOU KILL THE GIRL AT... BIRTH?
WE DIDN'T KNOW WHAT WE'D DONE UNTIL SHE--
SLADE WILSON IS A NO-GOOD, BACKSTABBING, TWO-FACED, BOOGER-EATING DEAD MAN!

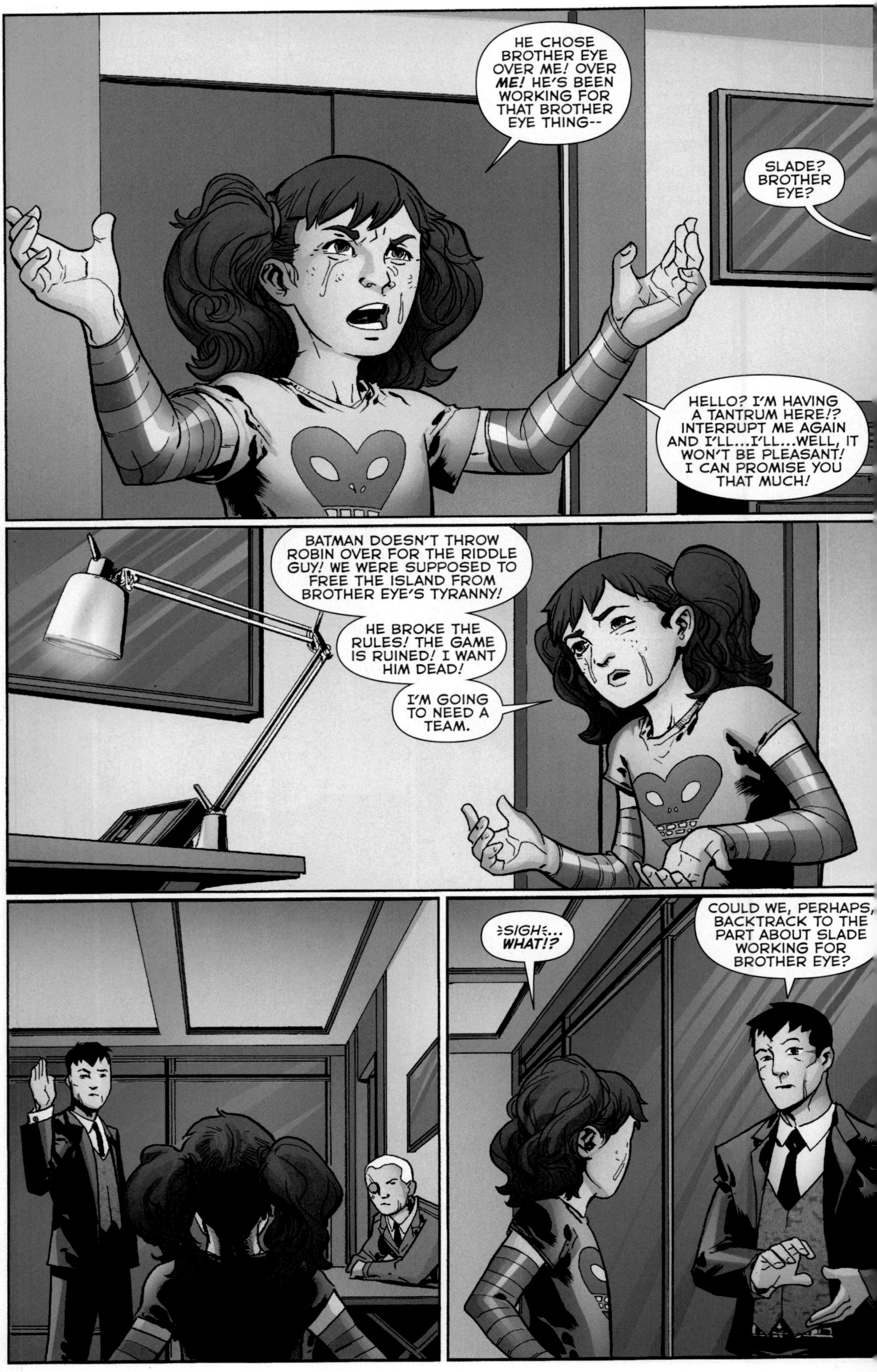
HE CHOSE BROTHER EYE OVER ME! OVER ME! HE'S BEEN WORKING FOR THAT BROTHER EYE THING--
SLADE? BROTHER EYE?
HELLO? I'M HAVING A TANTRUM HERE!? INTERRUPT ME AGAIN AND I'LL...I'LL...WELL, IT WON'T BE PLEASANT! I CAN PROMISE YOU THAT MUCH!
BATMAN DOESN'T THROW ROBIN OVER FOR THE RIDDLE GUY! WE WERE SUPPOSED TO FREE THE ISLAND FROM BROTHER EYE'S TYRANNY!
HE BROKE THE RULES! THE GAME IS RUINED! I WANT HIM DEAD!
I'M GOING TO NEED A TEAM.
SIGH... WHAT!?
COULD WE, PERHAPS, BACKTRACK TO THE PART ABOUT SLADE WORKING FOR BROTHER EYE?

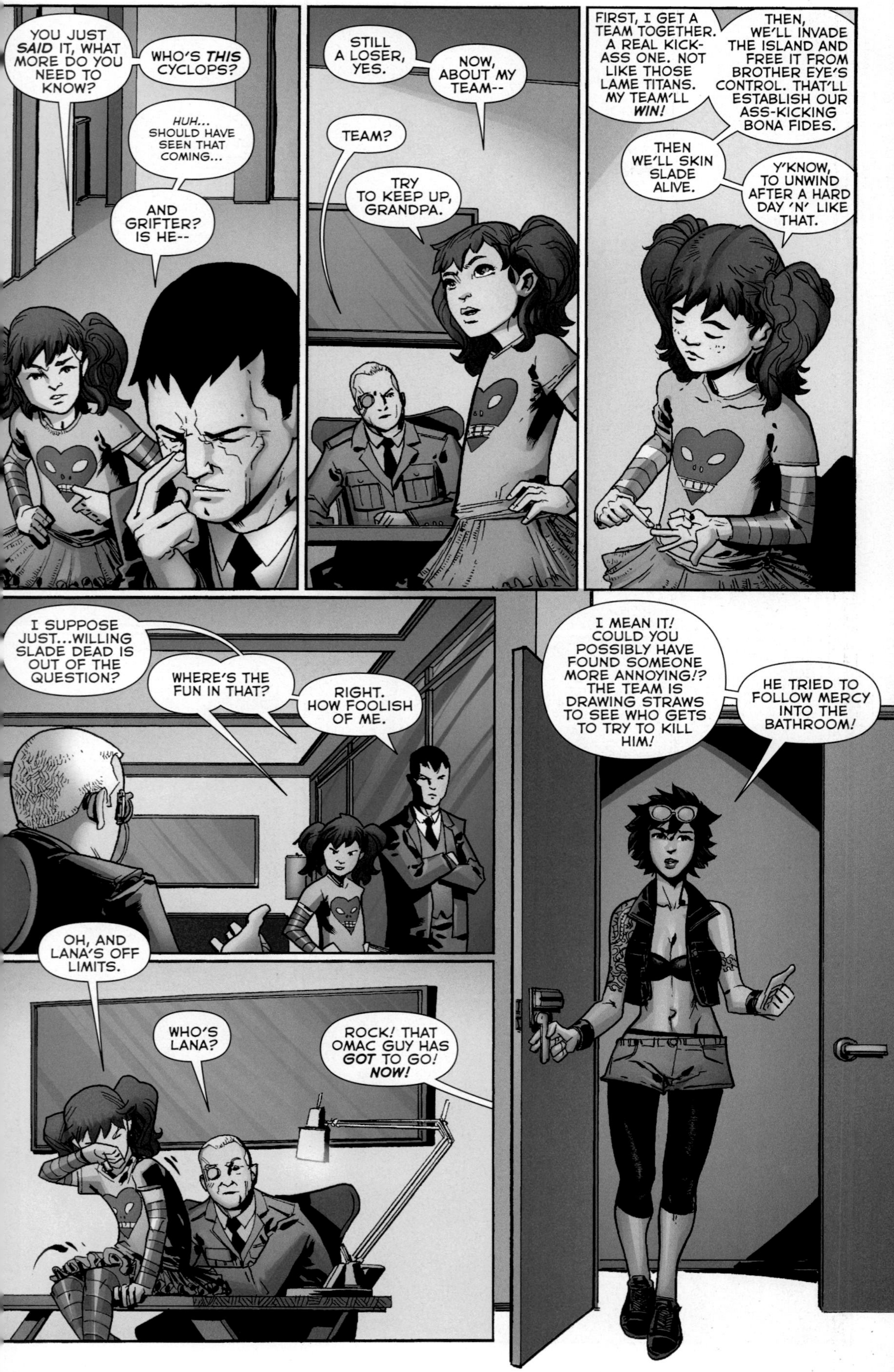
YOU JUST *SAID* IT, WHAT MORE DO YOU NEED TO KNOW?
WHO'S *THIS* CYCLOPS?
HUH... SHOULD HAVE SEEN THAT COMING...
AND GRIFTER? IS HE--
STILL A LOSER, YES.
NOW, ABOUT MY TEAM--
TEAM?
TRY TO KEEP UP, GRANDPA.
FIRST, I GET A TEAM TOGETHER. A REAL KICK-ASS ONE. NOT LIKE THOSE LAME TITANS. MY TEAM'LL *WIN!*
THEN, WE'LL INVADE THE ISLAND AND FREE IT FROM BROTHER EYE'S CONTROL. THAT'LL ESTABLISH OUR ASS-KICKING BONA FIDES.
THEN WE'LL SKIN SLADE ALIVE.
Y'KNOW, TO UNWIND AFTER A HARD DAY 'N' LIKE THAT.
I SUPPOSE JUST...WILLING SLADE DEAD IS OUT OF THE QUESTION?
WHERE'S THE FUN IN THAT?
RIGHT. HOW FOOLISH OF ME.
OH, AND LANA'S OFF LIMITS.
WHO'S LANA?
ROCK! THAT OMAC GUY HAS *GOT* TO GO! *NOW!*
I MEAN IT! COULD YOU POSSIBLY HAVE FOUND SOMEONE MORE ANNOYING!? THE TEAM IS DRAWING STRAWS TO SEE WHO GETS TO TRY TO KILL HIM!
HE TRIED TO FOLLOW MERCY INTO THE BATHROOM!

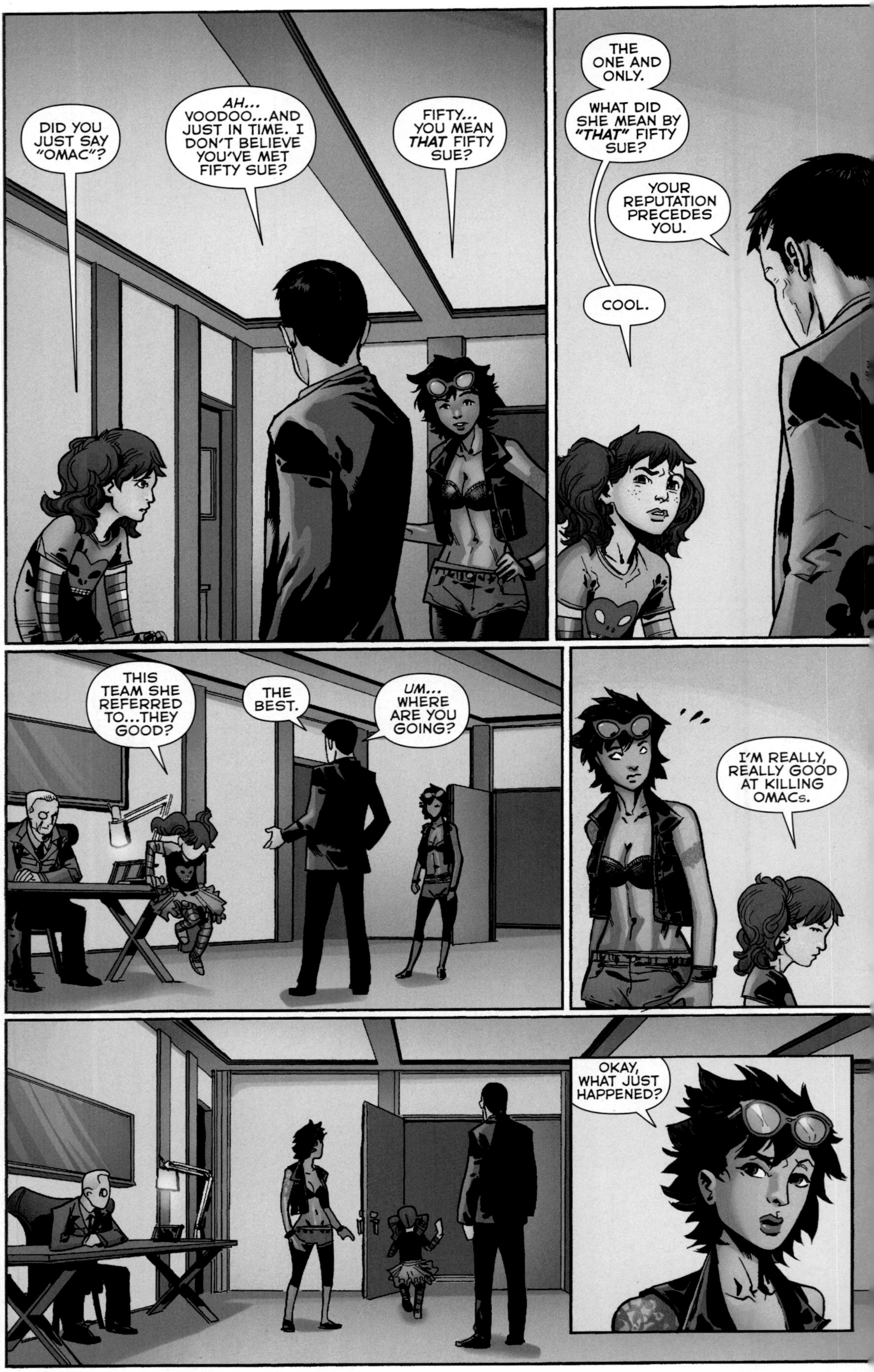

DID YOU JUST SAY "OMAC"?
AH... VOODOO...AND JUST IN TIME. I DON'T BELIEVE YOU'VE MET FIFTY SUE?
FIFTY... YOU MEAN THAT FIFTY SUE?
THE ONE AND ONLY.
WHAT DID SHE MEAN BY "THAT" FIFTY SUE?
YOUR REPUTATION PRECEDES YOU.
COOL.
THIS TEAM SHE REFERRED TO...THEY GOOD?
THE BEST.
UM... WHERE ARE YOU GOING?
I'M REALLY, REALLY GOOD AT KILLING OMACs.
OKAY, WHAT JUST HAPPENED?

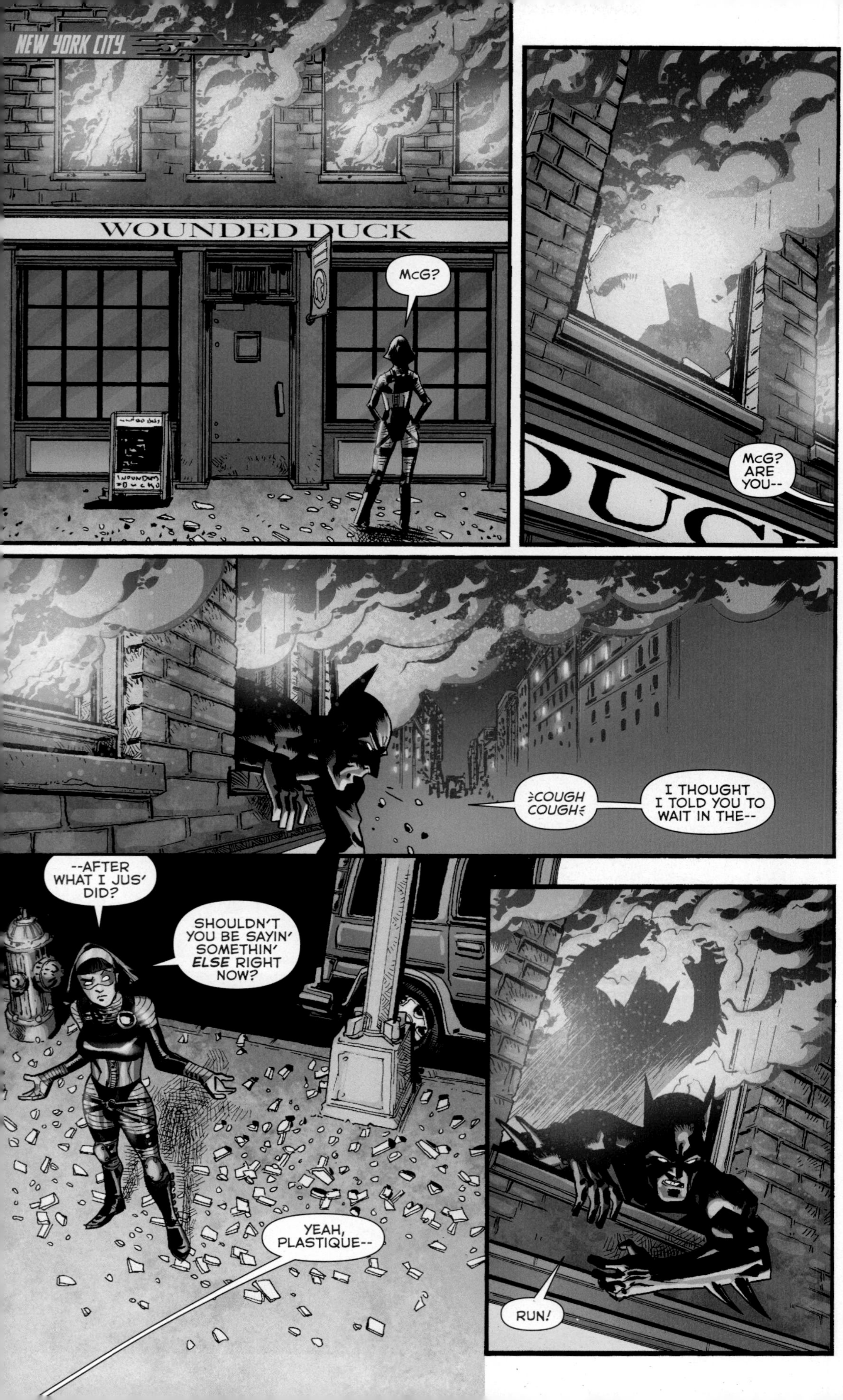
NEW YORK CITY.
WOUNDED DUCK
McG?
McG? ARE YOU--
DUC
COUGH COUGH
I THOUGHT I TOLD YOU TO WAIT IN THE--
--AFTER WHAT I JUS' DID?
SHOULDN'T YOU BE SAYIN' SOMETHIN' ELSE RIGHT NOW?
YEAH, PLASTIQUE--
RUN!

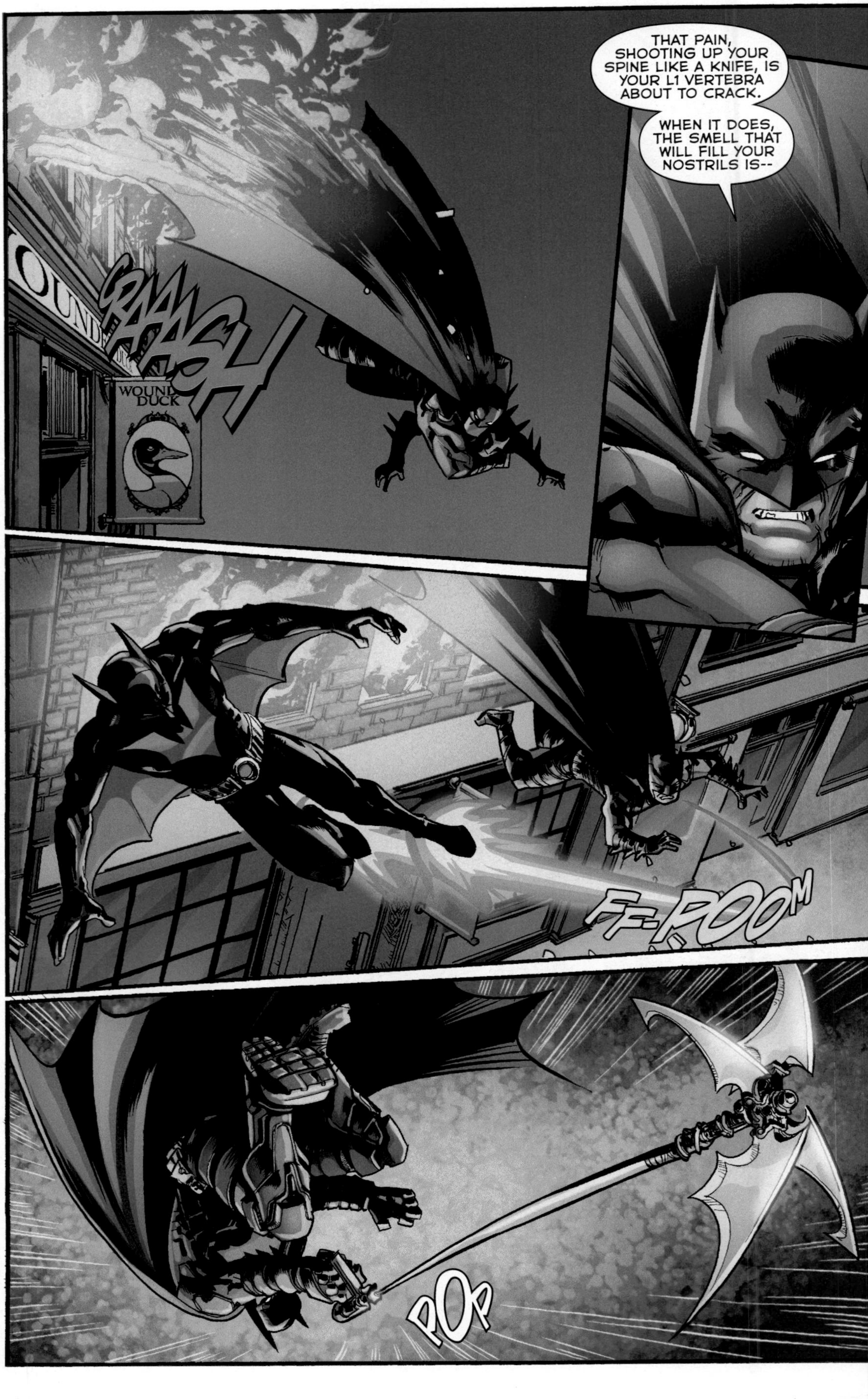

THAT PAIN, SHOOTING UP YOUR SPINE LIKE A KNIFE, IS YOUR L1 VERTEBRA ABOUT TO CRACK.
WHEN IT DOES, THE SMELL THAT WILL FILL YOUR NOSTRILS IS--
WOUND DUCK
CRAAACH
FF-POOM
POP

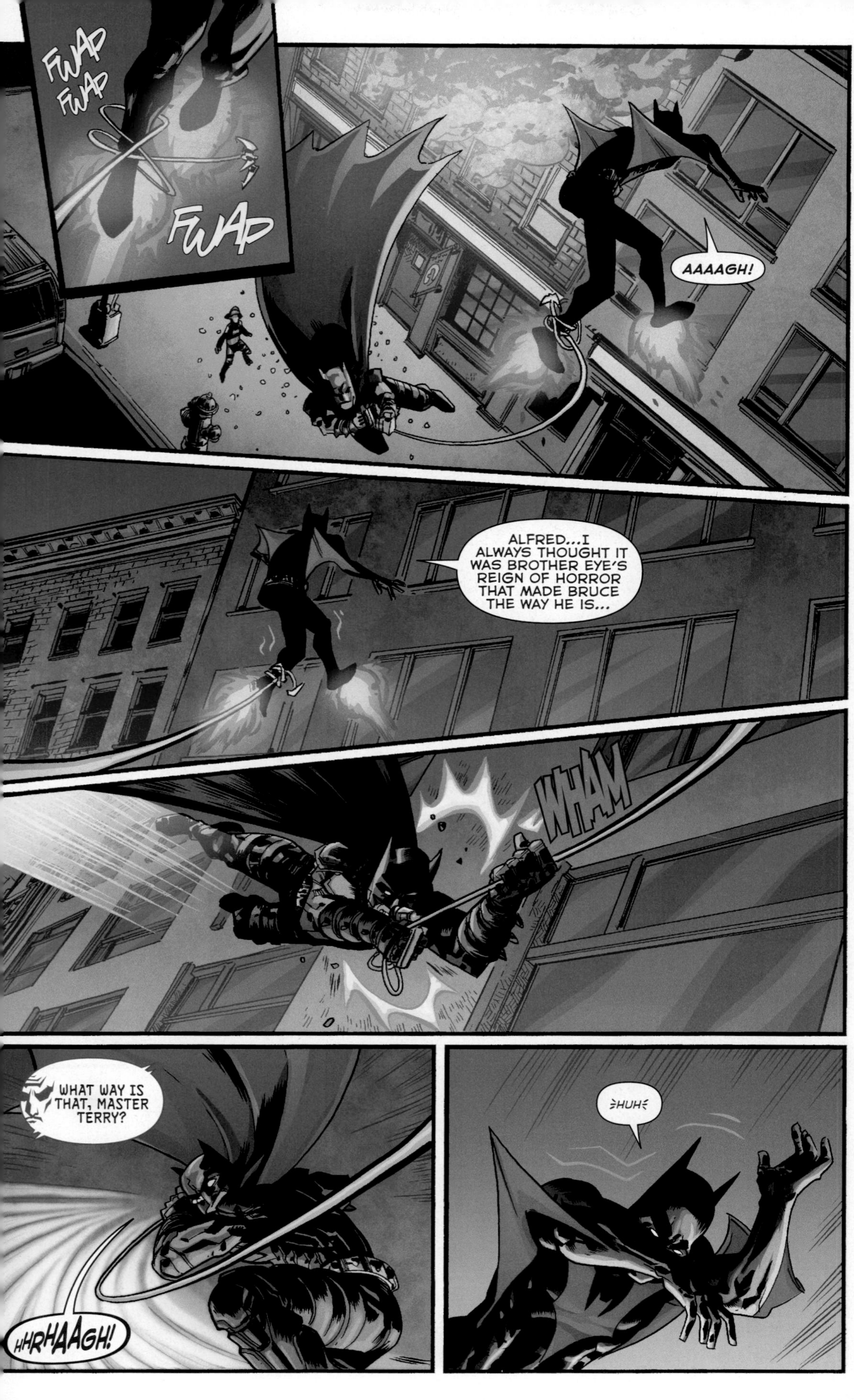
FWAP
FWAP
FWAP
AAAAGH!
ALFRED...I ALWAYS THOUGHT IT WAS BROTHER EYE'S REIGN OF HORROR THAT MADE BRUCE THE WAY HE IS...
WHAM
WHAT WAY IS THAT, MASTER TERRY?
HHRHAAGH!
HUH

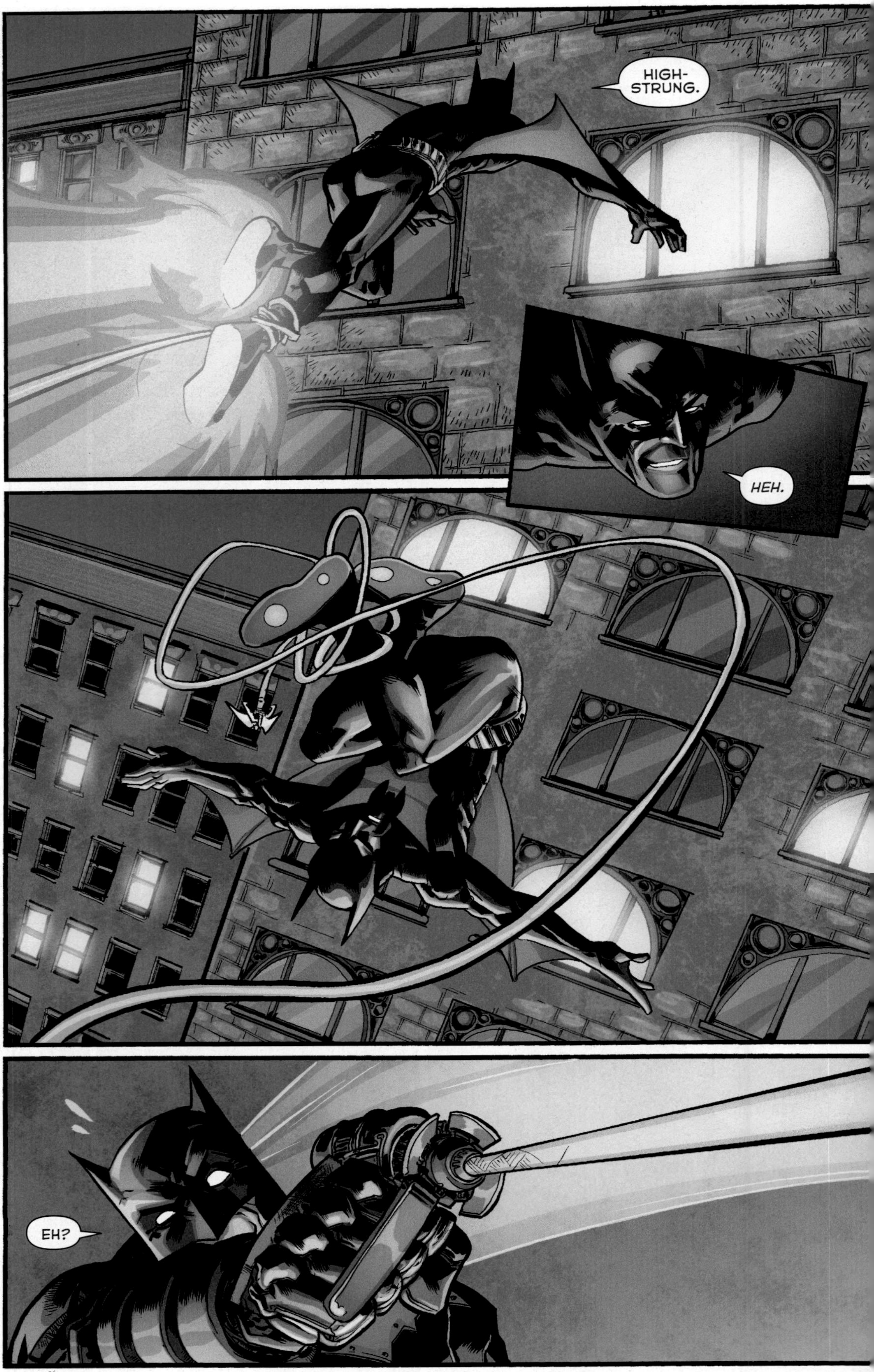
HIGH-STRUNG.
HEH.
EH?

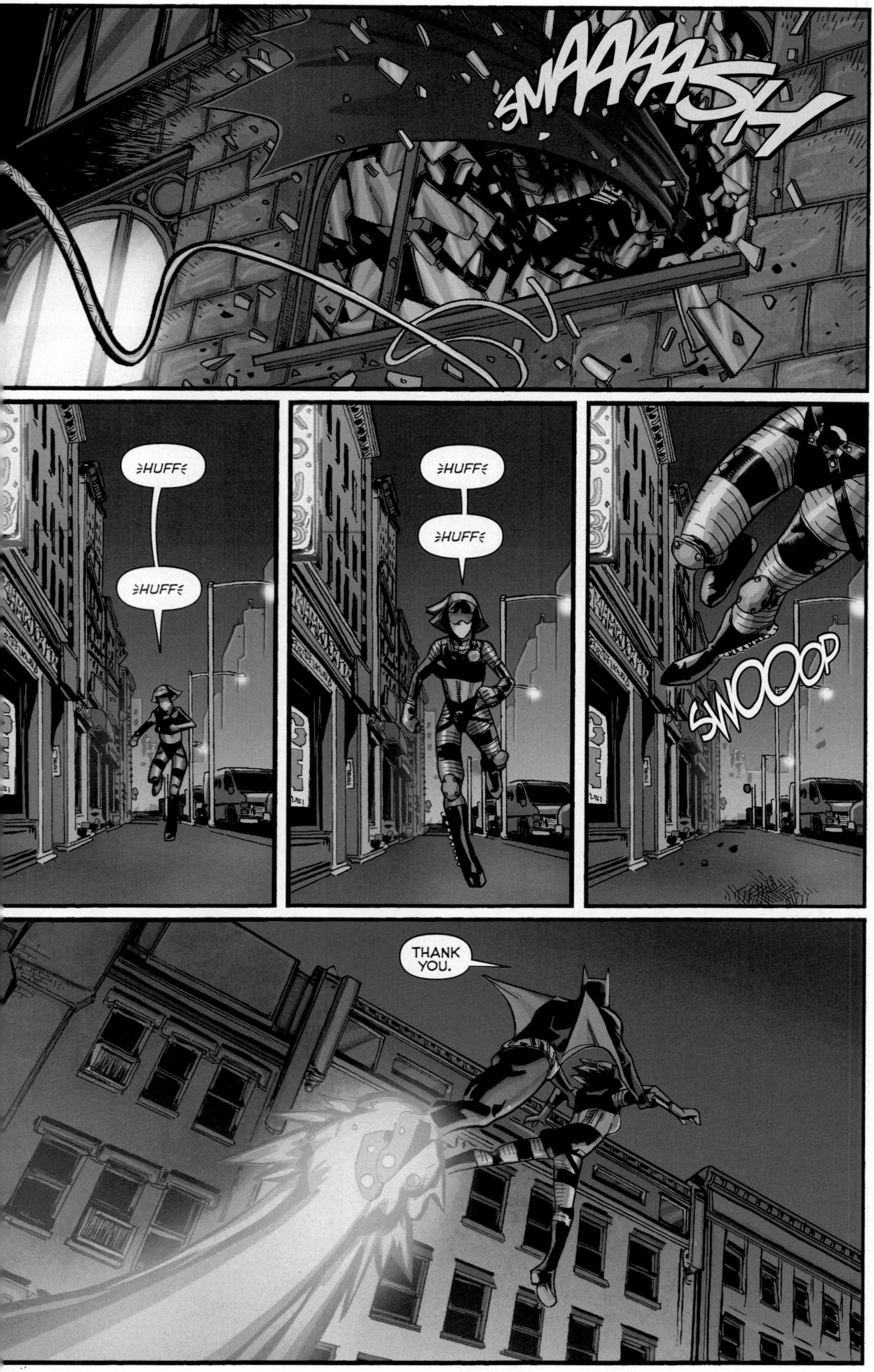
SMAAAASH
HUFF
HUFF
HUFF
HUFF
SWOOOP
THANK YOU.

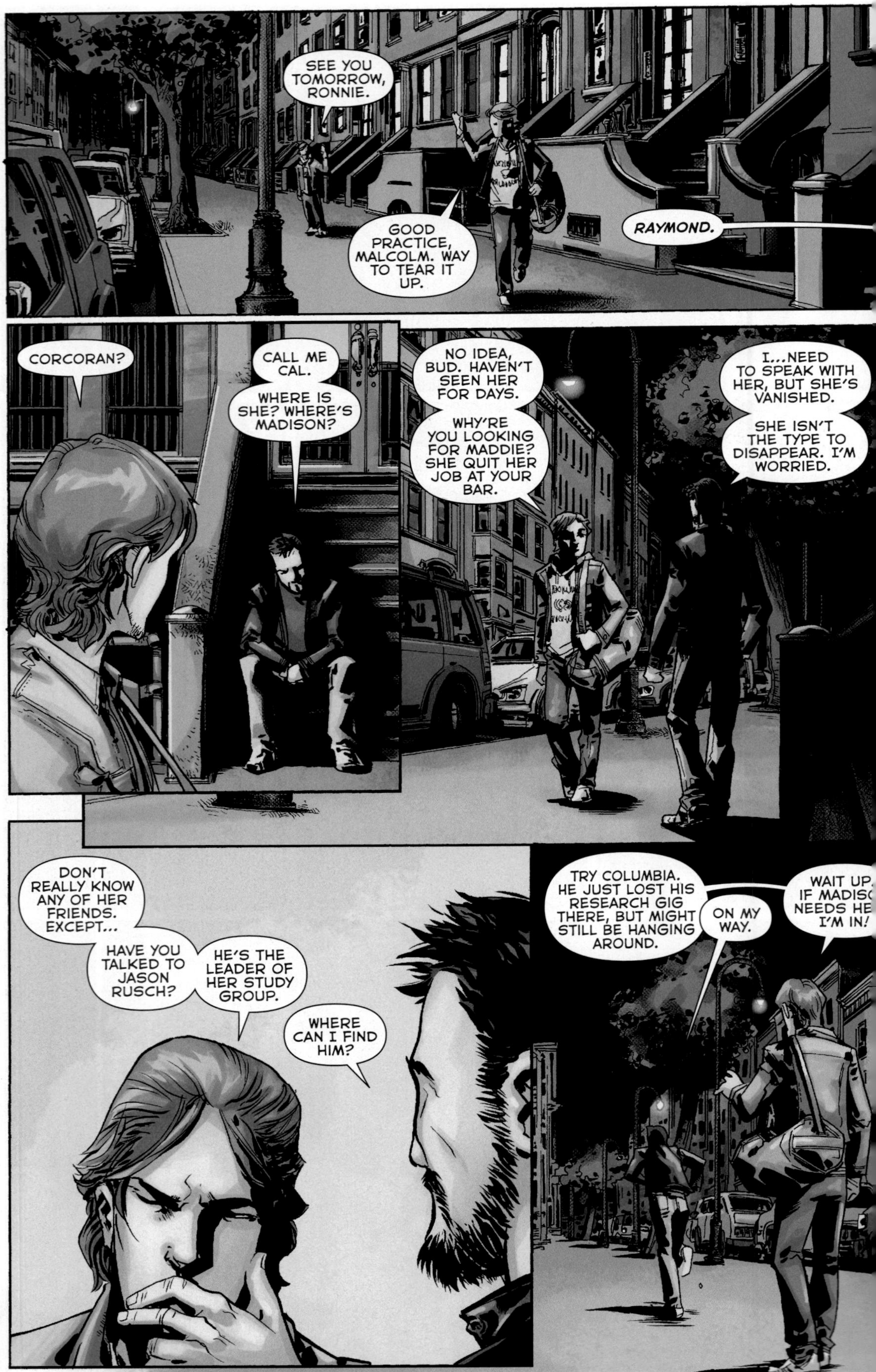

SEE YOU TOMORROW, RONNIE.
GOOD PRACTICE, MALCOLM. WAY TO TEAR IT UP.
RAYMOND.
CORCORAN?
CALL ME CAL.
WHERE IS SHE? WHERE'S MADISON?
NO IDEA, BUD. HAVEN'T SEEN HER FOR DAYS.
WHY'RE YOU LOOKING FOR MADDIE? SHE QUIT HER JOB AT YOUR BAR.
I...NEED TO SPEAK WITH HER, BUT SHE'S VANISHED.
SHE ISN'T THE TYPE TO DISAPPEAR. I'M WORRIED.
DON'T REALLY KNOW ANY OF HER FRIENDS. EXCEPT...
HAVE YOU TALKED TO JASON RUSCH?
HE'S THE LEADER OF HER STUDY GROUP.
WHERE CAN I FIND HIM?
TRY COLUMBIA. HE JUST LOST HIS RESEARCH GIG THERE, BUT MIGHT STILL BE HANGING AROUND.
ON MY WAY.
WAIT UP. IF MADIS
NEEDS HE
I'M IN!

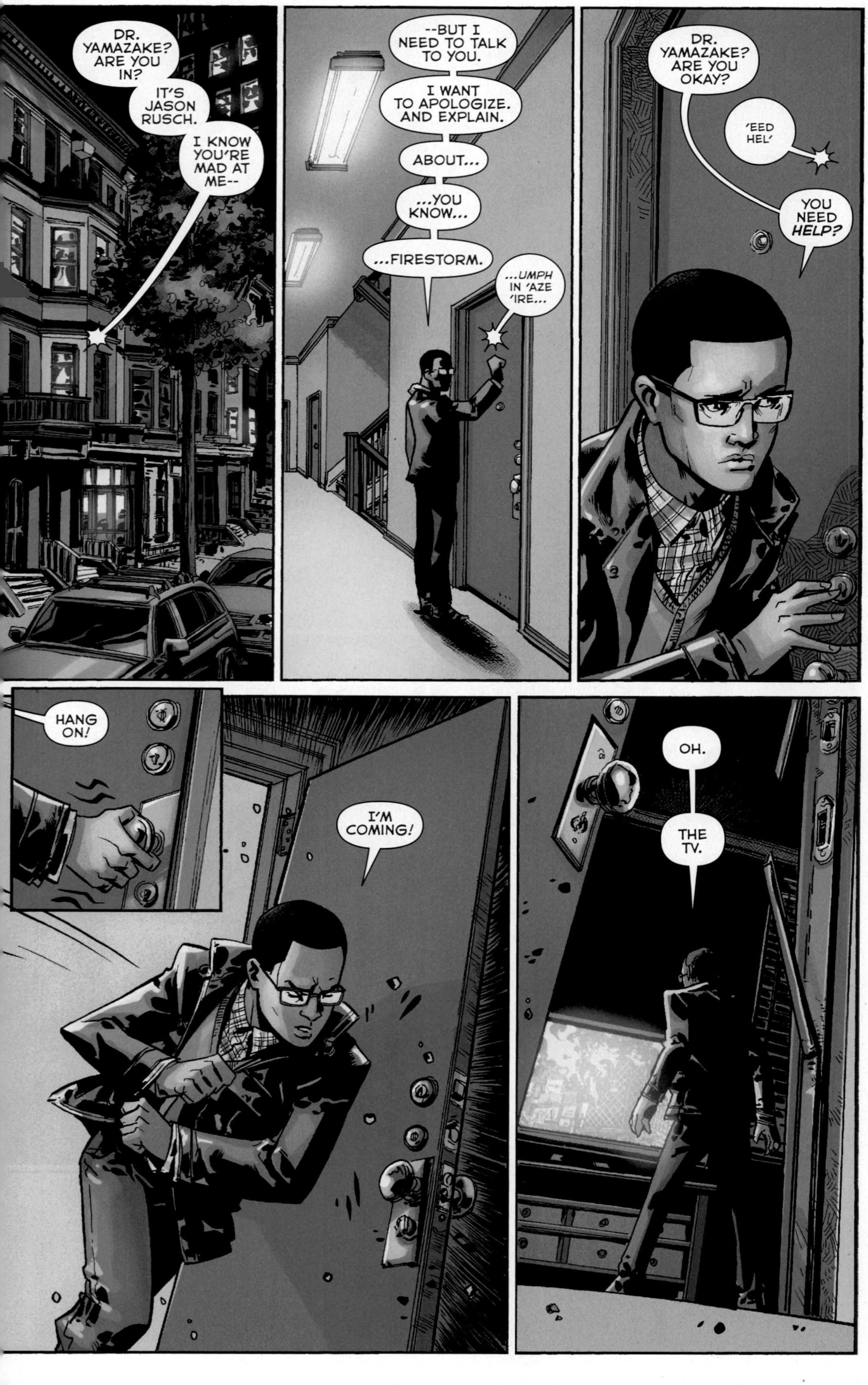
DR. YAMAZAKE? ARE YOU IN?
IT'S JASON RUSCH.
I KNOW YOU'RE MAD AT ME--
--BUT I NEED TO TALK TO YOU.
I WANT TO APOLOGIZE. AND EXPLAIN.
ABOUT...
...YOU KNOW...
...FIRESTORM.
...UMPH IN 'AZE 'IRE...
DR. YAMAZAKE? ARE YOU OKAY?
'EED HEL'
YOU NEED HELP?
HANG ON!
I'M COMING!
OH.
THE TV.

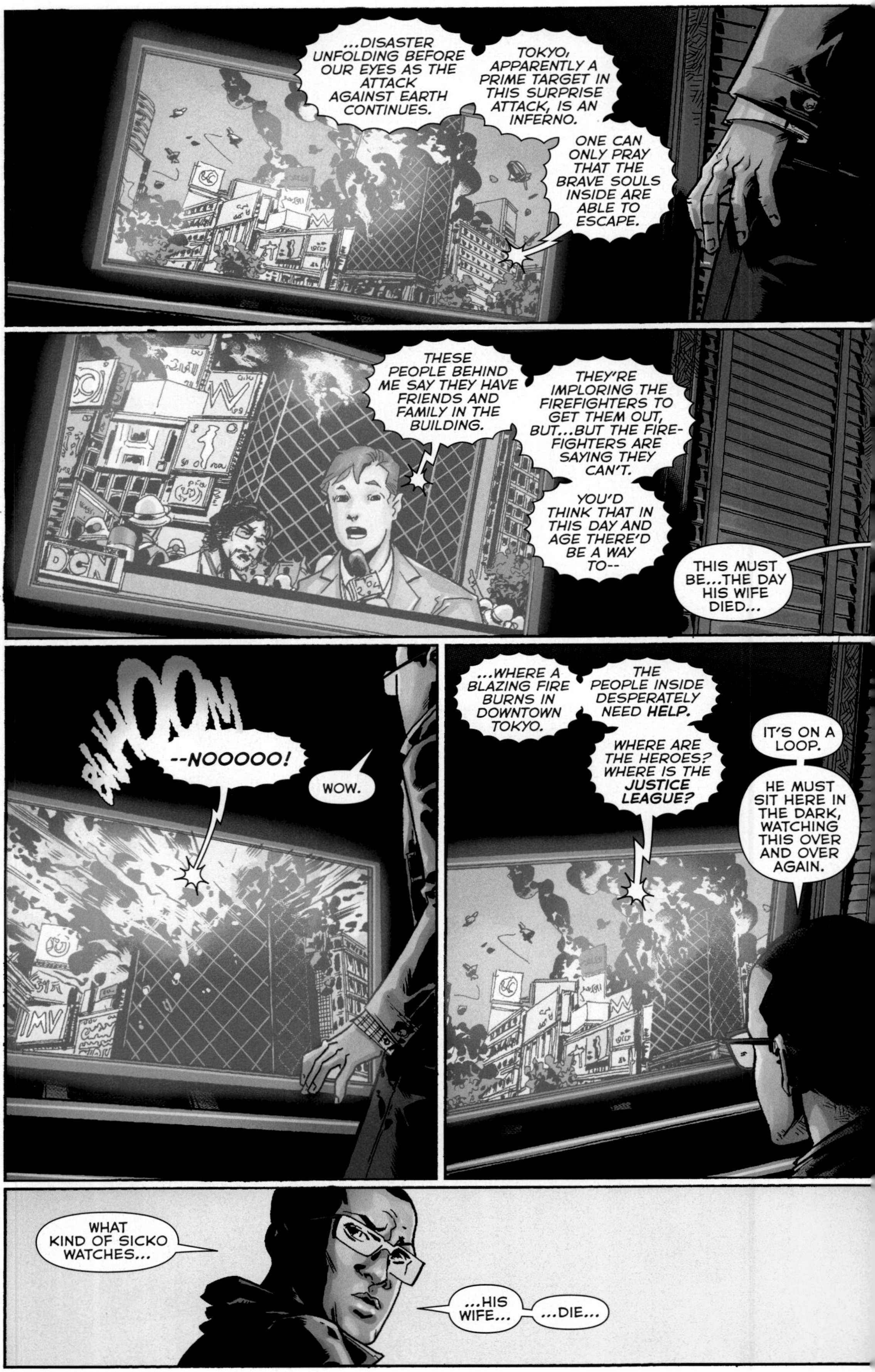
...DISASTER UNFOLDING BEFORE OUR EYES AS THE ATTACK AGAINST EARTH CONTINUES.
TOKYO, APPARENTLY A PRIME TARGET IN THIS SURPRISE ATTACK, IS AN INFERNO.
ONE CAN ONLY PRAY THAT THE BRAVE SOULS INSIDE ARE ABLE TO ESCAPE.
THESE PEOPLE BEHIND ME SAY THEY HAVE FRIENDS AND FAMILY IN THE BUILDING.
THEY'RE IMPLORING THE FIREFIGHTERS TO GET THEM OUT, BUT...BUT THE FIRE-FIGHTERS ARE SAYING THEY CAN'T.
YOU'D THINK THAT IN THIS DAY AND AGE THERE'D BE A WAY TO--
THIS MUST BE...THE DAY HIS WIFE DIED...
BWOOM
--NOOOOO!
WOW.
...WHERE A BLAZING FIRE BURNS IN DOWNTOWN TOKYO.
THE PEOPLE INSIDE DESPERATELY NEED HELP.
WHERE ARE THE HEROES? WHERE IS THE JUSTICE LEAGUE?
IT'S ON A LOOP.
HE MUST SIT HERE IN THE DARK, WATCHING THIS OVER AND OVER AGAIN.
WHAT KIND OF SICKO WATCHES...
...HIS WIFE...
...DIE...

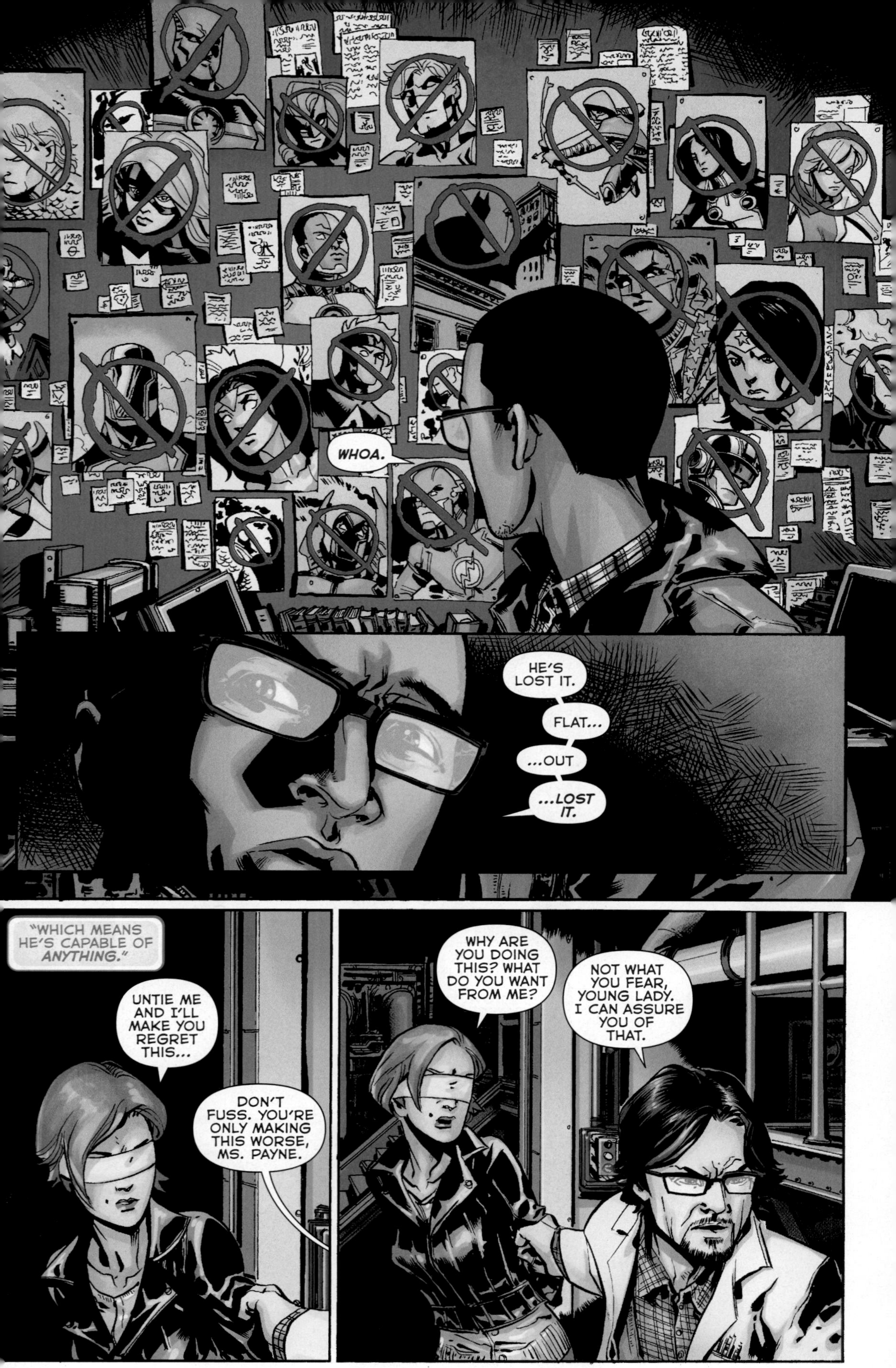
WHOA.
HE'S LOST IT.
FLAT...
...OUT
...LOST IT.
"WHICH MEANS HE'S CAPABLE OF *ANYTHING.*"
UNTIE ME AND I'LL MAKE YOU REGRET THIS...
DON'T FUSS. YOU'RE ONLY MAKING THIS WORSE, MS. PAYNE.
WHY ARE YOU DOING THIS? WHAT DO YOU WANT FROM ME?
NOT WHAT YOU FEAR, YOUNG LADY. I CAN ASSURE YOU OF THAT.

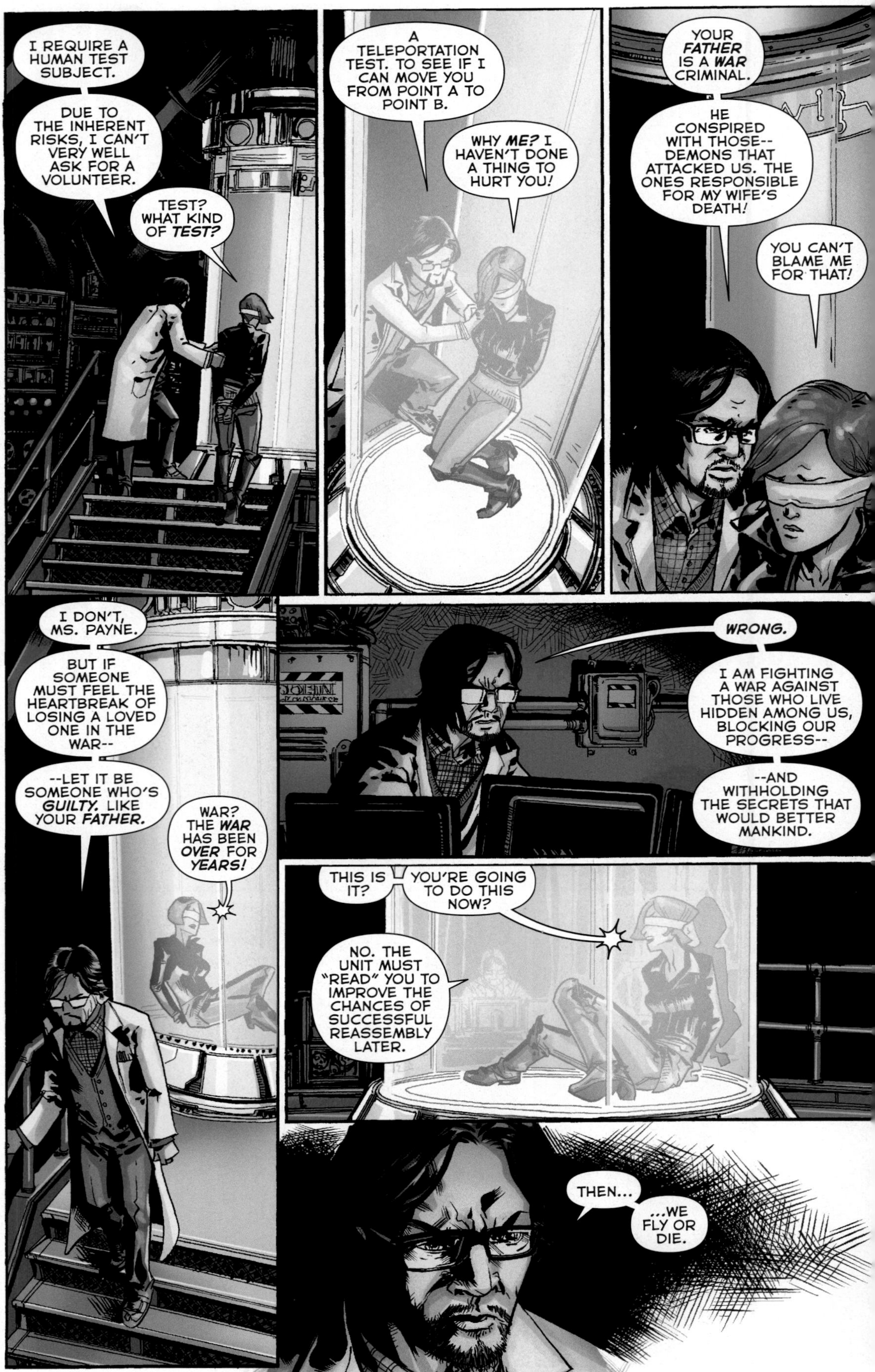
I REQUIRE A HUMAN TEST SUBJECT.
DUE TO THE INHERENT RISKS, I CAN'T VERY WELL ASK FOR A VOLUNTEER.
TEST? WHAT KIND OF *TEST?*
A TELEPORTATION TEST. TO SEE IF I CAN MOVE YOU FROM POINT A TO POINT B.
WHY *ME?* I HAVEN'T DONE A THING TO HURT YOU!
YOUR *FATHER* IS A *WAR* CRIMINAL.
HE CONSPIRED WITH THOSE-- DEMONS THAT ATTACKED US. THE ONES RESPONSIBLE FOR MY WIFE'S DEATH!
YOU CAN'T BLAME ME FOR THAT!
I DON'T, MS. PAYNE.
BUT IF SOMEONE MUST FEEL THE HEARTBREAK OF LOSING A LOVED ONE IN THE WAR--
--LET IT BE SOMEONE WHO'S *GUILTY.* LIKE YOUR *FATHER.*
WAR? THE *WAR* HAS BEEN *OVER* FOR *YEARS!*
WRONG.
I AM FIGHTING A WAR AGAINST THOSE WHO LIVE HIDDEN AMONG US, BLOCKING OUR PROGRESS--
--AND WITHHOLDING THE SECRETS THAT WOULD BETTER MANKIND.
THIS IS IT?
YOU'RE GOING TO DO THIS NOW?
NO. THE UNIT MUST "READ" YOU TO IMPROVE THE CHANCES OF SUCCESSFUL REASSEMBLY LATER.
THEN...
...WE FLY OR DIE.

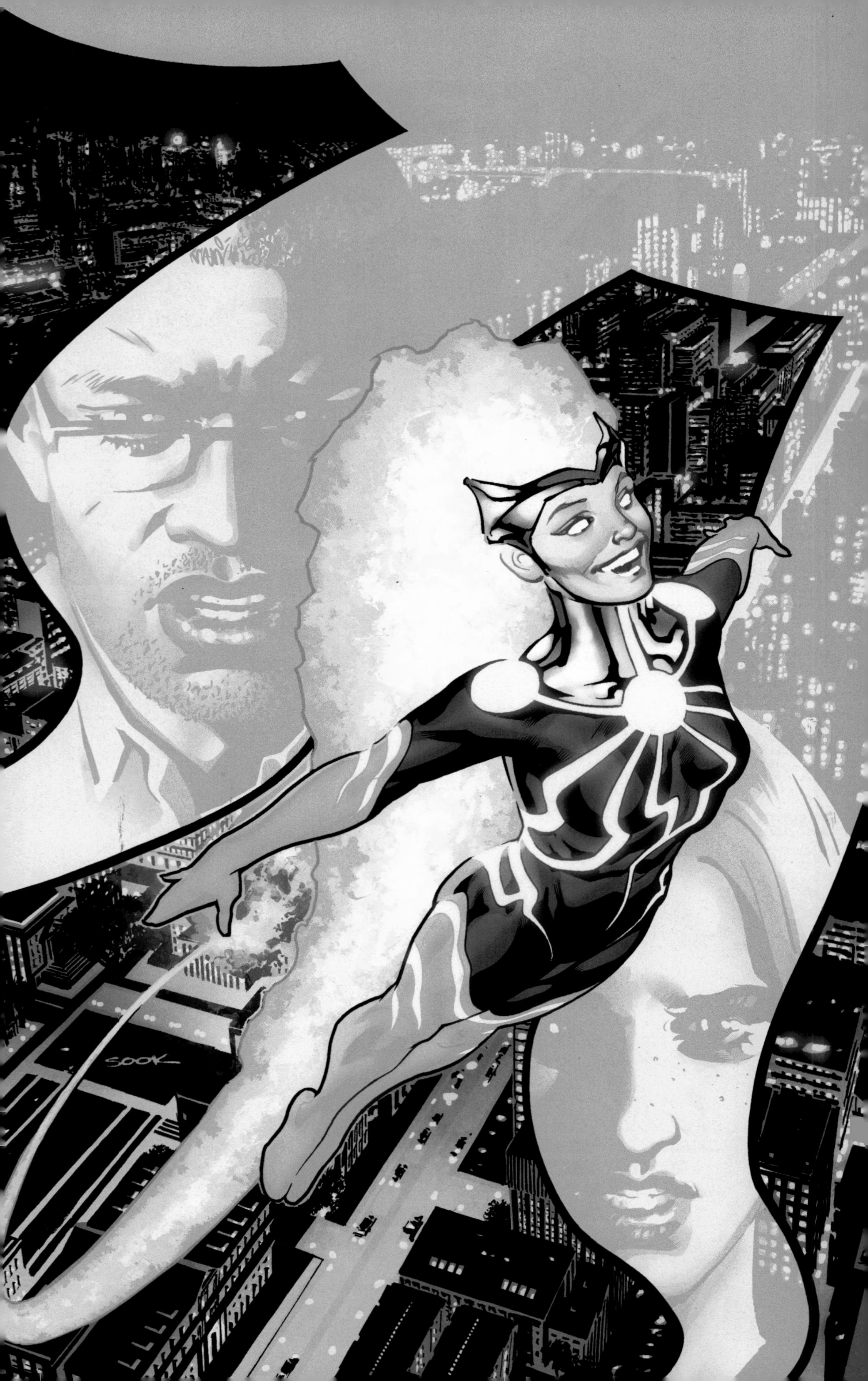
SOOK

INTO THE FUTUR

WRITERS
- Brian Azzarello
- Jeff Lemire
- Dan Jurgens
- Keith Giffen

ARTIST
- Patrick Zircher

COLORS
- Hi-Fi

LETTERS
- Dezi Sienty

COVER
- Ryan Sook

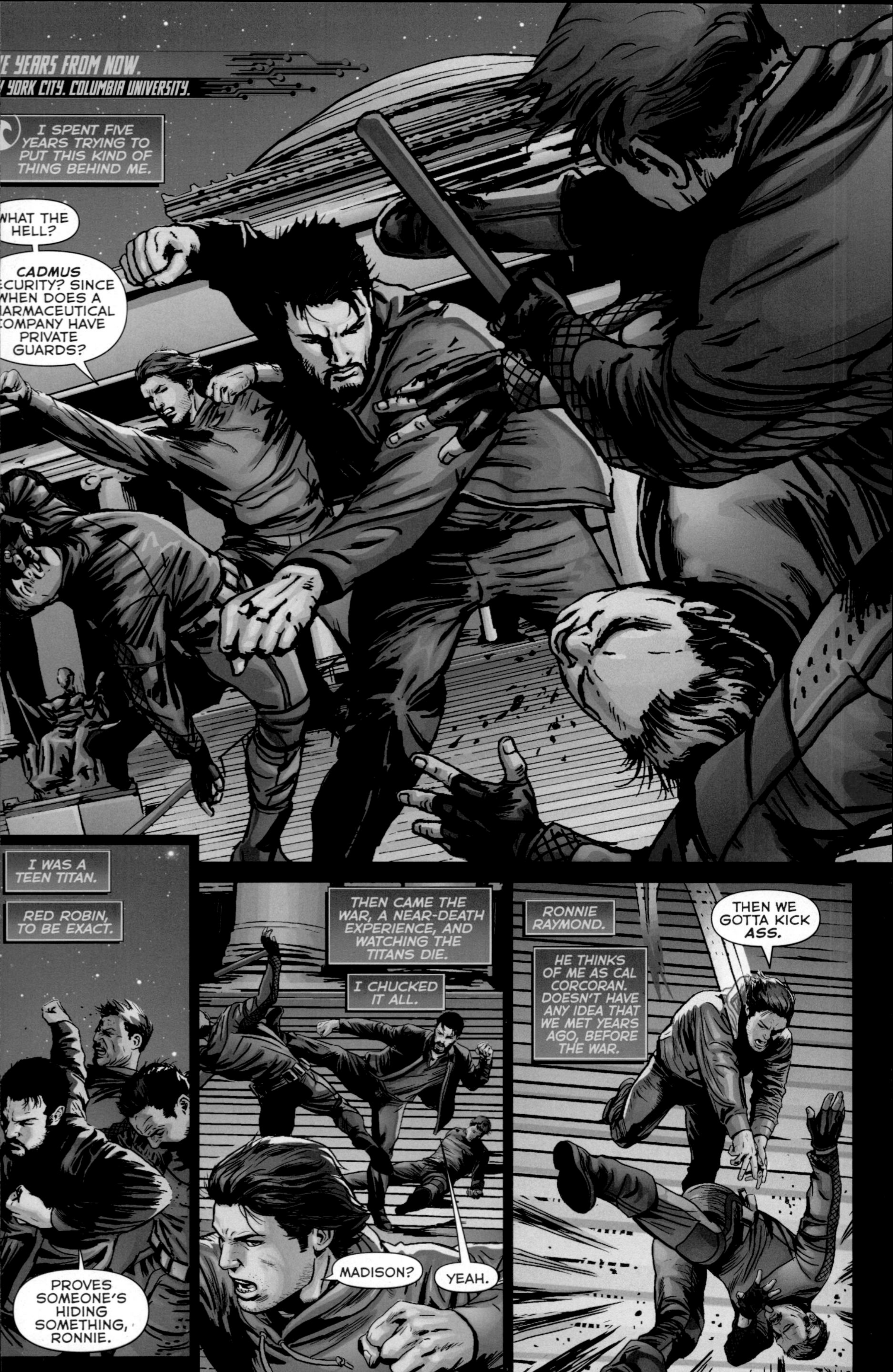

E YEARS FROM NOW.
Y YORK CITY. COLUMBIA UNIVERSITY.
I SPENT FIVE YEARS TRYING TO PUT THIS KIND OF THING BEHIND ME.
WHAT THE HELL?
CADMUS ECURITY? SINCE WHEN DOES A ARMACEUTICAL COMPANY HAVE PRIVATE GUARDS?
I WAS A TEEN TITAN.
RED ROBIN, TO BE EXACT.
PROVES SOMEONE'S HIDING SOMETHING, RONNIE.
THEN CAME THE WAR, A NEAR-DEATH EXPERIENCE, AND WATCHING THE TITANS DIE.
I CHUCKED IT ALL.
MADISON?
YEAH.
RONNIE RAYMOND.
HE THINKS OF ME AS CAL CORCORAN. DOESN'T HAVE ANY IDEA THAT WE MET YEARS AGO, BEFORE THE WAR.
THEN WE GOTTA KICK ASS.

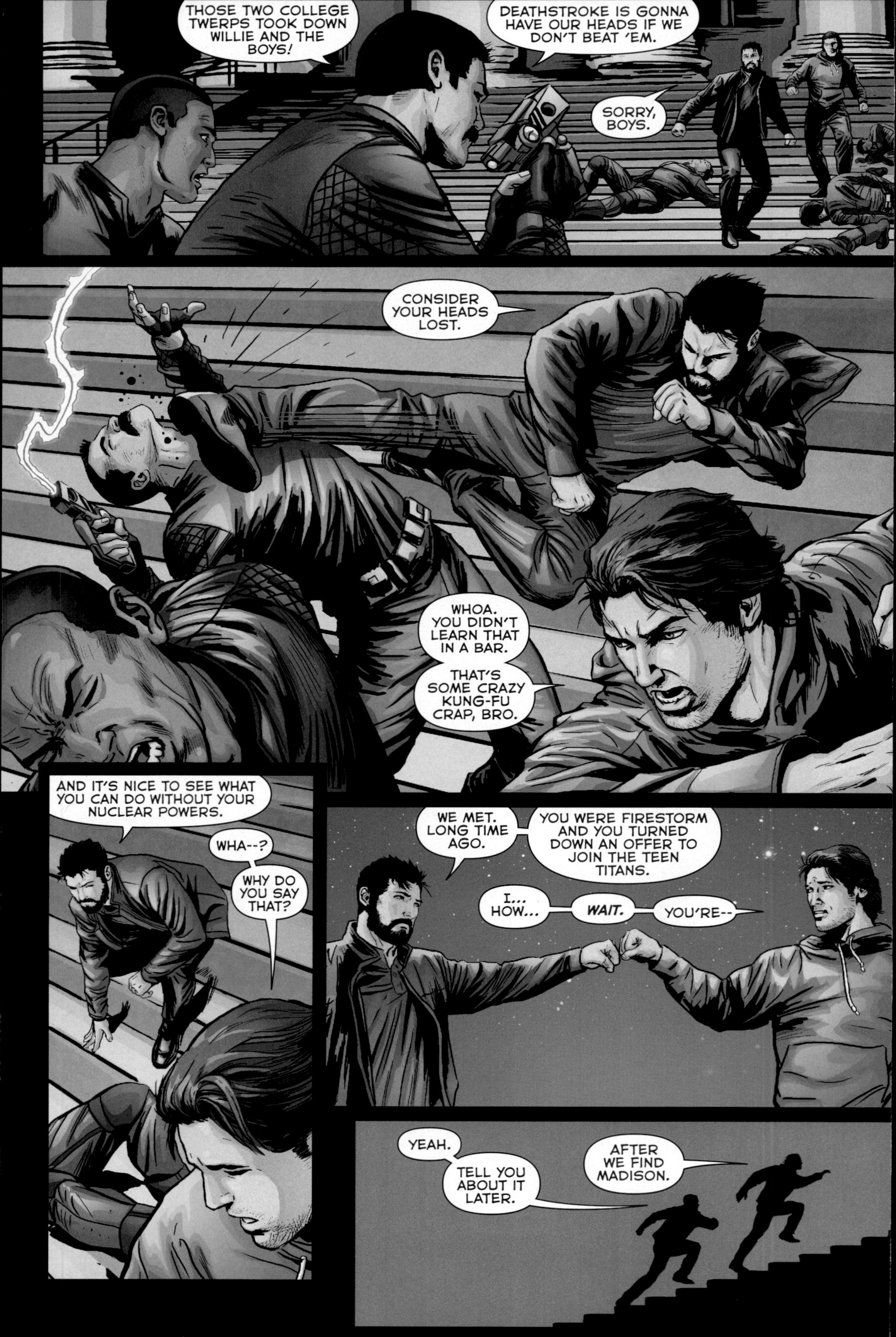
THOSE TWO COLLEGE TWERPS TOOK DOWN WILLIE AND THE BOYS!
DEATHSTROKE IS GONNA HAVE OUR HEADS IF WE DON'T BEAT 'EM.
SORRY, BOYS.
CONSIDER YOUR HEADS LOST.
WHOA. YOU DIDN'T LEARN THAT IN A BAR.
THAT'S SOME CRAZY KUNG-FU CRAP, BRO.
AND IT'S NICE TO SEE WHAT YOU CAN DO WITHOUT YOUR NUCLEAR POWERS.
WHA--?
WHY DO YOU SAY THAT?
WE MET. LONG TIME AGO.
YOU WERE FIRESTORM AND YOU TURNED DOWN AN OFFER TO JOIN THE TEEN TITANS.
I... HOW...
WAIT.
YOU'RE--
YEAH.
TELL YOU ABOUT IT LATER.
AFTER WE FIND MADISON.

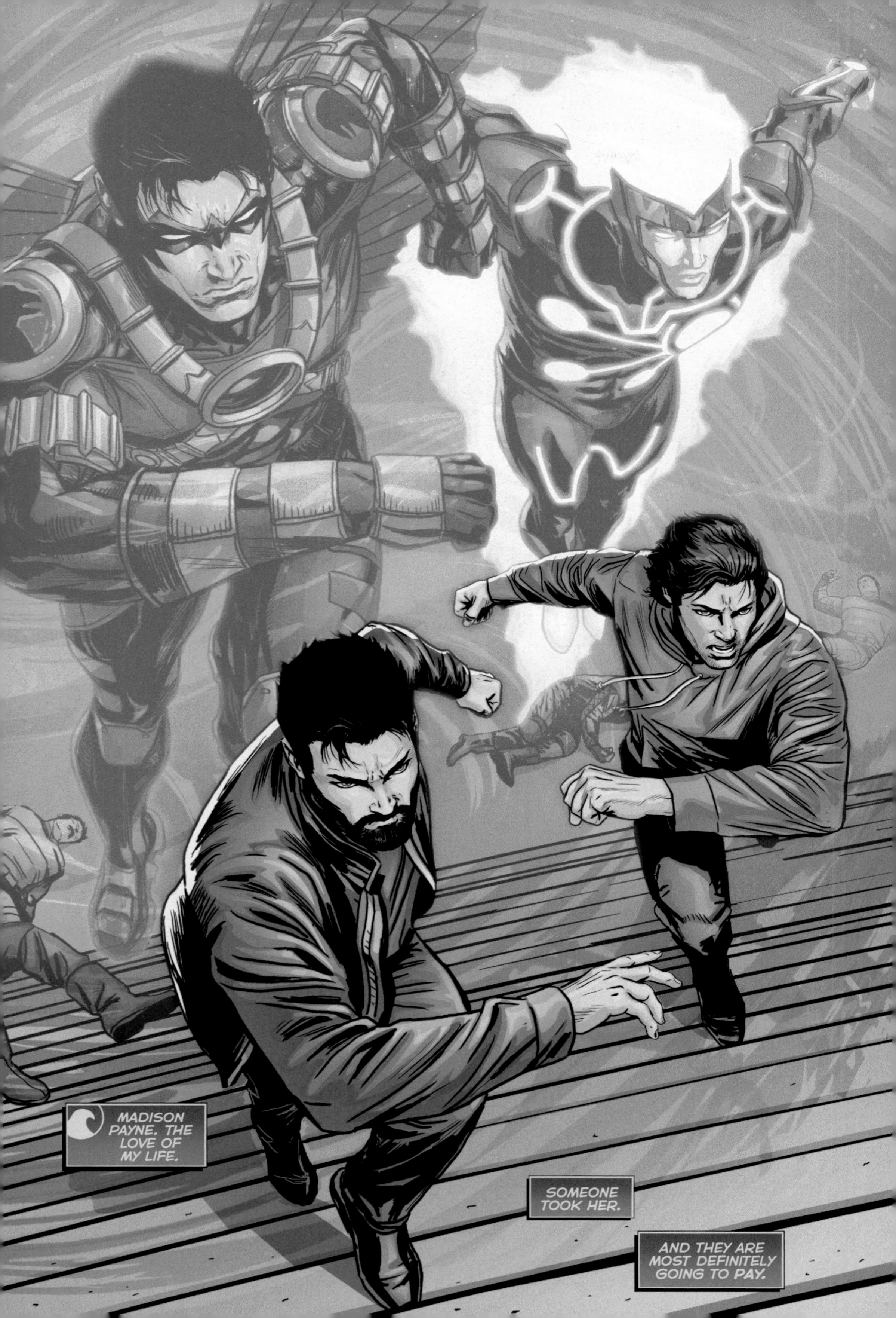
MADISON PAYNE. THE LOVE OF MY LIFE.
SOMEONE TOOK HER.
AND THEY ARE MOST DEFINITELY GOING TO PAY.

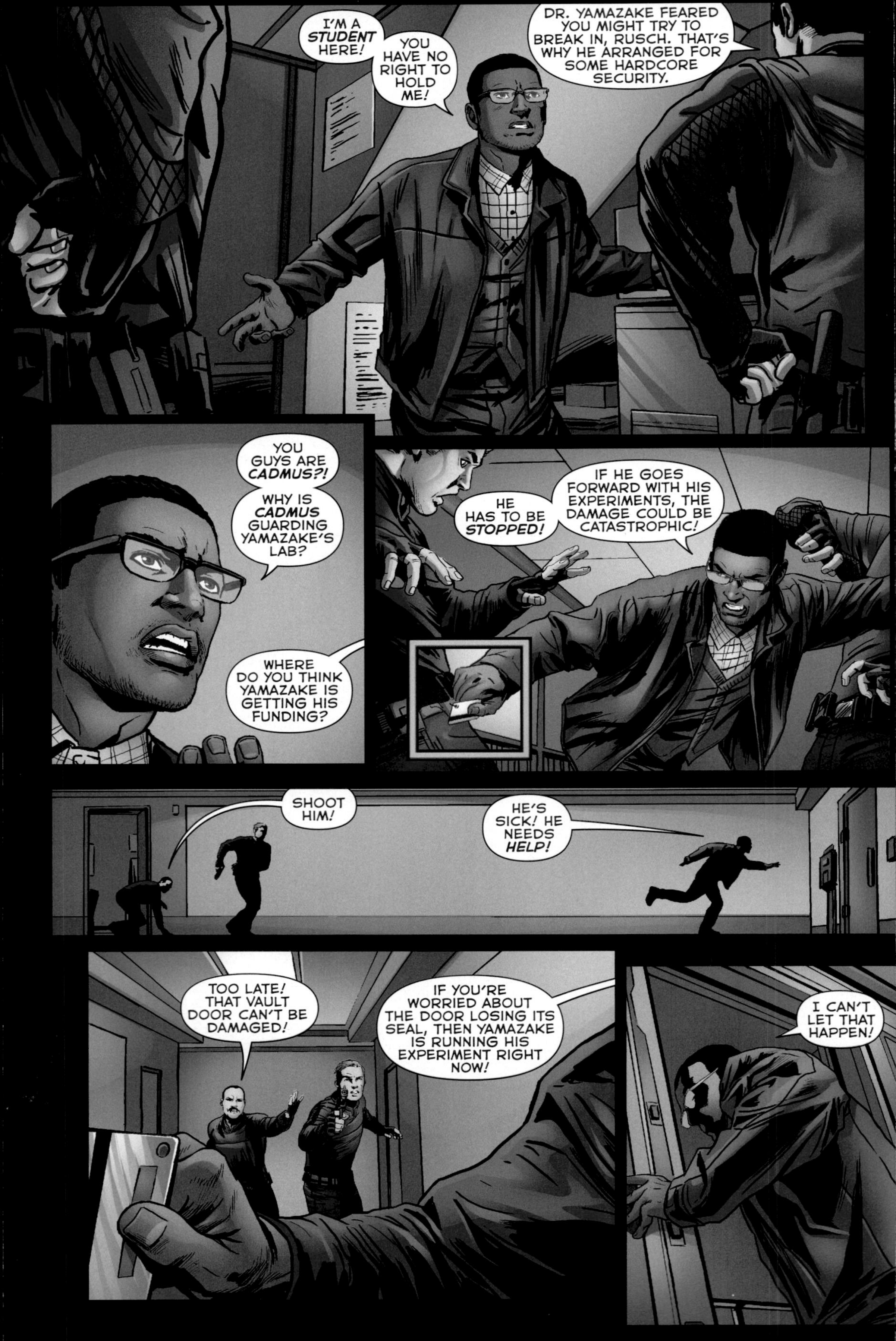
I'M A STUDENT HERE!
YOU HAVE NO RIGHT TO HOLD ME!
DR. YAMAZAKE FEARED YOU MIGHT TRY TO BREAK IN, RUSCH. THAT'S WHY HE ARRANGED FOR SOME HARDCORE SECURITY.
YOU GUYS ARE CADMUS?!
WHY IS CADMUS GUARDING YAMAZAKE'S LAB?
WHERE DO YOU THINK YAMAZAKE IS GETTING HIS FUNDING?
HE HAS TO BE STOPPED!
IF HE GOES FORWARD WITH HIS EXPERIMENTS, THE DAMAGE COULD BE CATASTROPHIC!
SHOOT HIM!
HE'S SICK! HE NEEDS HELP!
TOO LATE! THAT VAULT DOOR CAN'T BE DAMAGED!
IF YOU'RE WORRIED ABOUT THE DOOR LOSING ITS SEAL, THEN YAMAZAKE IS RUNNING HIS EXPERIMENT RIGHT NOW!
I CAN'T LET THAT HAPPEN!

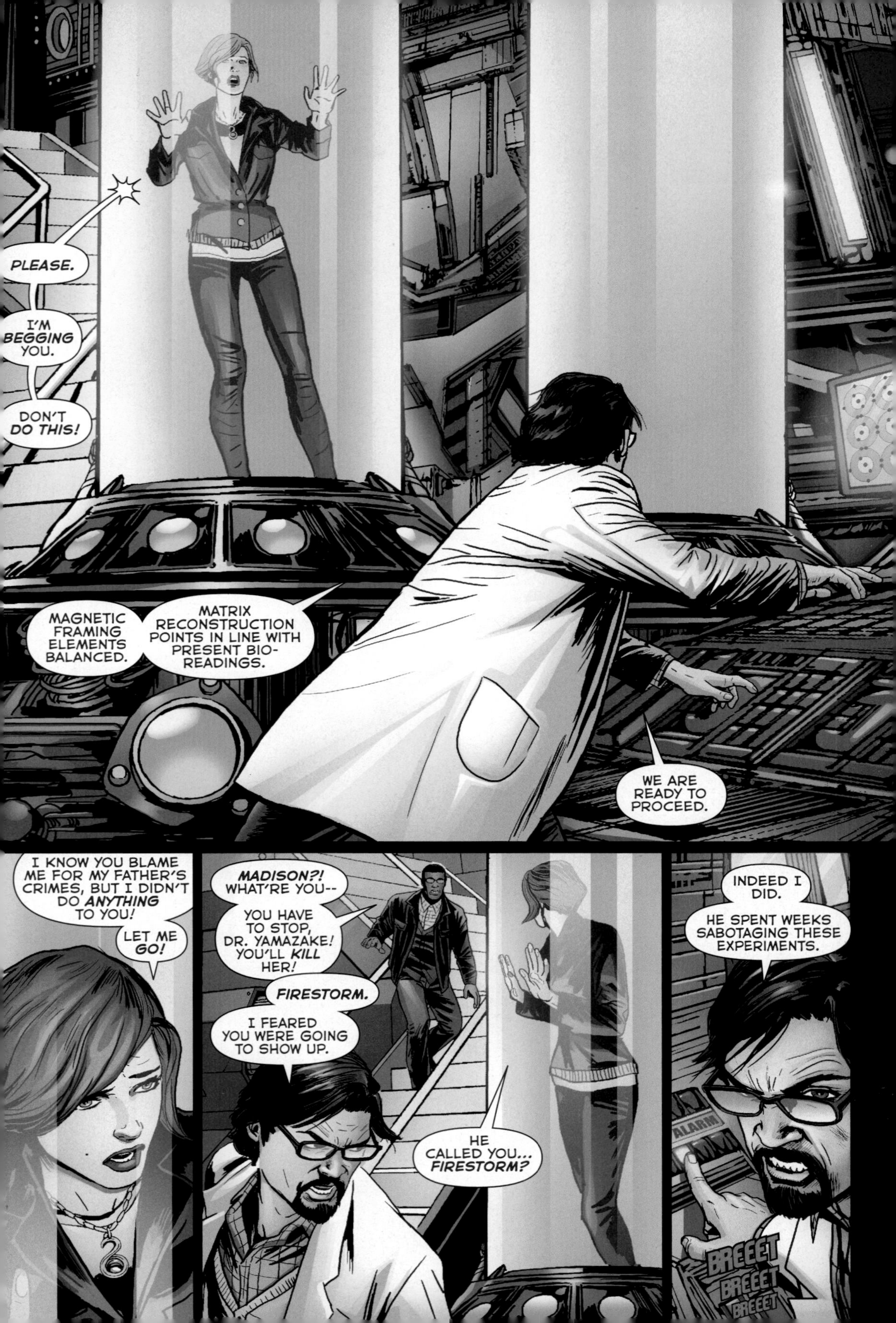
PLEASE.
I'M BEGGING YOU.
DON'T DO THIS!
MAGNETIC FRAMING ELEMENTS BALANCED.
MATRIX RECONSTRUCTION POINTS IN LINE WITH PRESENT BIO-READINGS.
WE ARE READY TO PROCEED.
I KNOW YOU BLAME ME FOR MY FATHER'S CRIMES, BUT I DIDN'T DO ANYTHING TO YOU!
LET ME GO!
MADISON?! WHAT'RE YOU--
YOU HAVE TO STOP, DR. YAMAZAKE! YOU'LL KILL HER!
FIRESTORM.
I FEARED YOU WERE GOING TO SHOW UP.
HE CALLED YOU... FIRESTORM?
INDEED I DID.
HE SPENT WEEKS SABOTAGING THESE EXPERIMENTS.
ALARM
BREEET
BREEET
BREEET

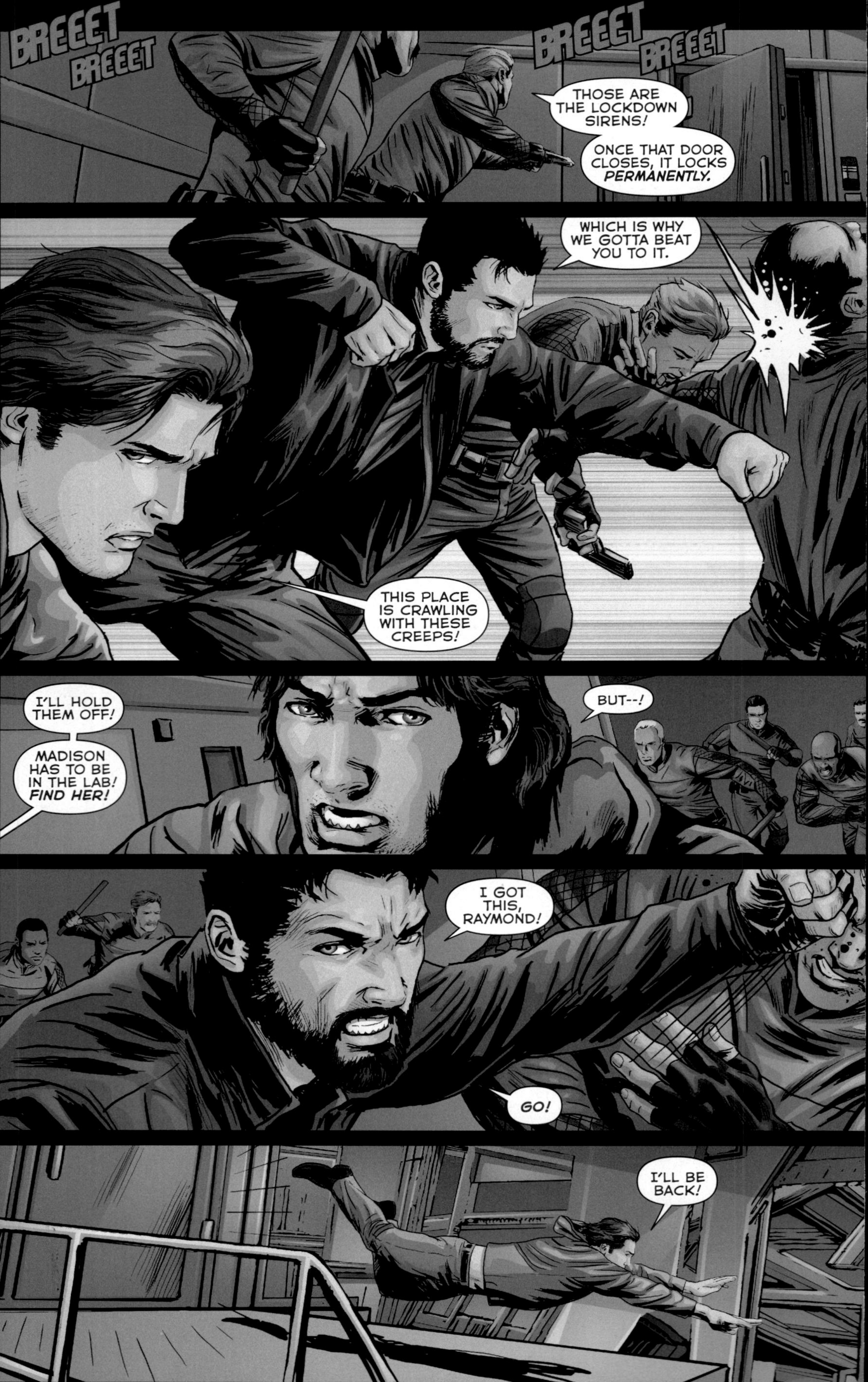
BREEET
BREEET
BREEET
BREEET
THOSE ARE THE LOCKDOWN SIRENS!
ONCE THAT DOOR CLOSES, IT LOCKS *PERMANENTLY.*
WHICH IS WHY WE GOTTA BEAT YOU TO IT.
THIS PLACE IS CRAWLING WITH THESE CREEPS!
I'LL HOLD THEM OFF!
MADISON HAS TO BE IN THE LAB! *FIND HER!*
BUT--!
I GOT THIS, RAYMOND!
GO!
I'LL BE BACK!

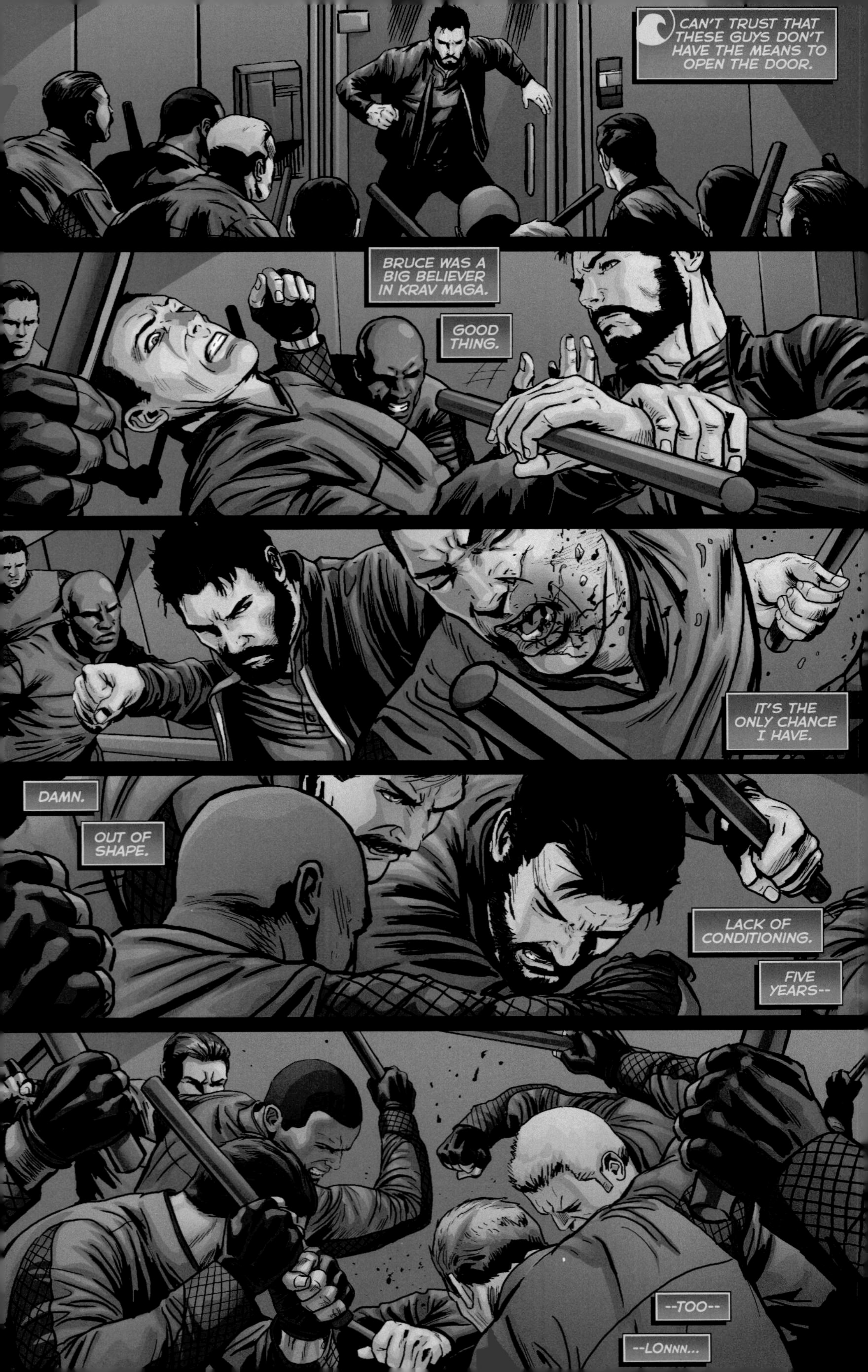
CAN'T TRUST THAT THESE GUYS DON'T HAVE THE MEANS TO OPEN THE DOOR.
BRUCE WAS A BIG BELIEVER IN KRAV MAGA.
GOOD THING.
IT'S THE ONLY CHANCE I HAVE.
DAMN.
OUT OF SHAPE.
LACK OF CONDITIONING.
FIVE YEARS--
--TOO--
--LONNN...

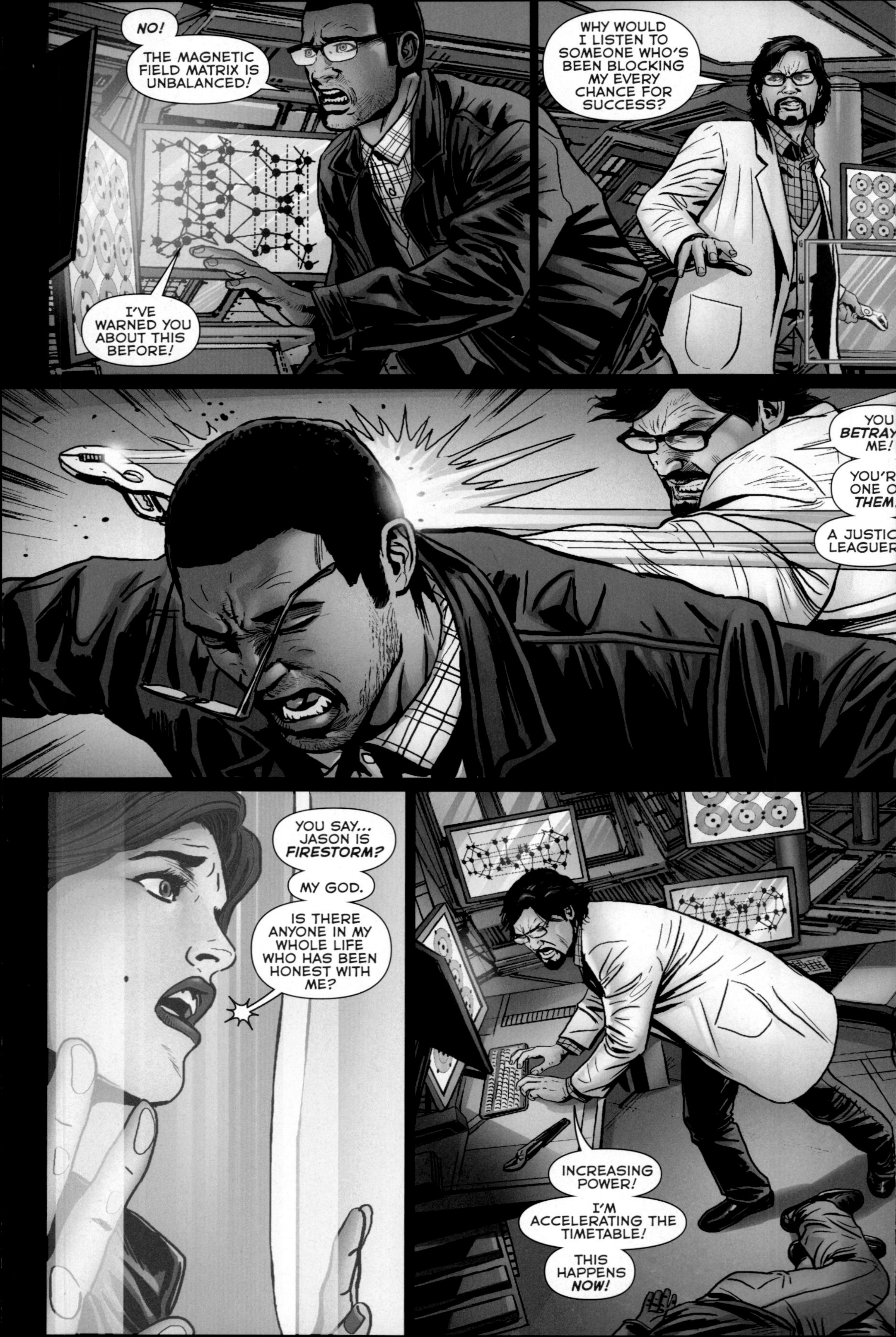
NO!
THE MAGNETIC FIELD MATRIX IS UNBALANCED!
I'VE WARNED YOU ABOUT THIS BEFORE!
WHY WOULD I LISTEN TO SOMEONE WHO'S BEEN BLOCKING MY EVERY CHANCE FOR SUCCESS?
YOU BETRAY ME!
YOU'R ONE O THEM
A JUSTIC LEAGUER
YOU SAY... JASON IS FIRESTORM?
MY GOD.
IS THERE ANYONE IN MY WHOLE LIFE WHO HAS BEEN HONEST WITH ME?
INCREASING POWER!
I'M ACCELERATING THE TIMETABLE!
THIS HAPPENS NOW!

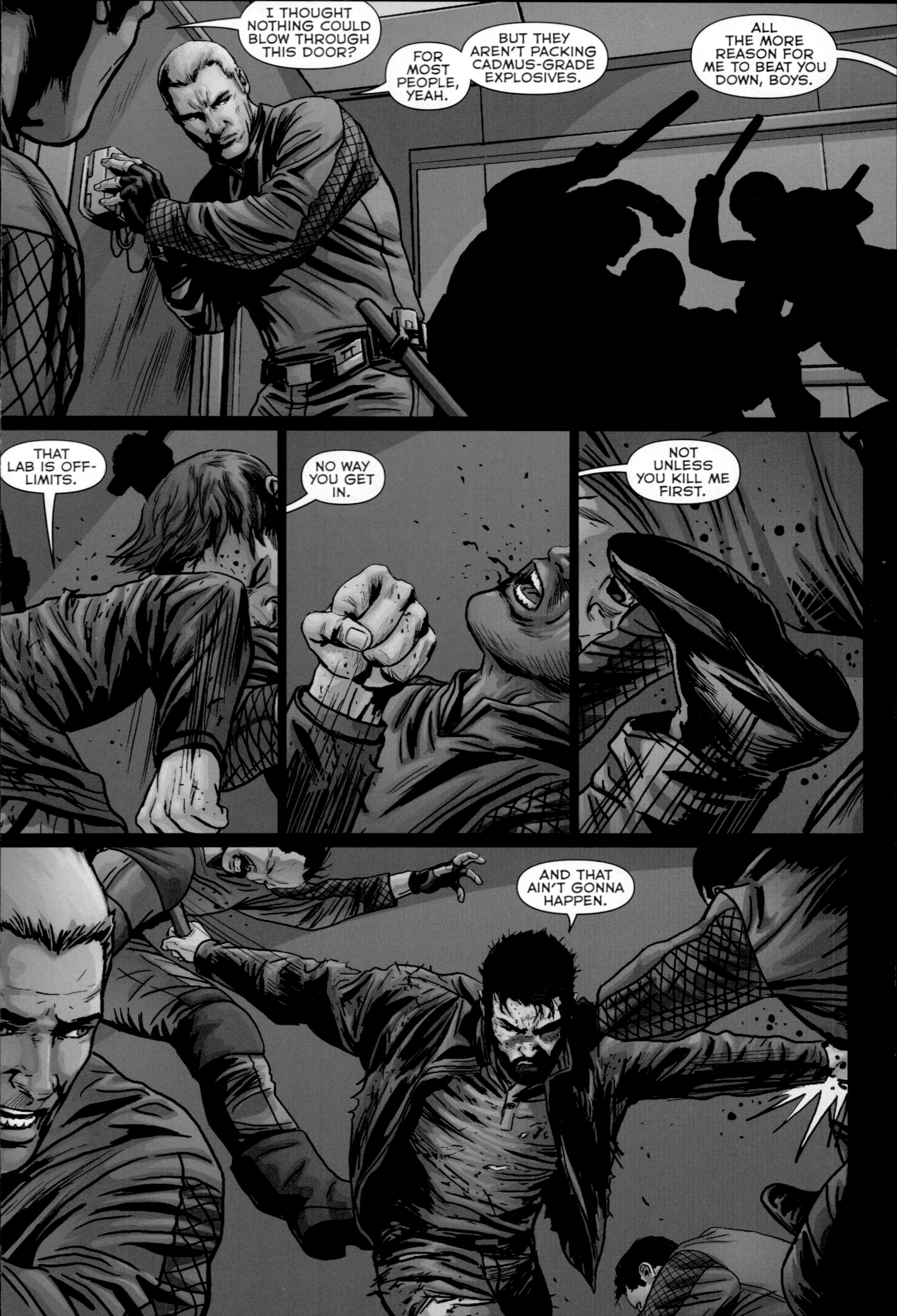
I THOUGHT NOTHING COULD BLOW THROUGH THIS DOOR?
FOR MOST PEOPLE, YEAH.
BUT THEY AREN'T PACKING CADMUS-GRADE EXPLOSIVES.
ALL THE MORE REASON FOR ME TO BEAT YOU DOWN, BOYS.
THAT LAB IS OFF-LIMITS.
NO WAY YOU GET IN.
NOT UNLESS YOU KILL ME FIRST.
AND THAT AIN'T GONNA HAPPEN.

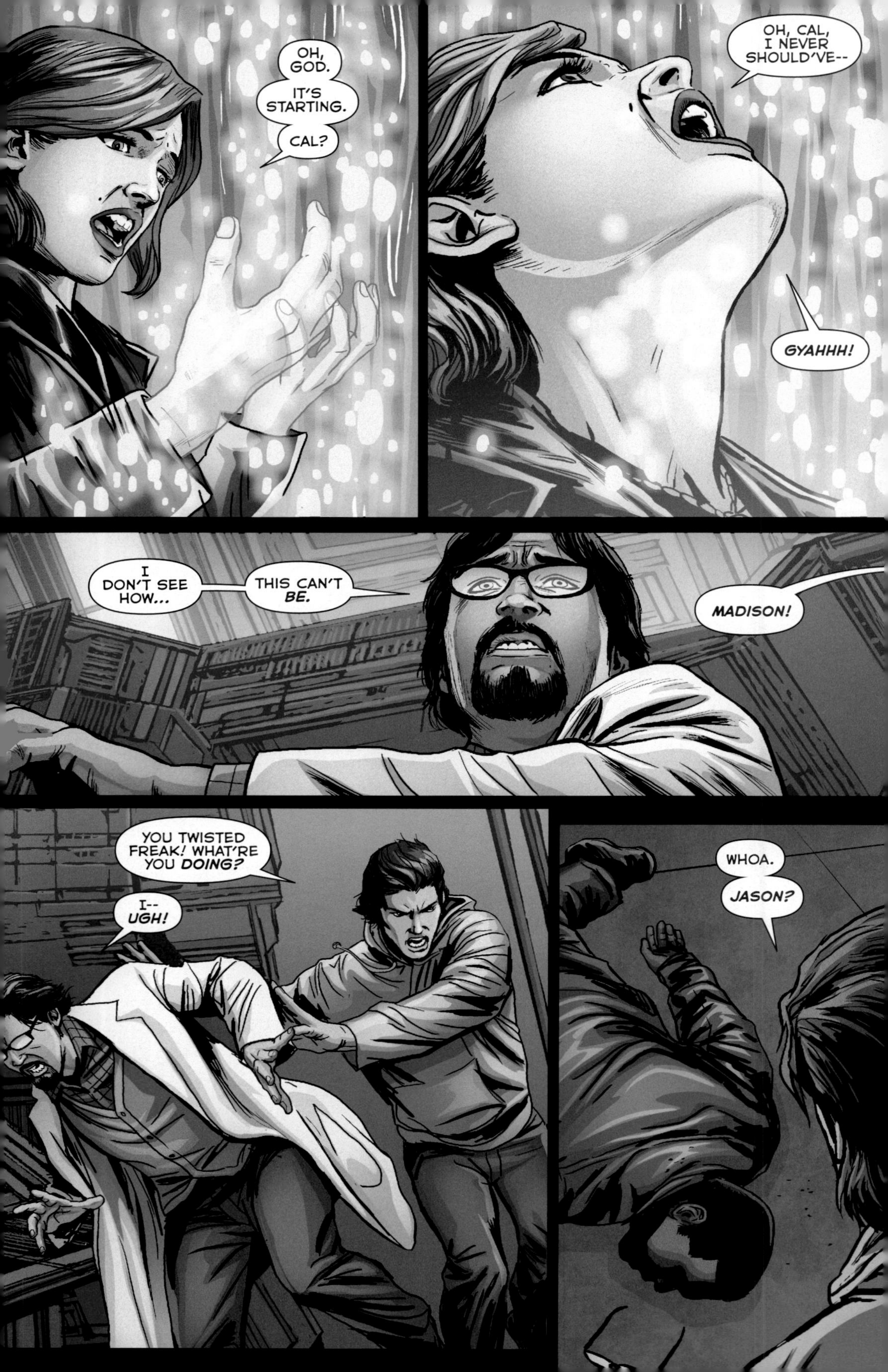

OH, GOD.
IT'S STARTING.
CAL?
OH, CAL, I NEVER SHOULD'VE--
GYAHHH!
I DON'T SEE HOW...
THIS CAN'T BE.
MADISON!
YOU TWISTED FREAK! WHAT'RE YOU DOING?
I-- UGH!
WHOA.
JASON?

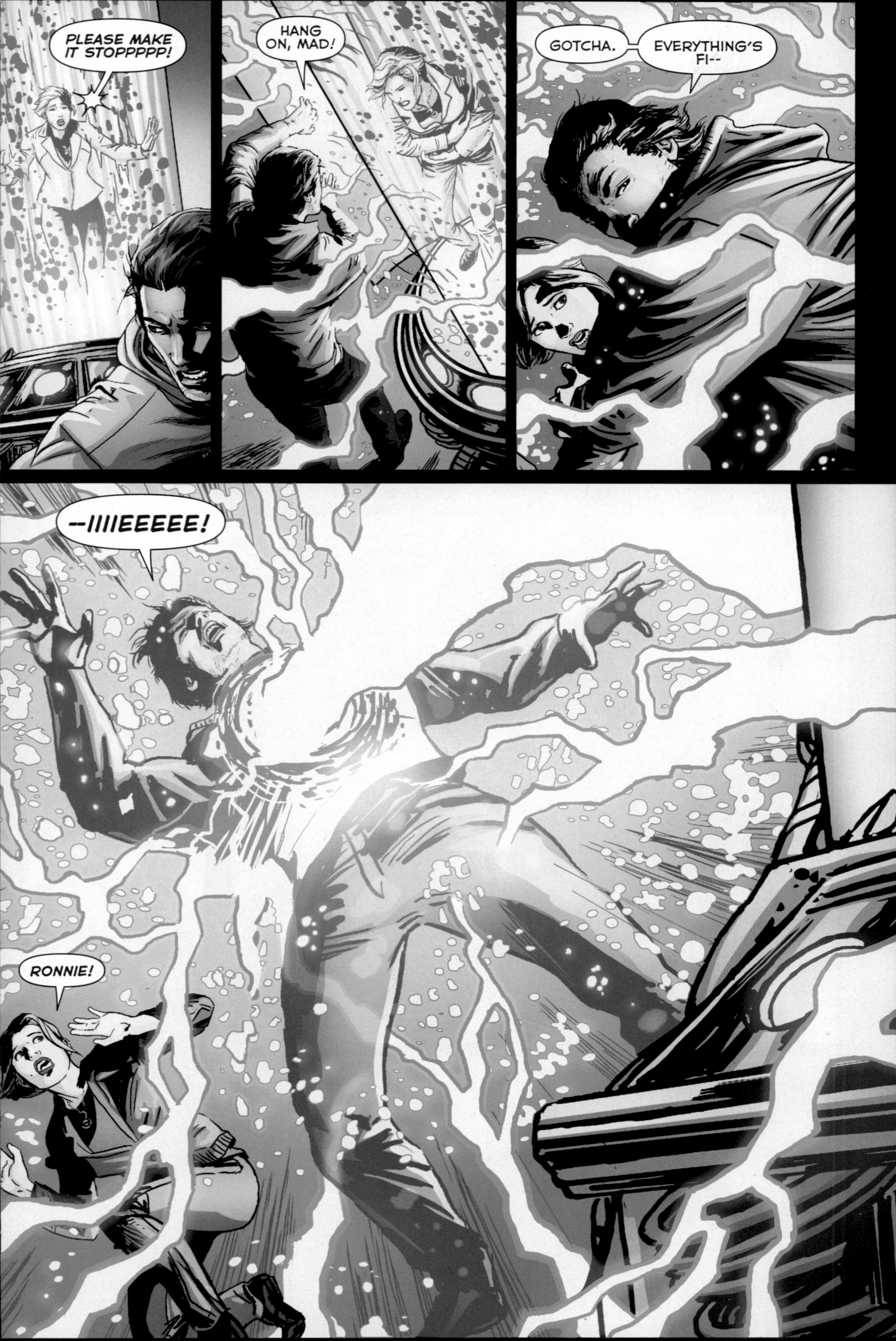
PLEASE MAKE IT STOPPPPP!
HANG ON, MAD!
GOTCHA.
EVERYTHING'S FI--
--IIIIEEEEE!
RONNIE!

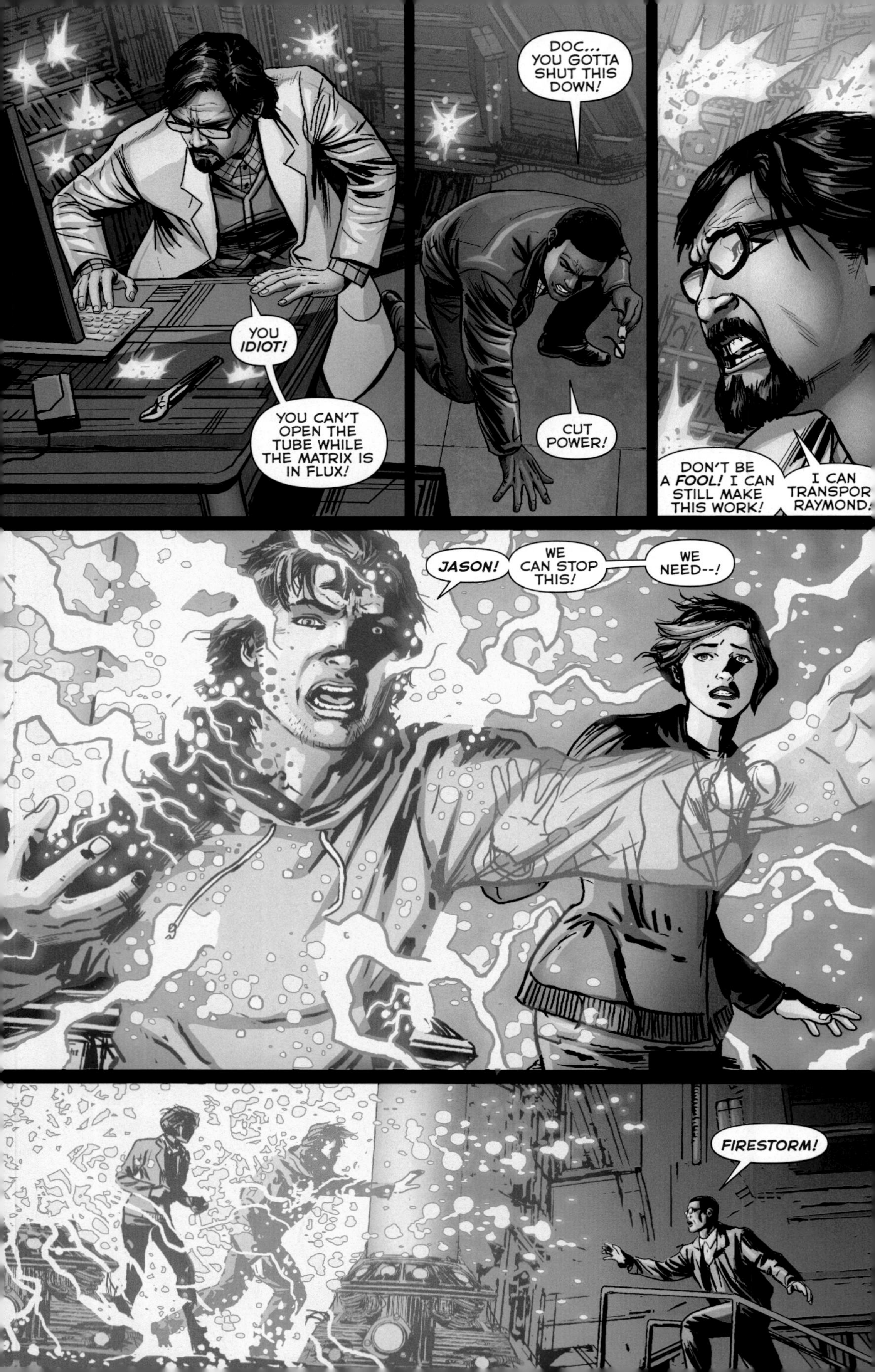
YOU IDIOT!
YOU CAN'T OPEN THE TUBE WHILE THE MATRIX IS IN FLUX!
DOC... YOU GOTTA SHUT THIS DOWN!
CUT POWER!
DON'T BE A FOOL! I CAN STILL MAKE THIS WORK!
I CAN TRANSPOR RAYMOND!
JASON!
WE CAN STOP THIS!
WE NEED--!
FIRESTORM!

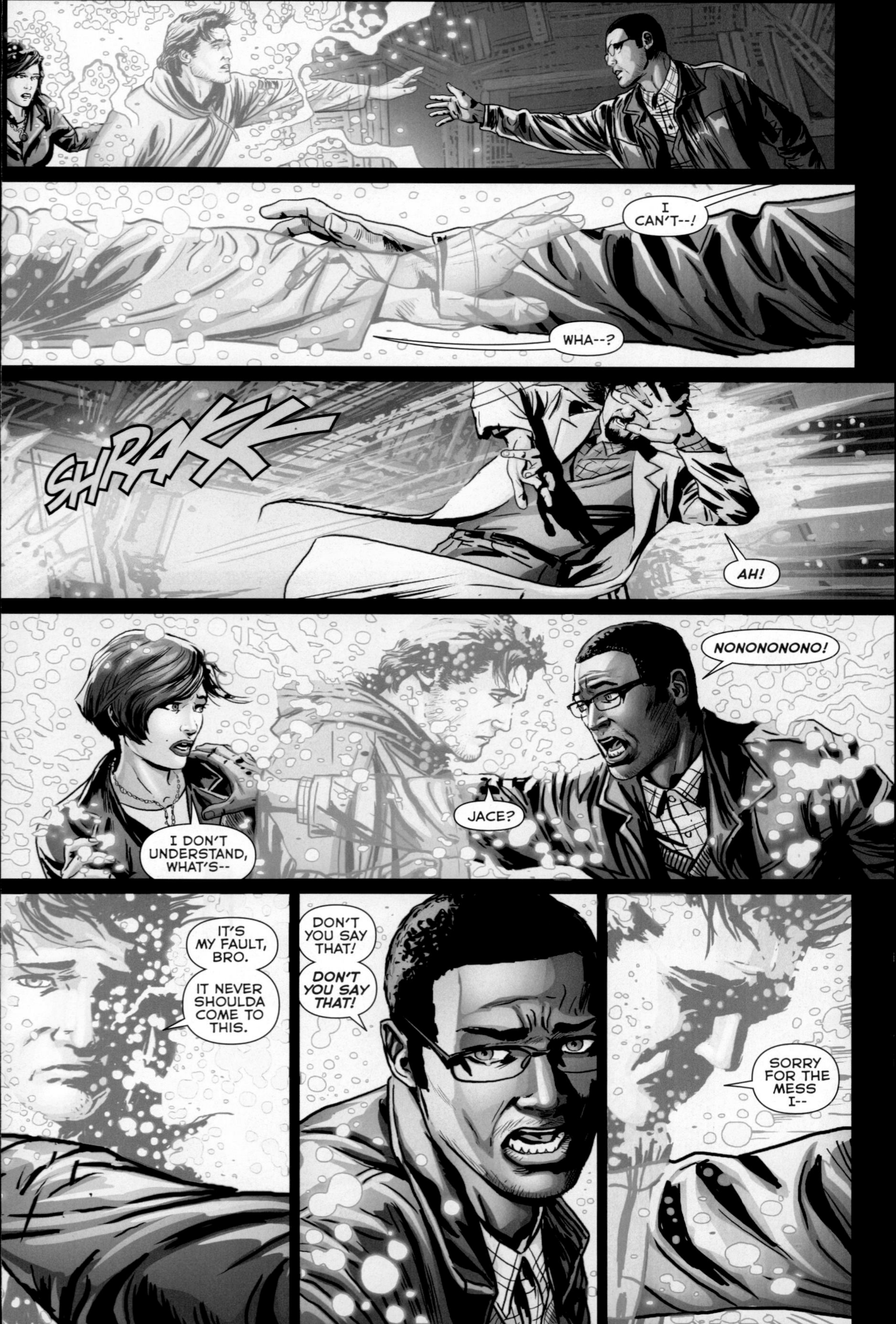
I CAN'T--!
WHA--?
SHRAKK
AH!
NONONONONO!
JACE?
I DON'T UNDERSTAND, WHAT'S--
IT'S MY FAULT, BRO.
IT NEVER SHOULDA COME TO THIS.
DON'T YOU SAY THAT!
DON'T YOU SAY THAT!
SORRY FOR THE MESS I--

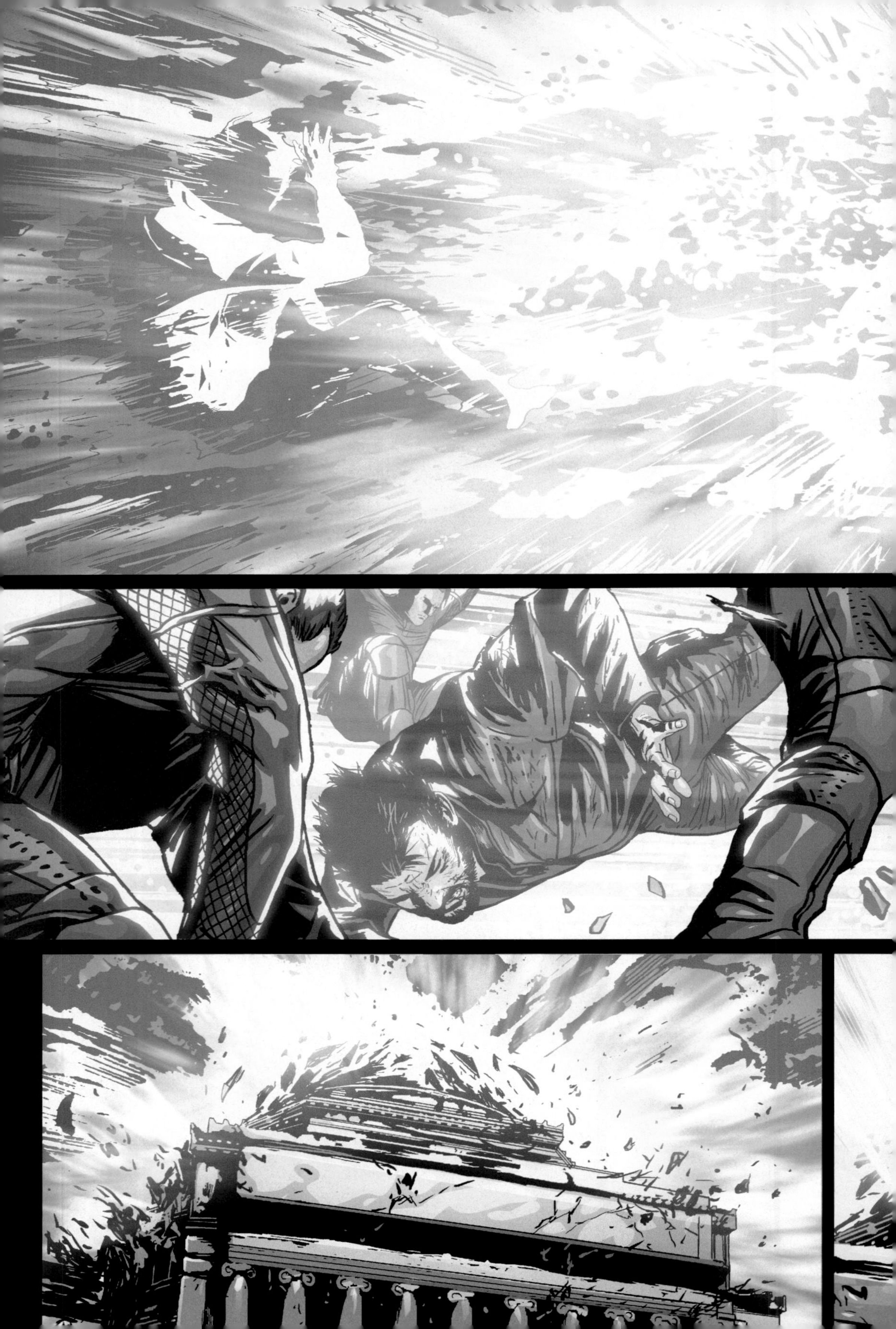

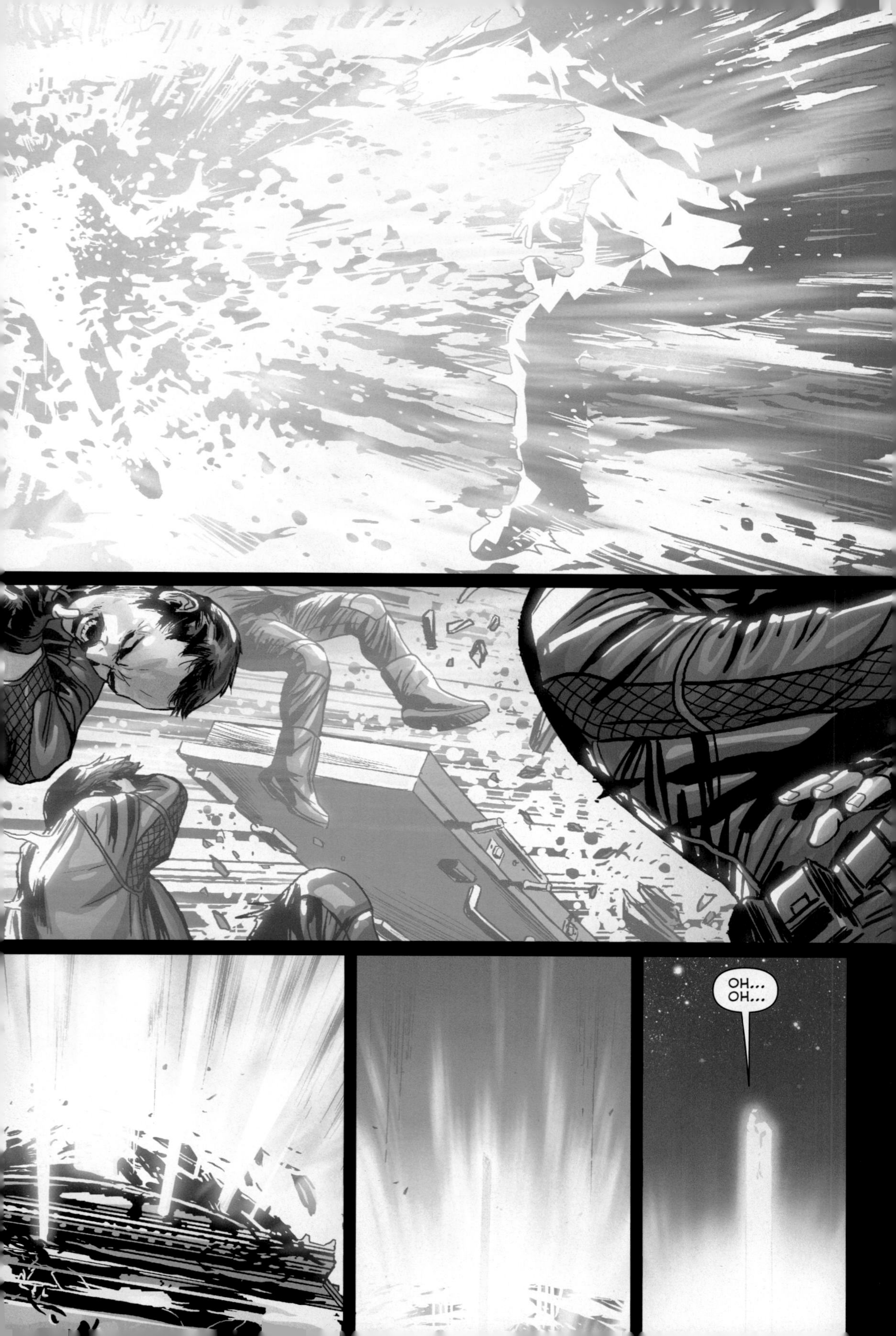
OH...
OH...

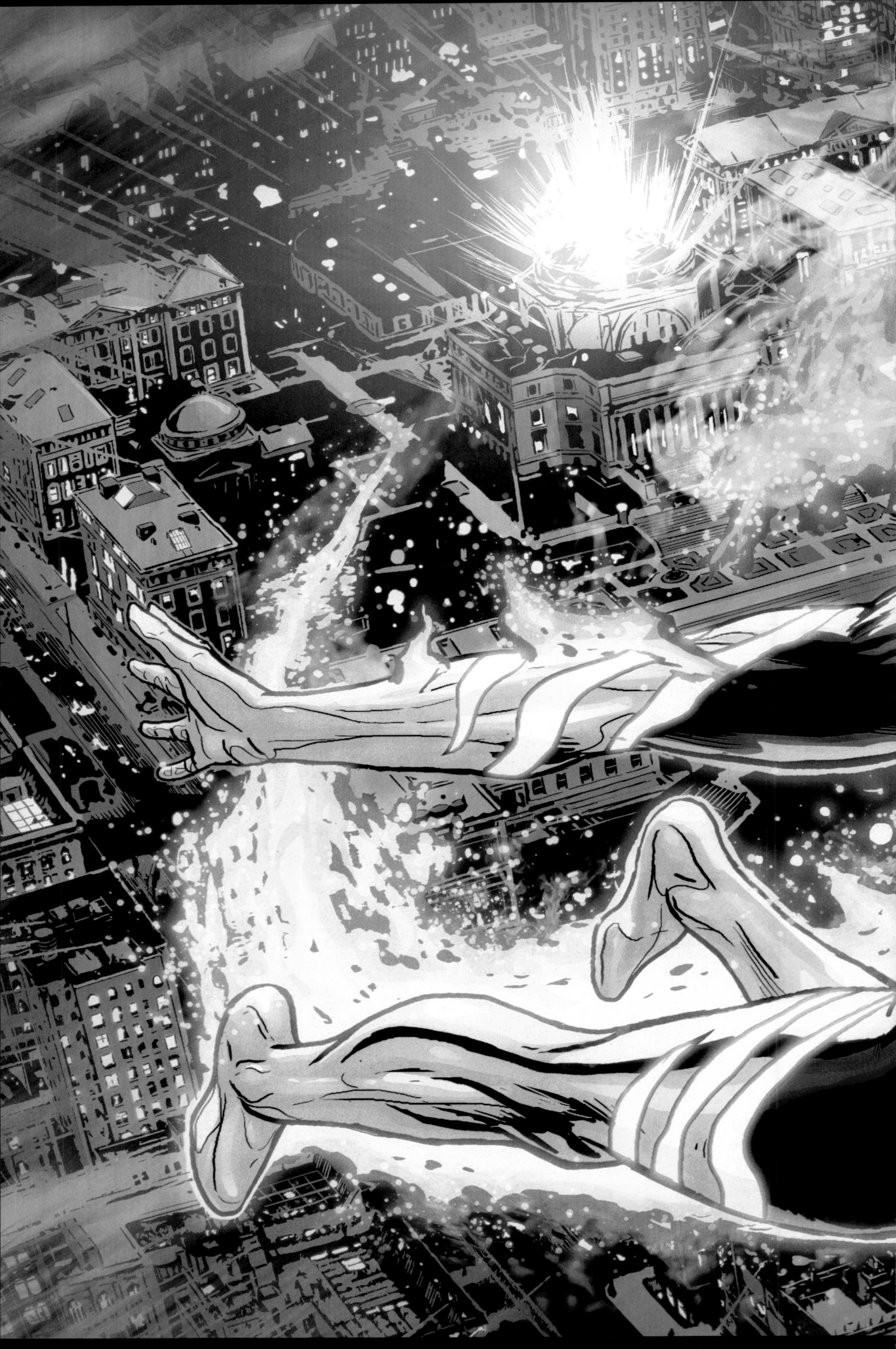

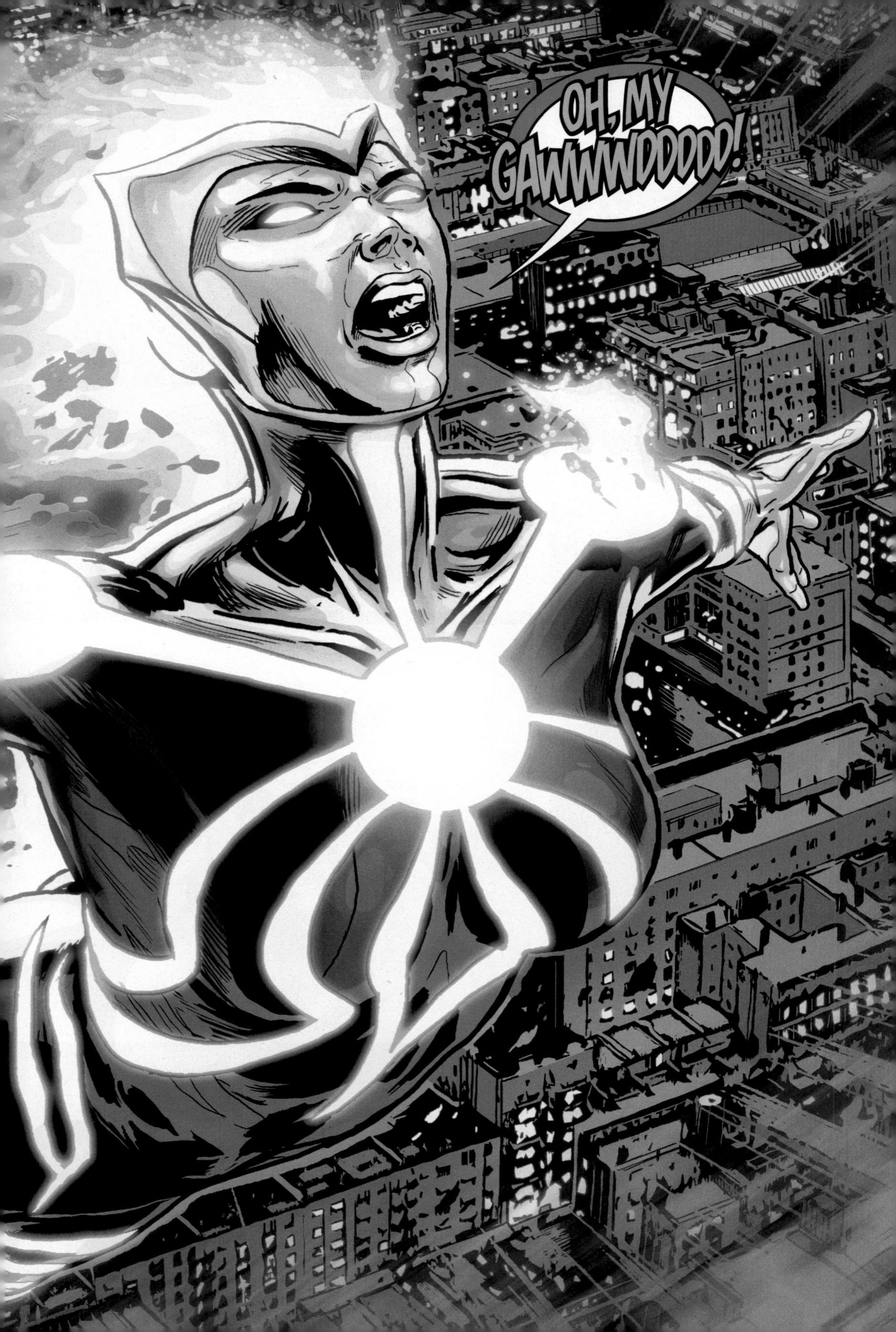
OH, MY GAWWWDDDDD!

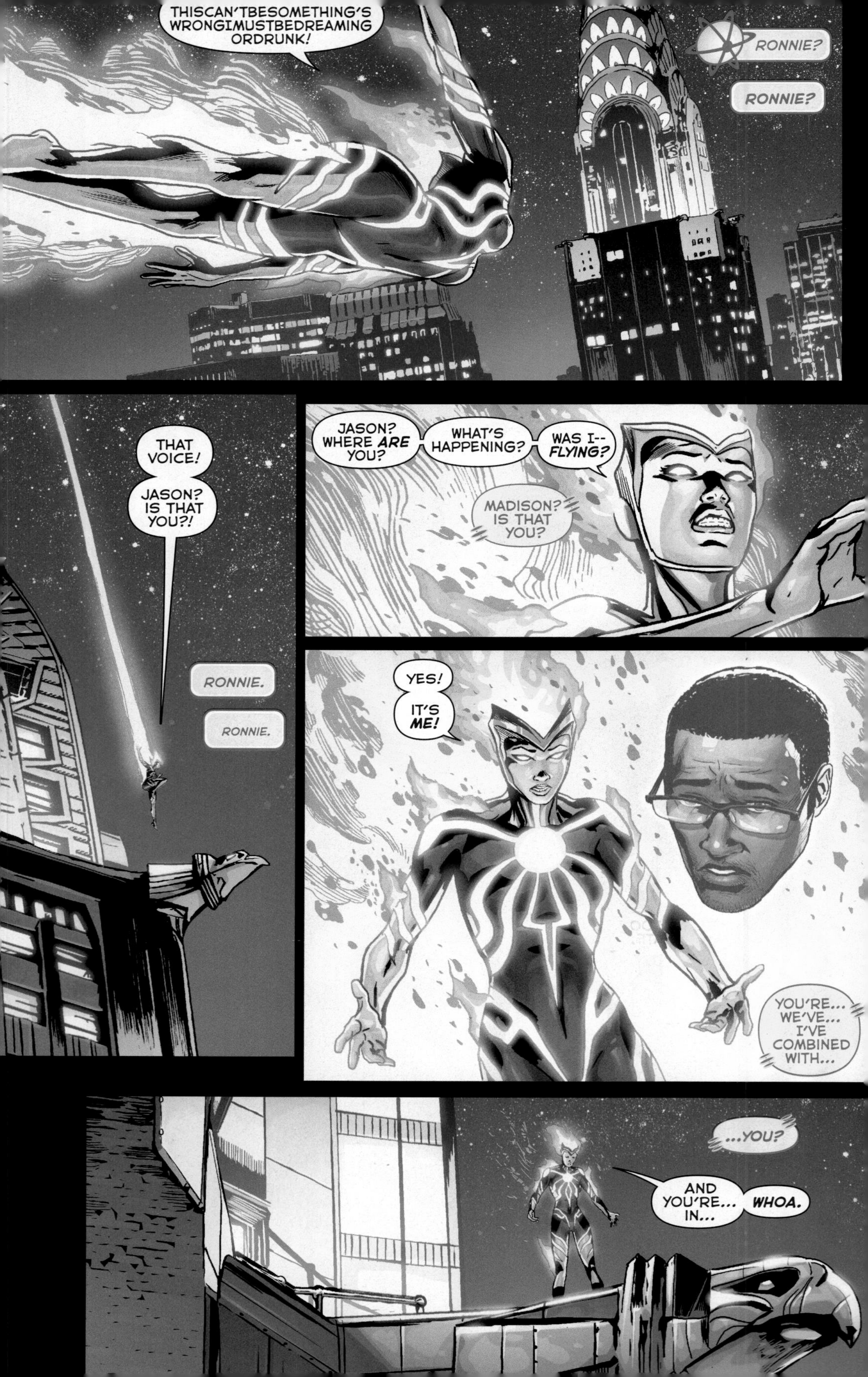
THISCAN'TBESOMETHING'S WRONGIMUSTBEDREAMING ORDRUNK!
RONNIE?
RONNIE?
THAT VOICE!
JASON? IS THAT YOU?!
RONNIE.
RONNIE.
JASON? WHERE ARE YOU?
WHAT'S HAPPENING?
WAS I-- FLYING?
MADISON? IS THAT YOU?
YES!
IT'S ME!
YOU'RE... WE'VE... I'VE COMBINED WITH...
...YOU?
AND YOU'RE... IN...
WHOA.

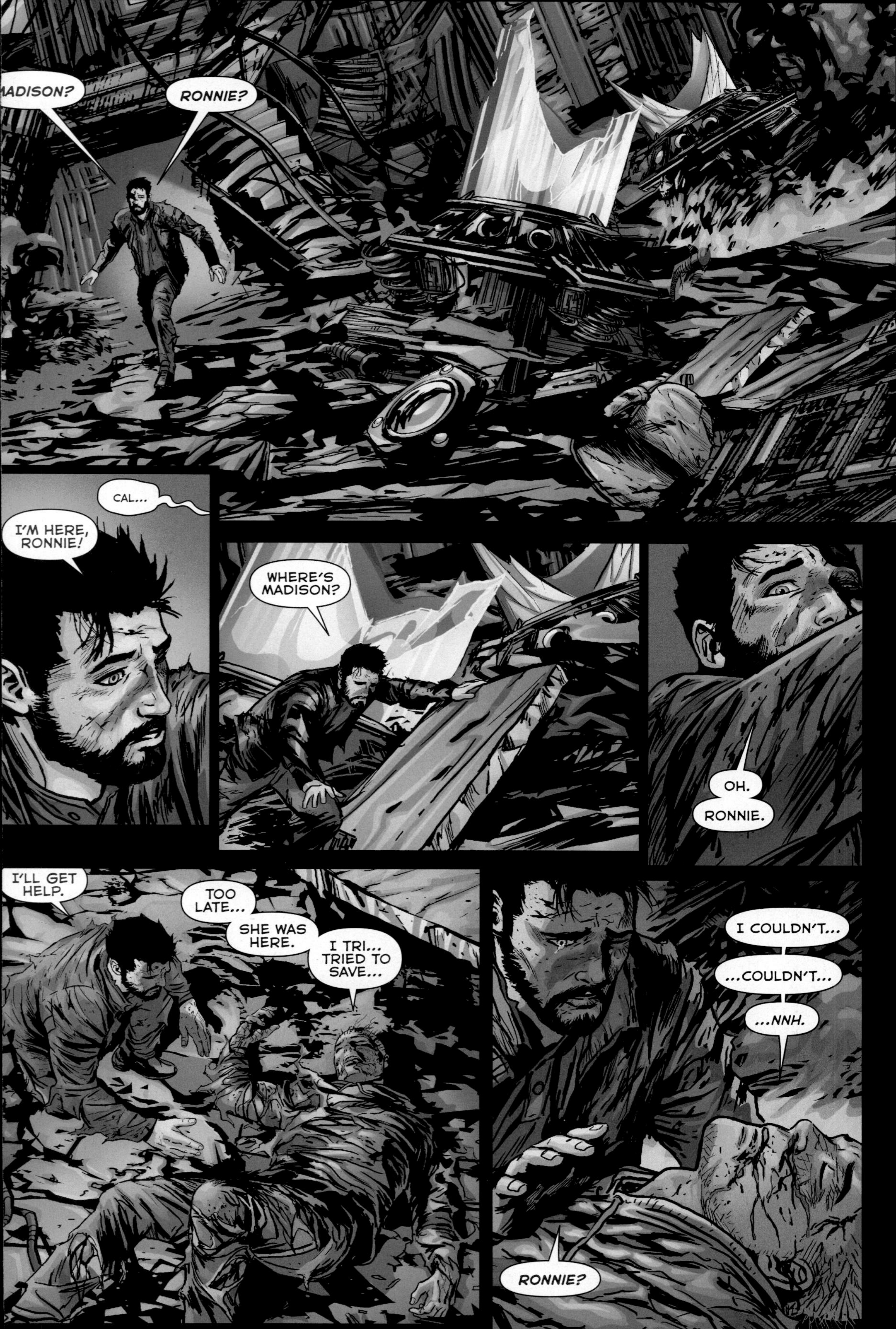
MADISON?
RONNIE?
CAL...
I'M HERE, RONNIE!
WHERE'S MADISON?
OH. RONNIE.
I'LL GET HELP.
TOO LATE...
SHE WAS HERE.
I TRI... TRIED TO SAVE...
I COULDN'T...
...COULDN'T...
...NNH.
RONNIE?

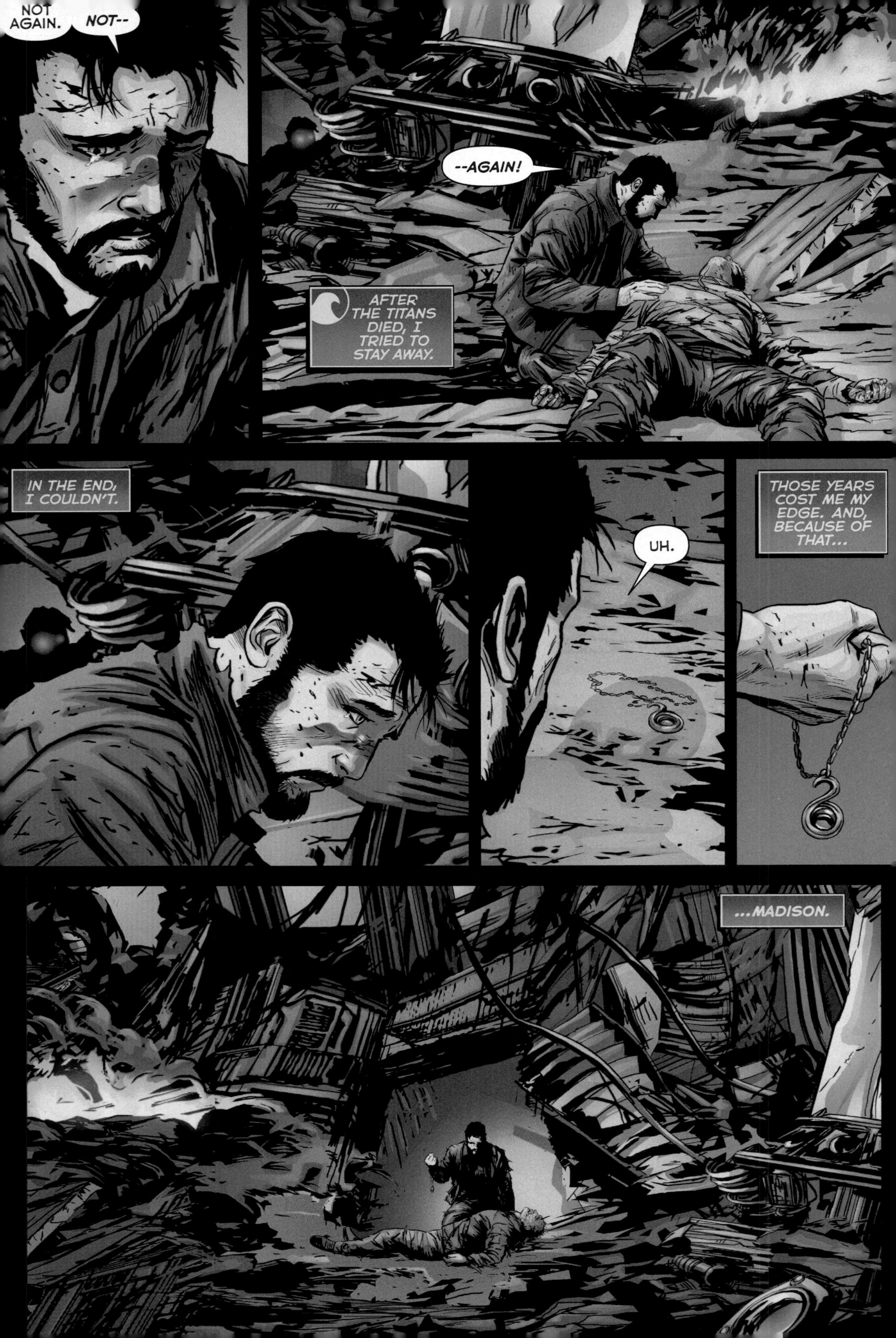
NOT AGAIN.
NOT--
--AGAIN!
AFTER THE TITANS DIED, I TRIED TO STAY AWAY.
IN THE END, I COULDN'T.
UH.
THOSE YEARS COST ME MY EDGE. AND, BECAUSE OF THAT...
...MADISON.

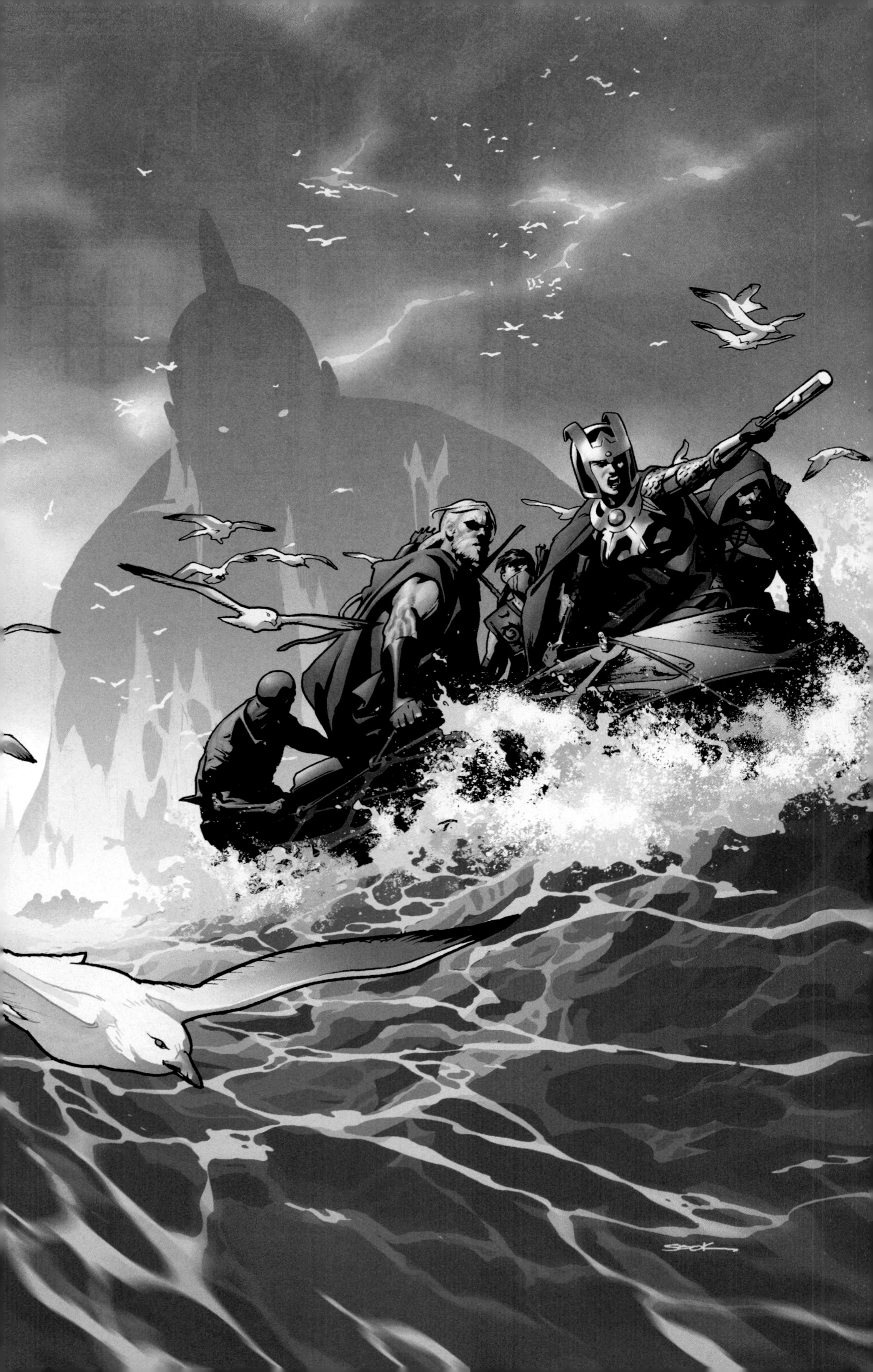

INTO THE FUTUR

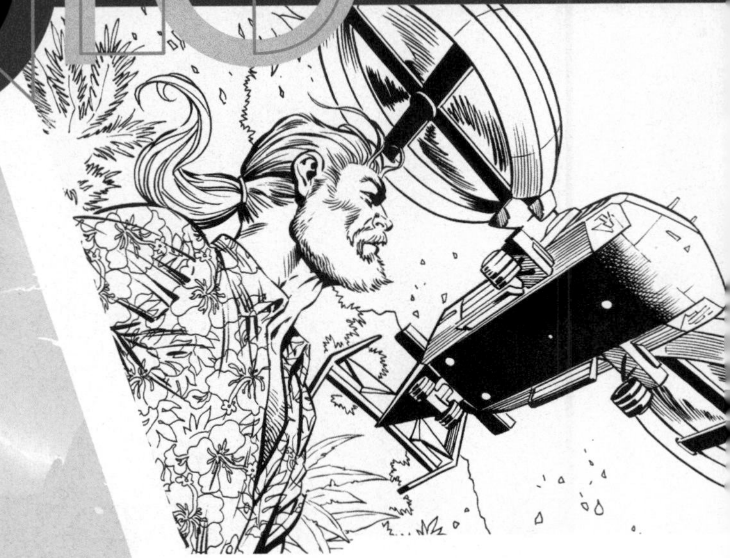

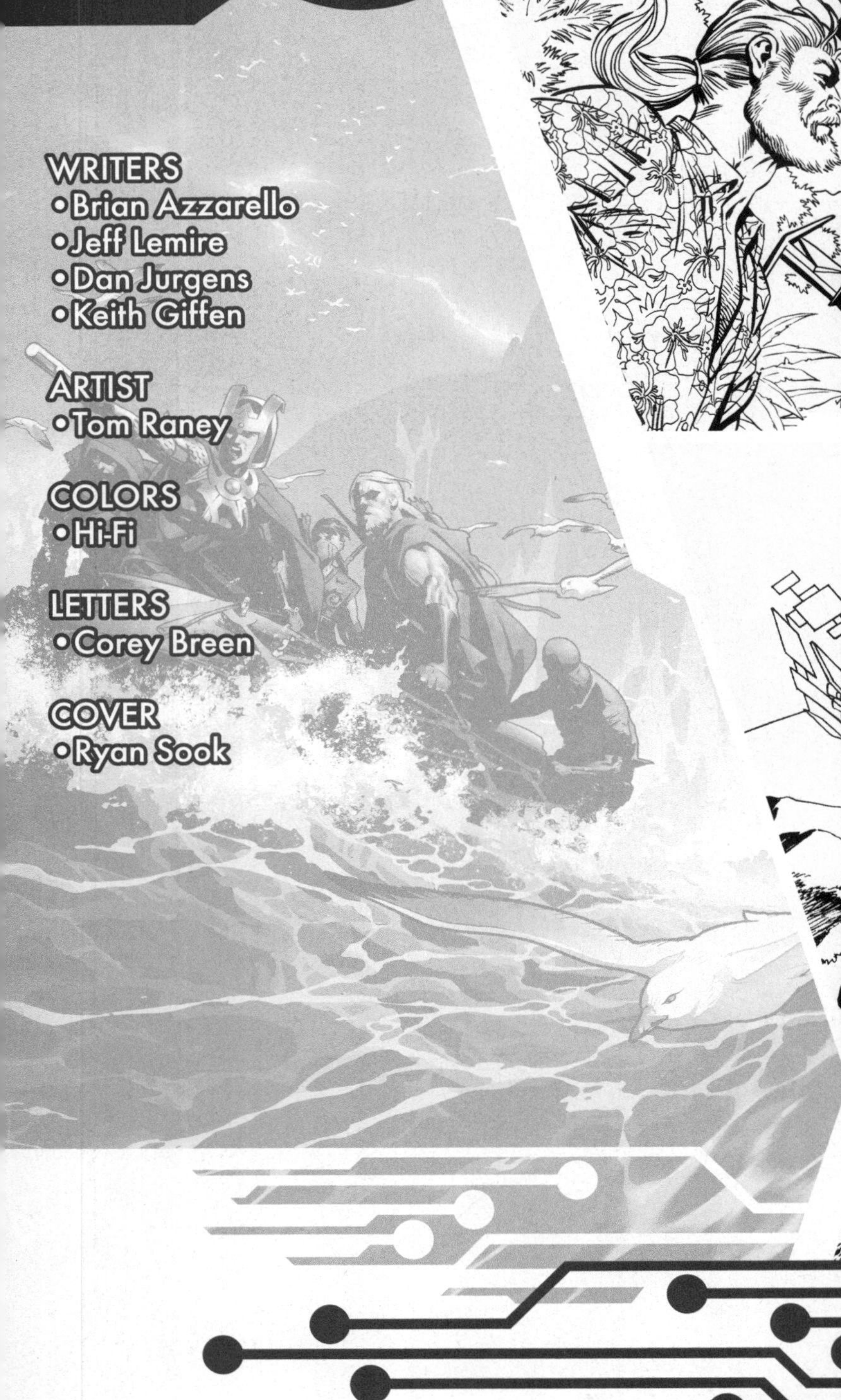

WRITERS
- Brian Azzarello
- Jeff Lemire
- Dan Jurgens
- Keith Giffen

ARTIST
- Tom Raney

COLORS
- Hi-Fi

LETTERS
- Corey Breen

COVER
- Ryan Sook

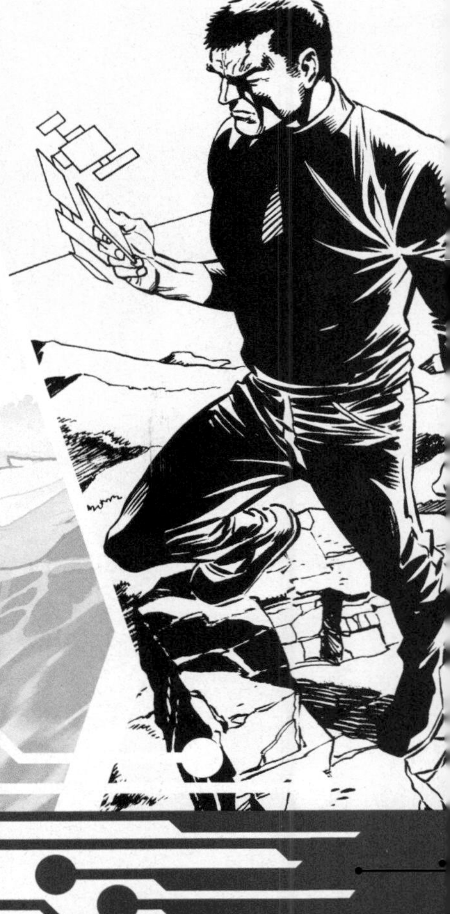

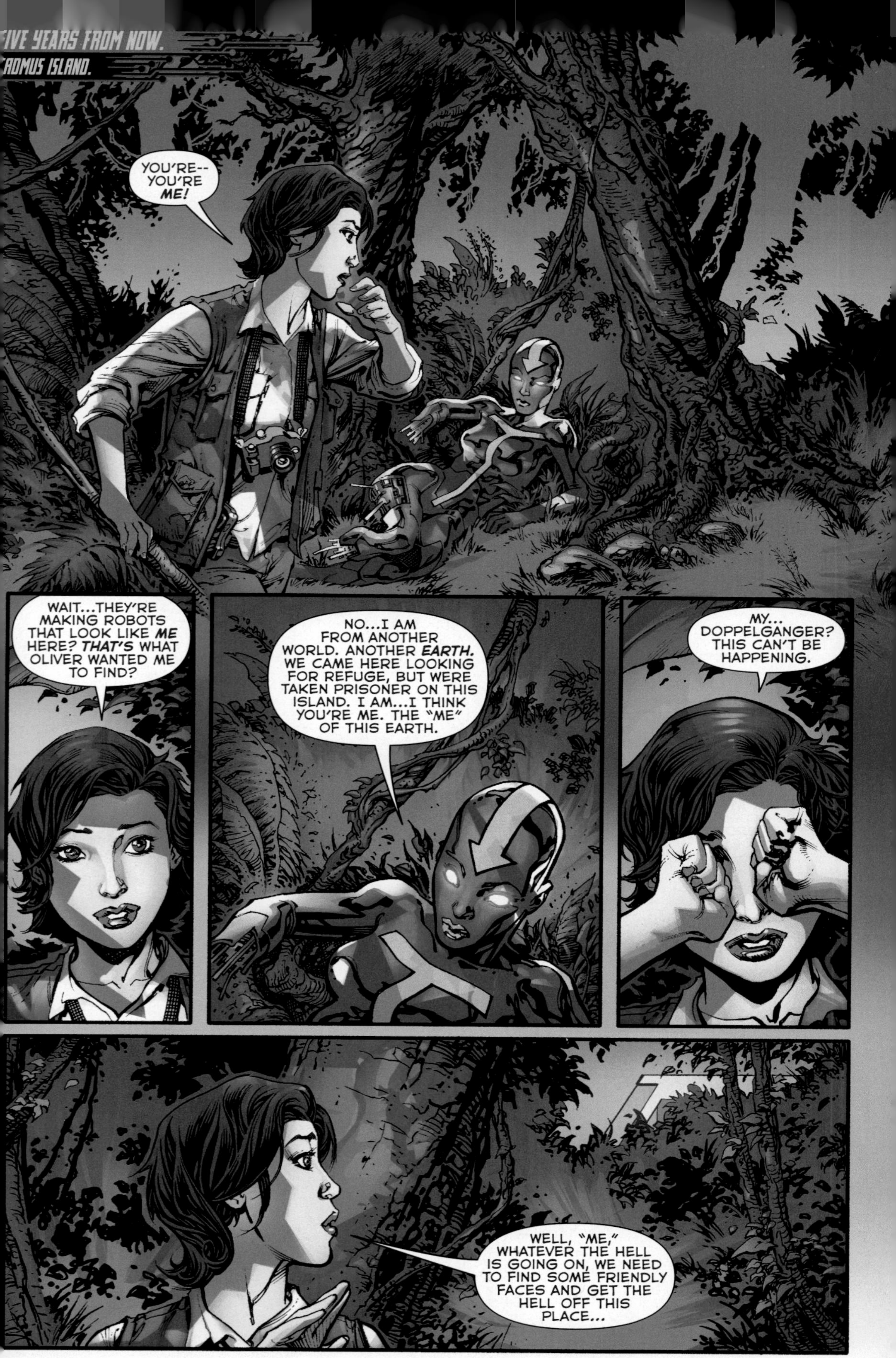
FIVE YEARS FROM NOW.
CADMUS ISLAND.
YOU'RE-- YOU'RE *ME!*
WAIT...THEY'RE MAKING ROBOTS THAT LOOK LIKE *ME* HERE? *THAT'S* WHAT OLIVER WANTED ME TO FIND?
NO...I AM FROM ANOTHER WORLD. ANOTHER *EARTH.* WE CAME HERE LOOKING FOR REFUGE, BUT WERE TAKEN PRISONER ON THIS ISLAND. I AM...I THINK YOU'RE ME. THE "ME" OF THIS EARTH.
MY... DOPPELGANGER? THIS CAN'T BE HAPPENING.
WELL, "ME," WHATEVER THE HELL IS GOING ON, WE NEED TO FIND SOME FRIENDLY FACES AND GET THE HELL OFF THIS PLACE...

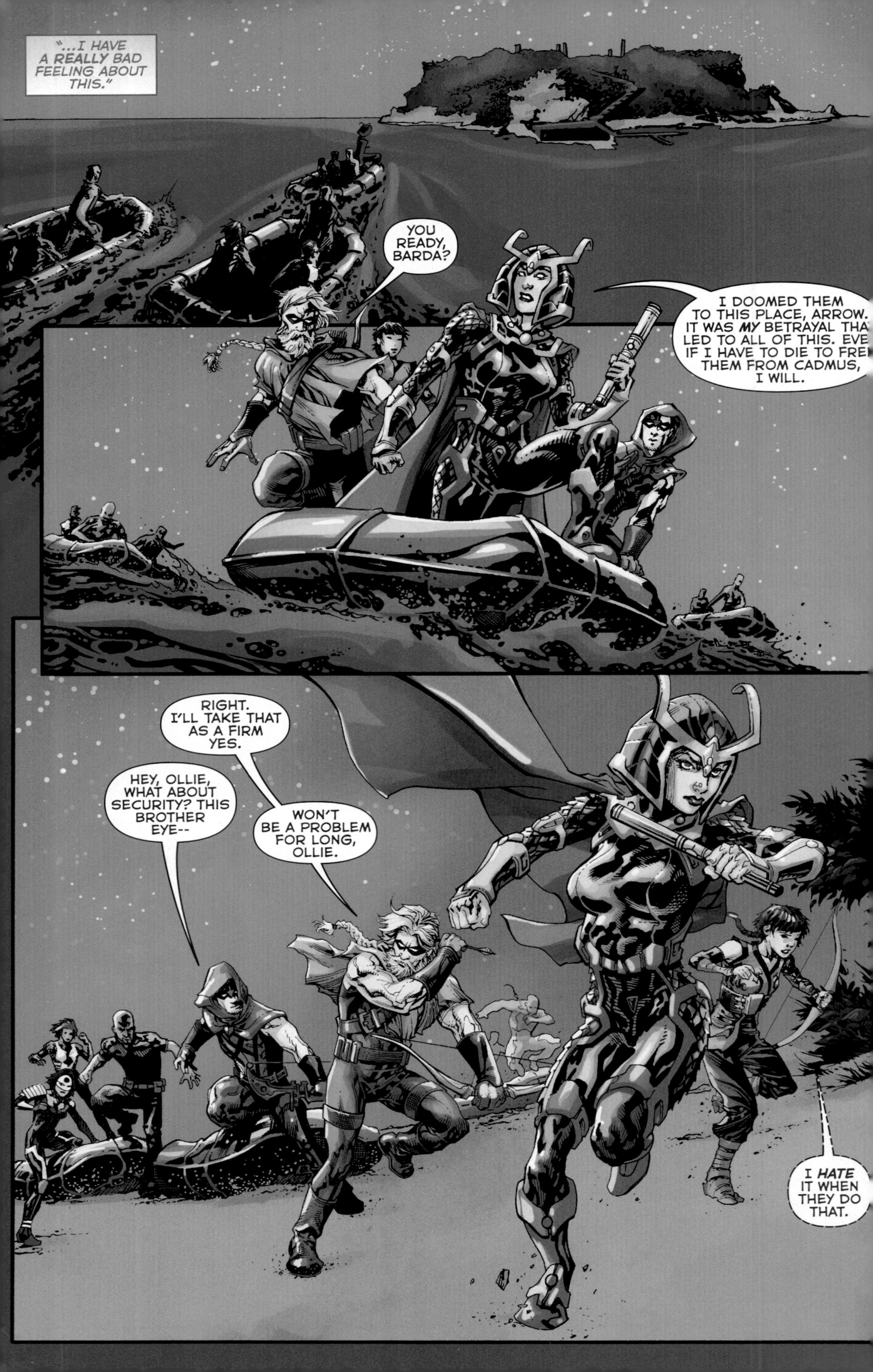
"...I HAVE A *REALLY* BAD FEELING ABOUT THIS."
YOU READY, BARDA?
I DOOMED THEM TO THIS PLACE, ARROW. IT WAS *MY* BETRAYAL THA LED TO ALL OF THIS. EVE IF I HAVE TO DIE TO FRE THEM FROM CADMUS, I WILL.
RIGHT. I'LL TAKE THAT AS A FIRM YES.
HEY, OLLIE, WHAT ABOUT SECURITY? THIS BROTHER EYE--
WON'T BE A PROBLEM FOR LONG, OLLIE.
I *HATE* IT WHEN THEY DO THAT.

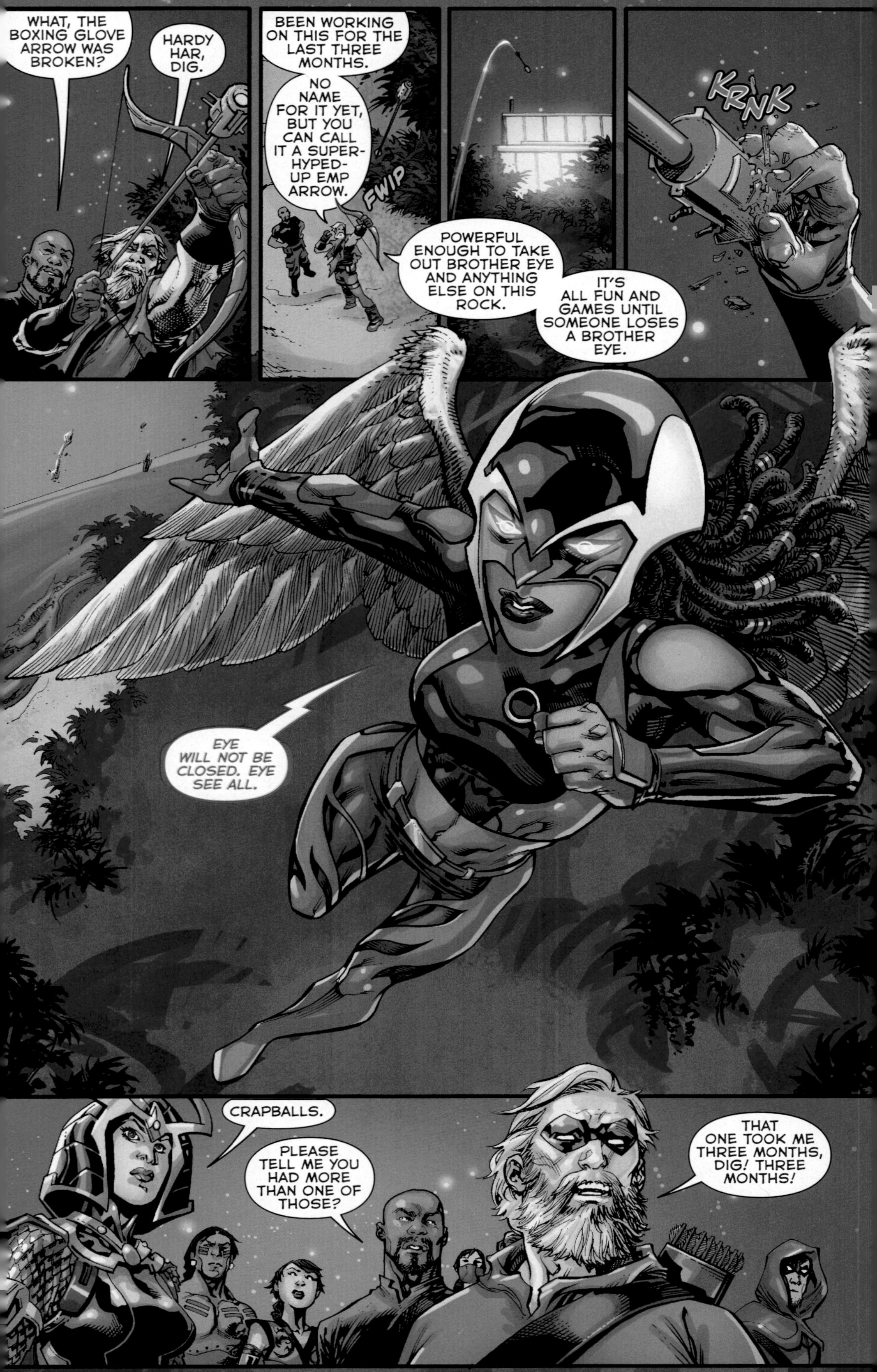

WHAT, THE BOXING GLOVE ARROW WAS BROKEN?
HARDY HAR, DIG.
BEEN WORKING ON THIS FOR THE LAST THREE MONTHS.
NO NAME FOR IT YET, BUT YOU CAN CALL IT A SUPER-HYPED-UP EMP ARROW.
FWIP
POWERFUL ENOUGH TO TAKE OUT BROTHER EYE AND ANYTHING ELSE ON THIS ROCK.
IT'S ALL FUN AND GAMES UNTIL SOMEONE LOSES A BROTHER EYE.
KRNK
EYE WILL NOT BE CLOSED. EYE SEE ALL.
CRAPBALLS.
PLEASE TELL ME YOU HAD MORE THAN ONE OF THOSE?
THAT ONE TOOK ME THREE MONTHS, DIG! THREE MONTHS!

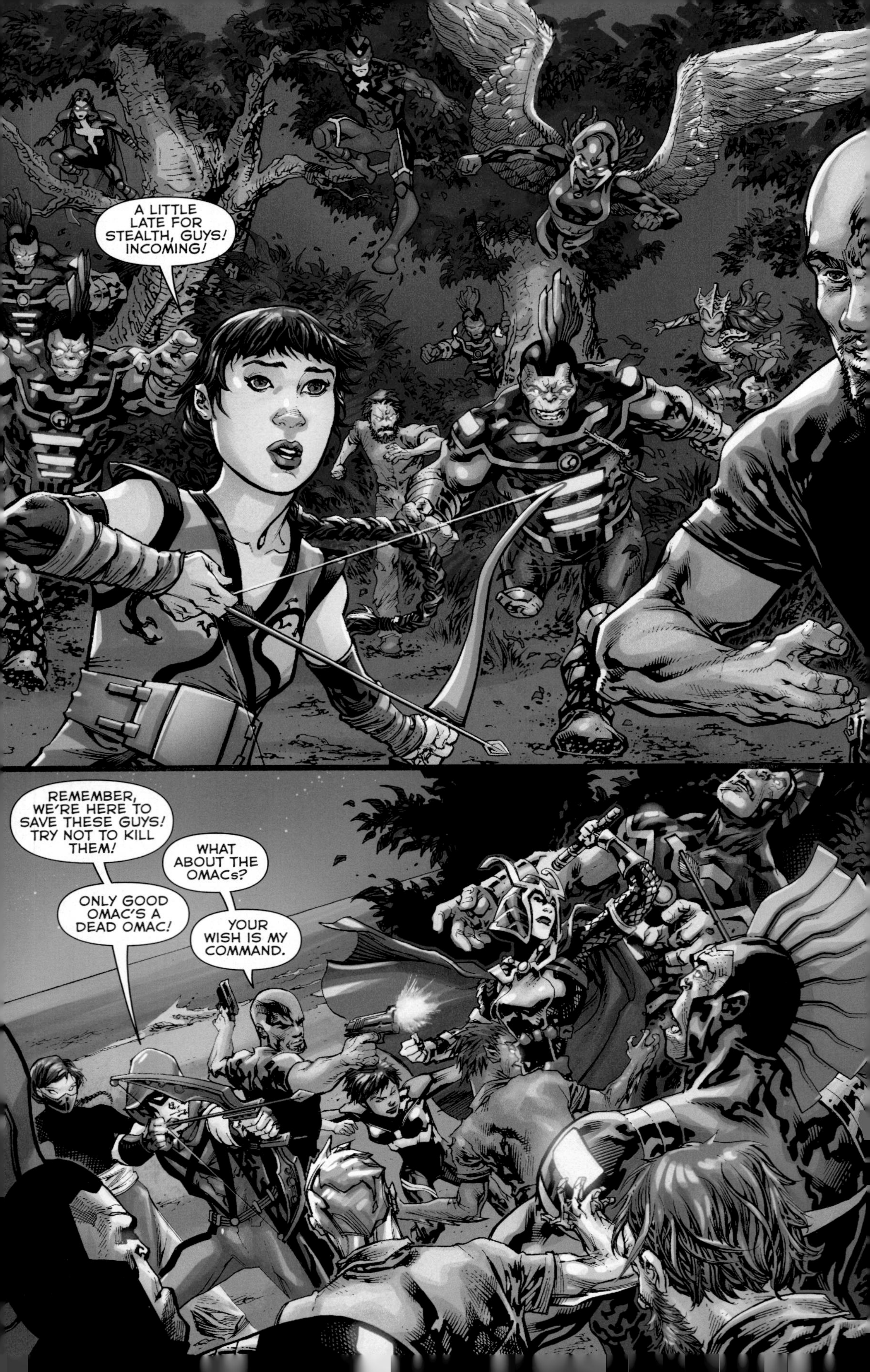
A LITTLE LATE FOR STEALTH, GUYS! INCOMING!
REMEMBER, WE'RE HERE TO SAVE THESE GUYS! TRY NOT TO KILL THEM!
WHAT ABOUT THE OMACs?
ONLY GOOD OMAC'S A DEAD OMAC!
YOUR WISH IS MY COMMAND.

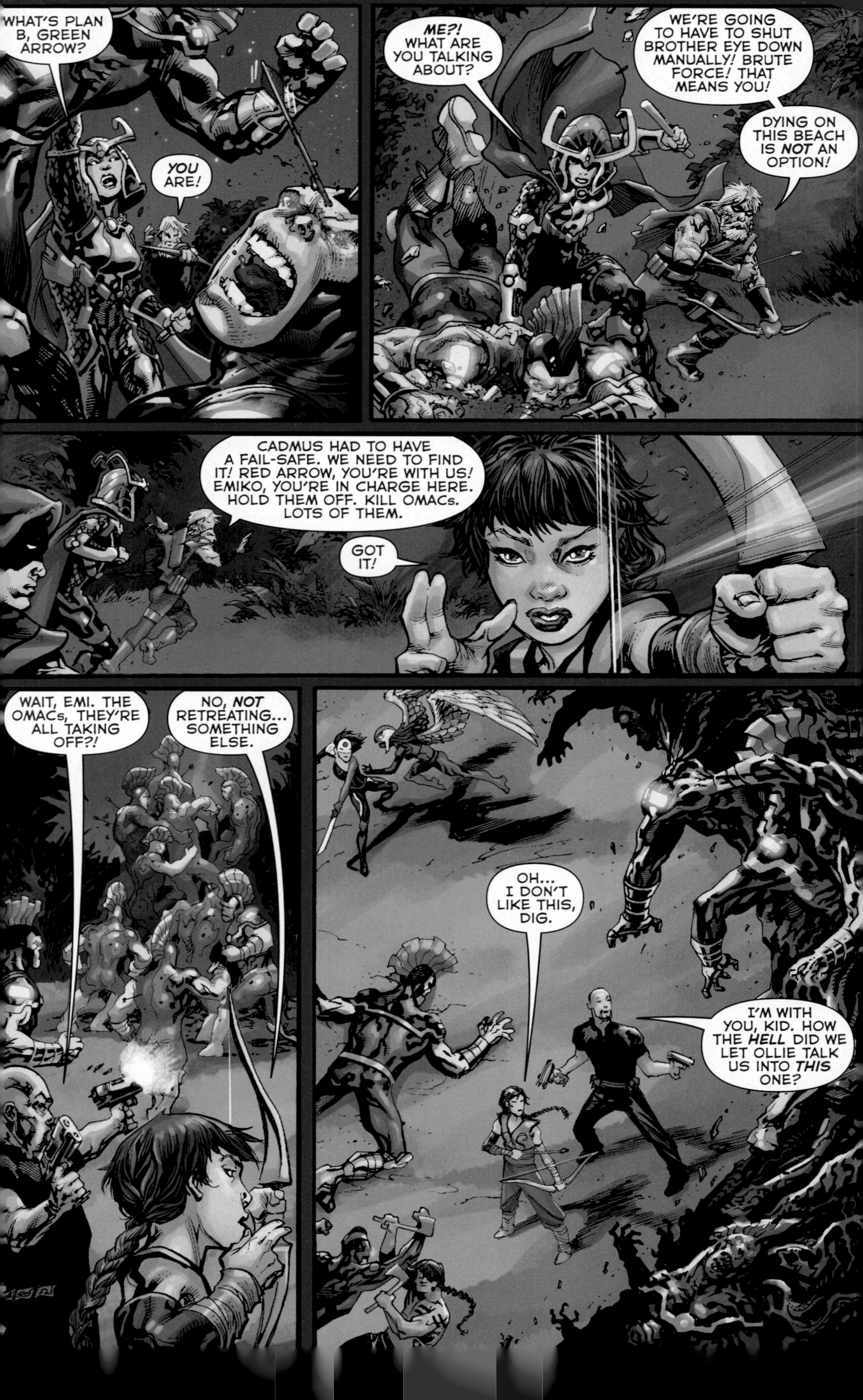
WHAT'S PLAN B, GREEN ARROW?
YOU ARE!
ME?! WHAT ARE YOU TALKING ABOUT?
WE'RE GOING TO HAVE TO SHUT BROTHER EYE DOWN MANUALLY! BRUTE FORCE! THAT MEANS YOU!
DYING ON THIS BEACH IS NOT AN OPTION!
CADMUS HAD TO HAVE A FAIL-SAFE. WE NEED TO FIND IT! RED ARROW, YOU'RE WITH US! EMIKO, YOU'RE IN CHARGE HERE. HOLD THEM OFF. KILL OMACs. LOTS OF THEM.
GOT IT!
WAIT, EMI. THE OMACs, THEY'RE ALL TAKING OFF?!
NO, NOT RETREATING... SOMETHING ELSE.
OH... I DON'T LIKE THIS, DIG.
I'M WITH YOU, KID. HOW THE HELL DID WE LET OLLIE TALK US INTO THIS ONE?

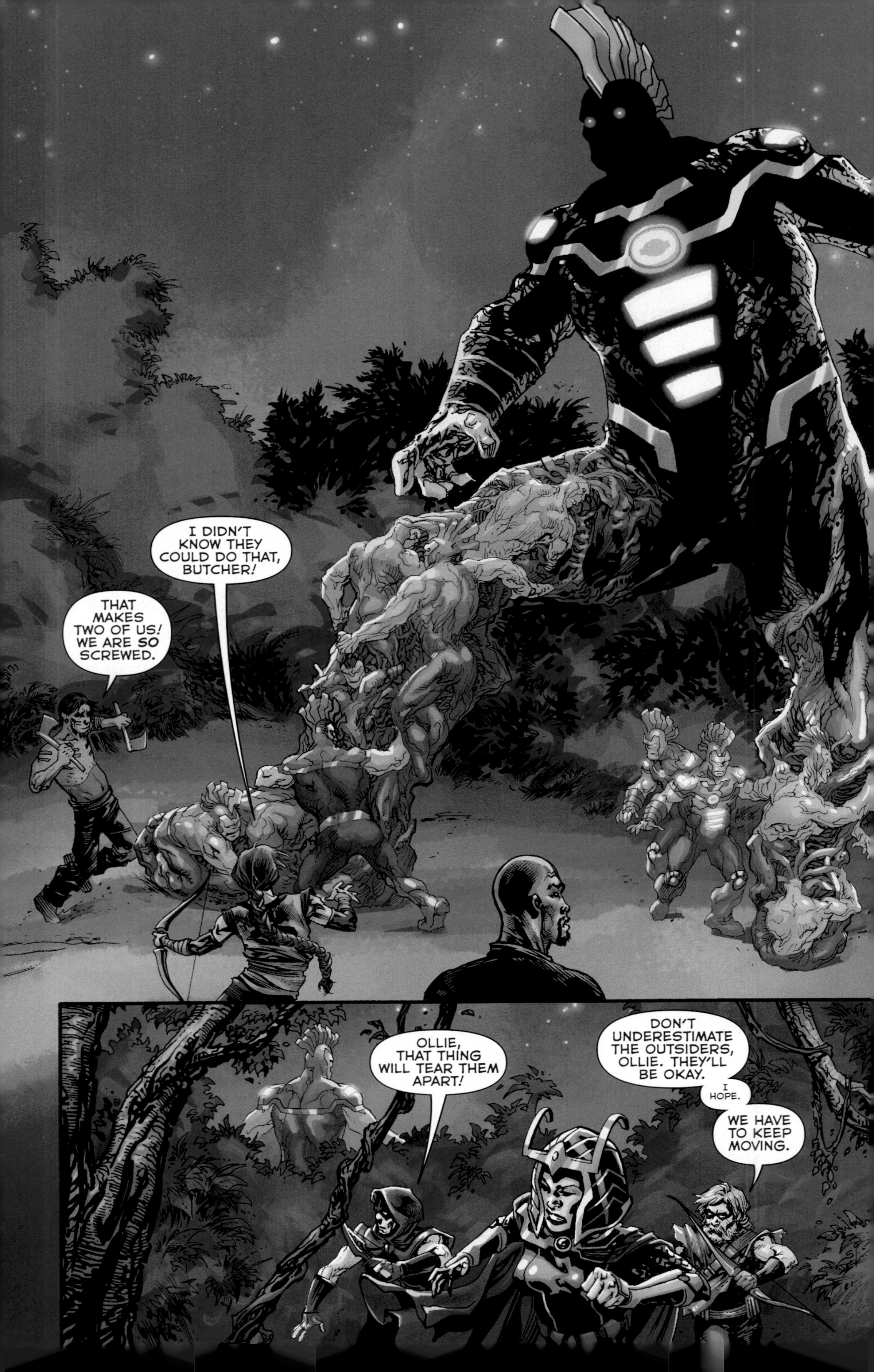

I DIDN'T KNOW THEY COULD DO THAT, BUTCHER!
THAT MAKES TWO OF US! WE ARE SO SCREWED.
OLLIE, THAT THING WILL TEAR THEM APART!
DON'T UNDERESTIMATE THE OUTSIDERS, OLLIE. THEY'LL BE OKAY.
I HOPE.
WE HAVE TO KEEP MOVING.

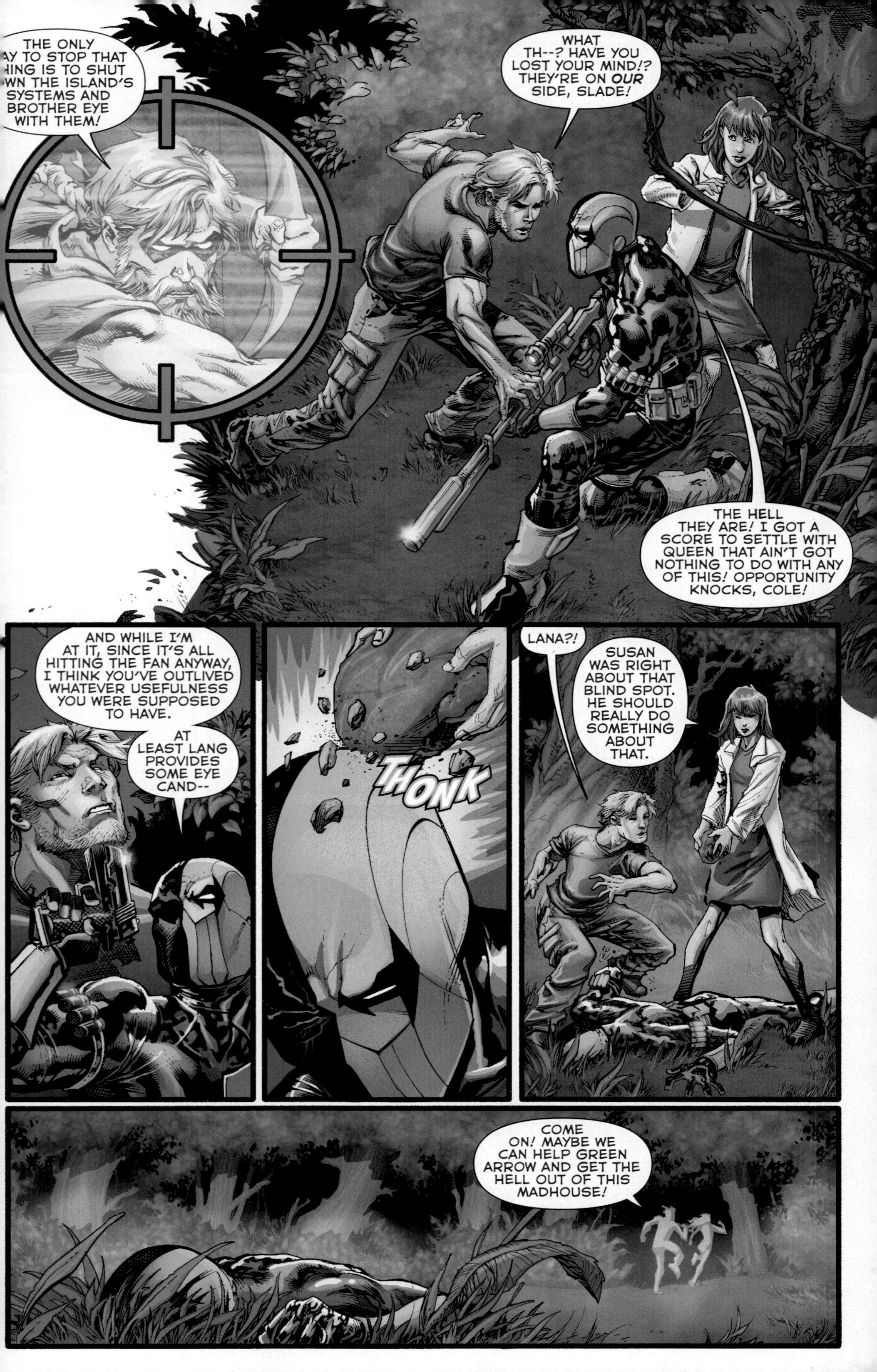
THE ONLY
AY TO STOP THAT
HING IS TO SHUT
WN THE ISLAND'S
SYSTEMS AND
BROTHER EYE
WITH THEM!
WHAT TH--? HAVE YOU LOST YOUR MIND!? THEY'RE ON OUR SIDE, SLADE!
THE HELL THEY ARE! I GOT A SCORE TO SETTLE WITH QUEEN THAT AIN'T GOT NOTHING TO DO WITH ANY OF THIS! OPPORTUNITY KNOCKS, COLE!
AND WHILE I'M AT IT, SINCE IT'S ALL HITTING THE FAN ANYWAY, I THINK YOU'VE OUTLIVED WHATEVER USEFULNESS YOU WERE SUPPOSED TO HAVE.
AT LEAST LANG PROVIDES SOME EYE CAND--
THONK
LANA?!
SUSAN WAS RIGHT ABOUT THAT BLIND SPOT. HE SHOULD REALLY DO SOMETHING ABOUT THAT.
COME ON! MAYBE WE CAN HELP GREEN ARROW AND GET THE HELL OUT OF THIS MADHOUSE!

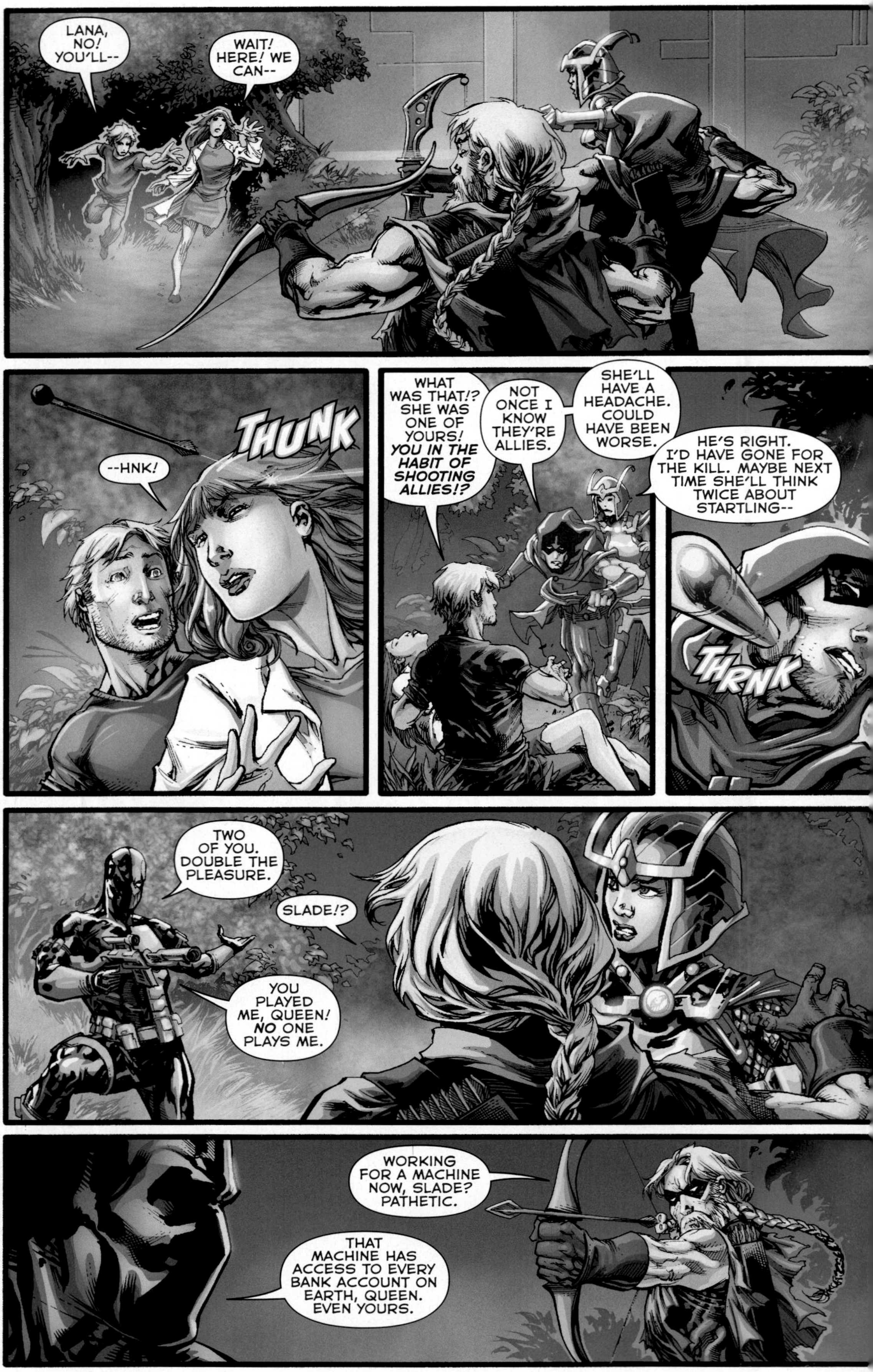
LANA, NO! YOU'LL--
WAIT! HERE! WE CAN--
THUNK
--HNK!
WHAT WAS THAT!? SHE WAS ONE OF YOURS! YOU IN THE HABIT OF SHOOTING ALLIES!?
NOT ONCE I KNOW THEY'RE ALLIES.
SHE'LL HAVE A HEADACHE. COULD HAVE BEEN WORSE.
HE'S RIGHT. I'D HAVE GONE FOR THE KILL. MAYBE NEXT TIME SHE'LL THINK TWICE ABOUT STARTLING--
THRNK
TWO OF YOU. DOUBLE THE PLEASURE.
SLADE!?
YOU PLAYED ME, QUEEN! NO ONE PLAYS ME.
WORKING FOR A MACHINE NOW, SLADE? PATHETIC.
THAT MACHINE HAS ACCESS TO EVERY BANK ACCOUNT ON EARTH, QUEEN. EVEN YOURS.

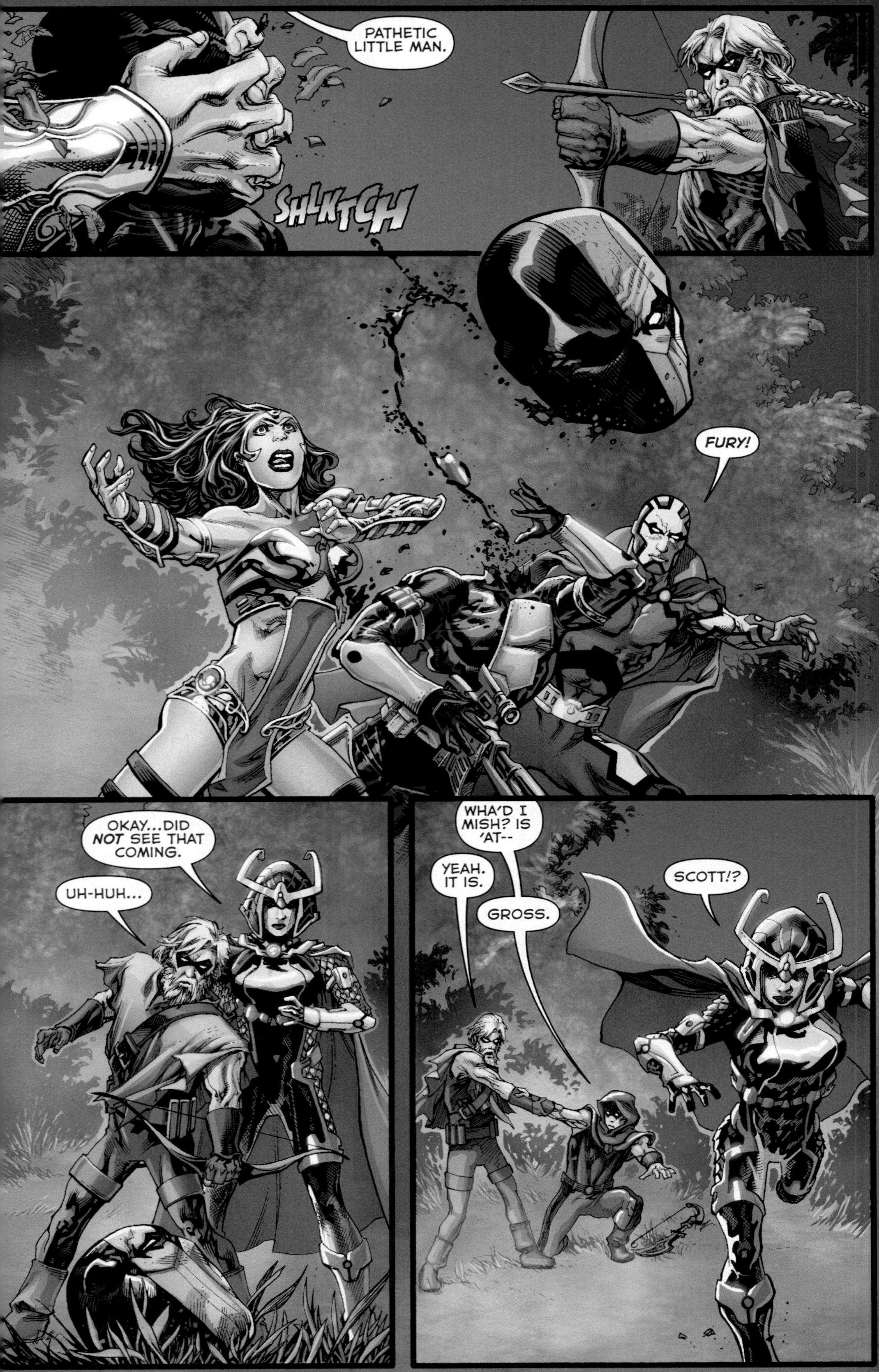
PATHETIC LITTLE MAN.
SHLKTCH
FURY!
OKAY...DID NOT SEE THAT COMING.
UH-HUH...
WHA'D I MISH? IS 'AT--
YEAH. IT IS.
GROSS.
SCOTT!?

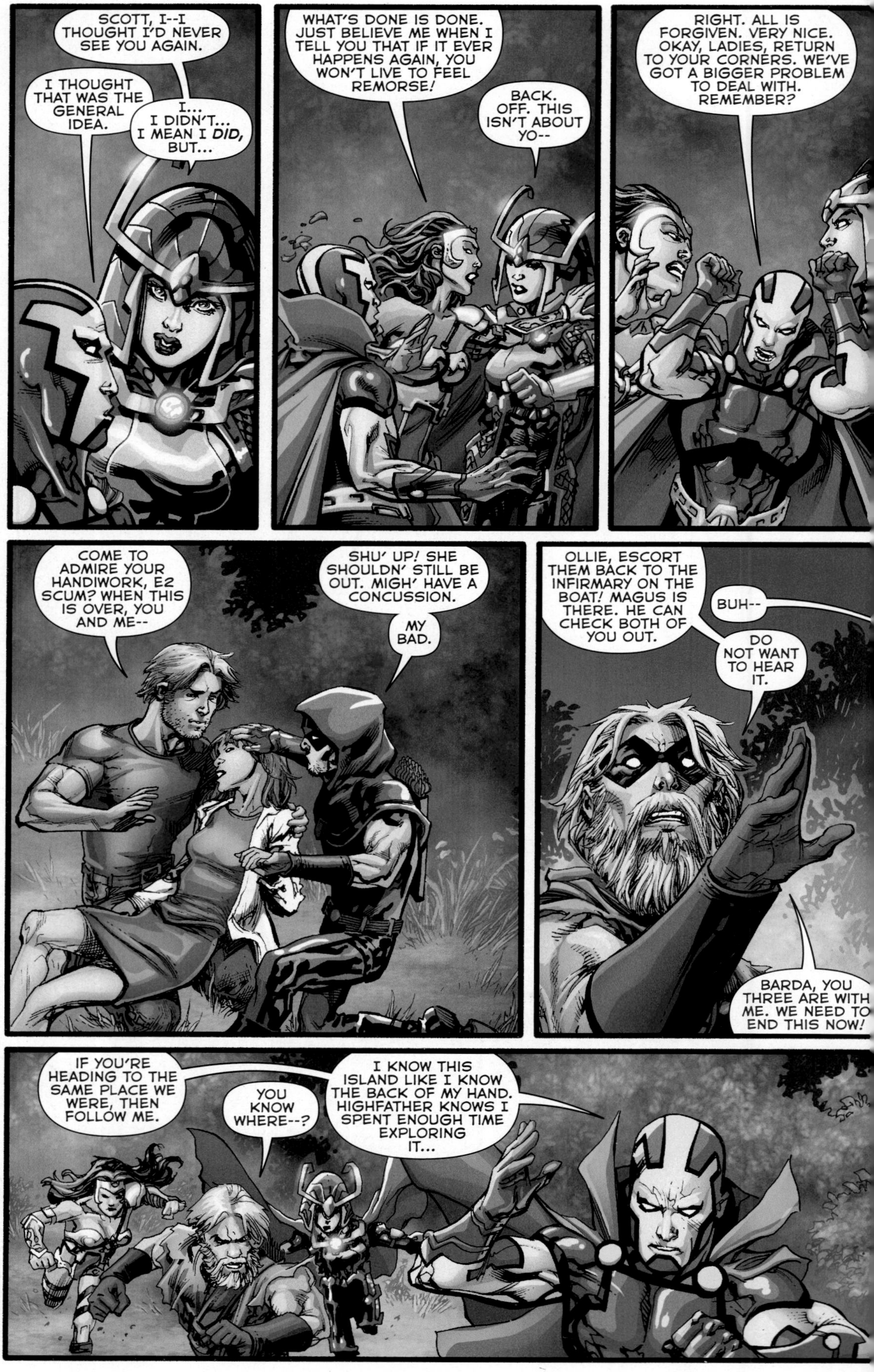
SCOTT, I--I THOUGHT I'D NEVER SEE YOU AGAIN.
I THOUGHT THAT WAS THE GENERAL IDEA.
I... I DIDN'T... I MEAN I DID, BUT...
WHAT'S DONE IS DONE. JUST BELIEVE ME WHEN I TELL YOU THAT IF IT EVER HAPPENS AGAIN, YOU WON'T LIVE TO FEEL REMORSE!
BACK. OFF. THIS ISN'T ABOUT YO--
RIGHT. ALL IS FORGIVEN. VERY NICE. OKAY, LADIES, RETURN TO YOUR CORNERS. WE'VE GOT A BIGGER PROBLEM TO DEAL WITH. REMEMBER?
COME TO ADMIRE YOUR HANDIWORK, E2 SCUM? WHEN THIS IS OVER, YOU AND ME--
SHU' UP! SHE SHOULDN' STILL BE OUT. MIGH' HAVE A CONCUSSION.
MY BAD.
OLLIE, ESCORT THEM BACK TO THE INFIRMARY ON THE BOAT! MAGUS IS THERE. HE CAN CHECK BOTH OF YOU OUT.
BUH--
DO NOT WANT TO HEAR IT.
BARDA, YOU THREE ARE WITH ME. WE NEED TO END THIS NOW!
IF YOU'RE HEADING TO THE SAME PLACE WE WERE, THEN FOLLOW ME.
YOU KNOW WHERE--?
I KNOW THIS ISLAND LIKE I KNOW THE BACK OF MY HAND. HIGHFATHER KNOWS I SPENT ENOUGH TIME EXPLORING IT...

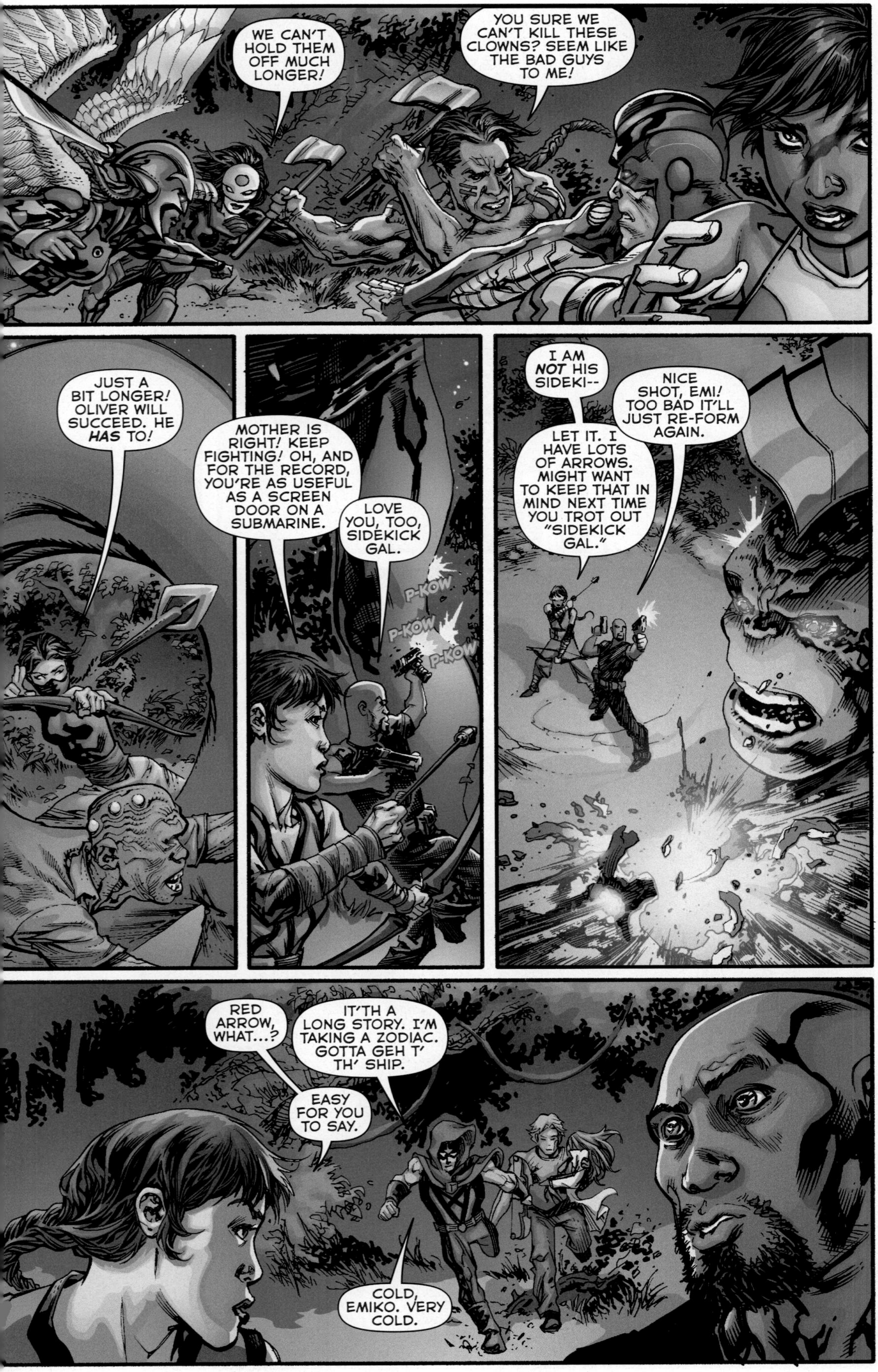
WE CAN'T HOLD THEM OFF MUCH LONGER!
YOU SURE WE CAN'T KILL THESE CLOWNS? SEEM LIKE THE BAD GUYS TO ME!
JUST A BIT LONGER! OLIVER WILL SUCCEED. HE *HAS* TO!
MOTHER IS RIGHT! KEEP FIGHTING! OH, AND FOR THE RECORD, YOU'RE AS USEFUL AS A SCREEN DOOR ON A SUBMARINE.
LOVE YOU, TOO, SIDEKICK GAL.
P-KOW
P-KOW
P-KOW
I AM *NOT* HIS SIDEKI--
LET IT. I HAVE LOTS OF ARROWS. MIGHT WANT TO KEEP THAT IN MIND NEXT TIME YOU TROT OUT "SIDEKICK GAL."
NICE SHOT, EMI! TOO BAD IT'LL JUST RE-FORM AGAIN.
RED ARROW, WHAT...?
IT'TH A LONG STORY. I'M TAKING A ZODIAC. GOTTA GEH T' TH' SHIP.
EASY FOR YOU TO SAY.
COLD, EMIKO. VERY COLD.

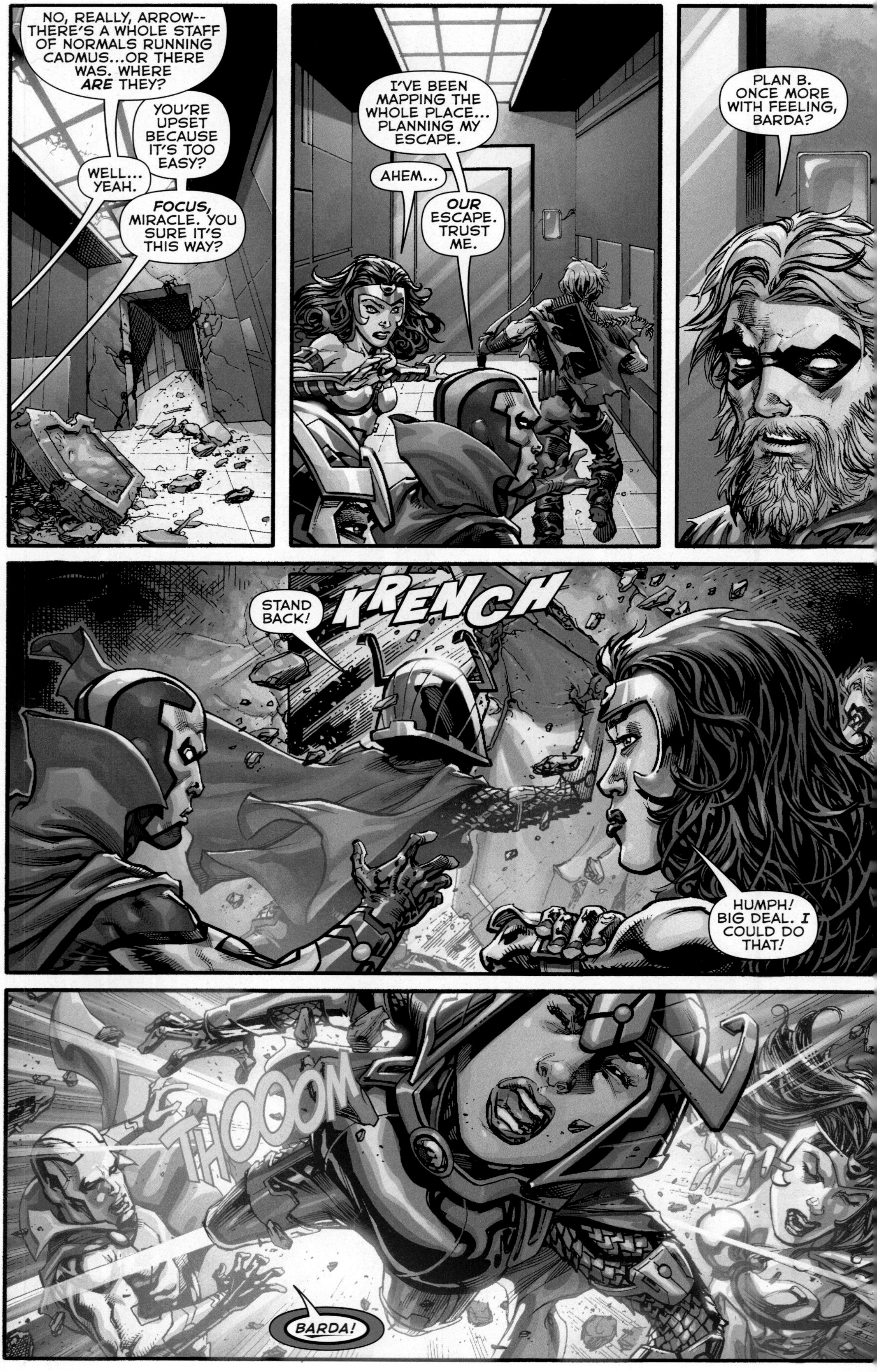
NO, REALLY, ARROW--THERE'S A WHOLE STAFF OF NORMALS RUNNING CADMUS...OR THERE WAS. WHERE ARE THEY?
YOU'RE UPSET BECAUSE IT'S TOO EASY?
WELL... YEAH.
FOCUS, MIRACLE. YOU SURE IT'S THIS WAY?
I'VE BEEN MAPPING THE WHOLE PLACE... PLANNING MY ESCAPE.
AHEM...
OUR ESCAPE. TRUST ME.
PLAN B. ONCE MORE WITH FEELING, BARDA?
STAND BACK!
KRENCH
HUMPH! BIG DEAL. I COULD DO THAT!
THOOOM
BARDA!

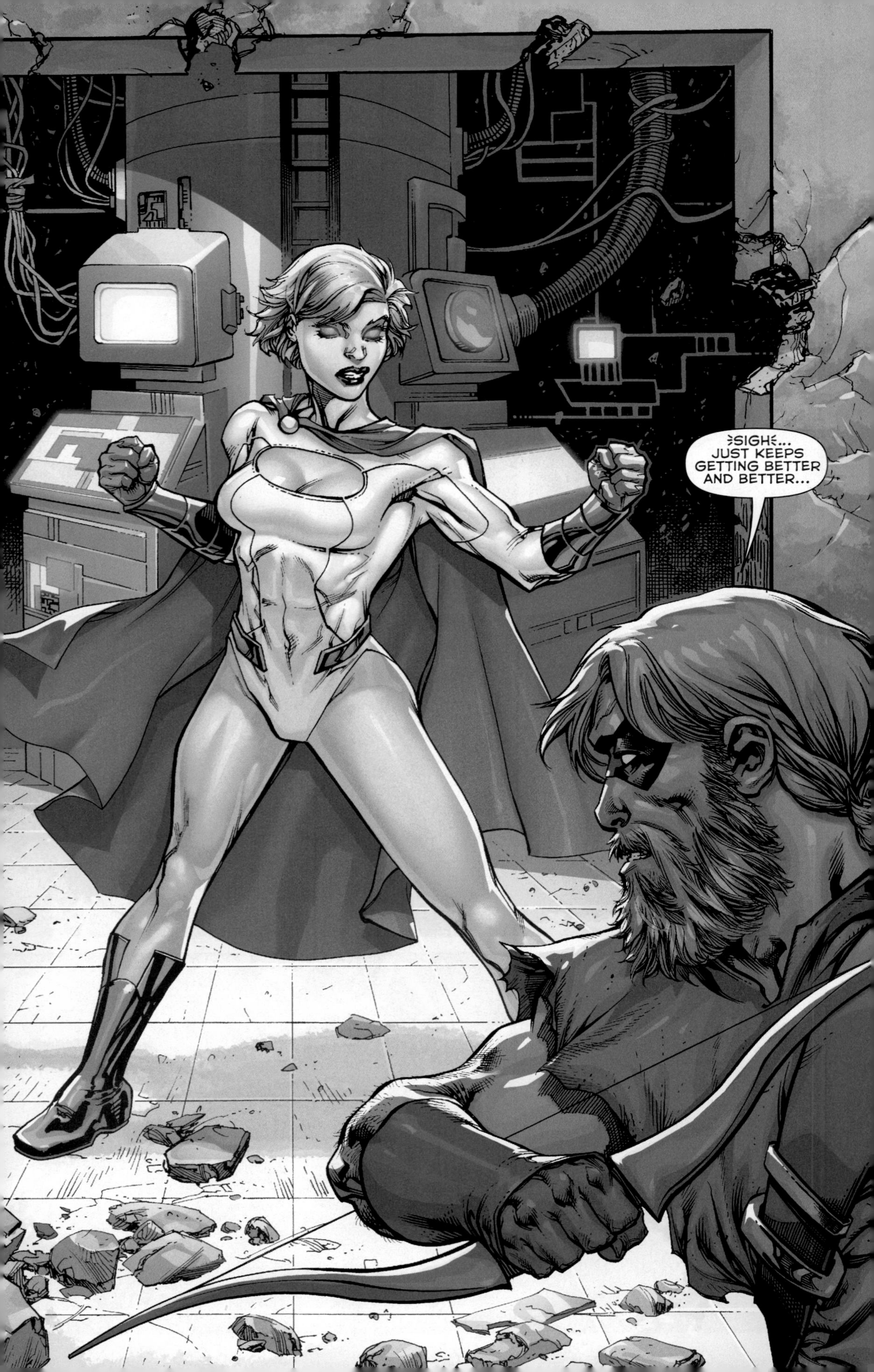

SIGH... JUST KEEPS GETTING BETTER AND BETTER...

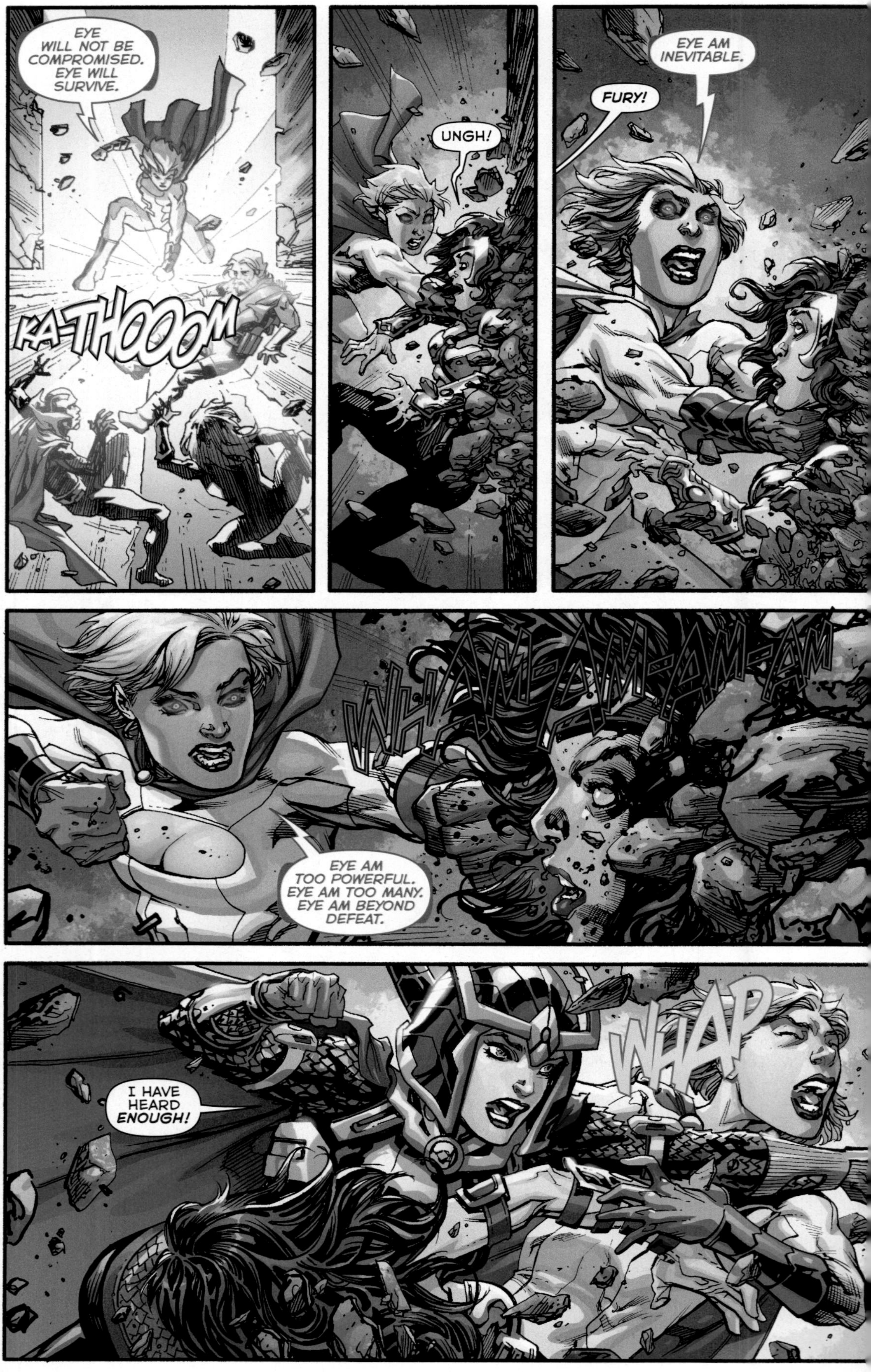
EYE WILL NOT BE COMPROMISED. EYE WILL SURVIVE.
KA-THOOOM
UNGH!
EYE AM INEVITABLE.
FURY!
WHAM-AM-AM-AM
EYE AM TOO POWERFUL. EYE AM TOO MANY. EYE AM BEYOND DEFEAT.
I HAVE HEARD ENOUGH!
WHAP

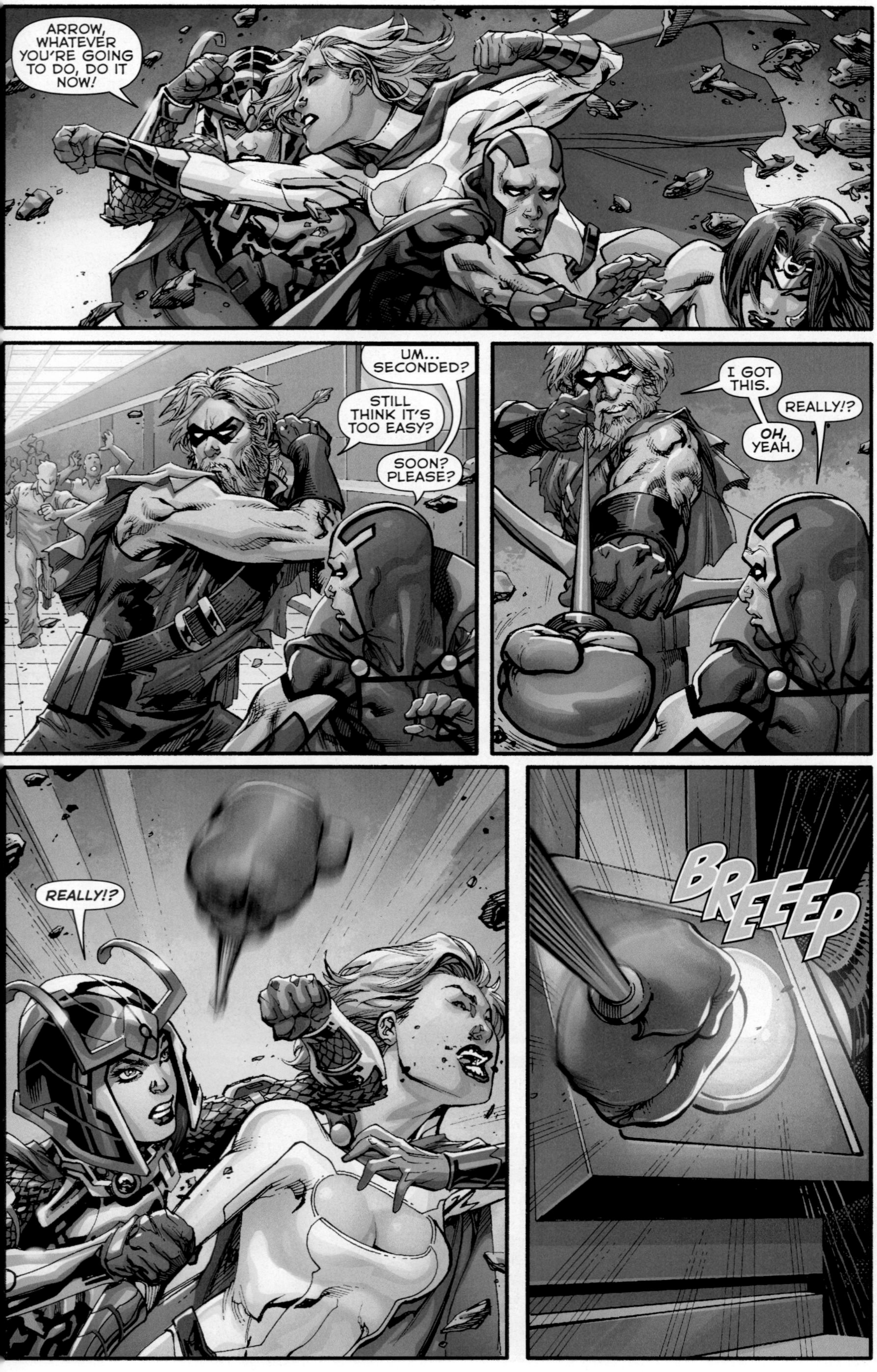
ARROW, WHATEVER YOU'RE GOING TO DO, DO IT NOW!
UM... SECONDED?
STILL THINK IT'S TOO EASY?
SOON? PLEASE?
I GOT THIS.
REALLY!?
OH, YEAH.
REALLY!?
BREEEP

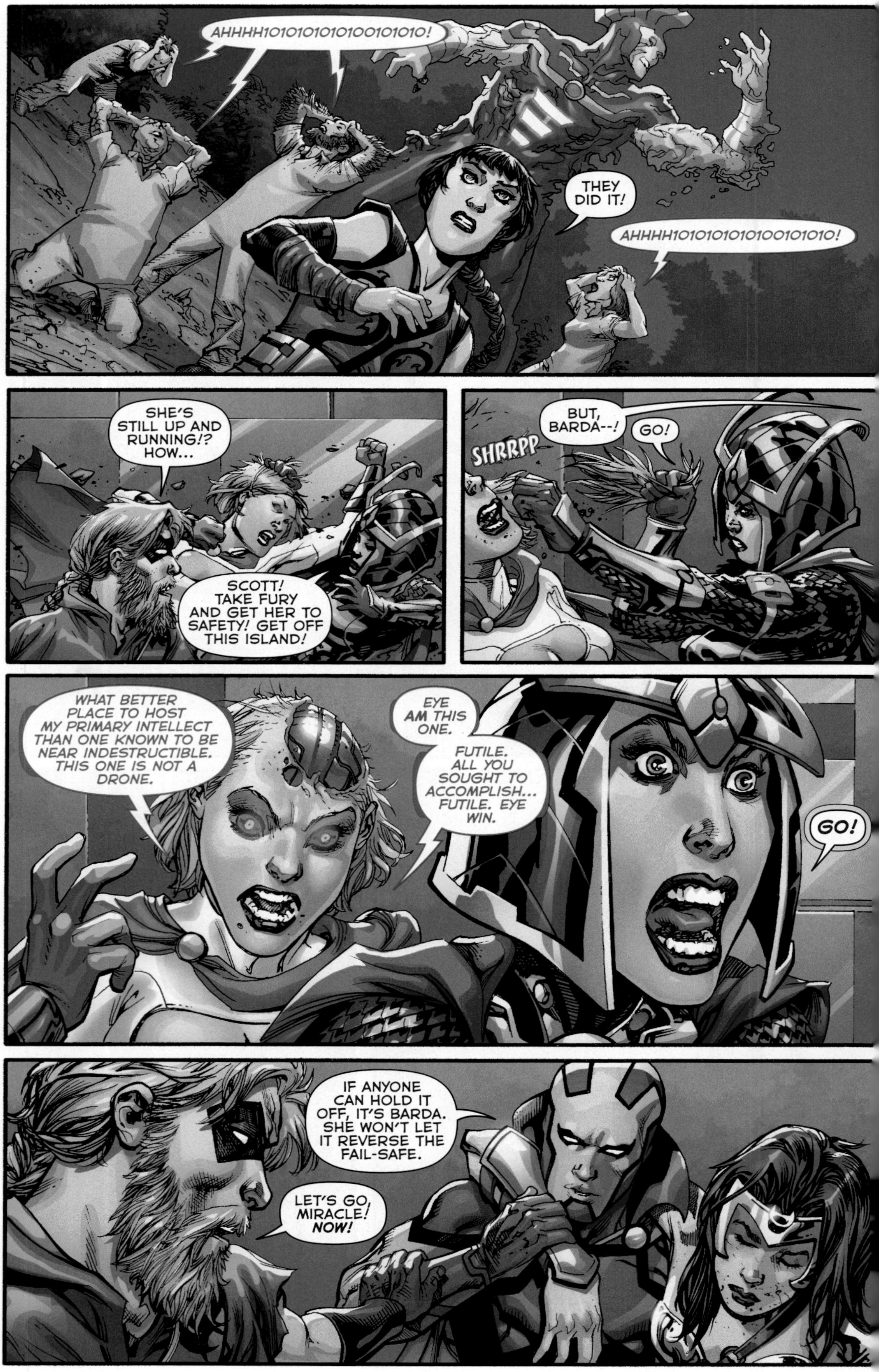
AHHHH10101010101010100101010!
THEY DID IT!
AHHHH10101010101010100101010!
SHE'S STILL UP AND RUNNING!? HOW...
SCOTT! TAKE FURY AND GET HER TO SAFETY! GET OFF THIS ISLAND!
BUT, BARDA--!
GO!
SHRRPP
WHAT BETTER PLACE TO HOST MY PRIMARY INTELLECT THAN ONE KNOWN TO BE NEAR INDESTRUCTIBLE. THIS ONE IS NOT A DRONE.
EYE AM THIS ONE.
FUTILE. ALL YOU SOUGHT TO ACCOMPLISH... FUTILE. EYE WIN.
GO!
IF ANYONE CAN HOLD IT OFF, IT'S BARDA. SHE WON'T LET IT REVERSE THE FAIL-SAFE.
LET'S GO, MIRACLE! NOW!

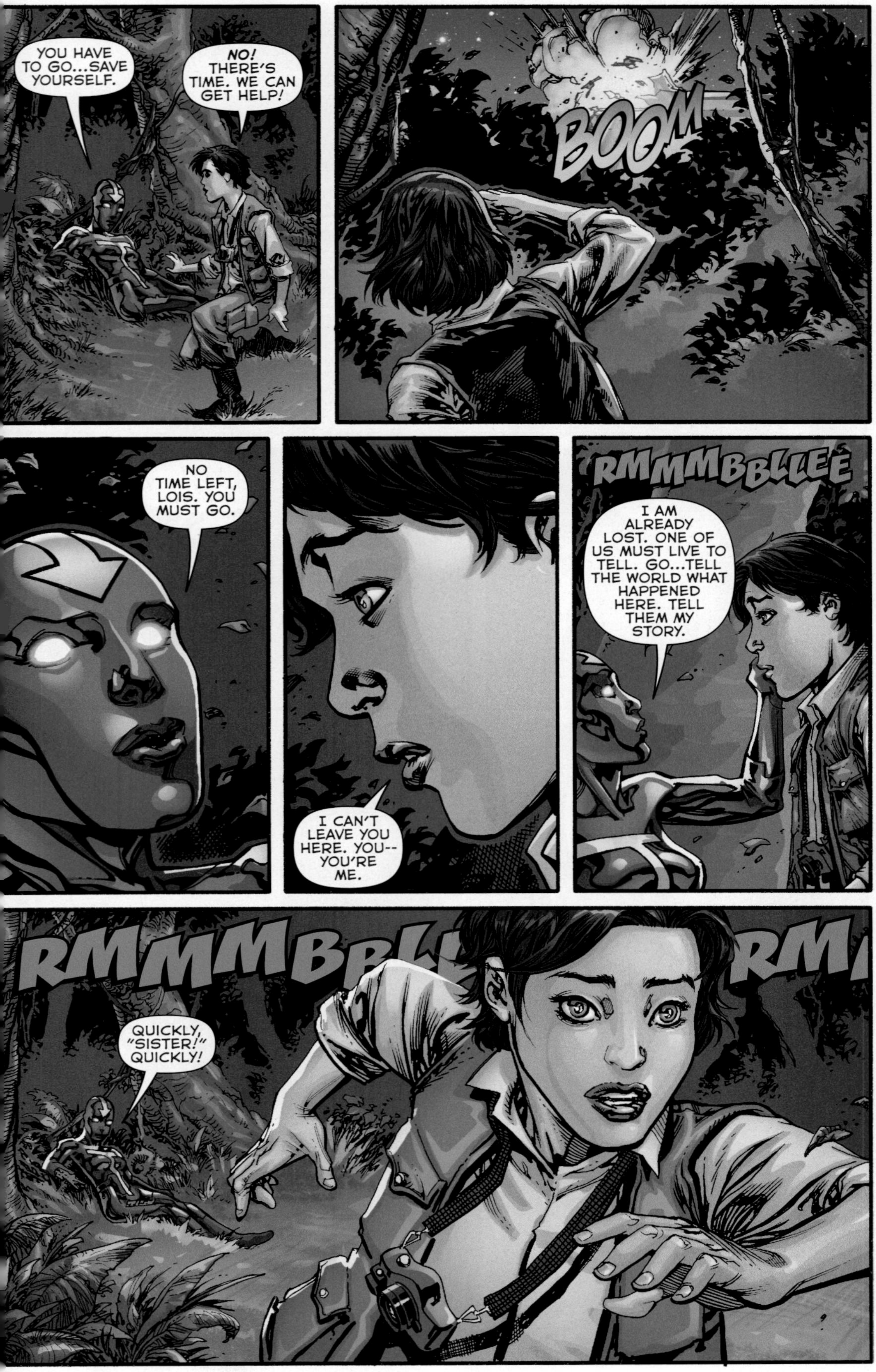
YOU HAVE TO GO...SAVE YOURSELF.
NO! THERE'S TIME. WE CAN GET HELP!
BOOM
NO TIME LEFT, LOIS. YOU MUST GO.
I CAN'T LEAVE YOU HERE. YOU-- YOU'RE ME.
RMMMBBLLEE
I AM ALREADY LOST. ONE OF US MUST LIVE TO TELL. GO...TELL THE WORLD WHAT HAPPENED HERE. TELL THEM MY STORY.
RMMMBBLL
RM
QUICKLY, "SISTER!" QUICKLY!

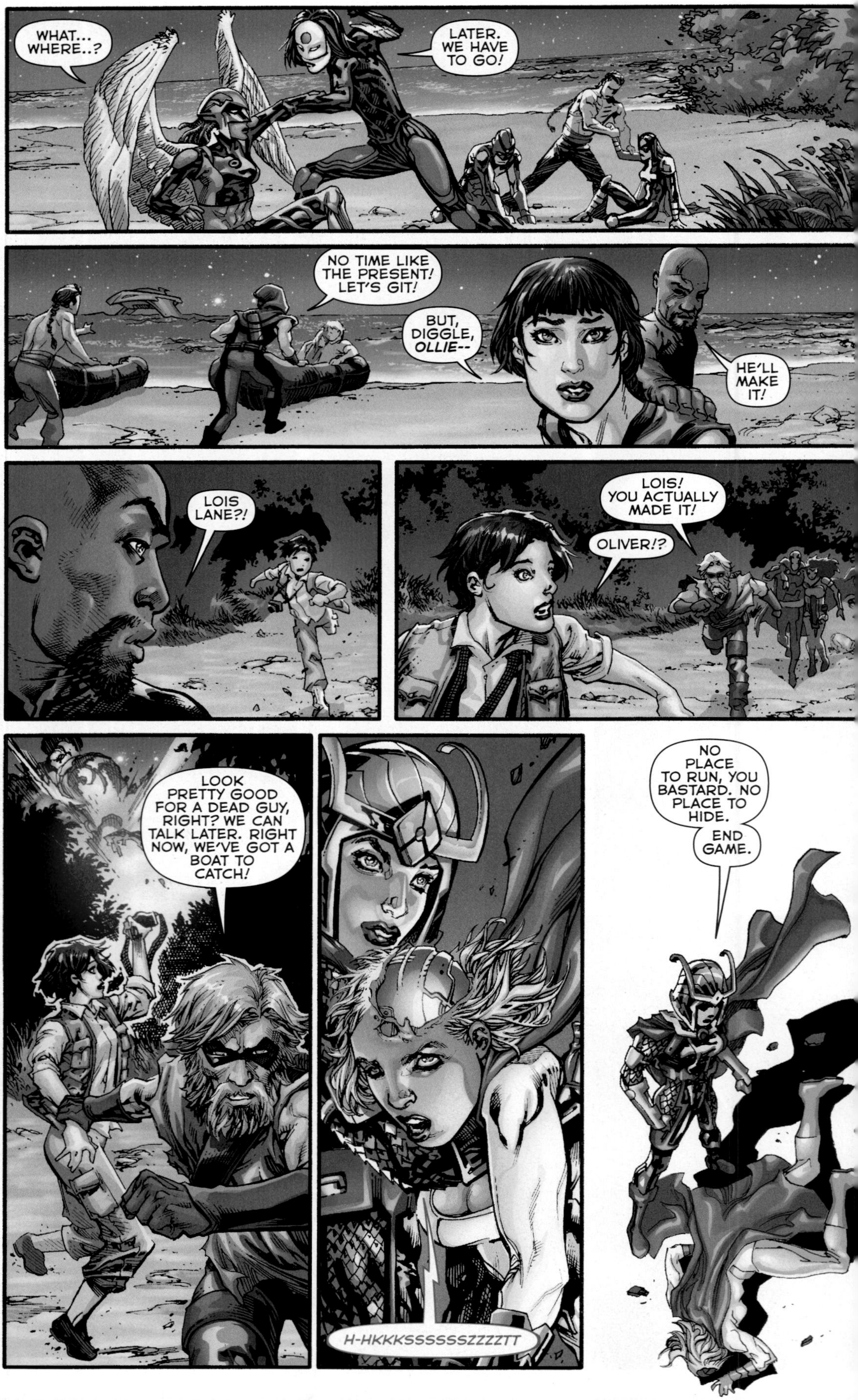
WHAT... WHERE..?
LATER. WE HAVE TO GO!
NO TIME LIKE THE PRESENT! LET'S GIT!
BUT, DIGGLE, OLLIE--
HE'LL MAKE IT!
LOIS LANE?!
LOIS! YOU ACTUALLY MADE IT!
OLIVER!?
LOOK PRETTY GOOD FOR A DEAD GUY, RIGHT? WE CAN TALK LATER. RIGHT NOW, WE'VE GOT A BOAT TO CATCH!
H-HKKKSSSSSSSZZZZZTT
NO PLACE TO RUN, YOU BASTARD. NO PLACE TO HIDE.
END GAME.

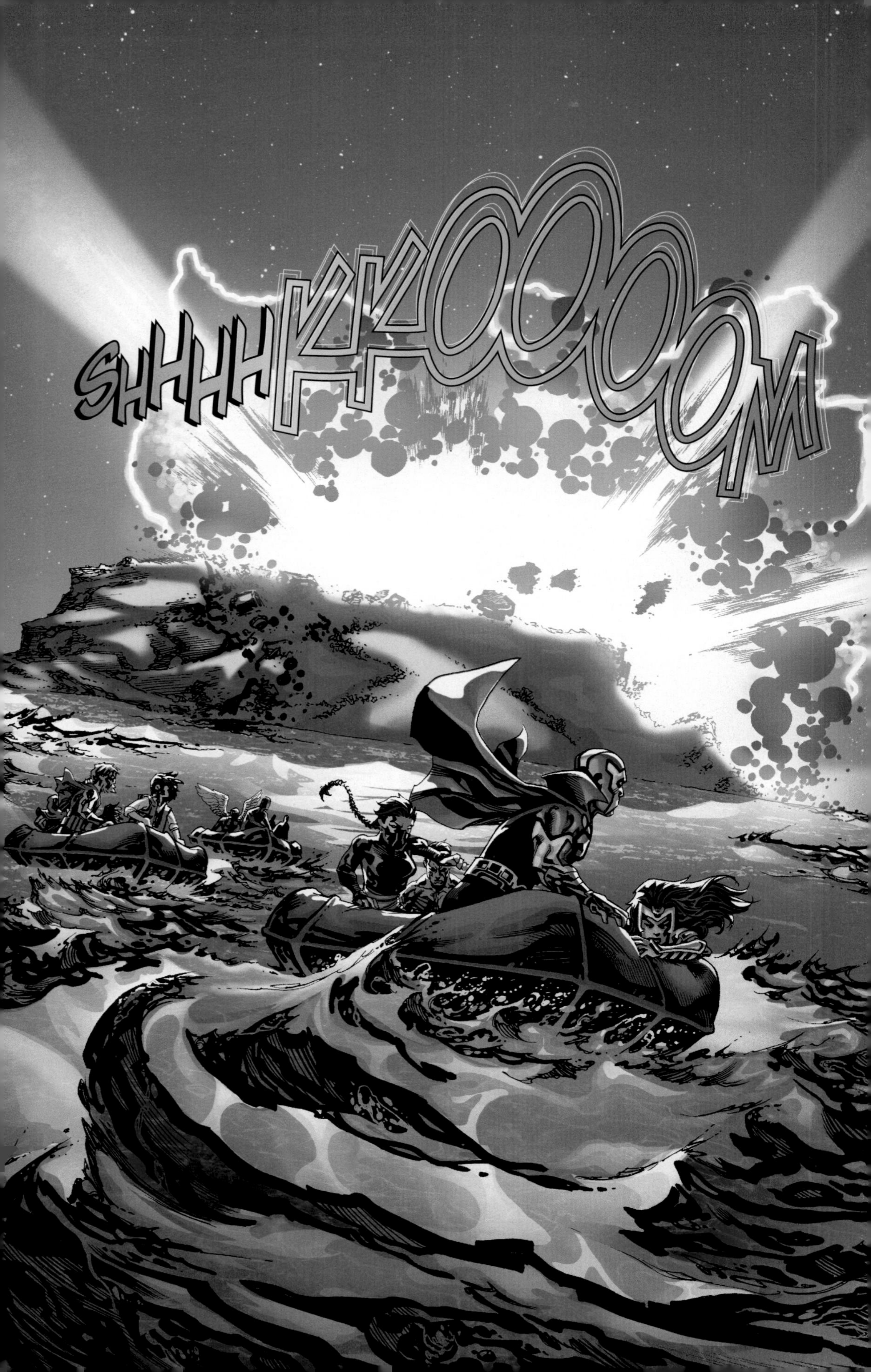
SHHHKKKOOOOOOM

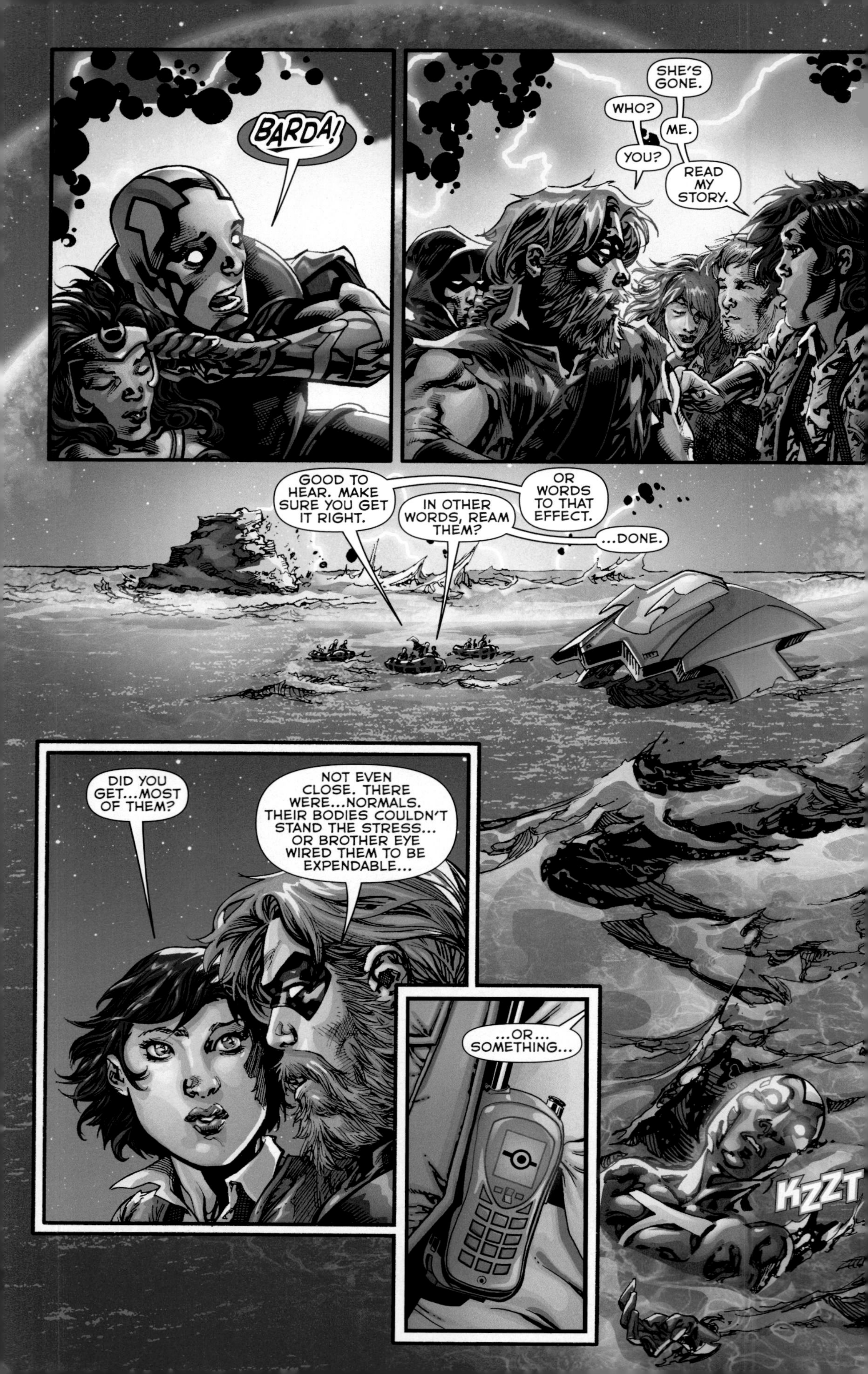
BARDA!
SHE'S GONE.
WHO?
YOU?
ME.
READ MY STORY.
GOOD TO HEAR. MAKE SURE YOU GET IT RIGHT.
IN OTHER WORDS, REAM THEM?
OR WORDS TO THAT EFFECT.
...DONE.
DID YOU GET...MOST OF THEM?
NOT EVEN CLOSE. THERE WERE...NORMALS. THEIR BODIES COULDN'T STAND THE STRESS... OR BROTHER EYE WIRED THEM TO BE EXPENDABLE...
...OR... SOMETHING...
KZZT

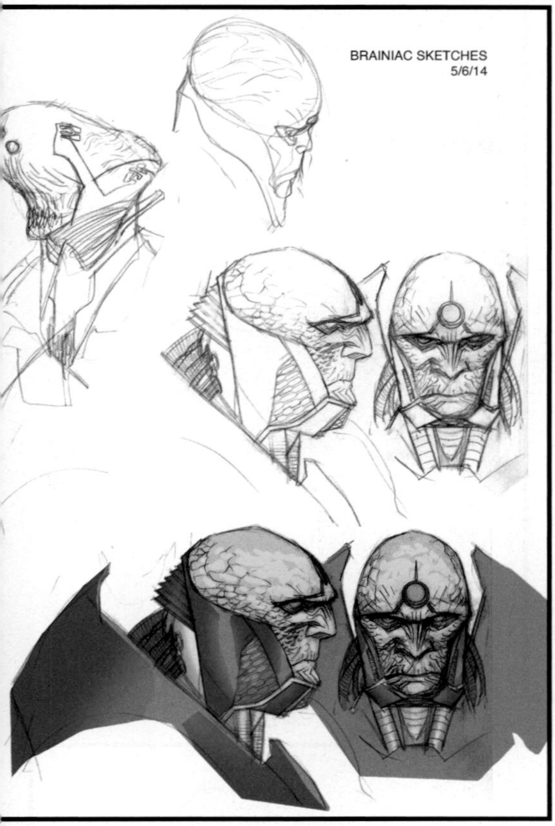
BRAINIAC SKETCHES
5/6/14

The look of Brainiac developed from his Kryptonian origins to a more otherworldly look seen in the final pages.

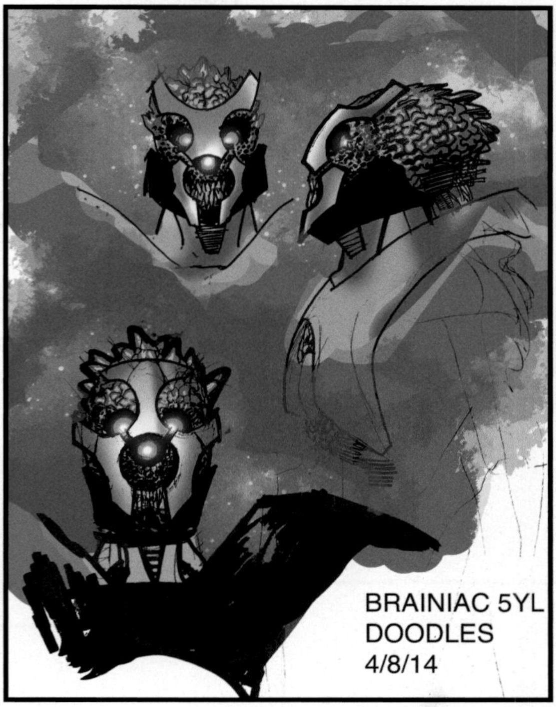
BRAINIAC 5YL
DOODLES
4/8/14

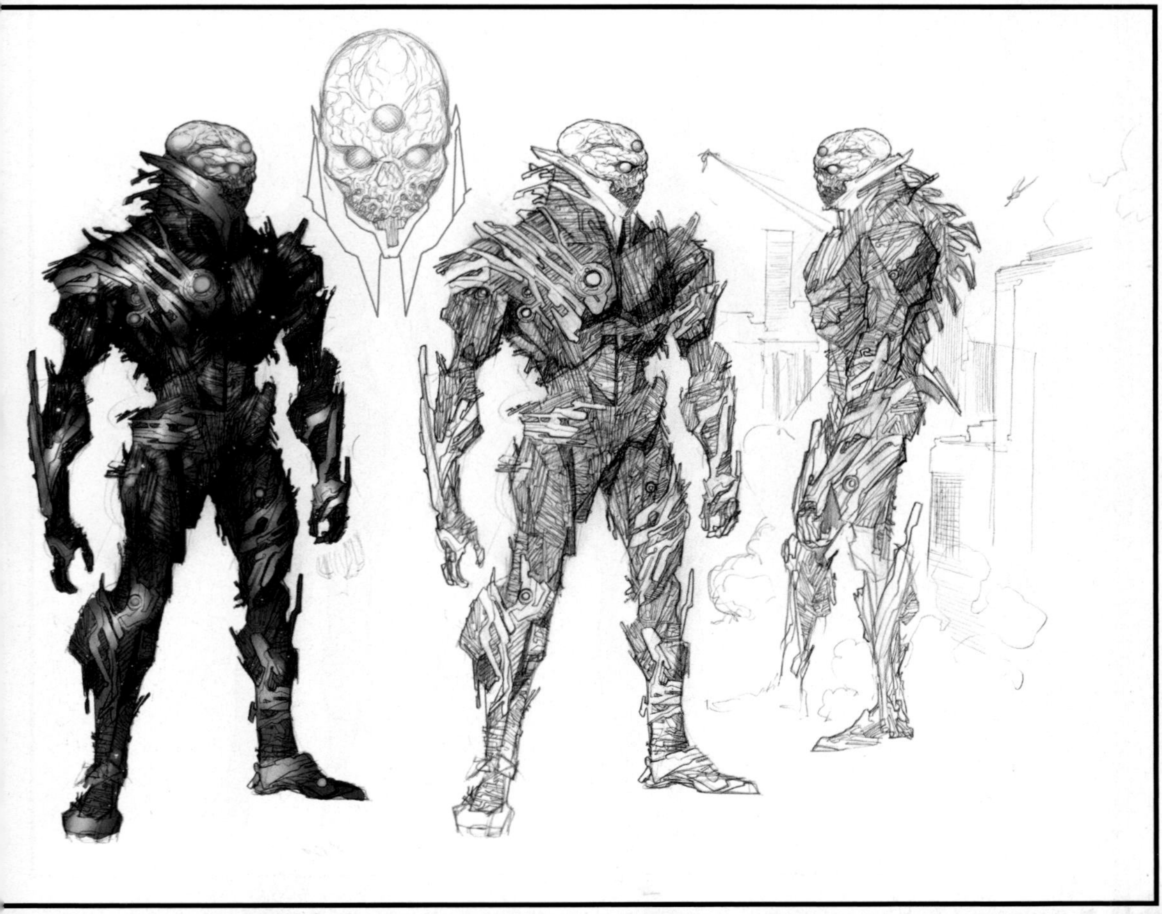

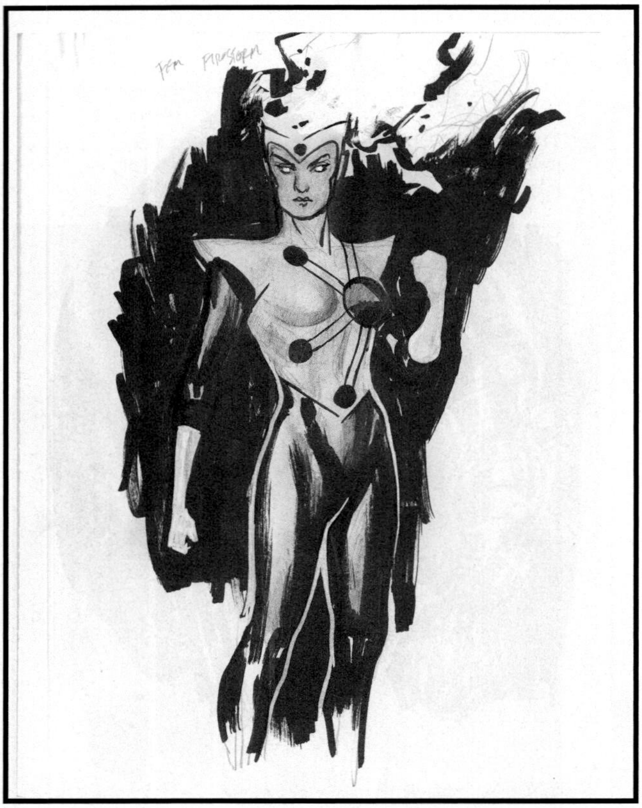
Fem Firestorm

The new female firestorm, a merger of Madison Payne and Jason Rusch.

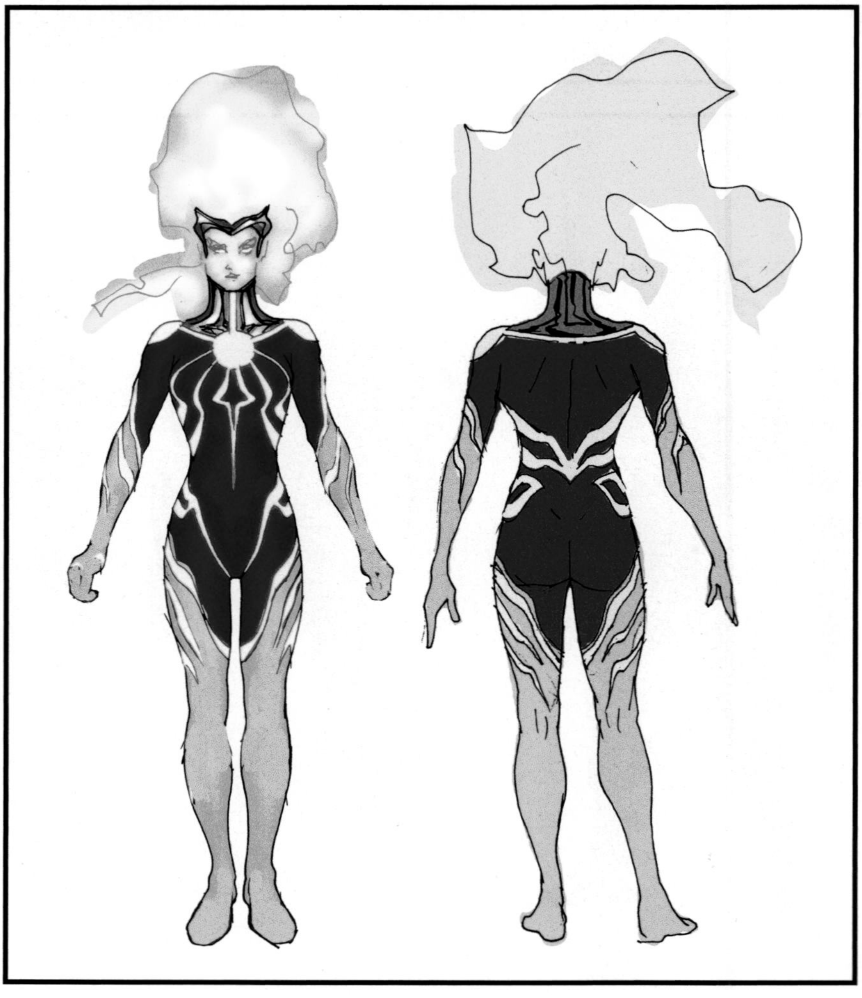

Even familiar heroes went through a change
and darker development in the five years.

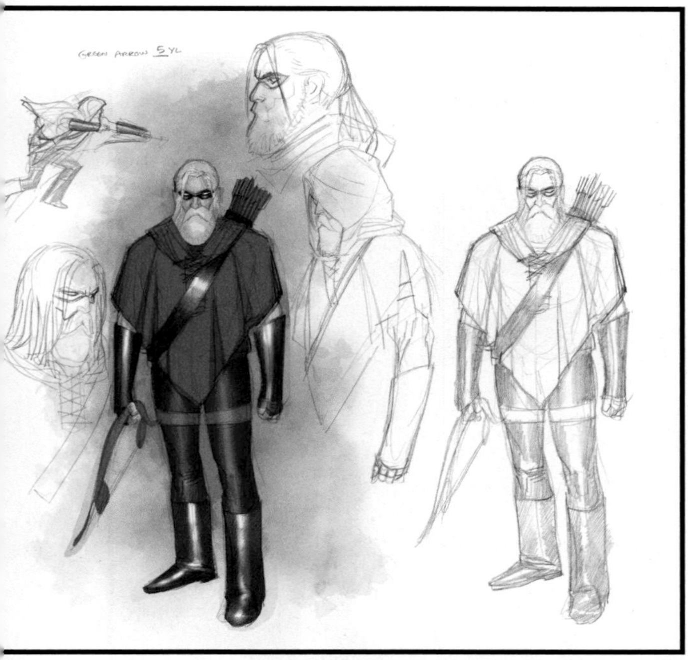
GREEN ARROW 5YL

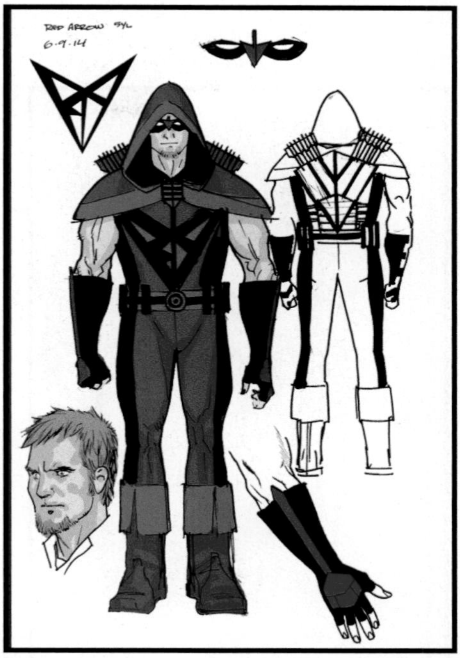
RED ARROW 5YL
6.9.14

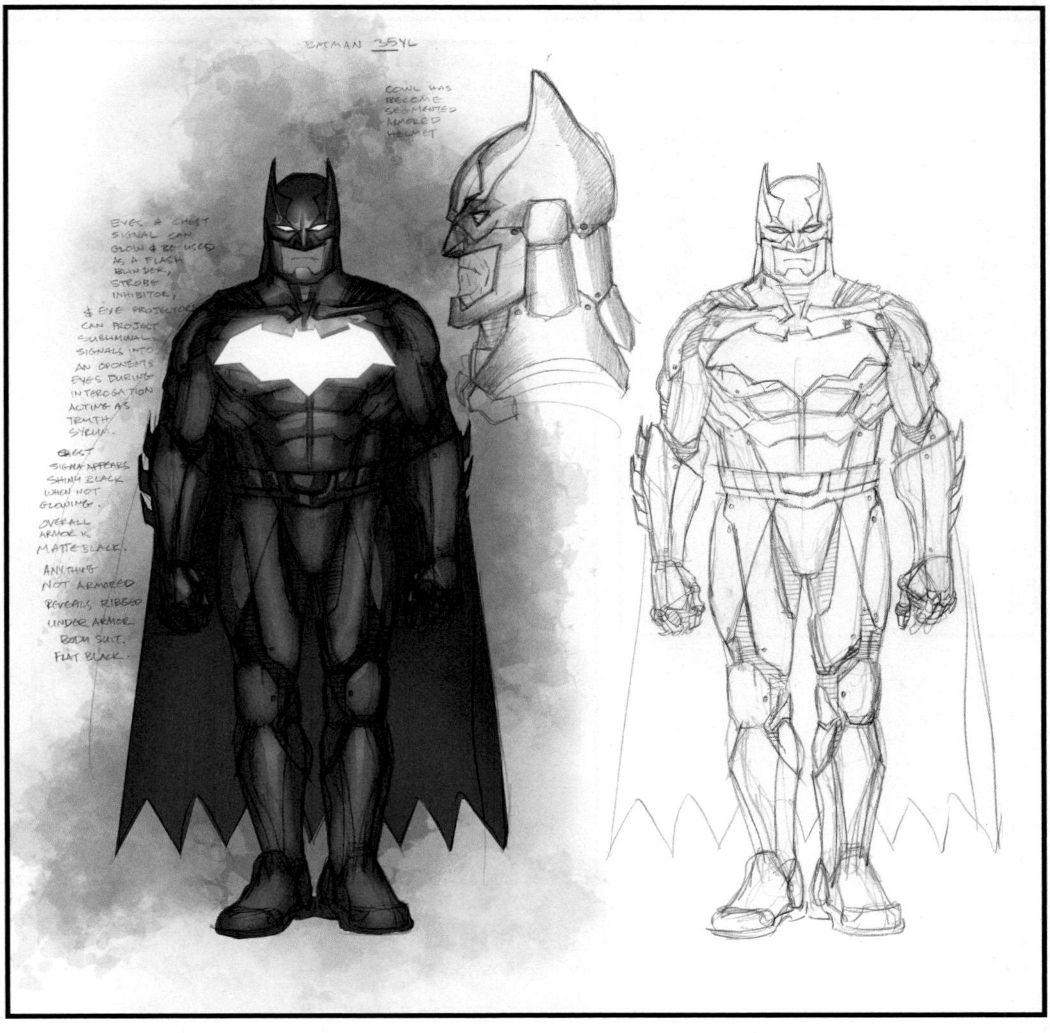
BATMAN 35YL
COWL HAS BECOME SEGMENTED ARMORED HELMET
EYES & CHEST SIGNAL CAN GLOW & BE USED AS A FLASH BLINDER, STROBE INHIBITOR,
& EYE PROJECTORS CAN PROJECT SUBLIMINAL SIGNALS INTO AN OPONENTS EYES DURING INTEROGATION ACTING AS TRUTH SYRUM.
CHEST SIGNAL APPEARS SHINY BLACK WHEN NOT GLOWING.
OVERALL ARMOR IS MATTE BLACK.
ANYTHING NOT ARMORED REVEALS RIBBED UNDER ARMOR BODY SUIT. FLAT BLACK.

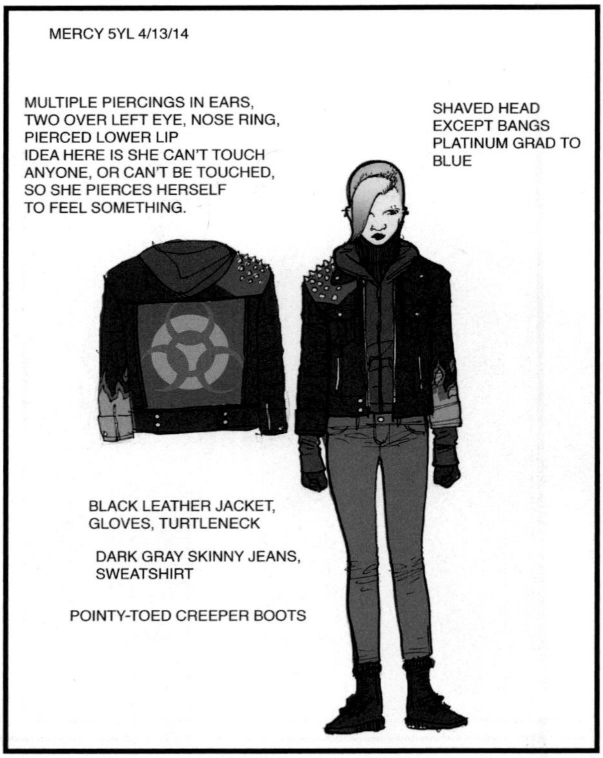
MERCY 5YL 4/13/14
MULTIPLE PIERCINGS IN EARS, TWO OVER LEFT EYE, NOSE RING, PIERCED LOWER LIP
IDEA HERE IS SHE CAN'T TOUCH ANYONE, OR CAN'T BE TOUCHED, SO SHE PIERCES HERSELF TO FEEL SOMETHING.
SHAVED HEAD EXCEPT BANGS PLATINUM GRAD TO BLUE
BLACK LEATHER JACKET, GLOVES, TURTLENECK
DARK GRAY SKINNY JEANS, SWEATSHIRT
POINTY-TOED CREEPER BOOTS

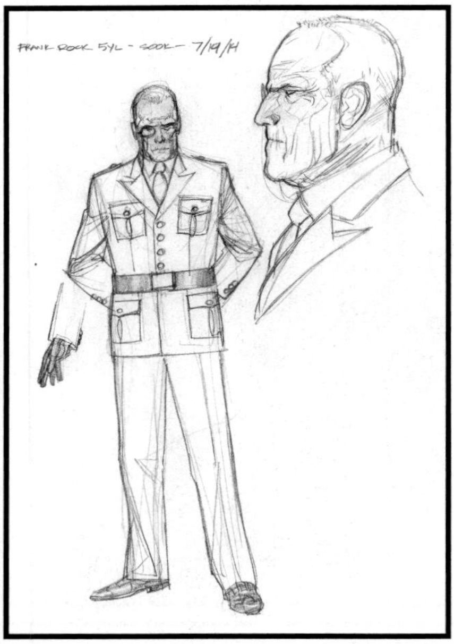
FRANK ROCK 5YL - SOOK - 7/19/14

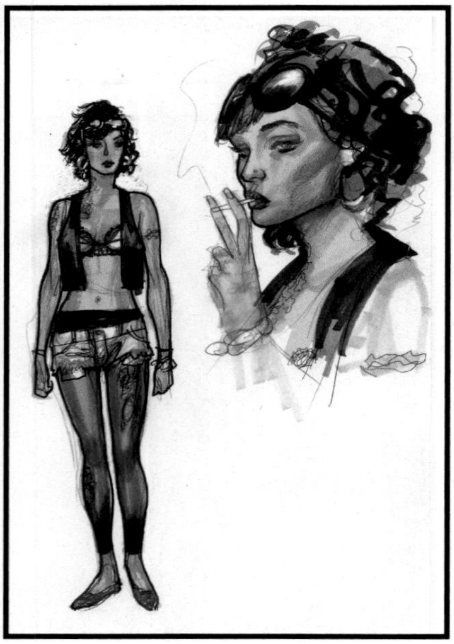

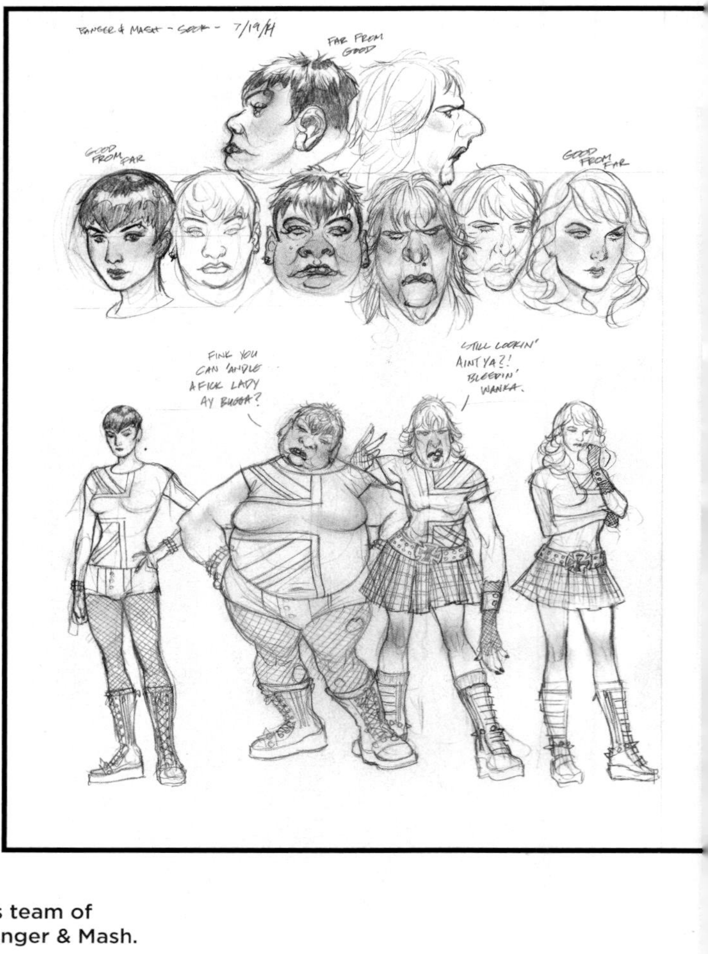
BANGER & MASH - SOOK - 7/19/14
FAR FROM GOOD
GOOD FROM FAR
GOOD FROM FAR
FINK YOU CAN 'ANDLE A FICK LADY AY BUGGA?
STILL LOOKIN' AINT YA?! BLEEDIN' WANKA.

An older but familiar Frank Rock and his team of troubled agents: Mercy, Voodoo, and Banger & Mash.

Batman's worst nightmare, sharing a
cyborg body with his archenemy, the Joker.

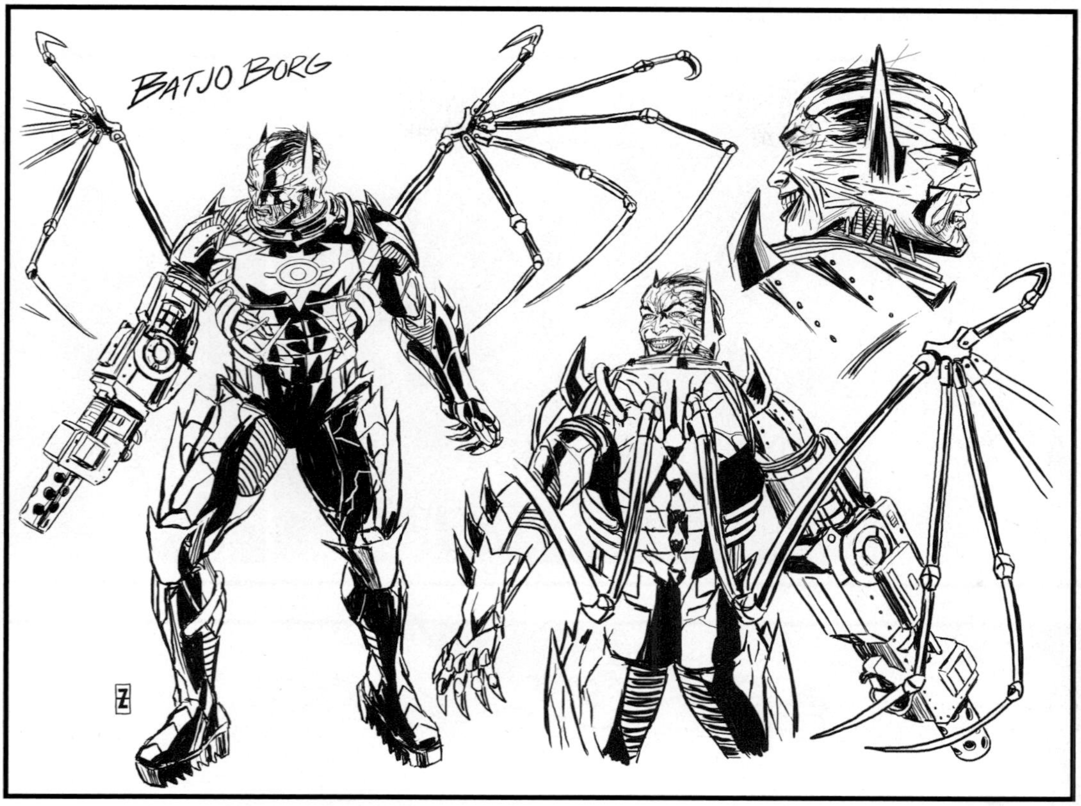
BATJO BORG

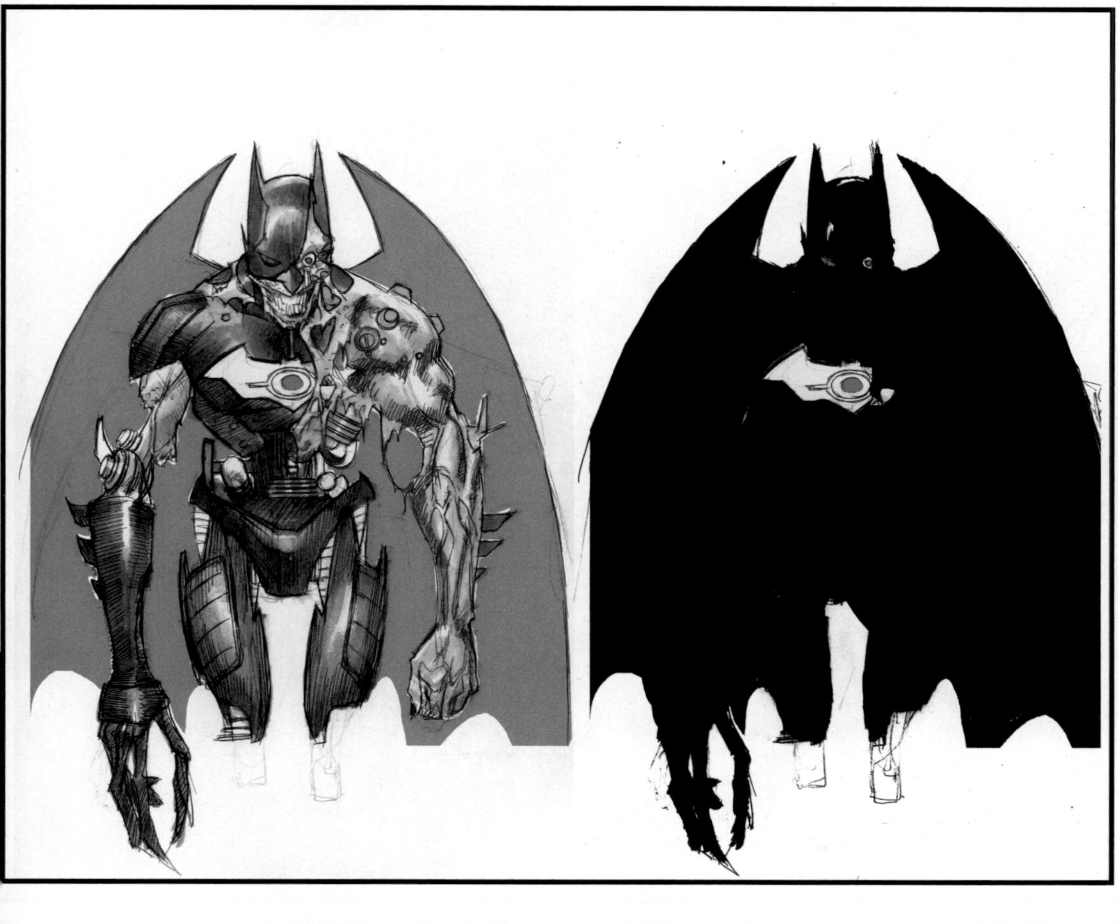

Preliminary sketches and pencils of the full cover spread to issues #23-25.

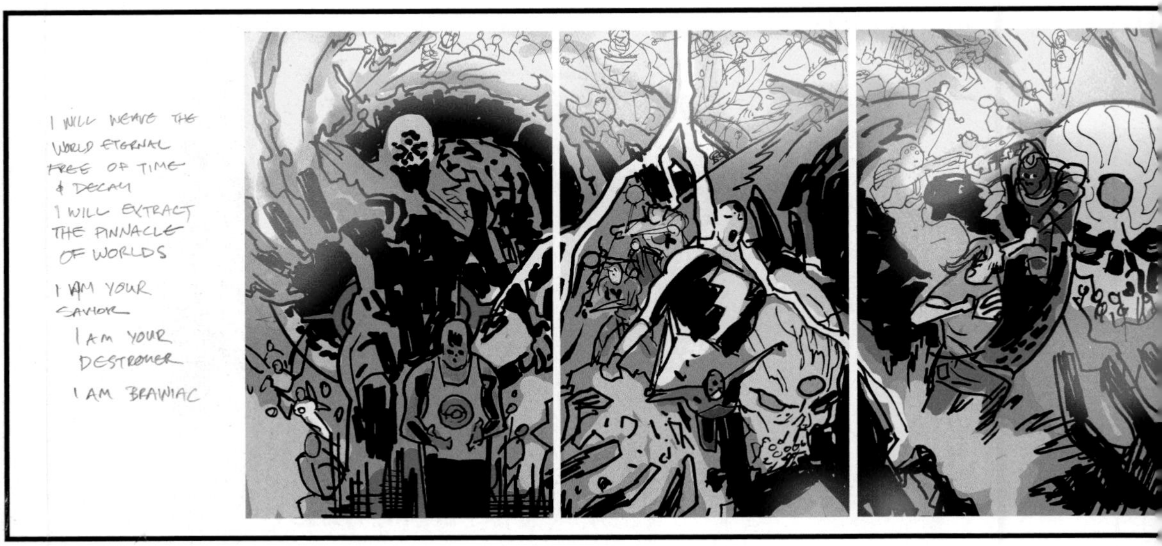
I WILL WEAVE THE
WORLD ETERNAL
FREE OF TIME
& DECAY
I WILL EXTRACT
THE PINNACLE
OF WORLDS
I AM YOUR
SAVIOR
I AM YOUR
DESTROYER
I AM BRAINIAC

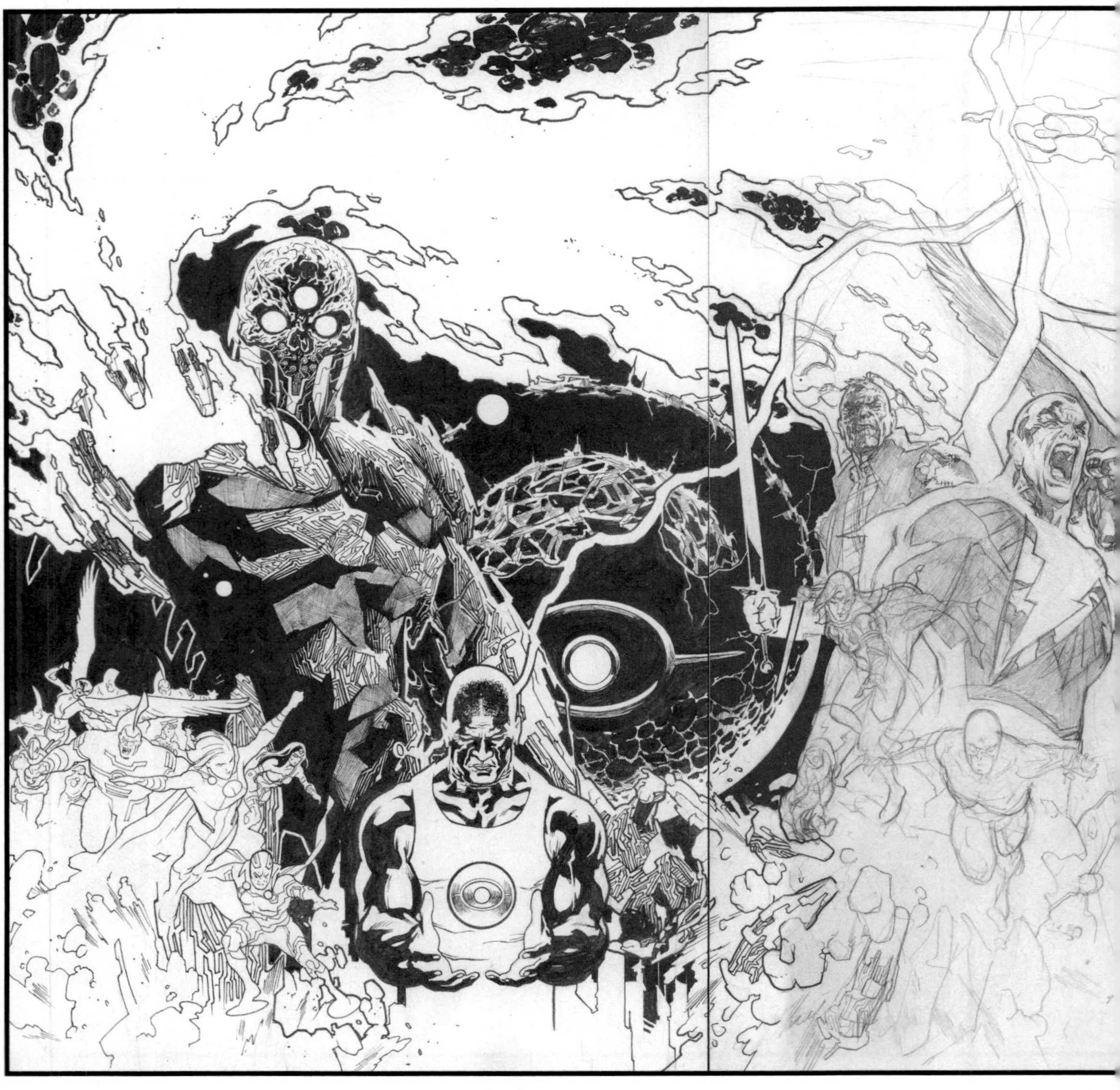

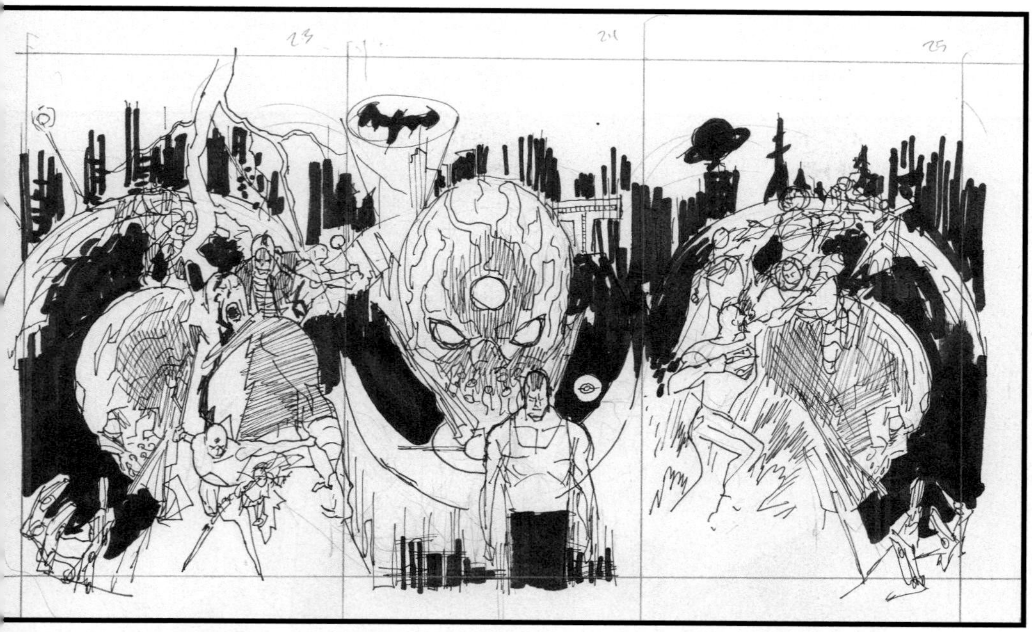

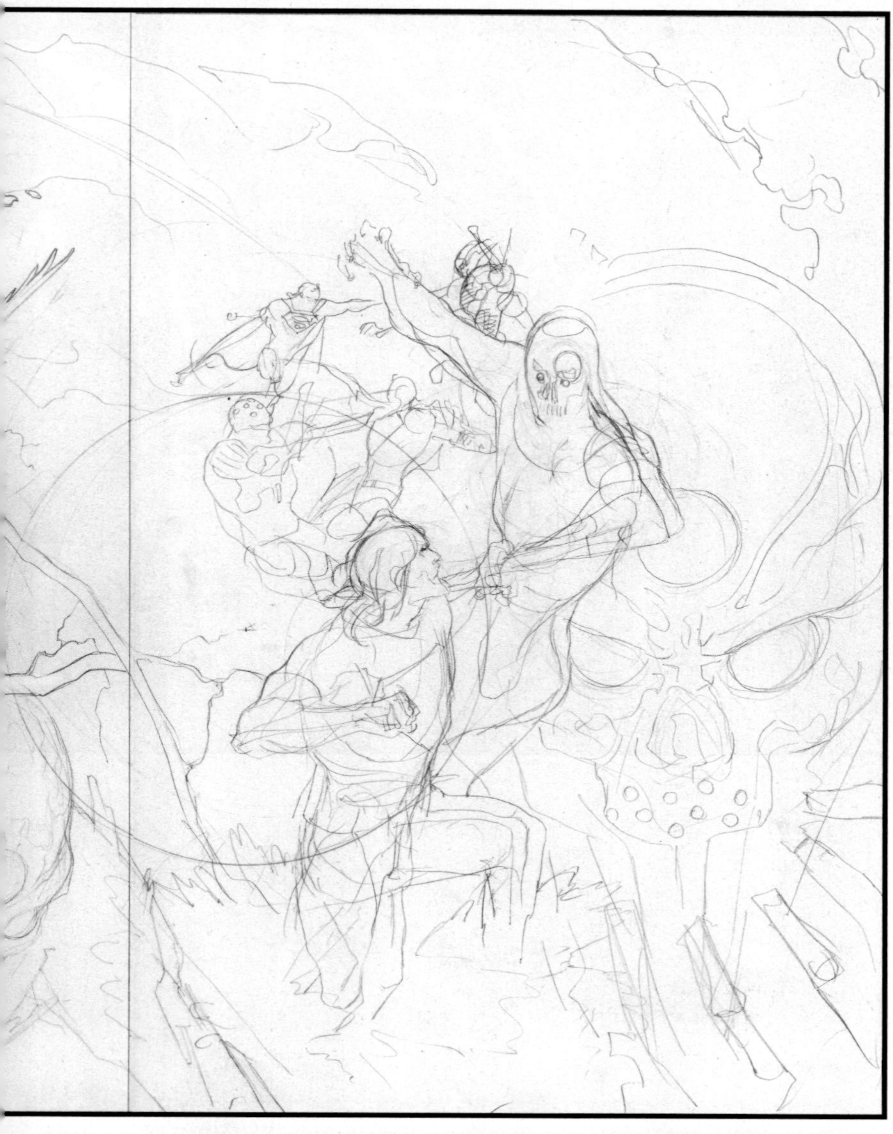

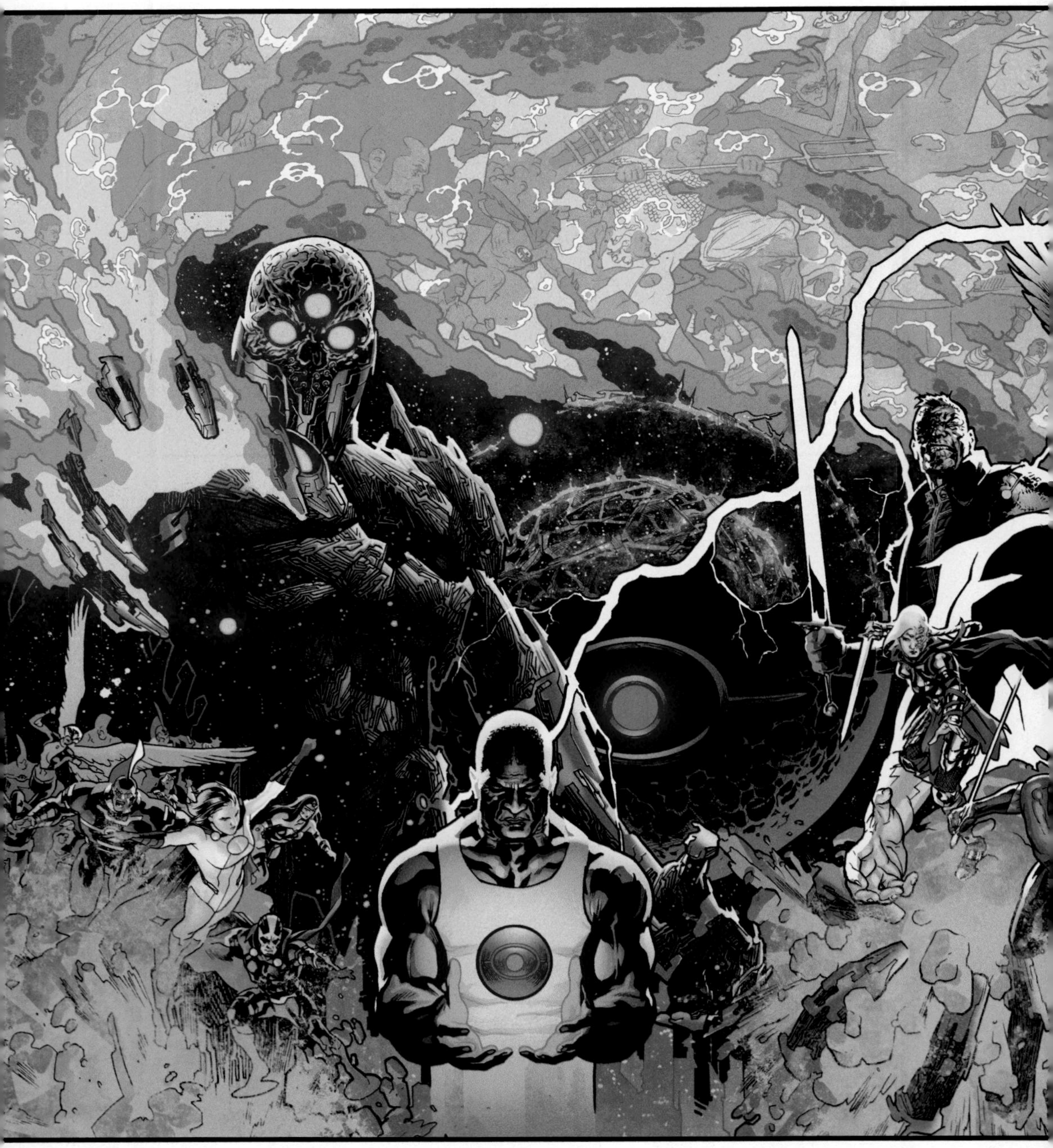

The final cover spread to issues #23-25

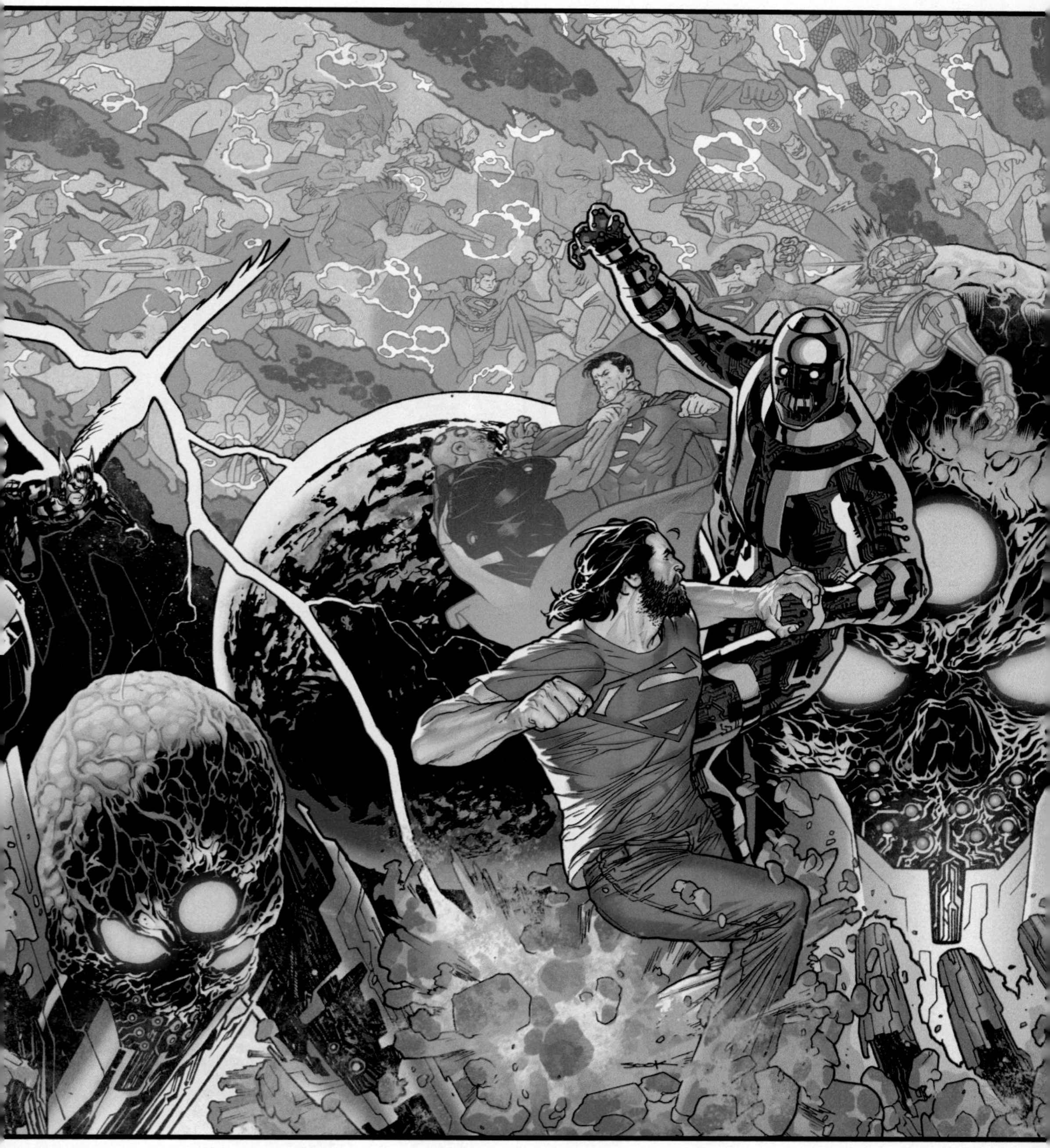

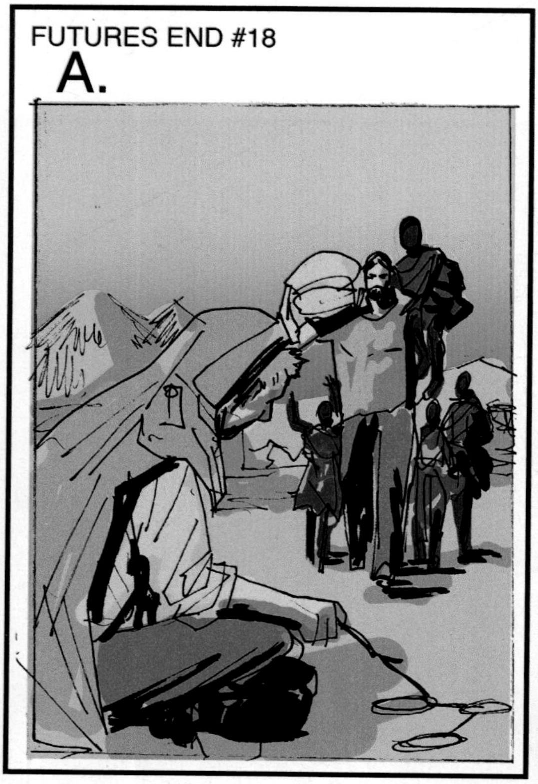
FUTURES END #18
A.

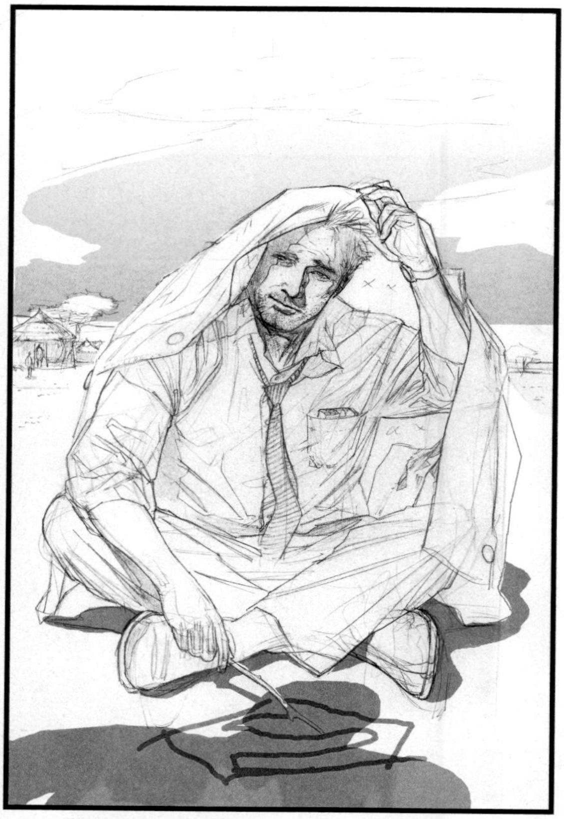

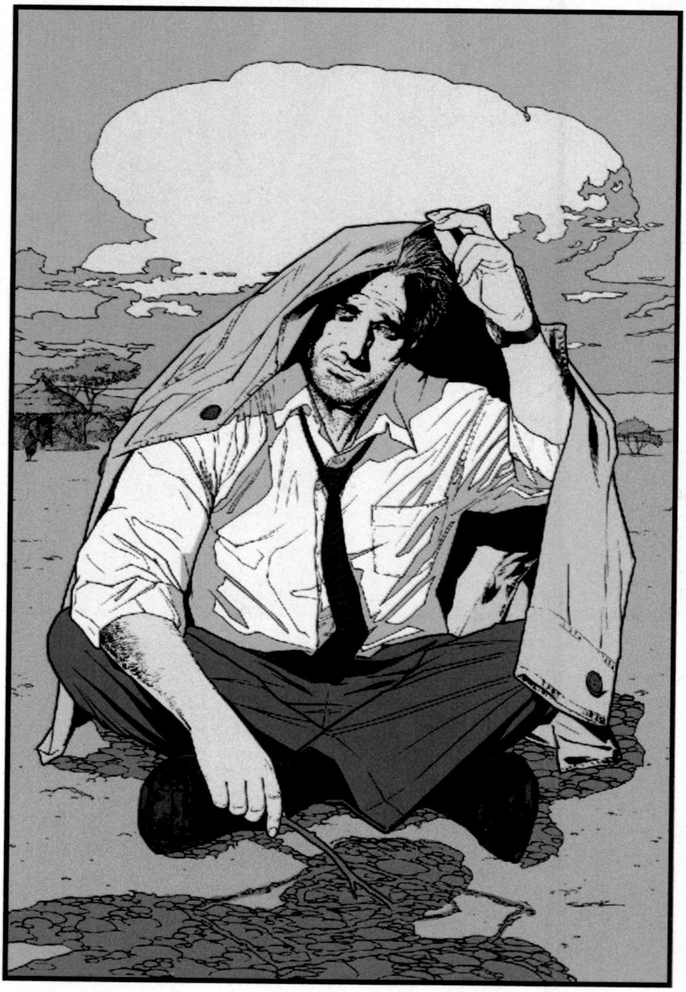

Preliminary cover sketches

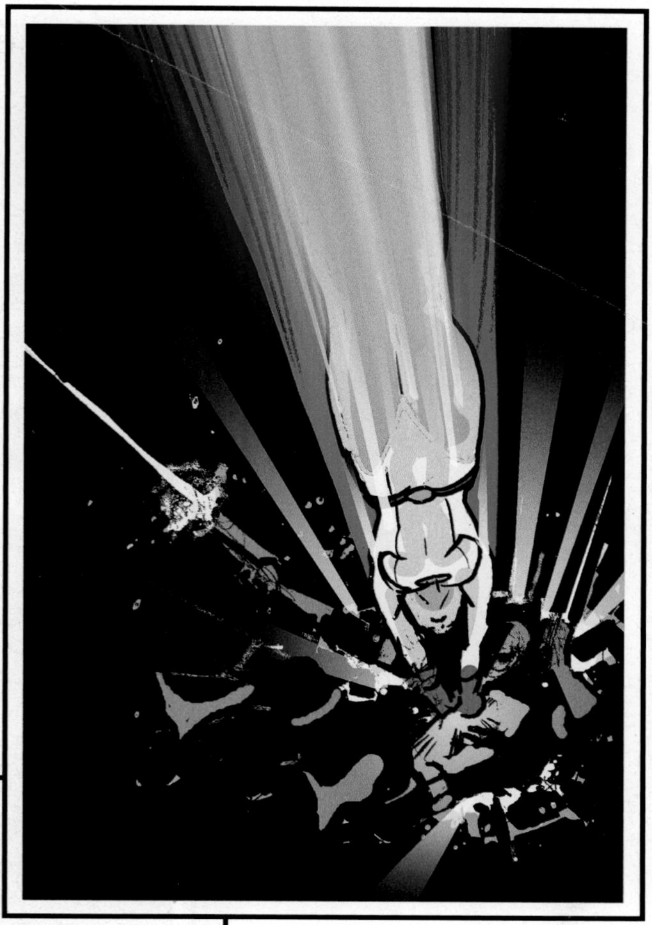

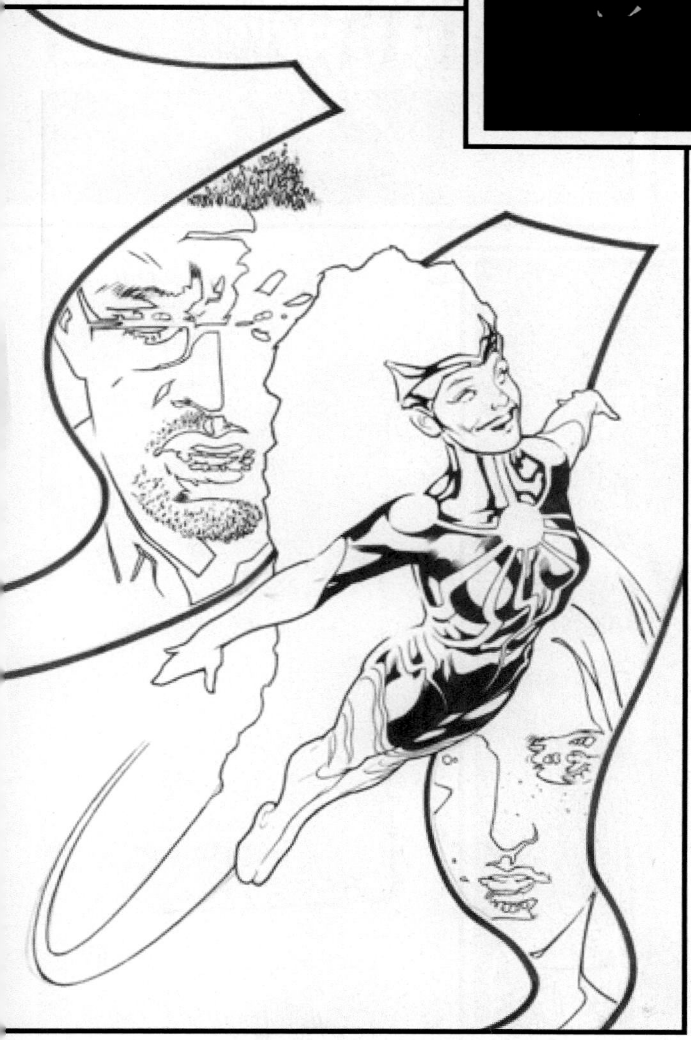